SOUTHERN BAPTIST THEOLOGICAL SEMINARY, 1859–2009

SOUTHERN BAPTIST THEOLOGICAL SEMINARY, 1859–2009

GREGORY A. WILLS

UNIVERSITY PRESS

2009

OXFORD

UNIVERSITY PRESS

Oxford University Press, Inc., publishes works that further
Oxford University's objective of excellence
in research, scholarship, and education.

Oxford   New York
Auckland   Cape Town   Dar es Salaam   Hong Kong   Karachi
Kuala Lumpur   Madrid   Melbourne   Mexico City   Nairobi
New Delhi   Shanghai   Taipei   Toronto

With offices in
Argentina   Austria   Brazil   Chile   Czech Republic   France   Greece
Guatemala   Hungary   Italy   Japan   Poland   Portugal   Singapore
South Korea   Switzerland   Thailand   Turkey   Ukraine   Vietnam

Published by Oxford University Press, Inc.
198 Madison Avenue, New York, New York 10016

www.oup.com

Oxford is a registered trademark of Oxford University Press

Library of Congress Cataloging-in-Publication Data
Wills, Gregory A.
Southern Baptist Theological Seminary, 1859–2009 / Gregory Wills.
p. cm.
Includes index.
ISBN 978-0-19-537714-9
1. Southern Baptist Theological Seminary—History.   2. Conservatism—
Religious aspects—Southern Baptist Convention—History.   I. Title.
BV4070.S86 W4 2009
230.07'36132—dc22   2009000775

1 3 5 7 9 8 6 4 2

Printed in the United States of America
on acid-free paper

PREFACE

Southern Baptists have remained stubbornly conservative in a culture whose democratic impulses have led American Christians to adapt their beliefs and practices to modernity's individualist values. These values have reoriented Christianity inward and disadvantaged the objective authority of scripture and traditional orthodoxy. Through most of the twentieth century, the Southern Baptist Theological Seminary was the denomination's chief promoter of adaptation to modernity. After about 1900 many of its faculty embraced progressive theology and aimed to influence Southern Baptists in this direction. E. Y. Mullins, president and professor of theology at the seminary from 1899 to 1928, effectively promoted a form of modern theology that made individual experience the source of religious authority and the mediator of the Bible's meaning. Southern Baptists broadly embraced the individualist reformulations of Baptist identity and abandoned such traditional commitments as Calvinist doctrine and church discipline. By the 1940s progressive theology spread dramatically in Southern Baptist colleges and seminaries.

But for most Southern Baptists, the adaptation went only so far. Throughout the twentieth century, most remained committed to traditional orthodoxy in such fundamental areas as biblical inspiration, creation, conversion, atonement, and miracles. Southern Seminary played a surprising role in restraining modernism and preserving orthodoxy.

Founding president and professor of theology James P. Boyce bound the seminary to an orthodox creed and committed its governance ultimately to popular control by Southern Baptists. When the inspiration controversy of the late 1870s and early 1880s challenged traditional beliefs, he and the faculty led the denomination to reaffirm orthodox views. Boyce and his faculty established the seminary with such great personal sacrifice, and led the denomination with such wisdom, that they attained a heroic status in denominational memory. The seminary's founding commitment to preserving orthodoxy was thus implanted in denominational memory in ways that strengthened the denomination's conservatism and limited the seminary's ability to stray from it.

The denomination's popular conservatism and the founding faculty's place in denominational memory limited the influence and reach of progressive thought. Through most of the twentieth century, progressive faculty members related to the denomination by means of a realistic policy in which they accommodated their teaching to the fact that Southern Baptists were incorrigibly conservative and expected their seminary to be the same. At the end of the century a majority of Southern Baptists nevertheless recognized that the seminary faculty was progressive, and they overhauled the school in order to reestablish traditional orthodoxy. Southern Baptist populism privileged orthodoxy over individualism. The seminary could not evade the symbolic power of its original commitment to orthodoxy and popular control.

This book is not about Southern Seminary alone—it is also about Southern Baptists. It shows how the denomination navigated the tension between the individualist values of modernity and traditional commitment to orthodoxy. The seminary's conflicts and transformations revealed Southern Baptists' most basic commitments and significantly shaped their identity. The story has a larger meaning also. It helps illuminate the course and character of religion in America, its conservative versions especially.

A few words about the sources are in order. This book relies heavily on manuscript sources, especially personal correspondence, but including also diaries, notebooks, and memoranda. I have in nearly every case regularized spelling, capitalization, and punctuation in quotations from the sources. Where the sources contained shorthand symbols or abbreviations, I have usually spelled out the words.

Several collections require comment. The Olin T. Binkley Papers and the Henlee H. Barnette Papers at the Z. Smith Reynolds Library at Wake Forest University were recent accessions and were not fully processed. The special collections staff kindly accommodated my request to conduct research in these valuable collections. Due to the fact that these collections were in process, references to items from these collections may lack box numbers.

Two unique sources document the 1958 controversy over the dismissal of twelve professors. The first is a 555-page transcript of interviews conducted by the school of theology committee of the board of trustees, April 28–30, 1958, in Louisville, Kentucky. The committee interviewed twenty-three members of the faculty and President Duke McCall and recorded its proceedings on nineteen tape reels. In 1974 the trustees had the recordings transcribed, then destroyed the recordings and placed the transcript under seal. Trustees removed the seal in 2007.

Another important source is Hugh Wamble's lengthy electronic manuscript, "Conflict between Authority and Conscience." Wamble was a professor of church history and was among those dismissed in 1958. Although some of the manuscript's statements are based on memories current when Wamble wrote it in 1990, it includes lengthy quotes from his contemporaneous notes and from other contemporary sources. Wamble's family graciously provided me an electronic copy for my research. When citing this work, I included the chapter number as well as the page number, since the page numbers may differ based on line spacing and margins. My copy was 787 total pages, with one-inch margins and single spacing. A copy has been placed in the archives of the James P. Boyce Centennial Library. Andy Rawls and media services provided copies of many audio recordings.

I conducted about twenty oral interviews in the course of my research and read twenty or thirty oral interviews conducted by others. Though oral histories are immensely valuable in many respects, I have treated them with less deference than contemporaneous sources. Memory is selective and naturally tends toward the self-serving. Oral histories do not often distinguish between beliefs that were based on hearsay at the time of their origin, and those based on sounder evidence. They may accurately reflect a belief that was held by an individual or group, and this is historically significant, but the belief gains little additional credibility thereby. Though they are often suggestive rather than probative, the suggestions are invaluable. I found them valuable also in interpreting or corroborating the contemporaneous records.

Trustee and faculty minutes are on deposit at the president's office of the Southern Baptist Theological Seminary.

Dozens of persons contributed in significant ways to the making of this volume.

Trustees and President R. Albert Mohler made this history possible by granting full and ready access to essential material: minutes of trustee and faculty meetings, the presidential papers of Duke K. McCall and Roy L. Honeycutt, and the transcriptions of faculty interviews of April 1958. I wish to thank R. Albert Mohler also for granting a candid and helpful interview, and above all for his perfect respect for the freedom to write the seminary's history without partisan constraints or institutional interference.

Russell D. Moore, Senior Vice President for Academic Administration and Dean of the School of Theology, supported this project in many ways and was a source of encouragement throughout. Without the generous provision of teaching relief and research support, this task could not have been completed for many more years.

Duke McCall gave generously of his time in answering my many questions and provided gracious hospitality during my visit in Florida. William Hull kindly sat for an interview and for additional hours of discussion concerning Southern Seminary. David S. Dockery on numerous occasions provided needed information or insight in response to many questions. Wayne Ward shared at length from his large store of memories of more than sixty years at Southern Seminary and was always ready to answer questions of detail or fact. Others who kindly assisted me by granting interviews were Heber Peacock, T. C. Smith, Ralph Elliott, Hargus Taylor, Marvin Tate, Clara McCartt, James Leo Garrett, Rick White, Jerry Johnson, Jim Chancellor, Scott Hafemann, Paul House, Ladislau Biro, and Edgar Hatfield. Without these interviews, my understanding of the people and events that make up this history would be greatly impoverished.

I owe special thanks to the many archivists and librarians without whose help I would not have had access to the rich store of sources that illuminate the seminary's history. Jason Fowler, Chris DeWease, and others at the James P. Boyce Centennial Library's archives and special collections department assisted me time after time. They not only had the foresight to modernize the organization and storage of the manuscript collections and to prepare extensive finding aids, including correspondence calendars, but also cheerfully fulfilled my requests for information, copies, and work space. They also provided invaluable aid in the scanning, selection, and captioning of photographs. Paul Roberts and the interlibrary loan staff always found the documents that I needed.

Bill Sumners, Kathy Sylvest, and Taffey Hall at the Southern Baptist Historical Library and Archives provided much valuable advice and assistance during many long visits. They also awarded the project a research grant that defrayed the expenses of one of those visits. Vicki Johnson and Julia Bradford in the special collections department of Wake Forest University's Z. Smith Reynolds Library were unstintingly helpful in affording access to their valuable collections over several weeks of research there. Librarians at Samford University, Furman University, Union Theological Seminary, Southwestern Baptist Theological Seminary, Southeastern Baptist Theological Seminary, Harvard University, Baylor University, the University of Virginia, Campbellsville University, the University of South Carolina, Meredith College, the American Baptist Historical Society, Duke University, and the University of North Carolina at Chapel Hill also provided valuable assistance.

Colleagues and friends supported this project in invaluable ways. Tom Nettles graciously provided a manuscript copy of his forthcoming biography of James P. Boyce, patiently discussed many questions with me, and loaned needed books. Josh Powell provided friendship, encouragement, and sound advice. Jason Allen provided space for research of trustee and faculty minutes in the president's office, helped me find needed sources, discovered a forgotten collection of John R. Sampey's papers, and was always eager to discuss various issues in the seminary's history. Mark Rogers, Adam Winters, Brandon Nygaard, John

Randolph, and Josh Green served as research assistants and did much yeoman's work. They took many of the 100,000 photographs of documents on which this history largely relies, entered many thousands of notes from them, and scoured long lists of newspaper microfilm for needed articles. Dan Stiver and Bart Tichenor graciously provided a copy of Hugh Wamble's manuscript history of the 1958 controversy, and Hargus Taylor and John Michael kindly provided copies of additional relevant materials. Tim Harrelson and Jeff Mayfield provided many helpful books.

Several colleagues and students read various drafts of the manuscript in part or in whole and provided helpful feedback. Kurt Wise defined neighborliness when he cleared our yard of trees felled by the remnants of Hurricane Ike while I was rushing through a second draft. Ingrid Buck, my mother-in-law, kindly provided a two-week writing retreat at a critical time. My wife, Cathy, not only encouraged the book's completion by many acts of patient sacrifice but also worked long hours entering indecipherable corrections and wielding her own editing pen with uncommonly good sense. Sam, Abby, James, and Maggie patiently shared their father with a project that must have seemed interminable.

A word about the author may also be in order. I am a Southern Baptist. I have worked and taught at Southern Seminary since 1994 and sympathize with its aims and commitments. Perspective inescapably affects interpretation, but I have attempted to avoid partisan judgments. It ill serves history and the present to recolor the past to suit the historian's predilections or institutional reputation. I have endeavored to let the actors in this drama speak in their own voices. It is hard otherwise to do justice to their arguments, interpretations, and perspectives. It is impossible otherwise to achieve historical understanding. The lessons of the past cannot be right if the history is wrong.

CONTENTS

REFERENCES AND NOTES

The following manuscript collections are held at Southern Baptist Theological Seminary, in the Archives and Special Collections Department of the James P. Boyce Memorial Library. In the notes I have omitted reference to their holding location.

James P. Boyce Papers
John A. Broadus Papers
Archibald T. Robertson Papers
Thomas T. Eaton Papers
Edgar Y. Mullins Papers
John R. Sampey Papers
Ellis A. Fuller Papers
Duke K. McCall Papers
Roy L. Honeycutt Papers
Letterpress Copy Books
Transcription of Trustee Interviews 28–30 Apr. 1958

Notes Abbreviations

ANTS   Franklin Trask Library, Andover Newton Theological Seminary, Newton, Massachusetts

HUA   Harvard University Archives, Harvard University, Cambridge, Massachusetts

LVA   Library of Virginia, Richmond

SBHLA   Southern Baptist Historical Library and Archives, Nashville, Tennessee

SBTS   Archives and Special Collections, James P. Boyce Centennial Library, Southern Baptist Theological Seminary, Louisville, Kentucky

SWBTS   Archives, A. Webb Roberts Library, Southwestern Baptist
         Theological Seminary, Fort Worth, Texas

UNC   Manuscripts Department, Wilson Library, University of North
         Carolina, Chapel Hill

USC   South Caroliniana Library, University of South Carolina,
         Columbia

UVA   Albert and Shirley Small Special Collections Library, University of
         Virginia, Charlottesville

WFU   North Carolina Baptist Historical Collection, Z. Smith Reynolds
         Library, Wake Forest University, Winston-Salem, North Carolina

SOUTHERN BAPTIST THEOLOGICAL
SEMINARY, 1859–2009

BOYCE'S SEMINARY

On the first day of October 1859, four young professors and nine students opened the Southern Baptist Theological Seminary.[1] It was an uncertain undertaking. Southern Baptists were not sure that they needed it, and many doubted its success. And opposition to it came from many quarters. By November Professor Basil Manly Jr. judged that the seminary's survival was already "drawing to a crisis," and he grieved at the prospect of seeing "so auspicious a movement for Southern Baptist interests come to naught."[2] The seminary survived the crisis. It survived others worse. From the beginning its success depended uniquely on one man, James P. Boyce. His remarkable determination to establish and preserve the seminary rescued it from failure time and again. Without his leadership it would have passed into extinction.[3]

James Petigru Boyce was born in Charleston, South Carolina, on January 11, 1827, the son of one of the South's wealthiest merchants, Ker Boyce. He grew up faithfully attending the Charleston First Baptist Church, where his mother was a member. In 1846, at the age of nineteen, he came under the conviction that he

---

1. John A. Broadus to Mamma [Mrs. Major Broadus], 1 Oct. 1861, box 17, Broadus Papers.

2. Basil Manly Jr. to Basil Manly Sr., 25 Nov. 1859, Manly Collection of Manuscripts, microfilm, reel 1, SBTS.

3. The two best sources on Boyce's life are John A. Broadus, *Memoir of James Petigru Boyce* (New York: A. C. Armstrong, 1893), and Tom J. Nettles, *James Petigru Boyce* (Phillipsburg, NJ: P and R Publishing, 2009).

was a sinner in need of the grace that could be found in Christ alone. He experienced conversion and was baptized shortly after.[4]

Boyce immediately applied himself with great earnestness to prayer, Bible reading, and evangelistic work among his friends at Brown University, where he was a student. After graduation in 1847, he resolved to apply himself to the ministry of the gospel. Eye trouble prevented him from pursuing theological studies immediately, and he agreed to serve temporarily as editor of the Charleston weekly, the *Southern Baptist*. In 1848 he and his wife, Elizabeth Ficklin Boyce, moved to New Jersey, where Boyce took the full theological course at Princeton Theological Seminary in two years, by taking the second- and third-year courses simultaneously. In 1851 the Columbia First Baptist Church ordained Boyce, and he served as its pastor for four years. When his father died in 1854, he became executor of his father's estate, a position that demanded considerable attention for the rest of his life.[5]

Furman University, a Southern Baptist school with a small theology department, elected Boyce as professor of theology in 1855. By this time he had already determined to do all he could to establish a full-fledged theological seminary for Southern Baptists. When he convinced South Carolina Baptists to take the lead in the effort in 1856, he became the recognized leader of the seminary movement. From that point Boyce gave himself to establishing and preserving the seminary. He made extraordinary personal sacrifices for its success. But it was not his determination alone that accomplished the design—it was vision. It was his proposal that won denominational support for the seminary, and it was his blueprint for the seminary's design that denominational leaders adopted.[6]

At the very heart of Boyce's vision was a commitment to subordinate the seminary to Bible truth and to the denomination. The seminary should always conform to scripture truth and always serve Southern Baptist churches. To accomplish the first he persuaded Southern Baptist leaders to adopt a confession of faith for the seminary and to require every professor to subscribe

4. Broadus, *Memoir of Boyce*, 34–35, 43–45.

5. Broadus, *Memoir of Boyce*, 46–47, 53–88, 93–95, 336. The terms of his father's will required that the estate remain in executorship until the youngest of his grandchildren entered majority, which did not occur until one month after James Boyce's death. The estate was reputed to be worth $17 million in 1854 ("Notes from the Life of a Southern Millionaire," newspaper clipping from Chattanooga paper, in box 16, Broadus Papers).

6. Broadus, *Memoir of Boyce*, 101–102, 106–107. Boyce was a Furman trustee but resigned ahead of his nomination as a professor. He opposed faculty serving on trustee boards and had before urged ending the practice at Furman. See James C. Furman to Edwin Mims, 3 Dec. 1851, quoted in Harvey Toliver Cook, *The Life Work of James Clement Furman* (Greenville, SC: Alester G. Furman, 1926), 140.

agreement with it. To accomplish the second he persuaded Southern Baptist leaders to establish a board of trustees controlled finally by the Southern Baptist Convention. The churches had the power, through their delegates to the Southern Baptist Convention, to determine the trustees who directly governed the seminary.

Boyce's design for the seminary centered in these two ideas, and he led the denomination to establish them permanently into the constitution of the seminary. On this basis he rallied Southern Baptists to support the seminary in that generation and in the generations following. Boyce's leadership so characterized the seminary that one critic objected that the school belonged to Boyce more than to the denomination.[7] The critic was in an important sense correct. Boyce's imprint made the Southern Baptist Theological Seminary Boyce's seminary.

THEOLOGICAL EDUCATION AND THE BAPTIST COLLEGES

By 1830 Baptists and Methodists were the most popular American denominations. They did not require formal education for ordination. Their preachers were farmers and mechanics rather than college or seminary graduates. However, both denominations broadly supported educating preachers, and their most popular preachers promoted the cause of education and led their churches to establish a multitude of colleges in the nineteenth century.[8] They lagged behind other denominations, however, in establishing seminaries.

Presbyterians established Union Theological Seminary in Richmond, Virginia, in 1812; Columbia Theological Seminary in Columbia, South Carolina, in 1828; and Danville Theological Seminary in Danville, Kentucky, in 1853. Episcopalians chartered Protestant Episcopal Theological Seminary in Virginia in 1823. Lutherans established Lutheran Theological Southern Seminary in South Carolina in 1830, and Concordia Theological Seminary in St. Louis in 1839. But Baptists had no seminary in the South.

Southern Baptists had only small theology departments at some of their colleges. In most cases Baptists had established these colleges for the purpose of training ministers, but they in fact taught little theology. The college curriculum consisted of the liberal arts and sciences, culminating in moral philosophy. Theology courses were outside the undergraduate curriculum and attracted

---

7. James P. Boyce, "The Two Objections to the Seminary, I," *Christian Index*, 16 Apr. 1874, 2.

8. See Archibald T. Robertson, "Southern Baptist Ministers of a Hundred Years Ago and Education," *Seminary Magazine* 4 (1891): 4–8.

few students. Even if they had attracted more students, the colleges could not afford to employ a sufficient number of professors to teach an entire theological curriculum.

Baptists in Ohio and Kentucky established the Western Baptist Theological Seminary in Covington, Kentucky, in 1849. It attracted few students, and Kentucky Baptists were dissatisfied with the faculty's rumored antislavery views. A few years later they divided its few assets between the two groups, and the Kentucky Baptists merged it with Georgetown College to create a theology department like those existing at other Southern Baptist colleges.

Georgia's Mercer University was founded to train men for the gospel ministry but had no theology professor until 1839, when trustees elected Adiel Sherwood. Sherwood found that the students were few and ill prepared. Upon his resignation in 1841, trustees suspended the theology department until 1844, when they elected John L. Dagg.[9] When Basil Manly Jr. graduated from the University of Alabama, his heart thrilled at the prospect of studying theology under Dagg's direction. But Dagg discouraged him from attending Mercer because he did not believe that Manly could get a thorough theological education there. Dagg advised him to go north, to Newton Theological Institute in Newton, Massachusetts, so that he could have "the best advantages and the fullest course" available.[10]

Newton was one of three theological seminaries that Baptists had established in the North by midcentury. They were Hamilton Theological Seminary (later Colgate) in New York in 1820; Newton Theological Institute in 1826; and Rochester Theological Seminary in Rochester, New York, in 1850. Until the establishment of the Southern Baptist Theological Seminary in 1859, many Southern Baptist ministerial students who wanted to take the full theological course matriculated at northern schools. When southerners began to suspect these northern Baptist schools of entertaining antislavery sentiments, some Southern Baptists preferred the Old School Presbyterians' Princeton Theological Seminary, where both James P. Boyce and Basil Manly Jr. matriculated.[11]

But Southern Baptists found northern seminaries unsatisfactory, and their dissatisfaction with them grew throughout the antebellum period. They worried that southern ministerial students who studied in the North would come under the influence of Yankee values, habits, and manners. More worrisome

9. See Spright Dowell, *A History of Mercer University: 1833–1953* (Macon, GA: Foote and Davies, 1958), 80–81.

10. Basil Manly Jr., "The Beginnings of the History of the Seminary," *Seminary Magazine* 5 (1891): 114.

11. See Manly, "The Beginnings," 114; Broadus, *Memoir of Boyce*, 65, 67.

was the growing antislavery sentiment in northern seminaries and the theological systems that seemed to nurture antislavery views. Southerners believed that the New Divinity and German theology had deeply tinctured many northern seminaries and had fostered antislavery sentiment. Their "peculiar dogmas" made them untrustworthy in theology and uncharitable toward southerners.[12]

Many southerners connected objectionable theology with antislavery views. The Presbyterians' Columbia Theological Seminary came under suspicion of fostering both the New Divinity and abolition in 1837. Samuel Weir, editor of Columbia, South Carolina's *Southern Times and State Gazette*, asked whether the seminary was "as free from all suspicions of a taint of the new divinity, and of abolitionism, as a southern school ought ever to be." Although the students publicly avowed their southern identity and their opposition to abolitionism, Weir warned that as long as any professor or student was a northerner, "it will be impossible to eradicate all apprehensions on this score from the public mind of this country."[13] The same year, William B. Johnson sought a theology professor for Furman University and fretted that the obstacles of "abolition and the German theology" made it impractical to "transplant northern professors into southern institutions."[14] Southern Baptists who wanted a full course in theology had two choices, a committee of Alabama Baptists said, "either to enter a pedobaptist seminary where erroneous views of divine truth are inculcated, or else go north, where they are continually exposed to insult."[15] Southern Baptists needed their own seminary.

THE MOVEMENT FOR A SOUTHERN BAPTIST SEMINARY

Earlier efforts to establish a Baptist seminary in the South had failed. In 1835 Basil Manly Sr., pastor of the Charleston, South Carolina, First Baptist Church, urged Southern Baptists to establish a southern seminary. He noted that South Carolina had already escrowed $20,000 for theological education. He called on the Baptists of North Carolina and Georgia each to contribute the same amount and to establish a board of trustees representing each state equally. The endowment would support three professors. Such an institution, with God's

---

12. R. B. C. Howell, "A Great Southern Theological School," *Monthly Miscellany*, Mar. 1849, 81, 83. Also published in the *Southern Baptist*, 2 May 1849, 625.

13. Samuel Weir, untitled, *Southern Times and State Gazette*, 24 Feb. 1837, 3.

14. William B. Johnson to James C. Furman, 2 Mar. 1837, William B. Johnson Papers, Special Collections, James B. Duke Library, Furman University.

15. "Report on Education," in Alabama Baptist Convention, *Minutes*, 1858, 20.

blessing, would attain an "importance and usefulness of which we can not now conceive."[16] Jesse Mercer, the leading figure among Georgia Baptists, encouraged Baptists in Georgia and the Carolinas to take the matter in hand.[17] An effort by some Virginia Baptists to establish such a school in Williamsburg failed due to opposition from prominent Baptists.[18]

In 1843 Joseph S. Baker, editor of Georgia's *Christian Index*, argued that the colleges could not provide adequate theological training. He called on Baptist educational leaders to subordinate their ambitions for state honor and to become partners in establishing a southern seminary. There was no other way to provide adequate theological education.[19] The Baptist conventions of Georgia and South Carolina each appointed a committee to discuss combining their efforts at theological education. They concluded in 1843 that Georgia and South Carolina could not support a theological seminary by themselves. The effort would require the other southern states to unite with them.[20]

The formation of the Southern Baptist Convention in 1845 gave renewed hope to proponents of a southern seminary. Southern Baptists withdrew from the northern-controlled boards for foreign and home missions when the southerners objected to the antislavery scruples of board members. These same objections applied to northern Baptist seminaries. Joseph S. Baker, for example, urged that the delegates who met to organize the Southern Baptist Convention in 1845 adopt among its causes the establishment of a southern seminary.[21] Although the convention did not take up the question, after it adjourned a number of delegates held a conference to discuss the matter. They decided to hold a similar conference after the Southern Baptist Convention meeting in Richmond in 1846. Richard Furman published arguments aimed to persuade them to adopt

16. Basil Manly Sr., "Theological Education in the Southern States," *Southern Baptist and General Intelligencer*, 14 Mar. 1835, 170–172. Also published in the *Christian Index*, 24 Mar. 1835, 2.

17. Jesse Mercer, untitled, *Christian Index*, 24 Mar. 1835, 2.

18. See Joseph S. Baker, "A Small Mistake," *Christian Index*, 30 May 1872, 85.

19. Joseph S. Baker, "Education amongst the Baptists," *Christian Index*, 28 Apr. 1843, 265.

20. Committee of the Georgia Baptist Convention, "The Georgia Baptist Convention," *Christian Index*, 2 June 1843, 347.

21. Joseph S. Baker, "A Southern Theological School," *Christian Index*, 25 Apr. 1845, 2. See also Henry Keeling, "Southern Theological Sem.—Southern Colleges," *Christian Index*, 11 Apr. 1845, 3. There was apparently some discussion of the issue at the 1845 Southern Baptist Convention meeting, perhaps in an informal meeting during the convention (*History of the Establishment and Organization of the Southern Baptist Theological Seminary*, [Greenville, SC: G. E. Elford, 1860], 3).

Furman Theological Institute as the great southern theological seminary, but the conference in Richmond did not take place.[22]

R. B. C. Howell, pastor of Nashville First Baptist Church, sought to revive the movement in 1847. When Nashville hosted the meeting of the American Indian Mission Association in that year, he invited the delegates to hold a conference to discuss the establishment of a Southern Baptist seminary. The conference recommended that the delegates to the 1849 Southern Baptist Convention take action to establish a theological seminary.[23] Howell promoted the cause in the months before the 1849 convention, arguing that Southern Baptists had a duty before God to equip and prepare preachers thoroughly and that the theology departments of Baptist colleges were inadequate to the task.[24]

College leaders agreed that their efforts in theological education fell short and that Southern Baptists needed a great theological seminary. Some South Carolina leaders believed that Furman University was the logical place for the new seminary. James C. Furman, the senior theology professor at Furman Theological Institute, pressed the claim that Furman should become the nucleus of the new seminary. "The theological department of Howard, the department of Mercer, and our own are the three claimants now before the churches. Among the three which is likely to succeed? Our Georgia brethren have as much as they can do to get the collegiate department of their university fairly afloat. . . . We have three professors [of theology]. . . . Let the young men from sister states swell our numbers."[25]

Others held that Mercer University was the logical place for the seminary. James L. Reynolds, who had served as professor of theology at both Furman and Mercer, had already urged Southern Baptists to adopt Mercer as the nucleus of the new seminary. He hoped in 1847 that the time would soon come "when all young ministers in the South will rally around Mercer University and contribute to the enlargement and growth of at least one theological seminary of which Baptists need not be ashamed."[26]

When Howell wrote college leaders ahead of the 1849 conference on theological education, the response was not encouraging. The chief obstacle was

22. William B. Johnson, "Furman Theological Institution," in South Carolina Baptist Convention, *Minutes*, 1847, 19–20.

23. R. B. C. Howell, "Proceedings and Report," *Christian Index*, 13 Jan. 1848, 10–11. The resolution called on the delegates to act but left open whether they should act through the Southern Baptist Convention or as a separate conference.

24. Howell, "A Great Southern Theological School," 81, 83.

25. James C. Furman to R. B. C. Howell, ca. Jan. 1849, quoted in Cook, *The Life Work of James Clement Furman*, 109.

26. James L. Reynolds, quoted in Cook, *The Life Work of James Clement Furman*, 108.

not outright opposition but the natural protectiveness of the state colleges. The general scheme for the new seminary was that the various state Baptist colleges should donate their individual endowments for theological education to endow a central theological seminary. And the most feasible approach would be to use the pooled endowments to build upon the foundation of the theology department at one of the existing colleges. This meant that one school would advance at the expense of the others.

But even if the new seminary was established independently of any college, so that none would benefit directly from it, many believed that the colleges would be injured. Most colleges had emphasized theological education and had significant theological endowments. The colleges struggled to raise what little money they had, and they relied heavily on the fact that they taught theology. Baptists supported them in large measure because they promised to train ministers for the churches. If the colleges gave up teaching theology, the churches would feel less obliged to support them. The Baptist leaders of each state felt too keenly the many sacrifices already made to establish their colleges to jeopardize them in this way. It was too much to ask. Thomas Meredith, president of North Carolina's Wake Forest College, argued that establishing a seminary would undermine support of the college because Baptist resources were insufficient to support both. Besides, he said, there were too few ministerial students to justify the enterprise, and the colleges themselves would still have a theology professor to train ministers.[27] The cost to the colleges was too high.

Even Richmond College, whose state charter prohibited it from teaching theology, opposed the scheme. Robert Ryland, president of Richmond College, argued that such a seminary could not attract sufficient funding or students, since there was no need for it. The state colleges were doing the job well already. As Ryland explained, "It is impracticable. It is not demanded. . . . My chief objection . . . is the certainty of its failure."[28]

FAILURE

Advocates of the seminary pressed forward despite opposition. William B. Johnson, president of both the Southern Baptist Convention and the South Carolina Baptist Convention, called a special session of the South Carolina

27. Thomas Meredith, "Theological Education in the Southern States," *Biblical Recorder*, 8 Apr. 1835, 2.

28. Robert Ryland, "A Great Southern Theological School," *Southern Baptist*, 2 May 1849, 625.

Baptist Convention in April 1849 in answer to the call of Howell's 1847 Nashville meeting. Johnson's opening address urged the necessity of establishing a full-fledged theological seminary for Southern Baptist churches. The convention responded by adopting a report urging that a "General Baptist Theological Institution for the South" was a matter of "great importance" and authorizing South Carolina's delegates to enter fully any conferences on the matter.[29] James P. Boyce also supported the movement. He argued that the state funds for theological education could be transferred to a cooperative seminary, and that such a seminary would attract especially the "most pious and intelligent" students. Predictions of failure were premature, Boyce felt, since the venture had never been attempted.[30]

Delegates to the 1849 meeting of the Southern Baptist Convention in Charleston responded to the Nashville call by convening a special conference on theological education during the second and third days of the meeting. The convention adjourned early each day to permit delegates to hold the conference, and delegates held a third session on theological education after the convention's adjournment.[31] They held these conferences outside the sessions of the Southern Baptist Convention, undoubtedly to avoid unnecessary questions about whether it was proper or expedient for the Southern Baptist Convention to take responsibility for theological education. The convention was a missionary organization, and some delegates wanted to avoid encumbering it with any agencies beyond its foreign and home mission boards. Proposals that the convention establish a publication board, a Bible board, a Sunday school, and an Indian mission board faced similar opposition.[32]

At the first session of the conference on theological education, A. M. Poindexter submitted a resolution urging that "this meeting consider the establishment of a theological institution of a high order by Southern Baptists." The resolution provoked an "interesting and exciting debate," which continued the following afternoon.[33] Advocates of the scheme argued that Baptists should rise above local

29. South Carolina Baptist Convention, *Minutes*, 1849, 1–2.

30. James P. Boyce, "Central Theological Institution," *Southern Baptist*, 28 Mar. 1849, 602.

31. See unattributed, "Baptist Triennial Convention," *Charleston Mercury*, 25 May 1849, 2; ibid., 26 May 1849, 2; D. K. Whitaker, "Baptist Convention," *Charleston Courier*, 26 May 1849, 2; ibid., 29 May 1849, 2; Southern Baptist Convention, *Minutes*, 1849, 38. Whitaker signed his articles "W.," but he is identified in Southern Baptist Convention, *Minutes*, 1849, 43.

32. For some discussion of the issues here, see, e.g., William B. Johnson, "The North and South," *Biblical Recorder*, 9 May 1846, 2.

33. D. K. Whitaker, "Baptist Convention," *Charleston Courier*, 26 May 1849, 2. Whitaker gave no account of the substance of the discussion.

interests in order to advance the greater common good. I. S. Tinsley of Virginia argued that a great central seminary would have a commanding influence far greater than that of the colleges. It would also strengthen the bonds of denominational union. This was a grand enterprise that called for noble sacrifice of local interests to the benefit of the whole. "Southern Baptists wanted no petty institution," Tinsley said, "where theology was doled out in small and scanty quantities, but they wanted an institution of a broad, high, and liberal character, and one suited to the demands of an enlightened age. They wanted an institution of which they might be proud, and which might become a bond of union and strength for the several states of the South."[34]

Basil Manly Jr. agreed in a carefully prepared speech. He pointed out that the theological education provided at the colleges was inadequate and inefficient. The theology professors at the colleges had to teach every subject of theology, since the schools had only one or two professors. But a central seminary would bring together the best-qualified professors, and each one could concentrate his efforts in specific disciplines. Bringing students together would unite their affections as well as stimulate their natural competitiveness and promote greater effort. Theological education in the colleges was expensive, and a central seminary would provide it more economically. The enterprise would succeed if only the colleges would transfer their theological education endowments to the new seminary.[35]

J. B. Jeter, pastor of the Richmond, Virginia, First Baptist Church, however, expressed grave doubts about the possibility of success. Jeter asked, "Could conflicting local interests, which interfered with the plan proposed, be reconciled, so that without heart burnings anywhere, the thing could be really accomplished?" He thought it unlikely. The only hope for success was if South Carolina's Furman Theological Institute, Georgia's Mercer University, and Alabama's Howard College agreed to donate their theological education endowments to the new seminary. But Jeter surmised that none of these was "so well satisfied with the utility of the plan proposed that they would be willing to part with what was now their own."[36]

At the final session, members appointed the Committee on Ministerial Education to try to persuade at least two of the state schools to contribute their funds to establish a common seminary. The committee was asked to promote any promising scheme by which to accomplish this.[37] It contacted the trustees

34. Quoted in Whitaker, "Baptist Convention," 2.
35. Quoted in Whitaker, "Baptist Convention," 2.
36. Quoted in Whitaker, "Baptist Convention," 2.
37. Whitaker, "Baptist Convention," 2.

of the various colleges to determine whether their endowments for theological education could be combined.

The committee's efforts were unavailing. The South Carolina Baptist Convention pledged that it would "unite with our brethren of other states, in the founding of a theological institution, to be located at such place as may be determined upon by a convention of all the states willing to cooperate in the enterprise," but it made no definite proposal and did not commit to donate its endowment for theological education.[38] Georgia Baptists expressed similar interest in a cooperative effort but likewise made no definite commitments.[39] Overall the response from the various states was discouraging. Most conventions commended the idea in general, but no definite proposal emerged.[40] The committee concluded in its 1851 report that it was not possible to combine the theological departments of the colleges.[41]

Howell's 1847 call had elicited considerable support for a Southern Baptist seminary, but nothing came of it. The Baptist leaders of the various southern states agreed that the cause of Christ in the South veritably demanded that they establish such a seminary, but they lacked a plan that both promised success in establishing the school and protected the state colleges from injury. Perhaps more important, no leader took the matter in hand. R. B. C. Howell and William B. Johnson had exercised the chief leadership. Howell had convened the special conference in 1847 and pressed the case for united action at the 1849 conference at the Southern Baptist Convention annual meeting. Johnson publicly urged action on the matter and called the special conference of the 1849 South Carolina Baptist Convention. But neither Johnson nor Howell made it a matter of personal duty to accomplish the thing.

Most leaders seemed convinced that the enterprise could not succeed on any terms. Even Johnson, who supported the effort, was sure Southern Baptists would not do it. Just ten days before the called meeting of the South Carolina Baptist Convention, he told James Mims that the seminary effort would fail: "I have no thought of its succeeding. . . . I apprehend that the effort will prove abortive, and that each state, having a theological institution must work on for a time longer, till one or the other will overshadow the rest." The chief obstacles, Johnson noted, were the "rival jealousies of state feeling" arising from the fact that each state naturally protected its own efforts and

38. South Carolina Baptist Convention, *Minutes*, 1849, 7, 16.

39. Broadus, *Memoirs of Boyce*, 114; Georgia Baptist Convention, *Minutes*, 1849, 17.

40. See, e.g., Mississippi Baptist Convention, *Minutes*, 1849, 22–23.

41. J. F. Dagg, "Report of the Committee on Ministerial Education," *Christian Index*, 1 May 1851, 70.

interests in theological education.[42] Johnson was right about the obstacles to success. The remarkable leadership of James P. Boyce would soon change the outcome.

BOYCE'S BOLD PROPOSAL

In 1856 James Petigru Boyce emerged as the leader of a new effort to establish a Southern Baptist seminary. By the time of his election as professor of theology at Furman University in 1855, Boyce had concluded that it was his duty under God to do all in his power to establish the seminary. Had he known in advance the full measure of the trials and personal sacrifices he would feel required to undertake for the establishment and survival of the seminary, he would likely have recused himself. But without his leadership and sacrificial devotion, the seminary would have failed to be established or, once established, would have suffered extinction. His energy, wisdom, and determination overcame the many great obstacles and crises that threatened the seminary's existence. In 1856 it became apparent to most Southern Baptist leaders that God had providentially raised up Boyce for this purpose.

At the age of twenty-two Boyce had seen clearly that Johnson's called meeting of the state convention in 1849 would harm the effort, because it would appear that South Carolina was trying to predetermine the outcome of the 1849 conference in favor of making Furman the nucleus of the new seminary. The special convention would produce the impression, Boyce said, "that the Carolina delegation have caucused at Aiken for the purpose of saddling the Furman Institution upon the convention as a central institution for the South."[43]

When advocates of theological education initiated another effort to establish a Southern Baptist seminary in 1855, Boyce's vision and commitment quickly propelled him to the front. In 1855 various friends of theological education met the day after the adjournment of the annual meeting of the Southern Baptist Convention in Montgomery, Alabama. After free discussion regarding establishing a seminary, the assembly resolved that "the interests of the cause of truth" demanded that Southern Baptists "unite in establishing a theological

---

42. William B. Johnson to J. S. Mims, 14 Apr. 1849, William B. Johnson Papers, Special Collections, James B. Duke Library, Furman University.

43. James P. Boyce, "Extra Convention: Our Correspondent Countryman," *Southern Baptist*, 11 Apr. 1849, 612.

institution of high grade." They appointed Boyce to the committee charged with publicizing and promoting the cause, and called Baptist leaders to a similar meeting in Augusta the following year.[44]

The 1856 Augusta meeting afforded little encouragement. Sixty delegates enrolled. Two-thirds were from Georgia and South Carolina, though eight other states sent representatives. The presidents of Baptist colleges in Mississippi, Kentucky, South Carolina, Georgia, Tennessee, and North Carolina sent reports to the convention. Just as in 1849, the leaders of the colleges were not keen to support the establishment of a Southern Baptist seminary. In the end the convention accomplished little. It concluded that the task was "embarrassed by difficulties at every point." Robert Ryland of the University of Richmond wrote John A. Broadus that "the theological education convention in Georgia was a failure, at least nothing was done."[45] But that was not entirely accurate. To be sure, many left discouraged. But they agreed to make one more push. They called for another convention to meet in Louisville, Kentucky, in 1857, and asked the Baptist colleges and theology departments in each of the southern states to appoint delegates and to report what funds they held for theological education and whether such funds could be appropriated to the use of a seminary for the whole South.[46]

What Boyce accomplished on July 30, 1856, earned him the leadership of the seminary effort and stamped the date as one of the most important in the seminary's history. At his suggestion, South Carolina Baptists pledged $100,000 for the seminary's endowment, provided that all the other southern states jointly raised an equal amount.

When Boyce was ordained to the gospel ministry in 1851, Thomas Curtis asked him if he planned to make preaching his life's work. Boyce replied, "Yes, provided I do not become a professor of theology."[47] When Furman's trustees elected Boyce to the chair of theology in 1855, he had already committed himself to the goal of establishing a southern seminary. Boyce declined his election to the presidency of Mercer University in Georgia in 1857 for this reason.[48] He told his close friend H. A. Tupper that his plans were either to study in

---

44. *History of the Establishment*, 3–4.

45. Robert Ryland to John A. Broadus, 7 May 1856, box 1, Broadus Papers.

46. "History of the Establishment," 4–6.

47. Broadus, *Memoirs of Boyce*, 88.

48. "Report of the Board of Trustees of Mercer University," in Georgia Baptist Convention, *Minutes*, 1858, 15.

James P. Boyce

Europe or "the establishment of a Central Institution."[49] His friend J. P. Tustin reported that Boyce refused the Mercer presidency because it seemed "to him, at present, to militate against cherished plans, long since formed—labored during many years—and apparently now within his reach."[50] God had called Boyce to lead Southern Baptists to establish the Southern Baptist Theological Seminary.

When Boyce accepted the position at Furman, he had already participated in the 1855 conference on theological education in Montgomery. He offered the resolutions at the 1855 South Carolina Baptist Convention that induced them to appoint ten delegates to the next conference in Augusta in 1856.[51] But it was at the 1856 meeting of the South Carolina Baptist Convention that Boyce

49. James P. Boyce to H. A. Tupper, Feb. 1857, quoted in Broadus, *Memoir of Boyce*, 107.

50. J. P. Tustin, "Southern Baptist Theological Seminary," *Southern Baptist*, 22 Sept. 1857, 2.

51. South Carolina Baptist Convention, *Minutes*, 1855, 8–9, 14.

earned leadership of the entire Southern Baptist effort to establish a theological seminary.

At the 1856 meeting of the South Carolina Baptist Convention, E. T. Winkler reported that the Augusta meeting on theological education had made a plea for information and proposals, but he offered no motion or proposal for convention action on the matter. The convention appointed a committee to consider its response to the Augusta plea. The committee consisted of John B. O'Neall, South Carolina's leading Baptist layman and from 1859 South Carolina's chief justice, James C. Furman, president of Furman University, and James P. Boyce. Boyce was convinced that the committee should make a definite proposal that Furman University would give its endowment designated for theological education to the new seminary, and that South Carolina Baptists would raise $100,000 in total for the seminary's endowment, provided that Baptists in the other southern states raised an equal amount.

Boyce felt that if one state took up the burden in a courageous and generous initiative, the seminary could be established. Anything short of this would mean delay and failure. Furman believed that a central seminary for Southern Baptists would not succeed and that it was in several respects unwise. And he might naturally hesitate to favor a plan that would diminish his university's endowment by more than 40 percent.[52] Furman opposed Boyce's idea, and O'Neall agreed. Boyce could not persuade them. The committee's report included no proposal, so Boyce prepared a minority report.

When Furman and O'Neall presented the committee's majority report, Boyce moved the substitution of his minority report. The convention debated the issues posed by the alternative reports for all of Tuesday afternoon and much of Wednesday morning, and Boyce ultimately persuaded the convention to adopt his proposal.[53] The delegates agreed to donate Furman University's theological education endowment, worth about $26,000, and to raise an additional $74,000 in South Carolina, for a total of $100,000 toward the new seminary's endowment, provided that it be located in Greenville, South Carolina, and that the other southern states raised jointly an additional $100,000.[54]

52. James C. Furman to E. T. Winkler, ca. 1856, quoted in Harvey Toliver Cook, *The Life Work of James Clement Furman* (Greenville, SC: Alester G. Furman, 1926), 164–165.

53. J. P. Tustin, "South Carolina Baptist State Convention," *Southern Baptist*, 12 Aug. 1856, 2; South Carolina Baptist Convention, *Minutes*, 1856, 9.

54. South Carolina Baptist Convention, *Minutes*, 1856, 18–19. Soon afterward Furman and O'Neall apparently came to support the plan. Furman was a founding trustee of the seminary.

"THREE CHANGES IN THEOLOGICAL INSTITUTIONS"

The South Carolina Convention adopted Boyce's proposal at the end of the morning session on July 30, 1856. That evening Boyce gave his inaugural address as professor of theology at Furman University, titled "Three Changes in Theological Institutions." The trustees had the year before assigned Boyce to present his inaugural address at this time. It was the night before Furman's commencement exercises. The audience comprised Furman's faculty, trustees, graduating students, as well as many delegates to the state convention just adjourned. Boyce took this opportunity to propose the three fundamental principles that should frame the new seminary's organization. In the morning he had put the seminary movement on a solid financial and denominational footing. In the evening he presented the blueprint of its essential principles. The seminary movement had its undisputed leader.[55]

In the address Boyce argued that a theological seminary needed to secure three things. The first was a curriculum that permitted students at every level of educational preparation to study there. The second was a curriculum that permitted the ablest students to pursue advanced studies. The third was a confession of faith that determined the boundaries of acceptable belief among the faculty.

Boyce proposed the first change because he judged that Baptists' theological education had failed in its promise to provide an adequate ministry for the churches. The main reason was that traditional theological education assumed that a "classical education" at college was prerequisite to ministerial training. But few Southern Baptist pastors had attended college and could meet the prerequisites for theological instruction. Boyce proposed to admit students without regard to previous college work, and to combine them in the same classes. This meant that all theology students should take instruction based on the English version of the Bible and English-language texts. College graduates and other able students could take advanced courses in interpreting the Bible in Hebrew and Greek, and in studying theology using Latin-language texts. But for most courses necessary for theological training, all students, from the least educated to the most advanced, would take the same courses. "Let us abandon," Boyce urged, "the false principle" of requiring a "classical education" of Greek and Latin, and establish an "English course of study for those who have only been able to attain a plain English education." Boyce proposed adopting a curriculum that relied first on the Bible in English.[56]

---

55. James P. Boyce, *Three Changes in Theological Institutions* (Greenville, SC: C. J. Elford, 1856). The following day the trustees formally requested the publication of the address.

56. Boyce, *Three Changes*, 17–18.

He proposed the second change because he judged that Baptists' theological education did not produce scholars who were able to meet the needs of Baptists or of the Christian faith generally. In areas of biblical studies and church history, Baptists had depended on German scholarship, much of it based on a "defective standpoint." One evil this had produced was that scholars had "overlooked, ridiculed, and defamed" Baptists, alternately ignoring them or classing them among "fanatics and heretics." To answer this need, Boyce proposed two remedies. First, the theological school needed an extensive library that collected not only rare books from the past but also the most advanced scholarship of the present. Second, the school should provide for advanced study of one or two years after graduation for the study of such languages as Arabic and Syriac, or for original scholarship. If Baptists made such provisions in a theology school, Boyce predicted, "a band of scholars would go forth" to make valuable contributions to theological study and to the defense of distinctive Baptist principles.[57]

He proposed the third change because he believed that a "crisis in Baptist doctrine" was approaching. Years before, while visiting the Baptists of Culpepper and Rapahannock counties in Virginia, he judged that the "current of the people" was strongly toward Arminianism, and that Baptist preachers, though at the time still sound, "may become Arminians." The beliefs of a "large portion of the ministry and membership" of Baptist churches was "either very much unsettled or radically wrong."[58] The errors of Campbellism, of Arminianism, and of the idea that all doctrine is mere opinion prevailed increasingly. To protect the theological school from such errors, Boyce proposed that they should adopt a confession of faith. He urged the adoption of the confession of the Charleston Baptist Association, which was called the Philadelphia Confession of Faith and was essentially the same as the Second London Confession, publish by London Baptists in 1677 and 1689.[59]

BAPTISTS, CONFESSIONS, AND THE THIRD CHANGE

Boyce knew that some Baptists opposed the adoption of confessions of faith. The most formidable opponent was the president of Furman's board of trustees, William B. Johnson. Johnson had the leading role in the organization of the first Baptist state convention in America, the South Carolina Baptist Convention, in 1821. He also had the leading role in the organization of the Southern Baptist

---

57. Boyce, *Three Changes*, 25, 28–29, 31.
58. James P. Boyce, untitled, *Southern Baptist*, 18 Sept. 1850, 2.
59. Boyce, *Three Changes*, 34, 38.

Convention in 1845. Although Baptist churches and the local associations that the churches organized adopted confessions, neither state conventions nor the Southern Baptist Convention did so.

The main reason was that state conventions and the Southern Baptist Convention were primarily missionary "societies" whose members consisted of any individual, society, church, or association that contributed money.[60] William H. Stokes, editor of Georgia's *Christian Index*, argued in 1843 that since the "single purpose" of a missionary convention was "to send the gospel," the basis of union was on this single point. Agreement on other points was unnecessary.[61] J. J. Finch, corresponding secretary of the North Carolina Baptist Convention, explained in 1846 that doctrinal agreement was inexpedient for missionary conventions because its object was the practical business of saving sinners. A "difference in doctrinal sentiments" should pose no barrier to cooperation in this object. "All who are friendly to this object are invited to cooperate, and this they may do consistently whatever may be their speculative opinions."[62]

This society model of membership traditionally invited contributions from persons who belonged to no church but who sympathized with missionary aims. All donors were entitled to membership. Confessional subscription was inconsistent with this giving-based principle of membership. Besides, confessions already secured sound doctrine through their pervasive use in churches and associations.[63] The Baptist colleges associated with Baptist state conventions had not adopted confessions either.

Baptist churches and associations in America had adopted confessions of faith with few exceptions. The vast majority of Baptists in America were either Particular Baptists, who withdrew from English Puritanism in the seventeenth century, or Separate Baptists, who withdrew from New England Puritanism in the eighteenth century. Both groups used creeds widely, although some

60. The Southern Baptist Convention and the state conventions later revised their constitutions to admit churches only as members.

61. W. H. Stokes, untitled, *Christian Index*, 29 Apr. 1842, 265–266.

62. J. J. Finch, "Our State Convention, No. 3," *Biblical Recorder*, 5 Sept. 1846, 2.

63. William B. Johnson argued that the state convention needed no confession to assure the orthodoxy of Furman University in part because the professors were members of Baptist churches, and the churches belonged to the association, both of which guarded the professors' soundness: "They cannot long be immoral or heterodox without detection and removal." No confession for the convention or university was therefore necessary. Johnson, "No. 1: To the Baptists of South Carolina in General, and to the Constituents and Correspondents of the State Convention of the Denomination in Particular," *Southern Baptist*, 18 Oct. 1848, 510.

early Separate Baptists were not convinced of their necessity. It was against this uniform practice that Alexander Campbell aimed his efforts to reform Baptist churches. He attacked the Baptists for their use of creeds and for the Calvinist doctrine contained in them. He drew many Baptists to his views until Baptist churches and associations expelled Campbell and his followers in the 1830s. Campbell's followers became known as the Disciples of Christ and the Churches of Christ. Baptists reasserted the scriptural grounds for their adoption of confessions of faith.[64]

When Furman University's professor of theology James Mims came under accusation of heresy in the late 1840s, the role of confessions of faith entered the controversy. William B. Johnson, chairman of Furman's board of trustees and the most respected Baptist leader in South Carolina at the time, defended Mims's orthodoxy and opposed the use of confessions in the school. At the 1849 meeting of the South Carolina Baptist Convention, Johnson successfully vindicated Mims's orthodoxy, in large part by arguing against creeds. A. M. Poindexter asked the convention to state whether it agreed with Johnson's views. It did not. The convention resolved that it was free to adopt a confession if it saw fit.[65]

Poindexter was probably just as concerned about the proposed central seminary as about Furman, especially since many hoped to make Furman the foundation of the seminary. The controversy over Mims's orthodoxy demonstrated the great difficulty the denomination had enforcing orthodoxy among theology professors. Poindexter was undoubtedly concerned that Johnson's anticreedalism might spread. He wanted assurance that South Carolina Baptists approved the adoption of confessions, and especially that they would not oppose adopting a confession of faith for any proposed seminary. William B. Johnson, however, expressed alarm at this prospect. He wrote Mims that "Poindexter is of opinion, I understand, that a creed, and from your knowledge of his views, a pretty hyper creed, must be adopted previous to action."[66] Poindexter felt that without some creed to protect against theological error, Southern Baptists would not support a central seminary. Johnson felt that the creed would hinder support.

Boyce agreed with Poindexter and the South Carolina Baptist Convention but argued that the Bible effectively commanded the use of creeds. Although scripture did not explicitly authorize their adoption, it taught in many places that the church had an obligation to reject false doctrine and false teachers. To do this, every church must determine what scripture teaches as truth. The

64. See, e.g., Elkhorn Baptist Association, *Minutes*, 1830.

65. South Carolina Baptist Convention, *Minutes*, 1849, 6.

66. William B. Johnson to J. S. Mims, 8 Oct. 1849, William B. Johnson Papers, Special Collections, James B. Duke Library, Furman University.

adoption of a summary or "abstract" of scripture teaching, Boyce concluded, "is but the best means taken by the church to meet these obligations." Boyce argued impressively in support of the common practice of adopting creeds. There could be no objection to adopting one for the new seminary.

A seminary indeed had greater need to require agreement with a creed. Its professors shaped the "conceptions of the doctrines of the Bible" for ministers of the gospel. If its professors were sound and orthodox, it would be a powerful instrument for the "production of a sound ministry."[67] If the trustees required conscientious subscription to such an "abstract of doctrine," they would prevent unsound teachers from spreading corrupt doctrine through the graduates. The creed was necessary to safeguard the orthodoxy of the faculty. It did not apply to students.

It was also a matter of trust with donors. Trustees had a solemn duty to donors to assure that "the ministers that go forth have here learned to distinguish truth from error" and to propagate in the churches "the same precious truths of the Bible" that they held.[68] Those who founded the school by their exertions and donations by right expected that the school would maintain the principles on which they established it. Those who managed the institution effectively promised to keep those founding principles secure.

Furman's trustees already required that professors submit a statement of their textbooks and course plans for trustee approval, and that churches recommending scholarship beneficiaries hold to the Charleston Baptist Confession, a version of the 1689 Second London Confession. Boyce argued in "Three Changes" that such provisions were no longer sufficient to protect the orthodoxy of theology instructors. When South Carolina Baptists established Furman thirty years earlier, "the denomination was then fully agreed in its doctrinal sentiments." But since "unanimity of sentiment does not so extensively prevail" as formerly, and since professors began to rely as much on their own lectures as on textbooks for instruction, trustees needed to require professors to subscribe to a confession of faith. "Let subscription to it on the part of each theological professor be required as an assurance of his entire agreement with its views of doctrine, and of his determination to teach fully the truth which it expresses, and nothing contrary to its declarations." This was the most effective means of assuring that the school's professors taught "in agreement with the sentiments of its founders."[69]

67. Boyce, *Three Changes*, 35, 44.

68. Boyce, *Three Changes*, 44. See also James P. Boyce, "The Two Objections to the Seminary, V," *Christian Index*, 25 June 1874, 2.

69. Boyce, *Three Changes*, 37–38. Most of this passage was omitted without notice from the edition of *Three Changes* published in *James Petigru Boyce: Selected Writings*,

THE RESPONSE

The audience must have recognized that Boyce had reference to the new denominational seminary that he proposed establishing in Greenville rather than to Furman. William B. Johnson took it as a matter of course that Boyce's address related to the plan of instruction for the "common theological institution now before the community, should it be established."[70] The Furman trustees would, however, play a crucial role. Without their support, the enterprise could hardly succeed in Greenville. And unless they approved the donation of their endowment for theological education, Boyce could not expect to raise all of South Carolina's $100,000 pledge. Boyce asked the trustees to sacrifice their ambitions for Furman in order to establish one central theological seminary for all Southern Baptists.

A. M. Poindexter, secretary of the Southern Baptist Convention's Foreign Mission Board, called Boyce's address "the ablest thing of the kind he had ever heard." Francis Wayland called it the "first common sense discourse on theological education I have yet seen."[71] J. P. Tustin, editor of South Carolina's *Southern Baptist*, thought Boyce's two-hour address outstanding. He was aware of its wide ramifications and commended it as deserving special attention. He observed also that it made a "marked impression" on the audience. Furman's trustees took immediate steps to secure its publication.[72]

A few, however, were less impressed. William B. Johnson thought that the first two changes of the address were not changes at all. He believed that Furman had always permitted students to take a partial course in theology if they could not take the full course. Although Furman and some of the other southern colleges taught theology to those whose education fell short, their plan of instruction assumed that students had passed through a college course. Less prepared students were exceptions to be accommodated. Boyce envisioned a curriculum designed to include both kinds of students in the same classes.

Furman University, like most other Baptist colleges, aspired to offer a curriculum, library, and faculty adequate to producing "full and compete theologians,"

ed. Timothy George (Nashville, TN: Broadman Press, 1989), 52. There were several such omissions. Compare Boyce, *Three Changes*, 27–28, 37–38, 40, 44–45, with George, ed., *James Petigru Boyce*, 45, 52, 53, 56.

70. William B. Johnson to James C. Furman, 16 Jan. 1857, William B. Johnson Papers, Special Collections, James B. Duke Library, Furman University.

71. Poindexter and Wayland quoted in Timothy George, "Preface," in George, ed., *James Petigru Boyce*, [b].

72. J. P. Tustin, "Prof. Boyce's Address," *Southern Baptist*, 12 Aug. 1856, 3.

Johnson said, "as soon as means could be commanded."[73] But none possessed the means to do so. Johnson knew this and for this reason had long supported the effort to establish a denominational seminary for Southern Baptists. But his natural defensiveness about Furman exemplified the feelings of many state leaders throughout the South. They had labored and sacrificed to sustain the existence of their colleges. Their protectiveness led them to fear that the establishment of a seminary would harm their beloved colleges.

But theological education at the colleges had failed. Few students availed themselves of the theological instruction available in the colleges, and Baptist leaders complained of this state of affairs.[74] By Boyce's count, sixty Southern Baptist students were enrolled in theological education in 1857, but only fifteen of them were in the colleges' theological departments. The other forty-five were attending seminaries in the North, or Presbyterian seminaries in the South.[75] The colleges were teaching liberal arts and very little theology.

But securing broad cooperation proved as difficult as it had in 1849. Joseph Walker, editor of Georgia's *Christian Index*, predicted in 1857 that regardless of the desirability of a Southern Baptist seminary, state loyalties would prevent Southern Baptists from uniting behind it. The "colleges that impart a partial course of theological instruction" would not, Walker wrote "relinquish these privileges with the funds created for that purpose." Even if the seminary gained sufficient support to open its doors, Walker doubted that it would "live" for long, since it would not attract a sufficient number of students. The "noble enterprise," Walker wrote, lacked feasibility. The state colleges would "plod along with the partial course" in theology.[76]

BOYCE'S PROPOSAL ADOPTED

When the theological educational convention met in Louisville in 1857, the first order of business was whether or not to accept the South Carolina proposal. In the end the South Carolina proposal was so generous that it forestalled alternatives and overwhelmed opposition.[77] No other state presented a proposal. The

73. William B. Johnson to James C. Furman, 16 Jan. 1857, William B. Johnson Papers, Special Collections, James B. Duke Library, Furman University.

74. See, e.g., Georgia Baptist Convention, *Minutes*, 1857, 9.

75. James P. Boyce, "Address of Rev. J. P. Boyce at Hampton," *Religious Herald*, 1 July 1858, 1.

76. Joseph Walker, "The Southern Theological Institution," *Christian Index*, 28 Jan. 1857, 14.

77. The delegation from the Georgia Baptist Convention apparently planned to present a proposal but, in view of the South Carolina proposal, withheld it. See *History of the Establishment*, 12.

delegates unanimously adopted the proposal. South Carolina Baptists carried the day by largesse.

The vote to approve the South Carolina proposal was without opposition, despite that fact that Landmark leader James R. Graves opposed it. Graves was quickly becoming one of the most influential Southern Baptist leaders, and the most notorious among them. Basil Manly Sr. judged that God had answered their prayers in the most wonderful way in bringing the delegates to one mind in support of the South Carolina plan: "God's hand was in it. Graves made every effort in private and made some loud and noisy efforts in public to prevent action, to distract counsels, but at last he was powerless, as limber as a rag— overborne and conquered. When it was done, I said a few words and we all knelt and bowed down and worshiped. I prayed and all wept. And what was my surprise before I could rise erect to find Graves grasping my hand and saying that he wanted to take it once, at least, before we unite in heaven." This dis-play of Graves's goodwill, as much as anything else that occurred, convinced Manly that "the hand of God has been signally manifest."[78] Most state con-ventions expressed approval of the plan for the seminary and pledged their cooperation.[79]

The 1857 theological education convention appointed three committees whose work would be critical to the success of the school. The most important was the Committee on the Plan of Organization, consisting of James P. Boyce, John A. Broadus, Basil Manly Jr., E. T. Winkler, and William Williams. The rest were, like Boyce, young, but all had experience in higher education. Basil Manly Sr. appointed these gifted younger men deliberately for this new ven-ture in theological education, explaining: "These young men have got to do the work—and let them draw the plans. We will be there, when they report, to cor-rect them if they are wrong."[80] Naturally Boyce was chairman. Everyone seemed to agree that the undeniable indications of divine providence pointed to Boyce as the man. As a matter of course the convention turned to Boyce. It pinned its hopes for the new seminary on him.

When the 1858 education convention met in Greenville, it soon became apparent that Boyce had been the right choice. As chairman of the Committee on the Plan of Organization, he presented the committee's report. Its proposals

---

78. Basil Manly Sr. to Sarah Manly, 9 May 1857, Manly Collection of Manuscripts, reel 1, SBTS.

79. See, e.g., Baptist General Association of Virginia, *Minutes*, 1857, 21; Mississippi Baptist Convention, *Minutes*, 1857, 6; North Carolina Baptist Convention, *Minutes*, 1857, 14.

80. Basil Manly Sr. to Sarah Manly, 9 May 1857, Manly Collection of Manuscripts, reel 1, SBTS; Broadus, *Memoirs of Boyce*, 148.

received careful attention and extensive discussion. With some amendments, the report met enthusiastic approval.

The report had been a daunting undertaking. The committee had to propose the seminary's curriculum, its confession of faith, and its plan of government. The proposal needed to impress the denomination with its soundness, wisdom, and practicality. Any missteps at the start would undermine denominational support of the seminary. And without highest confidence among Baptists, it would prove impossible to raise the endowment.

The convention made several important changes to the committee's report. The committee named the school the Greenville Theological Seminary. At the recommendation of J. P. Tustin, the convention altered it to the Southern Baptist Theological Seminary.[81]

CURRICULUM

The new curriculum introduced three significant innovations in theological education at that time. The first was the elective system. The second was the mixing of college and noncollege men in the same courses. The third was the reliance on the English Bible, rather than the Bible in the original Hebrew and Greek, to provide a thorough grounding in exegesis and interpretation of the Bible.

Boyce's vision, as delineated in his inaugural address, advocated one curriculum for all students who had at least a common school education. College graduates and noncollege men would enroll in the same courses, with the same requirements and expectations. Other seminaries did not place noncollege men in the same curriculum with college graduates and did not admit noncollege men to the theological curriculum. John A. Broadus proposed a curriculum that embodied Boyce's vision.

When Boyce gathered his committee members together upon their appointment in Louisville in May 1857, Broadus suggested that the curriculum structure of the University of Virginia could provide for the "apparently difficult matter of uniting all grades of theological students in the same institution."[82] So Boyce asked Broadus to propose a curriculum for the committee to consider. Boyce sent Broadus a plan of the theological curriculum he had sketched out

81. "Report of the Committee on the Plan of Organization," convention draft, in the container "Charters and Fundamental Articles of the Southern Baptist Theological Seminary," SBTS.

82. Broadus, *Memoirs of Boyce*, 150.

John A. Broadus

two years earlier and expressed his confidence in Broadus's ideas: "I think you can gather enough of my ideas here to judge as to our substantial agreement."[83] Broadus developed his vision for accomplishing Boyce's aims into an innovative elective system of theological education.

The committee agreed that "the chief object of this seminary is to prepare its students for the most effective service as preachers of the gospel and pastors of the churches." Though they made provision for the most advanced scholarship possible among the most intellectually capable students, the committee members pledged to direct their main efforts to preparing preachers and pastors.[84] Baptists agreed widely that God called men of different degrees of educational preparation and of widely different intellectual gifts. They believed that a divine call, sound scriptural beliefs, and giftedness in preaching were the fundamental prerequisites. To require also a college or seminary degree was unscriptural.

83. Archibald T. Robertson, *Life and Letters of John Albert Broadus* (Philadelphia: American Baptist Publication Society, 1901), 142.
84. *History of the Establishment*, 27.

Many Baptists nevertheless valued education for their ministers. Pastors especially felt the importance of education to their task. Baptists therefore established schools primarily to provide education for men whom God had called to the ministry of the gospel. But they had difficulty devising an effective curriculum. God did not seem to call very many college graduates, as there were few enough of them among Southern Baptists. He called many men of more modest education, and not a few whose education was starkly deficient. Although Baptist colleges were committed to training all the preachers who came, they had adopted the same model as the Presbyterians and Congregationalists, who required college education, replete with reading knowledge of Greek and Latin, before admission to a theological course. Those who could not meet this requisite first had to complete a college course. Those unready for college had to complete an "academy" course and a college course in order to begin theological studies. Such "preparatory" students often outnumbered the theological students. Such was the case at Furman in the 1840s, where the professors had theological education as "their primary duty," Professor James C. Furman wrote, but where the number of students "preparing for the theological course has been greater than the number of those actually engaged in that course."[85] If the college prerequisite was relaxed, the theology curriculum had to double, for the theology professors had to teach the same subject to an advanced class of college graduates and to a remedial class without the benefit of college training. This arrangement, Boyce felt, fostered jealousy and alienation among the ministers-in-training.

The committee met the first week of August 1857, though only Boyce, Broadus, and Manly attended. Boyce knew from experience the curriculum at Princeton, and Manly knew that of both Newton and Princeton. Broadus had studied the catalogs of various theological seminaries and proposed adapting the "elective" approach that he had known at the University of Virginia to the needs of theological education. After much discussion and some emendations, the committee approved Broadus's plan.[86]

Boyce wanted students of every level of preparation to study together in the same classes, and Broadus suggested that the elective system would achieve that end. It was an elective system not in the twentieth-century sense in which students chose from many courses, but in the sense that students could choose which departments of the curriculum they would pursue. It was a plan, Broadus wrote, that was "adapted to the best qualified students," while at the same time

---

85. James C. Furman, "To the Baptists of South Carolina," *Southern Baptist*, 24 Apr. 1850, 1.

86. Broadus, *Memoir of Boyce*, 150–151; Robertson, *Life and Letters of Broadus*, 144.

making provision for "those whose time, preparation, taste, etc.," induced them to select only certain subjects or pursue them only to a certain extent.[87]

The curriculum was divided into eight departments or "schools." Five schools offered one course each: Biblical Introduction, Polemic Theology and Apologetics, Preparation and Delivery of Sermons, Church History, and Church Government and Pastoral Duties. Three schools offered two courses each. The school of Interpretation of the Old Testament had a course based on study of the English text of the Bible, and a course based on study of the Hebrew and Aramaic texts. The school of Interpretation of the New Testament similarly had one course based on study of the English text and one based on study of the Greek text. And the school of Systematic Theology had a course in which students read English works in systematic theology and another course in which they read Latin works.

To satisfy the aims of combining college and noncollege men, the curriculum relied on instruction in the English Bible for the principal study of Old and New Testament. Other seminaries taught their courses on the books of the Bible using the Hebrew Old Testament and the Greek New Testament; they therefore required knowledge of Greek and Hebrew for admission to Bible courses. Since God inspired the authors of the original texts, who wrote in Hebrew, Aramaic, or Greek, Bible teachers were best equipped to interpret the inspired text if they knew those languages. To introduce the study of the Bible in English seemed to threaten the commitment to learn the ancient languages of the Bible. But Boyce, Broadus, and Manly saw that this requirement was impractical and inefficient, at least for Baptists. They required "full graduates" to pass the courses in the original languages, but their core Bible courses for all students relied on the Bible in English.

The seminary's curriculum in the English Bible became well known in theological education. Other seminaries acknowledged the success of the scheme and adopted it themselves. Students found the courses invaluable. One great advantage of the English courses was that students gained familiarity with the meaning and interpretive issues for the entire Old Testament and New Testament. The Hebrew Old Testament courses and the Greek New Testament courses could not in two years take students through the entire Bible in those languages.[88]

Students of different grades studied the Bible together in English, but students with college training and those with ability and ambition took also the courses in Greek New Testament, Hebrew Old Testament, and Latin theology. Because

87. *History of the Establishment*, 27.
88. Broadus, *Memoir of Boyce*, 158.

of the self-selection in these courses, students accomplished more thorough study than would have been possible if classes comprised also students who took them merely to fill curricular requirements.[89] This system meant that only the most ambitious students undertook the entire curriculum. Large numbers of students in the early years stayed for only one year and graduated in a few schools only.

The academic year or session was eight months long, with each course extending over the entire session. At the end of each session, students received diplomas in each school in which they received a passing grade. Those who graduated in each of the schools, typically a three-year endeavor, received a "general diploma" and earned the title of full graduate.

The curriculum required that standards for passing each course were generally high. Following the example of the University of Virginia, the seminary held to examination periods each year, lasting two weeks or more. "Intermediate examinations" occurred in December and January, and final examinations in May. The examinations lasted eight to ten hours each, which "usually occupies the students closely from early morning till toward sunset, or after."[90] The Senior Greek examination in 1878 went eight hours, David G. Lyon reported, but it was not enough time, as "many of the students did not finish the questions."[91] Some schools added an oral examination. Only in 1908 did the seminary move to quarterly exams of two hours each, which reduced the examination period to four days.[92] Many students failed the examinations. In A. T. Robertson's Junior Greek examination for 1898, more than one-third of the forty-two students failed.[93]

The faculty felt that the curriculum succeeded remarkably in achieving Boyce's goals. Men of different qualifications sat side by side in the same lecture hall, had the same recitation requirements, and sat for the same examinations. Those who were less prepared learned that hard work produced results—and that college preparation was a great advantage. The requirement of graduating in every school for a full diploma excited ambition to take advantage of the full curriculum. The rigor of the examinations prevented the better students from trying to undertake too much and stimulated all students to the hard work necessary to graduate.[94]

89. Broadus, *Memoir of Boyce*, 159.

90. Basil Manly Jr., untitled, *Southern Baptist*, 24 Apr. 1868, 2.

91. David G. Lyon, Diary 1878–1879, 10 Jan. 1878, box 6, David Gordon Lyon Papers, Harvard University Archives.

92. W. J. McGlothlin to W. O. Carver, 4 Dec. 1907, W. O. Carver Papers, SBHLA.

93. W. D. Bolton, "Seminary Notes," *Baptist Argus*, 10 Mar. 1898, 312.

94. Broadus, *Memoir of Boyce*, 160–161.

THE ABSTRACT OF PRINCIPLES

Boyce urged the adoption of a confession of faith to bind the seminary to evangelical Baptist orthodoxy. The seminary would have tremendous influence in shaping the denomination's doctrine. Boyce designed it to serve for the promotion of traditional evangelical orthodoxy and for the "maintenance of Baptist principles."[95] By adopting a confession, Boyce argued, the faculty would assure Southern Baptists that their teaching was orthodox and Baptist. Boyce was determined to establish a denominational school. He had no interest in establishing a seminary under private control or serving private interests. He felt that integrity and honesty demanded nothing less. He wanted also to afford a guarantee to donors that their money would be spent in accordance with their desires.

The difficulty was how high to pitch the confession. If it were too broad in its prescriptions, many would refuse to support the seminary because it erected insufficient safeguards against false doctrine. If it were too narrow, it would exclude the views of some Southern Baptists and discourage their support. But it needed to safeguard all essential points of both Christian doctrine and Baptist practice.

In 1874 Boyce described the three principles that had guided both the committee and the convention in drafting the confession:

> The abstract of principles must be: 1. A complete exhibition of the fundamental doctrines of grace, so that in no essential particular should they speak dubiously; 2. They should speak out clearly and distinctly as to the practices universally prevalent among us; 3. Upon no point, upon which the denomination is divided, should the convention, and through it the seminary, take any position.... The doctrines of grace are therefore distinctly brought out in the abstract of principles. No less true is this of Baptist practices.... While, however, it was deemed essential to avow distinctly and unreservedly the sentiments universally prevalent among us, both as to doctrine and practice, it was equally important that upon those questions upon which there was still a difference of opinion among Southern Baptists, the seminary articles should not bind the institution.[96]

95. James P. Boyce, "The Two Objections to the Seminary, II," *Western Recorder*, 18 Apr. 1874, 2.

96. James P. Boyce, "The Two Objections to the Seminary, V," *Christian Index*, 25 June 1874, 2.

Basil Manly Jr.

Manly's task, as the committee reported, involved "extreme delicacy and difficulty."[97] Manly needed to draft a statement that comprehended the affirmations important to virtually all the regular Baptists. The confession needed to be specific and definite enough to secure the integrity of all the "essential doctrines held among us." It also needed to avoid affirming teachings on which Baptists tolerated differences.

Manly wrote that he had relied primarily on the two earliest confessions of the English Calvinistic Baptists. "My notion is to make a brand new one but with a historical basis, drawing it up as far as is possible in the language of our oldest—which dates from 1643 [1644], and where this will not do, in that of 1689, which is mainly copied from the Westminster, but abridging both, and getting down to an essence."[98]

97. "Report of the Committee on the Plan of Organization," convention draft, 8, in the container "Charters and Fundamental Articles of the Southern Baptist Theological Seminary," SBTS.

98. Basil Manly Jr. to [Charles Manly], 1 Mar. 1858, Basil Manly Papers, Southern Historical Collection, no. 486, Manuscripts Dept., Library of the University of North Carolina, Chapel Hill, microfilm. Joseph P. Cox incorrectly identified the letter as addressed to James P. Boyce ("A Study of the Life and Work of Basil Manly Jr.," Th.D.

The 1689 confession was the more popular of the two in America. Calvinist Baptists in London developed the confession by adapting it from the Westminster Confession of Faith to Baptist views. In the decades after the Great Awakening, Baptists in America grew rapidly, and the vast majority were Calvinistic and evangelical. The Second London Confession expressed well their views. The first two Baptist associations in America adopted it, the Philadelphia Baptist Association no later than 1746 and the Charleston Baptist Association in 1752. Most Baptist associations, and the churches composing them, adopted it or a shorter abstract of it.

Even among the majority Calvinists, some differences were tolerated. A significant minority adopted the distinctive doctrines of the New Divinity, a set of revisions of Calvinism developed by the followers of Jonathan Edwards in New England between about 1750 and 1830. New Divinity teachers rejected the traditional view that Christ's death was a penal substitution in which Jesus bore the penalty required of sinners in their place. They held instead a moral government theory of the atonement in which Jesus suffered as a testimony of the dignity and holiness of God's law, and as a vindication of the righteousness of his moral government of the universe. New Divinity teachers also rejected the traditional Calvinist teaching that God imputed Adam's sin to his posterity and Christ's righteousness to believers. God did not punish anyone for another's sin, they taught, nor did he forgive sinners for someone else's righteousness, for neither act would be just. Several South Carolina Baptist leaders held New Divinity views, most prominently William B. Johnson and Edwin S. Mims. When James Reynolds led an effort to have such views declared heretical, the majority of the state's leaders affirmed their tolerance of such teachings and retained their fellowship with Johnson and Mims. Manly's draft affirmed Calvinist orthodoxy but left room for belief in general atonement and the New Divinity.

The Abstract went through several drafts. Manly hoped to have his first draft by August 1857, but when he, Boyce, and Broadus met in Richmond to submit their preliminary reports to each other, Manly evidently had little to report—he had not found time to do the work. In February 1858 Manly invited Broadus to come down to Richmond to spend a week with him so they could work on their assignments together: "If you will come down, we can have a chat about our work committed to us—that creed, schedule of theological studies, etc. I can't go to work at it, till I feel I have got it to do, because there is nearly always something else pressing. . . . I need the 'firecoal on my back' and if you'll come

dissertation, Southern Baptist Theological Seminary, 1954, 146). See also Manly's preamble to the Abstract of Principles, "Report of the Committee on the Plan of Organization," convention draft, 8, SBTS.

down, and spend a week with me, we can spend the time pleasantly, and do our work besides."[99] Broadus apparently did not go. On March 1, 1858, Manly told his brother Charles that he finally found time to work on the confession and had gotten as far as the doctrine of the fall before he had to stop.[100] Nearly two months later he told Boyce that he still needed a few more days to complete the creed.[101] Manly submitted his draft to the criticism of three Richmond Baptist leaders, J. B. Jeter, A. M. Poindexter, and Robert Ryland, adopted some of their suggestions, and sent it to Boyce barely ten days before the committee was scheduled to meet in Greenville to make final revisions to their reports.[102]

The committee, Boyce, Broadus, Williams, Winkler, and Manly, met at Boyce's residence at the end of April 1858. They invited A. M. Poindexter to join them in their deliberations. Boyce had prepared and printed galley sheets of the initial drafts of the three subcommittee reports. They discussed and revised the reports for two or three days.[103] Boyce then took the revised draft to the printer to produce clean working copies of the full committee's final report for distribution to the entire education convention.[104]

99. Basil Manly Jr. to John A. Broadus, 15 Feb. 1858, attached to ms. of "Life and Letters of John A. Broadus," box 6, Robertson Papers.

100. Basil Manly Jr. to [Charles Manly], 1 Mar. 1858, Basil Manly Papers, Southern Historical Collection, no. 486, UNC, microfilm.

101. Basil Manly Jr. to James P. Boyce, 13 Apr. 1858, box 1, Boyce Papers.

102. Basil Manly Jr. to Charles Manly, 20 Apr. 1858, Basil Manly Papers, Southern Historical Collection, no. 486, UNC, microfilm; Basil Manly Jr. to John A. Broadus, 20 Apr. 1858, box 1, Broadus Papers.

103. On Thursday, 29 Apr., the committee met until two o'clock in the morning. It may have met also on the morning of 30 Apr. The convention opened at 11:00 A.M. on 30 Apr. See Basil Manly Sr. to [Sarah Manly], 30 Apr. 1858, Manly Collection of Manuscripts, microfilm, reel 1, SBTS.

104. Two drafts survive in proofsheets, the initial "committee draft" that Boyce had printed for the Committee on the Plan of Instruction, and the final "convention draft" that the committee presented to the convention itself. The committee draft included the three subcommittee reports: Boyce on the "general regulations" and "fundamental laws," Broadus on the "plan of organization," and Manly on the "abstract of principles." The changes made by the full Committee on the Plan of Organization can be deduced by comparing the committee draft to the later convention draft. The changes made by the entire convention are reflected in the handwritten editorial marks, often including the name of the person who moved the emendation. The drafts are among the copies of the "Report of the Committee on the Plan of Organization" in the container "Charters and Fundamental Articles of the Southern Baptist Theological Seminary," Archives and Special Collections, James P. Boyce Centennial Library, SBTS. There may have been additional drafts that did not survive, between the initial committee draft and the final

The Committee on the Plan of Instruction then presented its report to the education convention's forty-two delegates, who discussed and revised the report for most of four days.[105] Basil Manly Sr. reported that the delegates had a "vast amount" of "earnest and sharp" discussion on the various parts of the constitution and "articles of belief."[106]

The committee and the convention made relatively few changes to Manly's draft, but they spent a long time discussing each point and adopted a number of revisions. Some of the revisions reflected a concern to preempt the two most common objections to Calvinist theology: that it made God unjust and that it destroyed human freedom. William Williams, a member of the committee and afterward elected to the faculty, noted in his theology lectures that these were the only objections that Calvinism faced: "It seems inconsistent with free agency and consequently with man's responsibility," and "it seems inconsistent with the goodness and justice of God."[107] The delegates struggled to include statements to address these two objections.

This was an intrinsic difficulty with short statements of doctrine. The confession's individual articles must be brief and compact, but they must be so precise that they are not easily misunderstood. The confession's articles on God's providence and on the fall could easily be misunderstood to deny human responsibility, and thus implicitly to charge God with injustice in condemning sinners to hell. The convention adopted changes to the articles on providence and on the fall in an effort to prevent such misreadings.

Manly's draft of the article on the doctrine of providence asserted God's sovereignty over all things and included the qualifications necessary to maintain God's justice and human responsibility: "God, from eternity, hath willed all things that come to pass, and perpetually upholds, directs, and governs all creatures and all events; and yet so as not in any wise to be the author or approver of sin, nor to destroy the free will and responsibility of intelligent creatures." The committee adopted this wording after dropping the word "hath." But the convention wanted more precision. Some delegates worried apparently that if

---

convention draft. Three decades afterward, Manly remembered three or four revised drafts. Basil Manly Jr., "The Beginnings of the History of the Seminary [second part]," *Seminary Magazine* 5 (1892): 208–209.

105. For an account of the proceedings of the convention and the full text of the report as adopted by the convention, see "Southern Theological Convention," *Southern Baptist*, 11 May 1858, 2–3.

106. Basil Manly Sr. to [Sarah Manly], 30 Apr. 1858, Manly Collection of Manuscripts, microfilm, reel 1, SBTS.

107. William Williams, quoted in George J. Hobday, Systematic Theology Notes, William Williams, 1872–1873, 64–65, George J. Hobday Student Notebooks, 1872–1874, WFU.

God "willed" all things, it could imply that God accomplished even the sinful acts of humans by his direct agency, which would contradict the article's affirmation of God's goodness and human freedom. The convention finally adopted Boyce's suggested phrasing that God "decrees or permits" all things that come to pass. The new phrasing upheld God's complete sovereignty but suggested the traditional distinction between God's agency as the final cause and human agency as the efficient cause. John L. Dagg, whose *Manual of Theology* Boyce assigned as a textbook, taught that "God exercises a perfect control over every sinful agent in all his acts," but he distinguished between "God's permission of sin" and "his being the efficient cause of it."[108] William Williams similarly taught students that "God is immediately and directly controlling and governing all events and actions," including "sinful actions," yet the Bible taught that God "permits them."[109]

More troublesome in this regard was the article concerning "the fall of man." The delegates struggled to squeeze all the elements of human depravity into a compact statement. They were agreed on the doctrine of total depravity, that the fall resulted in the guilt and thorough corruption of every human being. But the delegates seemed concerned to affirm that Adam introduced sin, not God, and that even though fallen humans were born with corrupt natures, God was just in condemning them.

Manly's draft was clear enough on depravity: fallen humans "are now conceived in sin, and by nature children of wrath, opposite to all good, servants of sin, and subjects of death and other miseries in this world, and forever, unless the Lord Jesus set them free." Manly only alluded to the original goodness of God's creative act. And his statement on depravity so emphasized the sinner's helpless corruption that it could imply that God condemned sinners for Adam's sin only, and not for their own.

The committee was dissatisfied and rewrote the article almost entirely. The new draft introduced a statement that "God originally created man in his own image," changed "our first parents . . . fell" to "man . . . fell," and summarized Manly's longer statement on depravity by explaining that Adam's posterity were "conceived in sin, and under the condemnation of the law, indisposed to good, and wholly inclined to evil." The revision made clear that God created humanity good, but it omitted any statement of fallen human's individual responsibility for their sinful actions.

108. John L. Dagg, *Manual of Theology* (Charleston, SC: Southern Baptist Publication Society, 1857), 131–132.

109. William Williams, quoted in George J. Hobday, Systematic Theology Notes, William Williams, 1872–1873, 73–75, George J. Hobday Student Notebooks, 1872–1874, WFU.

The convention rejected the committee's revised statement and adopted instead the statement of a seven-person committee appointed to revise it. It rephrased the statement on depravity without weakening it, and notably added a statement of individual responsibility for sin: Adam's posterity "inherit a nature corrupt and wholly opposed to God and his law, are under condemnation, and as soon as they are capable of moral action, become actual transgressors."

Other revisions reflected the convention's concern to accommodate the various hues of Calvinism existing in the southern churches. These differences were confined almost entirely within the doctrine of the atonement. Many held to particular redemption, the traditional view of English-speaking Calvinists that Christ's death on the cross satisfied God's wrath and made propitiation for the sins of the elect only. Others understood the atonement as a "general provision," intrinsically sufficient to make propitiation for the sins of all persons, but intended by Christ for the elect alone and therefore effective for them only. This view had some variations and was associated with the teachings of the English Baptist leader Andrew Fuller. Both of these views had large numbers of adherents among Southern Baptists. Some leaders argued that there was no significant difference between the two views other than the terminology employed to express them. A. M. Poindexter, who had criticized Manly's first draft in Richmond and participated in the revisions of the Committee on the Plan of Organization before the convention met, held to a general atonement.

But there was one other view prevailing among Southern Baptists, the New Divinity notion of a universal atonement based on a "moral government" view of Christ's death. Timothy Dwight's *Theology Explained and Defended* taught the New Divinity view of the atonement and was popular among Baptists. Two prominent Southern Baptists held this view, William B. Johnson and Edwin Mims, Boyce's predecessor at Furman. Johnson was a delegate at the education convention.[110]

Manly's draft statement attempted to accommodate the moral government view, even though the First and Second London Confessions taught a limited atonement. As presented to the committee, Manly's draft of the article on "the Mediator" made no explicit distinction between the two approaches. It

110. See A. M. Poindexter, "The Imputation of Sin to Christ," *Baptist Preacher* 9 (1850): 179–192; William Williams, quoted in Hobday, Systematic Theology Notes, 130 ("There are some who are Calvinists on all other points who hold to this universal atonement, e.g., Dr. A. M. Poindexter"); William B. Johnson, "On Imputation," *Southern Baptist*, 7 Mar. 1849, 590; Johnson, "On Imputation, No. V," *Southern Baptist*, 4 Apr. 1849, 606–607; Johnson, *Love Characteristic of the Deity: A Sermon Preached before the Charleston Baptist Association, Monday, November 4, 1822* (Charleston: W. Riley, 1823), 16–21.

did not define the extent of atonement or distinguish its character between the traditional penal substitution view and the New Divinity moral government view.[111] It said only that Jesus "suffered and died upon the cross for the salvation of all who believe in him." But in the context of traditional Baptist views, it rather suggested the doctrine of limited atonement. It seemed to say that Christ's intention was to die for the elect only. The committee changed "for the salvation of all who believe in him" to "for the salvation of sinners." The new phrase more effectively included both limited and general atonement views.

The article on election was traditional and went through both the committee and the convention unchanged. It read: "Election is God's eternal choice of some persons unto everlasting life—not because of foreseen merit in them, but of his mere mercy in Christ—in consequence of which choice they are called, justified, and glorified." The article on the fall affirmed total depravity. The article on regeneration affirmed effectual calling, or what is now known as "irresistible grace." In regeneration, the Abstract said, the Holy Spirit gave life to those who were "dead in trespasses and sin" and "enlightened" their minds "savingly" as a "work of God's free and special grace alone." And the Abstract affirmed the doctrine of the perseverance of the saints. It was a comprehensive statement of Southern Baptist Calvinist doctrine that included the traditional Calvinism, the general provisionist Calvinism, and the New Divinity Calvinism's moral government view of the atonement. In the terminology of TULIP, an acronym of the five points of Calvinism affirmed by the Dutch Church's 1619 Synod of Dort, this was four-point Calvinism.

The delegates considered these affirmations important for many reasons, first and foremost because they affirmed the central truths of salvation according to the Bible. These were, moreover, points that Baptists had been forced to defend against the Methodists, Campbellites, and Free Will Baptists. These doctrines separated Southern Baptists from these churches.

---

111. The article on justification, both in the two drafts and in its final form, spoke of "the satisfaction that Christ has made," which could comprehend either a penal substitution view or a satisfaction view of the atonement. Proponents of the moral government theory held that the atonement was in some sense a satisfaction rendering sufficient honor to God's holy law so that he could forgive sins without any punishment. There is no evidence of objection to the term, and it was broad enough to encompass the several theories prevailing among Southern Baptists. Johnson apparently urged some of his New Divinity views at the convention—Basil Manly Sr. noted that Johnson spoke to almost every issue, but that he seemed to carry no "weight" in the convention. In any case, Manly and the rest seemed content to comprehend some New Divinity views in the abstract (Basil Manly Sr. to Sarah Manly, 3 May 1858, Manly Collection of Manuscripts, reel 1, SBTS).

The revisions reflected concern with another critical area, ecclesiology. Baptists believed that the various aspects of ecclesiology had been revealed in scripture and that they were bound as disciples of Christ to implement them. The Abstract thus affirmed such Baptist beliefs as congregational church government, baptism by immersion of those only who professed faith, and the Lord's Supper as "designed to commemorate" Jesus' death, "confirm" the faith of believers, and be a "bond, pledge, and renewal" of communion with Christ and of their church fellowship. Baptists believed that the Bible taught and required these things. These practices were the distinctive Baptist principles that separated Baptists in varying degrees from other evangelical denominations.

The most controversial practice of Baptists, for most other denominations, was known as "close communion." It was a simple doctrine: only baptized persons were eligible to participate in the Lord's Supper. It was controversial because Baptists held that the immersion of professing believers was alone baptism. Because the Greek word *baptizein* meant "to immerse," by definition sprinkling and pouring were not baptism. And because only those who professed repentance and faith in Christ were proper subjects of baptism, applying water by any form to infants was not baptism. Baptists therefore viewed Methodist, Presbyterian, Episcopalian, Lutheran, and Congregationalist believers as unbaptized. They could not therefore invite them to participate in the Lord's Supper.

Manly's draft stated this principle indirectly by affirming that baptism was "prerequisite to church fellowship," and that the Lord's Supper was, in part, a "renewal" of their "communion" with one another. The committee and the convention opted for a more explicit statement: baptism "is prerequisite to church fellowship and to participation in the Lord's Supper." They also made it more explicit in the article on the Lord's Supper, changing "renewal of their communion . . . with one another" to "renewal . . . of their church fellowship."

But ecclesiology also divided the denomination. James R. Graves's Landmark movement among Southern Baptists would soon insist on the notion that the Bible never taught that there was any such thing as a universal or spiritual or invisible church. The word "church," wherever used in the New Testament, meant a local, organized, visible church. The Abstract in all drafts insisted on the biblical character of the local church's membership, worship, and government—Christ commanded all believers "to associate themselves" into "particular" churches. It also recognized, however, the notion of the universal church: "The Lord Jesus is the head of the Church, which is composed of all his true disciples." The Abstract's recognition of the doctrine of the universal church afterward attracted Landmark opposition to the seminary, an opposition that endured through much of the seminary's history.

The Abstract of Principles exerted influence immediately. Joseph Otis's defense of Baptist doctrine in Kentucky's *Western Recorder* in 1859 made appeal to the Abstract in justification of his contention that Calvinistic tenets were standard Baptist fare. He cited John Broadus's explanation that the Abstract deliberately excluded the beliefs of Campbellites, Arminians, and open communionists.[112]

James C. Furman predicted that the adoption of a doctrinal statement would result in division among the seminary's erstwhile supporters.[113] But Southern Baptists were largely united in their convictions concerning doctrine and church practices. Their prevailing differences were on minor issues. The confession became a bond of union.

THE FUNDAMENTAL LAWS, THE ABSTRACT OF PRINCIPLES, AND DENOMINATIONAL CONTROL

Boyce's report dealt with the seminary's "fundamental laws" or system of governance. It included three critical and troublesome issues. The first related to the manner of the professors' subscription to the seminary's articles of faith and to their enforcement. Boyce's initial draft indicated that the Abstract of Principles "shall be subscribed to by every professor elect, as indicative of his concurrence in its correctness as an epitome of Bible truth, and it shall be the imperative duty of the board to remove any professor of whose violation of this pledge they may feel satisfied." The convention adopted instead a version that did not explicitly require subscription but insisted that all professors conform their teaching to the Abstract: "All persons accepting professorships in this seminary shall be considered by such acceptance as engaging to teach in accordance with, and not contrary to, the Abstract of Principles, hereinafter laid down, any departure from which principles, on his part, shall be considered ground for his resignation or removal by trustees." Although the final statement emphasized the requirement that the teaching conform to the Abstract, it suggested also that "any departure" from the Abstract's "principles" also constituted just ground for dismissal. And because all professors "engaged" to teach in accordance with the Abstract, Boyce and his colleagues thought it best that all professors subscribe their names beneath the Abstract in an official subscription book, a practice that endures to the present.

112. Joseph Otis, "The Atonement," *Western Recorder*, 19 Sept. 1859, 2.

113. James C. Furman to E. T. Winkler, ca. 1856, quoted in Cook, *The Life Work of James Clement Furman*, 164.

The second critical issue related to the relative number of trustees from each southern state. Boyce wanted all the states represented, but he also wanted the greatest share of governance in the hands of those who contributed the most money. Thus he proposed combining both elements. Every state would get one automatic seat on the trustee board and an additional seat for every $10,000 contributed from that state. The convention made two changes. It made the automatic seat conditional; if any state did not contribute $5,000 within three years, it would lose its seat until it contributed that amount. It also made eleven the maximum number for each state.

The effect of this arrangement was to give considerable control to South Carolina and Virginia, the states that initially gave the most money, and very little control to the western states, which gave very little. Arkansas and Louisiana lost their automatic seats. When the seminary moved to Kentucky, and Kentucky Baptists gave largely to the new endowment, Kentucky displaced South Carolina as the most important state delegation, but the eastern states continued to dominate. This arrangement continued until 1926, when trustees adopted an amended charter basing trustee representation on geography, granting every state convention in the Southern Baptist Convention two seats on the board and establishing nine at-large seats.[114]

The third critical issue in the fundamental laws related to the means by which the denomination would control the school. Boyce was committed to denominational control, but he did not want the seminary subject to whiplash changes based on emotional controversies or the accidental majorities they could create in any given meeting of the Southern Baptist Convention. He recommended, and the committee adopted, that the board would ordinarily be "self-perpetuating," electing its own members whenever vacancies occurred. But he included a provision by which the Southern Baptist Convention could replace the entire board of trustees if the convention concluded that the trustees had neglected the seminary's constitution or had sustained professors "teaching doctrines contrary to the abstract of principles."

The convention apparently feared that it would be too easy for the Southern Baptist Convention to replace the whole board, subjecting the seminary to continual threat of disruption and untoward interference. It retained the language that "the Board shall be self-perpetuating," but instead of giving the Southern Baptist Convention the right to replace the whole board, it gave the Southern Baptist Convention the right to nominate "not less than three persons" to fill any vacancy. The board was in a sense still self-perpetuating—it elected new

114. Minutes, Board of Trustees, Southern Baptist Theological Seminary, 11–14 May 1926.

trustees from those nominated by the Southern Baptist Convention, or, if the Southern Baptist Convention failed to nominate, the board could elect new trustees on its own authority.

The convention typically did not bother to nominate persons to the seminary's board for a generation. In 1926 the trustees amended the charter to permit the convention to nominate only two persons for each vacancy, a change intended "to protect the interests of the convention" by moving closer to direct election of trustees by the convention, and to preserve "the direct control of the institution through the trustees." The trustees amended it again in 1965, permitting the convention to nominate for each vacancy only one person, whom the trustees then elected.[115]

THE FACULTY

Boyce and the convention delegates planned to open the seminary in October 1858, but they delayed opening until October 1859 because two professors declined election. The convention voted to elect the four men nominated by the committee on the faculty: James P. Boyce, Basil Manly Jr., John A. Broadus, and E. T. Winkler. Winkler, pastor of the First Baptist Church of Charleston, South Carolina, declined election from a sense of duty to his church. He judged that if he resigned his church, "it would be a calamity." And God's blessing of his pastoral labors was sufficient indication, he believed, that his duty was to stay in his place. He feared, moreover, that he would be impatient as a professor and grow restless for the pastorate. He enjoyed the relatively "speedy results" of pastoral work. "I had rather apply truth immediately," Winkler explained, "as a pastor than cast bread upon the water as a professor."[116]

Broadus, though only thirty years old when elected, had already gained a reputation among Virginia Baptists as an accomplished scholar and a remarkable preacher. He graduated from the University of Virginia with an M.A., reserved for those few students who took all the courses in the curriculum. He was pastor of the Charlottesville Baptist Church, and served also as the University of Virginia's chaplain. He was invited to take the chair of Greek at the university, and later the chair of moral philosophy, but felt that his duty was to preach the gospel rather than to teach.[117]

115. Minutes, Board of Trustees, Southern Baptist Theological Seminary, 11 May 1926; ibid., 16–17 Mar. 1965.

116. E. T. Winkler to John A. Broadus, 26 May 1858, attached to Archibald T. Robertson, "Life and Letters of John A. Broadus," ms., box 6, Robertson Papers.

117. Robertson, *Life and Letters of Broadus*, 55–74, 139.

Broadus's church members pressed him hard to remain at the church. They felt that his fruitful ministry in Charlottesville had greater value to the Christian cause than seminary teaching. William P. Farish, a prominent church member, told Broadus that seeking to make ministers by seminary training was wrongheaded. It would injure the cause of Christ, Farish said, "to take valuable ministers from prominent positions to teach twenty or thirty young men to become preachers, many of whom are made worse by it and none benefited."[118] A group of church leaders sent Broadus a plea to decline his election to the seminary, arguing that he already had the most extensive influence of any Baptist pastor in the South. His friends across the state agreed that his preaching ministry at Charlottesville, his appeal and influence to students at the University of Virginia, and his leadership in the Albemarle Female Institute would accomplish more for the gospel and for the denomination than a career at the new seminary. Other persons could be found to teach Greek and homiletics to young preachers, but "no other man in the denomination can at all fill" his unique position in Charlottesville.[119]

Broadus struggled with the decision for about ten days. He took counsel with "leading brethren" and friends in Charlottesville, Richmond, Alexandria, and Fredericksburg. He thought it his duty to remain pastor of the Charlottesville church. "I cannot leave here," he wrote Boyce. "If anything I can conceive could make one feel it right to leave this post, it would be the seminary, but I could not dare to go away."[120] Broadus refused his election to the faculty of the seminary.

Basil Manly Jr. struggled with similar questions of duty but came to a different conclusion. Manly professed faith in Christ at the age of fifteen and graduated first in his class at the University of Alabama three years later. The Tuscaloosa Baptist Church licensed him to preach, and he enrolled in the Newton Theological Institute in Newton, Massachusetts. When the Baptists in the South formed the Southern Baptist Convention in May 1845, the southern students at Newton withdrew. Manly enrolled at Princeton Theological Seminary in New Jersey, the bastion of Old School Presbyterian orthodoxy, to complete his course. After graduation in 1847 he spent three years preaching extensively in Alabama and Mississippi, especially to the slave population, among whom he thought his preaching was "much blessed." He prepared and published at

118. William P. Farish to John A. Broadus, 8 May 1858, attached to Robertson, "Life and Letters of John A. Broadus."

119. Alexander P. Abell, John W. Jones, C. H. Toy, et al., to John A. Broadus, 8 May 1858, attached to Robertson, "Life and Letters of John A. Broadus."

120. John A. Broadus to James P. Boyce, 15 May 1858, in Robertson, *Life and Letters of Broadus*, 152.

this time the *Baptist Psalmody*, a hymnbook that sold more than 50,000 copies. In 1850 he became pastor of the First Baptist Church of Richmond, Virginia, the leading Baptist pulpit in the South. In 1854 he resigned and accepted election as the founding president of the Richmond Female Institute, where he remained until joining Southern Seminary's faculty in 1859.[121]

In 1856 Furman University elected Manly as professor of theology and ancient languages to work alongside Boyce, but Manly declined. He thought that it was premature: "The cause of theological education is one dearer to me than almost any other and I esteem no sacrifice too great for its promotion. I am not a little in hopes that the Baptists of the South may be induced to concentrate their efforts on that subject, and if they do, Greenville stands an excellent chance of being selected as the location." But the future of Furman's theology department depended in large degree on how Southern Baptists resolved the question of establishing a theological seminary.[122]

Manly had established himself in the hearts of Richmond Baptists, who were convinced that his leadership was critical to the success of women's education among Baptists in Richmond. Manly himself thought it likely that if he abandoned the school in 1858 it would fail. He told Broadus initially that if Broadus accepted his professorship, and if A. M. Poindexter accepted his election as the seminary's fund-raising agent, he would feel it his duty to leave Richmond and join the seminary faculty. Manly had urged Broadus to accept election because of the critical importance of the seminary to the gospel ministry in the South, but he added that if Broadus declined, he would decline also.[123] When Broadus declined, Manly thought that it was a "death blow" to the seminary.[124] But he changed his mind and accepted, even though both Broadus and Poindexter had declined election.

Boyce pinned his hope not only on the acceptance of the other professors but also on the acceptance of A. M. Poindexter, the man whom the convention elected to raise $100,000 from the states outside South Carolina, which was the remainder of the endowment. If the seminary failed to obtain pledges for this amount, it would lose its South Carolina endowment funds also and would fail. Boyce and the committee felt that Poindexter was the one man capable of doing

121. See Basil Manly Jr. to Crawford H. Toy, 7 Feb. 1873, Letterbook II, Manly Family Papers no. 4409, Southern Historical Collection, UNC.

122. Basil Manly Jr. to J. B. O'Neal, 13 Sept. 1856, Manly Collection of Manuscripts, microfilm, reel 1, SBTS.

123. Basil Manly Jr. to John A. Broadus, 14 May 1858, attached to Robertson, "Life and Letters of John A. Broadus"; Manly to Broadus, 18 May 1858, ibid.

124. Basil Manly Jr. to John A. Broadus, 18 May 1858, attached to Robertson, "Life and Letters of John A. Broadus."

the job. But Poindexter declined. They finally secured William F. Broaddus, John Broadus's uncle, to raise funds in Virginia. They later appointed others for other states, while Boyce completed the South Carolina endowment and began the effort in North Carolina.[125] Throughout his life Boyce remained the seminary's most effective fund-raiser.

The 1858 Greenville convention appointed a provisional committee, with Boyce as chairman, with broad powers until the South Carolina legislature granted the seminary's charter and the board of trustees could organize in May 1859. The convention felt that the seminary's plan to open in October 1858 was stymied by the refusals of Winkler, Broadus, and Poindexter. It postponed opening the seminary to students until October 1859.[126]

In the fall of 1858 Manly urged Broadus to reconsider. His work in the Charlottesville church and in the University of Virginia had broad reach but could not compare with the reach of his ministry as a professor in the seminary. As Manly wrote, "The opportunities for permanent and extensive influence there are superior to any other situation in the South."[127]

Boyce too wanted Broadus to reconsider. He told Broadus in March 1859 that the provisional committee had resolved to renominate him and Winkler. He suggested that circumstances in Charlottesville had changed sufficiently "to point this out as duty now." When Broadus replied that he would reconsider election to the faculty, Boyce reminded him that as a seminary professor his influence would reach "every quarter of the globe" and "every class of men." The denomination desperately needed "educated men to aid in forming the public sentiment of the churches" and to forestall "the radicalism and the demagogism" then prevailing in many places. "Ought you not to make the sacrifice— are you not called to enter upon this work? If you fail me and Winkler fail me, I must give up." Boyce, who knew that Winkler was unlikely to accept unless Broadus did so, wrote, "Your simple name will be a tower of strength to us."[128] On April 21, 1859, Broadus wrote that after "much difficulty and much distress" he had determined that "if elected, I am willing to go."[129] Broadus and Boyce

125. Minutes, Board of Trustees, Southern Baptist Theological Seminary, 7 May 1859, 79–80. Broadus's uncles spelled their name Broaddus.

126. Minutes, Board of Trustees, Southern Baptist Theological Seminary, 7 May 1859, 79.

127. Basil Manly Jr. to John A. Broadus, 19 Nov. 1858, attached to Robertson, "Life and Letters of John A. Broaddus."

128. James P. Boyce to John A. Broadus, 29 Mar. 1859, attached to Robertson, "Life and Letters of John A. Broadus"; Broadus to Boyce, 4 Apr. 1959, box 11, Boyce Papers; Boyce to Broadus, 11 Apr. 1859, attached to Robertson, "Life and Letters of John A. Broadus."

129. John A. Broadus to James P. Boyce, 21 Apr. 1859, attached to Robertson, "Life and Letters of John A. Broadus."

labored together in the seminary for thirty years. Broadus proved indeed to be a "tower of strength" for Boyce.

When the trustees met and organized in May 1859, the most important matter they faced was electing two faculty members to join Boyce and Manly. Boyce and the provisional committee recommended the reelection of Winkler and Broadus, "believing that the call thus extended to them a second time will come with such force as can not be resisted."[130] Some trustees apparently doubted the wisdom of this course, but after "due consideration," and after Boyce assured them that he and Manly strongly desired this, they reelected Broadus and Winkler, along with Boyce and Manly.[131]

Two days later Broadus accepted, but Winkler could not be persuaded and declined again. The trustees then elected William Williams, professor of theology at Mercer University, in Winkler's place. Williams had studied law at Harvard and Yale but had given up law for the gospel ministry serving as a pastor in Auburn, Alabama, for about five years while he studied theology privately. Mercer University elected him professor of theology in 1856.[132] His fellow Baptists regarded him highly as a preacher, and his students acclaimed him as a remarkably effective teacher. Williams accepted. The vital matter of the composition of the faculty was finally settled: Boyce, Broadus, Manly, and Williams.[133]

Boyce's ambition to establish a Southern Baptist seminary was at last being realized. He had been busy. He had raised South Carolina's $100,000 portion of the endowment. As chairman of the provisional committee he had already secured the seminary's charter from the South Carolina legislature, arranged for fund-raising in Virginia and North Carolina, secured the use of the old meeting house of Greenville First Baptist Church for lecture rooms and a library, and made arrangements for receiving and augmenting the theological library of Furman University.

The trustees had confidence in Boyce's leadership and assigned him broad responsibility for seminary affairs. They elected him "chairman of the faculty." He was acting as treasurer for the provisional committee, and the board elected him as the seminary treasurer. They elected him to the board's five-member

130. Minutes, Board of Trustees, Southern Baptist Theological Seminary, 7 May 1859, 81.

131. Minutes, Board of Trustees, Southern Baptist Theological Seminary, 7 May 1859, 81–82.

132. C., "Dr. William Williams," *Religious Herald*, 5 Apr. 1877, 2. See also Samuel Henderson, "The Late Dr. Williams, D.D.," *Religious Herald*, 28 June 1877.

133. Minutes, Board of Trustees, Southern Baptist Theological Seminary, 7 May 1859, 83; William Williams to John A. Broadus, 30 May 1859, attached to Robertson, "Life and Letters of John A. Broadus."

William Williams

executive committee, which had broad responsibility for conducting seminary business on behalf of the board. The executive committee elected him committee chairman.[134]

OPPOSITION

In the wake of the 1858 Greenville convention, Baptist leaders around the South were delighted and optimistic at the prospects of success. Raising the initial endowment proved difficult. Boyce spent much of the next twelve months canvassing South Carolina Baptists to raise the additional $70,000 needed. They pledged generously, but Boyce came up $5,000 short of the total.[135] When Furman transferred its theological endowment, it came to $26,000 rather than $30,000.[136] The 1858 educational convention considered that South Carolina

134. Minutes, Board of Trustees, Southern Baptist Theological Seminary, 7 May 1859, 80, 85–86; ibid., 26 May 1860, 89; *History of the Establishment*, 35.
135. South Carolina Baptist Convention, *Minutes*, 1858, 9, 16–17.
136. South Carolina Baptist Convention, *Minutes*, 1858, 20.

had fulfilled its promise, provided that it closed the shortfall, and proceeded to organize. The other state conventions adopted resolutions urging the churches and their members to support the enterprise by raising the endowment and sending their young ministers to the school.[137] Virginia Baptists hoped to raise $25,000 for the endowment.[138]

Delegates to the Alabama Baptist Convention passed a resolution expressing the highest expectations for the usefulness and influence of the seminary: "This convention heartily approves of the objects sought to be accomplished by the establishment of the Southern Baptist Theological Seminary—that its location, Greenville, S.C., is satisfactory—that its basis of organization and doctrinal platform we fully endorse—that we regard this institution as one of the greatest and noblest enterprises in which the denomination has ever engaged, and destined to accomplish more for our Southern Zion than perhaps any other instrumentality—and hence we cordially commend it to the favorable regard and enlarged benevolence of our brethren in Alabama."[139]

But the seminary's prospects seemed to stir its opponents. William F. Broaddus, a respected preacher and the uncle of John Broadus, worked as the seminary's agent in Virginia. He told Boyce that "opposition to 'theological schools' has met me at every step."[140] He listed the common objections he encountered. The first class of objections was competition with the Baptist colleges. "Richmond College was popular" and should be supported; or the other way, "Richmond College was not popular" and should be supported. The second was jealousy for the Baptist cause in the state: "The seminary took [Broadus] out of Virginia." The third class was theological. Some thought the seminary too narrow: "Boyce was an ultra-Calvinist." Others thought it too liberal: Broadus "was not quite sound on close communion."[141] William Broaddus himself saw little merit in these objections, but they conform to the pattern of objections to the seminary throughout its history: it harmed the colleges, it harmed state interests, and it promoted error. One Georgian told Boyce that even apart from direct opposition, "there is at least a disposition on the part of many leading brethren in this state to give your enterprise the 'cold shoulder,' on account of their fears of injury to Mercer University."[142] Others seemed moved by little more than

---

137. See, e.g., "Report of the S. B. Theological Seminary," in North Carolina Baptist Convention, *Minutes*, 1858, 35.

138. Baptist General Association of Virginia, *Minutes*, 1858, 21.

139. "Report on Education," in Alabama Baptist Convention, *Minutes*, 1858, 21.

140. William F. Broaddus to James P. Boyce, 12 Dec. 1859, box 1, Boyce Papers.

141. William F. Broaddus to John A. Broadus, 28 Feb. 1860, box 1, Broadus Papers.

142. James C. Craft to James P. Boyce, 16 Apr. 1858, box 1, Boyce Papers.

prejudice. One North Carolina pastor considered the "seminary worse than a penitentiary and a curse."[143]

Much opposition was a kind of anti-intellectualism. This often had roots in suspicion of educated men, but often had more substance than mere prejudice. Many Baptists thought the "self-made man" superior to one manufactured in schools. And with regard to preachers, many felt that men with gifts of speech and earnestness of soul would find their way through their own study and experience. To send such men to school for several years and shut them away with books in darkened libraries would stifle their natural eloquence and quench their natural fire, either making them too embarrassed to preach or refining them into mere "literary preachers."[144] They were not opposed to education in general but felt that education often had bad effects on preachers. Others, like the editor of the Edgefield, South Carolina, *Southern Light*, supported college training for ministers but not seminary training. He held that ministers of the gospel needed not the specialized seminary curriculum but rather the broad college curriculum and a commitment to drawing their theology from the Bible.[145]

Some North Carolina preachers opposed the seminary because it would elevate seminary preachers "above the masses" and produce "strait-jacket reading men instead of preachers."[146] One opponent charged that an institution like the new seminary "tends to aristocracy." Its graduates would be prone to pride because of their superior attainments. "There is a common desire to be exalted—to be above our fellows . . . we should be at least careful how we entrust such distinction to the few."[147] J. F. B. Mays repeatedly encountered this objection as he traveled in North Carolina as the seminary's agent. Many feared that the seminary was intent on the centralization of the denomination by consolidating power around the seminary. The faculty, they believed, would "decide the faith and practice of Baptists" and "forbid freedom of thought."[148]

Implicit in such expressions was anxiety about the influence that a central educational institution would have over the denomination. Just as such institutions as the University of Virginia or the University of Alabama seemed to

143. J. F. B. Mays to James P. Boyce, 15 Aug. 1859, box 1, Boyce Papers. Mays convinced the pastor otherwise, and he gave ten dollars for the seminary endowment.

144. See William Whitsitt's description of his mother's objections to his plans for additional study (William H. Whitsitt to John A. Broadus, 12 May 1868, box 2, Broadus Papers).

145. Unattributed, "The Central Southern Theological Institution," *Christian Index*, 28 Feb. 1856, 34.

146. J. F. B. Mays to James P. Boyce, 1 Oct. 1859, box 1, Boyce Papers.

147. G. F. C., "The Great Southern Theological Institute," *Christian Index*, 12 May 1858, 2.

148. J. F. B. Mays to James P. Boyce, 1 Oct. 1859, box 1, Boyce Papers.

produce the leadership elite who dominated state and society, a central seminary would produce men who would dominate the denomination. It would produce a two-tiered ministry of those who were seminary trained and those who were not. The most influential pulpits and the most important leadership posts would fall to seminary men. They would become an elite corps of preachers with vast influence in the denomination.

Many others feared that the seminary would stray from orthodoxy and Baptist principles. One writer, G.F.C., opposed the seminary because of the "tendency to corruption in the theology of such institutions." Boyce had insisted that the seminary must adopt an orthodox confession of faith in order to forestall such a result. But G.F.C. found fault even with the seminary's confession. It failed to state that a "church is composed of immersed believers," and it failed to assert the qualifications of the administrator of baptism.[149]

The southeastern states had led the seminary movement. The Southwest—Kentucky, Tennessee, Mississippi, Louisiana, Arkansas, and Texas—had a somewhat different character and identity than the states of the seaboard South. These states tended to place higher value on individualism and the meritocracy of frontier pluck, labor, and self-reliance, and they were suspicious of centralization and the aristocracy of eastern wealth, education, and organization. They were populists. The seminary's leaders were easterners who seemed rather whiggish by comparison. The seminary had an uphill climb to win the respect and support of southwestern Baptists.

The most potent and enduring source of opposition was James R. Graves of Nashville, Tennessee. William C. Crane had worried in 1857 about the "private influence of Graves" and his supporters against the seminary.[150] It did not help that Boyce used John L. Dagg's *Manual of Theology* as the textbook for his English theology course. Dagg and Graves had clashed over Landmark ecclesiology. Landmarkers also found it irritating that Robert B. C. Howell, Graves's recent archnemesis, was a member of the board of trustees. Seminary agent J. F. B. Mays discovered that opposition to the seminary in Mississippi was "because of Dagg's *Theology* and Howell's being on the board."[151] When Mississippi Baptists rejected his appeals, as almost all did, they pleaded that besides the hard times and the danger of civil war, the seminary was "anti-Graves."[152] Landmark regions of North Carolina received agent J. F. B. Mays coldly. The pastors said Boyce was

149. G. F. C., "The Great Southern Theological Institute, No. 3," *Christian Index*, 2 June 1858, 2.

150. William C. Crane to James P. Boyce, 10 June 1857, box 1, Boyce Papers.

151. J. F. B. Mays to James P. Boyce, 26 Sept. 1860, box 1, Boyce Papers.

152. J. F. B. Mays to James P. Boyce, 24 Oct. 1860, box 1, Boyce Papers.

Graves's enemy. Even when they permitted Mays to address their association meetings, few responded. His conclusion was that "where the *Tennessee Baptist* is freely circulated, I get poor encouragement."[153]

Graves published his objections after the 1857 education convention in Louisville. He argued that the Baptists of Tennessee were committed to preparing ministers at their own Union University, where they had recently endowed a chair of theology to equip ministerial students in conjunction with their regular college curriculum. Tennessee Baptists would not abandon or endanger Union's program for theological education for the sake of "some new and untried scheme of instruction, in a far distant state." South Carolina, North Carolina, and Virginia were free to start their new venture at Greenville, he suggested, but Tennessee would support its own college's theological program.[154]

Graves apparently felt that the design of Southern Baptist Theological Seminary was to crush out all theological education at the state Baptist colleges. The leaders of the seminary movement claimed that there was room for both kinds to coexist, but Graves was not buying it. If the seminary were seeking to admit only college graduates who were "seeking a higher culture," then he would pledge cooperation with the new school. But since the new seminary would admit men who had not been to college, it must be seeking to draw them all away from their state colleges and to the seminary. The new seminary would gain a despotic monopoly over theological education. The movement seemed bent on creating a "great, grand colossal central school, that would put its mighty foot or cast its mighty sneer upon all theological instruction given in the state schools." Centralization threatened the destruction of all competitors.[155]

Graves finally objected that easterners were not likely to produce such ministers as the West needed. Union University was already preparing a "practical, commonsensical, efficient, energetic ministry for the West." But the new eastern seminary would likely "manufacture a sleek, dainty race of ministerial exquisites, who were to compose the literary aristocracy of our ministry." Union University prepared men; eastern seminaries manufactured effetes. Eastern theological education would not suit the West.[156]

Graves said that he raised these objections in a speech before the Louisville convention. Graves did not, however, vote against the South Carolina proposal—the vote was unanimous. He shrewdly explained afterward that he did not

153. J. F. B. Mays to James P. Boyce, 15 Aug. 1859, box 1, Boyce Papers; Mays to Boyce, 1 Oct. 1859, ibid.

154. J. R. Graves, "Convention Items—Odds and Ends," *Tennessee Baptist*, 6 June 1857, 2.

155. Graves, "Convention Items," 2.

156. Graves, "Convention Items," 2.

oppose the South Carolina proposal, only the "centralizing idea."[157] He thus supported the seminary in fact while opposing it in the abstract. In subsequent years he sometimes opposed it in fact and supported it only in the abstract. Each served in its turn.

Broadus warned that Graves could not be trusted to support the seminary: "Nashville will try to crush it like everything else Atlantic."[158] But the seminary had sufficient popular support to make Graves wary of attacking it aggressively. Instead he sowed doubts about its soundness. He watched for signs of weakness and sought to exploit them. He made trouble enough for the seminary over the next thirty years, but Boyce and the faculty answered his objections in ways that won increasing support among Landmark Southern Baptists.

157. Graves, "Convention Items," 2.

158. John A. Broadus to Basil Manly Jr., 21 Apr. 1859, quoted in "The Seminary's Troubles from Extreme Landmarkers under Boyce and Broadus," box 7, Robertson Papers.

2

MAKING BRICKS WITHOUT STRAW
War, Disruption, and Sacrifice

The seminary began with flattering prospects in 1859. South Carolina Baptists had nearly pledged their half of the endowment, and pledges for the other half were adding up. Payment on the pledges was encouraging. Boyce and the faculty could not foresee that the endowment would soon fall victim to ravenous war and that they would have to carry on their work scratching for money, teetering on the edge of insolvency for nearly two decades. Many who were willing and able to give held back from fear that the seminary would fail. Others opposed or obstructed the effort. Boyce had to keep the seminary going without any supply of funds. He likened his job to that of the Hebrew slaves who struggled desperately to make their quota of bricks when Pharaoh stopped supplying straw: "Poor as my bricks may be they are as well made and as many as I can accomplish and find the straw." Year after year, the fate of the seminary rested on Boyce's shoulders.[1]

Before the coming of the war, the seminary prospered. The faculty were gratified that the seminary's first session was "highly successful and encouraging."[2] Only nine students enrolled on the seminary's opening day, October 1, 1859, but soon the number swelled to twenty-six. This was more than had enrolled in theological education in all Southern Baptist colleges combined three years

---

1. James P. Boyce to Basil Manly Jr., 17 Jan. 1874, Manly Collection of Manuscripts, microfilm, reel 2, SBTS.

2. John A. Broadus, *Memoir of James Petigru Boyce* (New York: A. C. Armstrong, 1893), 175.

The seminary's first building, housing lecture rooms and the library

earlier, and it was more than any other seminary had enrolled in its first year. Classes met in the old Baptist "meeting house" in Greenville, after the seminary installed walls dividing it into two lecture rooms and a library for the 2,000-volume theological collection donated by Furman University. At the seminary's first commencement in 1860, students received degrees in each of the "schools" in which they achieved passing marks. Basil Manly composed "Soldiers of Christ in Truth Arrayed" for the occasion. It became the "seminary hymn" and has been sung at every subsequent commencement. During the second session, 1860–1861, the seminary enrolled thirty-eight students. At the 1861 commencement the seminary awarded its first full graduate degree to John A. Chambliss, who completed the three-year course in just two years.[3]

3. John A. Broadus to Cornelia Taliaferro, 18 Feb. 1860, quoted in Archibald T. Robertson, *Life and Letters of John Albert Broadus* (Philadelphia: American Baptist Publication Society, 1901), 171; John A. Broadus to Cornelia Taliaferro, 22 Jan. 1861, quoted in Robertson, *Life and Letters of Broadus*, 182; Broadus, *Memoir of Boyce*, 167–170, 175–176. Broadus reported the second session enrollment as thirty-eight in the 22 Jan. 1861 letter but put it at thirty-six in his *Memoir of Boyce*, 176. William Mueller put the second-session enrollment at thirty-seven (*History of Southern Baptist Theological*

The secession of the southern states and the onset of the Civil War in the first half of 1861 imperiled the seminary's existence. Many students returned home before closing ceremonies in May 1861 to prepare for war.[4] Only twenty students enrolled in the 1861–1862 session, and by March 1862 only eight students remained.[5] Most had abandoned their studies and joined the Confederate army as either chaplains or combatants. So few remained at the close of the session that the faculty thought it best to forgo commencement ceremonies. Boyce hoped to open the seminary in the fall of 1862, despite the paucity of students. He urged the Confederate secretary of war to include ministerial students in the clergy exemption from military conscription. When Boyce failed to secure the exemption, the faculty had no choice but to close the seminary until the war ended.[6]

The seminary barely escaped extinction. The threats to its survival multiplied during its first thirty years. The Civil War caused its suspension and annihilated its endowment. In the economic destitution of the Reconstruction South, Baptists had little ability to raise a new endowment. The seminary relocated to Kentucky in 1877 with promises of a new endowment, but securing the pledges and their payment was thwarted by a business panic and economic depression, and by opponents within the denomination who launched powerful attacks against the school. And from within the faculty arose a new theology that threatened the seminary's credibility with the churches.[7] At every juncture it was Boyce above all others who threw himself into the gap with energy and poise. In these thirty years of hardship and anxiety for the seminary, Boyce secured the school's existence. His leadership helped shape Southern Baptists in profound and enduring ways.

SECESSION AND SLAVERY

America's war over slavery nearly swept away the seminary in its devastating stream. Abraham Lincoln's election as the nation's president in November 1860 produced a crisis in southern political sentiment. The South Carolina legislature

Seminary [Nashville, TN: Broadman Press, 1959], 118). Boyce counted a total of fifteen students in all theology programs in 1856 (Boyce, "Address of Rev. J. P. Boyce at Hampton," *Religious Herald*, 1 July 1858, 1).

4. Basil Manly Jr., "Letter from Greenville, S.C.," *Christian Index*, 12 June 1861, 2.

5. John A. Broadus to James P. Boyce, 14 Mar. 1862, Boyce Papers.

6. James P. Boyce to John A. Broadus, 16 Mar. 1862, attached to Archibald T. Robertson, "Life and Letters of John A. Broadus," ms., box 6, Robertson Papers; Boyce to G. W. Randolph, 20 Aug. 1862, quoted in Robertson, *Life and Letters of Broadus*, 194–195; Robertson, *Life and Letters of Broadus*, 192, 196; Broadus, *Memoir of Boyce*, 179–180.

7. The story of Crawford H. Toy and the new theology appears in the next chapter.

acted first when it called an election of representatives to a December convention to decide whether to secede from the United States. Boyce and Broadus opposed secession; Manly and Williams favored it. Boyce ran for election to the secession convention as a member of the Greenville district delegation. He ran on the ticket for preserving the Union. Running against him on the secession ticket was fellow Baptist James C. Furman, president of Furman University. Furman and the secession ticket won the election.[8]

Once secession became reality, Boyce and Broadus understood their duty to join their fellow citizens in sustaining and defending the state. "I have at this hour no sympathy with secession," Broadus explained to a friend in Baltimore, but "I mean to do my duty as a citizen here."[9] At the 1863 meeting of the Southern Baptist Convention, Broadus offered a set of resolutions acknowledging that "our sins have deserved the terrible calamities that God has sent upon us," expressing confidence in their "ultimate success" through humble reliance on God's preservation, and pledging their "hearty support to the Confederate government." Boyce argued that it was unconstitutional for the convention to address purely political or social matters, and he argued against their adoption. After considerable debate, the resolution passed.[10]

Slavery was the issue that loomed largest in the secession of the southern states. Southern Baptist clergy spoke out in favor of secession and defended slavery. A month before South Carolina passed its secession ordinance, Charleston Baptist leaders unanimously adopted a resolution endorsing slavery and their duty to both God and country to resist the "encroachments of the enemies of our domestic institution."[11] Their position was nearly universal among evangelical pastors in the South.

Georgia governor Joseph E. Brown, who after the war saved the seminary from collapse by his gifts, persuaded the delegates at the 1863 Southern Baptist Convention to adopt Broadus's resolutions: "All must admit that the institution of slavery is one of the prime causes of the war, and that its perpetuation depends upon the success of our arms.... it is neither a moral, social nor political evil.

8. James A. Hoyt, "The Southern Baptist Theological Seminary in Greenville," *Baptist Courier*, 2 Apr. 1903, 6; C. H. Toy to John A. Broadus, 11 Dec. 1860, attached to Robertson, "Life and Letters of John A. Broadus"; Broadus, *Memoir of Boyce*, 177.

9. John A. Broadus to Cornelia Taliaferro, 22 Jan. 1861, quoted in Robertson, *Life and Letters of Broadus*, 181.

10. Southern Baptist Convention, *Minutes*, 1863, 13, 18–19, 54–55; Joseph E. Brown, "Speech of Gov. Brown in the Baptist Biennial Convention," *Christian Index*, 25 May 1863, 2.

11. Charleston Baptist Association, *Minutes*, 1860, 4.

Like every other relation in life it may be, and has been abused.... I believe, sir, that it is an institution of God, and that we have revealed to us in the Holy Bible clear and overwhelming evidence of its establishment by Him and of his intention to perpetuate it."[12] Samuel Boykin, editor of Georgia Baptists' *Christian Index*, summarized the convictions of most Southern Baptists: "Slavery is the only issue. The United States is fighting against the Confederate States for slavery."[13]

All four of the seminary's faculty were slaveholders. The 1860 census reported that Boyce had twenty-three slaves in Greenville, Manly had seven, Williams had five, and Broadus had two. Boyce and Manly had additional slaves on plantations elsewhere. This was not unusual. Many southern clergy, especially the educated ministers of towns and cities, were slaveholders.[14]

The faculty, like southern evangelical clergy generally, did not believe that slavery was intrinsically evil. The Bible, they held, did not condemn slavery as a mere institution. And they believed that in God's providence, it had been productive of much good. As an unintended consequence of African slavery, several million Africans were introduced to the gospel of redemption, and a large number of them had been converted and redeemed. Basil Manly Jr. wrote that "their introduction into this country has been, in the providence of God, instrumental in saving more of their race from heathenism, than the united membership of all the churches which modern foreign missions have planted."[15]

They recognized that the capture of Africans to enslave and sell them was sin—it was "man-stealing" or kidnapping and was forbidden by the

12. Joseph E. Brown, "Speech of Gov. Brown in the Baptist Biennial Convention," *Christian Index*, 25 May 1863, 2.

13. Samuel Boykin, "Slavery," *Christian Index*, 25 Dec. 1863, 1.

14. Bureau of the Census, manuscript census, Slave Schedule, Greenville District, South Carolina, NARA mf., series 653, reel 1231, pp. 448–449, ibid., Free Schedule, NARA mf., series 653, reel 1220, pp. 407–408. The value of the personal property of Manly ($43,700) and Boyce ($330,000) indicates that they owned more slaves than those reported on the slave schedule for Greenville District. Williams once referenced Boyce's "farm" (William Williams to John A. Broadus, ca. 29 June 1862, box 1, Broadus Papers). Manly owned twenty-one slaves in 1862, some in South Carolina and others in Alabama (Basil Manly Jr. to Basil Manly Sr., 26 Oct. 1862, Manly Family Papers, SBHLA). On southern town clergy, slavery, and wealth, see E. Brooks Holifield, *The Gentlemen Theologians: American Theology in Southern Culture, 1795–1860* (Durham, NC: Duke University Press, 1978), 28–31.

15. Basil Manly Jr., Report of the Committee on Suggestions and Queries, in Edgefield Baptist Association, *Minutes*, 1865, 7.

scriptures—and that the whole slave trade was rooted in greed.[16] They recognized also that many profound evils encumbered it. They criticized the failure of masters to honor the sanctity of marriage among slaves and to provide for preaching and Bible teaching among slaves. They criticized also the state laws and local ordinances that permitted or encouraged these evils. Boyce, for example, said that he was unreservedly proslavery in his sentiments, but he judged that southern whites had perpetrated and condoned great evils against the enslaved Africans. He believed that secession would result in the end of slavery, and that God was removing slavery from the land because of the sins of slaveholders: "I feel that our sins as to this institution have cursed us—that the negroes have not been cared for in their marital and religious relations as they should be."[17]

Some southern whites nevertheless held evangelical preachers in suspicion because they supported the education and spiritual equality of slaves. Southern Baptists held that in matters of religion, slaves and masters, blacks and whites stood on an equal basis. J. L. Reynolds, a Furman University professor and occasional teacher at the seminary, urged that all classes, including "master and servant," came together on the "common platform of equality in the sight of God."[18] Baptists did in fact accord the slave members a broad equality in the churches. When John Broadus gave an address in Richmond on the moral condition of slaves and on the obligation of masters to provide religious instruction for the slaves, the *Richmond Dispatch* refused to report on the event because of the editor's opposition to religious education of slaves.[19]

Samuel Boykin, editor of Georgia's Baptist weekly, told his readers as early as 1863 that southern whites had a duty to proclaim the gospel and that "neglect to carry out this duty in regard to the evangelization of our blacks is one of the causes of this war of punishment."[20] J. L. Reynolds blamed the Confederate government's treatment of chaplains, hoarding, speculation, extortion, and prostitution as causes of God's punishment of the South.[21]

16. John A. Broadus, "As to the Colored People," *Baptist Courier*, 15 Feb. 1883, 1.

17. James P. Boyce to H. A. Tupper, Dec. 1860, quoted in Broadus, *Memoir of Boyce*, 185.

18. J. L. Reynolds, "Southern Slavery," *Confederate Baptist*, 13 May 1863, 2.

19. J. B. Jeter to John Broadus, 21 Feb. 1859, attached to Robertson, "Life and Letters of John A. Broadus."

20. Samuel Boykin, "Duty to Our Slaves—Probable Cause of the War," *Christian Index*, 23 Mar. 1863, 2.

21. J. L. Reynolds, "National Declension," *Confederate Baptist*, 17 June 1863, 2; Reynolds, "Secular News," *Confederate Baptist*, 22 July 1863, 3.

CIVIL WAR AND SUSPENSION

When the seminary suspended in 1862, the professors had to look elsewhere for employment and income. Boyce paid the professors some salary during the war, but donations slowed to a trickle, and the seminary could not keep their salaries current. Preaching provided some income. The professors had preached often in area churches and at meetings of Baptist associations. Boyce encouraged the faculty to accept election as pastor to country churches, which generally met only one or two Sundays a month. It would aid the seminary's reputation and supplement the faculty's income.[22] Boyce himself had became pastor of Cedar Grove Baptist Church in 1860.[23] When the seminary suspended, Manly and Williams each accepted calls to two churches in the Abbeville district and moved to small plantations in the same area. Because the salaries they received from their churches were small, and in the distress of the wartime economy would grow smaller, the plantations might provide some cash as well as staples. In 1863 they sold their homes in Greenville.[24] Broadus remained in Greenville and became pastor of four country churches, each meeting once a month on a different Sunday.[25]

Manly persuaded the Southern Baptist Convention to establish the Sunday School Board in 1863. The war caused common schools across the South to close. Manly saw an opportunity for Southern Baptist churches to provide for basic literacy education for the South's children through Sunday schools and, at the same time, to educate them in the gospel for the salvation of their souls. The new board elected Broadus its corresponding secretary, for which he received a small salary, and elected Manly president. The two of them did much of the writing (under a variety of pseudonyms) and produced reading primers, catechisms, tracts, and other religious literature.[26] *Kind Words*, a religious newspaper for young people initiated in 1865, became their most popular work. *Kind Words* survived the many revolutions in Southern Baptist

22. See, e.g., William Williams to John A. Broadus, 15 Aug. 1860, box 1, Broadus Papers.

23. Broadus to Boyce, 11 Oct. 1860, box 1, Broadus Papers; Broadus, *Memoir of Boyce*, 173–174.

24. Broadus, *Memoir of Boyce*, 181; Edgefield (SC) Baptist Association, *Minutes*, 1864, 10–11; ibid., 1865; Lottie Broadus to John Broadus, 9 Sept. 1863, box 1, Broadus Papers.

25. Robertson, *Life and Letters of Broadus*, 209.

26. See Southern Baptist Convention, *Minutes*, 1863, 12, 14–15, 45–47; ibid., 1866, 24–26, 30; John A. Broadus, "Confederate Sunday School Publications," *Baptist Courier*, 9 Oct. 1890, 1; Broadus, "Address of Dr. John A. Broadus," *Seminary Magazine* 5 (1892): 315; Robertson, *Life and Letters of Broadus*, 209–210.

Sunday school work until it was shelved in 1929. The board could not compete with northern Sunday school publishers, which produced literature at lower prices and secured southern trust by paying southerners to write material intended for southern churches. The Sunday School Board moved to Memphis in 1868 and merged with James R. Graves's publishing company in an effort to gain financial viability. In 1873 the combined board was dissolved and its work remanded to the Southern Baptist Convention's Home Mission Board, which carried on the work until the formation of the modern Baptist Sunday School Board in 1891 (now Lifeway Christian Resources of the Southern Baptist Convention). The board's Broadman Press was named for Broadus and Manly's pioneering work. Broadus resigned his position in 1866—the board needed a secretary who could travel extensively and devote his full time. Manly resigned in 1868 to make way for the new consolidated board.

Concern for Confederate soldiers drove faculty and students to preach the gospel in army camps and hospitals as chaplains, evangelists, and colporteurs. As a chaplain Boyce preached to the men, gave away Bibles, books, and tracts, and visited the sick.[27] He expressed well the evangelical concern for the souls of soldiers who faced death without faith in Jesus Christ: "We are in the course of ten days to occupy James Island, where the battle is expected.... How tenderly my heart yearns over them. How many, after all, must go unprepared into the presence of God. I feel like preaching all the time.... Oh, that God might aid me and help me in what I can do! It would be enough to bring multitudes to him."[28]

Broadus spent three months in the summer of 1863 preaching to Confederate soldiers in Virginia, a period of deep religious interest in Lee's army.[29] His chief concern was to persuade unconverted soldiers to submit to Christ in faith. He addressed soldiers in a tract, *We Pray for You at Home*: "We pray that you may be inclined and enabled to commit your soul to the divine Savior, who died to redeem us.... We pray that the Holy Spirit may thoroughly change your heart, bringing you truly to hate sin and love holiness.... Whether it be appointed to you to fall soon in battle, or years hence to die at home, may God in mercy

27. Boyce to Broadus, 24 Dec. 1862, box 1, Broadus Papers.

28. Boyce to Broadus, 23 Dec. 1861, quoted in Robertson, *Life and Letters of Broadus*, 188–189.

29. Robertson, *Life and Letters of Broadus*, 198–209; J. William Jones, *Christ in the Camp, or Religion in Lee's Army* (Richmond, VA: B. F. Johnson, 1887), 312–315, 319–321, 326–327, 329–330. Broadus mentioned preaching to soldiers around Fredericksburg, Virginia, earlier in 1863 (ibid., 313).

James P. Boyce in his
Confederate uniform

forbid that you should live in impenitence and die in your sins."[30] Soldiers
attended preaching voluntarily in large numbers, and Broadus never enjoyed
preaching so much.[31]

Boyce resigned his chaplaincy in May 1862 and was twice elected to the
South Carolina legislature. Boyce proposed a bond-issue plan by which South
Carolina could raise $34 million, its share of revenue for the Confederate gov-
ernment. The state legislature adopted his bill.[32] Boyce's plan promised such success that the Confederate government's treasury secretary appointed Boyce as
the treasury department's commissioner to all the state legislatures to persuade

30. Broadus, *We Pray for You at Home* (Raleigh, NC: n.p., ca. 1862), quoted in
Robertson, *Life and Letters of Broadus*, 191.

31. Jones, *Christ in the Camp*, 326.

32. Boyce to Broadus, 30 Jan. 1863, box 1, Broadus Papers; Boyce to Broadus, 4 Feb.
1863, box 1, Broadus Papers.

each state to adopt similar bond-issue arrangements. From November 1864 to the end of the war, Boyce served as aide-de-camp to South Carolina governor A. G. Magrath. He was in the state house in Columbia when Union artillery began shelling the city on February 16, 1865. As acting provost marshal of Columbia, he lingered to oversee the city's evacuation and afterward "always declared that so far as he could ascertain, then or afterwards, he was himself the very last Confederate that rode out of Columbia as the invaders came up the street."[33]

Boyce returned to Greenville, where he did not escape the invaders. His grand home attracted the special attention of Union soldiers intent on looting. Broadus informed Manly that "Boyce lost a quantity of his own clothing, a valuable watch which he had kept and a few other things. They ransacked his house twice, threatened to burn it and to shoot him if they did not produce plate and jewelry, but found nothing. He had sent those things off and told them so." Broadus himself "lost nothing of importance."[34]

SHALL THE SEMINARY LIVE?

Boyce's losses as a result of the war extended far beyond a looted home, threatening to prevent the reopening of the seminary. He was a partner or shareholder in various businesses, and under the laws of the time, some creditors sought to hold him liable for the corporation's entire debt.[35] Boyce thought that under the circumstances he might be compelled to leave the seminary, for at least a year or two, to earn enough money to pay his debts and care for his family. The faculty recognized that if the seminary was to survive, it would have to rely on his leadership and his ability to loan funds to the seminary in the lean times ahead. "We ought to make the future of the seminary a matter of special daily prayer," Broadus urged Manly in May 1865. "We can't yet see what is to be feasible for the seminary. If Boyce's private fortune is spared, he will probably work it along. But all is uncertain."[36]

33. Broadus, *Memoir of Boyce*, 193–196; Boyce to Broadus, 16 Feb. 1865, Basil Manly Papers, no. 486, Southern Historical Collection, UNC.

34. John A. Broadus to Basil Manly Jr., 22 May 1865, Manly Collection of Manuscripts, microfilm, reel 2, SBTS; Broadus, *Memoir of Boyce*, 196–197.

35. G. G. Wells to John A. Broadus, 9 Nov. 1892, box 14, Broadus Papers; Broadus, *Memoir of Boyce*, 202–203.

36. John A. Broadus to Basil Manly Jr., 22 May 1865, Manly Collection of Manuscripts, microfilm, reel 2, SBTS.

Boyce proposed a plan for reopening the seminary in the fall of 1865. He told them that he would loan the seminary $3,000 so that each of the professors could receive $1,000 salary for the 1865–1866 session. Boyce knew that this would not be enough to pay all their bills, so he urged them to keep their country church pastorates. The two incomes would have to suffice. Because he would have to be absent most of the time seeking to recover something from the wreck of his business interests, the other three professors would have to do all the teaching without him.

Williams opposed returning to the seminary right away. He did not believe that he could support his family on Boyce's loan, and his Abbeville churches would pay him less if he moved away to Greenville. He planned to open a school to supplement what his churches paid him. And he thought the seminary would need only two professors, since it could not attract more than a half dozen students in the coming year.[37]

Broadus was "decidedly" in favor of accepting Boyce's proposal from the start. He urged Manly and Williams "to agree to it, by all means." But by the end of August 1865 the faculty still had made no final decision about reopening the seminary. Boyce was traveling about to ascertain the status of the properties of his father's estate and the extent of his debts, and to secure whatever could be saved. They needed to know whether Boyce would be able to stay in Greenville enough of the time to teach, or whether he would have to withdraw from teaching to attend to the estate. If Boyce could not return, and Williams refused to return, that would leave only Broadus and Manly. To reopen with only half the faculty intact would convey the impression that the seminary was crippled and unlikely to succeed. And if they did not instill confidence in the seminary's health, few students would matriculate, and donors were unlikely to give.[38]

Manly stood ready to make the venture, though he had doubts enough of its success. He thought he would return to Virginia. The trustees of the Richmond Female Institute elected Manly as president and urged him to return to his former position. He concluded that if the seminary did not reopen he would accept. But when the decision on the seminary was delayed into late August, he declined the Richmond offer. He had committed himself to the work of preparing an educated ministry for the churches and felt that it was his duty under God to do everything possible to preserve the seminary. If the seminary reopened,

37. Basil Manly Jr. to Parents, 21 July 1865, Manly Collection of Manuscripts, microfilm, reel 2, SBTS.

38. John A. Broadus to Basil Manly Jr., 10 July 1865, Manly Collection of Manuscripts, microfilm, reel 2, SBTS; John A. Broadus to Basil Manly Jr., 3 July 1865, quoted in Robertson, *Life and Letters of Broadus*, 212.

Boyce's loan and the salary from his Abbeville churches would provide enough to "eke out" an income sufficient for his family's necessities. If the seminary could not reopen, he had no prospects. As Manly wrote to J. B. Taylor, "Thus I launch upon the open sea, uncertain of my future. There is no other opening known to me, in case it should appear inexpedient to reopen the seminary."[39] Williams still declined to return, and Boyce planned to withdraw for a year or two, but Manly and Broadus were committed, in the hope, as Manly put it, that "by energy and sacrifice, Broadus and I can save the Seminary."[40]

Boyce returned to Greenville at the end of August. He renewed his proposal and argued the necessity of Williams's acceptance. He insisted that "the seminary must not fall below three professors." If Williams finally declined, Boyce would feel it his duty to stay in Greenville and teach in order to preserve the seminary, though his inability to attend to his business affairs would almost certainly involve him in "enormous losses." Boyce asked Williams to accept as a "favor to him personally." When the four of them met for a decision, Broadus extinguished all remaining reservations: "Suppose we quietly agree that the seminary may die, but we'll die first." In early September they announced that the school would reopen on November 1, 1865.[41]

The faculty was now intact. Students would be few, given the hard times and the short notice. Boyce was hopeful of saving enough from the wreck of his father's estate to provide for the families of his four sisters and two brothers.[42] But they could not save the seminary by themselves. They needed the support of individual Baptists throughout the South.

STRUGGLE FOR SURVIVAL IN THE RECONSTRUCTION SOUTH

Only seven students matriculated the first session after the war, but the professors were determined to maintain the full course and do their best work no matter the small classes. Broadus's homiletics class began the year with two

---

39. Basil Manly Jr. to J. B. Taylor, 28 Aug. 1865, Manly Collection of Manuscripts, microfilm, reel 2, SBTS; Basil Manly Jr. to Parents, 10 July 1865, ibid.; Basil Manly Jr. to Parents, 21 July 1865, ibid.

40. Basil Manly Jr. to Parents, 10 July 1865, Manly Collection of Manuscripts, microfilm, reel 2, SBTS; Basil Manly Jr. to J. B. Taylor, 28 Aug. 1865, ibid.

41. John A. Broadus to Basil Manly Jr., 25 Aug. 1865, quoted in Robertson, *Life and Letters of Broadus*, 214; Broadus, *Memoir of Boyce*, 200; Basil Manly Jr. to John A. Broadus, 9 Sept. 1865, box 2, Broadus Papers.

42. Broadus, *Memoir of Boyce*, 7–8, 31–32, 94–95, 202–203, 336; "Division of the Assets of the Principal of the Estate of Ker Boyce," Manuscript Items Relating to James P. Boyce," microfilm, SBTS.

Seminary Hall dormitory, also known as the Goodlett House

students, but one dropped out midsession, and the remaining student was blind. Broadus could not use his accustomed assigned reading and recitation method, so he developed lectures that gave the student the complete course. Several years later Broadus revised and published these lectures under the title *On the Preparation and Delivery of Sermons*. Broadus had to borrow more than $1,000 to publish the book.[43] The royalties quickly extinguished the debt. Reviewers praised the book, which was widely used as a textbook in American theological education even decades after his death.[44]

Students came in larger numbers in subsequent years until enrollment averaged sixty-seven students between 1873 and 1877. With borrowed money Boyce purchased the Goodlett House hotel in 1867 and refurbished it as a dormitory and dining hall, renaming it Seminary Hall. This reduced student expenses considerably, as the seminary charged nothing for the room and could offer board at half the cost students paid in boardinghouses. Boyce also secured ownership of the old Baptist meetinghouse building, which held the lecture rooms and

43. Charlotte Broadus to John Broadus, ca. 19 Sept. 1870, box 3, Broadus Papers; Charlotte Broadus to John Broadus, 22 Jan. 1871, box 3, Broadus Papers.

44. Crawford Toy to John Broadus, 16 Nov. 1870, box 2, Broadus Papers.

library, and bought the property adjoining Seminary Hall. Boyce rented parts of the buildings to pay the insurance and interest on the loans.[45]

In 1869 the seminary needed a fifth professor. Broadus was in poor health and had to give up teaching homiletics, with its heavy demands in correcting student sermons. Boyce's heavy responsibilities required him to give up teaching polemics. The faculty reassigned homiletics and polemics to the versatile Manly and asked him to continue teaching biblical introduction. They appointed Crawford H. Toy as professor of Old Testament and Oriental languages.[46] Toy, who had studied Semitic languages at the University of Berlin, was an impressive linguist and promising scholar who was loved by students. After Basil Manly resigned, the seminary appointed William H. Whitsitt to the faculty in 1872 as professor of Biblical Introduction and Polemic Theology. Whitsitt also relieved Broadus of part of his work in New Testament Greek, enabling Broadus to teach homiletics again. Like Toy, Whitsitt had studied two years in Germany.[47]

Despite the successful development of its facilities, faculty, and enrollment, the seminary's fate remained uncertain for many years. The demoralization of the South jeopardized the seminary's future. Southerners took the loss hard. So certain were they that their course had been just and right, and that the North had acted unjustly and unscripturally, that defeat seemed impossible. When defeat came, it called into question their assumptions about God, his justice, and his sovereignty.

Evangelical clergy provided the most popular and persuasive explanation: the war, defeat, and the abolition of slavery were God's chastisement on southern whites for their sins, especially in their treatment of the slaves. South Carolina Baptists, like most evangelical southerners, were confident of God's approval of the course of the southern states in forming the Confederate States of America. God's approval, they felt sure, meant success in this war. They believed that southern states acted justly in the defense of their "homes, liberties, and churches," and that God would lay the rod of his chastisement not against them but against those who pursued the "unrighteous" and "wicked" attack on southerners' "peaceful homes."[48] Samuel Boykin, editor of Georgia

45. Basil Manly, "Students' Fund of the SBTS," 1 Sept. 1871, box 3, Broadus Papers; Faculty Minutes, Southern Baptist Theological Seminary, 28 Dec. 1869; Broadus, *Memoir of Boyce*, 210–211. Broadus suggested that the seminary purchased the Goodlett House in 1869, but Manly's statement and the faculty minutes indicate that Boyce bought it in 1867.

46. Broadus, *Memoir of Boyce*, 211–212.

47. Broadus, *Memoir of Boyce*, 225.

48. South Carolina Baptist Convention, *Minutes*, 1861, 97–98.

Baptists' *Christian Index*, expressed the standard view: "The result of the contest depends upon the righteousness of our cause. If slavery be not of God, then we are fighting against him, and our cause will fail. If it be of God, then our enemies are fighting against him." [49]

The seminary shared the South's fate. The endowment apparently had been invested in state bonds. Reconstruction rulers brought the southern states to repudiate their state debts, wiping out the endowment.[50] All that remained was a gift of Georgia Railroad bonds from Boyce's brother-in-law and friend, H. A. Tupper, and Boyce's own gift of a parcel of land. Each was worth $5,000 before the war but could not be sold at anything approaching fair value for some time.[51] The seminary held the legal bonds of individual Southern Baptists who still owed on their five-year pledges to the endowment, but it would have been both unfeeling and futile to press for collection. The seminary's plan relied on earning interest from its endowment to pay the professors' salaries. Without an endowment, the seminary needed to raise a significant sum of money every year just to pay salaries and other current expenses. If it could not rebuild the endowment, the school would not long survive.

Raising money in the Reconstruction-era South was a poor business. Many Southern Baptists wished to help the seminary, but few were able. On every hand they pleaded their financial losses, debts, lack of income, and poverty. Andrew Broaddus, an uncle of John Broadus, tried to collect money owed to the seminary based on the pledges made before the war. Aside from Baltimore and Washington, he could collect little: "There is scarcely any money in the country. Some of those who gave bonds, have died and left no property. Many others have lost all, and will probably never pay." [52] After fund-raising for six months in Baltimore, Washington, Virginia, and Missouri, Broaddus had collected less than $5 in cash, net of expenses, and less than $3,000 in bonds.[53]

---

49. Samuel Boykin, "Slavery," *Christian Index*, 25 Dec. 1863, 1.

50. Broadus, *Memoir of Boyce*, 198. Of the Confederate states, only Texas did not repudiate its debts (Richard F. Bensel, *The Political Economy of American Industrialization, 1877–1900* [New York: Cambridge University Press, 2000], 94–96). See also C. Vann Woodward, *Origins of the New South, 1877–1913* (Baton Rouge: Louisiana State University Press, 1967), 86–106; and J. Mills Thornton III, "Fiscal Policy and the Failure of Reconstruction in the Lower South," in *Region, Race, and Reconstruction: Essays in Honor of C. Vann Woodward*, ed. J. Morgan Kousser and James M. McPherson (New York: Oxford University Press, 1982), 349–394.

51. Broadus, *Memoir of Boyce*, 200.

52. Andrew Broaddus to John A. Broadus, 29 Mar. 1866, box 2, Broadus Papers.

53. Andrew Broaddus to James P. Boyce, 20 Aug. 1866, box 2, Broadus Papers.

One Baptist apologized for sending only four dollars: "I am ashamed to send so little but money is so very scarce here that it is almost an impossibility to get hold of it. The Yankees took all of our horses and stock, so that we have been right hard put to it, to commence our farming operations again, we had them camping on us almost at our door, our loss was very heavy, they were with us three times, I feel very thankful that I have a home left."[54]

Boyce could well sympathize. The terms of his father's vast estate required him to act as executor for decades—he was still executor at the time of his death in 1888—making him responsible for the welfare of the families of his four sisters and two brothers. Creditors pressed legal claims against all that remained of the estate and of his own property. It required considerable labor and ingenuity to prevent complete loss to the estate. The threats to the solvency of the estate came from all directions. For instance, Boyce owned part interest in a factory in Lincolnton, North Carolina. When the factory became insolvent, all the stockholders became responsible for the debt. Because Boyce was one of the few stockholders with any assets, the creditors could seize his property to the full amount of the debt. Boyce's attorney, acting under his directions, succeeded in selling the factory to new owners who assumed the debt and saved Boyce and the others from this peril.[55]

Boyce faced many such perils in the years after the war. Most damaging of all, he had pledged himself as security on loans made to his brother and brother-in-law in New York, and when they could not pay their debts, the creditors claimed Boyce's assets.[56] At one point he feared being recognized in New York lest his creditors seek to seize him. Boyce later called this time "the days of my pecuniary troubles." At the point of greatest loss he intended to sell his prized library to provide for the needs of his family, though it had been his keen desire to leave the books to the seminary's library.[57]

Boyce's secretary assured a delinquent bondholder that Boyce sympathized with persons seeking to pay their debts: "At the close of the war he paid debts of that kind to the amount of $180,000.00.... But he paid it as well as his obligations to institutions of this kind, and we are satisfied that you will do the same."[58]

---

54. Marta [?] Harden to James P. Boyce, 9 Sept. 1867, box 1, Boyce Papers.

55. G. G. Wells to John A. Broadus, 9 Nov. 1892, box 14, Broadus Papers; James P. Boyce to John A. Broadus, 8 Nov. 1888, box 12, Broadus Papers.

56. See Broadus, *Memoir of Boyce*, 202–203; James P. Boyce to John A. Broadus, 10 Oct. 1860, box 1, Broadus Papers.

57. James P. Boyce to John A. Broadus, 31 Oct. 1888, box 12, John A. Broadus.

58. E. Woodruff to L. B. Helm [?], 14 Nov. 1882, Letterpress Copy Book 10, Sept. 1882–June 1883, 417.

Boyce set up a plan to save the seminary. The seminary needed a new endowment, but Boyce could not raise money for the endowment when at the same time he scrambled for donations just to meet operating expenses. So he solicited privately 100 pledges of $100 annually for five years. These payments would provide $10,000 annually and would pay the seminary's expenses for five years. This would give Boyce freedom to raise its endowment without the concern of meeting immediate expenses for five years. The trustees asked the Southern Baptist Convention to endorse the plan, and it did. Initially the plan was successful. From January 1869 to May 1870, enough money came in to pay all salaries through the end of 1870 and to eliminate most of the seminary's debt.[59]

But the prosperity was short-lived. By 1871 many felt that times were harder than they had been since before the war. The price of cotton was so low that selling prices would not even pay off the debts incurred to plant it. There was no money to be had, John Broadus's wife, Charlotte, lamented: "Nobody can collect money that is due, nobody can pay debts."[60] By the end of 1871, Boyce could not pay the professors' salaries.[61] Many of the subscribers stopped paying on their bonds.[62]

The professors, like so many southerners, were impoverished by the war and struggled to live. Life for the faculty and their families in Reconstruction-era South Carolina was, as professor William H. Whitsitt later called it, a "fiery trial…one long nightmare.…so much poverty and sorrow and humiliation."[63] Broadus, for example, fell ill in 1866 and pleaded for repayment from those who owed him anything, but he was "utterly unable to obtain any money." He had to beg a small loan from a friend who had nothing to spare. He would soon "have nothing at all to buy food for my children."[64]

During these difficult years the professors bought on credit from Greenville merchants, or they did without. They often spent much of their vacation raising money for the seminary instead of earning extra money by filling the pulpits of urban churches whose pastors spent a month or more on vacation, or instead of writing books that would produce a little income from royalties.[65] The struggle to live, for the professors and for the seminary, continued unabated for more than a decade.

59. James Boyce to John Broadus, 16 May 1870, box 3, Broadus Papers; Broadus, *Memoir of Boyce*, 206.

60. Charlotte Broadus to John Broadus, 13 May 1871, box 3, Broadus Papers.

61. J. William Jones to John A. Broadus, 19 Dec. 1871, box 3, Broadus Papers.

62. Broadus, *Memoir of Boyce*, 206.

63. William H. Whitsitt, "A New Year's Greeting," *Baptist Courier*, 2 Jan. 1902, 1.

64. John A. Broadus to [John H.?] Griffith, 5 Oct. 1866, box 2, Broadus Papers.

65. Broadus, *Memoir of Boyce*, 207–208.

Boyce consistently borrowed money at his own risk and loaned it to the seminary for the payment of the salaries of the other professors. Although he was paying interest on the money he borrowed, he refused to receive interest on the money he loaned to the seminary until the board of trustees ordered in 1870 that the seminary pay him interest at the same rate that it cost him.[66] At one point Boyce decided that if he stopped borrowing money to pay the salaries, perhaps Southern Baptists would appreciate the gravity of the situation and be induced to give. Professors received no salary for twelve months and had to buy their necessities on credit. They did "the work of two or three men on half the salary of one man, with that salary in arrears and no certainty of ever receiving it."[67]

Manly, Williams, and Broadus served as pastors of various country churches in Edgefield, Abbeville, and Greenville counties.[68] Broadus, the most accomplished preacher on the faculty, was able to earn additional income by preaching for churches in northern cities for one or two months. They paid well and made few demands except for preaching. Such engagements afforded Broadus opportunity to work on books and articles, to raise money in the North, and, on rare occasions, to get a little rest. He became a favorite of Baptist churches in New York, Chicago, and Detroit. He developed a special relationship with members of the Orange, New Jersey, Baptist Church, who contributed generously to all the seminary's needs for many years.

The faculty had opportunities to make more money elsewhere. In 1868 the South Carolina Railroad asked Boyce to be the company's president at an annual salary of $10,000. Similar offers came to Boyce across the years.[69] Louisville's Walnut Street Baptist Church pressed Boyce to be its pastor in 1875.[70] Manly received offers of the presidency of the Richmond Female Institute, the University of Alabama, Union University in Tennessee, and Georgetown College in Kentucky, as well as the Home Mission Board.[71] Missouri's William

66. James Boyce to John Broadus, 16 May 1870, box 3, Broadus Papers.

67. Broadus, *Memoir of Boyce*, 207.

68. See Basil Manly Jr. to Crawford H. Toy, 7 Feb. 1873, Letterbook II, Manly Family Papers no. 4409, Southern Historical Collection, UNC; Edgefield Baptist Association, *Minutes*, 1866; ibid., 1867; ibid., 1868.

69. Broadus, *Memoir of Boyce*, 208–209.

70. James P. Boyce to John A. Broadus, 9 Mar. 1875, box 6, Broadus Papers.

71. Basil Manly Jr. to J. B. Taylor, 28 Aug. 1865, Manly Collection of Manuscripts, reel 2, SBTS; Basil Manly Jr. to John A. Broadus, 13 July 1871, box 3, Broadus Papers; Manly to Broadus, 27 Dec. 1872, box 4, Broadus Papers; Manly to Broadus, 13 May 1875, box 6, Broadus Papers.

Jewell College wanted Williams as its president.[72] Richmond First Baptist Church pressed Whitsitt to become its pastor.

Broadus received the largest number of offers. Leading churches pressed him to become their pastor. First Baptist Church of Richmond pressed Broadus hard in 1875, at a time when he felt keenly his debts and sacrifices. Such churches as Richmond Second Baptist Church[73] also sought to secure him as pastor. Such institutions as Washington and Lee,[74] Richmond College,[75] Vassar,[76] and Rochester recruited Broadus to serve as president. A. H. Strong pleaded with him to become president of the proposed University of Chicago. He made only $2,500 as a professor at Southern Seminary, and some offers pledged four times as much, but he ever felt that his duty was to remain at Southern.[77]

The faculty felt that their duty, their divine call, was to advance the kingdom by establishing the seminary and teaching its students. In an 1867 appeal for funds, Boyce pleaded that "our professors have had scarcely any of their salary paid since the close of the war. Although offered other positions at much larger salaries and salaries that will be paid punctually, they prefer to stay at their present posts, if they can only get necessary food and clothing for their families." The faculty stood by Boyce and the cause of an orthodox and educated ministry.[78]

Only one of the professors left because of the hardships. Manly grew restive under the combination of hard work, low pay, and Reconstruction political realities. In 1871, in addition to his heavy duties teaching at the seminary, he taught between five and ten hours per week in the Greenville Female College, he was the preacher in three different churches (they met only once or twice a month), and he had to solicit gifts of several thousand dollars to the scholarship fund and make it sustain thirty students through the year. "This doing double and treble work is injustice to myself. . . . I am tired of it." In addition, his finances dogged him, and he was caring for his ill wife. The uncertainty of the seminary's future complicated his efforts to address these problems. He did not want to leave the seminary and in 1871 declined the presidency of both Union

72. Lottie Broadus to John A. Broadus, 4 June 1871, box 3, Broadus Papers.

73. H. K. Ellyson to John A. Broadus, 26 July 1866, box 2, Broadus Papers.

74. J. William Jones to John A. Broadus, 1 May 1867, box 2, Broadus Papers.

75. J. L. Burrows et al. to John A. Broadus, 24 July 1866, box 2, Broadus Papers.

76. Edward Lathrop to John A. Broadus, 17 Aug. 1878, box 8, 1878; J. R. Kendrick to John A. Broadus, 19 Aug. 1878, box 8, Broadus Papers.

77. Franklin H. Kerfoot to S. A. Hayden, 14 Aug. 1894, Letterpress Copy Book 18, July 1893–Dec. 1895, 452.

78. James P. Boyce to "Sister" [form letter], 1 July 1867, box 1, Boyce Papers; Broadus, *Memoir of Boyce*, 205–206.

University in Tennessee and Georgetown College in Kentucky. He felt deep affection for his fellow professors and preferred teaching preachers to teaching college students, but with the seminary's future so uncertain, he was "unwilling to pass through the mill of another year or two like the past." Later in the summer of 1871 he changed his mind and accepted the presidency at Georgetown.[79] He concluded that by taking the presidency of Georgetown College he could prepare the way for the seminary's move to Kentucky and "stave off" opposition in the state. This was the deciding factor for him.[80]

Not long afterward, however, he confessed to Broadus that he was not sure that he was right in leaving the seminary. "I loved that work, and the men that were associated with me in it, as I never expect to love any other. And probably I ought to have clung to it to the end, through thick and thin." His regret over leaving the seminary endured until he returned to his former post in 1879.[81]

NORTHERN BAPTISTS AND NORTHERN SEMINARIES

The gifts of Northern Baptists proved as critical to the seminary's survival as those of Southern Baptists. In the summer of 1868 the faculty debated whether Manly and Broadus should seek to raise funds among Northern Baptists. The main objection was, Williams observed, that it would alienate many Southern Baptists: "We might gain some little perhaps by going north for aid, but would probably lose more by the feeling which would be excited in the strong southern men that the seminary was too much inclined northwards." Boyce figured that Broadus could get more money by working the same time in Virginia, but he raised "no objection to your getting all you can" in the North.[82] Manly felt some "repugnance" at the idea but decided to make the effort nevertheless, explaining: "We must have some money for the aid of those who are needy among the students, and if the South won't give it, we must get it anyhow."[83]

79. Basil Manly Jr. to John Broadus, 13 July 1871, box 3, Broadus Papers; Basil Manly Jr. to James P. Boyce, 28 Aug. 1871, box 1, Boyce Papers.

80. Basil Manly Jr. to John Broadus, 26 Oct. 1872, box 4, Broadus Papers. See also J. C. Long to John A. Broadus, 12 Sept. 1871, box 3, Broadus Papers; unattributed, "Religious," *Working Christian*, 31 Aug. 1871, 4.

81. See Basil Manly Jr. to John A. Broadus, 28 Apr. 1875, box 6, Broadus Papers. The Home Mission Board elected Manly corresponding secretary (president) in 1875, but he declined (Basil Manly Jr. to John A. Broadus, 13 May 1875, box 6, Broadus Papers).

82. Basil Manly Jr. to John A. Broadus, 30 June 1868, box 2, Broadus Papers. Manly was summarizing Williams's opinion.

83. Basil Manly Jr. to John A. Broadus, 17 July 1868, box 2, Broadus Papers.

Manly solicited funds from Baptists in Philadelphia and New York and received generous contributions, while his efforts in Virginia, Tennessee, Kentucky, and Missouri netted almost nothing.[84] For the next thirty years the faculty sought and received gifts from Northern Baptists, as Manly, Boyce, and above all Broadus forged strong relationships among them.[85]

In 1870 Broadus spent about two months preaching in the Orange, New Jersey, Baptist Church.[86] Every summer pastors from New York and other northern cities vacationed for a month or more away from the urban heat and dust. Nearly every summer Broadus supplied such New York pulpits and received generous compensation. His salary was modest even when paid on time, and he needed the extra income to pay debts and to send his family in the summer to the springs in Virginia to recover their health. "With the present gloomy prospect as to seminary finances," Broadus wrote Boyce to explain his plans to supply the pulpit of New York's Calvary Baptist Church, "I shall be obliged to do something this summer for pay."[87] Boyce did not object—how could he—but encouraged him to get acquainted with "desirable men," and "we shall be greatly helped in our New York campaign."[88] Broadus would be unable to canvass southern regions to raise funds for the seminary, but his efforts among Northern Baptists paid large dividends. Their gifts contributed largely to the seminary's survival and success.

The relationship involved some delicacy. The experiences of the Civil War and Reconstruction deepened southerners' sense of regional identity. White southerners questioned the reasons for their defeat and subjugation. The answer came from the Bible—God punished them for their sins. But the judgment did not mean that God cast them off. It was, rather, a sign of God's solicitude for their souls, for "the great chastisement he has sent upon us" was God's call to repentance and trust in spiritual truth rather than in material things.[89] This became the prevailing understanding of the meaning of the war in the South and undergirded the Lost Cause ideology and a common sense of divine transcendence.[90]

84. Basil Manly Jr. to John A. Broadus, 8 Aug. 1868; Broadus, *Memoir of Boyce*, 208.

85. Broadus, *Memoir of Boyce*, 208.

86. John Broadus to James Boyce, 30 Apr. 1870, box 1, Boyce Papers; John Broadus to James Boyce, 23 May 1870, ibid.

87. John A. Broadus to James P. Boyce, 30 Mar. 1877, box 11, Boyce Papers.

88. James P. Boyce to John A. Broadus, 4 Apr. 1877, box 7, Broadus Papers.

89. Belton O. Mauldin to Charles E. Taylor, 1 Mar. 1866, box 1, Papers of Charles Elisha Taylor, UVA. See also Mauldin to Taylor, 7 Aug. 1865, ibid.

90. See Edward J. Blum and W. Scott Poole, eds., *Vale of Tears: New Essays on Religion and Reconstruction* (Macon, GA: Mercer University Press, 2005); Mark A. Noll, *The*

At the close of the war the faculty found themselves suddenly in an alien land. All seemed unsettled by the social, economic, and political revolutions that accompanied defeat and Reconstruction. Like most white South Carolinians, the faculty believed that the state's Republican government was ruining the state, and they supported the Democratic Party's bid for control of state government.

They feared the ruin especially of Baptist educational institutions. Furman University and Greenville Female College were ruined by the general financial collapse and narrowly avoided failure. The Republican state government reorganized the University of South Carolina, and the faculty had reason to fear that Southern Baptist Theological Seminary might face a similar fate.

When the seminary's trustees met for the first time after the war, they found they did not have a quorum. Many seats were vacant because trustees had moved to other states or died. The remaining trustees could not therefore administer the seminary's affairs legally. They could not gain a quorum without electing new trustees, but they could not elect new trustees, even if nominated by the Southern Baptist Convention, without a quorum. Boyce asked the delegates to the 1868 Southern Baptist Convention to nominate new trustees and to approve the seminary's petition to the civil court to ratify their election.[91]

Boyce petitioned the South Carolina Court of Equity to install the new trustees. The judge doubted his authority to act in the matter. Under ordinary circumstances, the judge said, the matter should be remanded to the South Carolina legislature, since that body granted the original charter that created the trust. But these were not ordinary circumstances. The judge feared that if the matter came before the current radical Republican legislature, it might take advantage of the opportunity and "radicalize the whole concern." It might decide to install radical Republicans as trustees, who could replace the entire faculty. After much testimony and urgent pleading from Manly, the judge "determined to strain a point and grant our petition. This fixes it, so that at any rate nobody will be likely to attempt to rip it up, or object to it."[92]

Civil War as a Theological Crisis (Chapel Hill: University of North Carolina Press, 2006); Randall M. Miller, Harry S. Stout, and Charles Reagan Wilson, eds., *Religion and the American Civil War* (New York: Oxford University Press, 1998); Harry S. Stout, *Upon the Altar of the Nation: A Moral History of the Civil War* (New York: Viking, 2006); Daniel W. Stowell, *Rebuilding Zion: The Religious Reconstruction of the South* (New York: Oxford University Press, 1998); Charles Reagan Wilson, *Baptized in the Blood: The Religion of the Lost Cause* (Athens: University of Georgia Press, 1980).

91. Southern Baptist Convention, *Minutes*, 1868, 14–16.

92. Basil Manly Jr. to John A. Broadus, 10 July 1868, box 2, Broadus Papers.

The faculty rejoiced when the Democratic Party gained control of the state government as a result of the 1876 elections. Wade Hampton's election as governor meant the overthrow of the Reconstruction government. Students and faculty gathered with "the great mass of rejoicing people" downtown to hear victory speeches. The last speaker was Broadus, who, after a solemn "Thank God," urged the people to use the victory "for the good of the people and for the glory of God." [93] Whitsitt ever afterward displayed prominently in his study an engraving of Hampton, despite the fact that it made some visitors uncomfortable: "It signifies a great deal to me. It is a memento of times that tried men's souls and of the noble man who brought us deliverance and set our feet in a large place. I shall never forget Hampton and his work." [94]

In this context, the faculty had to be careful in how they appealed to Northern Baptists for aid. They could not seem to approve the northern view of the war, lest they dishonor their fellow southerners. If the seminary's appeals in the North caused southerners to feel that "the seminary was too much inclined northwards," it would lose critical support in the South. [95]

The faculty felt deep affection and gratitude toward their brethren in the North, but they were not "much inclined northwards." They repudiated northern evangelicalism's defective religion. Broadus warned that "under Yankee rule, we may not expect to worship God but according to Yankee faith." [96] At the 1868 meeting of the American Baptist Home Mission Society in New York, Manly made a speech objecting to a report that committed the group to recognizing "all rights and duties of citizenship" for the freed slaves, because it introduced political partisanship and because "we at the South do not recognize the social equality of the negro." Southern Baptists supported "their advancement in morals, in education and everything that goes to make up the dignity of man," Manly said, but not suffrage. [97] Williams wrote an article for the *New York Examiner and Chronicle* repudiating all designs to reform southern religion. [98]

93. J. S. Dill, *Lest We Forget: Baptist Preachers of Yesterday That I Knew* (Nashville, TN: Broadman Press, 1938), 36–37.

94. William H. Whitsitt, "A New Year's Greeting," *Baptist Courier*, 2 Jan. 1902, 1.

95. Basil Manly Jr. to John A. Broadus, 30 June 1868, box 2, Broadus Papers.

96. John A. Broadus, quoted in Paul Harvey, " 'Yankee Faith' and Southern Redemption: White Southern Baptist Ministers, 1850–1890," in *Religion and the American Civil War*, ed. Randall M. Miller, Harry S. Stout, and Charles Reagan Wilson (New York: Oxford University Press, 1998), 176.

97. Basil Manly Jr., "Dr. Manly and the Colored Man," *South Carolina Baptist*, 5 June 1868, 2.

98. William Williams, *New York Examiner and Chronicle*, 25 Jan. 1866. See also William Williams to John A. Broadus, 11 June 1868, box 2, Broadus Papers.

The faculty, like most Southern Baptists, were as opposed to religious reconstruction as to political.

Northern Baptists pressed their efforts to reconstruct Southern Baptists and reunite the two groups. The American Baptist Publication Society sold its Sunday school literature in the South so successfully that it drove the Southern Baptist Convention's Sunday School Board out of business in 1873. The American Baptist Home Mission Society narrowly missed driving the Southern Baptist Convention's Home Mission Board to the same point. By 1868 one-third of its missionaries labored in the South, and over the next two decades they won formal cooperation with many southern state conventions. The northern board had money to appoint missionaries and construct church buildings; the southern board was in debt and moribund. Southern Baptist leaders saved the Home Mission Board only by arguing that the Southern Baptist Convention could maintain its independent existence only by resuscitating the Home Mission Board.

Southern Seminary had reason to fear that Northern Baptist seminaries would sap its remaining strength in similar fashion. Northern seminaries attracted many Southern Baptist students after the war. Crozer Theological Seminary in Chester, Pennsylvania, especially drew Southern Baptist students. Some Landmarkers urged ministerial students to study at Crozer because its professors did not support recognizing alien immersions, whereas one of Southern Seminary's professors did. Most important, James M. Pendleton, who gave the Landmark movement its initial character, taught there. Thomas T. Eaton convinced one Tennessee Landmark student to give up his plans to sit under Pendleton's teaching at Crozer and to attend Southern Seminary instead, but he confessed that many in Tennessee opposed sending students to Southern. "Some of our extreme Landmarkers," Eaton said, believed that Southern Seminary's professors were "unsound" and "dangerous."[99] In 1873 at least one Mississippi student planned to transfer to Crozer because of his state's opposition to Williams.[100] After Pendleton's death, however, Crozer more commonly attracted Southern Baptists who wanted a more progressive education than they could get at Southern Seminary, at least concerning the matter of alien immersion.

But most Southern Baptist students who attended Crozer did so for one simple reason—Crozer promised to pay their living expenses. Southern Seminary could not match Crozer's offers of support. The faculty appointed Manly to administer a "Students' Fund" to defray the living expenses of the neediest

99. Thomas T. Eaton to John Broadus, 26 July 1872, box 4, Broadus Papers.
100. Crawford H. Toy to John A. Broadus, 1 Aug. 1873, box 4, Broadus Papers.

students, but the money was never sufficient to meet all needs of the students who matriculated. Alabaman B. F. Riley wrote Broadus that his "sympathy is with the S.B.T.S.," but the "amount you offered me was insufficient to have sustained me." Riley decided to attend Crozer instead because the "inducements so generously offered" were sufficient to defray all his expenses.[101] Other northern seminaries offered similar inducements. One student planned to attend Rochester Theological Seminary rather than Southern because it offered enough money to support him and his family for three years.[102] William C. Lindsay decided to leave Southern Seminary and transfer to Crozer when his money ran out and only relented when Manly promised that somehow he would find money to support him.[103]

Money was not the only reason Southern Baptist students went to northern seminaries, but it usually played a critical role. Some students felt that it was too difficult to graduate at Southern or that Southern was overpopulated. Jabez L. M. Curry, president of Virginia Baptists' Richmond College, urged the school's graduating ministerial students to attend Southern Seminary. Most or all decided to attend Crozer because of "the ease of graduation and the pecuniary inducements held out." Men whose principles allowed them to attend Crozer for these reasons were best quarantined away from the South lest their infections spread to others. "Crozer is," Curry reflected, "I am sorry to say, becoming a sort of theological cholera hospital."[104] Broadus discovered in 1888 that "several Richmond College men are going to Rochester and Crozer (more money, easy to graduate, want to know the North, etc.), and some are beginning to say we have too many students."[105]

Southerners generally held that "Yankee" culture valued money more than personal relationships, efficiency and profits more than virtue or honor. Seminary alumnus Fred Eason reflected this belief in his dealings with a prospective South Carolina student who decided to go to Rochester Theological Seminary rather than to Southern. He chose Rochester because it offered him sufficient money to support himself and his family throughout his studies there. When Eason heard the man's reasons, he did not try to dissuade him, for he knew that Southern could not provide that much support. But

101. B. F. Riley to John A. Broadus, 7 Sept. 1874, box 5, Broadus Papers.

102. C. F. Anderson [?] to John A. Broadus, 16 Sept. 1879, box 8, Broadus Papers. See also J. P. Greene to Archibald T. Robertson, 1 Feb. 1895, box 1, Robertson Papers.

103. William Williams to John A. Broadus, 11 June 1868, box 2, Broadus Papers; William C. Lindsay to John A. Broadus, 7 July 1868, ibid.; Basil Manly Jr. to Broadus, 17 July 1868, ibid.; Lindsay to Broadus, 8 Aug. 1868, ibid.

104. Jabez L. M. Curry to John A. Broadus, 31 Oct. 1874, box 5, Broadus Papers.

105. John A. Broadus to James P. Boyce, 19 Sept. 1888, box 11, Boyce Papers.

even if Southern could have furnished sufficient aid, Eason said, he saw that the man was not suitable for Southern. "He will suit those Yankees far better, being decidedly of their stripe." [106] Money rather than loyalty had controlled him.

The question of the merits of attending seminary in the North has always plagued Southern Baptist ministerial students. The considerations changed somewhat across the years, but one remained constant. Southern Baptists were a people apart. Students who received their training in the North would naturally tend to develop the principles, manners, and tastes of Northern Baptists. Such training would unfit them for most Southern Baptist pulpits. Training in a non-Baptist northern seminary only increased the concern. Later, when most northern seminaries identified with the new theology, Southern Baptist churches raised another concern. They naturally expected that graduates of those schools were infected with liberal theology.

The seminary established its own scholarship fund in 1868. The faculty assigned Manly the task of raising the Students' Fund and disbursing it to the neediest students. The first year the money came from several Northern Baptists, and Northern Baptists continued to give liberally to the fund for many years. By its second year about half the student body received support from the fund, which continued for some sixty years to supply the needs in a similar proportion.[107]

Despite the differences and rivalries of Northern and Southern Baptists, Southern Seminary needed the support from the northerners. The northern support, added to Southern Baptist gifts, kept the seminary going. The seminary would have collapsed had not many southern and northern Baptists given sacrificially to its support. Donors managed to give enough to keep the seminary from failing.

But it was not enough. South Carolina was economically prostrate for many years. The state's Baptists were struggling to save Furman University from collapse by raising a new endowment. Manly concluded in 1871 that the prospects for saving the university were "slender." [108] Others agreed.[109] In the premises, the seminary could not look to South Carolina Baptists to do much toward a new endowment. In 1877 one South Carolina pastor attributed the "meager" contribution from his church to the people's desperate poverty: "It is a struggle

---

106. Fred Eason to John A. Broadus, 2 Sept. 1874, box 5, Broadus Papers.
107. Basil Manly, "Students' Fund of the SBTS," 1 Sept. 1871, box 3, Broadus Papers.
108. Basil Manly Jr. to John Broadus, 19 July 1871, box, 3, Broadus Papers.
109. See, e.g., William Williams to John Broadus, 25 July 1871, box 3, Broadus Papers.

with us, and a severe one, to live just now.... Many of us are literally living from hand to mouth." [110]

The state's political polarization held little prospect in the near future for social stability and economic growth. State politics was divided nearly evenly by race, most whites chafed under military occupation, and civil peace was fragile. The faculty found the political situation appalling. "We are helpless except to protect ourselves," Boyce concluded after the elections of 1870. [111] Manly told his colleagues that South Carolina was "doomed." [112]

"THE SEMINARY MUST LIVE SOMEWHERE"

By 1870 it was clear that unless the seminary took extraordinary action, it would die. Strenuous efforts to raise a new endowment had failed. Boyce had borrowed heavily on his personal credit to meet expenses and could borrow no more. Even if the seminary sold its Greenville property, the proceeds would scarcely cover the debt. Its only asset, it seemed to Manly, was Boyce's "earnest determination, the echo of his confidence and zeal." Remaining in Greenville would likely mean the seminary's failure, he thought, but they would not despair, for "the seminary must live somewhere." [113]

The best hope was to move. Other cities wanted the seminary and were prepared to raise money for a new endowment. Its presence would strengthen Baptist work, boost civic pride, and inject cash into the local economy. In 1870 the South Carolina Baptist Convention offered to release the seminary from all obligations to remain in the state if it agreed to release the convention from its obligations to the seminary.

Boyce thought it best to move the seminary to Atlanta, if Baptists and civic leaders there would give it $200,000 and those in the rest of the state $100,000. [114] Atlanta was attractive to Boyce because if the seminary moved there, he would not have to withdraw from it. In 1870 Boyce believed that he would probably have to leave the seminary because his father's estate remained in a desperately precarious condition. If the seminary moved to Atlanta, however, he could care

110. J. O. B. Dargan to James P. Boyce, 3 Apr. 1877, box 2, Boyce Papers.

111. James Boyce to John Broadus, 24 Sept. 1870, box 3, Broadus Papers.

112. Basil Manly Jr. to John Broadus, 22 Nov. 1871, box 3, Broadus Papers.

113. Basil Manly Jr. to Crawford H. Toy, 7 Feb. 1873, Letterbook II, Manly Family Papers, no. 4409, Southern Historical Collection, UNC, microfilm.

114. James Boyce to John Broadus, 24 Sept. 1870, box 3, Broadus Papers.

for the interests of the estate and keep up his teaching duties.[115] William Thomas, recently pastor of Greenville First Baptist Church, expected both Boyce and Manly to resign their posts at the seminary. He noted that unless Boyce had recently changed his mind, he "will leave the seminary so soon as its finances allow."[116]

Atlanta, however, was not alone in wanting the seminary. In 1871 Boyce began soliciting bids from interested cities and told Broadus that "our future location is very uncertain."[117] Most of the bids came from the "West," that is, Tennessee and Kentucky. Some talked of establishing a "grand university," perhaps by combining several of the struggling state colleges, at Chattanooga or Memphis, and placing the seminary at its center, but even if desirable it was not feasible.[118]

Boyce traveled to the various cities to investigate the desirability of their locations and the feasibility of their offers.[119] He then invited the friends of the seminary to convene an "educational convention" at Nashville in 1872 to help decide the issue. The convention heard offers from Memphis, Nashville, Murfreesboro, Knoxville, and Chattanooga in Tennessee, as well as Atlanta and Louisville, but gave no advice in resolving the question.[120]

The seminary entertained several generous offers. Georgia Baptists had promised $250,000 if the seminary moved to the state. Baptists in Memphis proposed moving the seminary to that city and establishing a great university with the seminary at its center, promising to raise $200,000 in the city.[121] Chattanooga offered not just promises but actual bonds, cash, and real estate amounting to $125,000. Tennessee Baptists promised another $100,000

---

115. James Boyce to John Broadus, 24 Sept. 1870, box 3, Broadus Papers. Boyce had to travel frequently to New York and Chattanooga to oversee the interests of the estate and defend it against creditors' suits. Greenville at the time was served by only one railroad with infrequent trains and an inconvenient route (another line was under construction). The additional time required for travel made it difficult for Boyce to get back to Greenville in time to meet with his classes. Atlanta, due to its nearness to Chattanooga and its superior connections, would have made it possible for Boyce to meet his classes often enough to do them justice.

116. James Boyce to John Broadus, 24 Sept. 1870, box 3, Broadus Papers; William Thomas to John Broadus, 14 Nov. 1871, box 3, Broadus Papers.

117. James Boyce to John Broadus, 25 July 1871, box 3, Broadus Papers.

118. Basil Manly Jr. to James P. Boyce, 21 May 1870, box 1, Boyce Papers.

119. Faculty Minutes, Southern Baptist Theological Seminary, 10 Mar. 1872.

120. "Baptist Educational Convention, Nashville," *Christian Index*, 14 Mar. 1872, 43.

121. Samuel Boykin, "Letter from Memphis," *Christian Index*, 7 Mar. 1872, 38.

for any Tennessee location.[122] Many persons assumed that Boyce would sway the committee to choose Chattanooga, since many of the assets of his father's estate were there and Boyce traveled there frequently to look after them. Largely for this reason, Boyce pointedly refused to tell trustees his opinion on the merits of the various locations and their proposals, though the trustees individually and as a body asked him repeatedly for his views.[123] Manly was skeptical of all the Tennessee locations and characterized them as molded in Graves's image. He told Broadus that it would be "in vain to depend on Tennessee. Big mules, big folks, and brag, but nothing else grows well there."[124] Boyce did not agree. He knew that Graves did not seem to want the seminary to move west, but felt nevertheless that after Louisville, Memphis was the most promising alternative.[125] Louisville Baptists envisioned raising $500,000 for the seminary's endowment. They promised to raise $300,000 in Kentucky for the seminary, provided that Baptists elsewhere gave an additional $200,000.

When the board of trustees met in May 1872, it concluded that the proposals from Atlanta, Chattanooga, Nashville, and Louisville were not sufficiently definite to take action. These four were, however, suited to the seminary's needs. A large portion of the endowment would have to come from the Baptists and philanthropists of the selected city. These four cities were sufficiently prosperous to give some assurance on that point. If the seminary moved to one of these cities, Boyce would probably be able to remain in his position. The board appointed a committee of seven trustees to visit the four cities in August and asked Boyce to accompany them. It also voted to give the committee power to choose the city on behalf of the full board. After its visits, the committee chose Louisville.[126]

The board presented the proposal for the relocation to the May 1873 meeting of the Southern Baptist Convention. The convention did not possess official authority to decide such a matter for the seminary; trustees possessed it. But because the seminary needed the endorsement, support, and goodwill of Baptists throughout the South, trustees asked the approval of the Southern Baptist Convention. Many delegates from Virginia, North Carolina, and South

---

122. James P. Boyce, "Southern Baptist Theological Seminary," *Western Recorder*, 3 May 1873, 1.

123. James P. Boyce, "The Two Objections to the Seminary, I," *Christian Index*, 16 Apr. 1874, 2.

124. Basil Manly Jr. to John A. Broadus, 22 Mar. 1873, box 4, Broadus Papers.

125. James Boyce to John Broadus, 25 July 1871, box 3, Broadus Papers; James P. Boyce to John A. Broadus, 17 Apr. 1873, box 4, Broadus Papers.

126. "Southern Baptist Convention," *Christian Index*, 23 May 1872, 82; Broadus, *Memoir of Boyce*, 202–203; Minutes, Board of Trustees, Southern Baptist Theological Seminary, May 1872.

Boyce and the trustee
relocation committee atop
Chattanooga's Lookout
Mountain, 1872

Carolina arrived at the meeting planning to vote against the relocation, but
Boyce's speech delineating the seminary's condition and prospects, and explaining the board's decisions and motives, was "irresistible" and "conclusive." Only
one delegate voted against the relocation to Louisville.[127]

The General Association of Baptists in Kentucky met in May 1873 also. A
committee of fifteen recommended endorsing the relocation and the conditions on raising the endowment. Boyce spoke of indications of God's providential favor of the seminary, of his confidence in securing the $500,000
endowment and more besides, and of the benefits of the seminary's relocation
for Kentucky Baptists. Broadus then explained how the seminary's plan and
curriculum were perfectly adapted to the Baptist denomination. "By his gentle
and persuasive manner, and his ardent expression of his devotion to the work

127. Unattributed, "Editor Mills and the Seminary," *Western Recorder*, 31 May 1873, 4;
unattributed, "Removal of the Seminary," ibid.; J. H. Luther, quoted in "Southern Baptist
Theological Seminary," ibid., 4; Broadus, *Memoir of Boyce*, 237–238.

of the ministry," one delegate wrote, he evoked tears across the audience and won the hearts of all.[128]

The board charged Boyce to act as the seminary's agent to raise the endowment. Boyce moved to Louisville in 1872. His plan was first to secure bonds worth at least $150,000 from Louisville's Baptists. He then planned to canvass the rest of Kentucky to secure bonds for another $150,000. Only after securing the state's allotment would he canvass the rest of the South for the final $200,000.[129] Both the Southern Baptist and the Kentucky conventions urged their constituencies to "contribute liberally" to the effort.[130] The prospects looked bright. The reality proved otherwise.

SHALL THE SEMINARY SUSPEND

No sooner had Boyce moved to Louisville and begun the effort to raise the new endowment than the seminary faced a new crisis. It ran out of money to pay current expenses. The seminary faced several financial problems. It needed to raise an endowment, which alone could sustain the school. The school's main operating expense was the professors' salaries, which amounted to about $12,000 annually.[131] Total annual expenses totaled less than $15,000. But until it had at least $250,000 in performing investments, the endowment interest would not be able to pay the salaries. Until that time, it needed the churches to give the money needed to meet current expenses, and needed to raise money each year for the Students' Fund, to provide room, board, and books to needy students who otherwise would not be able to attend.

Indeed, by October 1872 the endowment effort was going badly. Some of Louisville's leading Baptists opposed the seminary's move there. Boyce had hoped to raise $200,000 in Louisville but now expected only $150,000. Baptists throughout the state withheld their annual payment when due because they

128. George Hunt, "Southern Bapt. Theo. Seminary," *Western Recorder*, 28 June 1873, 2.

129. James P. Boyce, "Southern Baptist Theological Seminary," *Western Recorder*, 3 May 1873, 1; Hunt, "Southern Bapt. Theo. Seminary," 2.

130. Unattributed, "Southern Baptist Theological Seminary," *Western Recorder*, 24 May 1873, 4.

131. This did not include Boyce, who was working without salary at the time. In 1872 the salary was apparently $3,000 for each of the other four professors (James P. Boyce to John A. Broadus, 12 Oct. 1872, box 4, Broadus Papers). In 1873 the total salary for the four others was $11,500 (James P. Boyce to John A. Broadus, 3 Nov. 1873, box 5, Broadus Papers). Afterward regular salary was $2,500 (Franklin H. Kerfoot to S. A. Hayden, 14 Aug. 1894, Letterpress Copy Book 18, July 1893–Dec. 1895, 452).

feared Boyce would not raise the $300,000 needed from Kentucky as a condition of making the move. Many Baptists in the state believed that the total was set so high in order to guarantee the effort's failure. Boyce nevertheless remained "hopeful and determined," working unremittingly and trusting in God's help for success.[132]

Several important Louisville citizens opposed the seminary's relocation and refused to contribute.[133] J. Lawrence Smith, a wealthy and prominent Louisville resident, privately opposed the seminary in conversations with prominent citizens and Baptist ministers. He told one pastor that the clergy were foolish to support the seminary's relocation because when the "learned professors" sat in their churches, they would find themselves embarrassed by their modest learning and would preach poorly as a result. Smith told the pastors that the students would take over all the church work and push aside the lay workers. He said that the seminary professors would take leadership of the state Baptist causes and drive the current Kentucky Baptist leaders "out of office." Boyce thought him a good man and worked to discover the source of his opposition.[134]

Boyce discovered that many potential contributors in Louisville hesitated to give because they feared that Boyce would not succeed. Boyce therefore told them in 1873 that the seminary would not move to Louisville until he had raised at least $250,000. Arthur Peters, one of the seminary's most generous supporters in Louisville, insisted that the seminary should not relocate until it had raised the entire $500,000 endowment. Boyce saw little alternative but to accept this as a condition of relocating. This meant that the seminary would remain in Greenville indefinitely, since Boyce had raised scarcely one-fifth of the amount needed.[135] But Boyce found that when he established the condition of getting $500,000 before relocating, opposition began to dissolve: "Since I have declared that I have begun to conquer. The opposition in the state is dying out."[136]

Unfortunately, ability to pay died out at about the same time. The financial panic of 1873 precipitated an economic depression that lasted for years. Flood

132. James Boyce to John Broadus, 12 Oct. 1872, box 4, Broadus Papers.

133. Most prominent were Nimrod Long, J. Lawrence Smith, and William Caldwell. See James Boyce to John Broadus, 18 Nov. 1872, box 4, Broadus Papers; James Boyce to John Broadus, 17 Apr. 1873, ibid.

134. James P. Boyce to John A. Broadus, 6 Mar. 1873, box 4, Broadus Papers. At least one Louisville pastor to whom Smith spoke took such fear to heart: M. B. Wharton told William Whitsitt that he "couldn't preach before the seminary professors" (John A. Broadus to James P. Boyce, 18 Mar. 1873, box 11, Boyce Papers).

135. James P. Boyce to John A. Broadus, 6 Mar. 1873, box 4, Broadus Papers.

136. James P. Boyce to John A. Broadus, 17 Apr. 1873, box 4, Broadus Papers.

and drought destroyed crops, credit dried up, money was scarce, and gifts to the seminary were few.[137] A pastor in Raleigh, North Carolina, reported in 1873, "I have never seen our merchants so much depressed as they are at present."[138] The crisis continued and deepened throughout 1873. In January Boyce urged the churches throughout the South to take up an offering to meet the seminary's current expenses. Receipts did not match expenses, and he had to borrow $4,000. Banks would not loan any more money to him or to the seminary. As Boyce wrote, "I have no funds on hand to pay even the January salaries."[139] But only fourteen churches responded, and the offerings amounted to only $334. Receipts from bond payments due were also small. In May 1873 Boyce renewed the appeal, explaining the seminary's immediate need for $6,000 to pay the professors' salaries and meet loan obligations.[140] He received only $1,600 over the next five months. He had no money at his disposal, either the seminary's or his own. The banks in Louisville had suspended. He had already borrowed on his own credit to pay the professors' salaries, and he feared that as banks continued to tighten their credit, they might call in their loans to him. Then the seminary would have to sell all the Greenville property, including the dormitory, at unfavorable prices. He counseled the faculty to be as "contented as you can without money."[141]

In December 1873 he found the "times so tight now I can do nothing."[142] So he issued another public appeal. He explained that his two former appeals produced little response. Debt had therefore accumulated, and he could borrow no more. The banks were in fact calling due their loans. Two compelled payment in January 1874 of loans totaling $10,000.[143] The faculty had not been paid since July, and he still needed $6,000 to pay their salary. If no money came in, he would have to sell the Greenville property, but because of the hard times, he could get only about $15,000 for it, though it was worth $30,000. Boyce by temperament eschewed sensationalism and alarmism, but he warned Southern

137. William H. Williams to John Broadus, 29 Oct. 1872, box 4, Broadus Papers; William H. Williams to John A. Broadus, 14 Apr. 1873, box 4, Broadus Papers.

138. T. H. Pritchard to John A. Broadus, 30 Oct. 1873, box 5, Broadus Papers.

139. James P. Boyce, "Southern Baptist Theological Seminary, Greenville, S.C.," *Western Recorder*, 18 Jan. 1873, 2.

140. James P. Boyce, "Southern Baptist Theological Seminary," *Western Recorder*, 31 May 1873, 6.

141. James P. Boyce to John A. Broadus, 2 Oct. 1873, box 5, Broadus Papers.

142. James P. Boyce to John A. Broadus, 20 Dec. 1872, box 4, Broadus Papers.

143. James P. Boyce to John A. Broadus, 3 Nov. 1873, box 5, Broadus Papers; James P. Boyce to John A. Broadus, 9 Jan. 1873, box 5, Broadus Papers.

Baptists that "the very existence of the seminary is endangered by the tendency of so many to thrust upon others the whole work of supporting it."[144]

The Kentucky Baptists whose pledges were coming due at the end of 1873 were not paying either, preferring to wait and see whether Boyce could raise the entire endowment before they paid.[145] Churches refused to permit agents to come and preach and take offerings in the midst of the financial crisis, so Boyce spent his time meeting with individuals and writing letters requesting support.[146] He considered resigning and giving up the enterprise as hopeless: "I doubt even now the possibility of permanently endowing the Seminary, and fear we shall have to give up the whole work. Perhaps this is the will of the Lord."[147]

Banks called due more loans during 1874.[148] As usual, Boyce somehow managed affairs and kept one step ahead of insolvency. Boyce's reputation for business acumen worked at times like this to weaken his appeals for aid. Despite the fact that the seminary had no money, had mounting debts, and had only a trickle of donations coming in, some held off giving because they believed that Boyce was a financial wonderworker. Broadus told Boyce that "the people have come to think you can accomplish impossibilities, and so they are disposed to stand by and let you run the machine by your financial skill and influence."[149]

Boyce was now without wonders and without cash. Since he had moved to Kentucky he had been paying from his own pocket the expenses incurred in the endowment effort. By April 1874 he had exhausted his own cash resources: "I am forced to say plainly that I have not the means of my own to pay" the expenses of the endowment effort.[150] He had only one way to resolve the crisis—the seminary would have to close. With loans unavailable, creditors calling debts due, property devalued, and Baptists unable to give, there seemed no alternative. Boyce lamented: "I think however we shall have to recommend suspension of all work at Greenville, payment of indebtedness by sale of property there, and no reopening until the permanent endowment is raised and agency work by all the professors. This is the best. Sometimes I feel as though it were best to give up the whole thing there is so much apathy, and I am so exceedingly annoyed by the fear some of the best men in Kentucky have to pay their installments lest

144. James P. Boyce, "An Appeal for the Seminary," *Western Recorder*, 6 Dec. 1873, 8. See also James P. Boyce, "The Seminary Again," *Western Recorder*, 20 Dec. 1873, 5.

145. James P. Boyce to John A. Broadus, 23 Dec. 1873, box 5, Broadus Papers.

146. James P. Boyce to John A. Broadus, 14 Mar. 1874, box 5, Broadus Papers.

147. James P. Boyce to John A. Broadus, 19 Jan. 1874, quoted in Robertson, *Life and Letters of Broadus*, 293.

148. James P. Boyce to John A. Broadus, 4 Sept. 1874, box 5, Broadus Papers.

149. John A. Broadus to James P. Boyce, 29 Dec. 1873, box 11, Boyce Papers.

150. James P. Boyce, "To the Baptists of Kentucky," *Western Recorder*, 4 Apr. 1874, 2.

we should not make up the final amount."[151] Boyce knew that suspending the seminary was a perilous course and risked killing it. In 1870 he had refused to consider it because of this danger. "I'll spend every cent I have rather than suspend," he told a friend at the time.[152] Now he had, and suspension was the only option. If Southern Baptists began paying on their bonds, perhaps the seminary could reopen in a year or two.

The faculty opposed suspension. Broadus argued that suspending the seminary would doom it. Baptists would conclude that it had failed and would be unwilling to pay outstanding pledges or give new ones. If Boyce and the faculty could not raise sufficient money to meet current expenses by the early fall, Broadus proposed, "I should take it as a clear proof that the brethren won't sustain the seminary at all, and should prefer to quit and be done with it, rather than to die a dozen deaths before it is over."[153]

Boyce met with the faculty in Greenville and told them that "it is impossible to maintain the seminary on the present system, and he accordingly stated that he would feel forced to urge the executive committee to recommend to the board of trustees to suspend the seminary at the end of the present session till such time as the completion of the endowment or other arrangements may enable us to resume exercises." The other members of the faculty protested and asked Broadus to compose an appeal to the Baptists of the South to aid the seminary in its emergency. They asked Boyce to undertake a private campaign asking generous individuals to pledge gifts to meet current expenses.[154] Boyce wrote several hundred letters. He judged that he needed nearly a 100 percent positive response rate to raise enough money to sustain the seminary, but only about 50 percent signed the bonds he sent them.[155]

Just as Boyce had done beginning at the Baltimore meeting of the Southern Baptist Convention in 1868, he initiated a campaign for pledges to pay current expenses. He solicited bonds from donors who promised to give a specific amount each year for five years toward annual expenses.[156] So Boyce chose to make a public appeal and put the matter before Southern Baptists by publishing the facts in the Baptist newspapers of the South. He explained the seminary's

---

151. James P. Boyce to John A. Broadus, 15 Jan. 1874, box 5, Broadus Papers.

152. Boyce, quoted in Broadus, *Memoir of Boyce*, 212.

153. John A. Broadus to James P. Boyce, 9 Mar. 1874, box 11, Boyce Papers.

154. Faculty Minutes, Southern Baptist Theological Seminary, 30 Jan. 1874, vol. 1, 1868–1894; Boyce, "A Question for Every Baptist to Consider," *Christian Index*, 9 Apr. 1874, 2–3.

155. James P. Boyce, "A Question for Every Baptist to Consider," *Western Recorder*, 4 Apr. 1874, 2–3.

156. See James P. Boyce to John A. Broadus, 24 Mar. 1874, box 5, Broadus Papers.

situation and his intention to recommend that trustees suspend the school until the endowment was fully pledged. He presented also the faculty's objections to his recommendation.[157] If the effort failed, the seminary would close.

Boyce called on all members of the faculty to give up other plans for the summer of 1874 and help him meet the great crisis by canvassing the South for support.[158] Boyce said that "if we are to go on with the seminary," Broadus had to attend the Southern Baptist Convention, the General Association of Baptists in Kentucky, and the Mississippi Baptist Convention, as well as "do much work for me this summer" in fund-raising.[159] When students asked whether the seminary would be open in the fall of 1874, Broadus replied, "I hope that it will go on—that I don't know how we are to manage, but I hope and pray that God may put it into the hearts of the brethren to help manfully and immediately."[160]

The uncertainty and gloom soon turned to hope. Boyce and the faculty attended the state conventions that summer and laid the seminary's cause before the brethren. They canvassed the various states, holding services and private meetings with potential donors. Southern Baptists rallied around the seminary and pledged just enough to keep it going. Most significant, Kentucky Baptists pledged enough to the endowment fund to afford hope in the final success of the endowment campaign. Broadus, who spent most of the summer canvassing Kentucky with Boyce, summarized the summer's results: "Though the full amount for current support the next five years has not been reached, we are near it, and the result is sure. Dr. Boyce and I were sufficiently successful in Kentucky for permanent endowment, notwithstanding drought, to satisfy us that the thing can be carried through there, by hard work. I am now quite hopeful as to the seminary's future."[161] Northern Baptists met the crisis nobly as well. When Broadus attended the annual gatherings of the Northern Baptists in 1874, they showed their appreciation of Broadus and the seminary by "overwhelming applause" and, more important, by pledges of more than $2,100 a year for the current expense campaign, along with cash gifts and promises of more.[162] It took longer than expected to get all the pledges needed, but by November 1874

157. James P. Boyce, "A Question for Every Baptist to Consider," *Christian Index*, 9 Apr. 1874, 2–3.

158. John A. Broadus to James P. Boyce, 9 Mar. 1874, box 11, Boyce Papers.

159. James P. Boyce to John A. Broadus, 9 Jan. 1874, box 5, Broadus Papers. See also John A. Broadus to James P. Boyce, 6 Apr. 1874, box 1, Boyce Papers.

160. John A. Broadus to James P. Boyce, 21 Apr. 1874, Boyce Papers.

161. John A. Broadus to Carrie Davis, 4 Aug. 1874, box 5, Broadus Papers.

162. John A. Broadus to James P. Boyce, 26 May 1874, box 1, Boyce Papers.

the $75,000 in five-year bonds for current expenses came in.[163] These bonds, if paid, would sustain the seminary's operating expenses for five years and afford Boyce opportunity to spend his time raising the endowment rather than scrambling for funds to pay salaries.

Unfortunately, many of the bonds were not paid, and the money came in much smaller amounts than Boyce had hoped. The enduring business depression diminished donors' ability to give. Just as significant, however, it intensified the competition for donations. The various Baptist state conventions were struggling to maintain their colleges and missionary work, and they pressed their own desperate campaigns during these years. Virginia's "Memorial Campaign" of 1872, for example, was pushed with such a "fuss" that the state's Baptists "scarcely even hear of anything outside."[164] During such campaigns, state Baptist leaders discouraged fund-raising efforts on the part of the Southern Baptist Convention's southwide institutions, the seminary especially. South Carolina Baptists launched a "Centennial Campaign" in 1876 to raise $50,000 to be shared equally between Furman University and Southern Baptist Theological Seminary. The campaign committee secured William C. Lindsay, one of the state's most captivating speakers, to canvass the state for the cause. Money was still scarce, and few responded to Lindsay's appeals, despite the support of the state's leading Baptists. In the end, South Carolina Baptists gave only $700, less than the expenses incurred to employ Lindsay.[165] Other state conventions had similar experiences, though generally without any apportionment for the seminary. They did not generally welcome competition with their state fund-raising efforts.

The opposition, indifference, refusals, and hard times were a severe trial. Boyce despaired of accomplishing the task by his own strength. He initially placed too much confidence, he told Broadus, in the greatness of the cause and in his own ability: "I fear I came in too great self-confidence and conviction that so good a cause must commend itself. The Lord has taught me that all hope in man is vain and as I have been able to look to him alone I have some wonderful evidences of his aid."[166]

Although Boyce maintained good spirits and determination, he doubted that he would succeed. "I begin to fear lest I am not the man for this work. It requires more personal power of impressing oneself and more persistence and

163. Boyce reported $74,400 on 6 Oct. (James P. Boyce to John A. Broadus, 6 Oct. 1874, box 5, Broadus Papers.

164. J. M. Broadus to John A. Broadus, 31 Jan. 1873, box 4, Broadus Papers.

165. William C. Lindsay, "To the Baptist Pastors of South Carolina," *Working Christian*, 6 Jan. 1876, 2; William C. Lindsay to John Stout, 9 Jan. 1877, Lide-Coker-Stout Papers, USC; William C. Lindsay, "Centennial Report of South Carolina," *Working Christian*, 11 Jan. 1877, 2.

166. James P. Boyce to John A. Broadus, 10 Dec. 1872, box 4, Broadus Papers.

harsh treatment of others than I can feel to be gentlemanly."[167] Broadus knew Boyce, the seminary's situation, and the denomination's character intimately, and he blocked the advance of Boyce's doubts: "Nay, nay, no such word as fail. Somehow, somehow, you are bound to succeed. The seminary is a necessity. Our best brethren want it. God has blessed it thus far. It is your own offspring. You have kept it alive since the war—fed it with almost your own heart's blood. It must succeed, somehow, and you are the man that must make it succeed."[168] There was no one else. It was on Boyce's shoulders to succeed or fail.

Raising the Kentucky share of the endowment during the prolonged economic depression that began with the panic of 1873 proved far more difficult than Boyce had imagined it could be. Had he known in advance, he would not have undertaken it. "In securing this subscription in Kentucky," Boyce wrote a donor who was having second thoughts, "I have had because of the peculiar times to do a more Herculean task than I should have dared to attempt had I foreseen what I must do for success."[169] Boyce drew strength from his theology. Even in the depths of the financial crisis, without any money at his control, foreseeing at least two more years of hard effort, Boyce was confident in God's sovereignty and blessing: "It may be that terrible times are ahead which may engulf everything. Thank God all things work together for us, for his cause, and I believe shall work for his seminary."[170] Boyce persevered, with the aid and encouragement of the faculty, and trusting the cause to God's providential care, he finally accomplished the impossible.

CALVINISM

The theology that Boyce relied upon was Calvinism. It was the doctrine of the seminary's Abstract of Principles and the prevailing theology of Baptists in the nineteenth-century South.[171] A significant number rejected the doctrine of

167. James P. Boyce to John A. Broadus, 10 Mar. 1873, box 4, Broadus Papers.

168. John A. Broadus to James P. Boyce, 14 Mar. 1873, box 4, Broadus Papers.

169. James P. Boyce to J. C. McFerran, 22 Apr. 1879, Letterpress Copy Book 3, Jan.–Dec. 1879, 221.

170. James P. Boyce to John A. Broadus, 2 Oct. 1873, box 5, Broadus Papers.

171. See E. Brooks Holifield, *Theology in America: Christian Thought from the Age of the Puritans to the Civil War* (New Haven, CT: Yale University Press, 2003), 273–290; Thomas J. Nettles, *By His Grace and for His Glory: A Historical, Theological, and Practical Study of the Doctrines of Grace in Baptist Life* (Grand Rapids, MI: Baker, 1986); Anthony L. Chute, *A Piety above a Common Standard: Jesse Mercer and the Defense of Evangelistic Calvinism* (Macon, GA: Mercer University Press, 2004).

"limited atonement," and the rest did not make belief in it a condition of fellowship. But the churches and associations generally refused fellowship with pastors or churches that rejected other aspects of Calvinism.[172]

The non-Landmark leaders of the southeastern states drew on a well-established Calvinist tradition. Jeremiah B. Jeter, president of the Foreign Mission Board and a seminary trustee, explained to his readers that Baptists believed in predestination. God "elects or predestinates some to be saved," and others "are destined to be lost."[173] Samuel Boykin, editor of *Kinds Words* and other Sunday school publications, explained that since Christ's death was vicarious, it was "necessary to limit the extent of his atonement to the number of those for whom he died."[174] Henry H. Tucker, editor of Georgia's *Christian Index* and president of Mercer University, taught in striking terms the doctrines of total depravity, predestination, and particular redemption.[175] David Shaver, another editor of Georgia's *Christian Index*, wrote that the rejection of the distinctive teachings of Calvinism was a passage "to grievous forms of error—an avenue in which Henry Ward Beecher stands but midway."[176] C. T. Bailey, editor of North Carolina's *Biblical Recorder*, affirmed that he believed "in the doctrine of predestination and personal election."[177] The creeds adopted by the churches and associations reflected these commitments.

But the Baptist leaders of the Southwest, many of them Landmarkers, were just as keen to advance Calvinism. James R. Graves disavowed the label of Calvinism but nonetheless advocated traditional five-point Calvinism. When Graves was preparing to debate Methodist preacher Jacob Ditzler on baptism, communion, and perseverance in 1875, he asked Broadus's advice on defending "limited atonement" from objections based on 1 John 2:2 and 2 Corinthians 5:19. His argument, he told Broadus, was "wholly based on the covenant of redemption. Christ undertook to save those his Father gave him—for these he died. These he ransomed by his death."[178] Graves did indeed establish the

172. See, e.g., Minutes, Chattahoochee Baptist Association, 1871, in manuscript minute book, 76.

173. Jeremiah B. Jeter, "Queries," *Religious Herald*, 16 May 1878, 2.

174. Samuel Boykin, "Extent of the Atonement," *Christian Index*, 6 Mar. 1861, 2.

175. See, e.g., H. H. Tucker, "The Doctrine of Election," *Christian Index*, 29 Jan. 1880, 4; Tucker, "Election—Fatalism," ibid., 4 Mar. 1880, 4; Tucker, "The Divine Particularity in the Salvation of Sinners," ibid., 25 Mar. 1880, 4; Tucker, "Total Depravity," ibid., 15 Feb. 1883, 8.

176. David Shaver, "Calvinism," *Christian Index*, 26 Oct. 1871, 166.

177. C. T. Bailey, "Personal and Other Items," *Biblical Recorder*, 13 July 1881, 2.

178. James R. Graves to John A. Broadus, 1 Nov. 1875, box 6, Broadus Papers.

doctrine of perseverance on the covenant of redemption, including total depravity, unconditional election, limited atonement, and irresistible grace.[179] Jesus was the "surety, mediator, only for 'the seed of Abraham'—the elect of mankind." Their names "were put in the eternal contract," and none for whom Christ died would be lost. There was "no universal atonement."[180]

Landmark leader James B. Gambrell, editor of Mississippi's *Baptist Record* and later editor of Texas's *Baptist Standard* and executive secretary of the Texas Baptist Convention, assured Mississippi Baptists that he believed "most fully and firmly in predestination" and that "all the saved will owe their salvation to predestination."[181] He held that although men were "free agents," acting as they chose, their free agency "does not prevent God's governing men as he chooses." God "can cause men to do freely what he wishes them to do." Gambrell also taught particular redemption: "Those for whom Christ atoned must be pardoned.... If justice is satisfied, who shall lay any charge against God's elect, for whom Christ died? The sacrifice of the Lamb of God...makes the salvation of all for whom it is offered certain."[182] Jesus bore the sins of the elect only, Gambrell wrote, for "Christ pays with his blood...and gets all he pays for."[183] Landmark leader Thomas T. Eaton, editor of the *Western Recorder* from 1887 to 1907 and a seminary trustee, took it for granted that Baptists were Calvinists: "The essence of Baptist doctrine, called usually the great Calvinistic faith, is that it makes God great."[184]

The number of Southern Baptists who opposed Calvinism or were indifferent to it was sufficient to alarm many Baptist preachers. Boyce feared in 1850 that many of the Baptists in Virginia's Culpepper and Rappahanock counties were tending toward Arminianism.[185] This concern was one of the factors that induced him to establish the seminary. Few Southern Baptists were Arminians—perhaps none of the clergy—but many held "lax views" of the doctrine of election, most

179. James R. Graves, *The Graves-Ditzler, or, Great Carrollton Debate: Final Perseverance*, vol. 6 (Memphis, TN: Southern Baptist Publication Society, 1876), 1126–1142.

180. Graves, *Graves-Ditzler*, 1136, 1138.

181. James B. Gambrell, "Free Agency," *Baptist Record*, 8 Nov. 1877, 2; Gambrell, "Note," *Baptist Record*, 23 May 1878, 2.

182. James B. Gambrell, "Bro Everett on the Atonement," *Baptist Record*, 9 Jan. 1879, 2.

183. James B. Gambrell, "Eld. J. P. Everett on the Atonement," *Biblical Recorder*, 30 Jan. 1879, 2.

184. T. T. Eaton, quoted in A. J. S. Thomas, "Brag Will Out," *Baptist Courier*, 16 Mar. 1893, 2.

185. James P. Boyce, untitled, *Southern Baptist*, 18 Sept. 1850, 2.

commonly by teaching that God elected persons because he foresaw that they would repent and believe.[186]

William F. Broaddus, the seminary's Virginia agent, encouraged the faculty to write books while the seminary was suspended during the Civil War, but he warned that if they exported "more Calvinism than is meet to be written," it could do "mischief" among Virginia Baptists.[187] Broaddus considered preachers who leaned toward "the creed of Arminius" to be "defective" in their theology, but he knew also that some Virginia Baptists might find an unqualified statement of the faculty's Calvinism troubling.[188] G. T. Wilburn worried in 1874 that many Texas Baptists rejected the doctrine of election or made election dependent on God's foreknowledge, but he assured readers that many others were "faithful contenders of the truth" and preferred "to please God rather than men."[189]

The seminary faculty taught Calvinism because the Bible taught it. It was the doctrine of Jesus and Paul. The system of doctrine "commonly called Calvinism," Broadus wrote, "is believed by many of us to be really the teaching of the apostle Paul."[190]

Boyce taught a traditional five-point Calvinism. It was the doctrine of the founders of the Philadelphia and Charleston Baptist associations, and of such preachers as Richard Furman and Jesse Mercer, who initiated the great missionary and educational organizations of Baptists in the South. These facts made the doctrine more dear to Boyce, but they did not make it true. Above all, he held the doctrine because he found it in the Bible.

Boyce assigned Calvinist textbooks for his systematic theology classes, though none had the combination of readability, comprehensiveness, and compactness that he wanted. In his English-language course he assigned successively John L. Dagg's *Manual of Theology*, John Dick's *Lectures on Theology*, Charles Hodge's *Systematic Theology*, J. J. Van Oosterzee's *Christian Dogmatics*, Alvah Hovey's *Manual of Systematic Theology*, A. A. Hodge's *Outlines of Theology*, and finally his own condensed *Abstract of Systematic Theology*. In his Latin theology course he assigned Francis Turretin's classic statement of Calvinist doctrine, *Institutio*

---

186. B. W. Whilden, "Baptist Confession of Faith and the Doctrine of Election," *Baptist Sentinel* 2 (1871): 409. See also Shaver, "Calvinism," 166.

187. William F. Broaddus to John A. Broadus, 23 Feb. 1862, box 1, Broadus Papers.

188. William F. Broaddus to John A. Broadus, 8 Mar. 1869, box 2, Broadus Papers.

189. G. T. Wilburn, "Texas Baptists," *Christian Index*, 2 Apr. 1874, 2. See, similarly, E. F. T., "The Texas Baptist State Convention," *South Carolina Baptist*, 30 Oct. 1868, 2.

190. Broadus, *Memoir of Boyce*, 310; see also ibid., 73.

Theologiae Elencticae.[191] Boyce added his own lectures on various topics and gave his own ideas throughout the course. When Boyce traveled to New York and other places in 1860 to raise endowment and to attend to matters of business, Manly taught his theology class.[192] Williams taught systematic theology in 1861–1862, when Boyce was with the army, and 1871–1876, due to Manly's leaving and Boyce's move to Louisville.[193]

The other faculty evidently agreed pretty thoroughly with Boyce. Broadus undertook a study of Calvinism in 1857. He wrote Charles Hodge in an effort to acquire an edition of Calvin's works. He asked his uncle Andrew Broaddus, a veteran Baptist preacher, "how far Calvinism should be carried." His uncle affirmed both that God was completely sovereign and that humans were fully accountable to repent and believe in Christ, but their perfect compatibility was beyond human understanding: "I can not fathom the mystery connected with God's sovereignty and man's accountability."[194] Broadus concluded that the Calvinist approach was scriptural.

Throughout his career Broadus insisted that God was absolutely sovereign and humans were responsible. Broadus, like his colleagues, taught that God's sovereign election was consistent with human responsibility and agency. The contradiction was apparent rather than real, even though human intelligence could not grasp their consistency. "The scriptures teach an eternal election of men to eternal life, simply out of God's good pleasure," but those who attain salvation must "accept the gospel invitation and obey the gospel commandments." Christians cannot apprehend their consistency, but "we must not for that reason deny either of them to be true."[195] God's predestination unalterably secured the salvation of the elect, but none would be saved unless they voluntarily repented and believed. Like Boyce, Broadus appreciated Charles Hodge's three-volume

191. James P. Boyce to John A. Broadus, 10 Oct. 1860, box 1, Broadus Papers; John Stout to Fanny Coker, 18 Sept. 1869, Lide-Coker-Stout Family Papers, USC; James P. Boyce to John A. Broadus, 30 Aug. 1878, box 8, Broadus Papers; Broadus, *Memoir of Boyce*, 268, 304–307.

192. James P. Boyce to John A. Broadus, 10 Oct. 1860, box 1, Broadus Papers; John A. Broadus to James P. Boyce, 11 Oct. 1860, ibid.

193. James P. Boyce to John A. Broadus, 16 Mar. 1862, quoted in Robertson, *Life and Letters of Broadus*, 191–192. James L. Reynolds taught systematic theology in 1876–1877 while Williams was on sick leave.

194. Charles Hodge to John A. Broadus, 6 Jan. 1857, box 1, Broadus Papers; Andrew Broaddus to John A. Broadus, 3 Mar. 1857, attached to Robertson, "Life and Letters of John A. Broadus."

195. John A. Broadus, *Commentary on the Gospel of Matthew* (Philadelphia: American Baptist Publication Society, 1886), 450.

Systematic Theology and encouraged young ministers to read the "ponderous volumes." A young James M. Frost, later the founding corresponding secretary of the denomination's modern Sunday School Board, thanked him for it.[196]

In various places Broadus expressed his agreement with the Calvinist approach. He taught that each person's "natural depravity is absolutely total," [197] and that God's grace was "not bestowed blindly nor by chance, but in all wisdom and intelligence," according to God's "sovereign pleasure." It was the result of God's predestination, which was "antecedent to and the ground of election." [198] God had a sovereign right over "sinful creatures" and was "under no obligation to show favor" to them. God acted justly in "choosing and rejecting according to his own purpose." God chose them "not based upon faith as foreseen by God" but based rather on "the decree of God." [199] This was because "all are equally deserving of punishment," and "the decision between 'vessels of wrath' and 'vessels of mercy' must be left to God." [200] When Jesus praised the Father for hiding the gospel from the wise and revealing it to "babes" as the Son chooses (Matt. 11:25–27), Broadus explained that this was an act of "sovereign, electing grace." Jesus as the "sovereign Son reveals the Father only to such as he chooses." The proper response to God's sovereignty was not to demand explanations but to render praise, Broadus said, for Jesus did not explain "God's sovereign dealings with men," but rather taught the "propriety of the sovereign Father's course." [201] Many persons criticized the "terrible doctrine of predestination," Broadus said, but to the apostle Paul "this doctrine was the greatest consolation." Predestination, Broadus held, "is the foundation of our hope." [202]

Broadus seemed to teach also the doctrine of particular redemption. He held that the atonement's intrinsic value was sufficient "that all should be saved if they accepted it" by faith in Christ, but Jesus intended it for the elect only. "His death was never expected, nor divinely designed, actually to secure the

196. James M. Frost to John A. Broadus, 30 July 1877, box 8, Broadus Papers; Frost to Broadus, 28 Oct. 1885, box 11, Broadus Papers. To laypersons Broadus could recommend James M. Pendleton's *Christian Doctrines* (see, e.g., J. A. Miller to John A. Broadus, ca. 13 Jan. 1894, box 15, Broadus Papers).

197. John A. Broadus, "The Pauline System of Christian Doctrine, no. 3," 84, box 19, Broadus Papers.

198. John A. Broadus, "Notes on Ephesians," box 19, Broadus Papers.

199. John A. Broadus, "The Pauline System of Christian Doctrine, no. 11," 349, box 19, Broadus Papers.

200. John A. Broadus, "The Pauline System of Christian Doctrine, no. 10," 328, 332–333, box 19, Broadus Papers.

201. Broadus, *Commentary on Matthew*, 252–253, 256.

202. John A. Broadus, "Dr. Broadus on Predestination," *Baptist Courier*, 2 Oct. 1890, 1.

salvation of all, and so in the sense of specific purpose he came 'to give his life as a ransom for many.'" [203] Jesus died as a substitute, and "inasmuch as he bore the sins of others, they are discharged from guilt and punishment." He "purchased them by enduring the punishment of their sins." When Paul wrote that Jesus "died for all" (2 Cor. 5:14–15), it meant that he "endured the punishment instead of all believers," who are forgiven through faith because they have shared in the death of Christ, "their representative." [204]

Williams also argued the Calvinist distinctives in traditional fashion. He taught that God's decrees determined "whatever takes place" and included "all things." He taught that God imputed Adam's guilt to his posterity, resulting in "universal total depravity," in which all persons lacked the "moral ability to do what is spiritually good" and were "totally destitute of any love of God or any inclination to do his will or engage in his service." He explained that scriptural election was "God's eternal and unchangeable choice of certain persons to salvation of his sovereign will." He taught that Christ's death was a "limited atonement," because a "true substitution and satisfaction" necessarily involved specific "persons whose place is taken and not an indiscriminate mass," and because the Bible taught that the atonement actually purchased and procured repentance, faith, and salvation. He held that the Holy Spirit's work of "imparting spiritual life and renewing the will" was "irresistible grace" and was granted to "the elect only." He taught also that the "perseverance" of the saints was a "necessary inference from the doctrine of election" and from the "nature of the union between the Christian and Christ." [205]

Basil Manly evidently held similar Calvinist positions, but he published relatively little material explaining his views of doctrine. He affirmed his confidence in God's complete sovereignty in many places and drafted the seminary's Calvinist statement of faith, the Abstract of Principles. [206] Crawford H. Toy also left little record of his theological views, though he affirmed God's complete

203. Broadus, *Commentary on Matthew*, 419.

204. John A. Broadus, "The Pauline System of Christian Doctrine, no. 5," 148, 153, box 19, Broadus Papers.

205. William Williams, quoted in George J. Hobday, Systematic Theology Notes, William Williams, 1872–1873, 58–59, 65, 88–89, 132, 142, 166, George J. Hobday Student Notebooks, 1872–1874, WFU.

206. See, e.g., Basil Manly Jr., "Can We All Agree to Do It," *South Carolina Baptist*, 4 May 1866, 2; Basil Manly Jr. to John A. Broadus, 2 Oct. 1875, box 16, Broadus Papers. In Manly's personal copy of the 1850 *Baptist Preacher*, Manly or someone else wrote margin notes defending and affirming election and limited atonement. The orthography is quite similar to Manly's (ms. margin notes, in A. M. Poindexter, "The Imputation of Sin to Christ," *Baptist Preacher* 9 [1850]: 186–187, SBTS).

sovereignty and human responsibility in terms similar to those Broadus used. A student recorded that Toy told his Old Testament class in 1875 that they should preach both truths in equal measure and not attempt to reconcile them: "On one hand God's government is absolute—He controls everything, thought, actions, and everything. And on the other side we take the position that every divine message is conditioned on a certain moral quality and attitude of the heart." [207]

Whitsitt agreed with the Calvinist doctrine also. He frequently commended the solid orthodoxy of the Philadelphia Confession of Faith. He praised an English Baptist preacher because "his predestinarian orthodoxy was a real comfort." [208] He rejected Alexander Campbell's teaching that the Holy Spirit called everyone in the same way and left them to their free will. "Those called in the gospel sense," Whitsitt countered, "are the elect." [209] He taught his students that Baptists believed that "the salvation of men has its eternal foundation in the electing decree of God." [210]

Not all students graduated convinced of the faculty's Calvinism. Student A. W. Middleton expressed in class his opposition to Boyce's undiluted Calvinism, and later student Charles Kendrick agreed. [211] Some Baptist preachers, and perhaps even more Baptist laypersons, found Calvinism unscriptural and distasteful. But the Calvinism provoked little objection and no significant controversy. Its hold on the denomination was weakening, however, in the late nineteenth century. This was largely the result of a growing pragmatism and activism in church life in America, which relegated many traditional doctrinal commitments to neglect, though rarely to outright rejection. A small but influential group of leaders, many of them trained at Southern Seminary, rejected much of the old Calvinism under the inspiration of a new experientialist approach to Christianity. In the early twentieth century the seminary played a critical role in leading the denomination away from Calvinism. But until then it remained the faith of the denomination, and objections to the seminary focused on other issues.

207. Toy, quoted in A. J. Holt, "Lecture Notes of C. H. Toy's O.T. Class," 31 Mar. 1875, SBTS.

208. William H. Whitsitt, "Two Strict Baptist Churches," *Baptist Church*, 23 Nov. 1899, 1.

209. William H. Whitsitt, Journal, 324–325, Whitsitt Papers.

210. William H. Whitsitt, *Position of the Baptists in the History of American Culture: Inaugural Address, Greenville, S.C., Sept. 2, 1872* (n.p., 1884), 12.

211. C. E. W. Dobbs, "Our Second Session and the Trying Days of '61," *Seminary Magazine* 3 (1890): 124–125; C. A. Kendrick, "Dr. Williams and the Seminary," *Christian Index*, 4 Apr. 1872, 53.

JAMES R. GRAVES, ALIEN IMMERSIONS, AND THE SEMINARY

At the same time the seminary was raising its new endowment and preparing to move west, western critics attacked the faculty's soundness. They accused the faculty of holding unscriptural views regarding baptism, specifically that they taught open communion and the validity of "alien immersions." They suggested also that Southern Baptists could place no confidence in the seminary's orthodoxy, since the seminary was, they claimed, independent of denominational control.

The most serious opposition came from James R. Graves and other Landmarkers. Graves regularly sowed doubts concerning the seminary during the 1870s. Graves had been a polarizing figure in the denomination since the late 1850s. In 1859, as editor of the *Tennessee Baptist*, he published a statement that suggested that Robert B. C. Howell, pastor of Nashville First Baptist Church and president of the Southern Baptist Convention, had slanderously accused Graves of falsehood. Graves was a member of the church, which after investigation brought Graves before the church's discipline under a charge of slander. Graves raised a procedural objection and led a faction to withdraw and form their own church. The controversy attained immediate celebrity and polarized the denomination in the South. Joseph E. Brown, a prominent Georgia Baptist, said that "the name of a Baptist could scarcely be mentioned, but some one would ask which wing he belonged to—Is he a Graves man, or is he a Howell man?"[212] The denomination narrowly averted division. Howell received the denomination's vote of confidence when delegates elected him president of the 1859 Southern Baptist Convention, but he declined election as a conciliatory gesture. Graves persistently contended with his fellow Baptists and remained a controversial figure until his death in 1892. He sought to avoid formal breaches with his denominational brethren, but he took advantage of any opening to weaken their standing by attacking their views or actions, often by innuendo rather than explicit accusation. Graves relished the contention. His standing and power derived largely from his role as leader of minority dissent in the denomination. He could have led a splinter movement outside the denomination, but he preferred the larger stage afforded by remaining within. He needed, therefore, to temper his criticism with some show of support.

Graves sought to undermine confidence in Boyce and the seminary at the same time he claimed to support it. At the 1870 meeting of the Southern Baptist Convention, for example, Graves objected to a sermon that Boyce delivered

---

212. Joseph E. Brown, quoted in "Proceedings of the Georgia Baptist Convention," *Southern Baptist*, 5 May 1860, 1.

there on the suffering of Christ.[213] William F. Broaddus said that Boyce's arguments were "unanswerable."[214] When the sermon was published in denominational newspapers, it was well received throughout the South, Crawford Toy
said, and was a "timely vindication of the truth."[215] Graves preached a sermon
rebutting Boyce's that night.[216]

At the same meeting, Boyce explained the purposes and needs of the seminary and appealed for funds to support students who needed financial aid.
Boyce wanted fifty persons to pledge $200 each. Graves rose and demanded
the floor to raise a point of order. Graves said that "he would be one of the fifty
to give two hundred dollars each to this object." Graves and several others subscribed.[217] For more than ten years, however, Graves did not pay his pledge, and
on one occasion he "paid" interest on his pledge by charging the seminary for
notices, which his paper had previously published without charge. Boyce cred-
ited Graves with the interest but refused to send any more notices to Graves's
Tennessee Baptist, an outcome that no doubt suited Graves.[218]

In 1871 Graves saw another opening for attacking the seminary. Baptist newspapers in the North and the South that year opened their columns to discussions of open communion. The editors came out uniformly against the practice,
but a significant minority of Northern Baptist pastors approved the practice.[219]
Open communion was the practice of inviting all professing Christians to the
Lord's Supper without raising any question about whether they had been baptized. It held that baptism was not a necessary prerequisite to participation in
the Lord's Supper. But most Baptists in the North and almost all in the South
practiced close communion. Close communion was the position that baptism—
immersion subsequent to repentance and faith—was a necessary prerequisite
to participation in the Lord's Supper. And they held to close communion as an
essential element of New Testament church practice. Baptist churches typically
dismissed a pastor who embraced open communion sentiments. Associations
dismissed churches that embraced the practice. No Southern Baptist pastors

213. For the published version of the sermon, see James P. Boyce, "The Doctrine of the
Suffering Christ," *Baptist Quarterly* 4 (1870): 385–411.

214. William F. Broaddus, quoted in John Broadus to James Boyce, 23 May 1870, box
1, Boyce Papers.

215. Crawford Toy to John Broadus, 15 Nov. 1870, box 3, Broadus Papers.

216. James Boyce to John Broadus, 16 May 1870, box 3, Broadus Papers.

217. Unattributed, "Sayings and Doings," *Working Christian*, 26 May 1870, 2.

218. James P. Boyce to John A. Broadus, 25 Feb. 1873, box 4, Broadus Papers.

219. See Lottie Broadus to John A. Broadus, 25 Feb. 1871, box 3, Broadus Papers;
William D. Thomas to John A. Broadus, 26 Aug. 1871, box 3, Broadus Papers.

approved the practice, with one exception: John A. Chambliss, the seminary's first full graduate.

In August 1871 Chambliss resigned as pastor of the Richmond, Virginia, Second Baptist Church because he adopted open communion views. Within a year Chambliss reversed himself and rejected open communion, but in the meantime the seminary came under suspicion as the source his aberrant position.[220]

James R. Graves opened the columns of his *Tennessee Baptist* to attacks on the seminary. He published an article charging that Chambliss embraced open communion views under the influence of the professors at Southern Seminary. This charge had little effect, since all the faculty held to close communion. Boyce afterward pointed out that all the professors taught and practiced close communion. No professor who rejected close communion could in fact teach at the seminary. They pledged themselves to teach in accordance with and not contrary to the Abstract of Principles, which stated plainly that believer's baptism by immersion was "prerequisite to church fellowship and to participation in the Lord's Supper."[221]

Graves pressed at the same time a more promising line of attack. In the same article that charged the seminary with teaching open communion, the writer alleged that the faculty also taught the validity of alien immersions performed by pedobaptist clergy. William Williams did in fact recognize the validity of some alien immersions, and Graves pressed the issue. He wrote Williams asking him his views respecting alien immersions.[222]

Alien immersion referred to the practice of acknowledging the validity of immersions performed by non-Baptist clergy. Most Southern Baptists, whether Landmark or non-Landmark, rejected the validity of such immersions. "Landmarkers are generally opposed to alien immersions," Landmark leader James B. Gambrell explained, but so were "thousands who oppose Landmark doctrine."[223] But some preachers, especially in Virginia, recognized alien immersions as valid baptism in many instances. Graves encouraged attacks on the seminary for justifying alien immersions.

220. Unattributed, "Action of the Second Baptist Church," *Working Christian*, 17 Aug. 1871, 3; J. A. Chambliss, "Reconsidered," *Working Christian*, 23 May 1872, 3; William D. Thomas to John A. Broadus, 23 Aug. 1871, box 3, Broadus Papers; Thomas to Broadus, 26 Aug. 1871, box 3, Broadus Papers.

221. James P. Boyce, "The Two Objections to the Seminary, IV," 14 May 1874, 2.

222. See William Williams to John Broadus, 29 Nov. 1871, box 3, 1871.

223. James B. Gambrell, "Landmarkism and Alien Immersions," *Baptist Record*, 8 Mar. 1877, 2.

Baptist newspapers published Williams's response to the charges: "If a believer is immersed by a pedobaptist, or unbaptized minister of Christ, I am not able to prove from scripture, to my satisfaction, that the candidate has not materially and essentially obeyed the command....No Baptist holds to close communion, as it is called, more strictly and firmly than I do." [224] He recognized alien immersions as valid, but he upheld close communion.

For Landmarkers, an administrator who was not validly baptized himself could not on principle baptize others validly. Only a duly baptized person could baptize another. But just as important, Landmarkers held that baptism was valid only if it was authorized by a true gospel church. Since Landmarkers held that pedobaptist churches were not valid churches in any sense, such organizations could not authorize valid baptisms. On the basis of the Landmark argument, the validity of every baptism depended on the pedigree of the administrator. Unless the pedigree included an unbroken succession of administrators whose own baptisms had been at the hands of immersed men, it was not pure. There was no cure for a defective pedigree.

Williams identified the great weakness of this argument: "How will anyone know that he has been baptized?" Williams knew that the man who immersed him had himself been immersed, but "who immersed him I do not know." [225] In most cases, no one could ascertain any information about the quality of the baptism of the person who baptized one's own administrator. And even that information would not begin to meet the demand to know that an uninterrupted succession of valid immersions extended backward to the apostles.

But Williams did not credit the more traditional argument against recognizing as valid baptism those immersions performed by pedobaptist preachers. Non-Landmarkers agreed that the administrator himself should be baptized, but they held that an unbaptized administrator did not necessarily invalidate the act. They held that there was a more fundamental defect: pedobaptist clergy did not practice New Testament baptism even when they immersed because of their practice of infant baptism. New Testament baptism was a sign of the new believer's union with Christ in his death, burial, and resurrection. Presbyterians and Methodists acknowledged that baptism could not mean this when applied to infants. Roman Catholics and Campbellites taught that baptism accomplished the very things that it symbolized. But all of them,

---

224. William Williams, "Ordination, Church Ordinances, Alien Immersion, Etc.," *Christian Index*, 25 Jan. 1872, 14–15.

225. William Williams, "To Rev. J. S. Baker," *Christian Index*, 2 May 1872, 69.

traditional Baptists held, vitiated New Testament baptism by investing the ceremony with unbiblical meaning. So the issue for non-Landmark Baptists was not succession but the meaning of baptism, established in the doctrines and practices of the church.

In 1873 Boyce felt confident that the alien immersion controversy would not seriously injure the seminary and that Williams was free to fight back. He wrote to Broadus, "I do not fear the badgering of Williams. If any one badgers, let him fight. We need not fear the consequences. I think some eyes would be opened to see that much can be said on the other side of a question on which they speak so dogmatically." [226]

The most direct criticism of the seminary and Williams on this matter came from Mississippi. Boyce thought that it was critical for Williams to represent the seminary at the 1873 Mississippi Baptist Convention. He expected that Williams would be able to win the trust of many there and significantly weaken the opposition. But if they treated him badly, Boyce felt, it would help the seminary. "Soul liberty is worth more than alien immersion," Boyce judged, "even with Landmarkers." [227] But respected leaders defended Williams, even though they disagreed with his position on alien immersions. [228]

Williams alone believed that churches should recognize some alien immersions. J. William Jones, a graduate and agent of the seminary, replied that he knew positively that Boyce, Broadus, Manly, and Toy opposed the validity of such "baptisms." Williams, he said, did not teach that they were valid but gave no opinion on the question. [229] Broadus held that persons should not be received based on their alien immersions, but they should be baptized "for the sake of good order and to prevent any troublesome questions from afterward arising." [230] Whitsitt in 1872 agreed with Williams's principle that every case of alien immersion must be evaluated on its own merits, but in practice he apparently agreed with Broadus. [231] By 1875 Whitsitt apparently felt that alien immersions were invalid on grounds of principle. [232]

226. James P. Boyce to John A. Broadus, 25 Feb. 1873, box 4, Broadus Papers.

227. James P. Boyce to John A. Broadus, 21 Apr. 1873, quoted in Robertson, *Life and Letters of Broadus*, 290.

228. See, e.g., Joseph Baker, "Dr. Williams and His Raspers," *Christian Index*, 11 Apr. 1872, 57; E. B. Teague, "Dr. Williams and His Critics," ibid.

229. J. William Jones, "Alien Immersions," *Christian Index*, 14 Dec. 1871, 194.

230. John A. Broadus, "Alien Immersion," *Baptist Courier*, 25 Jan. 1894, 2.

231. William H. Whitsitt to John A. Broadus, 4 Mar. 1872, box 4, Broadus Papers.

232. William H. Whitsitt, Journal, ca. 1875, 352, 354, Whitsitt Papers, SBTS.

BOYCE AND THE TWO OBJECTIONS

Graves attacked the seminary on one other front, raising questions in 1873 about its control. The attacks on the seminary had been growing for several years. Several state conventions passed resolutions rejecting open communion and opposing the recognition of alien immersions as valid baptisms. Graves interpreted the actions as repudiations of the seminary. But Boyce's 1873 endowment campaign gave him a new hook.

Boyce was asking Southern Baptists to give in support of his campaign to raise $500,000 in endowment. Graves suggested that Southern Baptists would not sacrifice and give unless they had the "power to remove a professor" who began teaching "manifest and dangerous errors."[233] They questioned why they should feel compelled to endow $500,000 to secure the school's finances when they had no means of securing the orthodoxy of the school's teaching. Southern Baptists, whether Landmark or not, were unlikely to give much to a seminary without power to control it. Graves was suggesting that the seminary belonged more to Boyce than to Southern Baptists.

Graves's objection resonated well with many southwestern Baptists. James B. Gambrell, a young Mississippi pastor who later became one of Southern Baptists' most influential leaders, echoed Graves's sentiments. He doubted whether it was "safe policy for Baptists to endow, and thereby render entirely independent, institutions over which they never extend any positive control." The denomination needed guarantees that "if we endow it, it will remain faithful to the denomination." It needed remedies available "in the event that it does not continue to reflect the views of our people."[234] Gambrell was a warm supporter of the seminary, but without secure mechanisms for denominational control of the seminary, his support cooled.

In February 1874 Graves published an article by a Mississippi pastor summarizing the concerns about the seminary common in Landmark regions. He objected that the seminary taught doctrines "against which some four or five state conventions have protested," and that the denomination did not own or control the seminary.[235]

In 1874 Boyce decided to answer these concerns forcefully. It was time to place a full vindication of the seminary before Southern Baptists. Boyce had

233. James R. Graves, untitled, *Tennessee Baptist*, 5 July 1873, 4.

234. James B. Gambrell, "An Important Question Connected with the Southern Baptist Theological Seminary," *Tennessee Baptist*, 19 July 1873.

235. Quoted in James P. Boyce, "The Two Objections to the Seminary, IV," *Christian Index*, 14 May 1874, 2.

asked Broadus to canvass the faculty to learn their views on the relevant points so that he could be sure of his facts.[236] Then, in a series of five articles that coincided with the seminary's 1874 campaign to raise the five-year fund for annual expenses, Boyce refuted the objections made against the seminary.

In three of the five articles Boyce assured Southern Baptists that they controlled the seminary. The seminary, he said, belonged to the denomination in every proper sense, and the denomination controlled it through its power to nominate trustees.[237] The seminary's charter declared the board to be "self-perpetuating," but it also defined strict limitations. It limited the board to choosing persons nominated by the Southern Baptist Convention. The board had to elect one of at least three persons nominated by the convention for each vacant seat on the board. If, however, the convention failed to nominate anyone, the board had the power to elect persons on their own authority—though they had to be members of a "regular Baptist church."

The 1858 education convention gave the board the power of self-perpetuation because it had no authority to require the Southern Baptist Convention to appoint trustees or take responsibility for its operations in any way. Boyce believed that the convention did not invite the seminary to a direct connection to the convention because of the competing educational interests in various state colleges. The 1858 education convention recognized that the Southern Baptist Convention would not be likely to nominate the seminary's trustees even though it had the authority to do so. It adopted a charter, therefore, that gave the board the right to fill its own vacancies if the Southern Baptist Convention refused to nominate anyone.[238]

Boyce himself had not wanted a self-perpetuating board and insisted on the right of the denomination to control the institution. Boyce was "peculiarly sensitive that sound doctrine should there be perpetually taught" and believed that denominational control was the best security. The seminary would wield great influence, and Boyce was anxious that the influence "should be secured to the Baptist principles which I had learned to cherish as those of the word of God." He would not have supported a board that was independent of denominational control: "I for one, therefore, was unwilling that a self-perpetuating board should be established which could not be controlled should it depart from the faith." Denominational control protected the seminary's orthodoxy and gave

236. James P. Boyce to John A. Broadus, 7 Apr. 1874, box 5, Broadus Papers.
237. James P. Boyce, "The Two Objections to the Seminary, I," *Christian Index*, 16 Apr. 1874, 2.
238. James P. Boyce, "The Two Objections to the Seminary, II," *Western Recorder*, 18 Apr. 1874, 2.

the Southern Baptist Convention the power to control the board through its nominations. The board's power of self-perpetuation permitted the Southern Baptist Convention to remain unentangled with the seminary if it wished.[239]

Since 1858 the Southern Baptist Convention had exercised its power to nominate trustees only once. In 1868 the trustees discovered that they did not have a quorum and so could not conduct any business, including the election of trustees. They requested the convention to make nominations to the board. The convention did so, though it nominated only one person for each vacancy rather than three.[240]

In 1896, when controversy over seminary president William H. Whitsitt threatened to divide the convention, the board adopted a motion requiring the president to inform the Southern Baptist Convention of any vacancies on the board and "of the right of the convention to nominate." In 1897 the Southern Baptist Convention finally began to take advantage of its right to nominate at least three persons to fill vacancies on the board.[241] In later years trustees amended the charter, first to permit the convention to nominate two persons for each vacancy, and later, one person.

The charge that four or five state conventions protested certain doctrines taught at the seminary was based on the fact that the conventions in Georgia and Mississippi passed resolutions against open communion and alien immersion, and the West Tennessee and Arkansas conventions passed resolutions against alien immersion. But these resolutions had little direct bearing on the seminary, since all the professors rejected open communion, and four of the five professors rejected the validity of alien immersions. William Williams alone held that churches should in some instances admit persons to Baptist churches based on an alien immersion.

All the charges against the seminary then boiled down to this: one professor favored recognizing some alien immersions. Boyce pointed out that the conventions that passed resolutions against alien immersions also passed resolutions expressing their support of the seminary and recommending it to the state's ministerial students.[242] These conventions took the practical ground that although they rejected alien immersions, they would not break fellowship with

239. Boyce, "The Two Objections to the Seminary, II," 2.

240. James P. Boyce, "The Two Objections to the Seminary, III," *Western Recorder*, 25 Apr. 1874, 2.

241. Minutes, Board of Trustees, Southern Baptist Theological Seminary, May 1896, 214; ibid., May 1897, 227–228. In 1898 the convention did not nominate persons for vacancies, but asked the board to fill no vacancies that year. The board agreed, and in 1899 the convention nominated persons to all vacancies.

242. Boyce, "The Two Objections to the Seminary, IV," 2.

persons who recognized them. Boyce argued that toleration of alien immersion views had always been the position of Southern Baptists and that for this reason the Abstract of Principles said nothing about it.[243]

DENOMINATIONAL TRUST

During those long years of struggle for the seminary's life, Broadus was confident that as long as Boyce survived, the seminary would also. He wrote to Boyce: "By living for the seminary you will, I am right confident, save it; by dying for it you inevitably kill it—buried in your grave." [244] The seminary, Broadus said, "would have perished a dozen times" had it not been for Boyce's "exertions and sacrifices." [245] Southern Seminary's existence and survival rested to an unusual degree in the person of James P. Boyce. As a result, the denomination identified the seminary with his name above all others.

Boyce's labor and sacrifice made the seminary Boyce's school. Boyce himself recognized that he had a claim on the seminary even if he neither owned nor controlled it:

If to have longed for the existence of such an institution from before the time of my ordination to the ministry, if to have prayed and labored for it, for the past nineteen years, if to have urged it upon unwilling hearts, and to have argued for it with those who found objections to it in other theological seminaries which had no application here, if to have succeeded in developing a plan which had never before been adopted of combining all classes of our ministry in one institution without detriment to any, if to have sacrificed for it the ease and comfort which might otherwise easily have been mine, if to have spent days and years of humiliation in begging for it, stooping to do for this institution what I would not do for bread to eat if I were starving, if to have foregone numberless opportunities of bettering my pecuniary condition, and to have oftentimes incurred embarrassments that its credit might be sustained and its faculty paid, if to have subjected my family to deprivations which have caused my nearest friends to accuse me of injustice to them, if to have spent sleepless nights and to have more than once endangered my health and even my life, if to have done these things makes the seminary mine—and in what other sense is it

243. James P. Boyce, "The Two Objections to the Seminary, V," *Western Recorder*, 29 June 1874, 2.
244. John A. Broadus to James P. Boyce, 19 Mar. 1874, box 11, Boyce Papers.
245. John A. Broadus to James P. Boyce, 11 Oct. 1873, box 5, 1873.

so?—I accept it as such to make all that it is and all its glorious possibilities a free gift to the Baptist denomination of the South.[246]

But Boyce could not retain denominational trust alone. Much depended on the faculty, who won the trust of Southern Baptists by effective preaching and by wise public leadership of the denomination. Their public roles often meant raising money or making reports, the first essential to his institutional stewardship and the second to his denominational responsibility. The Southern Baptist Convention did not invite official seminary reports during Boyce's lifetime, but the denomination at large needed regular reports if it was going to give money and its endorsement to the seminary. Boyce and the trustees reported seminary affairs unofficially in addresses to state conventions, the Southern Baptist Convention, and in articles for newspapers. Preaching and denominational leadership beyond seminary affairs also played a critical role in winning denominational trust. When facing skepticism or criticism, Boyce generally wanted the faculty representative to preach rather than raise money. If by preaching they won the people's hearts, the gifts would undoubtedly come.

One of the important occasions for raising money, especially for the student scholarship fund, was to take an offering at the annual meeting of the various state conventions. In 1869 the faculty wanted to raise funds in Georgia. The faculty agreed that Boyce should attend the Georgia Baptist Convention "with the idea of not collecting money, but making an impression." He would seek to deepen the impression when the Southern Baptist Convention met in Macon later. Later in the summer, they hoped, they could "prosecute an agency in Georgia effectively." [247] For similar reasons the faculty by mutual agreement pursued a policy of writing regularly for various denominational newspapers.[248]

The seminary faculty needed the trust of the denomination to repel critics and enemies, to attract sufficient support, and to draw students. The trust was essential because the seminary played a critical role in denominational health. Its faculty served as the fountainhead for the spread of doctrine and church practice among the churches, so the churches naturally watched the seminary's movements carefully. They listened for unfamiliar accents and were quick to raise the alarm when suspicions of unsound teaching arose. When Professor Crawford H. Toy began promoting unsound doctrine in the late 1870s, it threw the seminary into crisis.

246. Boyce, "The Two Objections to the Seminary, I," 2.
247. Faculty Minutes, Southern Baptist Theological Seminary, 9 Apr. 1869, vol. 1.
248. See, e.g., Faculty Minutes, Southern Baptist Theological Seminary, 9 Apr. 1869, vol. 1.

3

MODERNISM'S FIRST MARTYR

Crawford H. Toy and the Inspiration Controversy

Southern Baptist Theological Seminary was the first American school to dismiss a teacher over the emerging liberal theology. Charles A. Briggs, professor of theology at Union Theological Seminary, who nearly suffered the same fate, correctly identified Southern Seminary professor Crawford H. Toy as modernism's first martyr: "The first to suffer for the higher criticism in the United States was C. H. Toy."[1] Toy's beliefs ran afoul of Boyce's vision of a seminary bounded by an orthodox creed and controlled by the denomination. When Toy began teaching the new theology's view of inspiration and its critical reconstruction of the history of Israel, the seminary dismissed him. Boyce's leadership in the dismissal, and the faculty's defense of traditional views of the Bible, established a historical precedent that has endured in denominational memory. It helped shape Southern Baptist identity and became an emblem of the denomination's commitment to orthodoxy and to the popular control of its institutions.[2]

1. Charles A. Briggs, *General Introduction to the Study of Holy Scripture* (New York: Scribner's, 1899), 286.
2. The literature on Crawford H. Toy is relatively thin. See Billy Grey Hurt, "Crawford Howell Toy: Interpreter of the Old Testament," Ph.D. dissertation, Southern Baptist Theological Seminary, 1965; Pope A. Duncan, "Crawford Howell Toy: Heresy at Louisville," in *American Religious Heretics: Formal and Informal Heresy Trials*, ed. George H. Shriver (Nashville, TN: Abingdon Press, 1966), 56–88; Pope A. Duncan, "Crawford Howell Toy (1836–1919)," in *Dictionary of Heresy Trial in American Christianity* (Westport, CT: Greenwood Press, 1997), 430–438; Paul R. House, "Crawford Howell Toy and the Weight of Hermeneutics," *Southern Baptist Journal of Theology* 3 (1999): 28–39.

This conflict represented a new state of affairs in American Protestantism. Southern Baptists were among the first American denominations to experience controversy over modernist or liberal theology, or, as many called it, the new theology.[3] The new theology sought to counter growing skepticism about the validity of traditional Christianity. Developments in philosophy toward an austere empiricism fostered the skepticism. On the principle of empiricist science, Christianity's claim to absolute truth and morality could not logically derive from finite historical experience—eternal and unconditioned truth could not derive from historically conditioned occurrences. On a popular level, the traditional Protestant approach to the Bible, with its plain literal approach to the Bible's historical accounts, seemed increasingly implausible to many Americans and Europeans as the nineteenth century went on. The parting of the sea, the slaughter of the Amalekites, and the cursing of the fig tree seemed not only an improper basis for moral absolutes but self-evidently fabulous.

Although the philosophical objections damaged the credibility of traditional Protestant Christianity, the greatest damage came from science, from developments in geology, biology, and historical criticism. Charles Lyell's *Principles of Geology* overturned the reigning catastrophist model of geological formation in favor of a uniformitarian approach that lengthened the age of the earth and discredited the Bible's chronology of creation. Charles Darwin's *Origin of the Species* (1859) similarly overturned the prevailing creationist models of the origin of living things in favor of the gradual evolution of all species from primeval organisms. This cast doubt on the Bible's account of God's immediate creation of full-orbed plant and animal kingdoms. The science of historical criticism applied naturalistic rules to the analysis of the Bible's historical accounts and discredited the supernaturalistic elements of its history.

Advocates of the new theology believed that liberalism afforded a stronger defense of Christianity than orthodoxy could manage. A critical element of this system was a new view of the inspiration of the Bible. These new theologians argued that many of the Bible's historical statements were mythological—false in their historical meaning but true in their religious meaning. The creation account in Genesis, they held, was historically false but religiously true. It taught nothing of the history of the earth or living things; it taught God's fatherly love for creation. This approach allowed them to be critical of the Bible and at the same

---

3. On the new theology, see Gary Dorrien, *The Making of American Liberal Theology: Imagining Progressive Religion, 1805–1900* (Louisville, KY: Westminster John Knox Press, 2001); William R. Hutchison, *The Modernist Impulse in American Protestantism* (Cambridge, MA: Harvard University Press, 1976); Kenneth Cauthen, *The Impact of American Religious Liberalism* (New York: Harper and Row, 1962).

time justify their indulgence of some of its traditional affirmations. Toy adopted this view because he thought the old view was inconsistent with the facts, with the new science of evolution and the new historical criticism of the Bible.

When trustees dismissed Toy in 1879, Southern Baptist pastors engaged in a long public controversy concerning the doctrine of inspiration. Toy submitted his resignation to the trustees. In the late 1870s and early 1880s the new view of inspiration spread rather alarmingly among the young ministers who studied at the Southern Baptist Theological Seminary. Boyce and Broadus set themselves against the new theology. Their labors kept the new theology out of the seminary for the next twenty years, and their example became a boundary marker for Southern Baptist identity for generations.

Although the orthodox view prevailed initially, the new view spread steadily, especially among seminary graduates. The Toy controversy proved only the first episode in a drama that characterized the seminary's life for about a hundred years. In the twentieth century the seminary's professors and many graduates believed and taught the new theology's view of inspiration, but they had to fight against the stigma it bore on account of Toy's dismissal. The trustees' stand against Toy's views became a symbol of the seminary's commitment to orthodox belief. More than two generations afterward, when one South Carolina Baptist urged president-elect Duke K. McCall to root out liberalism at the seminary, he reminded McCall of the "action of Dr. Boyce, Dr. Broadus fully concurring, with reference to Professor Toy."[4]

TOY'S CAREER AT SOUTHERN SEMINARY

Toy graduated from the University of Virginia in 1856 and had professed faith and joined the church under Broadus's ministry in Charlottesville. After three years teaching school, Toy gained appointment as a missionary to Japan with the Southern Baptist Mission Board. To prepare, he enrolled at Southern Seminary when it opened in 1859. He completed the most challenging half of the three-year curriculum in one year. He graduated in four of the eight schools: Old Testament Interpretation in English and Hebrew, New Testament Interpretation in English and Greek, Systematic Theology in English and Latin, and Ecclesiastical History.[5] The Civil War interrupted his missionary plans, and

4. John R. Jester to Duke K. McCall, 2 Aug. 1951, SBTS—Call folder, McCall Papers.

5. *Catalogue*, Southern Baptist Theological Seminary, 1859–1860, 37; ibid., 1860–1861, 6. By later standards Toy would have graduated in seven of the eleven schools, undoubtedly the basis of Broadus's statement that Toy completed two-thirds of the seminary course in one year.

Crawford H. Toy

he served in the Confederate army during the war. Afterward he decided to become a teacher of ancient languages and studied Semitic languages at the University of Berlin from 1866 to 1868. Furman University elected him professor of Greek in 1868. Southern Seminary elected him professor of Old Testament Interpretation and Oriental Languages in 1869. Toy taught Hebrew and Old Testament Interpretation, as well as special courses in Syriac and Arabic. He was secretary of the faculty and like the other professors was expected to make the rounds of the various annual denominational meetings to represent the seminary, and in the summer to raise support among pastors and interested laypersons wherever he should travel.

Toy's influence was noticeable from the start. Students found him at once charming and profound. Returning student John Stout met the new professor in August 1869 and came away deeply impressed: "He is so thorough, so true, so strong."[6] Toy's dignified demeanor and thoughtful, precise speech made him an impressive figure. He was reserved by temperament but was also so engaging,

6. John Stout to Fanny Coker, 31 Aug. 1869, Lide-Coker-Stout Family Papers, USC.

hospitable, and genuine that his students adored him. Stout rejoiced when he learned that his own Sunday school class at Greenville First Baptist Church had been disbanded, because it meant he was free to attend Toy's class, which had forty seminary students: "He takes such straight-along common sense views of the Sacred Scriptures."[7]

Toy began his career as a champion of the faith once for all delivered to the saints. His 1869 inaugural address argued that Baptists should support an educated ministry, interpreting the Bible through both the science of biblical interpretation and the illumination of the Holy Spirit. He assumed the Bible's inspiration. The Holy Spirit, he said, rendered "absolutely perfect guiding influence" on its authors, such that it is "in every iota of its substance absolutely and infallibly true."[8] Also in 1869 he published "The Tübingen School," an article bolstering traditional orthodoxy and criticizing German rationalism. In it Toy defended the reality of miracles, the historicity of the resurrection of Christ, the genuineness of 2 Peter, and the consistency of the parts of the New Testament.[9]

Both productions functioned to certify Toy's soundness. He had studied two years in Germany, the source of formidable rationalist critiques of the Bible and romanticist reconstructions of the faith. Southern Baptists might naturally suspect that these destructive theories had influenced Toy. With these two publications Toy pledged himself to orthodoxy. He had emerged from the German lion's den unscathed.

Or so it appeared. Most observers interpreted Toy's address as a defense of traditional views of inspiration and interpretation. In fact it staked out the mediating approach of such German theologians as Isaak August Dorner, with whom Toy had studied Schleiermacher's thought in Germany. Like the German mediating theologians, who combined the critical methods of F. C. Baur's Tübingen school with the reverent spirit of Halle's pietism, Toy argued for an approach to hermeneutics that harmonized scientific truths with spiritual truths. Rationalists interpreted only the human element. Allegorizers interpreted only the spiritual. True hermeneutics combined the principles of both, because the Bible had both a human and a divine element.[10]

---

7. John Stout to Fanny Coker, 23 Sept. 1869, Lide-Coker-Stout Family Papers, USC.

8. C. H. Toy, *The Claims of Biblical Interpretation on Baptists* (New York: Lange and Hillman, 1869), 44.

9. C. H. Toy, "The Tübingen School," *Baptist Quarterly* 3 (1869): 210–234. Toy also praised Isaac A. Dorner's alternative approach.

10. On the mediating theologians, see John E. Wilson, *Introduction to Modern Theology: Trajectories in the German Tradition* (Louisville, KY: Westminster John Knox Press, 2007), 101–122; Claude Welch, *Protestant Thought in the Nineteenth Century* (New Haven, CT: Yale University Press, 1972), 1:269–291.

Christianity's enemies used science to attack its claims, but like a good mediating theologian, Toy incorporated the insights of the same science to establish the proper interpretation of the Bible.[11] His interpretive conclusions may have been traditionally orthodox in 1869, but his approach to the character and interpretation of the Bible was more consistent with such mediating theologians.

The address in fact reflected some basic commitments that led Toy to his new view of inspiration. Most important, he divided scripture into internal and external elements. The division corresponded to Kant's analysis of reality into phenomenal and noumenal realms. The Bible, Toy said, had a "human" or "intellectual" element and a "divine" or "spiritual" element.[12] The external element was subject to the methods of scientific reason. It was part of the phenomenal realm. This aspect of the Bible was "a record of fact, thought, and feeling, written by men for men." The correct method for interpreting this aspect of the Bible was the application of the rules of grammar and logic according to human learning and science. True understanding of the spiritual element came through the rigorous application of scientific principles to the human element.[13] The internal element belonged to the noumenal or spiritual realm. This aspect of the Bible was "a revelation by the Spirit of God." The correct method for interpreting this aspect of the Bible was "to have the inspiration and guidance of the Holy Spirit."[14] Toy criticized allegorical and spiritual interpreters, including most Baptists, for ignoring the human element.

Scientific interpretation of the "human side" afforded access to the "divine side."[15] "The gems of truth are indeed divine, but the casket in which they are given us is of human workmanship and its key made and applied by human skill." The "truths of scripture are enclosed in outward facts," Toy wrote. Ten years later he characterized the relation of the Bible's two elements in essentially the same way: the Bible's "religious thought is independent of this outward form."[16]

Toy devoted most of the inaugural discourse to methods of interpreting the human element. That is partly because the human element yielded to

11. Toy, *Claims of Biblical Interpretation*, 23.

12. Toy, *Claims of Biblical Interpretation*, 52, 54, 60.

13. Toy, *Claims of Biblical Interpretation*, 31.

14. Toy, *Claims of Biblical Interpretation*, 9. See Paul House's similar argument in "Crawford Howell Toy and the Weight of Hermeneutics," *Southern Baptist Journal of Theology* 3 (1999): 28–39.

15. Toy, *Claims of Biblical Interpretation*, 42.

16. C. H. Toy, "Full Text of the 'Paper' Offered with the Resignation of Rev. C. H. Toy, D.D., as Professor in the Southern Baptist Theological Seminary," *Baptist Courier*, 27 Nov. 1879, 2.

the methods of empirical phenomena, to science. The method of interpreting the divine element was more straightforward. The "Christian consciousness," Toy said, was the key to correct interpretation of the spiritual element.
It afforded "deepening and especially realizing the truth thus gained." Read
sympathetically, like Kant's transcendental categories, Christian consciousness provided for both access and certainty regarding the Bible's spiritual
element.[17]

Toy recognized that his theory of inspiration determined his hermeneutical
principles, but his definition did little to clarify his view. The Holy Spirit, he said,
applied "absolutely perfect guiding influence" and preserved the Bible writers in
their human "personality of character and intellect and surroundings." And this
inspiration assured that the Bible was "in every iota of its substance absolutely
and infallibly true," provided only that "its real assertions" were known. Toy's
view here sounded like that of the rest of the faculty, and probably was. But he
soon came to understand its "substance" and its "real assertions" to mean the
spiritual element only.[18]

By implication Toy erected a kind of Nestorian division between the human
and divine elements in scripture. He made this quite clear regarding those Bible
passages that addressed matters in the realm of science: "At the point at which
the Bible touches secular science, we have absolutely nothing to do but to sit
still and wait for the interpretations of that science." Astronomers and geologists drew their careful conclusions, and theologians wisely adjusted their interpretations: "Let geology arrive at a satisfactory conclusion, and we may rest in
the assured conviction that it will not be in conflict with the inspired record." [19]
Geologists had determined that the earth was quite old—and "the facts of the
geologists were correct"—and the result was to "give a much grander character
to the first chapter of Genesis than had before been perceived in it." Nor did
Darwin's views evoke concern. When Toy accepted Darwin's views a few years
later, he again found that his view of inspiration could accommodate the conclusions of science. The human element relied on "phenomenal observation"
and used "all the array of worldly facts and experiences simply as framework
for the scheme of redemption." The truth of the framework became dispens-
able, and since it dealt with the phenomenal elements merely, its accuracy had
no necessary bearing on the truth of the spiritual elements. Toy intended this
schema to bridge the human and divine elements of scripture, but it drove them
apart. And as it did, it drove him away from traditional interpretations of the

17. Toy, *Claims of Biblical Interpretation*, 43.
18. Toy, *Claims of Biblical Interpretation*, 44.
19. Toy, *Claims of Biblical Interpretation*, 49.

Bible and away from Southern Baptist views. He left the seminary ten years later as champion of a more progressive faith.[20]

TOY'S THEOLOGICAL PILGRIMAGE

Toy's troubles began with Genesis. Since boyhood he had read books on geology. He especially liked Hugh Miller's works reconciling Genesis with the new geology. Before the 1830s, the reigning geological model held that the earth's geological features could be explained by violent upheavals and catastrophic change over a short period of time. This approach to geological development was consistent with the traditional interpretation of Genesis in which the earth was less than 10,000 years old. The new geology, promoted persuasively by Charles Lyell in the 1830s, held that the earth's geological features came about by gradual change at uniform rates over hundreds of thousands of years.[21] Toy was persuaded by Lyell's uniformitarian principles for deducing the earth's great age. Hugh Miller and others convinced Toy that the six days of creation in Genesis 1 represented geological periods of long duration.[22]

In 1869 Toy still held this view: "Moses did not necessarily mean days of twenty-four hours each; he might mean long periods."[23] Science and the Bible harmonized. But the harmony collapsed around 1872 when Toy could no longer square the Genesis account with an old earth. He became convinced that the Hebrew word for "day" in Genesis 1 could not refer to a geological epoch and that the order of creation in Genesis contradicted both reason and the geological strata of the fossil record.[24]

20. In his 1997 faculty address at Southern Seminary, Paul House analyzed helpfully the insight that the internal-external schema apparent in the inaugural address contributed to the developed view that resulted in his resignation. Pope Duncan noted this also. See Paul R. House, "Crawford Howell Toy and the Weight of Hermeneutics," *Southern Baptist Journal of Theology* 3 (1999): 28–39; and Duncan, "Crawford Howell Toy (1836–1919)," 431.

21. The first American edition of Lyell's *Principles of Geology* appeared in 1837; the first English edition appeared in 1830.

22. Hugh Miller, *The Old Red Sandstone* (Edinburgh: J. Johnstone, 1841); Miller, *Footprints of the Creator: Or, the Asterolepsis of Stromness* (Boston: Gould and Lincoln, 1850); Miller, *The Testimony of the Rocks: Or, Geology in Its Bearings on the Two Theologies, Natural and Revealed* (Boston: Gould and Lincoln, 1857).

23. Toy, *Claims of Biblical Interpretation*, 49.

24. C. H. Toy, "A Bit of Personal Experience," *Religious Herald*, 1 Apr. 1880, 1. See also C. H. Toy, quoted in A. J. Holt, Lecture Notes of C. H. Toy's O.T. Class, 28 Sept. 1874, SBTS ("The word day then can not mean a geological period").

But the problem was more than geology. In the early 1870s Toy adopted Darwinism. In 1869 he took a neutral position on Darwinism.[25] Broadus reported that Toy embraced evolutionary views after studying Herbert Spencer and Charles Darwin. In Greenville, Toy gave a popular lecture advocating Darwin's view of human evolution.[26] In 1874 he told his students that they should "not deny evolution on Christian grounds," for Christianity and evolution were compatible.[27] In 1877 the editor of the *Religious Herald* reported that in response to J. B. Hawthorne's attack on Darwin at the recent meeting of the Southern Baptist Convention, "Prof. Toy has some sensible views in reference to Darwin, which we hope to publish soon."[28]

Toy could no longer harmonize the Bible with science. If evolutionary views of geology and biology were correct, then the Genesis history of the origin of the earth and of living things was false. For some time he could not reconcile Genesis with the accepted science because he feared the consequences. He wrote, "What, then, would become of the Bible, its truthfulness, its helpfulness?"[29] He could not repudiate the new science, but he was loath to give up the Bible.

Around 1875 he solved the problem. He reconciled science and the Bible by practically divorcing the divine and human aspects of the Bible. The divine aspect was the internal spiritual meaning inspired by the Holy Spirit. The human aspect was the human language of the text. He so divided the Bible's outward meaning from its inward that its outward meaning could be false but its inward meaning true. He held that the Bible was wholly true because it was true in its "real" spiritual intent, even though its historical human assertions were in error. The Bible employed the primitive thought forms of the day to convey its inner spiritual truths. Genesis was wrong as science but true as religion. It erred on the when and the how of creation, but it was right on who was behind it all. With this new approach in hand he could embrace the scientific claims of gradualist geology and Darwinian evolution wholeheartedly and at the same time retain his faith in a Bible that was true in its spiritual meaning.

This approach came at considerable expense. It was akin to Kant's solution to Hume's skeptical critique of empiricism. Kant admitted that empirical

25. Toy, *Claims of Biblical Interpretation*, 49.

26. John A. Broadus, *Memoir of James Petigru Boyce* (New York: A. C. Armstrong, 1893), 260.

27. C. H. Toy, in quoted in Holt, Lecture Notes, 9 Oct. 1874, 155.

28. Unattributed, "News and Notes," *Religious Herald*, 28 June 1877. The paper evidently did not publish Toy's article.

29. Toy, "A Bit of Personal Experience," 1; Toy, "Genesis and Geology," *Religious Herald*, 6 May 1880, 1.

phenomena blocked reason's access to the essential truths of noumenal reality, but he opened an alternative route to knowledge of the noumenal by means of "practical" reason. Toy, by admitting the unreliability of the outward phenomena of scripture, endangered access to its inward noumena. But Toy had no alternative route to scripture's spiritual meaning. Historical criticism of the human message divorced the text from its ostensible religious meaning. By the end of his career, he seemed to feel that the spiritual message had passed beyond the horizon.[30]

This new view of inspiration also had great interpretive consequences, requiring a reconstruction and reinterpretation of the Bible. Toy adopted the reconstruction of the history of Israel advanced by the Dutch biblical scholar Abraham Kuenen.[31] "His critical conversion," Toy's Harvard colleague George F. Moore wrote, "was apparently wrought by Kuenen, and he accepted the views of the new school at once and completely."[32] Kuenen held that both Old Testament and New Testament religion were like the other religions of the world, just "so many manifestations of the religious spirit of mankind."[33] God's "never resting and all-embracing activity" in all humanity put every religion on a path from lower forms to the "higher form of religion."[34] The correct "starting point of modern theology" was the "rejection of supernaturalism" in favor of critical research of the religion of Israel based on the premise of its

30. Toy's approach was similar to that of his Berlin teacher, Isaac August Dorner, the great leader of the German mediating theology. Dorner, who greatly admired Kant and Schleiermacher, similarly placed great value on the distinction between scripture's true inward meaning and its unreliable outward form. He referred to the human element as relating to the "empirical" (empirischen), the "finite" (endlichen), the "outer" (aussere), "external" (ausserliche), and "non-spiritual" (nicht geistlichen). He referred to the divine element as relating to the "spiritual" (geistlichen), the "inner" (innere), the "eternal" (ewige), the "non-historical" (geshichtlose). Only the spiritual element, Dorner held, was necessarily free from error. More than Toy, Dorner seemed to appreciate the problem this distinction posed for such central Christian truths as the incarnation and the resurrection, in which their historical, empirical, or positive character was intrinsic to their inward or positive meaning. See Dorner, *A System of Christian Doctrine*, trans. J. S. Banks (Edinburgh: T and T Clark, 1881), 2:192–197; Dorner, *System der Christlichen Glaubenslehre*, 2nd ed. (Berlin: Wilhelm Herz, 1886), 1:630–634.

31. Broadus, *Memoir of Boyce*, 260.

32. George F. Moore, "An Appreciation of Professor Toy," *American Journal of Semitic Languages and Literatures* 36 (1919): 12.

33. Abraham Kuenen, *The Religion of Israel to the Fall of the Jewish State*, trans. Alfred Heath May (London: Williams and Norgate, 1874), 6.

34. Kuenen, *The Religion of Israel*, 9.

"natural development."[35] On these premises Kuenen sketched out the ostensible evolution of Israelite religion and redated the various Old Testament books based on the degree to which a book's perspective seemed to correspond to various points in the religion's historical progress.[36] By this method Kuenen concluded, for example, that the Pentateuch's historical setting was incorrect, since its perspective reflected later religious developments rather than those of the time of Moses, who cannot therefore have produced the laws ascribed to him, not even the Ten Commandments.[37] Kuenen concluded, therefore, that both the historical and the ritualistic material in the Pentateuch developed in the postexilic era.[38]

Toy repudiated the irreverent and skeptical criticism of the rationalist wing of German scholarship, but he viewed Kuenen's reconstruction of the Old Testament as reverent and constructive. The prophets and the psalter provided the materials for a reconstruction of the history of Israel and showed that the account contained in the Pentateuch and the historical books was not trustworthy as history. Over many centuries the prophets developed the religion of Israel: the strict monotheism, the "ethical" portrayal God as compassionate and personal, and the fierce patriotism. From this vital spiritual religion finally emerged the codified sacrificial system with its Levitical priesthood and liturgy. In the light of this new history, Toy saw the Old Testament in terms of the gradual development of spiritual religion, which consisted centrally in monotheism and an ethic of love and justice. The religious value of Old Testament texts inhered in their promotion of such spiritual truths.[39]

By 1874 Toy began teaching his students some of the conclusions of current historical criticism of the Old Testament. He taught them, for example, that the second chapter of Genesis had a different author than the first chapter because of differences of style and because each called God by a different name, the two chapters being gathered together by an unknown "editor."[40] Genesis, he said, was not written by Moses but derived from a Jehovist source and an Elohist source.[41] Leviticus was not written by Moses but was written later by someone

35. Kuenen, *The Religion of Israel*, 11–12.

36. Kuenen, *The Religion of Israel*, 13–14.

37. Kuenen, *The Religion of Israel*, 134–142.

38. Toy esteemed Kuenen's work highly (C. H. Toy, "Kuenen's Life and Work," *Christian Register*, 21 Jan. 1892, 4). For another contemporary estimate of Kuenen's role in Old Testament criticism, see T. K. Cheyne, *Founders of Old Testament Criticism* (New York: Scribner's, 1893), 185–194.

39. See Toy, "Kuenen's Life and Work," 4.

40. Holt, Lecture Notes, 151.

41. Holt, Lecture Notes, 168.

in the spirit of Moses: "The genius given by Moses was elaborated in the after history of Israel." In this sense, it could be called "the teachings of Moses."[42] He told his students to interpret the various particular passages in terms of concepts of spiritual redemption: monotheism, sin deserves punishment, the need for mediator, the promise of a messiah, God's intention to bless all nations. "All revelation is intended to develop redemption." This notion of "spiritual redemption" furnished Toy with his "canon of interpretation."[43]

Between 1874 and 1877 Toy revised extensively his understanding of the Old Testament's history and interpretation. In 1874 he arranged his Old Testament lectures in canonical order: Pentateuch, historical books and Psalms, and finally the prophets. He spent half the session lecturing on the Pentateuch. In 1877 he ordered them according to the critical reconstruction of Hebrew religion, broadly: historical books and Psalms, prophets, and then Pentateuch. He barely discussed the Pentateuch, which he now regarded as the work of the priests and of Ezra during the time of the exile, though Moses provided the germ.[44] The Law, Toy told students, represented declension from the pure religion of the prophets—the Law "imprisoned" spiritual religion and produced formalism.[45] In 1874 he defended the unity of Isaiah, but in 1877 he assigned portions to three different authors.[46]

In 1877 Toy taught students that the traditional messianic prophecies in the Psalms, Isaiah, Micah, and Joel did not refer to Christ, but that Christ was the fulfillment of all truly spiritual longings, and in this sense only the passages were messianic.[47] Over and over Toy told students that specific prophecies were not fulfilled and "never came to pass," but they were fulfilled in a general way by Christ, because he represented spiritual redemption.[48] The prophetic promises of Israel's national prosperity and the restoration of the Davidic dynasty were "not realized in fact." But such ideas reflected merely the "outward form," the "framework of the spiritual thought." The spiritual truth was underneath. The "true inward spiritual thought was wonderfully fulfilled in Christ."[49] Toy

---

42. Holt, Lecture Notes, 182. In 1874 Toy held that it was "morally certain" that Moses wrote Exodus, though Moses could not have written all of it (Holt, Lecture Notes, 168, 194).

43. Holt, Lecture Notes, 162.

44. Hugh C. Smith, Lectures in Old Testament English by C. H. Toy, 1877–1878, 130–132, Archives and Special Collections, SBTS.

45. Holt, Lecture Notes, 148–246; Smith, Lectures, 1–139, 132.

46. Holt, Lecture Notes, 239; Smith, Lectures, 68.

47. Smith, Lectures, 44, 49–51, 58–60, 67–69, 118–124.

48. Smith, Lectures, 48, 56–57, 65–68, 108.

49. Smith, Lectures, 108.

interpreted the individual and national experiences of the Hebrews typolog-ically, or rather allegorically: "Israel is the anticipation of Christ and his the fulfillment of Israel."[50] The "outward framework of spiritual idea" was irrele-vant, since the true spiritual thought conveyed within communicated God's plan for spiritual redemption, represented most fully in Christ.[51] This was the "great principle of exegesis," he told the students, to "pierce through the shell, framework" to discover the "real, religious, spiritual idea."[52]

In 1877 Toy also began cautiously to publish some of his conclusions based on the historical-critical reconstruction of the history of Israel. In an 1877 hom-iletical commentary, Toy wrote that Deuteronomy 17:14–17 probably originated in some oral tradition from Moses, but that 250 years later Samuel developed it into a constitutional form and wrote it down as law.[53] In lessons for Sunday school teachers he wrote that the laws restricting temple service to priests came into existence long after Moses, perhaps in the seventh century B.C.[54] Toy explained that an unknown writer drew upon existing materials and produced the book of Deuteronomy around 623 B.C.[55]

One consequence of divorcing the human and spiritual elements was that Toy began to reinterpret the Bible's accounts of supernatural events as natu-ral events. Toy maintained that God acted through ordinary natural law—he guided history by his providence. Traditional orthodoxy held this also but added that God sometimes accomplished his purposes apart from natural agency in a miracle. Toy, however, explained miracles as the spiritual interpretation of God's acting through natural causes. He suggested that where the scripture said that leprosy broke out on Uzziah's face while he burned incense beside the altar, perhaps in fact the leprosy was already there and the priests only then saw it for the first time and naturally regarded it as divine judgment.[56] He suggested also that the destruction of Sennacharib's army was not miraculous in the common

---

50. Smith, Lectures, 125.

51. Smith, Lectures, 124.

52. Smith, Lectures, 125.

53. Toy, translator's note, in C. F. D. Erdmann, *The Books of Samuel*, trans. and ed. C. H. Toy and John A. Broadus (New York: Scribner's, 1877), 136–137.

54. C. H. Toy, "Critical Notes," *Sunday School Times*, 9 Feb. 1878, 87.

55. C. H. Toy, "Critical Notes," *Sunday School Times*, 12 Jan. 1878, 23. As noted above, Toy held that Ezra gave Deuteronomy and the Pentateuch their final form around 400 B.C. See also C. H. Toy, *The History of the Religion of Israel* (Boston: Unitarian Sunday School Society, 1882), ix–x.

56. C. H. Toy, "Critical Notes," *Sunday School Times*, 9 Feb. 1878, 87.

sense, but that the "inspired writers" represented a "natural event as the work of an angel of God."[57]

Toy came to believe that most of the passages quoted in the New Testament to establish the fact that Christ was the Messiah were not messianic in a traditional sense. For example, the New Testament quoted Psalm 2 several times as proof that Jesus was the promised Messiah. Toy, however, argued that Psalm 2 had no reference to a messiah but rather spoke of God's promise of blessing to Israel through his "son," the king. Toy, however, wanted to save the truthfulness of the New Testament, so he concluded that although the New Testament writers erred regarding the meaning of Psalm 2, they nevertheless taught its spiritual meaning—"God's watchcare over his people"—and saw rightly that such spiritual truths had their fullest representation in Christ.[58] Toy interpreted Isaiah 42:1–10 and 53:1–11 as references to Israel, although New Testament writers understood them to refer to Christ. The New Testament authors misinterpreted the texts, Toy believed, but they still taught truth about Christ in a general way, for "Christ was by divine appointment the consummation of all God's revelation of truth in ancient Israel."[59] Indeed, for Toy the entire history of Israel was the "anticipatory, predictive picture of the Messiah."[60] In a broad sense, Toy made every passage in the Old Testament messianic.

Toy explained to a friend in 1879 that New Testament interpretations of the Old Testament were frequently wrong. The New Testament writers often quoted Old Testament passages in ways that were false to their original meaning. Toy wrote that Paul imposed on Old Testament texts meanings contradictory to their real meaning. When Paul quoted Deuteronomy 30:11–14, for example, to prove that sinners are saved by faith and not by works in Romans 10:6–9, Paul's interpretation was "not valid." The passage in Deuteronomy "means obedience to law; Paul makes it mean not obedience, but faith."[61] Toy held that such contradictions did not diminish the divine character of the Bible's spiritual message, which was "independent of all such externals. God permitted the prophets and psalmists to use the incorrect astronomy and geography of their day, and the apostles and other New Testament writers to use the incorrect translation and exegesis of their day, and in this human framework is the divine thought

57. C. H. Toy, "Critical Notes," *Sunday School Times*, 2 Mar. 1878, 135.

58. C. H. Toy, "Critical Notes," *Sunday School Times*, 8 Feb. 1879, 87.

59. C. H. Toy, "Critical Notes," *Sunday School Times*, 12 Apr. 1879, 231.

60. C. H. Toy, "Critical Notes," *Sunday School Times*, 19 Apr. 1879, 247.

61. C. H. Toy to John L. Johnson, 16 Dec. 1879, John Lipscomb Johnson Papers, Southern Historical Collection, UNC.

manifest and powerful. To insist on the framework is ritualism and fetishism." [62] The Bible's inner truth was independent of its outward form. Some years later Toy began to doubt whether one could derive the former from the latter.

In 1877 Toy wrote a letter congratulating Charles A. Briggs—the two had studied together at the University of Berlin—on his inaugural address as professor of Old Testament at Union Theological Seminary in New York: "I am glad to find that we are in accord as to the spirit of Old Testament study, and rejoice that you have spoken so earnestly and vigorously on behalf of the spirit of broad, free, spiritual minded investigation. There is much work in this country for the advocates of such a view, and it will require patient and wise effort to dislodge the traditional narrowness that has obtained so firm a foothold in some quarters." Both men would be charged with heresy. Briggs had the more celebrated trial. Toy was "the first to suffer." [63]

WHAT TO DO ABOUT TOY

When Boyce and Broadus had learned something of Toy's new views of inspiration, no later than the summer of 1876, they did not move immediately for his dismissal. Toy's views were changing. In response to their initial inquiries about his new views, Toy said that he retained full confidence in the fact of the inspiration of the Bible but rejected all theories of inspiration. In the context of Toy's piety and commitment to orthodoxy, this seemed reassuring. It seemed to fit with his rejection of the speculative theology of German rationalism in favor of Baconian realism. But as Boyce and Broadus began to learn the details and conclusions of Toy's views, they grew alarmed and labored to convince him of his errors. Toy's new view of inspiration drove him to reinterpret passage after passage. Over several years his rejection of traditional interpretations became extensive. The denomination found such reinterpretations highly objectionable and would not support a seminary that tolerated such teaching.

The only outcome favorable to the seminary was to restore Toy to orthodox views. Boyce and Broadus knew that Toy could not continue teaching with his new views; his views did not contradict a narrow reading of the Abstract of Principles, whose first article read: "The scriptures of the Old and New

---

62. C. H. Toy to John L. Johnson, 16 Dec. 1879, John Lipscomb Johnson Papers, Southern Historical Collection, UNC.

63. C. H. Toy to Charles A. Briggs, 19 Jan. 1877, Charles August Briggs Papers, series 31, ledger 5, letter 773, Archives, Burke Library, Union Theological Seminary, New York; Briggs, *General Introduction*, 286. In the same letter Toy expressed surprise that Briggs held that the "last redaction of the Pentateuch was made before the Babylonian Exile."

Testaments were given by inspiration of God, and are the only sufficient, certain, and authoritative rule of all saving knowledge, faith, and obedience." Boyce and Broadus recognized, however, that the implications and results of Toy's theory of inspiration were inconsistent with the common understanding of the article.

The matter remained quiet for two or three years, and few persons knew Toy's views beyond the circle of his students. Boyce began the effort to restore Toy to orthodox views. Boyce wrote him a letter in June 1876 in which he "broke into a gentle remonstrance and earnest entreaty on inspiration." [64] The following summer Boyce grew yet more concerned. Toy had apparently explained his views publicly in Virginia, and though this created no public outcry, it exposed Toy's views for the first time to the churches. Boyce apparently solicited an explanation, for Toy sent Boyce an account of his position in June 1877. Boyce felt that it was not necessarily wrong in general but was objectionable in the particulars. As Boyce wrote to Broadus, "I have a letter from Bro. Toy setting forth his theory, in itself well enough. In so doing, I do not know that he goes beyond the statements of others. The trouble is when he enters, as he did in Virginia, into the details and begins to knock away one part and another." Boyce hoped to persuade Toy of sounder views, but in the meantime the seminary had to weather criticism on the matter. Boyce continued: "I think however that the ice being broken we shall be able to keep all right." [65]

Boyce asked Toy in the spring of 1878 not to teach his new views, and Toy agreed. Boyce and Broadus hoped that by teaching his courses without introducing his new opinions, Toy "might ultimately break away from the dominion of destructive theories." [66] But Toy apparently understood this to mean that he would not teach his new theory of inspiration, for he certainly taught his new understanding of Israel's history and the reinterpretations that derived from it. And he could not fail to answer the questions that students naturally raised. Some students adopted his views and encouraged others to talk to Toy privately and he would help them arrive at a more satisfactory understanding of the Bible.[67] The more time passed, the more advanced his errors became, and

64. Boyce to Toy, quoted in Archibald T. Robertson, *Life and Letters of John Albert Broadus* (Philadelphia: American Baptist Publication Society, 1901), 301.

65. James P. Boyce to John A. Broadus, 22 June 1877, Broadus Papers. Toy's letter does not survive.

66. Broadus, *Memoir of Boyce*, 262.

67. David G. Lyon, Diary 1878–79, 8 Dec. 1878, David Gordon Lyon Papers, HUA. Lyon wrote: "Visited Bro. Scott of Penn [J. M. Scott, Saltsburg, Pa.], one of the students who is going to leave bec. he is troubled on the subjects of inspiration, atonement, origin of sin, etc. I strongly urged him to visit Dr. Toy before doing so. He is going now to spend some days with Rev. W. C. Brooks (Universalist), New Albany, Ind."

the more students adopted them. And they were failing to convince Toy of his errors. Time was running out.

In 1877 one of Toy's former students began a public campaign in favor of the new approach to the Bible. William C. Lindsay, pastor of the Columbia, South Carolina, First Baptist Church, began a series of articles promoting the new view in South Carolina Baptists' *Working Christian*. He wrote under the pseudonym Senex and did not mention Toy or the seminary, but persons close to the seminary knew of the close connection between Toy and Lindsay. Although Lindsay graduated before Toy adopted the new view, he moved back to Greenville in 1876 in order to lead the seminary's "centennial" fund-raising campaign. For eighteen months he spent much of his time in conversation with Toy and in Toy's library "devouring" its books.

Lindsay pressed the new view with considerable zeal. In the Senex articles he argued that the Bible contained many "obscurities and inaccuracies." Its historical and scientific statements were "frequently erroneous." Darwin was a safer authority in such matters. The Bible's inspiration was "concerned only with the religious element" in the scriptures. Books like Esther and the Song of Solomon had little inspiration. The traditional view of the Bible, "the dogma that all its utterances are inspired," produced confusion in some believers and induced others to abandon the faith.[68] The new view, Lindsay urged, was more biblical and better suited to defend the faith against its enemies.

Boyce attributed Lindsay's views to Toy's influence. "See articles of Senex in *Working Christian*," he told Broadus. "Some of the fruits of Toy's teaching." He was hearing reports of students adopting Toy's views. "I also heard in West Virginia that A. M. Simms had become unsound on inspiration. I asked about it and they said 'at least he was so regarded,' and they talked as though he would give up his ministry."[69] Many students did adopt Toy's views.[70] Most Southern Baptists did not know that Senex was Lindsay, that Toy shared Lindsay's views, or that other students were adopting the new view.

The faculty had already confronted the issue in a smaller way in 1876. When seeking instructors to teach in the place of Williams, who was ill, Toy advocated hiring Abraham Jaeger, a Jewish convert who had studied at the seminary and had aided Toy in teaching Hebrew. When Broadus raised no protest,

68. Senex [Lindsay], "Letters to My Friend—No. 1," *Working Christian*, 24 May 1877, 2; Senex, "Letters to My Friend—No. 2," 31 May 1877, 2; Senex, "Letters to My Friend—No. 3," 7 June 1877, 2.

69. James P. Boyce to John A. Broadus, 15 June 1877, Broadus Papers.

70. See David G. Lyon, Diary 1878–79, 8 Dec. 1878; George B. Eager to John A. Broadus, 8 Apr. 1878, box 8, Broadus Papers. See also discussion below on the ensuing inspiration controversy.

Boyce suggested that Jaeger's views on inspiration "are not accordant with our abstract of principles." When Toy tried to raise money from seminary donors for Jaeger's support and students petitioned the faculty to appoint him, Boyce firmly opposed the idea: "We must be very circumspect as to the position of influence which we give to a man not thoroughly sound. I had rather put an ignorant orthodox man in the chair of a professor than the most gifted of men if unsound. Dr. [E. G.] Robinson could not have done Rochester more harm than he did had he been the veriest ignoramus. And in Jaeger's case his unsoundness comes in the most serious direction for scholarship to dread, that of inspiration." Jaeger did not get the job.[71]

The faculty tried to counteract the influence of Toy's views on the students. William W. Landrum remembered an effort to bolster the students' orthodoxy by inviting T. T. Eaton to preach at the seminary's opening: "I remember when Dr. Eaton (at the suggestion of the faculty, doubtless) preached the introductory sermon [for the seminary] at Greenville. It was designed to stiffen the backbones of such men as Holmes, Eager, Smith (Richmond), Lindsay of Columbia, and our contemporaries."[72]

When Toy began to publish his views, he did so with great caution and in small parcels. In 1878 Toy wrote the critical notes on the Old Testament lessons for the *Sunday School Times*. In the January 12 lesson Toy wrote that the Pentateuch did not achieve its final form until late in the exilic period.[73] New York's *Independent*, whose editors promoted the new liberal theology and ridiculed the old, expressed their delight with Toy's statements. They praised Toy for

71. James P. Boyce to John A. Broadus, 11 Feb. 1876, box 6, Broadus Papers; Boyce to Broadus, 6 Dec. 1876, box 7, Broadus Papers; Minutes, Seminary Faculty, 27 Oct. 1873 and 30 Jan. 1874; Crawford H. Toy to John A. Broadus, 25 July 1874, box 5, Broadus Papers; Abraham Jaeger to Broadus, 11 Aug. 1874, ibid.; Toy to Broadus, 11 Aug. 1874, ibid.; Toy to Broadus, 21 Aug. 1874, ibid.; Jaeger to Broadus, 27 Aug. 1874, ibid.; Broadus to Boyce, 16 Feb. 1875, box 11, Boyce Papers. Jaeger joined the Episcopal Church and from 1878 to 1880 taught Hebrew at the University of the South; from 1880 to 1884 he taught Hebrew and Church History at Kenyon College in Ohio. Afterward he served a Virginia parish. See "News and Notes," *Religious Herald*, 12 Apr. 1877, 2; J. M. Broadus to John A. Broadus, 13 Apr. 1877, box 7, Broadus Papers; Mrs. Abraham Jaeger to John A. Broadus, 6 Apr. 1884, box 10, Broadus Papers; George R. Fairbanks, *History of the University of the South at Suwanee, Tennessee* (Jacksonville, FL: H. and W. B. Drew, 1905), 191, 209; *General Catalogue of Kenyon College, Gambier, Ohio* (Toledo, OH: Franklin Printing and Engraving, 1899), 122; *Journal of the Ninety-third Annual Council of the Protestant Episcopal Church in Virginia* (Richmond: William Ellis Jones, 1888), 9.

72. William W. Landrum to A. T. Robertson, 23 Feb. 1898, Robertson Papers.

73. Toy, "Critical Notes," *Sunday School Times*, 12 Jan. 1878, 23.

promoting the same liberal views of the Old Testament for which W. Robertson Smith was then under trial for heresy in Scotland. H. Clay Trumbull, editor of the *Sunday School Times*, defended Toy's orthodoxy but dodged the issue. He claimed rather gratuitously that the *Independent* misconstrued Toy's views and reminded his readers of the paper's commitment to "sound orthodoxy."[74]

Southern Baptist newspaper editors, who generally promoted discussion of theological issues in the denomination, hardly noticed. The two papers that took up the matter defended Toy. Missouri's *Central Baptist* announced that Toy believed that Moses did not write the book of Deuteronomy, but he dismissed the matter as an unimportant point of dispute among scholars.[75] J. C. Hiden, one of Toy's former students, replied in South Carolina's *Baptist Courier* that if Toy said it, it was worth hearing, but both papers dropped the matter.[76]

In August 1878 South Carolina pastor W. B. Carson warned Southern Baptists of the danger of the new view and implicated the seminary. He wrote in both the *Religious Herald* and the *Baptist Courier* that heretical views of inspiration were spreading. He had received a letter from a fellow pastor, C. C. Brown, defending the new view of inspiration. Brown predicted that in a few years all educated ministers would believe the new view of inspiration and that "this theory was now taught in the Southern Baptist Theological Seminary." In his letter to Carson, Brown identified Toy and Whitsitt as proponents of the new view, though Carson kept all names out of his article. Carson had written Broadus and Boyce months earlier asking whether Toy and Whitsitt taught this new view. Broadus did not reply, but Boyce wrote exonerating Whitsitt and affirming his own agreement with the old view: "Dr. Whitsitt teaches inspiration, but has taught no such thing, as far as I can learn. I am a firm believer in the position you take."[77] If Boyce discussed Toy's views, Carson kept it to himself. The editors of the *Religious Herald* echoed Carson's concerns and called the new theory of inspiration "subversive" of the "very foundations of Christianity."[78]

Matters took a more serious turn in December 1878 when "E.T.R." called attention to the matter in Virginia's *Religious Herald*. E.T.R. was the pseudonym of Josephine Eaton, principal and teacher of Latin at the Richmond Female Academy. She did not identify Toy by name but had him in mind. She said

74. Unattributed, "Editorial Notes," *Independent*, 17 Jan. 1878, 18; Trumbull, untitled, *Sunday School Times*, 26 Jan. 1878, 49.

75. Untitled editorial, *Central Baptist*, 24 Jan. 1878, 4; ibid., 21 Feb. 1878, 4.

76. J. C. Hiden, "Our Field Glass," *Baptist Courier*, 7 Feb. 1878, 2.

77. Boyce to Carson, quoted in Carson, "The Inspiration of the Scriptures," *Religious Herald*, 15 Aug. 1878, 1; Carson to Broadus, 2 Apr. 1878, Broadus Papers; Carson to Boyce, 11 June 1878, Boyce Papers.

78. Editorial note, *Religious Herald*, 15 Aug. 1878, 1.

that a professor in a Baptist seminary rejected "the inspiration of Moses" and of "various other parts of Scripture." She said that he was dishonest to teach thus under false pretense, since the denomination expected him to teach its view. But even if he pledged to keep his views to himself, she continued, injury entailed, since he could not teach persuasively those doctrines he privately dismissed. When he teaches Hebrew, "he will lack that reverence which all should be trained to as he reads Genesis." His own honor demanded resignation, she said, and if he should cling to his post, the churches should see to his removal. Otherwise their endorsement and support of the man made them complicit in poisoning the stream of truth and spreading death.[79]

Eaton's article set in motion the events that resulted in Toy's resignation. Broadus felt that she was "impudent and foolish" to broadcast these accusations. But Boyce and Broadus held that fairness to the denomination, to the seminary, and to Toy himself demanded that trustees investigate the matter and render judgment. Welcome or not, the time for decision had come. The very week of Eaton's article Broadus advised Toy's resignation and urged Boyce talk frankly with Toy about the matter: "I fear Toy will be obliged to go before the Board in May, and state what he holds and what he teaches. The point is not covered by our Articles of Belief, but his views differ widely from what is common among us, and it may be best, probably will be, that he should tell the Board so, and tender his resignation. If he cannot satisfy them he ought not to retain the position. If they are satisfied, we need not care for E. T. R. and company. If he determines to pursue that course, a note from you to Dr. [J. B.] Jeter might stop the sensation for the present. I think you ought to talk it frankly over with Toy at once. The question is a very difficult one, what exactly ought to be done."[80] Boyce apparently did as Broadus suggested. At the trustee meeting on May 7, 1879, in Atlanta, Toy resigned.

RESIGNATION

Toy did not believe that his resignation was necessary except as a means by which the trustees might vindicate his orthodoxy. Boyce and Broadus, like Eaton and the mass of orthodox Southern Baptists, held that persons who dissented from the denomination's fundamental beliefs, especially preachers and teachers, had

---

79. E. T. R., "E. T. R. Again: Honesty, False Teaching, Etc.," *Religious Herald*, 12 Dec. 1878, 3. Afterward one of Toy's former students identified E. T. R. as the one who exposed Toy (G. W. McLaurine [?] to W. H. Whitsitt, 1 Sept. 1896, Willian H. Whitsitt Papers, box 1, LVA). Eaton's regular articles were engaging and controversial, and had become popular.

80. John A. Broadus to James P. Boyce, 12 Dec. 1878, Boyce Papers.

a duty to resign or withdraw. They held their positions in trust with a commission to inculcate and promote orthodox doctrine. But Toy, like most proponents of the new theology, thought that they had an obligation to stay on. Orthodoxy was injuring the gospel and the churches, they believed, and they could lead the churches to greater health. Washington Gladden, a popular liberal minister, urged progressives like Toy to remain at their posts. It was "the duty of liberal men," Gladden said, "to stay in the churches to which they belong—if they can be tolerated there—and, by kindness and patience and fidelity to the truth as they see it, to do what they can to enlighten and broaden the fellowship of those churches."[81] Indeed, very few teachers and pastors who adopted the new theology resigned their positions. Their reliance on the persuasive power of bare facts, and their confidence that the facts were so demonstrably in their favor, led them to believe that by remaining in their positions they would lead the faithful to truer and more satisfying views of the Christian faith. They remained at their posts for the greater good of the churches. Toy was aware that his views were controversial and that most Southern Baptists found them objectionable; he did not feel that honor required him to resign. He believed that promoting his views would "greatly promote faith in the scriptures," as well as "truth and piety."[82]

Trustees brought no charge against Toy, but public sentiment in the Southern Baptist Convention charged him with heresy. In that era, when pastors, professors, and college presidents stood accused of heresy, ineffectiveness, or general complaints, as men of public trust they often resigned as a means of initiating public vindication. James Mims and James Boyce had resigned at different times at Furman University, and trustees rejected their resignations.[83] President N. M. Crawford and Professors John L. Dagg and P. H. Mell resigned at Mercer University, and trustees likewise rejected the resignations.[84] The resignations demonstrated their integrity, that they held honor, right, and justice above position and salary. In theory resignation also freed trustees to be finders of fact merely, unencumbered with anxiety about whether they should dismiss. In this context, the acceptance of the resignation in such circumstances amounted to dismissal.

The issue before the trustees was whether Toy's views were acceptable for a professor at the Southern Baptist Theological Seminary. Toy's resignation

---

81. Washington Gladden, *Recollections* (Boston: Houghton Mifflin, 1909), 230. See also "Comment on Current Discussion," *Andover Review* 11 (1888): 304–306; Gary Dorrien, *The Making of American Liberal Theology* (Louisville, KY: Westminster John Knox Press, 2001), 273, 278.

82. Broadus, *Memoir of Boyce*, 262.

83. On Mims, see South Carolina Baptist Convention, *Minutes*, 1849, 18; on Boyce, see ibid., 1857, 31–33.

84. Georgia Baptist Convention, 1856, 25–28.

letter therefore was an essay consisting of an extended defense of his views on inspiration. In the essay Toy suggested that the various theories of inspiration pretended to explain the manner of the Holy Spirit's operation on the human authors, when everyone should be content to accept the mere fact of inspiration. This missed the point of the objections to his approach. The traditional Protestant theory of inspiration, the plenary verbal view, was concerned chiefly with the results of inspiration, not the manner of it. The traditional view held that the scripture was so inspired throughout that its every part and its every word, though written by human authors, was precisely what the Holy Spirit intended. The resulting Bible was therefore God's very word, not in a general or spiritual sense only but also in its specific and historical statements. In Toy's theory, the Bible that resulted from inspiration was divine only in its inward spiritual truths, and was human in its outward historical statements. God revealed truth in the souls of the human authors, Toy believed, but they clothed these inward and eternal truths in the outward and temporal forms of human speech. The human and divine elements coinhered and generally resided in the same verses; the two elements did not form a unitary meaning. Toy's approach corresponded to Nestorian views of Jesus, in which the human and divine natures were effectively contiguous in the historical Jesus but did not quite form a unitary person.

In his essay to the trustees, Toy repudiated all theories of inspiration and claimed that he was guided by the facts alone. And the facts, he wrote, convinced him that the "outward form" of the Bible was subject to mistake but this did not jeopardize its religious message. Moses gave the Hebrews some basic laws that later generations developed into the "Mosaic" law of the Pentateuch. Certain prophecies of Isaiah and Hosea did not occur as they predicted, but these statements were the "mere clothing of their real thought." The Old Testament historical writers composed their histories as Christ composed parables, in order to teach religious truth rather than factual history. But the historical assertions constituted merely the "framework or vehicle of a religious truth." Such defects were of the human element only. The Bible was the outward record of Israel's inner experience of God's care and guidance. Because the Old Testament writers experienced God, their writings had religious power to inspire, encourage, and guide. Because they had this religious power, Toy recognized in them "a divine element."[85]

---

85. C. H. Toy to the Board of Trustees, May 1879, SBTS; Toy, "Full Text of the 'Paper' Offered with the Resignation of Rev. C. H. Toy, D.D., as Professor in the Southern Baptist Theological Seminary," *Baptist Courier*, 27 Nov. 1879, 2. Also Toy, "Dr. Toy's Address to the Board of Trustees of the Southern Baptist Theological Seminary," *Religious Herald*, 11 Dec. 1879, 1.

Toy claimed that his view was in full accord with the Abstract of Principles and that it established divine truth more firmly than the old interpretation. His teaching was "not only lawful for me to teach as professor in the seminary, but one that will bring aid and firm standing-ground to many a perplexed mind and establish the truth of God on a surer foundation."[86] This represented well the apologetic character of his emerging liberalism. For those who accepted evolution, uniformitarian geology, and the new critical view of the history of Israel's religion, such an understanding of inspiration was the only way to retain an authoritative Bible. Its inspiration and authority extended to spiritual matters and therefore did not interfere with science or history.

After Boyce read Toy's resignation essay to the trustees, they appointed a committee of five, which discussed the matter with Toy and learned his views in greater detail. They recommended that the board accept Toy's resignation because his interpretation diverged significantly from that commonly held among Southern Baptists. "After a full discussion" the board voted sixteen to two in favor of Toy's dismissal.[87] It made no attempt to prove the unsoundness of Toy's views. Seminary trustee John A. Chambliss wrote that Toy was "astonished" that the trustees accepted his resignation.[88]

JOB'S FRIENDS

In the period between Josephine Eaton's article and the board meeting, Toy must have felt how strangely altered matters had become. Broadus was his father in the faith and beloved mentor, and Boyce, his admiring benefactor and friend. Both were convinced that his errors were dangerous to the seminary, to the students, and to his soul. Both favored him presenting his resignation to the trustees.

As Toy looked toward the May meeting of the board, he identified with Job and rather transparently interpreted the book as a parable of his own recent experiences. In a March 1879 Sunday school lesson, he argued that Job's suffering

86. Toy, "Full Text," 2.

87. Minutes, Board of Trustees, Southern Baptist Theological Seminary, 7–13 May 1879; James C. Furman, chmn., "Report of Dr. Toy's Committee of Resignation," SBTS; The two who voted against dismissal, John A. Chambliss and D. W. Gwin, submitted a formal statement of protest against the board's action, which the board received. The statement apparently did not survive, as the trustee books of reports, with all such exhibits, were evidently lost for the period through 1888.

88. John A. Chambliss, "The Trustees of the Seminary and Dr. Toy's Resignation," *Baptist Courier*, 12 June 1879, 2.

resulted from the conflict between Job's emerging spiritual religion and the narrow creedalism of his friends. Job, like Toy, "had been floundering, as it were, in doubts arising from one-sided and insufficient conceptions of God." Job, again like Toy, fell into doubts and into "distressing darkness that drove him to the verge of despair." But even this was superior to the "cool dogmatizing of his friends," for it had a "genuine ring," a "passionate earnestness and realness." [89]

Just as God "pressed Job for an answer" and forced him to "sound the depths of his own knowledge," God's providence now pressed Toy to an answer and brought him to see "with what slight material he had been handling so freely" the question of divine inspiration. His former view had been "derived from others, it has been tradition and teaching, and I have accepted too readily and relied too confidently on insufficient views." Like Job, the new insight produced a "revolution in his thought"—his "whole religious position changes." The fundamental insight was that truth and piety derived from "personal knowledge of God" and not, by implication, from dogmatic theories and traditional systems. Job, like Toy, did not advocate "any theory" or "system of doctrines." Toy ascribed to Job the realization that he himself had attained.

The faculty acted rather in the role of the three friends. They had hectored Toy repeatedly concerning his views. The three friends were "good, pious, somewhat narrow men, who thought they understood the matter perfectly, and looked with complacent pity on the moral writhings of Job, only wondering and regretting that he did not accept their view of the case." They pressed their theory "in the teeth of obvious facts," but "their creed, the faith that they had been taught, demanded it." Though they were "good men," they fell into sin through their "undue confidence in their religious views" and zeal for "right doctrine." They held to a mechanical theory of religion and "for their theory's sake did injustice to their friend and to God, whom they thought they were defending." And, like Job, Toy was unmoved by his three friends.

Toy continued to love and respect Boyce and Broadus, but he felt unjustly dismissed. Boyce and Broadus indeed loved Toy and grieved over his tragic departure from orthodoxy. They felt the pain of this breach keenly, but they were unmoved from their duty to dismiss him from the faculty. Duty to God, truth, and the churches compelled them—they could do no other. But grief overwhelmed them. When Toy went to catch the train for his final departure from Louisville, Boyce and Broadus accompanied him to the station. While they waited, Boyce threw his left arm around Toy's neck and "lifted the right arm before him and said, in a passion of grief, 'Oh, Toy, I would freely give

89. Toy, "Critical Notes," *Sunday School Times*, 29 Mar. 1879, 199.

that arm to be cut off if you could be where you were five years ago, and stay there.'"[90] But there was no going back.

Toy moved to New York in October 1879 and began writing articles for the *Independent*.[91] Toy concluded at about the same time that the apostle Paul did not write 1 and 2 Timothy or Titus, though the letters claimed to be written by Paul. Alvah Hovey, president of Newton Theological Seminary, had asked Toy to write a commentary on these books. When Toy informed him of his new view concerning their authorship, he asked Toy to withdraw from the project.[92] In September the following year Toy accepted election to the chair of Semitic languages at Harvard University, where he remained until retirement.[93] He applied for membership in the Old Cambridge Baptist Church, but he withdrew his request when some church members objected to admitting him because of his new doctrines. In 1881 he wrote Broadus that he went frequently to hear Pastor Wayland Johnson's sermons, but that Johnson and the church were "not quite satisfied as to my orthodoxy."[94] Not long afterward he began attending the Unitarian First Parish Church of Cambridge.[95]

Toy continued to change. The reconstruction of biblical history and reinterpretation of biblical texts continued as consistency with science and his view of inspiration seemed to demand. Toy developed a deep interest in his later career in comparative religion. He seemed finally to find a resting place around 1907, when he came to understand himself as a philosophical pragmatist. He

90. Boyce, quoted in Broadus, *Memoir of Boyce*, 263–264.

91. C. H. Toy to John A. Broadus, 10 Mar. 1880, box 9, Broadus Papers; William D. Thomas to John A. Broadus, 30 Oct. 1879, box 9, Broadus Papers; J. H. Coghill to John A. Broadus, 29 Nov. 1879, box 8, Broadus Papers.

92. C. H. Toy to Alvah Hovey, 9 June 1879, Alvah Hovey Collection, ANTS; Toy to Hovey, 15 Aug. 1879, ibid.; John A. Broadus to Hovey, 8 Aug. 1879, ibid.; Alvah Hovey to John A. Broadus, 26 July 1879, box 8, Broadus Papers.

93. C. H. Toy to John A. Broadus, 8 June 1880, box 9, Broadus Papers. Harvard president Charles Eliot tried to persuade Aberdeen Old Testament scholar William Robertson Smith to take the position, but Smith felt that it would damage his liberal party in the Free Church of Scotland if he went over to a Unitarian divinity school. Smith recommended Julius Wellhausen for the position. See William Robertson Smith to Charles Eliot, 10 Mar. 1880, box 69, Charles W. Eliot Papers, HUA; Smith to Eliot, 4 June 1880, ibid.

94. C. H. Toy to John A. Broadus, 14 Dec. 1881, box 9, Broadus Papers. A church member wrote Broadus that Toy had applied for membership but that he was "not satisfied with his [Toy's] views on several questions of belief" and would not vote to receive him (A. M. Kendall to John A. Broadus, 16 Feb. 1882, box 9, Broadus Papers).

95. Toy, "Diary of 1900," 4, 11, 18, and 25 Mar. 1900, in Toy, Chest of 1900, HUA.

admired his friend and Harvard colleague William James, the great pragmatist philosopher. When Toy read James's lectures on pragmatism in 1907, he realized that he too was a pragmatist: "The book has cleared up some things for me. . . . It has given me a more satisfactory conception of 'truth.' My own categories have been simply the 'verifiable' and the 'unverifiable.' The latter I rejected for myself, though I admitted vaguely the right of others to hold things that seemed to me irrational if they found them helpful. I see now more clearly the real ground of my scarcely formulated view. And I find myself ready to accept the doctrine that 'truth' is not a static and stagnant thing, but a thing that we are constantly creating for ourselves. My faith has long been hedonistic, utilitarian, and your lectures have extended it and given it a firmer basis." [96] Toy had advanced beyond Unitarianism and perhaps beyond theism.

HERETIC OR MARTYR: INTERPRETING TOY'S DISMISSAL

Many Southern Baptists felt confused over Toy's ouster. Many knew and loved Toy, especially those who had attended the seminary. They may have disagreed with some of Toy's statements, but they saw little danger in them. They had heard him preach with persuasive power the Bible's redemptive truths. They had heard him pray and plead for the salvation of sinners. They felt they knew his heart, and they trusted the reality of its piety. But there was another reason for the confusion. Toy's public statements sounded rather traditional. He affirmed his reverence for the Bible, his abiding trust in its truth and power. He claimed that he differed from his brethren only in this, that he rejected all theories about the Bible, whereas his brethren held a "verbal theory" that was nowhere taught in the Bible. Rather than place his trust in theories, he preferred to rest on the facts of the Bible.

This position evaded the point at issue. Proponents of the "verbal theory" did not claim that the Bible taught the theory explicitly, but that it was a general statement of those facts that the Bible did teach on the subject. Of the same character were such doctrines as the Trinitarian nature of God or the "hypostatic union" of the human and divine natures in Christ. A careful examination of the facts of the Bible, traditionalists said, led to the conclusion that every word of the Bible was inspired alike and was the very word of God, and therefore without error.

Toy implied, however, that his opponents held to their view as a speculative theory, one adopted a priori, before examining all the facts, whereas he

96. Toy to William James, 22 July 1907, William James Papers, Houghton Library, Harvard University.

had abandoned all a priori theories in favor of fact. But, as some of his critics pointed out, Toy too had developed a theory. His theory was that the Spirit of God so indwelt the people of Israel that their religion grew purer and truer over time, culminating in the person of Jesus Christ. His claim to have no theory of inspiration was sincere, but it was special pleading. It lost its initial rhetorical power when the details of Toy's views became more widely known.

The Abstract of Principles did not address explicitly the questions raised by Toy's view of inspiration, but the trustees were competent to determine the doctrinal soundness of any professor and were not limited to the Abstract of Principles. They viewed the Abstract of Principles as the minimum standard of orthodoxy, not the maximum. The Abstract formed a permanent bulwark, but the fact that professors served at the pleasure of the trustees constituted another necessary defense of the soundness of the seminary's teaching. Trustees judged that Toy's views, whether contrary to the Abstract or not, were contrary to the Bible.

He felt therefore that the trustees would want to answer two questions: whether his views were consistent with the Bible, and whether they were consistent with the Abstract of Principles. These are the two questions he addressed in his defense of his views. But the trustees seem to have been most determined to avoid addressing either question. From respect for Toy's honor, they portrayed his departure as a mere difference of opinion. This placed the seminary at some disadvantage when Toy's friends protested his dismissal. Trustees could defend their action only by appeal to pragmatic considerations. They could not address the theological issues without accusing him of heresy. The result of this approach was unsatisfactory. Many Southern Baptists, especially among seminary alumni, wondered why the trustees dismissed so beloved a scholar absent a charge of heresy. But since trustees made no such charge, the dismissal appeared to be an unmanly capitulation to public feeling.

There was a genuine practical issue. If they had retained Toy, the resulting controversy would have damaged the seminary's efforts to secure the trust and support of the denomination, without which it would collapse. The trustee majority believed correctly that if Toy remained at his post, contributions to the seminary would decline. To retain him would imperil the school's very existence. In view of the seminary's precarious finances, if only a few donors stopped giving, the seminary might fail. Trustee J. B. Jeter explained it to readers of the *Religious Herald*: "There was however a conceded divergence in his views from those generally held by the supporters of the seminary; and the trustees deemed it inexpedient to subject it to the disadvantage which would inevitably arise from a protracted controversy on an important theological subject, especially while efforts are being made to obtain an endowment."[97]

97. J. B. Jeter, "The Southern Baptist Convention," *Religious Herald*, 22 May 1879, 2.

Most trustees, however, seem to have been convinced that Toy's view of inspiration was erroneous, inconsistent with scripture and damaging to the faith. When Lindsay published Toy's resignation letter in November 1879, renewing opposition to Toy's dismissal, trustees addressed the theological issues involved.

Jeter felt that Toy's views were inconsistent with the Abstract of Principles. Toy upheld the creed's first article, Jeter said, but only "according to the interpretation which he puts upon it." But the denomination interpreted the article differently. Most Southern Baptists understood the first article to mean that inspiration secured the truth of all scripture, whereas Toy's view limited the effective extent of inspiration. The first article was a general statement concerning inspiration, Jeter acknowledged, but "the details of the subject are comprehended in the general statement." [98]

But Jeter seemed to consider Toy's departure from scripture a more substantial matter than his inconsistency with the Abstract. The trustees, Jeter said, judged Toy's views as "diverging from the orthodox views on the subject of inspiration, and containing the seeds of dangerous errors." Among the "serious consequences" entailed was its denigration of the accuracy of the Bible's historical statements. Jeter explained: "It might seem a small matter for the geology or geography of the Bible to be false; but its history is inseparably associated with its doctrine. How can this be false without bringing into doubt the most momentous truths of revelation?... The resurrection of Christ is the central fact of Christianity. It is purely historical." If the historical statements of the Bible could be false, Jeter concluded, then so could the doctrine that was inseparably bound to the history. [99]

But others felt that Toy's views were consistent with the Abstract of Principles and the Bible, and that the faculty and trustees had sacrificed Toy to popular opinion. John A. Chambliss, one of the two trustees who protested Toy's dismissal, held that the trustees had established a poor precedent. The trustee majority dismissed Toy merely because his views were out of step with those commonly held among Southern Baptists. Toy's view of inspiration was within the boundaries of the Abstract narrowly interpreted. Chambliss and many of those who inclined to the new theology felt that the Abstract of Principles should be the maximum standard of orthodoxy for faculty. Any additional standard would stultify true scholarship and spiritual vitality. They held that forced conformity was a greater threat than heresy, fearing that under the majority's policy the seminary would become a "manufactory of music boxes, all shaped and pitched alike to give forth an invariable number of invariable tunes." The

98. J. B. Jeter, "News and Notes," *Religious Herald*, 13 Nov. 1879, 2.
99. Jeter, "News and Notes," 2.

antidote to conformity was freedom and toleration of differences of theological opinion. They yearned for "more independence and freedom of thought in the study of the Scriptures."[100] Boyce and the trustee majority also valued independence and freedom of thought, until it led to heresy.

THE INSPIRATION CONTROVERSY

Toy's dismissal precipitated a denominational controversy concerning the doctrine of inspiration. It began in earnest in late 1879 when the Baptist newspapers printed the text of Toy's resignation letter, and it lasted several years.[101] In Toy's resignation letter he presented his views in the least objectionable form. His views were more advanced than the public knew, but Boyce and Broadus felt constrained by honor to avoid public comment.

So many seminary graduates defended Toy that many Southern Baptists worried that the seminary was no longer safe for orthodoxy. Samuel Henderson suggested in the *Christian Index* that the seminary was weakening students' faith in the Bible, since so many seminary graduates were teaching that the Bible is a patchwork of human and divine elements.[102] James R. Graves made the most of the seminary's predicament. He suggested that the 1880 Southern Baptist Convention was notable for widespread dissatisfaction with the seminary. He accused Broadus and Whitsitt of being unsound, by his usual method of attributing the charge to unnamed informants: "It was affirmed by those who spoke from their personal knowledge that Profs. Whitsitt and Broadus fully sympathize with the views of Prof. Toy touching inspiration." He granted only that everyone admitted that Boyce and Manly were sound.[103] Boyce refuted the accusation: "I desire in your columns emphatically to deny the above affirmation. The informant of Dr. Graves is entirely mistaken."[104]

Boyce also confronted Graves personally about the accusation. Graves refused to name his informant, but Boyce deduced that it was only one person, and he

---

100. J. A. Chambliss, "The Trustees of the Seminary and Dr. Toy's Resignation," *Baptist Courier*, 12 June 1879, 2.

101. C. H. Toy, "Full Text of the Paper Offered with the Resignation of Rev. C. H. Toy, D.D., as Professor in the Southern Baptist Theological Seminary," *Baptist Courier*, 27 Nov. 1879, 2. The *Religious Herald* published it on 11 Dec. 1879.

102. Samuel Henderson, "A Word of Caution," *Christian Index*, 11 Mar. 1880, 1.

103. James R. Graves, "The Southern Baptist Convention," *Baptist* (Memphis, TN), 22 May 1880, 773.

104. James P. Boyce, "Statement in the Baptist about Professors Whitsitt and Broadus," *Western Recorder*, 8 July 1880, 4.

suspected that it was S. F. Thompson, who had been telling people that Broadus agreed with Toy for a year.[105] O. C. Pope, editor of the *Texas Baptist Herald*, felt certain that Broadus was sound, but he apparently was not as sure of Whitsitt.[106] Thompson apparently opposed Toy's dismissal and justified his opposition by claiming that Broadus and Whitsitt held the same view of inspiration.[107]

But the strongest criticism of the seminary came not from those who feared the seminary was becoming unsound. The faculty and trustees had taken a firm stand against Toy's views and in favor of orthodoxy. Rather, the most vigorous attacks came from those who felt the seminary had acted out of mere expedience, dismissing a sound and devout scholar to satisfy the protests of an uneducated and narrow constituency. Among these critics were some of the seminary's strongest supporters in the denomination, their own graduates.

Trustee William D. Thomas feared that Toy's supporters would make trouble for the seminary at the 1880 meeting of the Southern Baptist Convention. He wanted the board to justify dismissing Toy based on its concern for both the seminary and orthodoxy. He wrote Broadus: "I rather imagine that our brethren who have been dissatisfied with the action of board as to Toy will call upon the convention to require the board to report on the subject—if so, my idea would be not to resist the movement but to allow the convention to consider the matter and to call for a report. The board to report a very brief paper prepared before hand confining itself to the two points: (a) that the seminary could not prosper with agitation about an acting professor's views on such a subject—(b) that the subject itself could be best discussed and the interests of truth promoted by the course adopted."[108] Two years later seminary trustee J. L. M. Curry counseled similar preparation to repulse attacks on the orthodox view that might come to the floor of the Southern Baptist Convention in 1882. He urged Broadus to prepare a defense of the traditional view of inspiration of the Old Testament. William D. Thomas was preparing a general defense of inspiration, and another trustee, apparently Curry himself, was preparing to defend the board's action.[109]

Seminary trustee E. T. Winkler led the public critique of Toy's views. Inspiration of only one part or element of the Bible, Winkler argued, ultimately undermined the whole: "The trouble is found in what Dr. Toy denominates the human element of the Word of God.... He professes the utmost reverence for the Bible and at the same time he proposes to show that there are human infirmities

105. James P. Boyce to John A. Broadus, ca. 26 May 1880, box 9, Broadus Papers.

106. O. C. Pope to John A. Broadus, 25 May 1880, box 8, Broadus Papers.

107. See S. F. Thompson to John A. Broadus, 3 July 1879, box 8, Broadus Papers.

108. William D. Thomas to John A. Broadus, 29 Apr. 1880, box 9, Broadus Papers.

109. J. L. M. Curry to John A. Broadus, 8 Nov. 1881, box 9, Broadus Papers.

and errors in the Word of God.... Who can tell us what part is divine. Who can tell us what we are to believe and what we are to do as Christians?... We are dependent upon certain eminent scholars to know what is the Word of God— and none of these scholars agree in their decisions.... They give a thousand diverse answers.... And the result will be that we shall have just such a Bible as we choose to have. The only safe position that we as Baptists can hold, is that the Bible is free from error." [110] Winkler urged the professors to join the fight and write defenses of the orthodox view of inspiration. [111]

THE FACULTY AND INSPIRATION

Boyce and Broadus joined the fight. They knew Toy's position, but they felt some delicacy about criticizing their friend in public. They felt less delicacy in private. When Pastor Samuel M. Provence read Toy's resignation essay, he wrote Broadus expressing confusion over the board's action and sympathy for Toy. Broadus replied that Toy's letter gave "very little idea" of his actual views. [112] Broadus explained to others that Toy's view of inspiration left his religious convictions unanchored and that "there was no telling" whether he would become a Unitarian. [113] Boyce was making similar explanations. Provence heard from persons who traveled recently with Boyce that Boyce believed that Toy's beliefs were now "rotten to the core." [114]

After several years the faculty began to speak publicly on the matter and to publish defenses of the orthodox view. Broadus published a number a works supporting the traditional plenary theory of inspiration. At the 1883 meeting of the Southern Baptist Convention, he defended the traditional view in the convention sermon, "Three Questions as to the Bible." He argued that through the agency of men, the Bible says precisely what God intended it to say. God's use of human authors did not render the Bible liable to error any more than the incarnation rendered Jesus liable to error. [115]

---

110. E. T. Winkler, "Dr. Toy on Inspiration," *Baptist Courier*, 26 Feb. 1880, 1. This article appeared first in the *Alabama Baptist*.

111. Basil Manly Jr. to John A. Broadus, 27 July 1880, box 9, Broadus Papers.

112. John A. Broadus to S. M. Provence, quoted in Provence to Broadus, 7 Jan. 1880, box 8, Broadus Papers.

113. C. F. D. [Carrie F. Davis] to John Stout, 26 May 1880, Lide-Coker-Stout Family Papers, USC

114. Samuel M. Provence to John A. Broadus, 7 Jan. 1880, box 8, Broadus Papers.

115. John A. Broadus, *Three Questions as to the Bible* (Philadelphia: American Baptist Publication Society, 1883), 26–27.

Broadus sometimes urged caution concerning the terminology of "verbal inspiration," because many persons understood the phrase to imply a mechanical or dictation approach to inspiration, whereas instead the scriptures bear testimony to the fact its human authors retained the characteristic elements of human language and thought. Broadus held nevertheless that the human characteristics of the text did not mitigate or limit its inspiration. "The inspired writers not unfrequently report merely the substance of what was said, without aiming to give the exact words," Broadus said, but "the inspiration of the scripture is complete" and the "inspired writers have everywhere told us just what God would have us know." [116] The scripture writers employed human abilities and judgment "under the aid and control of the Holy Spirit, giving it just as God wished it to be given." Verbal inspiration did not mean mechanical dictation of God's speech in subversion of human freedom and consciousness, but the Holy Spirit controlled the writing concursively with human freedom and consciousness. The inspired writers were "moved by the Holy Ghost" so that they "will not only say what He wishes, but say it as He wishes." [117]

In 1887 Broadus presented "The Paramount and Permanent Authority of the Bible" as the doctrinal sermon of the annual gathering of the Northern Baptist societies. He warned against trying to make the Bible square with evolution—he preferred to "wait for evolution to evolve." He warned against appeals to "Christian consciousness" as the key to discerning the Bible's authoritative message. The approach derived from Schleiermacher's defective schema and suited erroneous notions concerning the progressive character of revelation. Once revelation ceased, Broadus said, there was no more progress in revelation. But there is progress in orthodoxy, a progress in knowing and doing. The Bible, Broadus said, "is the word of God" and does not merely contain the word of God, so that "wherever it undertakes to teach its teachings are true." [118] In one of his last statements concerning the Bible, his 1892 catechism, Broadus wrote that the Bible's authors "were preserved by the Holy Spirit from error" and that "there is no proof that the inspired writers made any mistake of any kind." [119]

Basil Manly Jr., who had replaced Toy and whose reputation for orthodoxy in the convention was well established, taught the traditional view of inspiration

116. John A. Broadus, *Commentary on the Gospel of Matthew* (Philadelphia: American Baptist Publication Society, 1886), 58.

117. John A. Broadus, "Quotations in Matthew," ms. notebook, 23, SBTS.

118. John A. Broadus, "The Paramount and Permanent Authority of the Bible," *Baptist Courier*, 23 June 1887, 1.

119. John A. Broadus, *Catechism of Bible Teaching* (Philadelphia: American Baptist Publication Society, 1892).

in the 1879–1880 session and began preparing a book on the subject.[120] In 1888 he published the *Bible Doctrine of Inspiration*, an able defense of plenary verbal inspiration. Manly rejected Toy's method of extricating the spiritual meaning from the external framework of human speech. The human and the divine elements, Manly held, make one inspired text and meaning. The Bible was "all written by man, all inspired by God." The divine and human elements, Manly said, could be distinguished, but they could not be separated. The "twofold authorship extends to every part of scripture, and to the language as well as to the general ideas expressed." Toy and the new theology assumed that the presence of the human element in the Bible necessarily subjected its message to human fallibility. But it was a fallacy, Manly said, to hold "that God can not inspire and so use a human being as to keep his message free from error."[121]

Boyce's view was similar. He held that God so inspired the Bible authors that they wrote "exactly" what God wished—"as if he had written every word himself."[122] He believed in the "verbal inspiration" of the Bible's writers, that they "were guided in their very language by Him to whom are 'known all His works from the beginning of the world.'"[123]

Whitsitt seemed to agree with Manly, Broadus, and Boyce. In his public statements in the 1880s and 1890s he identified strongly with traditional Protestant orthodoxy. With regard to Old Testament criticism, he aligned the seminary with the strict biblicism of Princeton Theological Seminary and professed a "critical attitude towards modern criticism."[124] But some suspected him of sympathy with Toy's views. He and Toy were close friends. Both were single; they had been roommates and became especially close during the seminary's first two years in Louisville.[125] Whitsitt, moreover, had been deeply troubled by Toy's dismissal. But if Whitsitt held Toy's views, he kept the fact to himself.

120. Manly taught inspiration that year in Biblical Introduction, a class he took over when Whitsitt became too ill to teach. See Jerome R. Baer, Notebook for Biblical Introduction 1879–80, SBTS.

121. Basil Manly Jr., *The Bible Doctrine of Inspiration Explained and Vindicated* (New York: A. C. Armstrong, 1888), 29, 90, 30.

122. James P. Boyce, *A Brief Catechism of Bible Doctrine* (Greenville, SC: Sunday School Board of the Southern Baptist Convention, 1864), 1.

123. James P. Boyce, *Three Changes in Theological Institutions* (Greenville, SC: C. J. Elford's Press, 1856), 27.

124. William H. Whitsitt, quoted in "Questions on Modern Criticism," *Baptist Courier*, 14 Apr. 1898, 6–7.

125. Crawford H. Toy to Edward B. Pollard, 1 Dec. 1911, box 1, Edward B. Pollard Papers, American Baptist Historical Society, Atlanta, Georgia.

Boyce and Broadus also took additional precautions to make sure that unsound views of inspiration did not intrude again on the faculty or spread further among the churches. Because of the prevalence of Toy's views among seminary graduates, whenever the faculty considered engaging tutors or instructors, they inquired carefully into each one's views of inspiration. Broadus, for example, wanted to know two things about alumnus Edwin C. Dargan to judge his fitness for joining the faculty—his pursuit of scholarship since graduation, and whether his "belief in inspiration has become in any respect relaxed."[126] Many of the ablest young graduates were found wanting on this account. When Boyce and Broadus wanted someone to help in Old Testament in 1880, they asked Toy for a list of the most capable students in that subject in recent years. Toy's list was a disappointment because most were unreliable on the doctrine of inspiration. Boyce "feared" them all with two exceptions.[127]

Boyce and Broadus refused to recommend seminary graduates to pulpits without knowing that their views of inspiration were sound. They had frequent opportunities to match pastors and churches, and they made it a point to ask a candidate his view of inspiration before recommending him to a church. This included established pastors considering a move and graduates whom they knew well. For example, when the pastor of Louisville's Broadway Baptist Church resigned in 1883, Boyce hoped that he and Broadus would have an opportunity to recommend the successor. They wanted a strong preacher who was orthodox and a loyal supporter of the seminary. Boyce asked Broadus to inquire quietly "about the inspiration views" of three men whom he had in mind as candidates.[128] Similarly, when William W. Landrum asked Broadus to recommend him to a church, Broadus first wanted to know what Landrum believed "in regard to certain rumors of my [Landrum's] heterodoxy."[129]

Broadus had scruples about recommending former student Henry A. Whitman even to teach English at the University of South Carolina because his views on inspiration were suspect. When Whitman had asked Broadus to recommend him to the chair of English, Broadus replied that he would do so, but that he would have to inform the school that Whitman was probably unsound on the doctrine of inspiration.[130]

126. Edwin C. Dargan to John A. Broadus, 4 Mar. 1879, box 8, Broadus Papers.

127. James P. Boyce to John A. Broadus, 23 Aug. 1880, box 9, Broadus Papers.

128. James P. Boyce to John A. Broadus, 25 Aug. 1883, box 10, Broadus Papers.

129. William W. Landrum to John A. Broadus, 12 Dec. 1882, box 9, Broadus Papers. See also J. A. Chambliss to John A. Broadus, 10 Jan. 1884, box 10, Broadus Papers.

130. Henry A. Whitman to John A. Broadus, 17 Jan. 1887, box 11, Broadus Papers. See also Whitman to Broadus, 25 Feb. 1881, box 9, Broadus Papers; Whitman to Broadus, 13 Apr. 1882, box 9, Broadus Papers.

Toy's followers all professed the belief that the Bible was fully inspired. But this did not satisfy Boyce. When they explained that inspiration applied primarily to the scripture's spiritual sense, Boyce suspected the soundness of their doctrine: "All the talk of such men about spiritual sense means no more than the rejection of plain statements from our creed because they are unpalatable." [131] Subsequent developments proved Boyce's assessment generally correct.

TOY AND HIS DEFENDERS

After his dismissal Toy gave counsel to his defenders and wrote a number of articles in support of his views. His dismissal raised the issue within the denomination, and it was now time to explain and advance the new view. Virginia's *Religious Herald* and South Carolina's *Working Christian* began the discussion in late 1879. Toy contributed a series of some seventeen articles for the *Baptist Courier* from January to June 1881. In them he cautiously promoted the superiority of interpreting the Bible for its spiritual meaning in preference to its outward historical meaning. Toy explained: "The Bible, like all other books, has not only an outside, but an inside, namely, its method and spirit, something vastly more important than historical, geographical, or chronological details." He gently undermined confidence in the inerrancy of the Bible's outward statements by representing David and other early Hebrews as having "crude notions" of God, by raising historical questions concerning the preservation of the biblical text and the limits of the canon, and by assigning the book of Daniel to the second century, long after many of its prophecies were fulfilled. Toy did not attack supernaturalism directly, but throughout the articles he emphasized the "naturalness" of the Bible. [132]

Toy encouraged his friend John L. Johnson to write articles on inspiration for Mississippi's *Baptist Record*. He recommended that Johnson establish the new view through a discussion of how New Testament authors misinterpreted the Old Testament, and he provided Johnson with an annotated list of pertinent

---

131. James P. Boyce to John A. Broadus, 4 Sept. 1883, box 10, Broadus Papers. By "creed" Boyce apparently had reference to the body of beliefs held by Baptist churches, not to the Abstract of Principles.

132. See, e.g., C. H. Toy, "Need of the Study of the Bible," *Baptist Courier*, 13 Jan. 1881, 1; Toy, "The Naturalness of the Bible," ibid., 27 Jan. 1881, 1; Toy, "The Ethical Naturalness of the Bible," ibid., 3 Feb. 1881, 1; Toy, "The Natural Growth of the Bible," ibid., 10 Feb. 1881, 1; Toy, "The Old Testament Text," ibid., 10 Mar. 1881, 1; Toy, "Settlement of the Old Testament Canon," ibid., 1; Toy, "The Object of the Book of Daniel," ibid., 2 June 1881, 1.

passages. Toy explained that such New Testament quotes derived variously from "rabbinical fancy," invented meanings, and incorrect interpretations.[133]

The captain of the campaign for the new view was William C. Lindsay, pastor of the Columbia, South Carolina, First Baptist Church.[134] Under the pseudonym Senex, he had begun pressing for acceptance of the new view of inspiration in 1877, fomenting considerable debate in South Carolina.[135] Inspiration, Lindsay said, "is concerned only with the religious element" of scripture.[136] The scripture's statements concerning physical phenomena, Lindsay said, were "frequently erroneous."[137] God gave "religious consciousness" to Christians to "detect" the religious element in scripture.[138] Toy encouraged Lindsay in 1877 that his approach was broadly correct.[139]

When the trustees dismissed Toy, Lindsay entered the fight under his own name and published a flurry of articles in defense of Toy and his followers. He recognized that the trustees did not dismiss Toy merely from expediency but because of his views of inspiration.[140] He was one of the first of Toy's defenders to recognize that the new view entailed extensive reconstruction of the Bible's history and considerable reinterpretation of its meaning. After several years of striving, he concluded that his efforts to enlighten the denomination were unavailing and that the only hope for advancing liberal views in the Southern Baptist Convention was making the seminary and college faculties more liberal.

Many others entered the fray, including graduate W. J. Alexander, who wrote "The Safety and Conservatism of Dr. Toy's Position."[141] F. C. Johnson, pastor of the Marietta, Georgia, Baptist Church, wrote that Toy's position was "impregnable"

133. C. H. Toy to John L. Johnson, 16 Dec. 1879, John Lipscomb Johnson Papers, Southern Historical Collection, UNC.

134. See especially Lindsay, "Dr. Toy's Paper," 2.

135. William C. Lindsay to John Stout, 20 May 1877, Lide-Coker-Stout Family Papers, USC.

136. William C. Lindsay, "Letters to My Friend—No. 1," *Working Christian*, 24 May 1877, 2.

137. William C. Lindsay, "Letters to My Friend—No. 2," *Working Christian*, 31 May 1877, 2.

138. William C. Lindsay, "Letters to My Friend—No. 3," *Working Christian*, 7 June 1877, 2.

139. William C. Lindsay to John Stout, 5 July 1877, Lide-Coker-Stout Family Papers, USC.

140. Lindsay, "Dr. Toy's Paper," 2.

141. W. J. Alexander, "The Safety and Conservatism of Dr. Toy's Position," *Baptist Courier*, 4 Dec. 1879, 2.

and thought that in that age of progress none were left who maintained the traditional verbal theory of inspiration.[142] R. W. Lide, pastor of the Darlington, South Carolina, Baptist Church, declared Toy's views "by far the most satisfactory that I have ever seen."[143]

The debate over inspiration was renewed in 1881 when Boyce interfered in the appointment of two missionaries who agreed with Toy's views of inspiration. In April 1881 the Southern Baptist Foreign Mission Board appointed two seminary graduates, John Stout and T. P. Bell, as missionaries to China. Stout was an established pastor and had been a classmate of Lindsay. Bell graduated in 1880. When the board announced their appointment, the board's secretary, Henry A. Tupper, began to receive complaints about their soundness. Neither Tupper nor the trustees had asked the men concerning their view of inspiration, even though Stout at the time proposed to send Tupper a statement about it. Tupper now asked Stout and Bell to communicate their beliefs on the subject.[144] Each aligned himself with Toy's view. The board rescinded their appointments.[145]

Boyce had discovered their views and felt that it was his duty to advise the board against their appointment. He participated in the examination of another missionary candidate, W. S. Walker, in Columbus, Mississippi, in May 1881. When Walker said he had no theory of inspiration, Boyce pressed him on the fundamental issue, the results of inspiration and the question of inerrancy: "But Brother Walker, do you think there are any mistakes in the Bible?" Walker replied, "Certainly not." But T. P. Bell, who was present at the examination and already under appointment by the board, told Boyce afterward that he could not answer as Walker had, and apparently implicated Stout in the same opinion.[146] Boyce wrote Tupper. Broadus told his wife that it was Boyce who "first insisted that the board should look into it," though she still wondered whether her husband had himself been the one.[147] When the mission board trustees discussed the matter in June 1881, Secretary Tupper "read a letter from Dr. J. P. Boyce and also letters from Brothers John Stout and T. P. Bell with reference

142. F. C. Johnson, "What Is the Baptist View of Inspiration," *Baptist Courier*, 4 Dec. 1879, 2.

143. R. W. Lide, "Dr. Toy's Paper," *Baptist Courier*, 11 Dec. 1879, 2.

144. H. A. Tupper to John Stout, 21 May 1881, Lide-Coker-Stout Family Papers, USC.

145. John Stout, "Appointment of Rev. John Stout and Rev. T. P. Bell Withdrawn," *Baptist Courier*, 7 July 1881, 2-3; H. A. Tupper to John Stout, 21 May 1881, Lide-Coker-Stout Family Papers, USC; T. P. Bell to H. A. Tupper, ca. 21 May 1881, ibid.; T. P. Bell, "Statement of Brother Bell," *Baptist Courier*, 14 July 1881, 2.

146. James P. Boyce to Matthew T. Yates, 13 July 1881, Letterpress Copy Book 7, June 1881-Nov. 1881.

147. Charlotte Broadus to John A. Broadus, 21 July 1881, box 9, Broadus Papers.

to their views on the inspiration of the scriptures."[148] Boyce's letter apparently exposed their views of inspiration and explained the reasons that their views were objectionable. Afterward Tupper asked Broadus to recruit two students to replace Stout and Bell, and Broadus found two with sounder theology.[149] Many Southern Baptists rightly suspected that Boyce was the leading voice among those who complained.[150]

Boyce and Broadus tried to win Toy's sympathizers to an orthodox view of inspiration. In some instances they failed notably, as in the case of David G. Lyon, a promising seminary student concerning whom Broadus and Toy both took an interest. Once Toy resigned, Broadus labored to prevent Lyon from following in Toy's steps. Lyon was an exceptional student who excelled especially in Greek and Hebrew. Broadus hoped that Lyon would teach in a Southern Baptist school and recruited him as a tutor in the seminary. Lyon aspired to study in Germany and in the weeks after Toy's resignation sought the advice of his two mentors. Toy advised him to go in order to gain advantage of the best scholarship. Broadus, who generally advocated study in Germany for the sake of scholarship, advised Lyon, however, to stay at the seminary because if he left at that time to go to Germany, it would embarrass the seminary, harm his reputation, and possibly injure his faith.[151] Broadus sensed Lyon's inclination to follow Toy's thought and hoped that by inviting him to return to the seminary as a tutor, Lyon could be prevented from adopting the new view of inspiration. When Broadus asked him whether his convictions would permit him "to teach, as to inspiration, in accordance with and not contrary to the opinions which prevail among intelligent American Baptists," Lyon answered in Toy's dialect. He said that he held no particular view of inspiration. "In general terms, I can say, that I view the Bible as the inspired Word of God, but in the details of the subject my opinions are not well enough matured for me to write anything

148. Minutes of the Foreign Mission Board of the Southern Baptist Convention, 6 June 1881.

149. The two students who replaced Bell and Stout were Cicero W. Pruitt and William S. Walker. See Cicero W. Pruitt, "Life of Cicero Washington Pruitt, Composed by Himself," 4, box 1, Ida Pruitt Papers, Schlesinger Library, Harvard University; Minutes, Faculty, Southern Baptist Theological Seminary, 18 Nov. 1881; Minutes, Foreign Mission Board of the Southern Baptist Convention, 19 Nov. 1881.

150. W. C. Lindsay to John Stout, 27 May 1881, Lide-Coker-Stout Family Papers, USC; George B. Eager to John Stout, 13 Sept. 1881, Lide-Coker-Stout Family Papers, USC. But others besides Boyce raised concerns (see T. P. Bell to John Stout, 28 June 1881, ibid.).

151. David G. Lyon to John A. Broadus, 7 June 1879 and 18 June 1879, box 8, Broadus Papers.

definite."[152] The faculty were not satisfied with this indefinite statement, and Boyce wrote Lyon for more detailed information.[153] Lyon's reply revealed that he held Toy's views and settled the question.[154] When Broadus wrote him the following year to discover "whether I have grown more conservative," Lyon responded, "I am not more conservative than I was a year ago." He relished the prospect of joining the faculty of Southern Seminary but knew that his views of inspiration precluded that: "You wish a man who can assent to the absolute infallibility of the biblical writers, and that I cannot do."[155] A year later Toy recruited Lyon for Harvard, where he established the Semitic Museum and spent his entire teaching career.[156]

There were other disappointments among seminary graduates. Broadus failed similarly to dissuade George W. Manly, another Toy sympathizer and the son of Basil Manly Jr., from his determination to study in Germany.[157] Lewis J. Huff withdrew from the ministry when he could no longer "preach what I did not believe" and joined Manly in studies at Leipzig.[158] William J. Alexander took up Toy's defense, embraced Darwinism and utilitarian moral philosophy, and then followed Toy into Unitarianism, for which last offense trustees of the University of South Carolina translated him from the chair of moral philosophy to English.[159]

In other instances, Boyce and Broadus had more success. J. O. Lowry returned to a more conservative position after Broadus's predictions about Toy's naturalistic trajectory started to become reality. Toy's participation in a Unitarian ministers' institute in 1881 caused Lowry to retract his statement of "moral and intellectual sympathy" with Toy.[160] Lowry recoiled before the

---

152. David G. Lyon to John A. Broadus, 22 May 1880, box 9, Broadus Papers.

153. James P. Boyce to John A. Broadus, 15 July 1880, box 9, Broadus Papers.

154. Basil Manly Jr. to John A. Broadus, 27 July 1880, box 9, Broadus Papers.

155. David G. Lyon to John A. Broadus, 28 Mar. 1881, box 9, Broadus Papers.

156. On Lyon, see "David Gordon Lyon, 1852–1935," *Journal of Biblical Literature* 55 (1936): iii–iv; "David Gordon Lyon, 1852–1936," *Biblica* 17 (1936): 389; David Gordon Lyon biographical card, in Biographical File, David Gordon Lyon, HUA.

157. See George W. Manly to John A. Broadus, 29 Dec. 1882, box 9, Broadus Papers; Manly to Broadus 18 Jan. 1883, ibid.; Manly to Broadus, 29 Jan. 1883, ibid.

158. Lewis J. Huff to John A. Broadus, 1 Jan. 1885, box 10, Broadus Papers; Huff to Broadus, 15 Mar. 1885, ibid.

159. See Gregory A. Wills, *The First Baptist Church of Columbia, South Carolina, 1809–2002* (Brentwood, TN: Baptist History and Heritage Society, 2003), 168–170; Gordon B. Moore to John A. Broadus, 16 Mar. 1888, box 12, Broadus Papers.

160. J. O. Lowry to John A. Broadus, 14 Sept. 1881, 4 Oct. 1881, 14 Oct. 1881, box 9, Broadus Papers.

practical consequences of Toy's views: "Dr. Toy's views and mine part company now...because of the practical destructiveness, the grief to which they tend."[161]

Boyce and the faculty kept up their insistence on orthodoxy and their opposition to the new theology while they lived. When Toy invited Broadus to preach in chapel services at Harvard Divinity School in 1886, Broadus doubted the propriety of accepting. Boyce advised that he decline: "There is great danger in any encouragement we give to Drs. Toy and Lyon. We do not know what harm we may do by making people think that their differences from us are not of importance. Besides I do not like to see the Unitarians helped by favors from others, and especially by sermons from which the 'gospel' must be left out so as not to say what would be unacceptable to Unitarians."[162]

Toy's writings and religious career did much to credit the faculty's position in the Toy affair. When Toy's views became known in greater detail, many of his followers faltered. In his *History of the Religion of Israel* (1882), he asserted that circumcision came not from the command of God but from the Egyptians, that Moses probably did not give any of the laws attributed to him, and that the law and the system of worship were invented hundreds of years after the scripture history supposed.[163] In his *Quotations in the New Testament* (1884), he argued at length that the New Testament authors interpreted the Old Testament in ways foreign to their original meaning, rendering their interpretations faulty and illegitimate. Their words were subject to error and defect, though their essential spirit and personality were true and trustworthy. The New Testament authors did not always report Jesus' words correctly, but even where they did, Jesus employed the same erroneous methods of interpreting the Old Testament as his followers. Jesus' interpretation of the Old Testament was not the final authority, but "the science of hermeneutics must be the final authority," Toy wrote.[164] Toy generally avoided discussion of the Bible's accounts of supernatural events.

Many who initially felt that his views were innocent in theory now judged them dangerous and false in fact. The editors of the *Religious Herald* pointed out with satisfaction that even some Unitarians objected to Toy's rough treatment of the Old Testament. Thomas Hill, former president of Harvard University, complained that in Toy's book "Abraham is reduced to a myth, Moses to a polytheist,

161. J. O. Lowry to John A. Broadus, 29 Oct. 1881, box 9, Broadus Papers.

162. James P. Boyce to John A. Broadus, 14 Aug. 1886, box 11, Broadus Papers.

163. C. H. Toy, *The History of the Religion of Israel* (Boston: Unitarian Sunday School Society, 1882), 16.

164. C. H. Toy, *Quotations in the New Testament* (New York: Scribner's, 1884), xxvii–xxix.

and Jesus to a very pure-minded Jew." Hill threatened to withdraw support for the Unitarian Sunday School Society for publishing such a book.[165]

Many of the young preachers who learned at Toy's feet sympathized with Toy's views and rejected the traditional view of inspiration. J. Hartwell Edwards had sympathized with Toy's views, but he assured Broadus that Toy's "recent writings have occasioned a reaction...in my own mind."[166] George B. Eager, who in 1900 would join the faculty of the seminary, rejected the traditional view of inspiration under Toy's influence, but he likewise grew alarmed at Toy's deliverances: "I came to see how far he was going and drew back amazed and startled."[167] J. A. Chambliss similarly sympathized with Toy's rejection of the traditional view but rejected what he called Toy's speculative opinions: "He is in his speculative opinions entirely out of harmony with Jesus and Paul."[168] Even William C. Lindsay, the most vocal proponent of the new theory of inspiration, drew back. He praised Toy's *History of Israel* but noted with concern that Toy's position eliminated all objective revelation. Lindsay felt that the solution should exist somewhere between Toy's "extreme naturalism" and "extreme supernaturalism."[169] These preachers saw the "danger of [Toy's] views," as Toy admirer George W. Manly put it, and followed only so far.[170] But Toy's influence endured. Such men did not follow Toy any longer, but they did not quite return to the old orthodox view either.

Most seminary graduates who accepted the new view of inspiration found churches and quietly pursued their pastoral labors, but they remained on the outside of denominational counsels. William W. Landrum reflected on his outsider identity: "I was branded a heretic at the time of the Toy controversy.... again at the time of the rejection of Bell and Stout as foreign missionaries. I was read out of the synagogue by eminent saints from all points of the compass."[171] But the tide was about to turn, and the seminary would lead the way. A large percentage of the next generation of seminary professors held a form of the new view of inspiration. William O. Carver, Edgar Y. Mullins, George B. Eager, Charles S. Gardner, and most of their successors took the new view of inspiration for

165. Thomas Hill, quoted in unattributed editorial, *Religious Herald*, 22 Feb. 1882, 2.

166. J. Hartwell Edwards to John A. Broadus, 20 Mar. 1883, box 9, Broadus Papers.

167. George B. Eager to John A. Broadus, 31 Dec. 1883, Broadus Papers.

168. J. A. Chambliss to John A. Broadus, 10 Jan. 1884, Broadus Papers.

169. William C. Lindsay, "History of the Religion of Israel," *Baptist Courier*, 26 Oct. 1882, 2; ibid., 2 Nov. 1882, 1. Lindsay finally could not "subscribe" to Toy's "theory that there is nothing in the Bible which requires different canons of interpretation from other books" (Lindsay to John Stout, 16 Apr. 1884, Lide-Coker-Stout Family Papers, USC).

170. George W. Manly to John A. Broadus, 29 Jan. 1883, box 9, Broadus Papers.

171. William W. Landrum to A. T. Robertson, 23 Feb. 1898, Robertson Papers.

granted. Carver observed correctly in 1954 that Toy's "views would today not be regarded as sufficiently revolutionary to call for drastic action." [172]

Toy left the South, left Baptists, and finally left the church. His efforts to enlighten Southern Baptists largely failed. They held firmly to their traditional narrowness. But a new generation of educated ministers drew encouragement from Toy's teachings and adopted the new liberal view of inspiration. They followed his example and sought by "patient and wise effort to dislodge the traditional narrowness."

172. William O. Carver, "Recollections and Information from Other Sources Concerning the Southern Baptist Theological Seminary," typescript, 27, SBTS.

4

ALL THINGS MADE NEW
The End of the Heroic Age

In March 1877 Boyce was discouraged and was talking again of suspending the seminary. Collections on bonds for endowment and for annual expenses were poor. It had been nearly five years since the trustees, with the endorsement of the Southern Baptist Convention, had determined to move to Louisville, on the condition of securing $500,000 in pledged bonds for the endowment. Boyce was still $27,000 short of reaching Kentucky's share of $300,000.[1] He was also well short of the South's additional $200,000. Subscribers had not yet begun to pay on their subscription pledges, since the first of their five-year installments would be due only after Boyce secured pledges totaling $500,000. The endowment movement was nearing a crisis. The extended delay in the move to Louisville was casting doubt on the seminary's ultimate success and was discouraging giving.

Money was still tight. Many of the Baptists who had given bonds in 1874 promising to pay in total $15,000 per year for five consecutive years were not paying. Only about half of the money pledged had come in. "The average collections for the past year," Boyce wrote Broadus in 1877, "have not been $8,000, while our expenses have been for salaries alone $12,400." The seminary still owed twice as much as its Greenville properties were worth. Boyce felt that "it would be prudent to stop the seminary" for a couple of years and let the professors take pastorates. "I am in great perplexity. The brethren will not and some cannot pay." Texas subscribers were "talking of repudiating their pledges...and

---

1. James P. Boyce to John A. Broadus, 26 May 1877, box 7, Broadus Papers.

others make no talk about it but just do it. May God guide us for I am blind and can see no longer." [2]

Broadus refused to consider suspension. Many students, he said, would transfer to northern seminaries or enter permanent work. The professors might sink in roots elsewhere and be hard to get back. Most important, Broadus said, "we can't get endowment unless we keep on." [3] In response to the crisis, the board of trustees voted to move the seminary to Louisville at once. The board and the faculty hoped that going forward with the move would "give a new impulse to the whole enterprise." [4]

Broadus noted that it was "no great task to remove the seminary.... There was nothing to move except the library of a few thousand volumes and three professors." [5] Boyce rented lecture rooms from the Public Library Hall. He rented the Elliott House as a dormitory and dining hall and rented additional dormitory space from the National Hotel. The move brought immediate benefits. Greenville was a village of about 5,000 persons and one Baptist church. [6] Louisville was a city of about 120,000 persons and seven Baptist churches. Seminary students had greater opportunities for gospel labor in the Sunday schools of the churches and in their various "mission stations," and streetcars could take students quickly to points all over the city. [7] Enrollment jumped immediately. Eighty-nine enrolled for the first session in Louisville, a jump of 31 percent over the previous high in Greenville. [8]

THE STRUGGLE FOR SOLVENCY

The seminary's removal to Louisville in 1877 did not solve its financial problems. Initially it made them worse. In Greenville the seminary did not have to pay rent for dormitories, lecture rooms, library, and offices, but in Louisville it

2. James P. Boyce to John A. Broadus, 23 Mar. 1877, box 7, Broadus Papers.

3. John A. Broadus to James P. Boyce, 27 Mar. 1877, box 11, Boyce Papers.

4. John A. Broadus, *Memoir of James Petigru Boyce* (New York: A. C. Armstrong, 1893), 248–249.

5. Broadus, *Memoir of Boyce*, 251.

6. Greenville's population was 2,757 in 1870 and 6,160 in 1880 (South Carolina Department of Agriculture, *South Carolina: Resources and Population, Institutions and Industries* [Charleston, SC: Walker, Evans, and Cogswell, 1883], 709).

7. Young Ewing Allison, *The City of Louisville and a Glimpse of Kentucky* (Louisville, KY: Committee of the Louisville Board of Trade, 1887), 8, 21; A. F. Ross to E. L. Compere, 26 Oct. 1877, box 5, E. L. Compere Papers, SBHLA.

8. Broadus, *Memoir of Boyce*, 251.

had to pay for all of these. The seminary had to raise more money for student aid to meet the needs of the larger student body. Indeed, the move to Louisville was less a symbol of success than an appeal for help. Boyce and Broadus knew that a great struggle remained ahead of them to establish the seminary securely. If those who had subscribed their bonds to the seminary would give what they owed, the seminary would have around $300,000 in invested endowment, and its finances would be entirely secure. But most subscribers had not paid. As late as 1879, most had not recovered from the great depression that followed the 1873 financial panic. The large sums that Baptists had promised to the seminary seemed to be the only hope of the seminary's survival. Boyce sought to enroll new subscribers to the endowment, but he was relying on the promises already made. He made every effort to collect, but the collections were entirely insufficient to save the seminary from insolvency and collapse.

Boyce employed agents of various types to collect on unpaid bonds and to enroll new subscribers. Employing full-time agents was expensive and in most instances brought only marginal returns. Boyce required agents to raise the money for their expenses and salary from cash donations above the subscriptions and bond payments they raised. In many cases agents failed in this requirement, and Boyce had to dismiss them. When he could, he relied on the volunteer labor of pastors who were friendly to the seminary. For example, he asked J. B. Taylor, pastor of the Wilmington, North Carolina, Baptist Church, to collect bonds of residents of that city. Boyce paid the pastors 5 percent of the money collected in commission for their labor on behalf of the seminary.[9]

Subscribers to such seminary bonds pledged payment in five annual installments. As difficult as it was to obtain the subscriptions, persuading subscribers to pay the money they had promised proved harder still. Boyce viewed a signed pledge as a solemn bond, a debt that subscribers were bound by honor and law to pay. Boyce expected subscribers to view their pledges the way he did. This is one reason that he insisted that subscribers sign legally binding bonds. He believed that few persons would sign such bonds frivolously. Such solemn pledges, Boyce figured, would suffer but little loss and would pay in at a high rate.[10] But the poverty of the postwar South and the distress consequent to the panic of 1873 rendered many subscribers unable to pay their bonds. And human nature being what it is, subscribers multiplied justifications for nonpayment, usually claiming that they signed the bond with some conditions, a thing Boyce emphatically prohibited his agents to do. The postwar bonds paid in at a

9. James P. Boyce to James B. Taylor, 14 Apr. 1883, Letterpress Copy Book 10, Sept. 1882–June 1883, 929.

10. See Broadus, *Memoir of Boyce*, 276.

low rate. In 1883, with all bonds due, and many long past due, only 52 percent had been paid.[11] Without Boyce's sagacity, and the sacrificial labors of Boyce, Broadus, and a few agents, the rate would have been much lower.

Boyce felt legally and morally justified in demanding payment of bond subscriptions. It made no sense, however, to press the legal claims of the bonds against those who signed pledges but had no money with which to pay. Every bond that failed of timely payment injured the seminary's prospects and encumbered its progress, but Boyce was sympathetic toward those in distress. "Sorry it is not convenient for you to pay the seminary bond," Boyce wrote one bondholder, "however we will cheerfully wait. It is a sad loss to us to have the bonds fail after we have secured them and cannot replace them."[12] He grieved over such losses to the seminary.

Boyce felt that to permit solvent subscribers to withhold payment was unjust to those who paid their bonds faithfully. It was unjust to the seminary also, since the seminary made long-term plans and commitments in reliance on pledged bonds. Boyce felt therefore that it was appropriate to sue some defaulters. Boyce reminded seminary agent M. B. Wharton in 1879 that the bonds were legally binding: "I will sue whenever parties refuse to pay from sheer meanness. Of course where parties are unfortunate and have not the ability to pay I will not oppress. In taking bonds be very careful not to use language that will convey the least idea that they are not binding, either legally or morally. I will sue whenever I find a disposition on the part of the giver to refuse or repudiate while he has the ability to pay."[13]

The board of trustees endorsed Boyce's policy and authorized him to sue defaulters. It told Boyce in 1881 that although in most cases it was inexpedient to sue, "in some cases it is the duty of the treasurer to sue."[14] The following year the board reminded Boyce of this duty: "The treasurer is hereby instructed to place such of the unpaid past due bonds of the seminary as he is unable to collect in the hands of attorneys for collection with instruction to sue whenever in the judgment of the treasurer it shall be necessary and expedient."[15] Boyce

11. "Notes Subscribed and Paid on Endowment," ca. May 1883, Letterpress Copy Book 10, Sept. 1882–June 1883, 899.

12. James P. Boyce to E. A. Cheek, 14 Mar. 1878, Letterpress Copy Book 1, Dec. 1877–July 1878, 250.

13. James P. Boyce to M. B. Wharton, 22 Jan. 1879, Letterpress Copy Book 3, Jan.–Dec. 1879, 72.

14. Minutes, Board of Trustees, Southern Baptist Theological Seminary, 4–9 May 1881.

15. Minutes, Board of Trustees, Southern Baptist Theological Seminary, 10–13 May 1882.

published a notice in the Baptist papers urging subscribers to make every effort to pay and reminding them of the solemn character of their pledge. Boyce was trying to avoid suing delinquents, but the board was pressing him to do so. He explained: "It is not our desire to sue any one and most certainly will not sue those who are not able. We were instructed at the last meeting of the board to sue delinquents, but instead of doing so we have been pleading, and appealing both publicly and privately and probably will be called to account at the next meeting of the board for not obeying instructions."[16]

Many took offense. Robert J. Willingham, pastor of the Chattanooga, Tennessee, First Baptist Church and a firm supporter of the seminary, complained that attorneys for the seminary had entered suits against several devout widows in indigent circumstances.[17] Some of his faculty colleagues considered this course a mistake. Broadus disagreed with bringing suit in such cases and felt that the policy brought unneeded criticism against the seminary for its apparent harshness. The irritation given outweighed the gain.

Boyce relied heavily on the faculty as fund-raising agents, though without additional pay. In the 1870s they sometimes spent much of their summers in the cause. Boyce apparently thought Toy effective only in Norfolk and other parts of Virginia, for he rarely asked him to go elsewhere. Manly and Whitsitt were effective agents, but each in turn had responsibility for raising money for the student aid on which most students depended. This required so much effort that they had little opportunity to solicit subscriptions for endowment or annual expenses.[18] He reserved the lion's share of fund-raising work for himself and Broadus, and no others were nearly as effective. He repeatedly sent Broadus to win support—when success was critical, he would have no one else. Broadus refused any compensation for his efforts until 1883, when his fund-raising labors and his need for rest restricted his ability to earn extra income from pulpit supply and writing. Boyce started paying him 5 percent commission generally, but only half that for his New York efforts in 1886.[19]

16. James P. Boyce to W. M. Howell [?], 9 Feb. 1883, Letterpress Copy Book 10, Sept. 1882–June 1883, 774. Trustees in 1883 reiterated their instructions regarding suing delinquent subscribers.

17. R. J. Willingham to John A. Broadus, 23 Oct. 1888, box 12, Broadus Papers. The widows were members of his former church in Talbatton, Georgia.

18. Charlotte Broadus felt that Boyce worked John Broadus to death in agency work, and perhaps implied that he asked too little of such work from Toy and Whitsitt (Charlotte Broadus to John A. Broadus, 13 June 1874, box 5, Broadus Papers).

19. John A. Broadus to James P. Boyce, 5 June 1883, box 6, Boyce Papers; James P. Boyce to John A. Broadus, 14 June 1883, box 10, Broadus Papers; James P. Boyce to John A. Broadus, 14 May 1886, box 11, Broadus Papers.

But pastors and the faculty could not cover the whole ground. Boyce had to employ full-time agents also. Agents faced enormous difficulties, struggling even to get an opportunity to plead the seminary's case before the churches. And when they got there, they discovered that another agent had just emptied the cupboard. College agents especially plied the churches and subordinated the value of the seminary's education to that offered by the state's Baptist college. In Missouri, for example, the agents of William Jewell College not only claimed priority for the state's interests but also pressed the claims of the college's theology department in competition with the seminary's course. Manly J. Breaker, the seminary's agent in Missouri, expressed his frustration: "I went up to our association to raise some money for the [seminary's] Student Fund, but the agents of William Jewell crowded me out. Two more 'colleges' open in our state this fall. What we are coming to, no one can tell, but I think it will never do for the seminary to wait on any local institutions. The theological department of William Jewell, which is an injury to the young ministers, is the mainstay of the college." [20] The seminary encountered similar problems in nearly every state.

The colleges were not the only competition for raising support. Dozens of interests plied the churches with appeals to worthy causes. The larger urban churches saw a veritable revolving door of agents seeking their donations. T. H. Pritchard, pastor of Raleigh, North Carolina's First Baptist Church, told Broadus that he was welcome to come and take an offering for the seminary, but he warned that the cupboard had been picked clean: "Two weeks ago, we raised money for Memphis [yellow fever epidemic]. Then came the quarterly collection for foreign missions. Home missions, education, and Sunday Schools having been honored before. On last Sabbath it was announced that a collection would be raised next Sunday for the orphan asylum at Oxford and before your letter was read yesterday I was waited on by the Young Men's Christian Association and the use of our church was asked for a general meeting of all the churches next Sunday night, to consider the condition of the poor of Raleigh. If you were to come the Sunday after, there would be five collections in as many Sabbaths." [21]

The seminary's support was unevenly distributed. Outside of Kentucky, most of the seminary's support came from the five Atlantic states of Georgia, North and South Carolina, Virginia, and Maryland. In accordance with the arrangement that brought the seminary to Louisville, Kentuckians had pledged $300,000. The other southern states had pledged some $200,000, with Georgia,

20. Manly J. Breaker to John A. Broadus, 12 Sept. 1879, box 8, Broadus Papers.
21. T. H. Pritchard to John A. Broadus, 30 Oct. 1873, box 5, Broadus Papers.

Virginia, and North Carolina accounting for more than half of that amount. Friends of the seminary in the North subscribed $45,000. The states of the "Southwest," Tennessee, Mississippi, Louisiana, Arkansas, and Texas, subscribed less than $10,000 combined.[22]

Many of these western Baptists read James R. Graves's weekly paper, the *Baptist*, and generally endorsed Graves's populist Landmark ecclesiology. Graves's attacks and slights against the seminary over the years made the seminary less popular among them. But Graves had followers in the eastern states also. When he attacked the seminary on account of William Williams's views on alien immersion in the early 1870s, contributions withered in Georgia. Not only the Graves men, seminary agent J. William Jones reported, but also "some good friends of the seminary" were disposed to make Williams's views a "pretext for not giving."[23] Graves professed to support the seminary in principle and printed many articles praising it. But he aimed criticism at its faculty and its graduates frequently enough to serve notice that his support of the seminary was less than heartfelt. Graves had pledged $500 to the seminary in 1878 but as of 1886 had paid nothing on the principal and only a fraction of the interest.[24]

During summer vacations and on special campaigns, Boyce and Broadus pressed just as hard as full-time agents, and they found the work just as grueling. Boyce felt the personal sacrifice, but his cheerful spirit and profound sense of the crucial importance of the work impelled him to it. Broadus found the work exhausting. It involved "the unavoidable necessity of much laborious preaching, and of anxious and embarrassing work in private." It meant embracing "every opportunity to preach in Baptist churches, before constantly new audiences." In order to be successful in each place, he had to feel "that a great deal depended on each particular effort," which he found was "the most trying" aspect of such preaching. In addition, during the week, "I must hunt up people, push myself in society, try to get hold of individuals in the most judicious way, etc., etc. It makes my head ache to think of it."[25]

Charlotte Broadus worried that her husband was sacrificing his health and perhaps his life on this altar: "I feel distressed that you cannot stop and allow yourself more rest. It makes me tired just to think how much you are going all the time. Well! I suppose it is fated that you are to wear yourself out anyhow,

22. "Receipts by State from Mar. 1, 1882 to Mar. 1, 1883," Letterpress Copy Book 10, 1 Sept. 1882–20 June 1883, 899.

23. J. William Jones to John Broadus, 28 Mar. 1872, box 4, Broadus Papers.

24. James P. Boyce to J. R. Graves, 1 Jan. 1883, Letterpress Copy Book 10, 1 Sept. 1882–20 June 1883, 563; James P. Boyce to James S. Mahaffey and Co., 3 Feb. 1883, ibid., 750; James P. Boyce to J. R. Graves, 23 Feb. 1886, Letterpress Copy Book 13, 1884–1886, 689.

25. John Broadus to James Boyce, 30 Apr. 1870, box 1, Boyce Papers.

and I'd as well learn to submit to the idea.... I don't feel cross, I feel troubled. In despair about my own health. In despair about my children, they will do wrong, and I can never do my duty towards them. In despair about my work, and about what people expect of me. I want to rest, and I can't, and can not have the comfort of seeing that you get any rest either." [26] In the summer of 1874, John Broadus spent the summer raising money, and Boyce had him preaching and meeting prospective donors in one community after another. Charlotte recognized that nothing else could be done to save the seminary— "you pledged yourself to the seminary and to Dr. Boyce"—but she wondered at the cost to her husband's and her own health. [27] The "incessant appointments are enough to kill you." [28]

Broadus had similar fears concerning Boyce. They both needed to stay healthy for the sake of seeing the seminary permanently established. "I am useful to it," Broadus told Boyce, "even very important to its best success, but you are indispensable." Broadus added that "we must both try to keep alive till, if it please God, we can see the seminary strong, and as safe as such things can be made." [29] Boyce and Broadus developed an unusual bond, having suffered and sacrificed together, and having laid themselves out for the cause in crisis after crisis. They knew how to encourage each other. In the darkest days after the 1873 panic, when Boyce saw little hope of saving the seminary and recommended suspending it, Broadus refused to let Boyce give up: "I do not wonder that you sometimes feel discouraged, painfully. The task is difficult, and the kind of opposition encountered is very depressing. But life is always a battle. My dear fellow, nobody but you can do this thing. I believe you can do it, and it will be, all things considered, one of the great achievements of our time. To have carried it through will be a comfort and a pleasure to you through life, a matter of joy and pride to many who love and honor you, an occasion of thanksgiving through all eternity. Opposition—every good thing encounters opposition." [30] They had placed the weight of the seminary's prosperity on their own shoulders. The seminary teetered on the edge of insolvency time after time. Experience had shown that without their labors, the seminary would not survive. But even with all their labors and sacrifices, the outcome still remained in doubt in the late 1870s. The move to Louisville and the increased enrollment did not stimulate renewed interest in giving. By 1878 the seminary again stood on the verge of failure.

26. Charlotte Broadus to John A. Broadus, 18 June 1871, box 3, Broadus Papers.
27. Charlotte Broadus to John A. Broadus, 8 June 1874, box 5, Broadus Papers.
28. Charlotte Broadus to John A. Broadus, 13 June 1874, box 5, Broadus Papers.
29. John A. Broadus to James P. Boyce, 14 July 1877, box 11, Boyce Papers.
30. John A. Broadus to James P. Boyce, 14 Mar. 1873, box 4, Broadus Papers.

JOSEPH E. BROWN AND THE RESCUE OF THE SEMINARY

Broadus traveled to Baltimore in 1878 in an effort to raise a substantial offering. He preached in the various churches and met with pastors and laypersons. The effort culminated in a "mass meeting" at the Eutaw Place Baptist Church. The seminary was in desperate financial straits, and its future appeared to hang on Broadus's success. Boyce reminded Broadus that failure would be disastrous: "I shall look anxiously for the result.... Brethren will find out when it is too late that I have not exaggerated the necessity of present success, and that too at Baltimore."[31] Charlotte Broadus was apprehensive: "I feel like that trip will be the Gettysburg of the seminary's fate. I mean to hope that our side will win."[32] Broadus failed to get support from wealthy individuals but received generous support from the people at the mass meeting. "The rich men all failed us.... The people did nobly" and pledged over $10,000. Broadus extended his Baltimore campaign to twenty days and ended with $12,000, mostly in pledges.[33] The results were less decisive perhaps than at Gettysburg. "This is not success," Broadus told Boyce, "but it is far from being failure. Few people imagined we should do so well.... But that other $6000. We cannot do without it."[34]

Broadus sent out a "touching appeal" to sustain the seminary in 1878, but few responded. The hindrances were the same as always, poverty amid hard times. One alumnus apologized that his church could take no offering: "It gives me pain to say that my little church can render no assistance just now.... My own salary is but half paid and I know from personal contact with the people that they are doing their utmost."[35] Georgia pastor Patrick H. Mell, who afterward succeeded Boyce as president of the Southern Baptist Convention, similarly regretted that he had little hope that his country churches could answer Broadus's appeal. They had not recovered from the prior year's drought. "Besides, they are just now appealed to by three boards of missions; and have not yet paid all the last year's due to their pastor."[36]

By late 1879 Boyce recognized that financially the seminary "was going to ruin," with less than $50,000 in invested endowment.[37] By the end of 1880 Kentucky subscribers to the new endowment campaign had paid less than 10

31. James P. Boyce to John A. Broadus, 12 Dec. 1878, box 8, Broadus Papers.

32. Lottie Broadus to John A. Broadus, 10 Dec. 1878, box 8, Broadus Papers.

33. David G. Lyon, Diary 1878–79, 26 Dec. 1878, David Gordon Lyon Papers, HUA.

34. John A. Broadus to James P. Boyce, 16 Dec. 1878, box 11, Boyce Papers.

35. George Hobday to John A. Broadus, 8 Mar. 1878, box 8, Broadus Papers.

36. Patrick H. Mell to John A. Broadus, 15 Apr. 1878, box 8, Broadus Papers.

37. "Cash and Securities Received," Feb. 1880, Letterpress Copy Book 6, Jan.–June 1881, 680; "Trial Balance," 19 Nov. 1881, Letterpress Copy Book 8, Nov. 1881–Sept. 1882, 272.

percent on the $100,000 already due.[38] Subscribers to the seminary's annual expenses were paying at a similarly low rate, and the seminary did not have sufficient revenue to pay salaries. To raise more endowment and to collect on payments already due, Boyce was compelled to employ agents, whose salaries sapped much of the money they collected. Seminary operating expenses could not be reduced further—faculty were already severely overburdened and woefully underpaid. Boyce saw no alternative to using some of the endowment money to pay annual expenses, but he knew that spending endowment funds was equivalent to the tolling of the seminary's death knell.

Boyce believed that the only hope for saving the seminary lay in a single gift so large as to restore public confidence in its prospects and to give new impulse to the endowment movement. Payment on pledged bonds and securing additional subscriptions was proceeding too slowly to pull the seminary into solvency in time to save it. Incremental increases would not do it. The seminary needed a new hope. Boyce set his heart on receiving a donation of $50,000 from an individual donor, which would "stimulate others" to give and "awaken a new interest" in the endowment movement. Boyce hoped to use the gift to attract other donations to raise at least $200,000 in new endowment funds. Boyce began praying earnestly to this end and asked his colleagues to pray likewise. On the seminary's missionary day, when all students gathered for prayer, he explained the financial crisis and asked them to pray that God would raise up such a donor.[39]

In December 1879 Boyce published another appeal. "I think it my duty to warn the brethren of the danger to our seminary," Boyce began. He described the seminary's financial condition frankly. Unless money came in, the seminary would have to suspend, and "this must be our last session for some years to come." He had borrowed money to pay professors' salaries for the past six months and had no means for borrowing more and would not be able to pay the salaries due in January. He urged subscribers to pay what they owed and asked every church to take a special offering for the seminary in December.[40]

Some supporters thought that the notice was unwise and that it would discourage giving because it suggested that the seminary was about to fail.[41] Boyce in any case thought that the churches should know the school's true condition.

38. George W. Norton et al., "Southern Baptist Theological Seminary: To the Givers of Bonds in Kentucky," *Western Recorder*, 3 Feb. 1881, 3.

39. John A. Broadus, "Hon. Joseph Emerson Brown," *Seminary Magazine* 7 (1894): 206.

40. James P. Boyce, "The Danger to the Seminary," *Baptist*, 6 Dec. 1879, 409.

41. See A. F. Fleet to John A. Broadus, 6 Dec. 1879, box 8, Broadus Papers.

Others renewed their gifts and urged others to do so.[42] By January 15, 1880, Boyce reported that seventy-nine churches and a number of individuals responded to his appeal by sending a total of $2,672. Too few had responded. "Unless every effort be made at once," Boyce told the public, "the prospect before is only ruinous."[43]

Small gifts were not going to prevent the seminary's suspension. In the December appeal Boyce added a line expressing his hope that God would raise up a donor to give $50,000. When Joseph E. Brown, former governor of Georgia, railroad president, and finally U.S. senator, read Boyce's notice, he felt immediately that he was the individual. He wrote Boyce at once and told him that "if he could be satisfied as to the financial condition and prospects of the seminary," he would give the money. Boyce visited Brown in Atlanta and explained in detail the seminary's financial history and the current conditions. Brown was convinced of the soundness of the seminary's stewards and of the worthiness of the enterprise—he gave Boyce $50,000 in cash and securities.[44] With the money trustees endowed the Joseph Emerson Brown Professorship of Systematic Theology.[45]

Brown's gift saved the seminary. It bore no conditions, but Boyce determined to make it part of a campaign to raise $200,000 in invested endowment. Boyce persuaded donors to contribute to the campaign on the condition of raising a total of $200,000.[46] To better assure donors of the safety of their gifts, Boyce and George W. Norton persuaded trustees to amend the seminary charter to prohibit inviolably the spending of endowment principal and to establish a financial board to oversee the management of the endowment. Boyce solicited $50,000 from the seminary's Louisville benefactors.[47] Broadus raised more than $40,000 in New York City. With help from various others, Boyce succeeded in raising the additional $150,000, making $200,000 in new endowment funds deriving from Brown's initial gift.[48] "The seminary is now safe—humanly speaking," Boyce exulted.[49]

42. See William C. Lindsay, "Thunderstruck," *Baptist Courier*, 18 Dec. 1879, 2.

43. James P. Boyce, "The Seminary—What Success," *Baptist*, 31 Jan. 1880, 524.

44. Broadus, "Hon. Joseph Brown," 206–207; William Whitsitt, "The Ordering of Providence," *Seminary Magazine* 5 (1892): 472–474.

45. Minutes, Board of Trustees, Southern Baptist Theological Seminary, May 1880.

46. James P. Boyce to John A. Broadus, 8 Feb. 1881, box 9, Broadus Papers; Minutes, Board of Trustees, Southern Baptist Theological Seminary, May 1881.

47. John A. Broadus to William Rockefeller, 22 Feb. 1881, box 9, Broadus Papers.

48. Broadus, *Memoir of Boyce*, 273–274.

49. James P. Boyce to M. T. Yates, 13 July 1881, Letterpress Copy Book 7, June–Nov. 1881, 434.

Brown's gift marked a turning point in the seminary's history. The seminary's survival was no longer in doubt. Boyce could now begin to strengthen the operational resources—building the library's collection, adding desperately needed faculty, and erecting buildings for dormitory and classroom use. For Boyce, the faculty, and the friends of the seminary, it stood as an instance of God's extraordinary providence. Some years later Boyce reflected on this: "With all our anxiety and hopes and fears how true it is that in our agony of trouble as to what will occur we find that God has found us ways of which we have never dreamed. Witness the gift of Governor Brown. We were praying for help and crying out in our despair and without our lifting a single finger almost it came from a quarter to which we had never looked for such a sum."[50] God had crowned their labors, sacrifices, and sufferings with success at last.

It was time for a new phase in the seminary's career. Boyce turned his attention to building up the faculty and erecting buildings to meet the seminary's needs.

EXPANDING THE FACULTY

Just months before the seminary moved to Kentucky, one of the founding professors died. In February 1876 William Williams became too ill to continue his classes. The faculty granted Williams a leave of absence to recover his health. They had done the same for Broadus in 1870, when they sent him to Europe for nearly a year for the purpose of recovering his health. Williams did not recover and died of tuberculosis in February 1877.

Many persons felt that Williams was the most effective teacher on the faculty. His expression was terse, and his thought was ordered and lucid, both in his classroom lectures and in his preaching.[51] His two "schools" were Ecclesiastical History, and Church Government and Pastoral Duties. When Boyce wanted him to teach homiletics in 1871, it resulted in a sharp conflict between them. Two years previously the seminary had appointed Crawford H. Toy in part to relieve Broadus of the burden of teaching homiletics, which required the careful marking of student sermons regarding both criticisms and recommendations for improvement. Broadus was in poor health and could not carry the burden of

50. James P. Boyce to John A. Broadus, 31 Oct. 1888, box 12, Broadus Papers.

51. See, e.g., J. William Jones, "Reminiscences of the Frist Session of Our Seminary," *Seminary Magazine* 3 (1890): 43–44; C. E. W. Dobbs, "Our Second Session and the Trying Days of '61," *Seminary Magazine* 3 (1890): 125; Joseph Willet, "Rev. William Williams, D.D.," *Seminary Magazine* 5 (1892): 361–364.

the two demanding departments. Toy would teach Old Testament and Hebrew, which freed Manly to take up homiletics, as well as polemics and biblical introduction. When Manly resigned in 1871, Boyce proposed a plan for the reassignment of professors to cover all departments. Boyce wanted Williams to take homiletics. He was an accomplished preacher and was the natural choice after Broadus. Broadus felt that Williams had few equals for clarity, cogency, and earnestness, and his gifts of analysis and style promised that he could teach students how to preach well.[52]

But Williams refused. He was convinced that he would make a poor homiletics professor, believing that although he himself could construct a sermon, he did not know how to teach a student to do it. "I can't tell him how to make his sermon better," he explained. Broadus tried to resolve the conflict by offering to teach the subject as he had done until 1869, but Boyce refused, fearing that the heavy workload would wreck Broadus's health. Broadus remembered that "Boyce urged his plan with growing vehemence, until Williams rejected it with decided heat." Boyce acquiesced. He quietly stated that he would teach homiletics. The conflict was intense but brief. It and the Toy controversy were the only significant conflicts among the faculty between 1859 and 1895.[53]

The following year, when the seminary added William H. Whitsitt to the faculty, the faculty accepted Boyce's proposal for reordering teaching assignments. Whitsitt took over teaching junior Greek, freeing Broadus sufficiently to take up homiletics again. The most notable change was that Boyce surrendered to Williams the department he loved—systematic theology. The subject was Williams's favorite also, and he taught it well. Boyce also took advantage of the opportunity to move Williams out of teaching church government, since so many Southern Baptists objected to his position regarding alien immersions. Boyce took up Williams's former departments of church government and church history. When Boyce moved to Louisville, the faculty divided Boyce's subjects among them, and Williams took up church history again in addition to theology. Williams was the professor of systematic theology until his death.[54]

He took the greatest delight in teaching systematic theology, Broadus said, and taught it well: "The old Calvinistic theology was drawn from the Scriptures with loving pains, stated with marvellous clearness and force, and defended with keen and cogent argument and all his own intense earnestness of tone

52. Broadus, *Memoir of Boyce*, 211–213, 224.

53. Broadus, *Memoir of Boyce*, 224–225.

54. Broadus, *Memoir of Boyce*, 225–227. Williams did not teach theology, however, during the 1876–77 session, since he was on a leave of absence—James L. Reynolds taught it in his place.

and manner. These were life-or-death truths with him, and he put his whole soul into the discussions."[55] The end of theology, Williams held, was to honor Christ in his church and to save sinners. Graduate Clinton C. Brown never forgot Williams's encouragement to faithful service to the gospel in his parting words to the class: "If we save one soul in our whole life, then our life has been a success."[56]

The move to Louisville meant that Boyce was to resume his share of the teaching and restore the faculty to four. The seminary still needed another professor but could not afford to pay a professor's salary. Landmark leader James B. Gambrell urged Boyce to replace Williams with a Landmarker in order to win their support of the seminary, but Boyce apparently had no such intention.[57] He invited F. H. Kerfoot to join the faculty as an instructor to teach church history, though he apparently held the same position on alien immersions that Williams did. Kerfoot initially accepted the post but afterward changed his mind. Despite increasing enrollment, financial strain prevented the seminary from adding another professor for several more years.

From 1869 to 1877, the faculty numbered five, though for much of that period only four were actually teaching because Boyce was absent in Louisville and because they granted sick leave to Broadus in 1870 and to Williams in 1876. In 1881 the faculty still included only four professors, though the student body had grown to nearly 100. With the addition of the $200,000 in invested endowment deriving from Brown's gift, the seminary was able slowly to increase the size of the faculty. Boyce and the rest of the faculty made sure that the men they recommended to the trustees were both scholars and conservatives. They had to be able students of languages, text criticism, and the latest historical criticism, but they also had to reject the new liberal view of inspiration and historical criticism's reinterpretation of scripture.

In 1881 the trustees approved the appointment of George W. Riggan, a seminary graduate, as assistant instructor in Hebrew, Greek, and homiletics.[58] In 1883 trustees elected him assistant professor in the same subjects. Riggan showed great promise as a scholar and was convinced of the traditional orthodox view of the Bible. He urged the young Baptist preachers who had become enamored of the new historical-critical view of the Bible to be wary of its conclusions. He argued for a "clear presumption in favor of old views," especially since the

---

55. John A. Broadus, "The Late Dr. Williams," *Religious Herald*, 15 Mar. 1877.

56. C. C. Brown to John A. Broadus, 27 Feb. 1877, box 7, Broadus Papers.

57. James B. Gambrell to James P. Boyce, 28 Mar. 1877, box 2, Boyce Papers.

58. On Riggan's life, see J. W. Loving, "Prof. George Washington Riggan," *Seminary Magazine* 7 (1893): 65–70.

critical scholars' disagreements made their findings doubtful. He suggested also that the critical conclusions could hardly be true with consequences so false to piety, since they tended to sweep away things "infinitely sacred to your own minds and to the minds of the people." If some critics remained "devout and humble Christians," it was because "their character was formed under the influence of old beliefs," which kept them "on the right track in spite of the logic of their creeds."[59]

Riggan defended the unity of Isaiah in articles to the *Religious Herald* in 1884. He acknowledged that his supernaturalist presuppositions and his crediting of the authority of the New Testament witness regarding the Old Testament shaped his arguments no less than the antisupernaturalism of the historical critics shaped theirs. He singled out seminary graduate David G. Lyon, by then teaching at Harvard, for criticism. Lyon, like most critical scholars, dated chapters 40 through 66 during the exile, much later than Isaiah's time, because of differences in style and the section's clear application to Israel's experience in the exile. But, Riggan argued, chapters 1 through 39 had many prophetic references to exilic conditions, and chapters 40 through 66, on the other hand, showed no influence of the Aramaic language and had no exilic allusions or local references, both of which would be expected if the section was written in the exilic period. Riggan concluded that "hostility to the supernatural is the mainspring to these attacks upon the authorship of Isaiah."[60] The faculty had great hopes regarding Riggan's future. In 1885, however, he contracted meningitis and died suddenly.[61]

Over the next seven years the trustees elected five others, all Southern Seminary graduates, who had the same conservative instincts as Riggan. In 1885, at the faculty's recommendation, they elected John R. Sampey in Riggan's place as assistant instructor of Hebrew, Greek, and homiletics.[62] In 1887 they made him assistant professor. They chose Archibald T. Robertson as the other assistant professor. In 1888 the trustees gave the faculty freedom to appoint another assistant professor. Broadus gave Sampey the choice of being his assistant in Greek and New Testament, or being Manly's assistant in Hebrew and

---

59. George W. Riggan, "What Is the Proper Attitude towards Recent Biblical Criticism," *Religious Herald*, 18 Jan. 1883, 1.

60. George W. Riggan, "Prof. Lyon on the Authorship of Isaiah," *Religious Herald*, 15 May 1884, 1; Riggan, "Prof. Lyon on the Authorship of Isaiah, No. 2," *Religious Herald*, 29 May 1884, 1.

61. John R. Sampey, *Memoirs of John R. Sampey* (Nashville, TN: Broadman Press, 1947), 32.

62. Carter Helm Jones, "Prof. John R. Sampey," *Seminary Magazine* 6 (1893): 377–379.

Old Testament. Sampey judged that his Hebrew was stronger than Robertson's, and that Robertson's Greek was stronger than his, so he chose Hebrew.

Sampey kept to a decidedly conservative path. Like Riggan, and like so many of the seminary's professors over the next generation, he held a strong presumption in favor of the traditional conservative views of the Bible and its meaning, and judged historical-critical views in part based on their consequences for the faith. He had a deep love for the missionary task and made several preaching tours of Brazil. He was a popular preacher among Southern Baptists and delighted in leading revival services in churches and colleges. Some of his younger colleagues later criticized him for his popular preaching style and for his failure to engage scholarship in his publishing. He served for several decades on the interdenominational International Sunday School Lesson Committee, taking a conservative line in determining the Bible passages of its widely used lesson plans.[63] In 1892 Sampey succeeded Manly in the chair of Hebrew and Old Testament interpretation. He became president of the seminary in 1929 and resigned in 1942.

In 1887 the seminary trustees also elected Franklin H. Kerfoot as Boyce's coprofessor of systematic theology.[64] Ten years earlier Kerfoot had agreed to join the faculty as a tutor, and he had already declined calls to teach at Crozer Theological Seminary and at the University of North Carolina.[65] But before the new session started, the Eutaw Place Baptist Church in Baltimore called Kerfoot as pastor, and he resigned his seminary tutorship to accept the church's call.[66] When Boyce announced to the faculty that he had determined to resign in the spring of 1888, Broadus asked him his opinion regarding his replacement in the chair of theology. He expressed some reluctance to give an opinion but told Broadus that his choice would be Kerfoot.[67] Upon Boyce's death, Kerfoot succeeded Boyce in the chair of systematic theology and of church government and pastoral duties. Kerfoot was decidedly conservative regarding the doctrine of inspiration and historical criticism. He taught systematic theology using Boyce's textbook and agreed generally with Boyce's Calvinism, though some

63. See William O. Carver, "Recollections and Information from Other Sources Concerning the Southern Baptist Theological Seminary," typescript, 36, Archives and Special Collections, SBTS; Carver to Kyle M. Yates, 28 Nov. 1952, box 10, Carver Papers, SBHLA.

64. See Fred Eberhardt, "Professor F. H. Kerfoot," *Seminary Magazine* 6 (1893): 319–322.

65. James P. Boyce to John A. Broadus, 9 July 1877 (apparently indexed as 2 July), box 11, Boyce Papers.

66. Faculty Minutes, Southern Baptist Theological Seminary, 1877.

67. James P. Boyce to John A. Broadus, 4 Nov. 1888, box 12, Broadus Papers.

interpreted his approach as seeking to shave off some of its sterner features.[68] Kerfoot resigned in 1899 to become the president of the denomination's Home Mission Board.

In 1888 trustees elected Archibald T. Robertson as assistant instructor in Greek and homiletics; they promoted him to assistant professor the following year.[69] In 1895 he succeeded Broadus as professor of interpretation of the New Testament, where he remained until his death in 1934. Robertson was outspoken in his criticism of historical-critical views and maintained traditional conservative views of the Bible's inspiration and interpretation. Robertson's encyclopedic *Grammar of the Greek New Testament in the Light of Historical Research* (1914) achieved for him a worldwide reputation among biblical scholars. He became a prolific author of books and articles and bolstered the seminary's reputation for both scholarship and orthodoxy.

In 1892 trustees elected Edwin C. Dargan as associate professor of homiletics, church government, and Latin theology.[70] He was already an experienced and popular preacher. He later dispensed with Latin theology and began teaching a course in ecclesiology. In 1895 he succeeded Broadus as professor of homiletics. He was a popular and successful teacher. And he was decidedly conservative. He rejoiced that a northern paper described an address by Robertson as "hyperorthodox" and hoped that "you and I and all the rest" would always merit the title.[71] On inspiration he recommended above all Manly's *Bible Doctrine of Inspiration* and taught that "the Bible is free from error."[72] He resigned in 1907 to become pastor of the Macon, Georgia, First Baptist Church, and afterward accepted appointment as editor of the Southern Baptist Convention's Sunday School Board.

In 1893 trustees elected William J. McGlothlin as assistant instructor of Hebrew and Greek. They promoted him to assistant professor of Old Testament two years later. In 1899, however, he succeeded Whitsitt as professor of church

68. See, e.g., Dale Moody, Oral History, in Walter D. Draughon, "A Critical Evaluation of the Diminishing Influence of Calvinism on the Doctrine of the Atonement in Representative Southern Baptist Theologians: James Petigru Boyce, Edgar Young Mullins, Walter Thomas Conner, and Dale Moody," Ph.D. dissertation, Southwestern Baptist Theological Seminary, 1987, 246.

69. J. W. Loving, "Professor Archibald Thomas Robertson, A.M.," *Seminary Magazine* 6 (1893): 437–439.

70. See John A. Broadus, "Professor Dargan," *Seminary Magazine* 6 (1893): 1–2.

71. Edwin C. Dargan to Archibald T. Robertson, ca. 20 June 1892, box 1, Robertson Papers.

72. Edwin C. Dargan, *The Doctrines of Our Faith* (Nashville, TN: Sunday School Board of the Southern Baptist Convention, 1905), 18, 22.

history. McGlothlin seems to have concurred with the traditional orthodoxy of Broadus and the founding faculty. He wrote an article in 1894 affirming the historical accuracy of the Genesis narratives and asserting that a ninth-century writer would have no reason for including many of its statements, whereas Moses would have had clear reasons.[73] McGlothlin resigned his professorship in 1919 to accept the presidency of Furman University.

BUILDING A PERMANENT CAMPUS

By 1883 the seminary had about $300,000 in invested endowment. It was not enough to pay all annual expenses, and Boyce still struggled at times to make ends meet. In 1884 Boyce reported that he had not paid the professors' salary for the past two months.[74] Nearly $300,000 in additional endowment was pledged but not paid, and the seminary still depended on gifts to its current expense account to operate. But the interest from the endowment provided about $12,000 and was closing in on annual expenses totaling from $16,000 to $18,000.[75] But the seminary was otherwise healthy. "Aside from the want of money," Boyce reported in 1884, "the seminary is doing well. We have over 100 students. The board hall is full and overflowing. If the friends of the seminary who have subscribed and given bonds so liberally would only pay them we would have but little complaint to make."[76] The endowment effort, however, was coming along well enough that Boyce added another goal to fund-raising. It was time to build.[77]

Boyce and Broadus would face similar trials in raising funds to buy property and erect buildings. Boyce had been watching downtown properties for years. He believed that it was unwise to purchase property unless it was a good business investment in addition to meeting the needs of the seminary. When he had

73. William J. McGlothlin, "Genesis an Historical Exhortation," *Seminary Magazine* 8 (1894): 121–126.

74. James P. Boyce to George Eager, 1 Dec. 1884, Letterpress Copy Book 11, 20 June 1883–26 Dec. 1884, 936.

75. "Notes Subscribed and Paid on Endowment," ca. May 1883, Letterpress Copy Book 10, Sept. 1882–June 1883, 899. See also James P. Boyce to Paul Willis [?], 10 Jan. 1882, Letterpress Copy Book 8, Nov. 1881–Sept. 1882, 503.

76. James P. Boyce to George Eager, 5 Dec. 1884, Letterpress Copy Book 11, 20 June 1883–26 Dec. 1884, 945.

77. The seminary had received pledges for about $85,000 in land also, but even when deeds came in a timely fashion, it could take years before the seminary could sell the land at a reasonable price and receive any money from the gift.

opportunity in 1885 to purchase a prime property for the seminary's permanent location, he bought it. But when he went around to Louisville's wealthy Baptists in July 1885, he received very little. Most told him no. He confessed to Broadus, "I get sick at heart when I see brethren so perfectly indifferent to the position in which they leave me. I am like a man sinking in a quagmire or quicksand and seeing others to whom he cries for help walking off quietly to eat their supper."[78]

While Boyce struggled to find a way to pay for the lot, Boyce sent Broadus to New York City in March 1886 to raise money for the building. They planned to erect a dormitory and estimated that the building would cost a minimum of $60,000. John D. Rockefeller promised $25,000, and J. A. Bostwick promised $15,000. Broadus hoped to get $10,000 each from Charles Pratt and William Rockefeller.[79] When these initial promises left Broadus about $10,000 short, the word came from Louisville not to return without the $60,000. Boyce wrote: "George Norton urged me earnestly to beg you not to return without getting that money now. I told him I thought you would not if practicable. I say plainly that I think you can do no better service than stay two weeks longer should you see any opening."[80] Within days Broadus reported that he had secured $60,000.[81]

Broadus's successes in New York coincided with Boyce's success in Louisville. The Norton brothers carried the day. George promised $10,000, and William $7,500. Many others gave smaller gifts. Boyce could now pay off the debts on the property already acquired and buy additional lots needed to build an entire campus.[82] Joseph E. Brown quietly gave an additional $5,000 as provision for cost overruns or other needs.[83]

The seminary moved into its new building in February 1888 and named it New York Hall in honor of the New York donors. It furnished dormitory and dining facilities for about 200 students, as well as lecture rooms, faculty offices, and a library, which were converted to additional dormitory rooms after the erection of Norton Hall in 1893.[84]

78. James P. Boyce to John A. Broadus, 20 July 1885, box 10, Broadus Papers; Broadus, *Memoir of Boyce*, 302.

79. John A. Broadus to James P. Boyce; 15 Mar. 1886, box 11, Boyce Papers.

80. James P. Boyce to John A. Broadus, 19 Mar. 1886, box 11, Broadus Papers; Boyce to Broadus, 26 Mar. 1886, ibid.

81. Caroline C. Bishop to John A. Broadus, 31 Mar. 1886, box 11, Broadus Papers.

82. James P. Boyce to John A. Broadus, 19 Mar. 1886, box 11, Broadus Papers.

83. James P. Boyce to John A. Broadus, 12 Aug. 1886, box 11, Broadus Papers.

84. Faculty Minutes, Southern Baptist Theological Seminary, 21 Feb. 1888; Broadus, *Memoir of Boyce*, 262; A. J. Dickinson, "The New Building," *Seminary Magazine* 1 (1888): 27.

Memorial Library

The library arrangements were nevertheless inadequate. Mrs. J. Lawrence Smith, who had already given generously to the seminary, surprised the faculty in 1888 when she told Broadus that she wanted to give $50,000 to build and equip a library.[85] The stately Memorial Library was completed in 1891.

In Boyce's last report to the trustees he urged the seminary's need for more adequate classrooms and for an additional $100,000 in endowment. George F. Norton and Ann E. Norton, widow of William F. Norton, made a written contract to give the seminary the $60,000 needed to erect a new building for classrooms, provided that the denomination raised the $100,000 in additional endowment. With this generous inducement, Southern Baptists responded enthusiastically. Trustee Joshua Levering gave $5,000, and his Baltimore firm matched it. Minnie Caldwell, daughter of George W. Norton, also gave $5,000. Delegates to the Southern Baptist Convention also raised large offerings. The additional endowment was secured, and in 1893 Norton Hall was completed. The new building was an impressive example of German Renaissance Revival architecture, with rich ornamentation, elaborate gables, and finials. It housed

85. John A. Broadus to James P. Boyce, 17 Oct. 1888, box 11, Broadus Papers; Minutes, Seminary Faculty, Southern Baptist Theological Seminary, 25 Sept. 1888, and 25 Oct. 1888, SBTS.

Norton Hall

six lecture rooms, including one that seated 200 and another that seated 300. It had also a 500-seat chapel, offices for faculty and staff, forced-air heat, and electric and gas lights.[86]

The faculty wanted one additional building, a gymnasium. The professors urged students to get daily exercise in order to maintain their health against the stress of rigorous study. They used a rented gymnasium for some years and then set up a makeshift gym in New York Hall. Joshua Levering, chairman of the board of trustees, gave $10,000 for the construction of a gymnasium completed in 1897.[87] The seminary now had a complete and attractive campus on Broadway in downtown Louisville.

STUDENTS, STUDY, AND SEMINARY LIFE

Students attended classes for eight months straight. The seminary held recitations and lectures six days a week. On Sundays students were encouraged to preach or teach Sunday school or both. In 1894 thirty-six students were serving

---

86. F. H. Kerfoot, "Norton Hall," *Seminary Magazine* 6 (1893): 484–486.

87. Minutes, Board of Trustees, Southern Baptist Theological Seminary, May 1897.

as pastors, and forty-eight others were preaching and teaching in Louisville-area mission points.[88] Baptists put little store by such holidays as Christmas and Easter, and the seminary was no exception. By 1875 students got one day of rest on Christmas.[89] In 1894 the faculty rejected a student petition to observe Christmas Eve also as a vacation day.[90]

Intermediate examinations arrived in January, and final examinations in May. Examinations were notoriously difficult. David G. Lyon recorded that his midterm examination in Senior Greek was eight hours long, and yet "many students did not finish the questions."[91] Final exams lasted a month. In 1878 they began on April 5 and ended on May 3. In 1884 they lasted from May 2 to June 2. The faculty passed a rule that they could not extend past 8:00 P.M.[92] Students had eight hours to complete Basil Manly's final examination in Biblical Introduction in 1888, covering inspiration, hermeneutics, typology and the relation of the Bible to astronomy, geology, and evolution.[93]

Standards for passing examinations were high, and failure was common. Adoniram J. Holt failed homiletics in 1875 even though he had considerable experience preaching already and did well in classroom recitations. Holt recalled: "After final examinations, Dr. Broadus came to my room...and said to me, 'I had hoped to put you through, Brother Holt, in homiletics, but while you were almost perfect in your recitations, you had formed such habits of speech, that we felt we could not afford to let you go out as a graduate in our most characteristic department.' This so distressed me that...I wept. Dr. Broadus was all tenderness, and comforted me by saying that I had made more real progress than any member of the class.... It was well that I failed that year, for I took homiletics over another year, and passed all right." Ever afterward Holt regarded Broadus as his mentor and the greatest figure he ever met.[94]

The high standards diminished the number of men who could complete all the courses and graduate in each "school" or department. Initially students received diplomas for passing in each department of the seminary separately.

88. C. M. Truex, "Local Department," *Seminary Magazine* 8 (1894): 164.

89. Richard T. Vann to Tat, 22 Dec. 1875, R. T. Vann—Correspondence, College Years 1871–1875, box 1, Harriet Vann Holmes Collection, Archives, Carlyle Campbell Library, Meredith College; Percy G. Elsom, "Seminary Notes," *Christian Index*, 9 Jan. 1890, 3.

90. Faculty Minutes, Southern Baptist Theological Seminary, 21 Dec. 1894.

91. David G. Lyon, Diary 1878–1879, 10 Jan. 1878, David Gordon Lyon Papers, HUA.

92. Faculty Minutes, Southern Baptist Theological Seminary, 15 Mar. 1878; ibid., 10 Apr. 1884. See also Basil Manly Jr., untitled, *South Carolina Baptist*, 24 Apr. 1868, 2.

93. Basil Manly Jr., "Final Examination in Biblical Introduction," 11 May 1888, box 12, Broadus Papers.

94. Adoniram J. Holt to Archibald T. Robertson, 13 Sept. 1928, Archibald T. Robertson Papers, WFU.

In 1876 the faculty added the degree of English graduate for those who passed all eight English courses. In 1890 they added the degree of eclectic graduate for those who passed at least nine courses, including both Junior Greek and Junior Hebrew. The highest degree from 1859 to 1892 was full graduate, for those who passed all the seminary's courses.[95]

In 1892 the trustees adopted the faculty's recommendation revising the seminary's degrees. Graduate in Theology (Th.G.) replaced English graduate. Bachelor in Theology (Th.B) replaced eclectic graduate. Master in Theology (Th.M.) replaced full graduate. And the seminary introduced as its highest degree the Doctor of Theology (Th.D.), for students who had received a Th.M., and who spent an additional year of study at the school, passed at least five "special" courses, and wrote an acceptable thesis in an area of original research. The first four Th.D. students graduated in 1894.[96]

The faculty expected students to live by the highest standards of deportment and tolerated no conduct that reflected poorly on Christianity, the ministry, or the seminary. In an 1891 faculty meeting, the faculty asked President Broadus to announce to the students that several of their fellows had been expelled: "The case of Jasper Harris was taken up again, he having confessed to the crime of cheating in the examination. On motion it was resolved that the president take away from Mr. Harris all his diplomas, and announce to the assembled students that on this account the connection of Mr. Harris with the seminary has ceased. On motion it was also resolved that the president be directed to state in the presence of the assembled students that John O. Rust of Bardstown, Ky., Wm. F. Shute of Washington City, and W. F. Jordan of Pana, Ills., had been guilty of drunkenness and that their connection with the seminary had also ceased."[97]

The faculty wanted to promote missionary zeal and set aside the first day of each month as "Missionary Day," when students gathered for study of missions, prayer for missionaries, and special guest speakers. Students organized literary societies, similar to those at many colleges. The Andrew Fuller Society was apparently the oldest. Tennessee students formed the Ten Club. Others formed the Shakespeare Seven, or the Shakes. Later still came the Browning Club and Dodeka, which endured into the 1990s. Membership in the clubs was by invitation only. Members were college graduates and were among the most gifted

95. Faculty Minutes, Southern Baptist Theological Seminary, 16 and 23 Sept. 1875; John A. Broadus to James P. Boyce, 16 Sept. 1875, box 11, Boyce Papers; Crawford H. Toy to John A. Broadus, 16 May 1876, box 7, Broadus Papers; Archibald T. Robertson, "The New Arrangement about the Degrees," *Seminary Magazine* 6 (1893): 32–33.

96. Faculty Minutes, Southern Baptist Theological Seminary, 19 Apr. 1892; ibid., 2 Mar. 1893; ibid., 26 May 1894.

97. Faculty Minutes, Southern Baptist Theological Seminary, 1 June 1891.

and influential students. The clubs' exclusivity tended to breed the resentment of other students.[98]

THE OFFICE OF THE PRESIDENT

In 1887 Boyce and the faculty petitioned the trustees to establish the office of the presidency in the seminary. It mattered little to Boyce personally—he judged that within two years either he would retire due to poor health or he would already be dead.[99] Few people understood what "chairman of the faculty" represented, but everyone understood the title "president." Securing reduced fares on railroads, for example, was a necessary part of Boyce's work. When making requests for railroad passes and reduced fares, the title of president carried more weight than chairman of the faculty. When the president of the railroad was a Baptist and already knew Boyce, as in the case of Joseph E. Brown, it made little difference. Brown was president of the Western and Atlantic Railroad and could give a free pass to the bishop of each denomination—Brown designated him "the Railroad Bishop of the Baptist Church."[100] But many did not know Boyce and would not know his successor. The title of chairman did not communicate the position's great responsibility and trust. Recognition as a seminary president would afford readier access to those prominent persons who were best situated to help the seminary, and it would likely help in a dozen secondary ways to make his job more effective.

Boyce was theoretically merely the chairman of the faculty, but in fact he was much more. He made decisions respecting property, buildings, and finances. He placed great confidence in Broadus's advice and generally sought it, though he did not always follow it. On matters concerning additions to the faculty and teaching assignments, he consulted the faculty. They managed faculty affairs rather informally in faculty meetings, discussing matters freely and generally arriving at consensus. There was no question, however, that Boyce was more than a faculty peer—he was their leader. Once they had opportunity to discuss

98. See John R. Sampey, *Memoirs of John R. Sampey* (Nashville, TN: Broadman Press, 1947), 31–32, 175–176.

99. James P. Boyce to the Board of Trustees, 9 May 1887, in Minutes, Board of Trustees, Southern Baptist Theological Seminary, May 1887. By October 1888, Boyce had decided that his poor health required him to retire as president, treasurer, and professor: "I shall positively resign my positions next May." James P. Boyce to John A. Broadus, 5 Oct. 1888, box 12, Broadus Papers.

100. Joseph E. Brown to James P. Boyce, 16 Jan. 1875, box 1, Broadus Papers; Brown to Boyce, 12 Jan. 1874, ibid.

the merits of any question, they tended to trust Boyce to take all the arguments into consideration and make the decision that seemed best to him for the interest of the seminary. When discussing the suitability of David G. Lyon as a tutor in 1880, for example, the faculty finally authorized Boyce to make the final decision.[101] When the rest of the faculty wanted to appoint Abraham Jaeger to the faculty in 1876, Boyce opposed it, and they fell in behind Boyce.[102] They did not each agree heartily with every decision, but they subordinated their differences to the common good and submitted to emerging consensus. The consensus that emerged was usually the position Boyce assumed. His word was law, not by office but by stature, out of respect for his exertions, sacrifices, and wise leadership. Broadus referred to him once as the seminary's "commander in chief."[103] Broadus deferred to Boyce and gave him the preeminence just as if he were president.

Broadus's role was in some respects scarcely second to Boyce's. He exercised leadership of the school that was nearly equal to that of Boyce. The denomination admired them both, students loved them, and other professors trusted them. They trusted each other's judgment, maintained remarkable accord, and complemented each other. It is not surprising that A. F. Fleet, professor of Greek at the University of Missouri, remarked that the seminary had "two presidents."[104]

But the seminary needed an official president. Most colleges and seminaries already had a president. Charles Eliot at Harvard and Noah Porter at Yale had exercised such active and successful leadership that it reshaped expectations for leadership in higher education. The many challenges facing educational institutions in the late nineteenth century—growing enrollment required larger faculties and larger facilities—were better met by a true chief executive rather than a *primus inter pares* chairman of the faculty. A president could press matters, but a chairman was usually "powerless to push things."[105] Boyce's successor, he and the faculty believed, needed appropriate executive authority. Boyce and the other founders had established the seminary largely on the pattern of the University of Virginia, which was governed by the faculty and had no president. Two Baptist colleges abolished the presidency in favor of a faculty chairman, pressed by financial stress and appealing to the example of the University of Virginia and of the seminary. But as enrollment and faculty grew, and with

101. Faculty Minutes, Southern Baptist Theological Seminary, 10 May 1880.
102. See James P. Boyce to John A. Broadus, 6 Dec. 1876, box 7, Broadus Papers.
103. John A. Broadus to James P. Boyce, 11 Oct. 1873, Boyce Papers.
104. Alexander F. Fleet to John A. Broadus, 26 Jan. 1884, box 10, Broadus Papers.
105. Alexander F. Fleet to John A. Broadus, 26 Jan. 1884, box 10, Broadus Papers.

them demand for money, the need for a strong chief executive was inescapable. Missouri's William Jewell College in 1892 and the University of Richmond in 1894 each reestablished the office of president. The University of Virginia itself finally elected its first president in 1904.[106]

Broadus supported the change. In May 1887 he asked the other professors to sign a petition to name Boyce president rather than chairman of the faculty.[107] They all endorsed the idea and included it in the faculty report to the board of trustees. The trustee committee assigned to report on the faculty letter endorsed the idea and recommended "changing the name of the presiding officer of the seminary from chairman to president."[108] The trustees, however, did not initially favor the change. They expunged the committee's recommendation and appointed a committee to investigate the question.[109] C. H. Judson, chairman of the committee, acknowledged that Boyce had effectively exercised presidential leadership all along: "Are we not indebted to him, far more than to anyone else, for raising and investing the endowment, for the organization of the seminary, for the selection of the present faculty etc. etc." But Judson and the committee felt the model had worked so well that it seemed unwise to change it. They worried also that Boyce's successor might use his office to domineer the faculty and dictate policy to the harm of the seminary. Judson explained to Broadus: "Is it not just possible that the noble generosity of the faculty, their love and reverence for Dr. Boyce, has warped their judgment, in regard to a principle of government of the seminary? I hope that, if the recommendation should not be adopted, both the faculty and Dr. Boyce will see that our apprehensions are as to the successors of Dr. Boyce and not as to himself."[110] Trustee John L. Johnson opposed the change but recommended that Boyce be named president, provided that the office be abolished when Boyce died.[111]

By the time of the May 1888 trustee meeting, the committee had decided in favor of the change. It did so, however, on the premise that it was a change

106. See G. W. Hansbrough to John A. Broadus, 30 Aug. 1883, box 10, Broadus Papers; David O. Moore, "The William Jewell College Story," *Baptist History and Heritage* 34, no. 3 (1999): 131–129.

107. William H. Whitsitt, Diary, 2 May 1887, quoted in "Excerpts from the Diary of William Heth Whitsitt, Made by Mary Whitsitt Whitehead, for W. O. Carver," SBTS.

108. Minutes, Board of Trustees, Southern Baptist Theological Seminary, May 1887.

109. Minutes, Board of Trustees, Southern Baptist Theological Seminary, May 1887.

110. C. H. Judson to John A. Broadus, 17 Apr. 1888, box 12, Broadus Papers. See also John L. Johnson to John A. Broadus, 23 Apr. 1888, box 12, Broadus Papers; C. H. Judson to John A. Broadus, 28 Apr. 1888, box 12, Broadus Papers.

111. John L. Johnson to John A. Broadus, 23 Apr. 1888, box 12, Broadus Papers.

in title only, not one that would "enlarge the power" or "increase the responsibilities" of the executive officer. It left "the administration and government of the seminary as heretofore in the hands of the faculty with equality of rank and position." The board adopted the recommendation and made Boyce president.[112] In reality Boyce functioned as a president with significant executive authority, but he did so with the goodwill of the trustees and the faculty. So did most presidents who followed him. But the ideal of faculty government "with equality of rank and position" endured for nearly a hundred years. The effective executive authority of the seminary's presidents clashed time and again with this ideal. In the most serious instance in 1958, it resulted in the dismissal of thirteen professors.

THE SEMINARY AND DENOMINATIONAL LEADERSHIP

It was essential to the seminary's success to retain the confidence of Southern Baptists. When the faculty stood before denominational gatherings or wrote for denominational newspapers, they were acquainting the denomination with the seminary and seeking its confidence. Boyce especially symbolized the seminary, for the institution owed its existence to him to a peculiar degree, and he had stamped it with his vision from the beginning. But the presidents who followed him played a similar role before the convention, and the seminary's prosperity depended in unusual measure on their success on the platform of denominational meetings.

The Southern Baptist Convention elected Boyce president of its annual meetings nine times, 1872–1879 and 1888. Two subsequent seminary presidents served as convention president, Edgar Y. Mullins (1922–1924) and John R. Sampey (1936–1938). Two professors, after leaving the seminary, also served as president of the Southern Baptist Convention, Edwin C. Dargan (1911–1913) and William J. McGlothlin (1930–1932).

Boyce was an accomplished moderator. He had earned such respect of Southern Baptists that even when he ruled contrary to the will of the body, they sustained his ruling in honor of his leadership. Boyce had strict notions concerning which matters were constitutionally permissible for the convention to consider. At the 1888 meeting of the Southern Baptist Convention, Boyce refused to permit the temperance cause to come before the convention. Lieutenant Governor John E. Massey of Virginia introduced resolutions in favor of temperance, and Boyce rule them out of order. Another delegate introduced

112. Minutes, Board of Trustees, Southern Baptist Theological Seminary, May 1888.

a different set of temperance resolutions, which Boyce likewise ruled out of order. Someone appealed to the floor to overturn Boyce's ruling. "A long discussion followed," and finally the floor sustained his ruling.[113] His ruling led some to conclude that he favored moderate consumption of alcoholic beverages.

A similar instance occurred years before at the General Association of Baptists in Kentucky. When the state convention met in 1857, many delegates argued against the introduction of the topic of temperance because of "their views as to the constitutionality of discussing it" in the convention. The editor of the *Louisville Journal* interpreted this sentiment to indicate that the delegates did not support temperance societies. They adopted, however, a resolution contradicting the editor's interpretation and a report that urged Kentucky churches to exclude from membership "all those who will persist in drinking, making, and selling of spiritous and malt liquors as a beverage."[114]

Boyce sought to keep out all matters unrelated to the convention's constitutional powers. In 1877 T. T. Eaton, a strong supporter of the seminary, reported himself to the convention as the representative of the Southern Historical Society, whose president, J. William Jones, was a good friend of the faculty and the seminary's agent. The society's mission was to preserve the memory of southern honor and valor in the Civil War. When Eaton took the floor, Boyce "ruled him out of order on the ground that the society was political."[115] Boyce considered all such voluntary societies to be "political," since they represented policies beyond the strict divine commission to the church and beyond the convention's constitutional authority, strictly interpreted. He included temperance societies in the ban.

Baptists supported temperance for the same reason they supported smallpox inoculation and public sewers—they conduced greatly to the public welfare. The Charleston, South Carolina, Baptist Association commended it in 1839 as a "cause inseparably connected with the welfare of mankind."[116] Baptists believed that a minister who drank alcoholic beverages was disqualified to preach, much less to be a teacher of preachers.

They excepted medicines.[117] During much of the nineteenth century, physicians, medical guides, and popular opinion advocated the use of whiskey, brandy, and wine for treatment of a variety of ailments, from teething and poor

---

113. Unattributed, "The Southern Baptist Convention," *Religious Herald*, 17 May 1888, 2.
114. General Association of Baptists in Kentucky, *Minutes*, 1857, 4, 6, 8, 24.
115. Unattributed, "News and Notes," *Religious Herald*, 24 May 1877.
116. Charleston Baptist Association, *Minutes*, 1839, 4. See also, ibid., 1832, 7.
117. See, e.g., Charleston Baptist Association, *Minutes*, 1836, 8.

digestion to fever and tuberculosis.[118] In the 1870s, when William Williams contracted tuberculosis and Broadus's wife and mother-in-law had chronic sicknesses, Boyce sometimes bought whiskey for them in New York or Louisville, where it was cheaper and better than that available in Greenville.[119]

Boyce's ruling at the 1888 meeting of the Southern Baptist Convention caused trouble in Mississippi. Opponents of prohibition in the state claimed that the seminary faculty ridiculed prohibition in their lectures as "foolish fanaticism," and that "Boyce, Broadus, and Manly, three of the smartest preachers the Baptists have, are down on this prohibition nonsense."[120] The same problem erupted in Texas, wrote Pastor Philip T. Hale: "The *Waco Advance* accuses you and your colleagues in the seminary of being 'anti-prohibitionists.' This opinion is gaining ground in the state, and so far as I am able to judge needs to be corrected or explained. Dr. Boyce's recent ruling in the convention has added greatly to confirm this opinion." Hale, who attended the seminary from 1879 to 1883 and was a full graduate, asked Broadus for an explicit response. Hale did not know how the faculty felt about prohibition legislation but was sure that he knew their opinion regarding temperance: "They wore the blue ribbon," he said, in reference to the popular lapel symbol that they had taken the temperance pledge.[121]

118. See, e.g., John Moore Neligan, *Medicines, Their Uses, and Mode of Administration,* 6th ed. (Dublin: Fannin, 1864), 454–455; Austin Flint, *A Treatise on the Principles and Practice of Medicine* (Philadelphia: Henry C. Lea, 1866), 254; National Convention for Revising the Pharmacopoeia, *Pharmacopoeia of the United States of America: Fourth Decennial Revision* (Philadelphia: J. B. Lippincott, 1864), 51–52.

119. W. A. Gellatly to John A. Broadus, 2 May 1872, box 4, Broadus Papers; Charlotte Broadus to John A. Broadus, 12 June 1872, ibid.; Annie Broadus to John A. Broadus, 21 Nov. 1873, box 5, Broadus Papers; John A. Broadus to James P. Boyce, 16 Feb. 1875, box 11, Boyce Papers; Boyce to John A. Broadus, 17 Nov. 1875, box 6, Broadus Papers; William Williams to John A. Broadus, 29 Jan. 1876, box 6, Broadus Papers. See also Broadus to Boyce, 31 Aug. 1860, box 11, Boyce Papers; Charlotte Broadus to John A. Broadus, 8 June 1861, box 1, Broadus Papers; Charlotte Broadus to John A. Broadus, 5 Sept. 1863, ibid.; H. C. Townsend to John A. Broadus, 12 Mar. 1870, box 3, Broadus Papers; Lottie Broadus to John A. Broadus, 30 July 1870, box 3, Broadus Papers; John A. Broadus to Basil Manly Jr., 27 June 1871, box 3, Broadus Papers; Annie Broadus to John A. Broadus, 19 Feb. 1876, box 6, Broadus Papers; Annie Broadus to John A. Broadus, 10 July 1876, box 7, Broadus Papers.

120. J. H. Gambrell to John A. Broadus, 14 June 1888, box 12, Broadus Papers.

121. Philip T. Hale to John A. Broadus, 26 June 1888, box 12, Broadus Papers. See also Timothy Yates, "Blue Ribbon Movement," in *Alcohol and Temperance in Modern History: An International Encyclopedia,* ed. Jack S. Blocker, David M. Fahey, and Ian R. Tyrrell (Santa Barbara, CA: ABC-CLIO, 2003), 107–109.

Broadus answered that the faculty had not ridiculed or opposed prohibition in their classrooms. In Virginia Broadus had been active in the Sons of Temperance, a popular national temperance organization.[122] In 1887 Broadus voted in favor of prohibition in Louisville under the state's "local option" law. Manly voted for the Prohibition Party candidate, John P. St. John, in the 1884 presidential election.[123] Boyce's opposition to introducing the policy question of prohibition into Baptist conventions produced the misapprehension that he and the faculty opposed voluntary temperance and legal prohibition. It is possible that Boyce thought legal prohibition inexpedient—there is no evidence either way.[124] But all the faculty were apparently committed to temperance.

THE SEMINARY, NORTHERN BAPTISTS, ROCKEFELLER, AND EVANGELICALISM

The popularity and influence of the faculty went far beyond the borders of the Southern Baptist Convention. They were frequent contributors to Northern Baptist newspapers, whose editors sought to contract their regular services. Such nondenominational papers as the *Sunday School Times* and the *Independent* did the same. They were frequent speakers at meetings of Northern Baptists. But their greatest popularity was on the platforms of those characteristic conferences of late nineteenth-century evangelicalism—the Chautauqua, the YMCA, and D. L. Moody's summer conferences at Northfield, Massachusetts.

Boyce, for example, spoke at the New York Chautauqua in 1880 and 1881. Basil Manly gave lectures on inspiration at the Worcester Summer School of Hebrew in 1884. John R. Sampey taught at William Rainey Harper's Summer School of Hebrew in 1890. Broadus, however, became one of the most noted speakers in such venues and attained extraordinary popularity among Northern Baptists and evangelicals. Broadus gave the doctrinal sermon at the annual gathering

122. Broadus was a "Grand Worthy Patriarch" in the order, gave addresses in various meetings, and was elected to represent Virginia in the group's national meeting. See Minutes, Grand Division of the Sons of Temperance of the State of Virginia, 1855, 97, 105–107, 111–113; John W. Wooden to John A. Broadus, 6 Apr. 1850, box 1, Broadus Papers; James L. Jones to Broadus, 19 Apr. 1856, ibid.; Jones to Broadus, 23 Oct. 1858, ibid.

123. John A. Broadus to J. H. Gambrell, ca. 18 June 1888, copied on obverse of Gambrell to Broadus, 14 June 1888, box 12, Broadus Papers.

124. Some evangelicals supported voluntary temperance but did not believe that social reform efforts lay within the church's divine commission. See, e.g., Thomas Meredith, "Query," *Biblical Recorder*, 28 Aug. 1847, 2.

of Northern Baptists in 1887.[125] Also in 1887 Broadus spoke at Moody's summer Bible conference. This was the second year of the conference, and the first year that it was at Northfield.[126] He became a regular Bible teacher at the Northfield conferences. Reuben A. Torrey recruited Broadus to teach also at the summer conference of the Moody Bible Institute in Chicago.[127] Broadus accepted John R. Mott's invitation to give several lectures to the annual meeting of the North American Young Men's Christian Association.[128]

Broadus's popularity brought him requests to accept nomination for leading pulpits and colleges or seminary presidencies in the North. He resisted pleas that he accept the presidency of the new University of Chicago. When Augustus H. Strong persuaded John D. Rockefeller to underwrite an effort to establish a great Baptist university, Strong pressed Broadus hard to accept nomination as president of the proposed school.[129] He had already recruited a young Baptist scholar, William Rainey Harper, to take a leading role, and now he felt he needed only Broadus's consent to be the head. Strong argued that Southern Baptist Theological Seminary was now established, and Broadus was needed for a bigger enterprise: "There is no man in the country who has at once the confidence of Mr. Rockefeller and of the denomination like yourself. There is no man whose wisdom and experience are more needed or would be more influential, than your own, in the moulding and shaping of such an institution as I have in mind, even as there is no man who could exert a stronger influence in favor of its establishment. I ask you favorably to consider the proposition to give yourself for the remainder of your life to this work rather than to the more limited work of the Southern Baptist Theological Seminary."[130] Rockefeller summoned Broadus to his Cleveland estate to discuss the matter in 1887.[131] Broadus afterward told Strong that he could not be considered for the post; his work at the seminary was too important. Strong's repeated pleas were unavailing.[132] Broadus remained at Southern Baptist Theological Seminary and became

125. Benjamin Griffith to John A. Broadus, 16 Feb. 1887, box 11, Broadus Papers.

126. L. D. Wishard and C. K. Ober, "College Students' Summer School for Bible Study," advertising sheet, box 11, Broadus Papers.

127. Reuben A. Torrey to John A. Broadus, 5 July 1892, box 14, Broadus Papers.

128. John R. Mott to John A. Broadus, 5 Feb. 1891, box 16, Broadus Papers.

129. Augustus H. Strong to John A. Broadus, 13 Oct. 1887, box 17, Broadus Papers.

130. Augustus H. Strong to John A. Broadus, 25 Oct. 1887, box 17, Broadus Papers.

131. John D. Rockefeller to John A. Broadus, 5 Oct. 1887, box 17, Broadus Papers; Rockefeller to Broadus, 10 Oct. 1887, box 12, Broadus Papers.

132. Augustus H. Strong to John A. Broadus, 5 Nov. 1887, box 17, Broadus Papers; Strong to Broadus, 6 Nov. 1887, ibid.; Strong to Broadus, 12 Nov. 1887, ibid.; Broadus to Strong, 18 Nov. 1887, ibid.

president two years later. William Rainey Harper accepted the presidency of Rockefeller's new Baptist university, the University of Chicago, in 1891.

William Rainey Harper was the principal of the Chautauqua's school of religion. Every year he pleaded with Broadus to teach and promised him top pay. In 1889 Harper promised to pay him $750 for three weeks' work, equal to three months of his seminary salary.[133] Broadus and Harper were already friends and shared similar aspirations for strengthening scholarship among Baptists. Harper organized Chautauqua schools of religion and recruited Broadus to teach in them summer after summer. Broadus became a regular on the Chautauqua platform during the last years of his life. His participation was problematic. Harper was becoming the most popular and effective proponent of the new historical criticism in America. Broadus and the seminary stood for the traditional orthodox approach.

HISTORICAL CRITICISM, THE NEW THEOLOGY, AND THE ISOLATION OF SOUTHERN SEMINARY

Harper never made it his intention to become a leader of the movement toward liberal theology. He intended to be an advocate of education and led a remarkably effective movement in the education of laypersons in theology, Bible, and even Hebrew and Greek. His inclinations were always to give preference to the conservative side of things, but scholarship was a higher value than conservatism. Over time, as scholarship tended toward liberal theology, Harper's views of the Bible became more liberal. In 1889, when Rockefeller tapped Harper to lead the new university in Chicago, few suspected his orthodoxy. T. T. Eaton, who with his sister, Josephine Peck, ran Kentucky's *Western Recorder* with remarkable sensitivity to the least aberration from orthodoxy, ran a series of articles from Harper on the study of the Old Testament.[134]

Broadus was caught in the middle. He admired John D. Rockefeller, and their friendship was genuine. He felt the same about Harper. Broadus respected Harper and many other historical-critical scholars and wanted to avoid rupturing his relationship with them personally and institutionally. Broadus rejected Harper's methods and conclusions but maintained cordial cooperation with him and other historical-critical scholars. Open antagonism to Harper's beliefs would have jeopardized his warm relationship with Rockefeller. Broadus

---

133. William R. Harper to John A. Broadus, 23 Feb. 1889, box 12, Broadus Papers. See also Harper to Broadus, 21 Dec. 1889, box 13, Broadus Papers.

134. T. T. Eaton to John A. Broadus, 8 Aug. 1889, box 12, Broadus Papers.

therefore distanced himself from the new views of inspiration, but he did not distance himself from the scholars and leaders who taught it.

An incident in Chicago illustrated well these tensions. At a Bible conference of some 1,500 pastors and college students, Harper and Charles A. Briggs, professor of Old Testament at Union Theological Seminary in New York, argued for their historical-critical approach, for example, rejecting the Mosaic authorship of the Pentateuch. T. T. Martin, a Southern Baptist evangelist, portrayed Broadus as the valiant and faithful witness who stood against these errors. Martin said that many in the audience felt some reservations concerning what they had heard. They knew that Broadus was in the audience and demanded to hear from him on the subject. He arose and gave an impromptu speech. He praised the University of Chicago and extolled the benefits of historical criticism, but he concluded by expressing his disagreement with Harper and Briggs. Quoting John 5:46, he repeated twice: "Beware, my brethren—Jesus said, 'Moses wrote of me.'"[135] Possibly Martin dramatized the incident. Briggs and Harper had in fact taught that the Bible erred in many particulars, though without affecting its divine message. Broadus did indeed teach that Christ's testimony regarding the Old Testament was authoritative and that the Bible did not contain errors.[136] For Broadus, as for most evangelicals, the testimony of Jesus was final for his followers. Since Jesus attributed the Pentateuch to Moses, so did he.

Archibald T. Robertson followed Broadus's example in a more aggressive way, and with less regard for the danger of rupturing relationships with historical-critical scholars and their schools. He criticized Harper's historical-critical methods in the *Examiner* in 1894, comparing Harper's approach to Abraham Kuenen's and concluding that Harper's methods were the same as Kuenen's. The only difference was that Kuenen rejected the admission of the supernatural, whereas Harper admitted it inasmuch as he asserted that the Bible was inspired. Robertson judged that Harper's version of inspiration was unworthy of the name, since it did not preserve the inspired authors from error. The vast majority of Baptists, Robertson said, believed in plenary inspiration. Harper's version of inspiration was in fact no more than illumination.[137]

135. T. T. Martin, *Viewing Life's Sunset from Pike's Peak: The Life Story of T. T. Martin* (Louisville, KY: A. D. Muse, 1939), 18–19. Martin claimed that one of those present in the audience gave him this account.

136. See Augustus H. Strong to John A. Broadus, 10 Feb. 1891, box 13, Broadus Papers; John A. Broadus to William Rainey Harper, 9 Feb. 1891, box 54, folder 26, Presidents' Papers, 1889–1925, Special Collections Research Center, University of Chicago; Robertson, *Life and Letters of Broadus*, 391–392.

137. Archibald T. Robertson, "Dr. Harper's Lectures on Genesis and Kuenen's Theory of Old Testament History," *Examiner*, 6 Sept. 1894, 1. See, similarly, Robertson, "Dr. Harper's Lectures on Genesis," *Standard*, 1 Nov. 1894, 2.

Harper was also inconsistent, Robertson said, in accepting the authority of the New Testament and at the same time rejecting the historical accounts of Genesis. Jesus spoke of the "blood of the righteous Abel," bearing "unmistakable testimony to the historical reality of Abel." Paul explained Christ's relation to believers in connection with Adam's relation to the entire race, indicating that Paul "treats Adam as a historic reality." Jesus and the New Testament writers interpreted the stories of Genesis as historically true. The authority of the New Testament therefore established the historicity of the Genesis stories. Kuenen was more consistent, Robertson wrote. He recognized that the New Testament opposed his methods, and he therefore chose to "forever cease to acknowledge the authority of the New Testament in the domain of the exegesis of the Old." Harper had adopted Kuenen's premises, Robertson warned, just as Crawford H. Toy had done, and sooner or later consistency would require him to follow them in adopting their conclusions.[138]

Many Northern Baptist scholars praised the article, but it seemed to make Broadus uneasy, though he acknowledged that it was just and measured. He wrote Robertson: "I felt well satisfied with the article in reading it. I am very glad of the commendations you have received. You are severe on Harper, but in a thoroughly fair and courteous way." [139] He had no reservations about identifying such serious errors. He perhaps recognized that the time when conservative and progressive scholars could work together would not last.

Broadus had another reason to be reserved in his criticism of such men as Harper. He seemed ever hopeful that they could be reclaimed to sounder views. In 1889 he had told Augustus H. Strong, president of Rochester Theological Seminary, that although Harper's views were "of hurtful tendency," yet he hoped that Harper was coming to more conservative views: "I am satisfied that his dominant sympathies and strongest present tendencies are towards conservative opinions of the matters involved, and that the supernatural in the Old Testament has greatly grown upon him of late years." [140] Broadus believed that as long as Harper held to the supernatural element, there was reason to hope for his return to orthodox views. Public criticism from his friends would drive him to plant his foot decidedly "in favor of the destructive side" of historical criticism. Such critics as Toy and Lyon were "far gone in the destructive views

138. Robertson, "Dr. Harper's Lectures," *Examiner*, 6 Sept. 1894, 1.

139. John A. Broadus to Archibald T. Robertson, 15 Sept. 1894, box 1, Robertson Papers.

140. John A. Broadus to A. H. Strong, 16 Mar. 1889, box 1, John D. Rockefeller Collection, University of Chicago, cited in Jeffrey P. Straub, "The Making of a Battle Royal: The Rise of Religious Liberalism in Northern Baptist Life, 1870–1920," Ph.D. dissertation, Southern Baptist Theological Seminary, 2004, 217.

already," but, Broadus hoped, Harper still had opportunity "for renewed consideration of a matter so important."[141]

A number of the seminary's brightest graduates were following Harper rather than Broadus, Manly, or Robertson. Edwin M. Poteat, who later served as president of Furman University, argued with A. T. Robertson in 1892 concerning inspiration and theology. Poteat embraced the new view of inspiration during doctoral studies at Yale University. He scouted the "fatal weaknesses" of Manly's arguments on inspiration and announced that his goal was to free the Bible from the shackles of traditional orthodoxy: "The chief concern for myself for the scholarship of this generation is that I may throw off the yoke of traditional interpretation and theology—both of which are largely Greek and Latin—and come again to unbiassed study of the New Testament."[142]

Southern Seminary's faculty wanted Poteat's Yale classmate Edward B. Pollard to accept a position as assistant professor of homiletics at the seminary.[143] Pollard's work was in Old Testament, and he had been studying Arabic, Assyrian, and Aramaic. He was a very gifted student and preacher. Broadus had been warning him of the dangers to his faith at Yale and urging him to extreme caution regarding the liberal views he encountered there. Now Broadus needed to know whether he passed muster on the doctrine of inspiration. When Broadus asked whether he found himself "embarrassed as to inerrancy of scripture," Pollard shrugged off the question as inconsequential. There were "impetuous critics" on both sides of the question, and the Bible would "succeed in vindicating itself against both false attacks and false defenses."[144] He neither affirmed nor denied inerrancy. Poteat believed that Pollard had embraced liberal views, but Pollard only positioned himself as more conservative than his Yale environment. Pollard's vague answer seemed evasive. His language and mode of argument should have marked him either as unsettled in his views or as a conservative liberal along the lines of Toy's resignation letter or Harper's view. But Broadus and the faculty thought him sufficiently conservative to invite him to the faculty.[145] Just as in the case of Harper, Broadus seemed to trust

141. John A. Broadus to William Rainey Harper, 17 Feb. 1891, box 54, folder 26, Presidents' Papers, 1889–1925, Special Collections Research Center, University of Chicago; Broadus to Harper, 9 Feb. 1891, ibid.

142. Edwin M. Poteat to Archibald T. Robertson, 22 Feb. 1892, box 1, Robertson Papers. See also Edwin M. Poteat, "Theology—Old and New," *Seminary Magazine* 5 (1892): 453–455.

143. Faculty Minutes, Southern Baptist Theological Seminary, 15 Mar. 1892.

144. Edward B. Pollard to John A. Broadus, ca. 1 Mar. 1892, box 14, Broadus Papers.

145. Edward B. Pollard to John A. Broadus, 22 Mar. 1892, box 14, 1892, Broadus Papers.

his general professions to take a conservative approach to the Bible. Pollard accepted nomination.[146]

The board of trustees, however, rejected the faculty's recommendation of Pollard. There is no record of the opinions of the trustees regarding Pollard's nomination. It is possible that the board wanted a more experienced preacher. It is likely that it wanted a proven conservative rather than an uncertain one. The board knew that the person it elected would be in line to succeed Broadus as professor of homiletics. It was the first time the board had rejected the faculty's nomination to the teaching staff. The trustees instead elected Edwin C. Dargan, a gifted pastor and Southern Seminary graduate, even though they had to subscribe personally to subsidize his salary.[147] They trusted Dargan's conservative reputation. By the time of Dargan's resignation in 1907, the faculty had begun to polarize into progressive and conservative camps, and Dargan remained on the more conservative wing. Pollard later became professor of homiletics at Crozer Theological Seminary and wrote frequently in favor of liberal theology.

THE END OF THE HEROIC AGE

Boyce's health deteriorated in 1887 and 1888. Boyce traveled to the West in the summer of 1887 to seek to recover his health.[148] He decided to travel with his family to Europe to restore his health in 1888. His physician told him that it was imperative for him to give up all responsibilities, and Boyce announced to Broadus his determination to resign effective May 1889.[149] He told Broadus that the faculty needed to begin making preparations for his resignation. Someone else would have to take over the seminary's financial affairs and replace him as treasurer.[150] Boyce died in Pau in southern France on December 28, 1888.[151]

Students loved and admired Boyce. He was a master of public ceremony and a delightful companion. Students valued his prayers before each lecture.

---

146. Edward B. Pollard to John A. Broadus, 2 Apr. 1892, box 14, Broadus Papers; Faculty Minutes, Southern Baptist Theological Seminary, 19 Apr. 1892.

147. Edward B. Pollard to John A. Broadus, 12 May 1892, box 14, Broadus Papers; William O. Carver, "Recollections and Information from Other Sources Concerning the Southern Baptist Theological Seminary," 49–50, SBTS.

148. See, e.g., James P. Boyce to John A. Broadus, 28 Aug. 1887, box 11, Broadus Papers.

149. James P. Boyce to John A. Broadus, 5 Oct. 1888, box 12, Broadus Papers; Boyce to Broadus, 19 Oct. 1888, ibid.

150. James P. Boyce to John A. Broadus, 5 Oct. 1888, box 12, Broadus Papers.

151. See Broadus, *Memoir of Boyce*, 341–342.

One student who was not expected to return for a second year nevertheless returned. When some students asked him why he returned, he said, "I came back to hear Dr. Boyce pray." [152] Some mistook his natural reserve for distance. Broadus attributed this to his dislike of small talk and thought him remarkably genial and open. Many students experienced his extraordinary generosity of spirit as he aided and advised them in numerous ways. Alumnus John Adams testified that "most of you professors in the seminary seemed to me like fathers but Dr. Boyce was my friend, not only in my marriage, but also in my time of need." [153] Another student remembered vividly Boyce's "ever thoughtful tenderness. The Dr. did me several favors while in China. One of which was to lend me more than a hundred dollars for several months, for which he would have no compensation. I greatly love Dr. Boyce." [154] G. W. Samson represented the feelings of many who knew him: "Boyce was in every respect the noblest spirit I ever met." [155]

Broadus, no less than Boyce, was a rare character. He was an accomplished scholar, having prepared the revised translation and critical edition of Chrysostom's homilies on the apostle Paul's letters to the Philippians, Colossians, and Thessalonians, published in Schaff's monumental edition of the patristic writings in English. [156] He gave the prestigious Beecher Lectures on Preaching at Yale University in 1889. He accepted Daniel C. Gilman's invitation to give a series of lectures at Johns Hopkins University in 1890.

Students loved and admired Broadus no less than Boyce, and many felt closer to Broadus. Broadus seemed to make the deepest impression on students of all the professors. Archibald T. Robertson professed the highest regard for Broadus. When Broadus was seriously ill in 1888, Robertson confided to his diary, "No man has left such a deep impress upon my life and cast of thought as he. I shall bear his mark upon me as long as I live. His personality is intense." [157]

Broadus and Boyce developed a unique friendship, a brotherly love forged in common ideals, shared labors, and sympathetic suffering. Broadus's testimony to Boyce echoed in denominational memory:

---

152. Quoted by H. H. Tucker, "Memoir of Dr. Boyce," *Christian Index*, 7 Feb. 1889, 9.

153. John Adams to John A. Broadus, 26 Jan. 1889, box 12, Broadus Papers.

154. J. M. Joiner to John A. Broadus, 6 June 1889, box 12, Broadus Papers.

155. G. W. Samson to John A. Broadus, 5 Feb. 1889, box 12, Broadus Papers.

156. *Saint Chrysostom: Homilies on Galatians, Ephesians, Philippians, Colossians, Thessalonians, Timothy, Titus, and Philemon*, vol. 13 of *A Select Library of the Nicene and Post-Nicene Fathers of the Christian Church*, ed. Philip Schaff (New York: Christian Literature, 1889).

157. Archibald T. Robertson, Personal Journal, 4 Mar. 1888, box 11, Robertson Papers. See, similarly, Robertson to John A. Broadus, 2 July 1890, box 1, Robertson Papers.

If I were to talk to you for hours and tell you of all he went through you could but half conceive it. I do not think the strongest type of character is the man who stands unmoved amid difficulties and trials, but he who does feel, and feels keenly and deeply, feels depressed and at times almost overwhelmed, and still does not give up. And such was the history in this case. Many times it seemed impossible to go on, and but for his heroic efforts the seminary would have been closed. That was what wore out this life ten years too soon, that long, sore, terrible struggle. He had lost by the war the greater part of his fortune. He had many opportunities to recover it with his wonderful business talents, and they were often pressed upon his acceptance, but he had made up his mind that, God helping him, this enterprise to which he had given his life should not fail....James P. Boyce was a genuine man, that he was made out of good timber all the way though. Who ever found a flaw in his make-up?...And I bear that testimony personally as one who knew him better than I knew my own brother....What an adviser he was. Ah, there were so many occasions when no counsel but his would do....He had great knowledge of character, great insight. I thought he was prejudiced sometimes, as everyone is likely to be, but oftener than otherwise, it would turn out that he was right, for good or ill.[158]

When Broadus died in 1895, none of the seminary's founders remained. His death marked the end of the institution's first age. The founding faculty steered the seminary through the severest trials. Time after time, when the death of the seminary was at hand, they refused to abandon it, and God blessed their stubborn faithfulness with sufficient support to continue the enterprise, at least until the next crisis. They chose to remain at their posts, with meager and uncertain income, when they could have left for positions of greater prominence and larger salaries. Finally, by the early 1890s, their labors and sacrifices succeeded in establishing the seminary on a permanent foundation, with a secure endowment and a marvelous campus. And they had withstood the advance of heresy, even at the cost of losing their beloved Toy. They established the school for the defense and promotion of orthodox doctrine and maintained their resolve to keep it there. Not long after, the seminary established its Founders' Day, observed annually on Boyce's birthday, as an occasion for recalling their gracious character and mighty deeds. The founding faculty's long struggles, great sacrifices, and latter success cemented their place in denominational memory.

158. John A. Broadus, "The Address of Jno. A. Broadus at the Funeral of Jas. P. Boyce," *Seminary Magazine* 2 (1889): 50.

Subsequent generations of Southern Baptists learned to revere them through the oft-repeated stories of their sacrifices and triumphs. Southern Baptists ensconced their ideals, beliefs, and judgments as the standard by which denominational faithfulness should be measured. Theirs was an epic tale that shaped Southern Baptist identity. For the denomination no less than for the seminary, theirs was the heroic age.

5

WILLIAM H. WHITSITT, ACADEMIC FREEDOM, AND DENOMINATIONAL CONTROL

William Heth Whitsitt succeeded Broadus as president of Southern Seminary in May 1895. His tenure was short and tumultuous. The controversy he precipitated cost him his position. The presenting issue in the controversy was Whitsitt's claim that in 1641 Baptists invented immersion as the mode of baptism. Most Southern Baptists found the claim troubling, and many thought it contrary to scripture. But Whitsitt's ultimate offense was betrayal of denominational trust—common Baptists could not get past the sneering tone with which he corrected his own denomination. He was president of a seminary established as a guardian of Baptist orthodoxy, but he had disparaged Baptist views in a way that broadly discredited the denomination.

Whitsitt seemed deaf to such concerns. He seemed to believe that the promotion of truth meant there could be no allowances for human feeling or popular prejudice. He seemed to stand for the truth at any cost, truth in the full glare of relentless reason, without smoothing or varnishing. Any who failed to grasp or who took offense were unfortunate casualties. "Truth is mighty," Whitsitt said, "and will prevail."[1] The truth must out, at any cost. In the end Whitsitt could not understand how Southern Baptist leaders, and even his own colleagues, refused to support him. Failure to support him was disloyalty to truth and reason.

But the significance of the controversy went deeper. The Whitsitt controversy was a battle for far more than a question in Baptist history. It was a struggle for

1. William H. Whitsitt, "Dr. Whitsitt's Address to the Students," Correspondence—Whitsitt Controversy, B. H. Carroll Collection, SWBTS.

the character of the denomination and divergent visions of the future. Whitsitt's friends battled for openness, tolerance, freedom, enlightenment, education, and progress. His foes fought for popular control and the conservation of orthodox Baptist doctrine. It signified the advance of a new progressive spirit. The progressives took an accommodating posture toward historical criticism and thought that historical-critical methods would not damage the Bible's divine message; traditionalists believed that they would. Progressives thought that historical-critical study of the Bible still led persons to Christ; traditionalists believed that it led to perdition.[2] Under Whitsitt's successors, traditionalists on the faculty became fewer and the progressives multiplied. Seminary graduates took this spirit into the leading pulpits and top denominational offices. Whitsitt himself did little to promote such progressive views, but he came to represent the progressives' struggle to promote truth and enlightenment in the Southern Baptist Convention. In denominational memory, Whitsitt was a martyr to freedom.

By 1898 most of Whitsitt's erstwhile supporters were convinced that continuing to defend Whitsitt as president would inflict permanent injury on the seminary and on the denomination. It was creating division, defection, and demoralization. It also threatened permanent schism. In all respects it diminished the denomination's effectiveness in advancing the gospel of Christ Jesus. Whitsitt did not, it seems, ever grant that such considerations were just or reasonable. He did not recognize the right of popular control in such matters. He would not sacrifice principle to preserve the seminary. He fought for freedom to teach truth, to enlighten a backward denomination. He lost the battle, but his martyrdom strengthened the resolve of progressive Southern Baptists and discredited the traditionalists.

ELECTION

Broadus's death in March 1895 gave the board of trustees about two months to consider what to do about a new president. As trustees prepared to meet in Washington, D.C., in May, two candidates had emerged: William H. Whitsitt and Franklin H. Kerfoot. The faculty elected Whitsitt as the chairman of the faculty, which made him the moderator of the faculty meetings. He was the longest-tenured faculty member and the most popular among students. The majority of the faculty wanted Whitsitt as president.[3]

2. See unattributed, "The Cranfill-Harper Interview," *Baptist Courier*, 6 Feb. 1896, 2.

3. Most seem to have preferred Whitsitt strongly. Even Dargan, who seemed in closest agreement with Kerfoot, preferred Whitsitt (Edwin C. Dargan to Mrs. P. [Josephine E. Peck], 31 Jan. 1899, Dargan Papers, SBHLA).

Franklin H. Kerfoot was also a credible candidate. He believed that he was the handpicked successor to Boyce in the presidency and claimed that he had assurance of this when he agreed to join the faculty. It is unlikely that either Boyce or Broadus gave him such assurance, not least because it was not in their power to do so. It is possible that some trustees pledged that they would press his name for the presidency upon Boyce's death.[4]

He had been Boyce's choice to succeed him in the chair of systematic theology. Kerfoot also succeeded Boyce as seminary treasurer and financial agent. He was probably the most eloquent and popular preacher on the faculty, after Broadus's death, and his brethren had put him at the front of denominational affairs. He had been intimately involved with the seminary's management for six years. He had the trust and support of a number of trustees. Most important, he had the support of Joshua Levering, chairman of the board of trustees and the seminary's most important living benefactor. Kerfoot was more popular in the denomination than Whitsitt and was perhaps the denomination's most gifted preacher.

There was one other credible candidate, Thomas T. Eaton, who appealed not only to Landmarkers but also to those traditionalists who feared that the orthodoxy of the seminary was vulnerable after the deaths of Boyce, Manly, and Broadus.[5] Eaton was a formidable figure. He was pastor of the large Walnut Street Baptist Church in Louisville and editor of the *Western Recorder*. Since James R. Graves's death in 1892, Eaton was the most influential Landmark leader in the denomination. He was also a longtime seminary supporter and trustee. Whitsitt was suspicious of Eaton and believed that Eaton opposed his election as president. Whitsitt believed that he had alienated Eaton because Whitsitt supported the creation of the Southern Baptist Young People's Union, whereas Eaton opposed it.[6] Eaton was an unlikely choice as seminary president. The only prevailing reason to chose him would be to avoid a breach among the faculty or trustees. But no breach emerged, and no trustee nominated him.

Eaton himself had a different concern. He knew that several trustees strongly favored Kerfoot, and that board chairman Joshua Levering would almost certainly vote with them. Kerfoot had been Levering's pastor in Baltimore. In 1890

---

4. William O. Carver, "William Heth Whitsitt: The Seminary's Martyr," *Review and Expositor* 51 (1954): 462; William O. Carver, "Recollections and Information from Other Sources Concerning the Southern Baptist Theological Seminary," typescript, 37–38, SBTS.

5. See William H. Whitsitt, Diary, quoted in R. Inman Johnson, "From the Diaries of William H. Whitsitt," 11, R. Inman Johnson 1982–84 folder, McCall Papers.

6. Whitsitt, Diary, quoted in Johnson, "From the Diaries of William H. Whitsitt," 13, R. Inman Johnson 1982–84 folder, McCall Papers.

Levering had offered to pay the expenses for Kerfoot and his family so that he could spend a year in Europe to restore his health.[7] Since other trustees, probably a majority, favored Whitsitt, Eaton feared division on the board. He felt that it would be wiser to delay the election a year or two while Whitsitt's service as chairman of the faculty convinced the Kerfoot supporters to vote for Whitsitt. "It would be hard, at the best, for any man to succeed Dr. Broadus and I wanted Dr. W[hitsitt] to have the practically unanimous support of the trustees and of the friends of the seminary generally.... He would in the interregnum so demonstrate his fitness for the presidency, that he would be unanimously chosen when the election was held." By the time of the trustee meeting, however, he had decided that delay was not necessary and that he would support Whitsitt.[8] I. T. Tichenor reported later that during the debate on electing a president Eaton was "Whitsitt's warm supporter."[9]

William E. Hatcher was the leader of the "Virginia forces" on the board. They represented the more progressive wing. Hatcher nominated Whitsitt as president. J. W. Warder, conservative leader of the Kentucky convention, nominated Kerfoot. Members made ten speeches. Kerfoot lost. In standard procedure, those who voted for Kerfoot apparently agreed to make the vote unanimous. It is probably testimony to the animosity that afterward developed between Whitsitt and Kerfoot that someone struck through the passage in the minute book recording Kerfoot's nomination in an effort to obscure it.[10]

LANDMARKISM

Whitsitt was an apostate Landmarker. He grew up in the grip of Landmarkism and abandoned it as a young adult. At the seminary, he sought to persuade Landmark students to follow his example and aimed some ridicule at the system. He came to believe that Landmark views of the church were akin to Roman Catholicism and that Baptists ought to overthrow them. He finally became fixated on a fated conflict with Landmarkism.

When Whitsitt was young, Landmarkism produced in him "a kind of fanaticism." His family attended the Mill Creek Baptist Church in the heartland of Landmarkism near Nashville. His family heard Landmark leader James R. Graves preach many times in the church, and they read Graves's *Tennessee*

---

7. Franklin H. Kerfoot to John A. Broadus, 4 June 1890, box 13, Broadus Papers.

8. Thomas T. Eaton to Archibald T. Robertson, 5 Dec. 1896, box 1, Robertson Papers.

9. I. T. Tichenor, "Dr. Eaton Wasn't Prosecutor," *Atlanta Constitution*, 15 May 1897.

10. Minutes, Board of Trustees, Southern Baptist Theological Seminary, May 1895, 2:198.

William H. Whitsitt

Baptist. Whitsitt admired Graves and his protégé, A. C. Dayton. The Whitsitt family hosted Graves and Dayton in their home. Whitsitt joined the church in 1855 and thrilled at his participation in Graves's great work of reformation. He attended Landmark-oriented Union University and became close to James M. Pendleton, the theologian of Landmarkism. When Nashville First Baptist Church excommunicated Graves in 1859, Whitsitt sided with Graves. And when the Mill Creek church ordained Whitsitt in 1862, Graves, by Whitsitt's request, served on his ordination council and preached the ordination sermon. Whitsitt wrote, "I considered that Graves and Dayton, by abolishing the universal spiritual church, and bringing in the Catholic system of theology, had rescued the Baptists from destruction, introducing a new and almost divine era of power and development." [11]

Whitsitt's service in the Confederate army weakened his commitment to Landmarkism. He met many non-Landmark Baptists and was impressed by their piety and good sense. By the time of the war's end he questioned the correctness of Landmark doctrine and concluded that Graves was too severe

11. William H. Whitsitt, "The Whitsitt Controversy—1896–1899," typescript, 10–14, box 1, William H. Whitsitt Papers, LVA.

toward non-Landmark Baptists. John Broadus convinced Whitsitt to attend Southern Seminary, where his study of Dayton's *Theodosia Earnest* convinced him that Landmarkism's distinctive doctrines were unscriptural, in particular, its repudiation of the notion of a "universal spiritual church."[12] During his time as a student, he rejected Landmarkism and began to tell Landmark students that their belief in church perpetuity had no proof from church history.[13]

Whitsitt alienated Landmarkers not merely because he opposed their views but especially because he communicated an attitude of superiority. Indeed, Whitsitt felt a natural superiority even toward his faculty colleagues. Outwardly cordial and genuinely friendly, he tended to view his colleagues and friends as vain, incompetent, or disloyal. He could be scathing toward his friends in his journal. His sense of superiority seemed natural and unself-conscious, but it greatly deepened as a result of his experiences in his great controversy with the denomination. He tended to view others' motivations in terms of either jealousy or vanity, making them strangely petty. He generally attributed noble motives, however, to those who stood faithfully by him.

Whitsitt's sense of superiority resulted in conflicted feelings toward his faculty colleagues. When Whitsitt read the speech that Toy delivered at a national Baptist educational convention in 1872, for example, he could barely stomach the piece: "My colleague Dr. Toy is a very learned pedant. . . . The man's pedantry crops out at every point. Anything so utterly destructive to the interests of learning has never come under my notice from so respectable a quarter. Indeed the idea all the way along seems to be, 'Behold, ye pigmies, how much more learned I am than ye are.'" Whitsitt thought that it was a "foolish tribute to personal vanity."[14] Whitsitt felt similarly superior to Boyce and other colleagues.

WHITSITT'S DISCOVERY AND SCIENTIFIC HISTORY

Whitsitt's own approach was "scientific history." He had great confidence in its methods and results. This confidence only heightened his sense of superiority, leading him to conclude that those who opposed his conclusions were misled by ignorance or prejudice rather than guided by reason. He therefore viewed their opposition as persecution rather than enlightened disagreement. His were the travails of a scientific historian. His study of history in Germany rather predisposed him to view himself as a scientist and to view history as governed

12. Ibid., 15–18.

13. E. B. Hardie to William H. Whitsitt, 10 Aug. 1896, box, William H. Whitsitt Papers, LVA.

14. William H. Whitsitt, Journal, ca. 1 Jan. 1873, 207–208, Whitsitt Papers, SBTS.

by natural laws. But it also rendered him nearly incapable of self-criticism. As Whitsitt recalled, "I was profoundly impressed by the lectures and methods of Johann Gustav Droysen, Professor of History in the University of Berlin. In particular I gave a great amount of study to a small work of Droysen, entitled *Grundriss der Historik*, and have often taken time to review it while I occupied the chair of ecclesiastical history in the theological seminary." Droysen taught that history was a science. "Historical truth" inhered in the "moral forces" that drove human history in its upward progress. Historical occurrences were the "perpetual actualization of these moral forces." [15] These moral forces were, like natural laws in the physical sphere, the elemental truths that explained "the advancing movement of the moral world." Whitsitt wrote, "Through the influences of Droysen I adopted the modern methods of historical research, and applied them to Baptist history in the same way as to other sorts of history. That fact is the Iliad of all my woes in connection with the Whitsitt controversy." [16] Whitsitt felt that his only offense had been to publish scientific conclusions. Facts were facts. All else was ignorance or prejudice.

In 1877 Whitsitt made his great "discovery" that English Baptists did not practice immersion until 1641. In 1880 he confirmed its truth by research in England and published his conclusions anonymously in the *Independent*. Whitsitt afterward took offense that such historians as Henry Dexter and A. H. Newman published his ideas but gave him no credit. Whitsitt described his discovery:

During the autumn of 1877, shortly after I had been put in charge of the School of Church History at the Southern Baptist Theological Seminary, in preparing my lectures on Baptist History, I made the discovery that, prior to the year 1641, our Baptist people in England were in the practice of sprinkling and pouring for baptism. I kept it to myself until the year 1880, when I had the happiness to spend my summer vacation at the British Museum. There I assured myself, largely by researches among King George's pamphlets, that my discovery was genuine, and established it by many irrefragable proofs from contemporary documents. Upon my return to New York, in September 1880, I felt so sure of my ground that I made known my discovery in the columns of the "Independent." It was received with much disapproval and sneers from many quarters. [17]

15. Johann Gustav Droysen, *Outline of the Principles of History (Grundriss der Historik)*, trans. E. Benjamin Andrews (Boston: Ginn, 1893), 16, 33.

16. William H. Whitsitt, "The Whitsitt Controversy—1896–1899," typescript, 18, box 1, William H. Whitsitt Papers, LVA.

17. William H. Whitsitt, "Baptist Baptism," *Cumberland Presbyterian*, 7 May 1896, 680. This article first appeared in the *Examiner*.

Dexter, Whitsitt suggested, ignored Whitsitt's role as the first one to discover this fact: "Dr. Dexter was interested in my explanation and proofs, for he shortly found his way to the British Museum, where he also convinced himself that my view was correct and my citations authentic. As a fruit of these researches he issued, near the close of 1881, more than a twelve-month after my discovery had been declared in the *Independent*, the well-known volume entitled 'John Smith, the Se-Baptist,' wherein he adopted my thesis, defended it by many citations, and entirely ignored my discovery, as set forth in the *Independent*." Whitsitt's one satisfaction was that twenty years afterward most historians had adopted his conclusion concerning the adoption of immersion by English Baptists in 1641.[18]

Other historians were initially divided concerning Whitsitt's conclusions. Nearly all supported him on the principle that Christian scholars should have freedom in their denominations to prosecute historical research and publish their conclusions. Henry C. Vedder, professor of church history at Crozer Theological Seminary, and A. H. Newman, professor of church history at Toronto's McMaster University, agreed with him that the evidence indicated that Particular Baptists in England adopted immersion in 1641. They did not agree with all his conclusions. Vedder agreed to help Whitsitt and wrote articles in his support, but he believed that the evidence could not sustain Whitsitt's emphatic conclusion that no Baptists immersed until 1641. He felt also that the evidence concerning English Particular Baptists could not answer the question for Roger Williams's baptism in Rhode Island in 1639. He believed further that some General Baptists probably did immerse before that time, but the evidence was not conclusive.[19] A. H. Newman had similar reservations.

Some historians felt that the evidence was insufficient to establish Whitsitt's main conclusion concerning the introduction of immersion in 1641. Historian Eri Hulbert of the University of Chicago Divinity School thought Whitsitt's conclusions uncertain.[20] Jesse B. Thomas, professor of church history at Newton Theological Seminary, agreed with the evidence that the Particular Baptists began immersing in 1641, but he rejected Whitsitt's broader conclusion that none of the Baptists in England or Holland immersed before 1641.[21]

---

18. Whitsitt, "Baptist Baptism."

19. Henry C. Vedder to Thomas T. Eaton, 19 Aug. 1896, box 1, Thomas T. Eaton Papers; Vedder to William H. Whitsitt, 29 Aug. 1896, box 1, William H. Whitsitt Papers, LVA.

20. Eri Hulbert to Thomas T. Eaton, 25 Aug. 1896, box 1, Thomas T. Eaton Papers.

21. Jesse B. Thomas, "Dr. Whitsitt's Question," *Western Recorder*, 17 Dec. 1896, 4. Thomas wrote this as the first in a series of nine articles contesting this point. The last article appeared on 4 Mar. 1897.

Whitsitt had long viewed himself as a reformer of his denomination and entertained visions of leading the heroic charge of reform. He dreamed of giving the opening sermon at the 1875 Southern Baptist Convention and striking boldly for reform: "I should like to be appointed to preach the introductory sermon (D.v. [Deo volente, i.e., God willing]) before the Southern Baptist Convention in 1875. I would take up the subject which has recently given me such sore trouble and discuss it before the whole denomination....But how far would I go?"[22]

Upon reflection he calculated that Southern Baptists "would crucify me if I attempted a work of reformation," and he refrained.[23] Melodrama aside, Whitsitt was not suited to the work of reformation in a populist denomination. Whitsitt's scientific approach to history, his discovery of the renewal of immersion, and his interpretation of American Baptist history in terms of a conflict between the Protestant spirit and the Catholic spirit prepared him to press the battle, but his inability to appreciate the human context of truth and knowledge prepared him to lose it. And his unwillingness to grant the justness of popular authority in denominational concerns prepared him for martyrdom.

In 1894, before Whitsitt assumed the presidency of the seminary, he became convinced that open warfare between Landmark and non-Landmark Baptists would soon commence. He was equally convinced that the time had long since passed that Southern Baptists should have fought this war: "In the years 1859 and 1860 Graves commenced an attack upon the Southern Baptist Convention that proved to be formidable...yet the movement was nipped in the bud by the war between the states. The time is coming on when the conflict will be fought over again, or to speak more correctly, when the conflict that was adjourned by the war between the states must be fought to a finish." The time had come, Whitsitt believed, to rid the denomination of its "Roman Catholic" wing.[24]

The shock to Southern Baptists came not just from the historical issue. They were disturbed that he had presented his teaching in a manner that rather demeaned Baptists for their traditional beliefs. Mississippi alumnus N. W. P. Bacon predicted that "your method of giving to the world your 'new discovery' gave the brethren a shock from which they are not likely soon to recover."[25] Whitsitt did not seem to appreciate how his course had injured the

22. William H. Whitsitt, Journal, 20 Mar. 1874, 251, Whitsitt Papers.

23. William H. Whitsitt, Journal, ca. Jan. 1874, 249, Whitsitt Papers, SBTS.

24. Whitsitt, Diary, 1 Sept. 1894, quoted in Johnson, "From the Diaries of William H. Whitsitt," 13, R. Inman Johnson 1982–84 folder, McCall Papers.

25. N. W. P. Bacon to William H. Whitsitt, 30 June 1896, box 1, William H. Whitsitt Papers, LVA.

feelings of the denomination. As a scientific historian, he did not seem to think it mattered. His apologies and explanations therefore did little to diminish the alienation he created. He failed to earn the denomination's trust.

WHITSITT'S OFFENSES AND THE START OF THE CONTROVERSY

In March 1896 New York's *Examiner* opened the Whitsitt controversy with an article by Henry M. King, pastor of the Providence, Rhode Island, First Baptist Church, criticizing Whitsitt's article in *Johnson's Universal Cyclopaedia*. The article appeared in 1893 in the first volume of a new edition of the encyclopedia.[26] In it Whitsitt claimed that English Baptists did not baptize by immersion until 1641, that Roger Williams, who established the first Baptist church in America, was not immersed, and that Baptists in America did not begin immersing until 1644.[27] Baptists therefore could not claim to receive their baptism in direct succession from the apostles. Others had recently argued that English Particular Baptists began immersing in 1633. Whitsitt's 1641 date, and his conclusion that no Baptists could have practiced immersion before this date, were new ideas. Whitsitt claimed them as "my discovery."[28]

Whitsitt was among the first to argue that the English Baptists initially baptized by pouring, or affusion, and only afterward introduced immersion. The Dutch Anabaptists baptized by pouring, with the exception of one sect. John Smyth and Thomas Helwys became Baptists about 1608 in Holland and baptized by pouring. They adopted Arminian doctrine and were known as General Baptists. In 1633 some English Puritans became Baptists. They retained their Calvinist doctrine and were known as Particular Baptists. They soon became convinced that since the apostles practiced baptism as immersion, other "modes" were invalid. They began immersing in 1641. Once the contemporary evidence became known, most Baptist historians accepted the conclusion.[29]

But these facts were unknown before the 1860s, when the history of baptismal practice among Dutch Anabaptists and English Baptists began coming

26. William H. Whitsitt, Diary, 5 Mar. 1892, quoted in Mary Whitsitt Whitehead, "Excerpts from the Diary of William Heth Whitsitt for W. O. Carver," SBTS.

27. William H. Whitsitt, "Baptists," in *Johnson's Universal Cyclopaedia*, new ed., vol. 1, ed. Charles Kendall Adams (New York: A. J. Johnson, 1893), 489-490.

28. William H. Whitsitt, untitled, *Examiner*, 23 Apr. 1896.

29. Many objected, however, to Whitsitt's conclusion that Roger Williams therefore could not have introduced immersion in Rhode Island before the English Particular Baptists did.

to light. All historians before this, both Baptist and non-Baptist, assumed that the first English Baptists practiced immersion. When Whitsitt's arguments became known among Southern Baptists, the fact that he disagreed with all the respected historians before him made his views appear implausible to most Baptists.

They seemed implausible also because he claimed that they were Baptists even before they practiced New Testament baptism. Baptists in the nineteenth century all believed that baptism required the act of immersion by very definition, since the Greek word literally meant an immersing. They held that to substitute sprinkling or pouring was disobedience to the command and in no sense baptism. If these early "Baptists" in fact sprinkled for baptism, then they had no true baptism and were not therefore genuinely Baptists. The idea that there were Baptists without true baptism seemed preposterous to virtually all Baptists at the time.

But what troubled them most of all was that Whitsitt's discovery threatened Baptists' understanding of their place in history. The vast majority of Baptists believed that Baptist churches had received their immersion baptism in unbroken succession from the early English Baptists through the Continental Anabaptists, who had received it in a succession of various churches outside the Roman Catholic church and originating in the apostolic churches. For most Baptists, this was simply an unexceptional fact of history, since non-Baptist scholars had long argued for it. There was no reason to doubt its accuracy.

For Landmark Baptists this unbroken succession of true baptisms was more than a historical question; it was a divinely prescribed condition for the existence of true churches. James R. Graves, Landmarkism's great leader, taught that the kingdom of God was coextensive with the visible church and that the only visible churches were those that had true baptism, namely, immersion. An unbaptized minister could not validly baptize others, and without baptism there could be no church. And since sprinkling was not baptism, if the early English Baptists sprinkled, theirs were not true churches, and all who derived their baptisms in succession from them were not baptized and had no churches. Hence, if no churches practiced immersion baptism before 1641, then the kingdom of God had for a time disappeared from the earth, contrary to the entire thrust of the New Testament teaching on the kingdom of God and in breach of Christ's promise that the gates of hell would not prevail against his church. For many Landmarkers, therefore, Whitsitt's historical teachings seemed to conflict directly with the Bible. For them it was little different than saying that history proved that Moses never parted the Red Sea or that Jesus did not walk on the water. It was preposterous.

But for non-Landmark Baptists it was a purely historical question. They could adjust themselves readily enough to Whitsitt's conclusions, if the historical evidence sustained them. They held that the validity of a church was based on its conformity to the apostolic doctrine and practices, and did not depend on direct succession. A true church had divine authority to baptize and, in the extraordinary circumstance of having no baptized person among them, could appoint someone to administer it. Upon reviewing the historical evidence, most were prepared to lose their claim to their unbroken succession, but they could not escape the feeling that they had lost something vital. It was disconcerting because the polemical contest between Baptists and other Protestants ranged largely over historical ground. Right or wrong, Baptists had used these arguments to advantage and drawn comfort and confidence from them. The loss could be borne, but it seemed real enough. Right or wrong, Whitsitt was implicated in that loss.

Shortly after King's article in the *Examiner*, Baptists in the South began raising their objections to Whitsitt's views. Baptist newspapers in the South opened their columns to writers on both sides of the issue. Non-Landmark editors could not ignore the controversy but wanted to contain it as much as possible in order to prevent alienation and anger toward the seminary. Landmark newspapers encouraged contributions from both sides, and the controversy dominated their columns for three years. Kentucky's *Western Recorder*, edited by Landmark leader Thomas T. Eaton, led the train.

On April 23, 1896, the controversy began in earnest. On that date the *Western Recorder* published its first article attacking Whitsitt's position. J. H. Spencer, one of Kentucky Baptists' elder statesmen, honored the seminary's faculty for their "uncompromising orthodoxy" but charged Whitsitt with going beyond the pale when he asserted immersion's late introduction into English and American Baptist churches. His views were, Spencer said, "directly contrary to those of the Southern Baptists, who own and support the seminary in which they are taught." Whitsitt's errors, he urged, were "not so vital as were those of Professor Toy," but they were "just as heretical."[30]

Whitsitt and his friends believed that the whole thing had been orchestrated by Eaton and his sister in a conspiracy to secure Eaton's election as seminary president in 1895.[31] As might be expected, there is no evidence for such a conspiracy. Eaton and Peck denied that they desired Whitsitt to resign or that they organized any effort to force him out. It was a year too late to be effective, since Whitsitt was elected in 1895, and King's article appeared in 1896. Peck thought privately that two faculty members would resign in due time— Whitsitt because of his reproaches against Landmarkers, and Kerfoot because

30. J. H. Spencer, "Dr. Whitsitt on Baptist History," *Western Recorder*, 23 Apr. 1896, 2.
31. See, e.g., [T. T. Eaton], "They Will Do Neither," *Western Recorder*, 14 Jan. 1897, 8.

he was an unpopular teacher with students.[32] But Eaton and Peck also thought that Whitsitt's statements were indefensible and that his plea for immunity based on freedom of research only exacerbated the offense. They felt that since the denomination had built and sustained the seminary by its donations, and entrusted its young preachers to its instruction, it had at the least a right of advice and consent to its faculty and teachings. The best interest of the seminary, in addition, entailed maintaining the goodwill of the denomination, not alienating a large portion of it.[33]

Shortly after the controversy over the encyclopedia article began, it came to light that Whitsitt was the author of several unsigned articles on baptism in the New York *Independent* in 1880. The *Independent*, probably the nation's most widely read religious newspaper, pressed progressive theology and toleration of new ideas in the churches. Crawford H. Toy had developed a friendship with the editor and wrote book reviews for the paper at the time that Whitsitt's articles appeared. The articles took an irreverent tone. In them Whitsitt argued that "prior to the comparatively recent date of 1641 none of the people who are known as Baptists were immersed.... The English Baptists never dreamed of the possibility of immersing an adult person as a religious ceremony before the year 1641."[34] He quoted from a number of contemporary documents to establish his conclusions.[35] Whitsitt argued that Roger Williams could not have been immersed, although "all the Baptists of America so assume." The introduction of immersion among English Baptists in 1641, Whitsitt said, was "the invention of immersion."[36] This phrase, and the condescending tone, suggested that the Baptist position on baptism was without foundation in history or scripture. Southern Baptists, when they discovered that Whitsitt was the author, did not understand how a Baptist minister and theology professor could take such a posture if he actually believed the Baptist position.

Articles in the *Western Recorder* accused Whitsitt of another offense, of saying that if a Baptist woman married a pedobaptist, she should join her husband's church. Several persons claimed that they had heard Whitsitt assert that "it was a Baptist wife's duty to forsake her own denomination and join the church of a pedobaptist husband, inasmuch as the family is older than the church and should take precedence wherever they may clash." Whitsitt denied

32. Josephine E. Peck to Archibald T. Robertson, 22 Oct. 1896, box 1, Robertson Papers; Peck to Robertson, n.d., box 6, Robertson Papers.

33. See, e.g., [T. T. Eaton], "The Situation," *Western Recorder*, 6 May 1897, 3.

34. [William H. Whitsitt], untitled, *Independent*, 24 June 1880, 15.

35. [William H. Whitsitt], "The Proof Supplied," *Independent*, 9 Sept. 1880, 16–17; [Whitsitt], "More Proofs," *Independent* 7 Oct.1880, 17.

36. [William H. Whitsitt], "The Proof Supplied," *Independent*, 9 Sept. 1880, 16.

the charge emphatically: "I have referred to the fact that the family is older than the church, ... but I have never claimed that the family is entitled to precedence over the church, or that a Baptist wife should follow her pedobaptist husband or do any other act against her conscience." [37]

When these protests of Whitsitt's views began in the spring of 1896, he saw it as the beginning of the epic battle he had long anticipated. But he was not optimistic about the outcome, at least for the hero of the contest, noting in his diary: "The great storm that has burst upon me at this juncture fills me with grave apprehensions. Our days in the president's house are likely to be few and full of trouble." [38]

WAITING FOR WHITSITT'S REPLY

Most Landmarkers believed that Whitsitt had disqualified himself as president or as professor at the seminary. Most non-Landmarkers initially stood by him from love for him and loyalty to the seminary, but many were not enthusiastic in his defense. The seminary's leading alumni were the most zealous in their support of Whitsitt. The denomination polarized over the issue. The battle for Southern Baptist public opinion had two fronts, the state newspapers and the annual meetings of local associations, state conventions, and the Southern Baptist Convention.

The pro-Whitsitt strategy entailed preventing Whitsitt's opponents from introducing resolutions against him in these annual meetings. Their chances of success would improve, they felt, if they could appeal to a strong statement from Whitsitt vindicating his views. The longer he delayed replying to the charges, the more difficult was his defense. To his opponents, silence implied that the charges could not be answered. But it also left his supporters without any ammunition with which to answer the substance of the charges. In fact Whitsitt was preparing a careful response to the charges. His supporters asked Baptist groups to wait for Whitsitt's reply before they acted. In many instances this plea forestalled condemnation by various associations and conventions. [39]

But it was not easy. Virtually every association and state convention meeting in 1896 was a potential battleground on the matter. Indeed, nearly any meeting of Baptists was liable to have someone offer resolutions addressing the issue.

---

37. William H. Whitsitt to J. W. Perry, 28 Mar. 1898, box 1, Thomas T. Eaton Papers.

38. Whitsitt, Diary, 15 Apr. 1896, quoted in Whitehead, "Excerpts from the Diary of William Heth Whitsitt for W. O. Carver," SBTS.

39. See, e.g., I. J. Van Ness to William H. Whitsitt, 12 June 1896, box 1, William H. Whitsitt Papers, LVA.

J. O. Rust, a Whitsitt supporter, reported he had led the Nashville, Tennessee, pastor's conference to pass pro-Whitsitt resolutions and had accomplished similar work at the Central Tennessee Sunday School Convention.[40] Whitsitt's supporters drew up plans and organized to make sure that pro-Whitsitt pastors attended every general meeting and were prepared to offer resolutions in support of Whitsitt and to rebut and defeat any proposed resolutions against him.

The first major meeting after the controversy broke was the Southern Baptist Convention, which met in Chattanooga in May 1896. Many delegates wanted the convention to condemn Whitsitt's errors, but most thought condemnation would be premature, since Whitsitt had not yet presented his evidence in full. They decided to wait until he published his defense later that year. Whitsitt's opponents nevertheless put the seminary on notice. J. S. Coleman commended the "newly awakened interest" among Southern Baptists concerning the "teachers and teachings" of the seminary. He wanted to know whether the convention controlled the seminary. He moved that the convention appoint a committee to report on whether the convention had any control over the seminary's faculty and teachings.[41]

B. H. Carroll, a Landmark trustee and the most influential leader of Texas Baptists, read the committee's report to the convention. It reported that the convention had no legal right to remove any professor or trustee, but that it had the right to nominate at least three persons for each vacancy on the seminary's board of trustees, one of whom the trustees must elect. The convention in fact had exercised this right only once. The committee concluded, however, that the denomination exercised a moral control that was even greater than its legal control: "So broad and deep and far-reaching are these moral and denominational relations, that we regard them as fundamental and the well-being of the seminary dependent on them."[42] This was the deeper issue that the Whitsitt controversy tested. Most Southern Baptists believed that the seminary had a moral obligation to respond to the denomination's control. Whitsitt and his most ardent supporters resisted such control and argued that the seminary needed scholarly freedom rather than denominational control.

Whitsitt's supporters succeeded in preventing the state conventions of Georgia, South Carolina, and Tennessee from addressing the issue.[43] His

40. J. O. Rust to William H. Whitsitt, 22 June 1896, box 1, William H. Whitsitt Papers, LVA.

41. Southern Baptist Convention, *Minutes*, 1896, 18.

42. Southern Baptist Convention, *Minutes*, 1896, 29.

43. Rosalie Beck, "The Whitsitt Controversy: A Denomination in Crisis," Ph.D. dissertation, Baylor University, 1984, 181–186.

supporters failed, however, in the state convention meetings in Louisiana, Texas, and Arkansas. The Louisiana Baptist Convention passed resolutions asserting their dissent from Whitsitt's views. Arkansas Baptists passed the strongest anti-Whitsitt resolution of any state convention in 1896: "While we love the seminary, we not only deplore but repudiate" Whitsitt's views. The only consolation for Whitsitt and his friends was that the convention expressed its continued general support of the seminary. That changed the following year.[44]

The response of the Texas convention was critically important, since Texas Baptists were predominantly Landmarkers, and since the convention was so large and influential in the Southwest. Delegates at the 1896 convention were preoccupied with their own distressing controversy regarding Samuel Hayden's accusations against convention leaders. But delegates were also distressed by Whitsitt's statements and took up the matter. A delegate introduced resolutions critical of Whitsitt, but he withdrew them after B. H. Carroll said that he feared the damage to the seminary and after seminary professor H. H. Harris asked them to wait until they had time to consider all the evidence. Carroll then introduced and the convention adopted a resolution calling for trustee action. It characterized Whitsitt's statements as "offensive and unjust to our people," and as "at variance with the generally accepted history." It placed proper "jurisdiction over the case" with the seminary trustees and asked them to investigate the matter carefully and to issue a "clear cut deliverance on the merits of the whole case" at the 1897 meeting of the Southern Baptist Convention in Wilmington, North Carolina.[45]

When the General Association of Baptists in Kentucky met in June 1896 in Bowling Green, Whitsitt's opponents proved less patient than those in other states. Before the meeting, Eaton, John T. Christian, and J. H. Spencer kept the columns of the Western Recorder filled with anti-Whitsitt copy. Pressure was building for a resolution. Whitsitt's opponents and supporters had urged attendance in support of their cause. Christian introduced resolutions objecting to Whitsitt's article in Johnson's Cyclopaedia as unproven and as "an injustice to our denomination." Two messengers argued for adopting the resolutions. One spoke against them because "the evidence was not all in hand." Then Whitsitt rose to speak in his own defense. He marshaled his historical evidence. The

44. Beck, "The Whitsitt Controversy," 187–190.

45. Unattributed, "The Houston Convention," *Texas Baptist and Herald*, 15 Oct. 1896, 8. See also Beck, "The Whitsitt Controversy," 187–190. A Whitsitt supporter suggested that the convention passed the resolution only because most delegates had gone home, but given Carroll's influence, it probably would have passed in any case (W. S. Splawn to William H. Whitsitt, 24 Oct. 1896, box 2, William H. Whitsitt Papers, LVA).

partisan assessment of the *Bowling Green Courier* may have exaggerated but captured the effect of Whitsitt's speech on many delegates: "Whitsitt's presentation of the case was overwhelmingly strong and seemed impossible to escape.... A more complete vindication of position assumed has rarely been heard, and its unanswerableness was clearly evinced in the withdrawal of the resolutions by their author so soon as the mists of tradition were cleared away by the unanswerable arguments offered by the fruits of learned and honest research."[46]

The delegates were nevertheless nearly evenly divided. The convention initially voted in favor of the resolutions by a slender majority. A motion to reconsider the adoption of the resolutions passed, however, indicating that some who initially voted in favor of the resolutions now opposed them. Apparently Whitsitt's speech made an impression. Christian then withdrew his resolutions. On the motion of Christian the convention, however, expunged the whole matter from the minutes.[47] Defeating Christian's resolutions was an important victory for Whitsitt and his supporters, though expunging the whole affair from the minutes left them with no record of it. Whitsitt's supporters interpreted the affair as an important victory and spread the news of Whitsitt's triumph at Bowling Green. He had overcome Eaton and Christian in open battle. Robertson said that it was a "signal triumph" and "the beginning of the end" of the conflict.[48] A. J. S. Thomas, editor of South Carolina's *Baptist Courier*, encouraged Whitsitt that "we feel sure victory is yours."[49]

The battle in the local associations was more difficult. In Landmark areas, many associations passed resolutions more or less critical of Whitsitt. The Cisco Baptist Association in Texas, for example, resolved that Whitsitt either retract his views or resign, and called on trustees to see to it.[50] Associations throughout Texas, Arkansas, Kentucky, and elsewhere followed suit. In other areas, by careful planning pro-Whitsitt pastors kept anti-Whitsitt resolutions out. The

46. Unattributed, "Dr. Whitsitt's Teachings," *Bowling Green Courier*, 26 June 1896.

47. William H. Whitsitt, note on back of leaf 1, in E. S. Alderman to Whitsitt, 11 June 1896, box 1, William H. Whitsitt Papers, LVA. For the full text of the resolution and the account of the debate, see "The General Association," *Western Recorder*, 25 June 1896, 4. The association's clerk was careful to expunge every part of the matter—no evidence of it remains in the minutes (see General Association of Baptists in Kentucky, *Minutes*, 1896, 10–11).

48. Archibald T. Robertson to William H. Whitsitt, 2 July 1896, box 1, William H. Whitsitt Papers, LVA.

49. A. J. S. Thomas to William H. Whitsitt, 2 July 1896, box 1, William H. Whitsitt Papers, LVA.

50. Cisco Baptist Association, *Minutes*, 1896.

strategy, for example, succeeded well in most Alabama associations in 1896.[51] But the critical association was Louisville's Long Run Baptist Association.

When the Long Run association met in early September 1896, men on both sides of the question came prepared for another battle like that in the state convention three months earlier. The church and galleries were packed with delegates and spectators. The anti-Whitsitt forces knew that it would be difficult to pass resolutions against Whitsitt directly. Their major strategy seems to have been to lock up debate on any pro-Whitsitt resolutions by giving many long speeches to win a motion to lay the matter on the table indefinitely. Whitsitt's opponents could then say truly that Whitsitt's own association refused to commend him. Initially the scheme worked even better than planned. A Whitsitt supporter moved the approval of a resolution expressing broadly their affection for Whitsitt and their confidence in him. Whitsitt's opponents replied that since so many leading men came prepared with long speeches to fight the issue, the resolutions should be laid on the table indefinitely. For the sake of peace, they said, the association should not take any action regarding Whitsitt. They persuaded the body first to table the resolution and then to expunge the whole matter from the minutes. This turn of events was better than silence, for now Whitsitt's opponents could say that the association expunged from its records all efforts to commend Whitsitt.[52]

Some of Whitsitt's supporters recognized that they had been outmaneuvered and that something needed to be done before the meeting adjourned. If the association remained silent and refused to rebut the accusations against Whitsitt, it would give credibility to the charges, especially since the charges found their chief support in the pages of Louisville's *Western Recorder*, edited by Whitsitt's longtime pastor T. T. Eaton. And now Whitsitt's association was going to make no answer. It was too much to bear. An outraged John R. Sampey demanded the floor, jumped "over the pulpit," and delivered an impassioned speech in defense of Whitsitt and against expunging the record, with wit and backbone rebuffing all efforts from the floor to force his silence.[53]

He argued that it was time for the association to face the Whitsitt matter squarely. Everyone knew that "there are people who don't want him to be

51. B. D. Gray to William H. Whitsitt, 24 Oct. 1896, box 2, William H. Whitsitt Papers, LVA.

52. For descriptions of the association meeting, see Carter Helm Jones, "Notes on the Whitsitt Controversy," news clipping, box 7, Robertson Papers.

53. Sampey acknowledged the following day that it was improper for him to "jump over the pulpit," make the "wild gestures" he did, and "get as mad as I was yesterday." John R. Sampey, quoted in Transcript of Long Run Baptist Association meeting, 3 Sept. 1896, 33–34, box 3, Thomas T. Eaton Papers.

John R. Sampey

president of the seminary." Eaton and others had attacked Whitsitt in the *Western Recorder*, and those articles could not be expunged from the record. Therefore, the association was bound by honor to take a stand: "The time has come for us to run up our flag and fight under it." If it expunged the whole matter, it would appear too timid to take a stand, and the effect would be to "have this man sacrificed simply for the sake of some brethren that don't want to be in the row. But, I tell you, Mr. Moderator, we want separation in some things. We want everybody to stand out and fight open and above board. There is no use in saying 'Peace' when there is no peace." Whitsitt stood accused before the denomination, and the association ought to speak in Whitsitt's defense.

Sampey argued that peace could not come at the cost of Whitsitt's resignation, because a fundamental principle was at stake: "After careful study and patient research Dr. Whitsitt has reached certain conclusions on a historical matter, and he has expressed them. . . . I say Dr. Whitsitt has a right to speak on this subject. . . . He has explained it, he is not going to take it back, because it is for principle. That is the principle that our fathers went to the stake for.... Let us all stand for freedom of research and freedom of speech."[54]

When the association met the following day, Kerfoot introduced resolutions that were designed to affirm Whitsitt without inflaming his opponents unduly. The resolutions avoided the historical question and dealt only with Whitsitt's character and the seminary's soundness.

The majority called for a rising vote. It would be easier to note who voted against the resolutions, who would mark themselves as Whitsitt's firm enemies. The resolutions passed with only two persons standing against them.[55]

A QUESTION IN BAPTIST HISTORY

When Whitsitt's reply, a little book called *A Question in Baptist History*, appeared in September 1896, the controversy entered a new phase. His most earnest supporters devoured the book and rejoiced at the power of his arguments.[56] Others who had been skeptical of his claims were convinced by the arguments.[57] But Whitsitt's Landmark opponents found the book unconvincing, and they proceeded to write article after article seeking to prove that Whitsitt misconstrued some evidence and overlooked other evidence. His conclusions, they argued, were implausible.

Historians offered a mixed assessment of Whitsitt's work. They agreed with many of its conclusions but thought them too broad and too confident. Albert H. Newman of McMaster University in Toronto, for example, criticized Whitsitt for shamelessly promoting his "discovery" that English Baptists began immersive baptism in 1641, when other historians taught and published this opinion before Whitsitt's research in 1880. Newman regretted that Whitsitt took such an "exaggerated view of the importance of his contributions to Baptist history." As to Whitsitt's contention that English Baptists first practiced immersion in 1641, Newman held that this was probably correct. But he

---

54. John R. Sampey, quoted in Transcript of Long Run Baptist Association meeting, 2 Sept. 1896, 9, 11, 13, 15–17, box 3, Thomas T. Eaton Papers.

55. Transcript of Long Run Baptist Association meeting, 3 Sept. 1896, 33, box 3, Thomas T. Eaton Papers.

56. Ernest Cook to William H. Whitsitt, 19 Sept. 1896, box 1, William H. Whitsitt Papers, LVA; S. M. Provence to William H. Whitsitt, 21 Sept. 1896, ibid.

57. H. H. Hibbs to William H. Whitsitt, 24 Sept. 1896, box 1, William H. Whitsitt Papers, LVA; Issac J. Van Ness to William H. Whitsitt, 25 Sept. 1896, ibid.; Fred Hale to William H. Whitsitt, 26 Sept. 1896, ibid.; G. A. Lofton to William H. Whitsitt, 27 Sept. 1896, ibid.

felt that Whitsitt discounted several important facts. First, immersion was far more prevalent among European Anabaptists than Whitsitt admitted. Second, Leonard Busher, apparently an English Baptist living in Holland, wrote in 1614 that baptism meant being "dipped." Third, Roger Williams's 1639 baptism was described by a contemporary, William Coddington, as the practice of "being plunged into the water." Fourth, if Williams was not immersed, surely there should be evidence that colonial Baptist churches changed their practice from pouring to immersion.[58] Newman felt that Whitsitt's opponents adduced insufficient evidence to establish a pre-1641 date, but much of Whitsitt's evidence was insufficient also. He thought Whitsitt's argument stood entirely on what was known as the Kiffin manuscript, the reliability of which was impossible to ascertain.[59] Henry C. Vedder of Crozer Theological Seminary offered a similar assessment with his own set of qualifications.[60]

Methodists and Presbyterians understood Whitsitt to credit the validity of sprinkling and pouring as proper baptisms. The *Arkansas Methodist*, for example, ran advertisements for Whitsitt's *Question in Baptist History* and urged its readers to learn from "Baptist authority that the Baptists once practiced sprinkling."[61] Tennessee Landmark pastor J. T. Oakley may have exaggerated, but he represented that "every Methodist and Presbyterian in this county, most, have Whitsitt's book and how they crow."[62] A South Carolina Baptist reported that a Methodist preacher near Spartanburg was quoting Whitsitt's writings to prove that Baptists did not immerse in their early history.[63] And when Baptists read Whitsitt's views, they had to agree that their pedobaptist neighbors understood him correctly. A South Carolina pastor wrote Whitsitt that "both Methodists and Baptists in this section...hold that you teach sprinkling as the primitive form and immersion an after thought."[64] L. O. Dawson told Whitsitt

58. Albert H. Newman, "A Question in Baptist History," *Independent*, 8 Oct. 1896, 17–18.

59. Albert H. Newman to William H. Whitsitt, 23 Nov. 1896, box 2, William H. Whitsitt Papers, LVA.

60. Henry C. Vedder to Thomas T. Eaton, 21 Nov. 1896, box 1, Thomas T. Eaton Papers; Vedder to Whitsitt, 2 Jan. [1897], box 2, William H. Whitsitt Papers, LVA. The letter is dated 2 Jan. 1896, but internal references make clear that it is 1897.

61. Newspaper clipping, in [William B. Caldwell] to William H. Whitsitt, ca. Oct. 1896, box 1, William H. Whitsitt Papers, LVA.

62. J. T. Oakley William O. Carver, 8 Feb. 1897, box 4, William Owen Carver Collection, SBHLA.

63. J. A. Bell to William H. Whitsitt, 16 Mar. 1897, box 2, William H. Whitsitt Papers, LVA.

64. G. M. Davis to William H. Whitsitt, 24 June 1896, box 1, William H. Whitsitt Papers, LVA.

that Texas Baptists were "greatly disturbed over your historical teachings," and "pedobaptists" there were using Whitsitt's arguments against Baptist views.[65]

J. D. Hufham, a seminary trustee from North Carolina, represented well the non-Landmark opposition to Whitsitt. He told Robertson that he had not the "slightest leaning of inclination or sympathy" toward Landmarkers, but after discussing the matter with Hatcher during a week as roommates, he still could not support Whitsitt. "Dr. Whitsitt is unfit to be at the head of the seminary. By his own acknowledgment he wrote editorially for a pedobaptist journal, wrote 'as a Pedobaptist' and 'from a Pedobaptist stand-point,' antagonizing opinions which are held by very many Southern Baptists. It was...dishonorable to the last degree. All the water of the ocean can not wash out the shame of it. He calls it a mistake; it was a dishonor."[66]

"HOLY GROUND AT WILMINGTON"

Whitsitt's foes were committed to placing the issue before the Southern Baptist Convention when it met in Wilmington, North Carolina, in May 1897. Their prospects of success seemed good. Many Southern Baptists were unhappy with Whitsitt's deliverances and wanted him to retract them or to resign. In the Southwest the vast majority felt this way. B. H. Carroll surveyed the situation in September 1896: "Texas is practically a unit against Dr. Whitsitt's views and the feeling is too deep for dispassionate judgment. I do not believe that any one less wonderful than an angel from heaven could carry any association in Texas in favor of the *Independent* editorials and the encyclopedia article, with or without explanations. It is a great mistake that only scholars and experts are interested in these matters."[67]

J. B. Riddle, a pastor in Waxahachie, Texas, explained the feelings in his association: "Until your statements were cleared up they would never urge another young man to attend our seminary or send it another dollar....You may not expect much more men or money from our section until you explain your statements."[68] Trustees, especially those west of the Appalachians, received many such letters from concerned pastors. They sought to register their "solemn

65. L. O. Dawson to William H. Whitsitt, 30 June 1896, box 1, William H. Whitsitt Papers, LVA.

66. J. D. Hufham to Archibald T. Robertson, ca. 1897, box 6, Robertson Papers.

67. Benajah H. Carroll to Thomas T. Eaton, 11 Sept. 1896, box 1, Thomas T. Eaton Papers.

68. J. B. Riddle to William H. Whitsitt, 6 June 1896, box 1, William H. Whitsitt Papers, LVA.

protest against the position of Dr. Whitsitt and against his being retained as president of the seminary, unless he retracts and apologizes in such a manner as to prove satisfactory."[69]

Non-Landmarkers were initially disposed to support Whitsitt against the bullying of a few Landmark editors. Isaac J. Van Ness, editor of Georgia's *Christian Index*, for example, told Robertson that "Eaton should be dethroned" and that "it was a fight to the death" that should "be pressed and with vigor."[70] But as the controversy progressed, many of them felt that Whitsitt had blundered seriously in his articles and his explanations. Many in Georgia and in North and South Carolina came to feel that for the good of the seminary, Whitsitt should resign.

Eaton studiously avoided direct criticism of Whitsitt, though he stated his disagreement with Whitsitt's conclusions and was clearly troubled by them. He managed somehow to convey disapproval more by what he did not say than by what he did. He was also committed to denominational populism and wanted to make certain that rank-and-file Baptists had their say in the matter. Most of what they said was critical of Whitsitt. The trustees were going to meet in Wilmington just prior to the Southern Baptist Convention, and Eaton wanted to know how Kentucky Baptists generally viewed the Whitsitt matter. He wrote a letter to all moderators of the Baptist associations in Kentucky, asking their opinion regarding what the trustees should do and regarding the general sentiment among the churches in their association.[71] Almost every moderator indicated that Whitsitt should resign and that the pastors in the association unanimously shared the sentiment.[72] Eaton then began to call openly for Whitsitt's resignation.

As the Wilmington convention approached, Virginia trustee William E. Hatcher assumed leadership of the pro-Whitsitt forces and directed their campaign strategy. He made A. T. Robertson his party whip. Robertson proved an astute and able operative, and Hatcher consulted him frequently regarding conditions and strategy, and gave him directions for executing their plans.

Hatcher believed that the key to success at the Wilmington trustee meeting was the Texas delegation. He proposed that they could co-opt B. H. Carroll by urging him to lead the convention to a conciliatory position. "Let us capture

---

69. J. R. Miller to Benajah H. Carroll, 12 June 1896, Whitsitt Controversy Correspondence, B. H. Carroll Collection, SWBTS.

70. Isaac J. Van Ness to Archibald T. Robertson, 28 Aug. 1896, box 1, Robertson Papers.

71. Thomas T. Eaton, circular letter to association moderators, 19 Mar. 1897, box 1, Thomas T. Eaton Papers.

72. [T. T. Eaton], "The Situation," *Western Recorder*, 6 May 1897, 3.

Dr. Carroll. And in this way, surely we can carry things in our way in trustee meeting. Now let us get Haralson, Levering, Northen, Kerfoot, and myself in a private way to persuade him to act as pacificator in convention. If the thing is brought into convention, let Carroll offer a substitute something like this: 'Resolved that the trustees, having made a deliverance on the Whitsitt matter the convention accept their action as final and cordially urges the brethren throughout the South to rally to the support of the institution, etc. etc.'"[73] With Carroll's help they could win the contest both in the trustee meeting and in the convention.

Hatcher also wanted to keep the convention from having a debate on the Whitsitt matter. Floor debates were risky affairs, and the outcome could not be guaranteed. Hatcher met and wrote the leading Baptists in each state, feeling out where various men stood and seeking to persuade them of the inadvisability of introducing resolutions. He wanted them to use their influence with other preachers. Hatcher's main argument was that the convention was not the proper place to deal with charges against Whitsitt. Such matters belonged constitutionally to the trustees—the convention had no direct responsibility in such cases. But Hatcher and the pro-Whitsitt men also gained support for Whitsitt by arguing effectively that Whitsitt was preferable to Eaton. Eaton had great respect and influence in the denomination, especially among Landmarkers, but many leaders thought him too ambitious and were wary of him. If the denomination forced Whitsitt out, many would see it as Eaton's victory, and he would gain considerable power in managing denominational affairs, especially in regard to the seminary. Leaders who disagreed with Whitsitt's views and actions nevertheless supported him in the controversy lest Eaton gain additional influence.[74] Hatcher urged Whitsitt supporters to make sure all pro-Whitsitt men should make certain their attendance at the convention, and he sought to influence the appointment of delegates.

Trustees met at Wilmington before the meeting of the Southern Baptist Convention and took up the "Whitsitt matter." B. H. Carroll thought that the board should respond to the petitions of associations in Texas and Kentucky requesting trustees to investigate the *Independent* editorials, the encyclopedia article, and whether Whitsitt advised a Baptist wife to join the church of her pedobaptist husband. After these petitions were read to the board, Carroll reported that the Baptist General Convention of Texas petitioned them also,

73. William E. Hatcher to Archibald T. Robertson, 29 Apr. [1897? 1898?], box 6, Robertson Papers.

74. See, e.g., J. W. Bailey to Archibald T. Robertson, 21 Apr. 1897, box 1, Robertson Papers; William E. Hatcher to Archibald T. Robertson, 12 Apr. 1898, box 1, Robertson Papers.

"earnestly requesting the trustees to consider the case, pronounce upon it clearly and report their actions to the convention." Carroll then moved resolutions that the board consider these matters of concern, "pronounce upon them clearly," and report their finding to the convention.[75] Carroll had resisted Hatcher's efforts to co-opt him.

Hatcher's trustee caucus was prepared for this. William J. Northen, past governor of Georgia, immediately offered a set of substitute resolutions declaring the whole affair a matter of academic freedom. They discussed Northen's substitute until 1:00 A.M. Eaton, Warder, Kilpatrick, Hatcher, and Hudson all made speeches. B. H. Carroll also spoke, Eaton reported, and gave a "masterly speech." Carroll argued that many associations and conventions had refused to pass resolutions or pronounce censure against Whitsitt because they trusted the trustees to consider the matter. For the board to refuse to consider the matter was to break faith with them.[76] The board adopted Northen's resolutions.

The first resolution affirmed the trustees' commitment to enforce orthodoxy. They pledged their "adherence to the fundamental articles adopted at the time when the seminary was established" and their "steadfast purpose" always to require the seminary's professors to uphold "the fundamental laws and scriptural doctrines embodied in these articles." The second resolution proved most problematic. It affirmed the faculty's freedom of research by rejecting trustee authority to take notice of any teachings beyond the seminary's Abstract of Principles and denominational consensus: "We can not undertake to sit in judgment on questions in Baptist history which do not imperil any of those principles concerning which all Baptists are agreed, but concerning which serious, conscientious and scholarly students are not agreed. We can however, confidently leave to continued research and discussion the satisfactory solution of these questions." The third and fourth resolutions asked professors to use their freedom with sensitivity to denominational concerns—to "exercise the greatest discretion of utterance"—and assured Southern Baptists that they could "safely trust us" to keep the seminary sound.[77]

Trustees wanted to hear from Whitsitt and asked him to come before the board the next morning. He read a prepared statement in which he denied that

75. Benajah H. Carroll, "The Whitsitt Case at Wilmington," *Baptist Standard*, 20 May 1897, 1.

76. Thomas T. Eaton to Alice [Eaton], 7 May 1897, box 1, Thomas T. Eaton Papers; Carroll, "The Whitsitt Case at Wilmington," 1.

77. Minutes of the Board of Trustees, Southern Baptist Theological Seminary, 6 May 1897. See also unattributed, "Great Ovation to Dr. Whitsitt in the Southern Baptist Convention Yesterday," *Louisville Dispatch*, 8 May 1897.

he taught that the family was superior to the church and apologized for the objectionable articles:

> In regard to the articles written as editorials for the *Independent*, I have long felt that it was a mistake....What I wrote was from a pedobaptist standpoint, with a view of stimulating historical research, with no thought that it would injure the Baptists and with no intention to disparage Baptist doctrines or practices. The article in *Johnson's Encyclopedia* has probably passed beyond my control, but it will be pleasing to me if I can honorably procure the elimination from it of whatever is offensive to any of my brethren. On the historical questions involved in the discussion I find myself out of agreement with some honored historians, but what I have written is the outcome of patient and honest research, and I can not do otherwise than to reaffirm my convictions and maintain my position.[78]

The statement satisfied the board, even Eaton.[79]

The board then read its resolutions and Whitsitt's statement to the delegates of the Southern Baptist Convention. The convention did not need to take any action, and none was taken. But some delegates drew the whole convention into singing "Amazing Grace" while some of Whitsitt's supporters surrounded him on the floor and offered him congratulatory handshakes.[80] Hatcher felt that the result was "most glorious."[81] Dargan called it a "glorious victory" for the seminary.[82] Whitsitt basked in his victory: "The convention gave me such an ovation on Friday afternoon the seventh of May as was never previously bestowed on one of its members."[83]

Wilmington was Whitsitt's great triumph, and he returned to Louisville as the conquering hero. He believed that he had won a contest of epic proportions. He told the student body: "We have just passed in safety the most threatening crisis in the history of Southern Baptists....We were delivered from our peril

78. Minutes of the Board of Trustees, Southern Baptist Theological Seminary, 7 May 1897. William Hatcher drafted the statement, and Whitsitt revised it.

79. Thomas T. Eaton to Alice [Eaton], 7 May 1897, box 1, Thomas T. Eaton Papers.

80. Carroll, "The Whitsitt Case at Wilmington," , 1; Thomas T. Eaton to Alice [Eaton], 7 May 1897, box 1, Thomas T. Eaton Papers.

81. William E. Hatcher to Archibald T. Robertson, 7 May 1897, box 1, Robertson Papers.

82. Edwin C. Dargan to Archibald T. Robertson, 7 May 1897, box 1, Robertson Papers.

83. William H. Whitsitt, Diary, quoted in R. Inman Johnson, "From the Diaries of William H. Whitsitt," 14, R. Inman Johnson 1982–84 folder, McCall Papers. See also unattributed, "Peacefully the Whitsitt Case Was Ended Yesterday," *Louisville Courier-Journal*, 8 May 1897.

at Wilmington through fervent and faithful prayers of the people of God." For delivering Whitsitt, Southern Baptists deserved highest praise. Their vindication of him showed their "broad sense and sound wisdom," and the "dignity and elevation of their character." The occasion was redolent of "the noblest passages in our Baptist history. We all felt that we stood on holy ground at Wilmington." It was his greatest victory: "The experiences at Wilmington were more than I could ask or think. The action of the board of trustees was what I had hoped for, but the scene in the convention on Friday afternoon was beyond all my dreams. It constituted the most memorable incident in my life." [84]

Hatcher and his allies believed that the overwhelming show of affection for Whitsitt would convince his opponents that further opposition was futile. But the smug claims of victory, together with Whitsitt's clumsy explanation, not only inflamed Whitsitt's opponents but turned many supporters against him. Claims of victory, B. H. Carroll afterward explained, were specious: "A trial was denied and yet an acquittal claimed. The convention was asked to take no action and took none, and yet an endorsement was claimed." [85] It would take more than a hymn and handshakes to settle the matter. Whitsitt's admission that he had written from a "pedobaptist standpoint" was an indefensible position for a Baptist theologian. As John R. Sampey pointed out decades later, "It sealed his doom." [86] Thirteen months after his Wilmington victory, Whitsitt resigned.

POPULAR AUTHORITY AND DENOMINATIONAL TRUST

In the weeks following the Wilmington convention, Hatcher was confident that the pro-Whitsitt forces had won a great victory and could make it last. He counseled silence. But the Wilmington victory did not last. It could not. The board's resolutions were broad enough to be acceptable to most trustees, but they did not address the main issue in the controversy. The point at which they came closest to the controversy was in declaring the board unfit to decide matters of history. This is the point that agitated B. H. Carroll to reopen the whole matter. Carroll insisted that the trustees were competent to judge matters beyond the Abstract of Principles and denominational consensus, and that they were responsible to the churches and to donors to govern the institution in all important matters.

84. William H. Whitsitt, "Dr. Whitsitt's Address to the Students," Correspondence—Whitsitt Controversy, B. H. Carroll Collection, SWBTS.

85. Benajah H. Carroll, "The Real Issue in the Whitsitt Case," *Baptist Standard*, 5 Aug. 1897.

86. John R. Sampey to Reuben E. Alley, 22 Dec. 1941, box 13, Sampey Papers.

Carroll had stayed out of the controversy before the Wilmington meeting because he assumed that the trustees would take up the matter, and as a trustee, he did not want to be a disputant. But now he reignited the newspaper controversy. In an article entitled "The Whitsitt Case at Wilmington," he argued that the board committed a grave error when it denied jurisdiction over the matter at controversy. Interpretation and representation of historical fact were critically important to both secular and religious history. Many errors of the new historical criticism arose from questions that were purely historical. If the trustees rejected any jurisdiction over historical questions, it might be impossible to dislodge a professor who adopted the historical criticism. As Carroll saw it, when the trustees refused to address the Whitsitt matter, they effectively remanded the case to the churches, associations, and conventions that had initially expected them to take up the case. In "Back to the Realm of Discussion," Carroll argued that if trustees granted such wide freedom of research that they could not cure theological maladies that arose there, then the seminary was without protection from error and the churches were mistaken in thinking that it was their seminary.[87]

The cure, Carroll said, was Whitsitt's resignation. The sum of Whitsitt's actions "disqualified him, in my judgment, for his position."[88] Whitsitt's retractions and apologies before the board may have resolved the most serious concerns about his character and beliefs, but the denomination's loss of trust was too deep to be repaired by the explanations in his *Question in Baptist History*. "The book alone," Carroll said, "would never have produced the shock and created the offense [that was] naturally produced by the other documents."[89]

Whitsitt had inflicted great injury on the seminary and should be held accountable. Carroll reflected, "When Dr. Broadus died, so very short a time ago, the seminary was in the hearts of all our people. At least there was no open opposition. Its faculty were welcomed at every state convention in the South. In two years' time under the present executive, and by his own course, what a sad change! The wisdom of thirty years reared an imposing structure, a veritable lighthouse, and two years of unwisdom threatens it with overthrow."[90]

---

87. Benajah H. Carroll, "The Whitsitt Case at Wilmington," *Baptist Standard*, 27 May 1897, 1, 5; Carroll, "Back to the Realm of Discussion," *Baptist Standard*, 27 May 1897, 12–13. See also Carroll, "A Word in Passing on the Seminary Issue," *Baptist Standard*, 9 Sept. 1897.

88. Benajah H. Carroll, "The Whitsitt Case at Wilmington," *Baptist Standard*, 20 May 1897, 5.

89. Carroll, "The Whitsitt Case at Wilmington," 5.

90. Carroll, "The Real Issue in the Whitsitt Case."

Carroll was not sure that it was possible to restore the denomination's confidence in the seminary, but he was not willing to give up. Whitsitt's resignation would be a necessary part of the solution, and so he was "for joining the issue in tenderness, courtesy, and love, but also with firmness and pluck." He was "not prepared to surrender the work of Boyce, Broadus and Manly without a struggle."[91]

If history had been the only issue, Whitsitt could have survived. Landmarkers, who were most disturbed by Whitsitt's historical conclusions, already supported the seminary weakly, with a wariness that caused them to withdraw support with every rumor of unsoundness. The seminary's strongest and most reliable support came from non-Landmarkers scattered throughout the South, but concentrated in the states of the Atlantic seaboard. Whitsitt's failure to retain the confidence of non-Landmarkers sealed his fate. Some were disturbed by the historical arguments, but they could get over that well enough. What they could not get over was the insensitivity, and above all, the apparent dishonesty, with which Whitsitt published his discovery in 1880. J. B. Miller, who had accompanied Boyce throughout Kentucky to assist him in raising the endowment, complained that he lacked confidence in Whitsitt's fitness to lead the seminary: "If Dr. Whitsitt wrote those editorials for the *Independent*, . . . I cannot see how he can be regarded as a just man, much less a Christian and a Baptist. . . . You see very plainly how very weak is the defense of Dr. Whitsitt. So far as I have seen neither he nor his friends have attempted any defense of the fatal blunder, not to say grave crime, in writing those articles in the *Independent*. . . . The time for action has come. Warmly as I love the seminary, much as I have done for it, in helping Dr. Boyce raise the $300,000 in Kentucky, I calmly, deliberately, and emphatically assert it as my decided conviction that the denomination ought not and will not support the seminary, unless Dr. Whitsitt is speedily removed."[92] Whitsitt bungled his opportunity to make amends.

Many other leaders shared Carroll's outlook. Whitsitt's statement at Wilmington spread resentment, and many who supported him before Wilmington changed their minds afterward. T. P. Bell, coeditor of Georgia's *Christian Index*, described the change: "This feeling against Dr. W[hitsitt]'s remaining in the seminary is deeper and more widespread than it was before Wilmington. Quite a number of our best men in Georgia, some of whom have stood squarely for him and will now oppose his being turned out, feel that he

91. Benajah H. Carroll to Coleman, 29 May 1897, Whitsitt Controversy Correspondence, B. H. Carroll Collection, SWBTS.

92. J. B. Miller to Benajah H. Carroll, 3 July 1896, Whitsitt Controversy Correspondence, B. H. Carroll Collection, SWBTS.

ought to resign. The feeling is almost universal that he has blundered fearfully; and that sentence in his statement, that he wrote those *Independent* articles from a pedobaptist standpoint has stuck in the gizzards of many good men." State convention leaders in Alabama, Florida, North Carolina, and Texas reported the same thing. The feeling grew that Whitsitt "had betrayed the Baptists who had honored him. This feeling is strong in the hearts of the common people, especially our plain preachers. They cannot understand how a man could say what Dr. W[hitsitt] has said and can you and I blame them?"[93]

When the associations and state conventions met in late 1897 and early 1898, a large number passed resolutions calling for Whitsitt's resignation. Louisville's Long Run Baptist Association was among them. At the September 1897 meeting fewer than 200 messengers enrolled, but nearly 3,000 visitors gathered to watch the association fight it out. When a pastor presented resolutions urging Whitsitt's removal, the floor erupted in near pandemonium. Whitsitt's supporters demanded the floor in order to oppose the resolutions and rebut the accusations. His opponents shouted, "Question! question!" and succeeded in moving directly to a vote without any debate. Messengers voted 73–36 in favor of Whitsitt's removal.[94] The next day messengers adopted a report suggesting that the seminary had strayed from denominational orthodoxy and the founders' vision, and expressing the "hope that ere long it will come into full harmony with the denomination of the South and that it will do the great work for which the founders designed it."[95] At their state convention meeting, Kentucky Baptists followed Long Run's example. The Arkansas Baptist Convention similarly voted to withdraw all "moral and financial support" of the seminary until Whitsitt departed.[96]

Most state conventions were deeply divided on the question. In Alabama, for example, Whitsitt's supporters could not keep the matter from being introduced, but they prevented the convention from passing a resolution condemning his view. The convention debated the Whitsitt question for more than three hours. A majority of the convention's resolution committee proposed a statement that the whole matter should be left in the care of the seminary trustees. A minority of the committee proposed censuring Whitsitt's actions and calling for his resignation. The convention seemed to favor Whitsitt by about two to one. A majority of the convention finally voted to table the matter.[97]

93. T. P. Bell to Edwin C. Dargan, 30 June 1897, Dargan Papers, SBHLA.

94. Unattributed, "Whitsitt Censured by the Long Run Association," *Louisville Courier-Journal*, 2 Sept. 1897; unattributed, "Ashamed: Details of the Whitsitt Scene Stricken Out," *Louisville Courier-Journal*, 3 Sept. 1897.

95. Unattributed, "Ashamed."

96. Unattributed, "Arkansas Convention," *Baptist Argus*, 25 Nov. 1897, 77.

97. L. O. Dawson, "The Alabama Convention," *Baptist Argus*, 23 Dec. 1897, 140.

Edwin C. Dargan

After Wilmington the faculty divided also. The faculty's opinion was critically important in shaping trustee opinions. Robertson and Sampey were the faculty leaders in the effort, and initially the faculty had defended Whitsitt as a unit. After the publication of Whitsitt's *Question* in 1896, for example, they drafted and signed a statement in his support.[98] Sampey rather notoriously took up Whitsitt's cause in the Long Run Baptist Association. Robertson was the most active worker in Whitsitt's forces as Hatcher's able lieutenant in the campaign. Dargan's support was qualified. He defended Whitsitt in general, but he thought that his intransigence was unhelpful. He apparently argued for greater toleration of the Landmark position and greater charity toward Landmarkers. But Whitsitt would not hear of it. Like Rehoboam rejecting Ahithophel's counsel, he relented not an inch. He later referred to Dargan's spurned counsel: "I don't want any of Dargan's 'toleration' or 'charity.' What I want is the 'faith once delivered to the saints,' and to be rid of these Catholic corruptions that have been brought in unaware." [99] By the summer of 1897, Dargan was convinced

98. Faculty Minutes, Southern Baptist Theological Seminary, 29 Sept. 1896.

99. William H. Whitsitt to Archibald T. Robertson, 27 Aug. 1908, box 2, Robertson Papers.

that Whitsitt should resign and told him so "in the warmest affection and with brotherly candor." [100] Whitsitt disagreed and told Dargan that he would not resign but must "fight it out, believing in God that he was doing his duty." [101]

Dargan and Kerfoot began to wonder whether the seminary could survive with Whitsitt as president. When Robertson saw that Dargan was wavering in July 1897, he tried to steady him. Robertson argued that he supported Whitsitt because the matter involved the very life of the seminary. If it were only about Whitsitt, Robertson said, "I could be willing to see him go for the sake of the seminary." But Whitsitt's resignation, Robertson argued, would enthrone Eaton such that he would then dominate the seminary. He would remake the seminary in the image of recondite Landmarkism and destroy its precious heritage. Robertson and Sampey felt certain that if the trustees dismissed Whitsitt, Eaton would subsequently drive off Robertson and Sampey, who played such a central role in Whitsitt's defense. Robertson wrote, "Eaton would instantly claim it as a triumph and vindication by the denomination of his orthodoxy and that he represents the denomination in his positions. He would then crack his whip over us with redoubled force." Eaton would overturn the seminary's ideal of "enlightened theological education" as Boyce and Broadus had established it. The seminary's truest friends and "real constituency both as to money and students" would "desert us forever." If Whitsitt "goes, as things are now, does not the seminary as we know it and treasure it, go too?" By saving Whitsitt, "we preserve the seminary in its course to fulfill its destiny." [102]

Dargan, however, was unsure. He told Robertson that he disagreed with him on many points in the matter. He was receiving mail from many loyal friends of the seminary who counseled Whitsitt's resignation. The way out was not clear, but the fact was that "the friends of the seminary were divided, some believing that we ought to make a fight, even at the peril and almost certain prospect of disruption in the denomination; others believing just as firmly that sacrifices ought to be made for the sake of denominational unity." [103] Dargan's flagging support helped bring a resolution to the controversy but opened a rift in the faculty that never completely healed.

By August Kerfoot shared Dargan's doubts. He also began to suggest to some of his friends that if Whitsitt should resign, he would be willing to serve as president himself. J. W. Bailey reported that "it has come to my knowledge that

---

100. Edwin C. Dargan to Archibald T. Robertson, 29 July 1898, box 1, Robertson Papers.
101. Edwin C. Dargan to Mrs. P. [Josephine E. Peck], 31 Jan. 1899, Dargan Papers, SBHLA.
102. Archibald T. Robertson to Edwin C. Dargan, 11 July 1897, Dargan Papers, SBHLA.
103. Edwin C. Dargan to Archibald T. Robertson, 12 July 1897, box 1, Robertson Papers.

Franklin H. Kerfoot

Bro. Kerfoot is quietly 'laying pipes' to succeed Bro. Whitsitt—writing letters."[104] When Robertson and Sampey learned of this, they viewed him as a traitor.

As the May 1898 meeting of the Southern Baptist Convention approached, the support for Whitsitt's resignation gained momentum. William W. Landrum summarized the majority opinion among Georgia Baptists: "Dr. Whitsitt is no leader; he blunders; he has not the holy tact of Boyce or Broadus and is liable to get the denomination into trouble again. His judgment does not equal his scholarship or his piety."[105]

Carroll worked to gather assurance that western Landmark leaders would cease their attacks once Whitsitt resigned. He asked Eaton, "If Dr. Whitsitt resigns, are you willing to join me in calling for peace and cooperation with the seminary?" Eaton replied: "Certainly I am. That certainly would close

104. J. W. Bailey to Benajah H. Carroll, 8 Aug. 1897, Whitsitt Controversy Correspondence, B. H. Carroll Collection, SWBTS.

105. William W. Landrum to Archibald T. Robertson, 16 Sept. 1897, box 1, Robertson Papers.

the 'Whitsitt controversy,' and there would be no further reason for strife."[106] Carroll wrote J. W. Bailey, "giving the strongest assurance" that the fight would stop upon Whitsitt's resignation and "that Eaton agreed with him."[107]

Despite the growing pressure across the South for Whitsitt's resignation, trustees took no action when they met in Louisville in May 1898. After considerable debate, the board adopted Louisville trustee Arthur Peter's resolution refusing to take any action in the matter: "We feel constrained by our convictions of duty to reaffirm our adherence to the action then [in 1897] taken."[108] In their address to Southern Baptists, they explained that "they have found it simply impossible to adopt any course of action which would be satisfactory to all the friends of the seminary."[109] Trustees could not resolve the controversy.

Delegates to the 1898 Southern Baptist Convention likewise discovered no solution and passed no resolutions on the Whitsitt question. Landmark and non-Landmark leaders had no sympathy with the attacks recently published in the *Western Recorder* charging Whitsitt with dishonesty and impugning his character. Few wanted to take any action that might be construed as endorsing Eaton, Christian, or the *Western Recorder*. But more important, they feared the division of the denomination. Had they passed pro-Whitsitt resolutions, the western states might have seceded. Had they passed anti-Whitsitt resolutions, some of the eastern states might have seceded. To preserve the unity of the convention, they kept the matter out the convention's deliberations. This was not an endorsement of Whitsitt. It represented the hope that somehow trustees could resolve the matter or that Whitsitt would take the initiative and resign. If neither occurred, many believed that the convention would divide in 1899.[110]

RESIGNATION

In the weeks following the 1898 meeting of the Southern Baptist Convention, the dissatisfaction with Whitsitt and the seminary grew so great that some of his closest advisers, including Robertson and Sampey, began to recommend

106. Thomas T. Eaton to Benajah H. Carroll, 30 Aug. 1897, Whitsitt Controversy Correspondence, B. H. Carroll Collection, SWBTS.

107. J. W. Bailey to Archibald T. Robertson, 1 Sept. 1897, box 1, Robertson Papers.

108. Minutes, Board of Trustees, Southern Baptist Theological Seminary, May 1898, 232–234, 236.

109. Minutes, Board of Trustees, Southern Baptist Theological Seminary, May 1898, 243.

110. See, e.g., Franklin H. Kerfoot to Benajah H. Carroll, 4 Apr. 1898, Whitsitt Controversy Correspondence, B. H. Carroll Collection, SWBTS; unattributed, "SBC at Norfolk," *Baptist Standard*, 19 May 1898.

his resignation. Whitsitt's aggressive posture in maintaining those positions, and his bumptious handling of the controversy injured the seminary's influence among many churches in the denomination. The farther west, the more pervasive the suspicion of the seminary.

Many denominational leaders favored Whitsitt's resignation because the widespread dissatisfaction with the seminary jeopardized all denominational organizations. When it began to appear that retaining Whitsitt as president would weaken the denomination broadly, they began to counsel his resignation.[111]

I. T. Tichenor, secretary of the Home Mission Board, wanted the controversy to cease, but the only means he could see was for Whitsitt to resign. The longer the controversy continued, the more it harmed the denomination's common enterprises: "I think it has done, and if protracted will continue to do great harm to our mission work, and to every other public interest of the denomination."[112]

By the summer of 1898, B. H. Carroll's outlook represented the prevailing sentiment. He summarized his reasons for opposing Whitsitt:

1) My utter inability to comprehend how one at heart a Baptist could have written the *Independent* editorials or said what he did concerning wife and husband, from any standpoint. And particularly as the lame explanations given were not voluntary or speedy, but tardy and under pressure. (2) My profound conviction that he does not possess the historic mind and hence a misfit in the chair of history. (3) His retention will permanently alienate many thousands from the seminary and strain the bond of Southern Baptist Convention unity. (4) It would blast one of my most cherished hopes, i.e., to see the seminary become the unique representative of orthodoxy and the mighty barrier against the drift southward of northern looseness of doctrine.[113]

Whitsitt was still unmoved. He had "done nothing to deserve" such treatment and would "endeavor to endure it with patience and humility." He would resign, he said, only if Hatcher endorsed it. But Whitsitt did not think Hatcher would do so. Whitsitt's friends in Virginia, South Carolina, and elsewhere did not wish it. Carter H. Jones, pastor of Broadway Baptist Church in Louisville, told

---

111. Isaac J. Van Ness to Archibald T. Robertson, 17 May 1897, box 1, Robertson Papers.

112. I. T. Tichenor to Thomas T. Eaton, 4 Feb. 1898, box 1, Thomas T. Eaton Papers.

113. Benajah H. Carroll to Thomas T. Eaton, 15 Jan. 1898, box 1, Thomas T. Eaton Papers. See also J. H. Kilpatrick to Thomas T. Eaton, 7 Feb. 1898, box 1, Thomas T. Eaton Papers.

Whitsitt that his church and Louisville Baptists firmly supported him. Pastor J. B. Hawthorne was already drafting a pro-Whitsitt report for the Southern Baptist Convention in 1899 that for some reason he believed would gain the favor of 90 percent of Southern Baptists. Hawthorne wrote Whitsitt that resignation would be a "calamity."[114] For Whitsitt's part, he asserted that resignation would mean "total surrender and absolute disgrace."[115]

In early July Robertson and Sampey became convinced that there was no way to save Whitsitt without dividing the Southern Baptist Convention and crippling the seminary. They concluded that Whitsitt should resign. Sampey met with Whitsitt and told him that the faculty believed that he should resign. Whitsitt admitted that "without his faculty solid behind him he is sure to meet defeat." But he wanted some time to consider this development. Despite all Sampey's arguments, Whitsitt could only see it in terms of a matter of a principle on which he could not yield. And Whitsitt thought that the solution was "to divorce the convention and the seminary" entirely. At times he vacillated, however, now hearkening to Hatcher, now to someone else. Robertson and Sampey wrote Hatcher letters in an effort to convince him that resignation was best, and that it should be done soon. Whitsitt had "put himself entirely in Hatcher's hands," and Hatcher preferred to delay consideration of resignation to "repeat the campaigns of former years." But neither Hatcher nor Whitsitt could "understand the changed conditions" that induced so many of Whitsitt's friends to favor resignation. Sampey wrote, "Carter Jones, Hunt, Prestridge, Carver, McGlothlin, Eager—in fact everybody I meet—thinks the time for a resignation is come." Few, however, had the courage to tell him.[116]

Carter Helm Jones, pastor of Broadway Baptist Church, called a meeting with Whitsitt's most loyal supporters, especially the Louisville trustees, and explained to them the situation. Most "strongly opposed" resignation initially but after much discussion changed their minds.[117] Robertson was the chief actor in securing Whitsitt's resignation. He had consolidated support for Whitsitt for the prior two years, and he played the same role in the new campaign for

114. J. B. Hawthorne, quoted in William H. Whitsitt to Archibald T. Robertson, 11 July 1898, box 1, Robertson Papers.

115. William H. Whitsitt to Archibald T. Robertson, 10 July 1898, box 1, Robertson Papers; William H. Whitsitt to Archibald T. Robertson, 11 July 1898, box 1, Robertson Papers.

116. Isaac J. Van Ness to Archibald T. Robertson, ca. 12 July 1898, box 1, Robertson Papers; John R. Sampey to Archibald T. Robertson, 5 July 1898, box 1, Robertson Papers; Sampey to Robertson, 8 July 1898, ibid.; William E. Hatcher to Robertson, 11 July 1898, box 7, ibid.

117. Carter H. Jones to Archibald T. Robertson, 14 July 1898, box 1, Robertson Papers.

resignation. McGlothlin explained it to Dargan: "Dear impulsive, vigorous, earnest Robertson was working as hard for the resignation as he had formerly worked to prevent it. He sent telegrams and letters flying all about and accomplished the matter in short order. Things are very quiet here. Practically everybody, including the students now here and the Nortons, had concluded that it was the only thing to do."[118]

On July 13, 1898, Sampey met with Whitsitt, who began at last to feel the weight of the fact that the faculty, local trustees, and trusted supporters counseled resignation. Sampey "told him he must bear this cross for our sakes, and he consented." Sampey reported to Robertson: "Whitsitt has written out his resignation."[119] The following day, Whitsitt wrote Robertson that "I have sent my resignation to Mr. Levering to take effect at the close of the session in 1899."[120] He would remain in office for eleven more months, since trustees would not ordinarily meet and elect a replacement until May 1899.

Within days Whitsitt reversed himself. He received letters from all over the convention objecting to this resignation and expressing indignation that the faculty should have requested it. Florence Whitsitt expressed their shared opinion that he had been overcome by the faculty's joint recommendation: "Of course he could do nothing when the faculty had become frightened and disheartened. Mr. Whitsitt has been unnecessarily sacrificed."[121] Whitsitt now thought that public opinion was against his resignation, but it was too late: "From the tone of letters that have reached me I am persuaded that I made a mistake in resigning the presidency of the seminary. But that mistake cannot now be remedied."[122] For the rest of his life Whitsitt remained convinced that a great injustice had been imposed upon him in the entire affair, and the faculty's role at the end was as painful as it was unfortunate.[123]

Whitsitt placed most of the blame for the faculty's defection on Kerfoot, as did Whitsitt's closest supporters. Kerfoot had never been a strong supporter of Whitsitt's aggressive strategy in defense of his historical views and tried to maintain neutrality. Kerfoot was the first on the faculty to conclude that Whitsitt should resign. His refusal to join the partisan efforts of his colleagues led to considerable alienation.

118. William J. McGlothlin to Edwin C. Dargan, 15 July 1898, Dargan Papers, SBHLA.

119. John R. Sampey to Archibald T. Robertson, 13 July 1898, box 1, Robertson Papers.

120. William H. Whitsitt to Archibald T. Robertson, 14 July 1898, box 1, Robertson Papers.

121. Florence Whitsitt to Archibald T. Robertson, 18 July 1898, box 1, Robertson Papers.

122. William H. Whitsitt to Archibald T. Robertson, 19 July 1898, box 1, Robertson Papers.

123. See William H. Whitsitt to Archibald T. Robertson, 14 Aug. 1898, Robertson Papers.

Robertson too changed his mind. He wrote a letter to the board of trustees explaining that several denominational leaders had so pressured him to urge Whitsitt to resign that he was misled and capitulated. James Frost told him that denominational sentiment had shifted since the Norfolk meeting of the convention, that most now wanted Whitsitt to resign, and that if he did not do so, the trustees would force him out. Isaac J. Van Ness told him that if Whitsitt did not resign soon, he would begin a crusade in the *Christian Index* to force Whitsitt out. Kerfoot especially influenced him: "Dr. Kerfoot said that the trustees would be glad to see Dr. Whitsitt resign, although they had not wished to expel him. He said that Dr. Whitsitt ought to save his dignity and not be driven out. He represented that prominent trustees who had stood by him wished him to go. He said also that Dr. Sampey and I saw only one side of the situation and were young and rash. He insisted that his conservatism was necessary for the saving of the seminary. He talked at length and I became much distressed."[124] Having repented of his role in securing Whitsitt's resignation, he entered upon a campaign to convince trustees to reject the resignation.[125]

This began a whole new round of conflict. Robertson led the campaign this time rather than Hatcher. He enlisted Samuel C. Mitchell, professor at Richmond College and son-in-law of John A. Broadus, to promote the effort. Mitchell published a fifteen-page pamphlet urging trustees to reject the resignation in order to sustain the fundamental principles of academic freedom and Baptist independence. This new campaign brought new dangers. It convinced Whitsitt's opponents that the resignation had been merely a political trick to forestall further attacks. Then the convention would appear to be at peace, and trustees would feel free to reject the resignation. If trustees rejected it, the controversy would have erupted with unprecedented force and probably would have divided the convention.[126]

The new campaign introduced deep division in the faculty. Kerfoot became a pariah to the pro-Whitsitt faction of Robertson, Sampey, and McGlothlin. Dargan fared hardly better. He remained convinced that it would be best for Whitsitt, the seminary, and the denomination for the trustees to accept Whitsitt's resignation. His position alienated him somewhat from the rest of

124. Archibald T. Robertson to Gentlemen of the Board of Trustees, ca. May 1899, box 6, Robertson Papers.

125. See, e.g., S. C. Mitchell to Archibald T. Robertson, 12 Jan.1899, box 1, Robertson Papers; Mitchell to Robertson, 18 Jan. 1899, ibid.; Mitchell to Robertson, 20 Jan. 1899, ibid.

126. See, e.g., J. W. Bailey to Archibald T. Robertson, 8 Jan. 1899, box 1, Robertson Papers; T. P. Bell to Edwin C. Dargan, 28 Jan. 1899, Dargan Papers, SBHLA; J. P. Greene to Dargan, 16 Feb. 1899, ibid.

the faculty and from many of his friends, who accused him of going over to the enemy.[127]

The campaign failed. Had the board rejected the resignation, it would have torn the convention in two or forced the sacrifice of the seminary in order to save the convention. When the board met in Louisville in 1899, board chairman Joshua Levering presented Whitsitt's letter of resignation. After several hours of debate, the board voted to accept his resignation as president. Nearly half the board wanted to retain him as a professor of church history, but the board voted 22–20 to accept his resignation as professor also.[128]

THE TRAGEDY OF WHITSITT'S CAREER

Whitsitt himself became more obsessed with the critical importance of destroying Landmark influence. The entire denomination was caught up in a contest between the traditional Baptist doctrine of the spiritual church and the recently devised Landmark doctrine of the exclusively visible church. The recognition of the spiritual character of the church, Whitsitt held, was nothing more than the fundamental Protestant insight that drove the break with Roman Catholicism. The rejection of the spiritual character of the church was nothing less than the Roman Catholic doctrine that undermined the gospel by making the church a sacramental institution. Whitsitt therefore interpreted most conflicts and disagreements within the Southern Baptist Convention as part of an epic contest between Protestantism and Catholicism.

In succeeding years, Whitsitt generally reduced all conflicts within the denomination to various phases of the great controversy over the doctrine of the spiritual church. He viewed the positions taken by Southern Baptist Convention agencies in terms of this issue. When agencies agreed with the seminary's position on issues that came before the convention, they were defending the spiritual church, but when they stood against the seminary's position on any issue, they were capitulating to Landmark pressure and bolstering Landmark doctrine.[129]

127. Joshua Levering to Edwin C. Dargan, 24 Jan. 1899, Dargan Papers, SBHLA; Edwin C. Dargan to Mrs. P., 31 Jan. 1899, ibid; John D. Robertson to Archibald T. Robertson, 27 Feb. 1899, box 1, Robertson Papers.

128. Minutes, Board of Trustees, Southern Baptist Theological Seminary, May 1899, 248–250.

129. See, e.g., William H. Whitsitt to Archibald T. Robertson, 22 June 1900, box 1, Robertson Papers; Whitsitt to Robertson, 14 July 1900, ibid.; Whitsitt to Robertson, 24 Feb. 1902, box 2, Robertson Papers; Whitsitt to Robertson, 14 May 1903, ibid.; Whitsitt to Mrs. Broadus, 2 Mar. 1903, box 17, Broadus Papers.

In the weeks after his resignation took effect, Whitsitt undertook a careful study of Landmarkism. Whitsitt set out in September for Europe to make new discoveries. The things he learned from his study, he noted, "will be of service to me and to the cause." He had retired from the field of battle, but he would not relent and hurled his shells through the *Religious Herald*. His role now was purely scholarly, shoring up truth by his efforts as a scientific historian.[130] In 1901 Whitsitt accepted the chair of philosophy at Richmond College, where he remained until his death in 1911, but he did not give up the fight.

When Robertson indicated the current strategy of resistance against Landmarkism, Whitsitt suggested that it was a strategy of proven failure. He felt that the Woman's Missionary Union, the Home Mission Board, and the Sunday School Board were already doing the bidding of the Landmarkers: "The Catholic party has gained ground every year, until now they talk of 'rooting up the corrupt tree planted by Huss and Luther' with as much decision as any other Catholics. It has been constantly a losing game. They make the issue and we do not meet it. Anyhow it seems to me that there are Catholics enough in Mexico and South America without our sending others there."[131]

Whitsitt urged Robertson to press the battle. The seminary, in Whitsitt's view, had been fated to play the leading role in the contest. Despite the fact that he was forced out by the "Lords of the Catholic Party," the seminary could still lead the denomination to victory. It was time for the faculty to "stand together for the ancient faith of the Baptists" and "lead us farther from the Catholic wilderness in which we have lost our way. This is the indispensable service which the institution must perform."[132]

He was stuck in the role he cast for himself, that of the tragic hero. He had by dint of effort and by applying scientific methods to historical research discovered the fatal weakness of Landmarkism. He seemed ordained to lead the anti-Landmark forces. But his fate was to labor on in obscurity, disgraced and ignored. He sarcastically blamed his careful use of the methods of "scientific history" that he had learned in Germany. Like Abelard he viewed his sufferings as persecution purely.

The Whitsitt controversy revealed a deepening rift within the denomination. Although tensions between Landmarkers and non-Landmarkers set the

130. William H. Whitsitt to Archibald T. Robertson, 8 July 1899, box 1, Robertson Papers.

131. William H. Whitsitt to Archibald T. Robertson, 28 Mar. 1903, box 2, Robertson Papers.

132. William H. Whitsitt to Archibald T. Robertson, 25 Apr. 1903, box 2, Robertson Papers.

controversy in motion, this rift was of a different character. It was a rift between traditional orthodoxy and the new progressive evangelicalism of many seminary graduates. Many were "evangelical liberals" who demanded freedom from denominational and creedal constraints. Whitsitt became the accidental martyr to their cause. The controversy set the trajectory of twentieth-century theology at the seminary in a progressive direction.

As a result, Whitsitt lost the confidence of the denomination. He had criticized a point held as scripture truth among a large percentage of Southern Baptists. He might have survived this readily enough had he cultivated brotherly feeling toward Landmarkers. Instead, he communicated an elitism that was scornful of common Baptists. To make matters worse, many Baptists, including many of his friends, felt that he had been dishonest in publishing an anonymous attack on Baptist views. Full confession of all his faults might still have saved him, but convention progressives appointed him their standard bearer and pressed the controversy with Landmarkism into a battle for freedom for progressive thought.

6

E. Y. MULLINS, SOUTHERN SEMINARY, AND PROGRESSIVE THEOLOGY

Edgar Y. Mullins followed Whitsitt as president of Southern Seminary and committed the seminary to the very principles for which Whitsitt had suffered expulsion. But Mullins succeeded where Whitsitt had failed because he was able to cultivate brotherly feeling toward Whitsitt's enemies and win the trust of rank-and-file Southern Baptists. He achieved remarkable popularity across the Southern Baptist Convention. As a result, he was free to promote progressive theology at the seminary. He led Southern Baptists away from traditional orthodoxy in significant ways and reshaped Southern Baptist theology. He did so while maintaining a reputation for conserving the orthodoxy of Boyce, Broadus, Manly, and Williams. He, for example, established an annual Founders' Day observance at the seminary, but it served more as a monument to the founders' memory than as a standard of measure. He no doubt recognized that the monument helped to cover the seminary's progressive values in the mantle of the founders.

Mullins viewed his approach to theology as "progressive as well as conservative."[1] It was in fact an outdated mediating theology, which had been the dominant theological approach in Germany from the 1840s until the 1880s. It agreed with Schleiermacher's privileging of experience as the source of revelation but differed with him by insisting on the objective character of that revelation. These two commitments formed the two fundamental commitments of Mullins's theology. But he elaborated on them in a unique way, arguing

---

1. Edgar Y. Mullins to Charles S. Gardner, 4 May 1907, Letterbook 31, 1906–1908, 340.

that Borden Parker Bowne's Personalist philosophy united the subjective experience to its objective meaning, and that William James's philosophy of pragmatism authenticated this union of experience and objectivity. Running through it all was a distinctly American privileging of the individual, whether in epistemology, ethics, or doctrine.

These commitments make Mullins one of the more difficult and most contested figures in American religious history. Progressive Southern Baptists have claimed Mullins as the chief originator of their movement, and conservative Southern Baptists have claimed him as an ally in theirs. Naturally, he rather belonged to both. Yale literary critic Harold Bloom called Mullins "the Calvin or Luther or Wesley of the Southern Baptists." He did not found the Southern Baptist movement, Bloom acknowledged, but he reformulated their faith. He was "their refounder, the definer of their creedless faith." [2] Historian Paul Harvey argued similarly that Mullins transformed the traditional Calvinist orthodoxy of Southern Baptist churches into a more progressive and experientialist faith.[3] Above all, it was a more individualist faith.

ELECTION

Trustees were divided regarding the choice of Whitsitt's successor. Most had two firm criteria. First, the new president could not be a Landmarker. To elect a Landmarker would be an admission of defeat, would imply that Landmarkers now controlled the seminary, and would provoke the seminary's most loyal supporters to abandon it. Second, the new president should be someone who stood above the fray of the recent controversy, which had so polarized the denomination that anyone who was an active participant would have little chance of uniting the whole denomination behind the seminary.

Many favored Franklin H. Kerfoot. He seemed the logical choice. He had been Boyce's pick to succeed him in the chair of systematic theology, and he had succeeded Boyce also as seminary treasurer. He was respected throughout the convention and widely acknowledged as one of its foremost leaders. He had the support of the chairman of the board of trustees, Joshua Levering, who was also the seminary's most important living donor. Many observers, including those

2. Harold Bloom, *The American Religion*, 2nd ed. (New York: Chu Hartley, 2006), 215. Bloom concluded that "pragmatically he is more important than Jonathan Edwards, Horace Bushnell, and the Niebuhrs."

3. Paul Harvey, *Redeeming the South: Religious Cultures and Racial Identities among Southern Baptists, 1865–1925* (Chapel Hill: University of North Carolina Press, 1997), 152–155.

trustees who opposed Kerfoot's election, believed that a majority of trustees favored him. His opponents saw him as the candidate of T. T. Eaton, the influential Louisville Landmark preacher, and feared that he would move the seminary toward Landmarkism.[4]

Kerfoot had tried to remain a nonpartisan in the Whitsitt controversy, except that in 1896 he moved the resolutions in support of Whitsitt and the seminary at the Long Run Association. He agreed with Whitsitt on the basic historical questions and had not opposed him publicly. His neutral public stance in the controversy suggested that few would view his election negatively, but in fact many seminary supporters disliked Kerfoot intensely. They took offense at his neutrality and thought that he should have defended Whitsitt publicly. Above all, they took offense because he had counseled resignation. Whitsitt, Robertson, and others believed that Kerfoot had secretly conspired to convince such denominational leaders as James M. Frost to support Whitsitt's resignation.[5] They blamed Kerfoot more than Eaton or anyone else for the loss of Whitsitt.

Kerfoot wanted to succeed Whitsitt. Robertson reported that Kerfoot told him in 1898 that "he thought the succession of the presidency was his by right and he could get it if a few others would support him."[6] After Whitsitt's resignation Kerfoot permitted his supporters on the board of trustees to press his candidacy. This was a mistake. His candidacy for the presidency convinced Whitsitt and most of the faculty that his course in the controversy had been self-serving, that he had counseled Whitsitt to resign in order to become president himself. Prominent alumnus J. William Jones expressed the common sentiment among Whitsitt's supporters: Kerfoot was "an incompetent and a traitor."[7] Had Kerfoot been elected in 1899, the faculty would not have accepted his leadership.

When trustees met in May 1899 to elect a new president, Kerfoot was nevertheless the leading candidate. He knew that many trustees favored making him president, but he became convinced that his election would alienate many

4. See, e.g., E. M. Poteat to Archibald T. Robertson, 2 Sept. 1898, box 1, Robertson Papers; A. J. S. Thomas to Archibald T. Robertson, 16 Jan. 1899, box 1, Robertson Papers.

5. See, e.g., James M. Frost to Archibald T. Robertson, 21 June 1899, box 1, Robertson Papers; Frost to Robertson, 22 June 1899, ibid.; Robertson to Frost, 23 June 1899, ibid.; Frost to Robertson, 24 June 1899, ibid.

6. Archibald T. Robertson to Gentlemen of the Board of Trustees, ca. May 1899, box 6, Robertson Papers. Robertson struck through this sentence—he apparently removed it from the copy that he actually transmitted to the board.

7. J. William Jones, quoted in William H. Whitsitt to Morton B. Howell, 3 May 1899, box 1, Thomas T. Eaton Papers.

Whitsitt supporters from the seminary and would demoralize and divide the faculty. He withdrew his name from consideration before trustees began deliberation on the matter.[8]

The trustees then unanimously elected John P. Greene, president of Missouri Baptists' William Jewell College and a seminary trustee. Greene had supported Whitsitt during the controversy but took no active part. After two weeks of counsel and reflection, Greene declined.

Joshua Levering then ordered a called meeting of the board to consider again the election of a president. The board met on June 29 in Atlanta. Many trustees felt that feelings were still too strong to expect any man elected as president to win acceptance from both parties in the Whitsitt controversy. They therefore wanted to defer the election for at least one year and appoint someone as "chairman of the faculty" to manage seminary affairs in the interim. Henry McDonald, pastor of Atlanta's Second Baptist Church where the trustees were meeting, nominated Kerfoot as chairman of the faculty. McDonald had been outspoken among the trustees in favor of Whitsitt's resignation. A. J. S. Thomas, editor of South Carolina's *Baptist Courier* and a loyal Whitsitt supporter, nominated Sampey.

William Northen, former governor of Georgia, instead convinced the board that a temporary settlement would not be in the seminary's best interest and that the board should elect a permanent president. McDonald then amended his nomination to make Kerfoot a candidate for president. William E. Hatcher, who had directed the pro-Whitsitt forces in the Whitsitt controversy, came prepared for this moment. He had a candidate in mind and had organized a small caucus of supporters. He now nominated Edgar Y. Mullins, pastor of the Newton Center Baptist Church in Newton, Massachusetts, as president. After lengthy discussion it became apparent that a majority favored Mullins. McDonald withdrew his nomination of Kerfoot, and the board elected Mullins unanimously.[9]

Edgar Y. Mullins seemed the perfect candidate. He was a native of Mississippi, was a seminary graduate, and was scholarly, eloquent, and urbane. Because he agreed with Whitsitt's views and was no Landmarker, he was in a position to earn the support and trust of Whitsitt's supporters in the faculty and in the convention. And because he had avoided entanglement in the Whitsitt

8. Franklin H. Kerfoot to the Board of Trustees, 12 May 1899, in Minutes, Board of Trustees, Southern Baptist Theological Seminary, 13 May 1899, 253. He sent a copy to others also (Kerfoot to Brethren, 12 May 1899, box 1, Robertson Papers).

9. Minutes, Board of Trustees, Southern Baptist Theological Seminary, June 1899, 264–265.

Edgar Y. Mullins

controversy, he could begin to earn the support of Landmarkers and Whitsitt's opponents from a neutral position. The board recognized that it needed a president with this background but had nearly despaired of finding such a man.

But Mullins had not been entirely nonpartisan. He had spent the four years of the controversy in Massachusetts, well away from the battlefield, and he did not attend the association and convention meetings where the battles were fought. But early in the Whitsitt controversy, Mullins wrote a couple of articles defending Whitsitt in the *Religious Herald*. Most trustees either had not read them or had forgotten them. Hatcher and the Virginia trustees knew the fact but said nothing.[10]

Robertson knew that Mullins sided wholeheartedly with Whitsitt. Mullins wrote Robertson on April 24, 1899, commending him for his article defending Whitsitt and urging trustees to reject the resignation. Mullins explained, "You expressed what I had felt so strongly that I cannot refrain from dropping a line to say so."[11] Robertson no doubt assured Hatcher of Mullins's support of Whitsitt.

10. See Edgar Y. Mullins, "A Roman Catholic Party among the Baptists," *Religious Herald*, 16 July 1896, 1; and Mullins, "Notes and Comments from Newton Centre," *Religious Herald*, 8 Oct. 1896, 1.

11. Edgar Y. Mullins to Archibald T. Robertson, 24 Apr. 1899, box 1, Robertson Papers.

In the weeks before the Atlanta meeting, Hatcher and R. H. Pitt, editor of Virginia's *Religious Herald*, had discussed the election several times and agreed that Mullins was the "best man in sight." When Pitt was about to run an article in the *Religious Herald* advocating the election of Mullins, the print foreman reminded him that Mullins had written articles in the *Herald* "very severe in their criticism" of Whitsitt's foes. To publicize Mullins's candidacy in advance might have induced anti-Whitsitt editors to recall and criticize Mullins's articles, which could have scuttled his candidacy. Pitt and the Virginia trustees had kept quiet.

When the trustees at the Atlanta meeting had been discussing Mullins's nomination for some time, some trustee "asked in a vague sort of way if it was not true that Dr. Mullins had written somewhat strongly in the Whitsitt controversy…and Hatcher with ready wit laughed the matter out of court, saying that if we were to follow up everything that had been said and done, that probably no member of the board itself would be eligible." [12] After a week of meetings with trustees and faculty, Mullins accepted.

Whitsitt hailed the election of Mullins as a "great triumph" for the cause in which he had fought.[13] Anti-Whitsitt leaders remembered that Mullins had in fact been a partisan on the Whitsitt controversy and sought to ignite a controversy over it. The *American Baptist Flag*, a Missouri paper dedicated to promoting Landmarkism, reprinted one of Mullins's 1896 pro-Whitsitt articles. The major Southern Baptist newspapers, including some of the Landmark papers, refused to give any notice to the matter. Mullins heeded advice to remain silent, and the danger quickly blew over.[14]

The division on the faculty did not fully heal. Robertson, Sampey, McGlothlin, and Carver viewed Kerfoot and Dargan as not fully devoted "to the seminary and its ideals." Mullins apparently shared their point of view. They counseled one another that they could now "afford to be generous" toward Kerfoot and Dargan and seek reconciliation. But such an attitude undoubtedly seemed rather patronizing. It tended inevitably to align Mullins with Sampey and Robertson and put him somewhat out of joint with Kerfoot and Dargan. Kerfoot's defeat placed him in an embarrassed position. Mullins and the faculty would naturally view him as a rival to Mullins. When the board of

12. R. H. Pitt to William O. Carver, 6 Mar. 1929, box 6, Carver Papers, SBHLA. Pitt had not attended the Atlanta meeting, but some of those present reported the proceedings to him.

13. William H. Whitsitt to Archibald T. Robertson, 9 Aug. 1899, box 1, Robertson Papers.

14. William H. Whitsitt to Archibald T. Robertson, 27 July 1899, box 1, Robertson Papers; Whitsitt to Robertson, 22 Aug. 1899, ibid.

trustees of the denomination's Home Mission Board elected Kerfoot president in July 1899, he decided to accept.[15] The faculty, with the exception of Dargan, were pleased at his departure. Dargan adapted well enough but apparently was not again accepted into the full fellowship of the faculty. He resigned in 1907. Despite good intentions on both sides, the personal feelings were not amenable to goodwill.[16]

In rearranging teaching assignments, the faculty agreed initially that Mullins would teach church history and William O. Carver would teach systematic theology. But Kerfoot and Dargan argued that they should not entrust so important a subject as systematic theology to the youngest member of the faculty. Mullins was persuaded by the argument. He initially suggested that Dargan take over systematic theology.[17] Two weeks before the term started, the faculty took systematic theology from Dargan and gave it to Mullins.[18]

Mullins's election represented two important ideas. First, Landmark leaders would not control the school. Mullins was not a Landmarker, nor did he have any sympathy with Landmark distinctives. He saw no benefit for the seminary or the denomination in trying to appease Landmarkers. Whenever Eaton insinuated that the seminary was not sound, Mullins opposed the charge aggressively in private and, if necessary, in public. Until Eaton's death in 1907, Mullins repeatedly rebuffed Eaton's insinuations.[19] His relationship with B. H. Carroll was similarly strained at times. They engaged in an extensive correspondence discussing their major disagreement over a minor point related to baptism. More important, when Mullins planned to raise endowment for the seminary in Texas during the entire calendar year in 1909, Carroll opposed it. Mullins needed the cooperation of the Baptist General Convention of Texas, and the convention asked Carroll to work it out with Mullins. Carroll told Mullins that he would not try to stop him if he started his campaign in January 1909, but he would find only the gleanings left by agents of Baylor. Mullins, Carroll said, would be wise to wait until December. This upset Mullins's plans. December

15. William H. Whitsitt to Archibald T. Robertson, 9 Aug. 1899, box 1, Robertson Papers; John R. Sampey to Edwin C. Dargan, 21 July 1899, Dargan Papers, SBHLA.

16. John R. Sampey to Archibald T. Robertson, 12 July 1899, box 1, Robertson Papers; Sampey to Edwin C. Dargan, 1 Aug. 1899, Dargan Papers, SBHLA; Sampey to Robertson, 7 Aug. 1899, box 1, Robertson Papers; Franklin H. Kerfoot to Dargan, 9 Aug. 1899, Dargan Papers, SBHLA; Kerfoot to Dargan, 6 Sept. 1899, ibid.; Isaac J. Van Ness to Robertson, 2 Nov. 1899, box 1, Robertson Papers.

17. Edgar Y. Mullins to Edwin C. Dargan, 3 Aug. 1899, Dargan Papers, SBHLA.

18. Faculty Minutes, Southern Baptist Theological Seminary, 18 Sept. 1899; Edwin C. Dargan to William O. Carver, 21 Sept. 1899, box 4, Carver Papers, SBHLA.

19. Mullins believed that their relationship was improving in 1907.

was too late if the Texas campaign was going to play the important role Mullins had envisioned.[20]

Mullins's election also represented a new kind of academic freedom at the seminary, at least in principle. Most of the faculty interpreted Whitsitt's battle with Eaton and the Landmarkers as a battle for scholarly freedom. The faculty discovered that Mullins interpreted it the same way. They internalized this as one of the central values of the seminary. Mullins assured faculty candidate Charles S. Gardner in 1907 that the seminary now granted more freedom for progressive theology. They faced less danger from denominational watchdogs than in the past, and Mullins interpreted the Abstract of Principles broadly: "I do not anticipate that the seminary is going to encounter any serious difficulty in doctrinal matters. I think there is greater freedom than there used to be in this regard, and less attention is paid to the would-be mischief makers. While our general attitude in this regard is one of conservatism, it is nevertheless not reactionary. We are progressive as well as conservative."[21] The freedom had limits, for Mullins was too realistic to permit the faculty to press their freedom too far. When the faculty promoted ideas in public that offended Southern Baptists, Mullins counseled reserve. As his tenure lengthened, his insistence on caution seemed to intensify.

SCHLEIERMACHER, JAMES, AND BOWNE: THE CENTRALITY OF RELIGIOUS EXPERIENCE

Mullins reshaped Baptist theology by combining the central idea of modern theology with the denomination's conservative heritage, and by building a faculty who agreed with these principles. The new theology built upon religious experience. Calvin represented the old theology's emphasis on God's transcendence and objective doctrine. Friedrich D. E. Schleiermacher represented the new theology's emphasis on subjective religious experience. According to Mullins, "Calvin and Schleiermacher are the two great names which stand forth in the doctrinal history as most significant for these two standpoints."[22] Christianity needed both. Like Germany's mediating theologians of

20. Edgar Y. Mullins to B. H. Carroll, 11 Mar. 1909, Correspondence—E. Y. Mullins 1909, B. H. Carroll Collection, SWBTS; Carroll to Mullins, 16 Mar. 1909, ibid.; Mullins to Carroll, 15 Apr. 1909, ibid.; Carroll to Mullins, 20 Apr. 1909, ibid.

21. Edgar Y. Mullins to Charles S. Gardner, 4 May 1907, in Letterpress Copy Book 31, 1906–1908, 342.

22. Edgar Y. Mullins, "Southern Baptists and the Changing Viewpoint," *Biblical Recorder*, 22 Apr. 1903, 2.

the prior generation, Mullins constructed a theology that united the objective knowledge of God with individual religious experience. Schleiermacher provided the central insight that religious consciousness connected human experience with divine reality. But Mullins sought a more secure basis for the objectivity of the knowledge that derived from experience by incorporating the insights of two of America's great philosophers, William James and Borden Parker Bowne.

Mullins had deep appreciation for William James. James taught philosophy at Harvard University and established his own philosophical tradition, pragmatism. James did what Mullins thought Christian apologists should do—he took the data of Christian experience seriously as a proper field of scientific study. James stopped short of concluding that human experience revealed anything other than the internal operations of the human consciousness. God, for James, was an important idea in human consciousness that provided the integration, hope, courage, and industry in religious individuals that made them healthy and productive members of society.

Mullins did not see pragmatism as a philosophy or a worldview. It had a more modest role. It was a test of truth claims. Mullins valued pragmatism as a method for evaluating truth claims because it considered personal experience and volition as valid data for determining truth. Mullins held that used this way pragmatism established a theistic worldview, establishing the validity of the Christian's claims of assurance of salvation and of future blessedness in heaven. Jesus, Mullins said, "was the greatest of pragmatists," for "his approach to the whole question of truth and reality was pragmatic." Modern pragmatism was "simply catching up" with Jesus.[23]

Mullins appreciated James in particular for his analysis of the role of religious beliefs in the psychological health and personal welfare of religious persons. James demonstrated that people's religious beliefs had measurable impact on their well-being. For a large class of persons, James argued, their religious beliefs answered the most basic needs of their soul and integrated their consciousness for meaningful and healthy existence in society. Mullins appreciated the popular liberal theologian Albrecht Ritschl for similar reasons. Ritschl's analysis of the role that doctrine played in the experience of Christians provided a compelling basis for doctrine in individual experience. Because the doctrines had personal value, Ritschl argued, Christians naturally held them to be true. But James's pragmatism had the advantage of a scientific basis, Mullins felt. James's analysis of religious experience was empirical and scientific. It examined the facts of experience. It had great apologetic value, Mullins

23. Edgar Y. Mullins to Carl Murchison, 24 Sept. 1912, in Letterpress Copy Book 42, 27. Jan. 1913–28 Oct. 1913.

thought, because when viewed correctly it provided empirical evidence of the truths behind Christian experience.

But Mullins found both James and Ritschl deficient because they did not see this. Both accepted the limits of human knowledge imposed by Immanuel Kant's critique of reason. Ritschl did not move beyond religious belief as personal value. James, with minor exceptions, did not move beyond religious belief as pragmatically beneficial. Mullins, however, held that the religious experience of the Christian was a genuine encounter with the self-revealing God and that it bridged the gap between personal experience and divine realities. "In religious experience," Mullins said, "we have direct knowledge of the noumena."[24] The Christian's religious experience involved essentially direct knowledge of eternal reality.[25] Mullins needed a philosophic basis for ultimate truth, which was more than James or Ritschl could provide.

The philosopher who had established the viability of this approach was Borden Parker Bowne, the founder of the Boston Personalist school. Bowne, who taught philosophy at Boston University from 1876 until his death in 1910, argued for a brand of idealism that began with the empirical data of personal experience and personal relationship, and united all reality in the personal mind of God. Belief in the existence of a personal God was warranted, Bowne taught, because it provided the most convincing and the most practical explanation of human experience.[26]

Personalism was attractive to Mullins because it promised to solve the basic problem of empiricism, how to bridge the divide between the world of sense and the world of spirit. But it appealed to Mullins also because of its obvious apologetic value. It started with personal experience, with "the facts of life," and yet transcended fact. It deduced "ultimate truth from empirical facts," the facts of common human experience, of coexistence of persons, and of common reason. Finally, it led "directly to Theism."[27] It is not surprising that Mullins called Personalism the "highest stage in the development of philosophic idealism," or that he identified himself as an "ardent admirer" of Bowne.[28]

24. Edgar Y. Mullins, "Forty Years of Progress in Theology," ts., 20, box 39, Mullins Papers.

25. On Mullins's assessment of Kant, Ritschl, and James, see, e.g., Edgar Y. Mullins, *The Christian Religion in Its Doctrinal Expression* (Nashville, TN: Sunday School Board of the Southern Baptist Convention, 1917), 193–196, 201–202, 225–226.

26. See Gary Dorrien, *The Making of American Liberal Theology: Imagining Progressive Religion, 1805–1900* (Louisville, KY: Westminster John Knox Press, 2001), 378–381.

27. Edgar Y. Mullins, "Pragmatism, Humanism, and Personalism—The New Philosophic Movement," *Review and Expositor* 5 (1908): 510–512.

28. Edgar Y. Mullins to Frederick White, 22 Dec. 1913, in Letterpress Copy Book 43, 29 Oct. 1913–6 Oct. 1914, 176.

A NEW CALVINISM

In the 1890s many Baptist leaders defended Calvinism as Baptist orthodoxy. This was one of the few things that Whitsitt and Eaton had in common. Whitsitt frequently emphasized the Calvinist character of Baptist doctrine in his history classes and praised the soundly Calvinistic Philadelphia Confession of Faith.[29] Eaton identified the "essence of Baptist doctrine" as the "great Calvinistic faith."[30] When the editors of South Carolina's *Baptist Courier* began an aggressive crusade against Calvinism in the 1890s, many pastors wrote the paper defending Calvinist doctrine.[31] A. T. Robertson held that the fundamental Baptist doctrine was the necessity of the new birth, which included the doctrine of justification by faith and "acceptance of the system of doctrine known as Calvinism."[32] E. C. Dargan's *Doctrines of Our Faith* (1905) taught the traditional Calvinist view of election.[33] Edward B. Pollard in 1890 defended the continuing vitality of Calvinism among Presbyterians and Baptists and contradicted the predictions of its eminent demise: "Calvinism is too strongly imbedded in several large Christian bodies to be swept away. It is not likely that the Presbyterians or the Baptists will ever give up Calvinism."[34]

Pollard's optimism was misplaced. Baptists in the North were already trading in their Calvinism, and Baptists in the South followed not far behind. Southern Baptists relinquished Calvinism in the early twentieth century due largely to the influence of pragmatism, experiential theology, and a growing emphasis on the priority of individual freedom. E. Y. Mullins provided leadership in all three areas.

29. See, e.g., William H. Whitsitt, "Address to Students," *Baptist Courier*, 7 Oct. 1897, 4–5; Whitsitt, "Philadelphia Locuta Est; Causa Finita," ca. 1906?, ts., box 1, William H. Whitsitt Papers, LVA.

30. T. T. Eaton, quoted in unattributed, "Brag Will Out," *Baptist Courier*, 16 Mar. 1893, 2.

31. See J. W. Perry, "Questions Answered," *Baptist Courier*, 16 Feb. 1893, 2; J. E. Covington, "Bro. Covington Says a Few Things," *Baptist Courier*, 19 Oct. 1893, 1; I. W. Wingo, "Calvinism and Fatalism," *Baptist Courier*, 18 Jan. 1900, 9; Wingo, "Bro. Wingo Replies to Theodore," *Baptist Courier*, 21 June 1900, 3; R. E. Peele, "Election," *Baptist Courier*, 5 Apr. 1900, 6; T. C. Johnson, "Election," *Baptist Courier*, 19 Apr. 1900, 3; Johnson, "A Word in Response to Theodore," *Baptist Courier*, 31 May 1900, 1–2; O. J. Peterson, "Election," *Baptist Courier*, 24 May 1900, 8; Pike, "The Courier, Theodore, and Calvinism," *Baptist Courier*, 7 June 1900, 1–2.

32. Archibald T. Robertson, "The Distinctive Baptist Doctrine," *Biblical Recorder*, 16 Sept. 1903, 2.

33. Edwin C. Dargan, *The Doctrines of Our Faith* (Nashville, TN: Sunday School Board of the Southern Baptist Convention, 1905).

34. Edward B. Pollard, "Is Calvinism Dying," *Seminary Magazine* 3 (1890): 147–148.

Most Southern Baptists did not set out deliberately to repudiate or modify their inherited Calvinism—they never did repudiate it entirely, as most continued to insist on the perseverance of the saints as one of several beliefs that marked the boundaries of orthodoxy for Southern Baptists. For the most part Calvinism receded without direct assault on its doctrines.

More relevant was the weakening power of Landmarkism in denominational leadership. Landmark leaders had stood strongly for the traditional Calvinism of the Baptists. Landmark editor James B. Gambrell repeatedly defended Calvinist views of the doctrines of election, predestination, and particular redemption. And when the *Baptist Courier*, probably under the editorial influence of liberal G. B. Moore, engaged in a relentless attack on Calvinism in 1893, Landmark leader T. T. Eaton responded with proofs of the historical and biblical character of Baptist Calvinism in his *Western Recorder*. B. H. Carroll, the Landmark founder of the Southwestern Baptist Theological Seminary, taught Calvinism no less than Eaton or Gambrell. The deaths of Eaton, Carroll, and Gambrell between 1907 and 1921 left the movement without an influential voice in denominational leadership. In some state conventions it was otherwise. The state organizations in Arkansas, Oklahoma, Mississippi, Louisiana, Kentucky, and to some extent Texas could muster majorities for Landmark issues beyond the middle of the twentieth century. Gambrell was the last Landmarker with denomination-wide influence.

Another cause was the apparent irrelevance of Calvinist doctrine, or doctrine of any sort, in preaching. In the late Victorian era Southern Baptist preaching changed, becoming less doctrinal and more sentimental. Charles S. Gardner, who afterward became professor of homiletics at Southern Seminary, confessed that for years he preached no doctrinal sermon but now thought that an occasional doctrinal sermon might do good: "I preached a 'doctrinal' sermon the other day, the first one I ever preached in my life; and I believe it did good." [35] But doctrinal sermons remained occasional.

As Southern Baptist preachers came to emphasize pragmatic standards equally with doctrinal ones, they preached for results. Sermons reflected less about God's sovereignty and holiness and more about his love and fatherliness. It was not an explicit rejection of God's election or predestination, but it was an acknowledgment that such doctrines did not seem to move sinners to repentance and faith. Such late nineteenth-century and early twentieth-century evangelists as Billy Sunday and D. L. Moody kept their theology, such as it was, largely out of view. They had great success in converting sinners, and many

---

35. Charles S. Gardner, "What Constitutes Valid Baptism," in *Eleventh Annual Session of the Baptist Congress* (1893), 104.

preachers imitated their approach. Southern Baptist preachers were becoming pragmatists and adopted this revival theology. They were in the business of saving souls and had little use for any theology that did not seem to result in conversions.

Mullins's theology reflected these trends. He identified his views with Calvinism but thought his own softer form of Calvinism much more palatable to his contemporaries than the Calvinism of the prior generation.

MULLINS AND THE NEW SHAPE OF BAPTIST THEOLOGY

Mullins led Southern Baptists to adopt a new approach to theology. He reconstructed Christian doctrine on the basis of experience. "The Christian doctrinal system," Mullins wrote, "arises out of the facts of Christian experience." [36] This new basis for doctrine led him to recast many traditional beliefs. In his *Axioms of Religion* (1906), Mullins appealed to religious experience in a more limited way, as a proof of the validity of Christian truth claims. In his *Christian Religion in Its Doctrinal Expression* (1917), Mullins based all Christian theology on experience. The result was a shift in emphasis that altered the contours of Southern Baptist religion.

Mullins's "experiential method" for the construction of Christian theology was not new. Schleiermacher was the pioneer a century earlier. Mullins, however, like German mediating theologians and some contemporary personalist theologians, gave experience more power than Schleiermacher had—it revealed facts: "Religious experience is the starting point of religious knowledge. Of course the facts concerning which we obtain knowledge exist independently of us. But we acquire truth about these facts through experience." [37]

Mullins promoted his approach to religion as empirical. He analyzed human religious experience. In this he was following in the train of liberalism generally, which since Schleiermacher had claimed that religion consisted in human experience. To learn about religion, theologians had to study the religious subject, humans, not the religious object, God. This "turn to the subject" was the foundation of Christian liberalism.

But as many critics of liberalism had already pointed out, an analysis of human religion cannot logically yield any knowledge of God or spiritual realities. This was the critical weakness in reliance on human experience. There were two common solutions, and Mullins had recourse to both.

36. Mullins, *Christian Religion*, 68.
37. Mullins, *Christian Religion*, 180.

The first solution was the assertion that religious experience corresponded to and revealed eternal truths in the spiritual realm. The basis for this was the argument that the existence of spiritual realities was necessary to make sense of human experience. Human experience was rife with questions of meaning, longing for purpose, sense of conscience, recognition of good and evil, experience of sin and guilt, and the desire for forgiveness and redemption. These experiences were incomprehensible, even absurd, unless they corresponded to spiritual realities. The existence of God, the immortality of the soul, a divine standard of good and evil, and divine purpose and destiny for humanity—such things must exist if humans were to make sense of their experience. Mullins wrote, "Faith in Christ is an act which takes for granted that the universe answers to the soul's craving for deliverance from sin." [38] Indeed, even the more basic experiences of personhood and freedom were unintelligible apart from belief in the existence of such spiritual realities.

This went beyond Kant's a priori argument that it was practically necessary to postulate God's existence based on considerations of conscience and freedom. In Kant's argument, God's existence remained a postulate and was not strictly knowledge. Mullins taught that Kant's argument was valid, but that it fell short of what was needed, since it could establish only the phenomena or experiences of religion and not the noumena, the realities behind the phenomena. Kant's argument neglected consideration of the fact of the Christian experience of God. As Mullins explained, "Our experience of redemption through Christ brings knowledge of the reality behind the phenomena. It brings direct knowledge of God." The Christian's experience was knowledge of the divine realities. The noumena remained beyond the reach of Kant's pure and practical reason but were accessible to Christian experience.[39]

The second solution to the problem involved the doctrine of divine immanence. This approach, which Mullins shared with liberalism broadly, distanced doctrine. Traditional Protestantism placed true doctrine as one of the essential elements of the Christian religion, without which true religious experience was impossible. But for Mullins, as for liberal Protestants generally, religion was an experience rather than a doctrine. Doctrine was a natural development because religious experience yearned for expression. But the doctrine was derivative of religion, not constitutive. Religious experience was a fact, and doctrine was an expression of the meaning or personal value of the experience. "Facts are one thing, meanings are another," Mullins wrote, reflecting the popular Ritschlian

---

38. Edgar Y. Mullins, "The Meaning of Religion, No. II—Certainty in Religion," *Religious Herald*, 8 May 1919, 4.

39. Mullins, *Christian Religion*, 134–135.

distinction between fact and meaning. "The doctrines are simply the statement of the meaning of religion." [40] Mullins, however, unlike Ritschl, believed that the meaning in the theological statement was objectively true. Mullins, having placed doctrine on a new footing, now gave it a new cast.

THE BIBLE AND REVELATION

Mullins's approach to the Bible was novel for Southern Baptists. He understood the Bible as an essential source of religious knowledge, but it was correlated to the individual Christian's religious experience and, in some important respects, subordinate to it. Mullins derived Christianity's most important doctrines primarily from the individual religious experiences of Christians. He derived other doctrines variously from Christian history, the Bible, and individual experience. The Bible for Mullins was an essential source for knowing Christian truth, but it was not the exclusive source or even the primary one. When Mullins discussed the "sources of religious knowledge," for example, he made it clear that religious experience came first, and then acceptance of the Bible as an "authoritative record of his supreme revelation. "God's revelation of himself to us comes through his direct action upon our spirits." This was direct knowledge. After this, Christians received the Bible as an authoritative record of knowledge. [41] In principle and in practice, Mullins made the Christian's religious experience the chief source of religious knowledge, and the Bible corroborated and sustained experience. "The Bible," Mullins explained, "is the greatest of all books of religious experience." [42]

The Bible was also critically important as a historical record. It recorded the religious experiences of Israel and the early Christians in response to God's self-revelation. But, above all, the New Testament was the essential historical record of the life and teachings of Jesus Christ, who revealed God supremely. Jesus was, Mullins wrote, "the historical revelation of God to men," and the New Testament was "the indispensable source of our knowledge of the historical Jesus and his work for our salvation." [43]

His view of the Bible's inspiration was not the traditional one. He held that the Holy Spirit guided the Bible's authors in understanding, interpreting, and expressing their experiences of God's self-revelation. Such interpretation of their experiences constituted the Bible's theological statements. This theology

40. Edgar Y. Mullins, "The Meaning of Religion," *Religious Herald*, 1 May 1919, 4.
41. Mullins, *Christian Religion*, 38–41.
42. Mullins, *Christian Religion*, 3.
43. Mullins, *Christian Religion*, 4.

in the Bible was "the expression of their experience under the guidance of the Holy Spirit."[44]

The Bible was authoritative, Mullins held, for two chief reasons. First, it recorded the same experiences of salvation as Christians of all generations experienced. The Bible was therefore suited to the needs of all Christians. It proved itself in the experience of individual Christians to be effective in their striving to live for God. Mullins noted, "The Bible is a record of similar experiences of other saved men."[45]

Second, the Bible was the source of the historical knowledge of Jesus' life and teachings. The Old Testament, Mullins wrote, was a history of the many times that God revealed himself to Israel. The New Testament was the history of how God revealed himself in Jesus Christ and his apostles. These revelations occurred in history, and the Bible writers composed a historical record and interpretation of these historical revelations. The Bible was then the history of the revelation of God to persons in the Old and New Testament eras. It was "the record of God's revelation of himself."[46]

When Christians read the Bible, they experienced many of the spiritual realities described in it. This experience then served as a fact testifying to the Bible's divine authority and power. But the knowledge that the Bible conveyed, Mullins held, was not intellectual in character. It was an experiential encounter with God's personality. When revelation occurred, it was a "revelation of God himself rather than of truths about God…God entering human experience and man becoming conscious of his presence and power." Thus revelation was "an event in the soul" rather than the "communication of truth." Revelation was personal rather than propositional: "No bare truth about God can be a revelation of God."[47]

The persons who received these revelations experienced them as fact. The record of these revelations, the Bible, interpreted these facts of experience. "In the scriptures," Mullins wrote, "we find an interpretation of the facts."[48] The Bible, for Mullins, was not directly a revelation of God but was rather an interpretation of the meaning or value of those facts.

Mullins suggested that although the Bible writers generally considered the revelations they recorded as supernatural events, they were nevertheless revelations "mediated to them for the most part through their experience and needs."[49]

44. Mullins, *Christian Religion*, 3.
45. Edgar Y. Mullins, "The Meaning of Religion," *Religious Herald*, 22 May 1919, 4.
46. Mullins, *Christian Religion*, 142.
47. Mullins, *Christian Religion*, 141.
48. Mullins, *Christian Religion*, 137–138.
49. Mullins, *Christian Religion*, 138.

Thus Christians had a dual testimony to the scriptures. The first was their own confirming experience in reading it, seeing their own experience mirrored there in its accounts of ancient saints. The second was the Bible's status as a historical record of God's revelation to individuals in the biblical history. "The doctrine of revelation," Mullins concluded, "arises out of the facts of experience and of history."[50] Jesus revealed God by his redemptive actions in history, the disciples experienced transformation as a result of their encounter with Jesus, and they wrote the New Testament scripture as a record of their experience of God's redemptive power.[51]

Mullins claimed to reject all theories of inspiration. Inspiration, Mullins apparently believed, consisted primarily in the illumination that the Holy Spirit gave scripture writers for communicating their own experience of God's presence and power in such a way that it evoked consciousness of God in others. It was impossible to gain any definite knowledge concerning the manner of the Spirit's working.[52] The only things that could be known about inspiration were its effects "in the experience of Christians of the past and present."[53] Mullins concluded that among other things the revelation in the experience of Old Testament prophets was supernatural because God's personality, which "can not be confined within the chain of physical law," entered their own experience: "Their own self-consciousness was the proof of their God-consciousness."[54]

Mullins omitted any mention of other traditional effects or evidences of the Bible's character. Traditional views of the Bible held that inspiration resulted in both the communication of propositional truth and the power to redeem persons. Two traditional proofs of the Bible's inspiration were that its prophecies of the future actually came to pass, and that the Bible contained no actual contradictions. Mullins omitted them because he held that revelation was personal and experiential—properly subjective. The old proofs appealed to objective qualities of the Bible as well as to its power to save persons. But for Mullins, the Bible did not reach objective truth directly. It reached it through the historical experiences it recorded and the experiences it created. Revelation was the experience of God's personality, and the Bible was the historical record of such revelation, inspired or illumined by the Spirit to lead others into the experience of God.

50. Mullins, *Christian Religion*, 137.
51. Mullins, *Christian Religion*, 141.
52. Mullins, *Christian Religion*, 143–144.
53. Mullins, *Christian Religion*, 144.
54. Mullins, *Christian Religion*, 150–151.

DOCTRINE: COMMON SENSE PERSONALISM

Before Mullins, Southern Baptist theologians, with traditional Protestants generally, began with the reliability of the Bible and then established Christian doctrine from it. Its supernatural message produced Christian experience, but it stood over experience and judged it. Mullins derived Christian doctrine from experience. He began with individual Christian experience and then established the reliability of the Bible upon its correspondence with and contributions to that experience. Mullins's approach reflected the Copernican revolution in theology wrought by Schleiermacher, in which religious truth was mediated by the religious experience of the subject rather than by objective revelation in the Bible. Schleiermacher worked out an entire system of Christian doctrine derived from Christian experience in his *Christliche Glaube* (1822). The first American to do the same was William Newton Clarke, a Northern Baptist scholar, who published his *Outline of Christian Theology* in 1898. Mullins sought to work out the system in a more satisfactory fashion than Schleiermacher or his followers had done. To this end Mullins published his *Christian Religion in Its Doctrinal Expression* in 1917 and made it his textbook in his theology classes.

His arrangement of material reflected doctrine's basis in experience. He began *Christian Religion in Its Doctrinal Expression* with the standard prolegomena section discussing philosophy, epistemology, and the nature of the Bible and its authority. Traditional systematic theologies presented next the doctrine of God, followed by the doctrine of Christ, and then the doctrine of the Holy Spirit. Mullins presented the doctrine of Christ first, then the doctrine of the Holy Spirit, and finally the doctrine of God. This was the order in which Christian knowledge came through experience. Christians had a direct revelation of Jesus Christ in their experience of redemption. The Holy Spirit mediated the experience, and Christ revealed God the Father.

In traditional Protestant thought, theology constituted genuine religious knowledge. The facts of religion consisted largely in the theology. Religion was more than theology—it included the experiences of faith, repentance, love, and thanksgiving. But for Mullins, as for liberal theologians generally, theology was not properly a part of religious knowledge. Religious experience was genuine religious knowledge, but theology was something different. Theology was derivative of the experience. It was a secondary characteristic, one step removed from experience.

Theology, Mullins held, was an interpretation of religious experience. Religion consisted in the fact of religious experience—God's self-revelation to the soul, the soul's response of repentance and obedience, and the sense of redemption, meaning, and relatedness to God. These were the central religious facts. Theology was the effort to express what these facts meant to Christians.

Theology sought to interpret and explain the facts: "Religion has to do with the facts about God and man, and the relations between God and man. Doctrines are simply the expression of the meaning of these facts and relations." The Bible was a record of both the experiences of believers and their doctrinal explanations of them.[55] The doctrines were in an important sense necessary postulates of faith and therefore had an objective character. Christians affirmed these doctrines because they alone made sense of religious experience. Christian doctrines were essential to explain Christian experience, and to unify and complete Christian ideas of God. Without doctrine, the Christian's religious experience was unintelligible. But doctrine was still derivative. It was the thought-clothing of religious knowledge.

The Bible, Mullins believed, became a source of knowledge through experience. Because persons knew God and spiritual realities by experience, the Bible could not itself be a direct source of religious knowledge. But that did not mean that doctrine was objectionable. It was not even extraneous to the Christian life. Valid Christian doctrine derived from authentic Christian experience. Doctrine should not, however, be confused with the experience of revelation. Doctrine was a natural human response to religion, which was the experience of revelation, which was the experience of God's redemptive presence and power. Religious experience awakened a craving to apprehend its meaning, Mullins wrote, and "the doctrines of theology are the answer to that craving."[56] Christians "inevitably" interpreted the fact of their experience of religion in terms of doctrine, Mullins explained, "but the primal fact is God entering human experience, and man becoming conscious of his presence and power."[57]

Mullins held that the doctrine learned from experience was different than fact, and that the religious experience was the essence of religion and comprised its proper facts. Yet Mullins believed that the doctrine yielded from experience was true in an objective sense. At this point he agreed more with the mediating theologians than with either Schleiermacher or Ritschl. Christians could have confidence in the truth of doctrine because it integrated their religious experience as nothing else could, and because it explained the powerful transformative effects of the gospel in their experience.

Experience established the Bible's functional authority for Christians. Mullins's experientialist approach limited the sense in which the Bible could be the Christian's objective authority. Mullins asserted that his "construction of

55. Mullins, *Christian Religion*, 243.
56. Mullins, *Christian Religion*, 16.
57. Mullins, *Christian Religion*, 141.

Christian doctrine rests on a fact basis entirely." But Mullins distinguished the facts of religion from those of the physical realm. Religion had its own "order of facts." [58] They were facts of religious experience—the fact that scripture writers recorded their experience in the Bible, and the fact of the Christian's own experience. [59] Theology, Mullins wrote, was the "explanation of this order of facts." [60]

Mullins held, for example, that the doctrine of the deity of Christ was a "necessary" belief for Christians for five reasons. First, the Christian's personal experience of Christ was that he had redeemed the individual from sin and had revealed God the Father in the subjective consciousness. Second, this doctrine integrated the Christian's intuitions of right and wrong, truth and error, cause and effect, and self and other. Third, belief in Christ's deity unified and explained all the experiential and rational evidence. Fourth, the belief in the deity of Christ was the conclusion drawn from the experience of virtually all Christians throughout history, and Jesus stood at the "heart of the whole movement." Finally, Mullins said, Christians believed in the deity of Christ because the New Testament historical records showed that the early Christians everywhere "regarded" him as "Lord of the church and Redeemer of man." [61] This last reason was the sole and sufficient basis of the doctrine in traditional Christian thought. But for Mullins, experience was prior to the Bible, and the Bible's authority lay chiefly in the corroboration its records afforded experience.

Mullins repeated this pattern in shorter form in his discussion of many other doctrines. He announced that the proof of the doctrine was first how "Christian experience speaks," second that "Christian history agrees with our own experience," and finally that "the witness of the New Testament writers" agreed. [62] Even the doctrine of creation, Mullins said, did not come from either the Bible or science, but from the "redemptive experience of Christians," who infer from their own dependence on God "that the universe is dependent on God." [63]

One of the extraordinary results of this approach was that Mullins established many doctrines over many pages with little or no reference to scripture passages. In practice, some doctrines yielded better to this approach than others. He drew heavily on appeals to experience in discussing the doctrines of revelation, the person Christ, the Holy Spirit, the Trinity, and God. In his discussion of other doctrines, however, experience seemed to have little

58. Mullins, *Christian Religion*, 2.
59. Mullins, *Christian Religion*, 164.
60. Mullins, *Christian Religion*, 2.
61. Mullins, *Christian Religion*, 167–169.
62. Mullins, *Christian Religion*, 196. See, similarly, ibid., 216–217.
63. Mullins, *Christian Religion*, 251–252.

relevance, and the discussion consisted largely in how the New Testament writers understood the matter. But on the whole, Mullins's systematic theology relied but little on scripture proofs for its doctrinal statements.

In the end, the Bible could not attain to the kind of objective authority for doctrine and practice that traditional Protestants claimed for it. The Bible had the highest authority for Christians, Mullins believed. "It is final for us in all matters of our Christian faith and practice." But this was misleading if read in a traditional sense. It was authoritative, Mullins wrote, "as a source of information as to the historical revelation of God in Christ." The Bible did not contain religious facts but bore powerful historical testimony to religious facts. It conveyed the interpretations of the experiences of revelation of the Bible writers. It was history, not properly revelation, but its history had power to produce the same religious experience that the Bible writers had. This was its authority. All legitimate Christian doctrine must derive from the genuine redemptive experience and be consistent with it.

DOCTRINE OLD AND NEW

Mullins's experiential method resulted in some significant transformations in Baptist doctrine. His view of scripture and the experiential basis of Christian doctrine were in the liberal tradition. So was his view of the atonement. Mullins rejected all traditional theories of the atonement for an "ethical" atonement. The atonement, Mullins held, was the means that God adopted to exercise his love of sinful persons in forgiving sins and "perfecting men and women in a holy society." [64] The essential element in the atoning work of Christ, in Mullins's theory, was the fact that God was immanent in Christ. When Christ submitted to death on the cross, it was "God becoming immanent in the race...projecting himself into the life of the human race." [65] When Christ defeated his death in his resurrection, he overcame death for all humanity. Indeed, according to Mullins, death was the judgment of God upon the race, and in thus overcoming death, Christ did away with judgment and wrath.

This meant that Jesus did not endure God's wrath against sin, except to the extent that he acquiesced to die, which was God's judgment for sin. But it was not judgment on Jesus, for Jesus had not sinned. Jesus bore the "penal consequence of sin" only in the sense that he identified completely with humanity. [66]

64. Mullins, *Christian Religion*, 315.
65. Mullins, *Christian Religion*, 320.
66. Mullins, *Christian Religion*, 323.

Mullins explained, "We are not to conceive of God's wrath as poured out upon Christ's head." [67] Rather, Christ "endured death which is the expression of God's wrath and the penalty for their sin." [68] Christ's death was propitiatory only in the sense that by overcoming death for the whole race—since God was immanent in Christ, Christ's resurrection projected life into all humanity—he put an end to death, which was the expression of God's judgment.[69] His atonement was substitutionary, Mullins said, in the sense that "he did for us what we could not do for ourselves." [70] This was a thorough recasting of traditional Protestant and Baptist views of the atonement, though Mullins's explanations lacked clarity and probably left many readers in confusion.

Though he usually did not reach them by the traditional route, Mullins drew largely traditional conclusions in many areas of theology. He held firmly, for example, to the necessity of belief in the deity of Christ. He understood the doctrine of the Trinity in traditional fashion. He also took the traditional Calvinist position regarding the doctrine of election. He explained that God elected individuals to salvation as the best means possible for accomplishing God's purposes of redemption. Election, Mullins wrote, did not compel persons against their will to be saved. The Holy Spirit, rather, led them to salvation in a manner consistent with human rationality, will, and personhood. Mullins answered objections against individual election in traditional Calvinist fashion. He also argued in a traditional manner for the doctrine of the eternal condemnation in hell for those who lived according to their evil desires. He explicitly rejected such popular modernist alternatives as annihilationism and the various forms of restorationism.[71]

Mullins's great influence on the denomination endured for most of the twentieth century and in some respects was practically permanent. But his influence on the faculty was less durable. Harold Tribble, Mullins's successor in the chair of theology, continued to teach Mullins's theology and used his textbook. But after Tribble resigned in 1947 to become president of Andover-Newton Theological Seminary, new influences eclipsed Mullins's thought. William Mueller and Dale Moody taught a different kind of theology in the postwar years, one that was heavily influenced by neo-orthodoxy, especially by Emil Brunner. The postwar faculty increasingly reflected newer theological strains. Mullins's personalism was unconvincing and passé by comparison.

67. Mullins, *Christian Religion*, 323.
68. Mullins, *Christian Religion*, 323.
69. Mullins, *Christian Religion*, 324.
70. Mullins, *Christian Religion*, 325.
71. Mullins, *Christian Religion*, 205–213, 338–358, 488–503.

SOUTHERN SEMINARY AND LIBERALISM

Mullins and the more progressive Southern Seminary faculty embraced a mediating theology, but mediation was fundamental to liberalism. It sought to establish a viable path between rationalism and orthodoxy. Rationalism was the great enemy, but traditional orthodoxy was also defective, since it was unscientific and could not answer the challenges posed by rationalism. As a mediating approach, liberalism tended to spread out across the spectrum. Some forms seemed nearly to slide into rationalism. Other forms seemed relatively traditional. Mullins and the faculty rejected identification as liberals, instead calling themselves by such identifiers as "conservative-progressive." Mullins explained it this way: "I believe in progress in theological thought and statement, but I believe in the evangelical fundamentals."[72]

Many Southern Baptist scholars, especially those at Southern Seminary, followed this mediating approach. It was sometimes pietistic more than philosophical, especially in the case of students. It divided the realm of physical science and historical criticism from the realm of religion. Humans lived in both the physical and the spiritual world, but they knew the realities of these realms by different means. They knew the facts of nature and history by observation and its reasonable deductions. But they knew the facts of the spiritual realm by personal experience—freedom, personality, and, above all, consciousness of the divine.

What made them pietistic was their insistence that the two realms were entirely independent of each other. The facts of one realm could not challenge the facts of the other realm. This meant that scientists and historical critics of the Bible could have absolute freedom in their methods and conclusions, and they could never pose any threat to the facts of the spiritual realm in religious experience. The approach enabled them to accept such findings of science as evolution, and at the same time to accept unqualified the Bible's account of direct divine creation. The two beliefs belonged to different spheres of reality. The two realms were coherent because God was the ground of both. God was immanent in both. His presence in the world's course ensured that its development and destiny coincided with the spiritual development and destiny of humanity. Augustus H. Strong, the president of Rochester Theological Seminary whose career and thought paralleled Mullins's in many ways, expressed clearly what so many Southern Baptist scholars felt: "Neither evolution nor the higher criticism has any terrors to one who regards them as part of Christ's creating and education process."[73]

72. Edgar Y. Mullins to Albert Waffle, 29 Apr. 1914, Letterpress Copy Book 43.

73. Augustus H. Strong, *Outlines of Systematic Theology* (Philadelphia: American Baptist Publication Society, 1908), ix.

Mullins's wall of partition between scientific knowledge and religious knowledge introduced the profound tension between his acceptance of the methods of science and historical criticism, on the one hand, and his insistence on traditional doctrinal positions, on the other. At a popular level, Southern Baptists generally accepted Mullins's approach and erected the same wall, and they did not worry much over the apparent contradictions.

This was an attractive approach for the faculty's progressive conservatives, and for preachers in the conservative denomination who also valued the latest scholarship of the historical critics. Mullins himself erected a division between scientific and religious knowledge that encouraged the pietist approach.

The approach was vulnerable to devastating criticism. It implied above all that truth lacked unity. Both Carver and Gardner criticized Mullins for this approach. Carver described his own reaction:

> He [Mullins] adopted and vigorously applied the principle of partition in the fields of thought and learning, and insisted on the "rights of theology" to its own matter, method, and principles, as an autonomous sphere along with the philosophical and the scientific spheres, whose rights he was always ready to concede. I was myself, never able to use this method and in my department, and frankly said so. It was a method more useful for meeting conflicts current in the cultural thinking of the day and for adjusting progressive thinking to lagging conservatism than for what I regarded as the truer approach. For me, truth is a comprehensive unit. What is true in any sphere of thought and culture is to be recognized as actually true. No plea for "rights" in one field that conflict with "rights" in another field can yield true insight and permanent understanding. But for very many readers his method brought about a modus vivendi which enabled them to hold in suspension incongruities and even conflicts and contradictions between "truths" in different spheres.[74]

Carver was right. Educated Southern Baptist preachers widely adopted Mullins's division of the spheres of knowledge. It permitted them to affirm broadly the work of scientists and historical critics without requiring them to adjust their traditional theology. Carver rejected such mediating approaches.

For all that Mullins shared with modernist theology, he tried to distance himself from it. Mullins believed that modernism would destroy the life of Christianity. He was distressed when he heard from a New York Baptist leader that Rochester Theological Seminary was trending toward modernism, fearing

---

74. William O. Carver, "Recollections and Information from Other Sources Concerning the Southern Baptist Theological Seminary," SBTS, 80–81.

that it would "work disastrously to the school in coming years." Any school that "severs its connection" from the "great fundamentals" would fail in advancing the work of the kingdom of God. It would lose its message, and "a ministry without a message, in my judgment, is a useless ministry."[75] But Southern Seminary progressives generally misconstrued liberalism. They interpreted it as rationalism, as antisupernaturalism on its way to materialistic atheism. So construing liberalism had a benefit. It distanced Southern Baptist progressives from the left-leaning forms of liberalism.

Progressive and liberal professors at Southern Seminary rarely felt that they had abandoned or betrayed the ideals of the seminary's founders. That would have been revolution. They were reformers. Missions professor W. O. Carver protested that they had remained "loyal to the basic ideas and...historic principles" of the founders, but they felt responsible to change everything necessary to provide for the contemporary needs of the churches. Their loyalty to the founders was in fact more formal than substantive. The founders were innovators in their day, progressive faculty argued, and the best way to honor them was by imitating their innovative spirit rather than by binding themselves to their theological formulas. Carver explained their approach to change: "I gradually defined my conviction that we would be most loyal to our founders and fathers by doing what they had to do. They took account of the needs of a Baptist ministry and leadership under the conditions of their own day. They formulated courses and adopted methods which they were intelligently convinced would most adequately provide for efficiency and loyalty in this leadership. We must take the same attitude and be willing to modify and to vary their methods and disciplines which they provided for their students, so as to make our seminary the best possible instrument for a worthy Baptist ministry and for leadership in the Baptist, the Christian, and the cultural world of the twentieth century." Loyalty to the founders meant adopting methods best suited for producing a "worthy Baptist ministry" to meet the needs of Baptists and the world. It is unlikely that Boyce would have found Carver's arguments persuasive. The founders said that the doctrines that they taught would always be fundamental to producing a worthy ministry. Southern Seminary progressives agreed only in the broadest sense.[76]

Curricular changes often reflected changes in doctrinal views. The introduction of courses that taught the new historical criticism or emphasized the gospel's social bearings reflected new theological trends. Progressive faculty could introduce such courses only with great care and caution. Carver acknowledged that

---

75. Edgar Y. Mullins to Albert Waffle, 29 Apr. 1914, Letterpress Copy Book 43.
76. Carver, "Recollections," 78.

progressive reforms were necessarily slow because of the seminary's conservative constituency: "I think we have, all in all, moved in this direction about as rapidly as a constituency such as ours would approve or submit to. We have not always been to the degree in which some of us have thought we should be, the leaders of denominational progress and preparation for changes."[77]

The progressive faculty felt the tension between loyalty to the churches and faithfulness to the academy. They aimed to be both preachers and scholars, but the South's conservative churches were not prepared to tolerate many of the ideas that they derived from their scholarship. They sometimes felt that they could best serve the churches by prosecuting their academic pursuits without raising questions of their suitability or acceptance in the churches. Progressives tended to sympathize with this view. Carver said that "Whitsitt used to say in his day that we ought to belong to 'the republic of letters.' "[78] Progressives agreed that sound Christian scholarship always served the best interests of the church. Carver explained: "If this ideal is rightly related and adjusted to full membership in the gospel and kingdom of our Lord it is an ideal that must be cherished. I am happy to believe that at the present time we are overcoming any lag in this direction which may have overtaken us. A seminary ought always to reflect and to perpetuate the true convictions of its denomination. It ought also to provide a leadership in the thought life, in the evangelical fervor and the evangelistic practice of its people; and at the same time to inspire the leadership of its denomination for cultural, spiritual advance and for the widest Christian fellowship consistent with the integrity and the true meaning of our Christian faith."[79] But the most progressive faculty members were realistic about the dangers such a course posed for the seminary. Unless they were cautious, the denomination would rebel and either dismiss the faculty or abandon the seminary.

WILLIAM OWEN CARVER

The seminary was already gaining a reputation as a "liberal" school. When Arkansan Perry Webb Sr. planned to enroll in 1919, someone asked him why he was going to "that liberal school."[80] The teaching of W. O. Carver was an important source of that reputation.

77. Carver, "Recollections," 78.
78. Carver, "Recollections," 78.
79. Carver, "Recollections," 78.
80. Perry Webb Jr., in Transcript, SBC Peace Committee Meeting, 9–10 Jan. 1986, tape 4, 7, Honeycutt Papers.

William O. Carver

Carver exercised an extraordinary and enduring influence on the character of the seminary's teaching in the twentieth century. Carver's theology, like
Mullins's, held that our knowledge of religion comes through religious experience, which provides sufficient data for deriving reasonable conclusions about
God, humanity, and ethics. Carver's theology incorporated some personalist
elements but was basically Ritschlian in its framework. It was neoromantic,
neo-Hegelian, and historicist—which is to say that the Christian faith derived
from religious experience, God was immanent in the world's historical progress, and true knowledge is historical knowledge, since eternal truth always
arrives clothed in its historical conditions.

Carver's *Missions and Modern Thought* (1910) was an extended justification
of the missionary enterprise based on the new modernist form of Christianity.
Many scientists, philosophers, and sociologists argued that the era of religion
was ending, and that humans no longer needed religion to explain the mysteries
of the natural world—science had taken over that function. Humans no longer
needed religion to give wholeness and meaning to their lives—psychology now
did that. And humans no longer needed religion to form ethical values—sociology now did that. And anthropologists were arguing that the introduction of
nonnative Christianity into other cultures deeply injured societies whose ideals

and practices had been constructed on the basis of other religious views. As a result of these developments, many leaders, inside and outside the church, questioned the value, and even the morality, of the Christian missionary enterprise.

Carver agreed that the traditional approach to missions was no longer justifiable. The old justifications no longer convinced, Carver said. Christian missions were formerly based on the premise that persons who did not repent and believe in the gospel of Jesus Christ would spend eternity in hell under God's judgment of their sin. But many Christians were now beginning to understand that many around the world already knew God "in experience" and "in the processes of nature and history," and they could not believe that God would condemn anyone to eternal misery. Carver argued that Christians had "a sufficient motive for missions" apart from the desire "to rescue men from eternal doom" that characterized traditional missions.[81] Missions had to adjust to modern conditions of knowledge and society.

The solution, Carver proposed, lay in recognizing the new modern shape of Christianity and adapting missions to it. In modern Christianity the gospel was still deeply relevant to individuals, but the chief aim was the formation of a worldwide Christian social order. The modern church should promote the missionary enterprise "for the life of the nation, for the salvation of society, for the condition of the world." The Christian message would save the world—that is, the social institutions of this world.[82]

Religion alone, Carver felt, could muster sufficient resources to save the world from ignorance, hatred, and injustice. It, above all human institutions and ideas, promoted the "advance of the race." Christianity was the "highest religion" and was "adaptable" to the state of progress in every society. "Christian civilizations," Carver urged, "are the highest, the most ethical, the most spiritual." Therefore, he concluded, every person who cared about human progress should "seek to promote the extension of the Christian faith." Other religions made positive contributions by striving for goodness, but "it is the Christian spirit alone that brings to their destiny these scattered strivings of the human heart." Christianity alone could civilize the world and establish justice, peace, and human brotherhood among the peoples of the earth.[83]

Traditional Christian missions first set about evangelizing the peoples of the earth to save individuals from hell. This was a necessary stage of development so that "the individual man" might be "discovered, emancipated, and enlightened."

---

81. William O. Carver, *Missions and Modern Thought* (New York: Macmillan, 1910), 14.
82. Carver, *Missions and Modern Thought*, 22–23.
83. Carver, *Missions and Modern Thought*, 34–35, 37–39.

The old missions thus implanted among the nations "this principle of selfhood," of the worth of individual personality. From this "consciousness of true individualism" would spring that community and brotherhood that God intended as the goal of human existence.[84] But traditional Christianity, Carver argued, was outworn. Human history had outgrown it. But that was no discredit to Christianity. Christianity, Carver said, was universally adaptable and was adapting to the new conditions of the world.

Carver believed that history, which God always directed by his presence in it, clearly demonstrated the progress of missions and of the church along these lines. The Middle Ages, including the hierarchical institutionalism of the Roman Catholic Church and the political subordination of the Eastern churches, quashed human individualism. God spurred the Protestant Reformation to restore it. Thus the initial motive of missionary activity was evangelistic in order to awaken individuals to their worth in God's sight. The individualist motive, though still important, was now becoming subordinate. The motive and aim of modern missions was to Christianize the world, so that Christianity would become in truth the one great world religion, and the nations of the world one great brotherhood. Christianity was the engine of progress toward this "true civilization."[85]

Carver felt that the enemies of religion did not recognize that civilization was the result of Christianity's vital power, and that the future of the civilization of the world depended upon the universal spread and dominance of Christianity. The motive for missions was not lost, therefore, when traditional theology disintegrated. The urgent need of the day was in fact the Christianization of the world. Christianity would teach persons to be authentic and responsible individuals, which then would become the basis for world brotherhood. Carver called for missions, then, not because souls were perishing daily into eternal misery apart from Christ but because individual misery and social disintegration threatened to deepen in the modern world unless the world was Christianized.

But *Missions and Modern Thought* was not about missions only. It was also an apologetic for Christianity, for the new form of Christianity adapted to the conditions of the modern age—modernist Christianity.

The old theology, Carver said, had its origins in medieval social constructs. As human religion in the modern era drew closer to "the revelation of God in Christ Jesus," the reconstruction of theology became necessary.[86] The old theology was too provincial and nationalistic. The times demanded a universal religion that interpreted God as the "God of all humanity" who through

---

84. Carver, *Missions and Modern Thought*, 40, 66–67.
85. Carver, *Missions and Modern Thought*, 52–67, 136.
86. Carver, *Missions and Modern Thought*, 227.

Christ, the eternal Logos, "lighteth every man that comes into the world."[87] A new theology was therefore inevitable in the modern world. Christianity had always been the most adaptable of all religions, while at the same time it always remained true to its essence. Modern Christianity was "only tearing down her house to build a greater, because new conditions are present."[88]

The new theology recognized that religion was basic to human existence and consisted in human experience of God. "Man is essentially and so permanently religious," Carver wrote.[89] Carver described religion even as Schleiermacher had: "Religion is man's God-consciousness." God-consciousness consisted, Carver explained, of three basic sentiments: "a sense of dependence upon the super-human, the recognition of obligation to the super-human, and desire for fellowship with the super-human."[90]

Carver recognized that many Christians found the reconstruction unsettling and maintained a "stubborn resistance" against the new theology. It was nevertheless "necessary to argue from the modern viewpoint and to assume the premises of modern thought." Modern forms of thought, Carver believed, had demolished the old theology and engendered broad skepticism concerning the historical Jesus, his resurrection, miracles, and reliability of the Bible. Some of the leaders of the new theology went too far perhaps in their trust of "scientific reason and historical science," denying the rational possibility of the virgin birth and the physical resurrection. But even these, Carver suggested, were beginning to find that Jesus existed eternally in human experience. They had to acknowledge the Christ of human religion and "are offering us the 'value-judgment Christ,' the 'ideal Christ,' the 'living-Christ.'" They rejected evidence for Jesus' bodily resurrection, but the recognition of Jesus' "continuous existence" demonstrated a kind of "spiritual resurrection."[91] But Jesus was overcoming the skepticism by the proof of his life in the vital experience of vast numbers of persons. Modern biology and historical science had convinced many that the Gospel accounts of Jesus were neither "demonstrable" nor "credible," but modern psychology, Carver said, was validating the human experience of the "connection between the Ground of the world's being and humanity, proving the "essential truth" of the Gospel accounts. Modern Christianity was uncertain how to conceive and express "our gospel," but it had "more profound conviction" of its "essential truth." Jesus had "become such a force in history"

87. Carver, *Missions and Modern Thought*, 228–229.
88. Carver, *Missions and Modern Thought*, 231.
89. Carver, *Missions and Modern Thought*, 194.
90. Carver, *Missions and Modern Thought*, 122–123.
91. Carver, *Missions and Modern Thought*, 233–234.

through missionaries and "his perpetual presence with them that there is no way rationally to deny him."[92]

To reconstruct Christianity, theologians had to recognize and preserve its genuine essence. As Carver understood it, the essence of true Christianity was modernist. He contended that religion was, in its essence, the experience of God's love as the power to live for others. Although Carver held that God revealed himself in history by Jesus Christ, God had always been in the business of revealing himself in the hearts of humans, and did so still. Jesus was the Logos of God, the reason of God, and so enlightened every person. The Christian faith was fundamentally personal and experiential for Carver.

But this did not isolate humans from real knowledge of God. Ludwig Feuerbach and other critics of liberalism had argued that if all religion derived from human experience, then it could not transcend the merely human. It was trapped in its own subjectivity. But Carver, like Mullins and many liberals, overcame this criticism by asserting that God was immanent in human experience. Experience bridged the gap between thought and sensation, between spirit and matter. Religious experience and human freedom formed the ground of "personality," which transcended the limitations of physical science. "God is immanent in the world," Carver said, and therefore the forces of both natural and human evolution were "'a progressive manifestation of God.'"[93] The development of human knowledge and culture was therefore "the growth of religion." God was in all things and was bringing his purposes to pass through all things. The new understanding of religion, humanity, and Christ were but the "new unfolding of Himself" in the world.[94]

Carver therefore thoroughly subordinated the physical or the real to the spiritual or ideal. Practically, however, spiritual reality seemed nearly to slip beneath the surface of physical reality. "Man is supernatural," Carver explained elsewhere.[95] The natural order was thoroughly supernatural. What people called a miracle was merely an unusual and "unanticipated manifestation" of God. But miracles were "as natural as all the usual activity" of God. Because God

92. Carver, *Missions and Modern Thought*, 232–236. In psychology, Carver had in mind primarily William James's work *The Varieties of Religious Experience* (see 240). He elsewhere praised Josiah Royce's work (Carver, "The Faith Plea of Jesus," typescript, box 1, Carver Papers, SBHLA).

93. Carver, *Missions and Modern Thought*, 182.

94. Carver, *Missions and Modern Thought*, 196, 240.

95. Carver, "Declare the Christian Principles for Social Ethics," typescript, p. 16, in "The Function of Christianity in the Making of the World Order," Norton Lectures at Southern Baptist Theological Seminary, April 2–5, 1946, box 1, Carver Papers, SBHLA.

was immanent in all world processes, natural events, from a spiritual stand-point, had a divine basis and a divine purpose. And so "the highest function of religion," Carver wrote, "is supernaturalizing the natural."[96]

It meant also that all religions, despite their ignorance of the fact, were leading to Christianity. All religions, Carver argued, were "more or less successful movements toward God."[97] "The sacred writings of all the faiths" were "preparatory" to the full revelation of Christ. Missionaries saw first that the "Law of Buddha, the Analects of Confucius, the Bhagavad Gita" functioned in reference to Christianity in the same way that the Old Testament did.[98] Thus "we now think of the religions of the world…as approaches to God."[99] In sending out the gospel to all religions, God met "his own Spirit" leading people of "dim faith and imperfect religions unto himself."[100]

Every religion followed an evolution from primitive to more enlightened. "All religions begin with the impulsive stage," and their real growth and pure development occurred "under the guidance of the inspiration of God."[101] This was true because God was immanent in the world process and in human progress. Human "experience in all the life and movement of the world" is God's "immanent activity."[102]

Salvation in modern Christianity was living for God and his kingdom. God destined humans to establish a perfect society based on brotherhood and selfless service of others. But humans do not attain such brotherhood until they realize and acknowledge God's fatherly love. According to Carver, "Brotherhood can have no sure foundation except in fatherhood."[103] Christ redeemed persons by revealing God's fatherly love: "His Son becomes our savior by revealing the Father love of God."[104] To live in the knowledge of God's fatherly love is true faith. The cross became the "greatest principle in the rescue and development of human personality" and the "mightiest principle in the evolution of character." The cross produced faith in God's fatherly love, which resulted in salvation, living in brotherhood. It was God's purpose that humans should live in selfless service to each other, and the cross revealed "the principle that he who would

96. Carver, *Missions and Modern Thought*, 243–245.
97. Carver, *Missions and Modern Thought*, 315.
98. Carver, *Missions and Modern Thought*, 255–256.
99. Carver, *Missions and Modern Thought*, 288.
100. Carver, *Missions and Modern Thought*, 299–300.
101. Carver, *Missions and Modern Thought*, 124, 131.
102. Carver, *Missions and Modern Thought*, 158.
103. Carver, *Missions and Modern Thought*, 169.
104. Carver, *Missions and Modern Thought*, 155.

save his life must continuously lose it." [105] Jesus thus manifested God in his flesh, and for this reason he is called "Redeemer." [106]

The purpose of the whole divine scheme was the perfection of human society: "Christianity is the religion of the individual, redeemed for social service, to the end of realizing the perfect social order." [107] Jesus' "supreme" and "comprehensive work" was to implant his "life principle" in the individual soul so that individuals can fulfill their destiny in producing the "social ideal." [108]

Carver urged Christians to adapt their faith to the modern conditions. Christians who ascribed authority to the Bible were missing the point, Carver felt. The true authority was not the Bible but the God to whom the biblical records bore witness. Scripture was an indispensable historical record of God's revelation to men and recorded the writers' interpretations of God's revelation in their own hearts. The advance of Christian religion was well served by modern Christianity's "transfer of Christian authority from the Book to the soul." [109] Christians therefore did not need to fear the ravages of the historical criticism of the Bible. The "attacks on the New Testament" served only to make Christ "more resplendent and more certainly living." They proved that "Jesus Christ can not be taken away." [110]

The realization of Christ's universal love in a world Christianity cast doubt on the traditional doctrine of hell. The new theology did not yet have a final answer, Carver said, concerning the destiny of persons who rejected God's call to acknowledge his fatherhood and live in brotherhood, but a "generous and sympathetic understanding" toward the "problems of unbelief" would suggest a reasonable solution for modern theology. Carver suggested that it was time to dispense with the doctrine. Persons who supported missions from the belief that otherwise "the heathen are going to hell" needed to be shocked with such a denial as would lead them to rethink the subject. [111]

The truest conception of both the Old and the New Testament was in terms of its revelation of God's universal love for all persons. The Bible in fact did not associate the missionary duty with the doctrine of "eternal damnation," Carver argued. None of the apostles adduced "endless torment" as a "motive of his missionary endeavor." None were even "directly influenced by this." And although Jesus spoke of the "awful doom of hell," he "must have his true

105. Carver, *Missions and Modern Thought*, 164–165.
106. Carver, *Missions and Modern Thought*, 165.
107. Carver, *Missions and Modern Thought*, 207–208.
108. Carver, *Missions and Modern Thought*, 211.
109. Carver, *Missions and Modern Thought*, 250.
110. Carver, *Missions and Modern Thought*, 254.
111. Carver, *Missions and Modern Thought*, 296–297.

interpretation" translated into the "consciousness and consciences of all men." It seemed to Carver, apparently, that there would be no room for a doctrine of hell in the Jesus of the heart.[112] The loss of the doctrine of hell would not diminish the motive for the missionary enterprise. "What we have lost of the 'tragic realism' of a literal hell," Carver explained, was more than compensated by the "task of bringing whole nations into their destiny of moral life." Modern missionaries were no longer moved by the "emotional enthusiasm of snatching a few souls from the eternal burning." There was a truer conception of Christianity, of the "nature of the universalism of the Word of God."[113] All these modern developments were preparing the world for one universal religion for all men, a world Christianity, founded in the revelation of Christ in the hearts of all men and intended for the development of true personality and perfect society. "Christianity is just now coming," Carver said, to understand "Christ in terms of his true universalism." As this realization spread, Christianity would "speedily become actually universal."[114]

CARVER AND SOUTHERN BAPTISTS

Southern Baptists paid no attention to the book. James M. Frost, president of the denomination's Sunday School Board, told Carver that he could not grasp the meaning of much of the book but ventured that the parts concerning theology "do not strike me very favorably."[115] Evidently very few Southern Baptists read the book. It was in any case the clearest published expression of Carver's thought. But Southern Baptists did read and criticize some of Carver's other expressions of sympathy for liberal thought.

Carver was for many years the book review editor of the seminary's journal, the *Review and Expositor*. Carver gained quite a readership among the more progressive seminary graduates for his reviews. Walter Pope Binns, later president of William Jewell College, told Carver more than once that "your reviews are more valuable than the rest of the magazine combined."[116] In the context of a conservative Southern Baptist Convention, where self-censorship was the daily discipline of progressive faculty, book reviews afforded a rare opportunity to

---

112. Carver, *Missions and Modern Thought*, 301–306.

113. Carver, *Missions and Modern Thought*, 298–299.

114. Carver, *Missions and Modern Thought*, 282.

115. James M. Frost to William O. Carver, 2 Mar. 1911, box 4, Carver Papers, SBHLA.

116. Walter Binns to William O. Carver, 13 July 1925, box 6, Carver Papers, SBHLA.

advance progressive ideas. The writer of the review was not responsible for the progressive ideas advanced in the book under examination but could explain the ideas in ways that made them attractive. Carver was skillful in the art. For those who had eyes to see, he advocated liberal ideas. For others, he retained a position of plausible denial. He did not see this as deceit or compromise. It was merely a necessary mode of teaching in a traditionalist denomination. He desperately wanted to enlighten Southern Baptists by leading them to receive the assured conclusions of modern thought, especially regarding the character and teaching of the Bible. Impatience could end a modernist's career.

Conservatives around the convention suspected that Carver, and perhaps others on the faculty, had some modernist beliefs, but they found it difficult to pin them down.[117] J. M. Frost suggested that "the brethren are suspicious" because the faculty seemed to favor ecumenism over traditional Baptist commitments.[118] Majorities at Southern Baptist Convention meetings repeatedly expressed their opposition to ecumenical entanglements.

In 1914 Carver came under severe attack when he went too far in crediting liberal doubts concerning the virgin birth of Jesus. In a review of novelist Winston Churchill's *Inside of the Cup*, Carver stated that the virgin birth had no necessary relationship to Jesus' deity and that it was a relatively unimportant doctrine: "So far as his divinity is concerned, it is not needed." No less alarming was the means by which Carver discounted the doctrine's place in the Christian faith— he argued that it was based on later additions to Matthew and Luke. "The first edition of Matthew did not have the accounts of the birth and childhood," and the corresponding accounts in Luke "show evidence of having been wrought into the text." As a theological belief or "dogma," Carver said, "I would perhaps care no more for the virgin birth than would Mr. Churchill." He protested that he still believed in the virgin birth because it was a fact established by history.[119]

Baptist newspapers in Texas, Missouri, and Oklahoma published criticisms of Carver's statements. O. L. Hailey, in the *Baptist Standard*, took Carver to task for his statement and concluded that he "accepts the doctrine of the Virgin Birth, but on wholly insufficient reasons."[120] Carver replied that "the virgin birth

117. See, e.g., William O. Carver to R. K. Maiden, 21 Feb. 1914, box 5, Carver Papers, SBHLA.

118. William J. McGlothlin, Diary, 9 Mar. 1914, SBTS.

119. William O. Carver, review of *The Inside of the Cup*, by Winston Churchill, *Review and Expositor* 11 (1914): 290–295. For a review of the controversy, see Mark Wilson, "Sounding a False Alarm: W. O. Carver and the 1914 Controversy over the Virgin Birth," *Baptist History and Heritage* 39, no. 2 (2004): 81–89.

120. O. L. Hailey, "A Significant Review of an Epoch Making Book by Dr. W. O. Carver," *Baptist Standard*, 21 May 1914, 7, 11.

fits exactly into my theory of things" and asserted that it did not matter how he arrived at the truth of the virgin birth, but only that he agreed with it.[121]

J. W. Porter, editor of Kentucky's *Western Recorder*, suggested privately that it would be useful if Carver could affirm that he agreed with James P. Boyce's view of the virgin birth.[122] Carver replied that Porter could quote him immediately that "I am in full agreement with Dr. Boyce and all others who believe without question or quibble in the virgin birth of Jesus." But he admitted privately to Porter that "I do not now recall all that Dr. B[oyce] says on the subject and the line of argument he makes in connection with it."[123] When Carver had opportunity to examine Boyce's *Abstract of Theology*, he wrote Porter that he found "nothing on the subject from which I in any wise dissent" and authorized Porter to quote him thus in the *Western Recorder*.[124] Carver found nothing on the subject from which to dissent because he found nothing on the subject. In fact, Boyce said nothing about the virgin birth in his *Abstract of Theology*, except that the prophet Isaiah foretold that the Messiah would be born of a virgin.[125]

Carver's review and his replies left many Southern Baptists puzzled. Carver affirmed his belief in the virgin birth but at the same time minimized its importance. And he accepted the higher critical views of the origin and development of the New Testament books of Matthew and Luke. Ironically, Carver's critics missed the far more significant point that Carver recommended that all Southern Baptist preachers should read a novel that advocated a modernist program of adjusting traditional orthodoxy to modern beliefs.[126] Churchill's novel was an emotionally powerful argument for modernist Christianity. The novel's protagonist, John Hodder, confronted with the powerlessness of the traditional orthodoxy to convince and help modern men and women, painfully reconstructed his

121. William O. Carver, "A Significant Review of a Review," *Baptist Standard*, 28 May 1914, 12–13.

122. J. W. Porter to William O. Carver, 29 June 1914, "Heresy Material" folder, box 23, Carver Papers, SBHLA.

123. William O. Carver to J. W. Porter, 27 June 1914, "Heresy Material" folder, box 23, Carver Papers, SBHLA.

124. William O. Carver to J. W. Porter, 2 July 1914, ms. copy at bottom of Porter to Carver, 29 June 1914, "Heresy Material" folder, box 23, Carver Papers, SBHLA.

125. James P. Boyce, *Abstract of Systematic Theology* (Philadelphia: American Baptist Publication Society, 1887), 265. Boyce mentioned the virgin birth in one other place only, where he quoted Charles Hodge on the arguments between traducianists and creationists on the origin of the soul (209).

126. See, e.g., James B. Gambrell to William O. Carver, 18 June 1914, folder 49, box 23, Carver Papers, SBHLA.

theology. The result was a thoroughly modernist Christianity with "Personality" at the center, God's spirit as the guide, and happiness through selfless service as the end. Hodder posed the internal leading of God's spirit against the written words of the Bible—"it is by the spirit and not by the letter of our Lord's teaching that we are guided. The Spirit which we draw from the Gospels. And everything written down there that does not harmonize with it is the mistaken interpretation of men." Being born again entailed rejecting the written law and accepting guidance by God's spirit. Laws and rules were made for "those who were not reborn." The book ends with a justification of divorce "if love should cease." [127]

Around 1915 he thought that the time had perhaps come to promote liberalism openly, but he could not convince other denominational leaders that Southern Baptists would be receptive: "I tried to induce some of our leaders to begin a popular campaign in our denominational press for the education of our people in matters scientific and modern." He rightly feared that unless the people in the churches became more progressive in their ideas, denominational progressives would always be vulnerable to the election of conservative leaders who would cry out their denunciations of the progressive leadership. The only way to enlighten Southern Baptists, Carver recognized, was to acculturate them by a process of gradual education: "I think a campaign of moderate religious culture is the only way out." [128]

When New Testament professor Archibald T. Robertson could not go to China in 1923 on behalf of the fundamentalist Milton Stewart Evangelistic Fund, he recommended that it appoint Carver, for Carver was already planning on going to China that year. William Blackstone, a trustee of the fund, liked the idea but wanted to know whether Carver was "thoroughly sound on the fundamentals, is he outspoken in his defense of 'the faith once for all delivered.'" [129] Blackstone arranged to interview Carver to gain satisfaction on these points, but Carver neither had the "reputation for general conservative scholarship" nor was able to satisfy Blackstone in the interview. Carver seemed to take some satisfaction that Blackstone objected to Carver's amillennial eschatology and "was obviously very disappointed that I would not say I am eagerly expecting the early return of the Lord." [130] Robertson's agreement with more orthodox

---

127. Winston Churchill, *The Inside of the Cup* (New York: Macmillan, 1913), 259–261, 505–510.

128. William O. Carver to Livingston Johnson, 13 Aug. 1925, box 6, Carver Papers, SBHLA.

129. William E. Blackstone to Archibald T. Robertson, 23 Jan. 1923, box 4, Robertson Papers. See also Reuben A. Torrey to Robertson, 26 Feb. 1923, ibid.

130. William O. Carver to Archibald T. Robertson, 26 Feb. 1923, box 4, Robertson Papers.

views of the Bible made him popular with fundamentalists. Carver, however, could not pass muster.

Carver pointed to reviews he had written as indications of his own position. His review of Harry Emerson Fosdick's *Modern Use of the Bible* represented well his own assessment of modernism. Carver affirmed the basic character of Fosdick's modernism: "I am thoroughly convinced that Dr. Fosdick is profoundly devoted to Jesus Christ and his redemptive enterprise, and that he is rendering an enormous service to great numbers of people." Carver felt that most of the injury from Fosdick's teaching was due to "misrepresentations." He also felt that Fosdick's approach was in some respects "defective," though this probably referred to differences in approach to advancing modern religion—Carver was more patient toward those who insisted on retaining traditional forms of orthodoxy. But Carver affirmed that modernism was right in its emphasis on "vital, effective religion that works now." [131]

Carver had little choice but to be more patient than Fosdick. Southern Baptists were a very different kind of constituency than Fosdick's intellectual audiences in New York City. And Carver urged his colleagues and students of the necessity of patience. They had to learn to be content with gradual progress, though it seemed maddeningly slow. Intellectuals might accept the mythological meaning given to biblical texts by the historical criticism of mediating theologians and Ritschlians, but common Southern Baptists were not likely to be convinced of these alternatives. For them, the Bible was either straightforwardly true, or it was not. To propose that it might be true spiritually and at the same time false historically impressed most Southern Baptists as implausible.

Carver's student Norfleet Gardner reflected on this problem in a letter to his professor. He remarked that Fosdick seemed little troubled in preaching a definite and even aggressive modernism. But Gardner questioned the suitability of such preaching in most other places: "How can a man preach these views without destroying the faith of his hearers? What will it leave them to believe?" [132] Such preaching could also result in losing one's position, as liberal Southern Baptist preacher S. L. Morgan noted in 1917: "Nearly all of us are driven by the force of circumstances to be a bit more conservative than it is in our heart of hearts to be. I am frank to say to you that I have found it out of the question to move people in the mass at all, unless you go with a slowness that sometimes seems painful; and I have settled down to the conviction that it is better to lead people slowly than not at all." [133]

131. William O. Carver to Ivy Lee, 29 Apr. 1925, box 6, Carver Papers, SBHLA.

132. Norfleet Gardner to William O. Carver, 3 June 1925, box 6, Carver Papers, SBHLA.

133. S. L. Morgan to Hight Moore, box 3, folder 20, Hight Moore Papers, SBHLA, quoted in Harvey, *Redeeming the South*, 137.

Carver naturally had to be very careful concerning his published statements. In a testy letter to Texas Baptist leader James B. Gambrell, Carver said that the denomination's heresy hunters would have plenty of idle time on their hands because the faculty of the seminary would censor themselves. "Voluntary censorship is likely to be abundant enough." The seminary, Carver thought, "had never lacked" this virtue.[134]

TRADITIONAL CONSERVATIVES

Some members of the faculty were not so progressive and had little sympathy with the trends toward liberal theology in American Christianity. They seemed to interpret the progressive ideas of their colleagues as scholarship rather than as movement away from traditional orthodoxy. Edwin C. Dargan, Byron H. DeMent, H. C. Wayman, Archibald T. Robertson, and John R. Sampey represented the more conservative wing of the faculty.

Dargan left the faculty in 1907 to return to the pastorate and afterward served as president of the Southern Baptist Convention and as editor of the convention's Sunday School Board. Byron H. DeMent battled liberalism at a summer Bible conference at Monteagle, Tennessee, in 1911. After Herbert L. Willett, a University of Chicago Divinity School professor who popularized the historical-critical method, downgraded many of the miracles in the gospel accounts, DeMent stood up and opposed him. He told the audience that "personally I thought the New Testament records of the life and miracles of our Lord had been hammered down to very fine gold, and that I considered their integrity more precious than life."[135]

Robertson was the most widely recognized and accomplished scholar in the seminary's history. He established his reputation when he published his encyclopedic *Grammar of the Greek New Testament* in 1914.[136] The book was remarkably comprehensive. His ambition for accuracy and completeness caused him to despair of completing it. When he finally completed the three-foot-tall manuscript, a new set of obstacles deepened his despair. Robertson finally found a publisher willing to take on the book's unique challenges and the uncertainty

134. William O. Carver to James B. Gambrell, 24 June 1914, folder 49, box 23, Carver Papers, SBHLA.

135. Byron H. DeMent to William O. Carver, 28 Aug. 1911, box 4, Carver Papers, SBHLA; DeMent to Carver, 31 Aug. 1911, ibid.

136. Archibald T. Robertson, *A Grammar of the Greek New Testament in the Light of Historical Research* (New York: Hodder and Stoughton, 1914).

JUBILEE YEAR, 1859-1909

Faculty in 1909: (top, left to right) George B. Eager, Charles S. Gardner, Edgar Y. Mullins, John R. Sampey, William J. McGlothlin; (bottom, left to right) William O. Carver, Archibald T. Robertson, T. M. Hawes, Byron H. DeMent

of its sales, but the company demanded that Robertson pay for the typesetting. Robertson's handwriting was nearly indecipherable. The technical precision required and the many corrections Robertson made to his own text meant that in many places the type had to be reset multiple times, and the cost of typesetting rose far beyond initial expectations. He borrowed on the full value of his life insurance policy and from every other source available to him. When the expense brought him to the verge of bankruptcy, he wished the entire thing in the bottom of the Atlantic. Mullins and trustee George W. Norton initiated an endowed publishing fund to underwrite the costs.[137] George Norton and his two sisters gave $1,500 of the $10,000 fund.[138] Such pastors as J. C. Massee solicited

137. George W. Norton to Archibald T. Robertson, 11 Apr. 1914, box 3, Robertson Papers.

138. George W. Norton to Archibald T. Robertson, 13 Feb. 1914, box 3, Robertson Papers; William O. Carver, untitled typescript on Archibald T. Robertson, pp. 10.3–11.1, A. T. Roberston folder, box 24, Carver Papers, SBHLA.

Archibald T. Robertson's New Testament Interpretation class, 1906–1907

pledges to the fund, as did the seminary's agent, P. T. Hale.[139] Upon publication the grammar received the high commendation of Greek scholars.[140] During the final twenty years of his career, Robertson became quite popular as a lecturer, speaking at Northfield's summer Bible conferences many times.[141] Such fundamentalists as A. C. Dixon, William B. Riley, Curtis Lee Laws, J. C. Massee, Len Broughton, C. I. Scofield, W. H. Griffith-Thomas, J. Gresham Machen, and B. B. Warfield sought him out for counsel, articles, and lectures. When the fundamentalist Milton Stewart Evangelistic Funds sought

139. J. C. Massee to Archibald T. Robertson, 8 Apr. 1914, box 3, Robertson Papers; Robert N. Lynch to Archibald T. Robertson, 2 Mar. 1914, ibid.; P. T. Hale to Archibald T. Robertson, 17 Mar. 1914, ibid.

140. See, e.g., Edward J. Goodspeed to Archibald T. Robertson, 16 July 1914, box 3, Robertson Papers; Preserved Smith to Archibald T. Robertson, 19 Sept. 1933, box 5, ibid.; Henry J. Cadbury, Review of A Grammar of the Greek New Testament in the Light of Historical Research, *Harvard Theological Review* 8 (1915): 138–140.

141. See, e.g., W. R. Moody to Archibald T. Robertson, 9 Jan. 1914, box 3, Robertson Papers; Robert Speer to Archibald T. Robertson, 18 Jan. 1926, box 4, Robertson Papers.

Robertson's services in China for 1923, they offered him $1,000 plus expenses for himself and his wife. They wanted him to preach and lecture at the large summer assemblies of English-speaking missionaries there to combat the spread of liberalism among them.[142]

John R. Sampey, like Mullins, placed a wall of partition between scholarship and faith, but it made him uneasy. He would not surrender his conservative convictions even when his historical-critical scholarship seemed to contradict them. He preferred to distrust his scholarship rather than the traditional orthodoxy. His study of Isaiah reflected this division. Although Sampey agreed to write the Isaiah commentary for the American Bible Commentary series published by the American Baptist Publication Society, he stayed too busy teaching during the seminary session and too busy preaching during vacations to make much progress. But his haste may have been deliberately slow. He came to doubt whether Isaiah wrote all of the book ascribed to him. He told editor Alvah Hovey that "the unity of the book seems almost disproved by Driver.... I still believe that Isaiah wrote chs. 40–66, together with 13:1–14:23; 24–27; 34, 35, etc."[143] Hovey was willing for Sampey to take this position but cautioned him to express himself "wisely."[144] Like most of his colleagues in this era, Sampey held to the presumptive truth of the traditional view and to the need to evaluate a view based in part on its consequences for the faith, which in this case would seem to undermine the authority of Jesus and the New Testament generally, since they attributed the book's various sections to Isaiah. These considerations made him reluctant to teach multiple authorship for Isaiah. But Sampey was apparently convinced that critical arguments for multiple authorship could not be readily answered. He never resolved his ambivalence and never wrote the commentary. Sampey's temperament was sufficiently conservative that he hesitated to press for reform of the tradition at this point.

Mullins hired progressive men and supported them. But he disagreed with many of the conclusions of liberal theologians and was concerned to check liberalism's spread. He did not believe that the damaging forms of liberal theology would spread very far. He evidently equated liberalism with antisupernaturalist commitments and did not include his own personalist mediating theology. In 1900 he assured a worried pastor that even in the North the churches and pastors were disposed to traditional beliefs and preferred "the older forms of

---

142. See William E. Blackstone to Archibald T. Robertson, 29 Jan. 1923, box 4, Robertson Papers; Edgar L. Morgon to Archibald T. Robertson, 3 Mar. 1923, ibid.; J. W. Lowrie to Archibald T. Robertson, 19 Nov. 1922.

143. John R. Sampey to Alvah Hovey, 9 Jan. 1897, Alvah Hovey Collection, ANTS.

144. Alvah Hovey to John R. Sampey, 16 Jan. 1897, Sampey Papers.

theology." Mullins wrote that it was not "at all possible" for the new theology to gain wide acceptance, because "it is not scriptural, and can not do the work of saving men." Mullins held that orthodox doctrine, being true, need fear no peril: "I have the utmost confidence in the ability of the old theology to hold its own against all comers." [145]

By the early 1920s, however, Mullins grew anxious about the spread of liberal theology. He feared that false teachers were gaining ascendancy among the European Baptist groups within the Baptist World Alliance. As a result, he was more willing to make common cause with fundamentalists in blocking the advance of liberalism. His opposition to liberalism in the Southern Baptist Convention made him extremely popular in the denomination the last decade of his life. It earned him top denominational leadership, as well as the scorn of such denominational progressives as Carver. He left a legacy of progressive thought that reshaped Baptist theology, but he also charted a course to reassert orthodoxy in the denomination.

145. E. Y. Mullins to A. I. Justice, 13 Apr. 1900, Letterpress Copy Book 20, 17 Feb. 1898–1 Aug. 1901, pp. 606–607.

7

REASSERTING ORTHODOXY
Mullins and Denominational Leadership

Mullins appeared to grow more conservative in the second half of his tenure as president as he led the denomination to stand for traditional orthodoxy. The change was more apparent than real. In this period Mullins rose to leadership of the Southern Baptist Convention. Effective leadership in the populist denomination demanded sensitivity to the majority. Although he agreed with the conservative majority on many points, he also sought to express the majority views in ways that did the least harm to progressive aspirations. He sought to provide space for progressive theology in the seminary and did not want to drive progressives from the denomination. But he also needed to keep the denomination's trust in the seminary's orthodoxy and denominational loyalty. It was a difficult balancing act, and he drew the criticisms of progressives and conservatives alike. In the end Mullins accomplished as much to reassert orthodoxy as to promote progressive theology.

Mullins led Southern Baptists through their three most controversial issues of the 1920s. Under his leadership, Southern Baptists repudiated ecumenical alliances, rejected the theory of evolution, and adopted a creed to link Southern Baptist agencies to traditional orthodoxy. Mullins wrote or cowrote the statements adopted in all three actions and gained a sterling reputation as a champion of orthodoxy among Southern Baptists.

But the more popular he became, the more he lost the respect of progressives on the faculty. They felt that Mullins's efforts to bolster popular orthodoxy only encouraged Southern Baptists to reject progressive ideas. His efforts made it more difficult for the faculty to lead the denomination toward progressive thought and out of their traditionalism. The progressive faculty recognized that they had to be content with the gradual advance through cautious and patient pedagogy. They nevertheless longed for progress and believed that Mullins's efforts were hindering it.

A REALISTIC APPROACH TO DENOMINATIONAL CHANGE

Mullins was confident that commitment to progressive ideas would grow, even among Southern Baptists. Progress was inevitable, Mullins held, but it would have to be slow progress where Southern Baptists were in view: "We will undoubtedly continue to go forward, because all the modern educational conditions favor progress, but we will have to go slowly, beyond a doubt." Genuine denominational progress would require perfect "patience."[1]

Mullins and his progressive colleagues adopted a realistic approach to reforming the denomination. If they pressed for rapid change, they risked alienating the very constituency they sought to reform. Progressives chafed and grew restive at times under these constraints, but they could not evade their necessity. When faculty progressives had wanted to rebel against the popular Southern Baptist opposition to Whitsitt in 1898, Georgia editor Isaac Van Ness explained to A. T. Robertson that criticizing the denomination would hurt the seminary. The faculty had to be realistic: "You may sometimes feel that it would be more comfortable to be free from the convention, but facts are facts, and we must do our best with the facts."[2] Facing the facts meant a realistic appraisal of where the mass Southern Baptists stood and where they could be led.

Shailer Mathews, a leading liberal theologian at the University of Chicago Divinity School and a veteran of denominational reform efforts, explained the realistic approach:

Education has to begin where people are not where they ought to be. If this be recognized, conflict between the progressive and the reactionary elements in religious thought may not be avoided but it will at least be postponed long enough to make some type of cooperation between the two elements possible. Whether or not one calls it compromise, cooperation between liberals and conservatives will always be in the direction of the liberals. Progress may be slow but to one who takes a long view of social process it is certain. Those who take a realistic view of progress through

1. Edgar Y. Mullins to William J. McGlothlin, 24 June 1914, Letterpress Copy Book 43, 1913–1914.

2. Isaac Van Ness to A. T. Robertson, ca. Oct. 1898, box 6, Robertson Papers.

cooperation rather than through conflict must be educators rather than agitators. And education demands patience.[3]

This was the blueprint for Southern Seminary's progressives also, and they followed it for most of the twentieth century. It was the policy of realist denominational relations.

The commitment to a realistic denominational diplomacy was for the most part little more than a conspiracy of circumspection. From the beginning of his presidency, Mullins understood the necessity of the realist approach. Whitsitt's idealistic crusade had damaged the seminary's reputation and diminished its effectiveness as an agency of reform. The faculty had to avoid giving additional offense in order to repair the denomination's trust.

BETWEEN FUNDAMENTALISM AND LIBERALISM

Mullins was well suited to leading the seminary's realist denominational relations. He agreed with most of the old orthodoxy and sought to preserve it. But modern thought forced a new approach to orthodoxy. Mullins's great project was to reestablish orthodoxy on a new philosophical foundation that was more secure than the realist philosophy of Boyce and Charles Hodge. The old orthodoxy did not survive the transition entirely intact, but at many points it did. Mullins's ambition to conserve orthodoxy on a new foundation won him the trust and admiration of most Southern Baptists.

Although Mullins won the confidence of both fundamentalists and modernists, and although he sympathized with both, during the 1920s he identified increasingly with the fundamentalists. His leadership in the adoption of the Baptist Faith and Message, with its strong statement of the inerrancy of the Bible, won praise among many fundamentalists. Mullins seemed genuinely pleased that the Baptist Faith and Message "has met with the enthusiastic endorsement of every Fundamentalist who has retained his balance and poise."[4]

Mullins and most of the faculty had the trust of fundamentalist leaders and, with the exception of J. Frank Norris, maintained cordial relations with them. Southern Seminary graduates in fact filled the front ranks of the fundamentalist leadership. J. Frank Norris, William B. Riley, A. C. Dixon, J. C. Massee, and John Roach Straton were all alumni of Southern Seminary. J. M. Gray, president

3. Shailer Mathews, *New Faith for Old: An Autobiography* (New York: Macmillan, 1936), 77–78.

4. Edgar Y. Mullins to S. M. Brown, 15 Mar. 1926, box 34, Mullins Papers.

of Moody Bible Institute, invited Mullins to speak at fundamentalist Bible conferences in the North. In 1926 Mullins urged Curtis Lee Laws, editor of the fundamentalist weekly *Watchman-Examiner*, to give an address to the students.[5] When Laws needed an associate editor, he asked the faculty at Southern Seminary to recommend one of their young graduates, and he hired one.[6] At the height of the fundamentalist-modernist controversy in 1925, Laws ran a series of articles defending major fundamentalist doctrines—he asked Mullins to write them.[7] A. T. Robertson valued the scholarship of the liberals and was disturbed by the reactionary and ill-informed criticisms of many fundamentalists, but his convictions on most points aligned with the fundamentalists.

One of Southern Seminary's professors became a leader in the fundamentalist movement, if only briefly. H. C. Wayman, who taught Old Testament at Southern Seminary from 1915 to 1923, became president of the fundamentalists' ill-fated Des Moines University in 1928. At the end of Wayman's first year, T. T. Shields, president of the board and leading fundamentalist preacher, told Wayman to dismiss several professors for modernist tendencies. Wayman disagreed with Shields's assessment and refused. Shields then induced the board to fire Wayman and all thirty-eight faculty. Students rebelled, and the university did not reopen.[8]

PRESIDENTIAL AUTHORITY AND THE LIMITS
OF PROGRESSIVE THOUGHT

In 1911 several members of the faculty grew restive under Mullins and challenged his authority and his manner of administering the school. The conflict lasted several months, and several professors contemplated resignation. A number of factors provoked the controversy.

One factor was jealousy. The faculty grew alienated from Mullins because they believed that he followed egoist principles in how he treated the faculty and

5. Edgar Y. Mullins to Curtis Lee Laws, 30 Mar. 1926, box 34, Mullins Papers; Laws to Mullins, 5 Apr. 1926, ibid.

6. Curtis Lee Laws to Archibald T. Robertson, 10 Oct. 1925, box 4, Robertson Papers; Laws to John R. Sampey, 13 Sept. 1929, box 1, Sampey Papers; Sampey to Law, 20 Sept. 1929, ibid. In 1925 Laws hired Austen K. DeBlois; in 1929 he hired John Slemp. DeBlois was not a Southern Seminary alumnus; Slemp was.

7. Curtis Lee Laws to Edgar Y. Mullins, 21 June 1925, box 35, Mullins Papers. Mullins agreed to write the articles.

8. See George M. Marsden, *Fundamentalism in American Culture: The Shaping of Twentieth Century Evangelicalism* (New York: Oxford University Press, 1980), 190–191; unattributed, "Noble Inspiration," *Time*, 20 May 1929.

ran the seminary. The faculty judged that he was content to accept the generous salary that the trustees offered him, but that he would not support a trustee
effort to raise faculty salaries. They felt that he was unconcerned with their
careers and their livelihoods. At times they referred to him as the "Pope." [9]

Mullins was younger than most of the faculty, had no teaching experience,
and was relatively unknown when he became president. Within a few years
he advanced to leadership of the Southern Baptist Convention and the Baptist
World Alliance. It did not help that he carried himself with an aristocratic
air and exercised the president's prerogative of executive authority in making
decisions relating to the seminary. The faculty expected to participate in such
decisions. Inman Johnson, who taught voice at the seminary and came to know
Mullins well, reported that "there was a good bit of jealousy of Mullins in the
faculty." [10]

Another factor in the 1911 faculty rebellion was financial. The cost of living
had been going up since Mullins became president, and faculty salaries had
not kept pace. Mullins's stated salary was the same as the professors', $2,500
annually, but he received another $2,500 annually for his role in raising the
seminary's endowment. Trustees afterward made his salary simply $5,000 and
a home but did not raise the faculty's salaries.

Sampey begged Edwin C. Dargan, who had became a trustee since resigning as professor of homiletics in 1907, to lead an effort among trustees to raise
faculty salaries, which were "not enough to meet my reasonable expenses."
Mullins's extra sources of income set him apart from the faculty. As Sampey
wrote to Dargan, "Mullins is the only man making expenses.... The rest of us
still abide in 'Poverty Row.'" [11]

Mullins understood the 1911 tensions as a misunderstanding concerning
salaries merely. It was at the May 1911 meeting of the board of trustees that the
board voted to make Mullins's salary $5,000 plus a home. When one trustee
suggested that the faculty salaries ought to be raised to $3,500 with the use
of a home rent-free, Mullins agreed that this was what ought to be done, but
that "the future was beset by many uncertainties in our collections and that it
would be unwise to take such action then." The board voted to raise faculty
salaries to $3,500, but without the benefit of a home. When Mullins explained
these matters afterward to the faculty, they still were not satisfied. The raise

9. Inman Johnson to Timothy F. George, 19 Feb. 1988, Timothy George folder,
Honeycutt Papers.

10. Inman Johnson to Timothy F. George, 19 Feb. 1988, Timothy George folder,
Honeycutt Papers.

11. John R. Sampey to Edwin C. Dargan, 23 Dec. 1910, Dargan Papers, SBHLA.

came at the trustees' initiative. Had it been left to Mullins, their salaries would still be $2,500. The faculty were unimpressed when Mullins told them that he suggested to several trustees that his salary should be reduced to $4,500 and a home.[12]

Many on the faculty believed that there was an institutional purpose in making Mullins's salary so much greater than the faculty's. It represented the vesting of administrative authority in him. It tended to put the president in a class above the faculty and "to centralize the seminary government in the president." Mullins disclaimed any such intention on his part: "I am in hearty accord with the principle of faculty government. I have never desired to change it."[13] The faculty replied in an official statement that their memories of the facts and their interpretations of events differed from his: "We do not, therefore, accept the statement submitted to us as including all of the pertinent facts." Above all, the faculty emphasized their belief that they ought to operate the seminary by a "democratic faculty government." It was the "historic method" of governing the seminary, and it remained for them "the true ideal for the future." They professed to accept "in good faith" Mullins's statement committing himself to the principle, but they did not entirely trust him.[14] His actions in 1911 suggested that although he may have believed in shared government among the faculty in principle, he practiced presidential rule by executive authority.

Another factor was evidently Mullins's effort to restrict the faculty's promotion of liberal ideas. Although no record survives of what Mullins told them, the evidence suggests that he warned the faculty to avoid publishing any statements that Southern Baptists would construe as liberalism.[15] Carver had recently published his *Missions and Modern Thought*, which made the case for liberal Christianity. And early in 1911 A. T. Robertson published a commentary on the Gospel of Matthew that seemed to credit liberal views of the book. Shailer Mathews, the editor of the commentary series and dean of the University of Chicago Divinity School, knew that some of the material in the commentary posed a danger to Robertson: "If you have any suspicion that it might so

12. Edgar Y. Mullins to the Faculty of the Southern Baptist Theological Seminary, 25 Sept. 1911, box 24, Carver Papers, SBHLA.

13. Edgar Y. Mullins to the Faculty of the Southern Baptist Theological Seminary, 25 Sept. 1911, box 24, Carver Papers, SBHLA.

14. "Action by the Faculty with Respect to the Communication Submitted by Dr. Mullins," 12 Oct. 1911, box 24, Carver Papers, SBHLA.

15. See John R. Sampey to Edwin C. Dargan, 2 June 1911, Dargan Papers, SBHLA; William J. McGlothlin to Archibald T. Robertson, 28 June 1911, box 2, Robertson Papers; William O. Carver to Robertson, 17 July 1911, ibid.; Sampey to Robertson, 2 Aug. 1911, ibid.

thoroughly commit yourself to 'higher criticism' as to arouse trouble, I shall be very willing to omit it." Including the material might prove a "handicap in the splendid work you are doing in leading your constituency out into the bigger vision."[16] When the book appeared, it caused no public controversy, but some denominational leaders found it troubling.

Isaac J. Van Ness, president of the Southern Baptist Sunday School Board, was puzzled by Robertson's introduction to the commentary. Robertson seemed to say that the "gospel of Matthew was written by an unknown person at an unknown time, who took the *logia* of Matthew and the Greek Mark and various other documents" and from them produced the canonical gospel.[17] Van Ness disagreed "entirely" with this theory and thought that if it was true, it "would utterly destroy to me any real inspiration in the book."[18] He noted that several of Vanderbilt University's liberal professors were "greatly gratified over your stand."[19]

Princeton seminary's Charles R. Eerdman regretted that Robertson had agreed to write a volume in this commentary series. The series was "discreditable" because it was premised on "radical criticism" and yet was "designated 'the Bible for home and school.'" Robertson, Eerdman felt, should not have permitted "the weight of your scholarship and high Christian character to add influence to such a project." He criticized Robertson's analysis of the origin of the text of Matthew "in accordance with the radical critical theories."[20] All in all, Robertson had given aid and comfort to the liberal scholarship associated with Shailer Mathews and the University of Chicago.

Mullins recognized that the seminary faculty could not afford to encourage liberal theology in their published writings. Carver and Robertson published their objectionable books—Carver's was much more objectionable, but both avoided public controversy—shortly before Mullins applied his authority to limit the activity of the faculty. After this episode, neither Carver nor Robertson repeated the offense. Robertson apparently had little desire in this direction and had no genuine sympathy with liberalism. Carver could not avoid letting slip here and there some encouragement to liberalism, but he produced nothing akin to *Missions and Modern Thought* again.

16. Shailer Mathews to Archibald T. Robertson, 11 Apr. 1910, Archibald T. Robertson Papers, WFU.

17. Isaac J. Van Ness to Archibald T. Robertson, 5 May 1911, box 2, Robertson Papers.

18. Isaac J. Van Ness to Archibald T. Robertson, 2 May 1911, box 2, Robertson Papers.

19. Isaac J. Van Ness to Archibald T. Robertson, 10 May 1911, box 2, Robertson Papers.

20. Charles R. Eerdman to Archibald T. Robertson, 31 Oct. 1911, box 2, Robertson Papers.

A final factor in the faculty rebellion was Mullins's imposition of restrictions on the faculty regarding denominational participation and leadership. In 1911 he evidently suggested that the seminary was not well served by the faculty's denominational leadership. Denominational leadership was important for the seminary, but it needed to be the president and not the faculty in this role.

Mullins apparently felt that the seminary president alone should exercise significant denominational leadership. Mullins may have feared that his faculty would become more popular and influential in the denomination than he was. Robertson, Sampey, McGlothlin, and Carver were indeed becoming very popular. Robertson especially was growing in the esteem of the denomination for both his preaching and his scholarship. The seminary could not afford for the faculty to become the president's rivals for denominational leadership.

Robertson was especially troubled by Mullins's assertion of authority. He reflected on the situation to his wife in August 1911: "There is the dark

Archibald T. Robertson at his Norton Hall office in 1912

background of Dr. Mullins's jealousy and suspicions of us all, which I left in June. It is pathetic and tragic. I have reveled for some days in glorious fellowship with some of the choicest spirits of earth. I shall not let Dr. M[ullins] bring that shadow back. He may live in it himself with all his selfish narrowness if he wills. I have other and richer fellowship now. Sampey writes in a somewhat better mood, but with the sad strain of a lost love. So do McGlothlin and Carver. We are all four drawn closer together." [21]

An unexpected turn of events that summer of 1911 resulted in Robertson receiving invitations to preach at New York's Madison Avenue Baptist Church and at the Northfield Bible Conference. Robertson was delighted with the warm appreciation that New York Baptists and the Northfield evangelicals expressed toward him. It largely reconciled him to Mullins's strictures. "I feel now as if I have made a turn in my career," Robertson told his wife toward summer's end, "and have entered upon a new stage in my life. What may come now I cannot foresee. Anything good may happen." [22] Robertson settled into these new spheres of labor largely outside the Southern Baptist Convention and did not disturb Mullins's ambitions.

Carver later marveled at Robertson's adjustment to Mullins's ambitions:

Robertson devoted so much time to lecture engagements, very largely beyond the bounds of the Southern Baptist Convention. Early in his career he had envisaged a line of service in the field of denominational leadership. He was gaining some reputation and manifested some abilities in these lines when he definitely realized that the president of the seminary did not care to have any members of his faculty to become too prominent in denominational life and leadership. Robertson told me that when he came definitely to this conviction and knew that he could achieve his desire and ambition without getting into conflict with the president, he deliberately made up his mind to devote himself to writing and lecturing as his way of contribution to the Christian cause outside the seminary. He found increasing satisfaction in these forms of service and work and accepted without bitterness that he could not be in any large sense a convention "leader," and he loyally supported the ambitions and achievements of Dr. Mullins in his extraordinary efforts and successes in such leadership. [23]

21. Archibald T. Robertson to Ella Robertson, 11 Aug. 1911, box 2, Robertson Papers.

22. Archibald T. Robertson to Ella Robertson, 11 Aug. 1911, box 2, Robertson Papers. See also W. R. Moody to Archibald T. Robertson, 14 Aug. 1911, ibid.

23. William O. Carver, "Recollections and Information from Other Sources Concerning the Southern Baptist Theological Seminary," SBTS, 45.

William J. McGlothlin

Robertson became Mullins's warm supporter and promoter, and Mullins came to rely heavily on Robertson's counsel. He gave up aspirations to equality with the president and become instead his promoter and chief counselor.[24]

McGlothlin, however, apparently transgressed Mullins's restrictions inadvertently around 1914 or 1915, as McGlothlin attained the kind of leadership in the Southern Baptist Convention that had thus far eluded Mullins. Mullins would struggle for nearly two decades before he won the broad popularity among Southern Baptists he had sought. He had won great fame among Northern Baptists and among Baptists in Canada and England by his brilliant address on the "axioms of religion" in 1905 at the inaugural meeting of the Baptist World Alliance in London. The University of Chicago Divinity School had sought him to become its dean. The Rochester Theological Seminary had been seeking to convince him to accept the presidency there. But Mullins was facing some headwinds in his ambitions for denominational leadership in the South. At the 1914 Southern Baptist Convention, he ran for president and lost to Lansing Burrows.

24. Robertson, e.g., boosted Mullins for the presidency of the Baptist World Alliance in1922 (Curtis Lee Laws to Archibald T. Robertson, 10 July 1922, box 4, Robertson Papers).

McGlothlin, by contrast, was reaching a high pitch of popularity with both students and the denomination in 1914.[25] Kentucky legislators sought private conferences with him concerning prohibition legislation in 1916.[26] He led the statewide effort to add a course on the Bible to the state's high school graduation requirements and wrote the curriculum.[27] At the 1917 meeting of the Southern Baptist Convention, McGlothlin introduced an important motion to amend the convention's bylaws and preached a sermon that the convention voted to publish and distribute widely.[28]

Joshua Levering, president of the board of trustees and chairman of the denomination's war-era Food Conservation Commission, appointed McGlothlin rather than Mullins or Robertson to serve as Southern Baptists' representative to the Food Department in Washington, D.C., in 1917. The faculty could hardly deny McGlothlin a leave of absence in the patriotic cause, especially when the Southern Baptist Convention had asked him to do it. The Food Department kept McGlothlin occupied for many months.[29] He afterward served on Herbert Hoover's Commission for European Relief.

Richard Edmonds, editor of the *Manufacturer's Record*, urged McGlothlin to tour the country to devote himself "to making addresses on the war situation." The idea appealed to McGlothlin—"the greatest opportunity I shall now have to serve my country and the cause of civilization"—and Edmonds promised to pay all expenses.[30] Instead, the federal food administration asked McGlothlin to spend two months speaking on food conservation in the Midwest.[31] He addressed "large and enthusiastic" crowds in Ohio, Indiana, and Illinois.[32]

At the 1918 meeting of the Southern Baptist Convention, McGlothlin addressed a mass meeting with George Truett and James B. Gambrell.[33] Gambrell told him that McGlothlin's 1918 convention address was the most satisfying he had ever heard and that he considered McGlothlin the denomination's top educational leader.[34] Furman University, Mercer University, and Howard College (now Samford University) each pressed him to permit his election as president,

25. William J. McGlothlin, Diary, 17 May 1914, Archives and Special Collections, SBTS.
26. McGlothlin, Diary, 16 Feb. 1916.
27. McGlothlin, Diary, 28 Apr. 1916.
28. McGlothlin, Diary, 21 May 1917.
29. McGlothlin, Diary, 27 Aug. 1917.
30. McGlothlin, Diary, 22 Oct. 1917.
31. McGlothlin, Diary, 4 Jan. 1918.
32. McGlothlin, Diary, 2 Feb. 1918; 9 Feb. 1918.
33. McGlothlin, Diary, 19 May 1918.
34. McGlothlin, Diary, 2 Aug. 1918.

but he felt he could serve God more effectively at the seminary. Other Baptist leaders looked to McGlothlin as their leader in theological education, seeing him as the natural successor to Mullins. As McGlothlin noted in his diary, "Many men to whom I have spoken have said that I would certainly be elected president of the seminary if the present president should be removed."[35]

These were dangerous ideas, especially since McGlothlin was dissatisfied with his situation in the seminary. He felt that he was being treated unfairly. He spent the summer of 1914 in Europe in order to study, but the massive disruptions at the start of the war there frustrated his plans. This meant also that he had not been able to earn extra money by speaking at conferences and supplying pulpits during the summer, as his colleagues had. And when the faculty distributed courses in 1914, he alone ended up with a larger load.[36]

There may have been some rivalry between Robertson and McGlothlin. After 1911 Robertson became Mullins's favorite. When Mullins was too ill to represent the seminary at important occasions, he sent Robertson to represent him. McGlothlin felt that Robertson had unfairly prevented the graduation of one of McGlothlin's doctoral students. When McGlothlin had to be absent for two weeks in the 1916 school session, the work was assigned to a student fellow, but when Robertson was on "vacation" during the same session, McGlothlin and other professors had to teach his classes.[37] In a 1916 faculty meeting, Robertson directed an "outburst" against McGlothlin for aiding students in proving another student guilty of sexual immorality. Mullins naturally sided with Robertson and privately admonished McGlothlin. "I didn't relish the talk," was McGlothlin's only comment.[38]

Carver remembered McGlothlin's growing alienation: "McGlothlin early began to feel a call and to cherish an ambition for denominational leadership which began to come to him naturally. With the coming of the World War he was invited to accept membership on the Government Commission for European Relief headed by Herbert Hoover. In this capacity he came into important official and personal relationships and extended his reputation. By this time it was evident that he would not be content to limit his talents and time wholly to the seminary and the normal engagements which come to the seminary professor. He was serving on important convention committees, sometimes as chairman.... Dr. Mullins...was still unwilling that any of them [the faculty] should aspire to or attain to eminent leadership.... After the

35. McGlothlin, Diary, 24 June 1918; 6 Apr. 1919.
36. McGlothlin, Diary, 19 Dec. 1914.
37. McGlothlin, Diary, 17 May 1914; 20 Dec. 1914; 14 June 1915; 13 Dec. 1915.
38. McGlothlin, Diary, 17 Feb. 1916.

World War the wide recognition of McGlothlin and his obvious determination not to be deterred from this opportunity by his seminary connection, gradually developed tension between him and Mullins and Robertson."[39]

In 1919 Furman trustees again pressed McGlothlin to accept the presidency. The same year the Southern Baptist Convention enthusiastically elected him corresponding secretary (president) of the denomination's education board. McGlothlin confided in Carver, and Carver urged him to stay at the seminary. But McGlothlin found Mullins unable to sympathize with his situation.[40] At first McGlothlin was inclined to accept Mullins's requirement that he restrict himself to an "officially correct" role and "school myself to want nothing more."[41] But Mullins and Robertson distanced themselves from McGlothlin, no doubt hoping that he would accept one of the many employment offers that were coming his way. The estrangement became unbearable to McGlothlin, who wrote in his diary, "The attitude of Mullins and Robertson had been galling for a good long time and was constantly growing worse."[42] Since 1916 the situation had been "very unpleasant." McGlothlin confronted Mullins in May 1919 and described how Mullins had neglected, ignored, and repulsed McGlothlin for three years. McGlothlin recorded that Mullins "admitted it and justified himself by saying that he had been warned against me and was guarding himself against me." Mullins drove him away. McGlothlin interpreted it as jealousy: "Mullins is ambitious and a lover of money. I do not believe in him." McGlothlin accepted the presidency of Furman.[43] The Southern Baptist Convention elected him president three successive years, 1930–1932. McGlothlin remained at Furman until his death from an auto accident in 1933.

In 1914 Mullins drove Byron H. DeMent also from the faculty, apparently with Robertson's active counsel. Mullins had recruited DeMent from the faculty of Baylor's theology department in 1906, which two years afterward became the Southwestern Baptist Theological Seminary. B. H. Carroll had assured DeMent of his hope that DeMent would succeed him as Southwestern Seminary's president. At Baylor, DeMent taught Hebrew, homiletics, apologetics, and ecclesiology.[44] His department at Southern was Sunday School pedagogy, later called religious education. This was a new discipline, and he had to develop his own curriculum in a department that could never earn the

39. Carver, "Recollections," 56–57.
40. McGlothlin to Carver, 25 June 1918, box 5, Carver Papers, SBHLA.
41. McGlothlin to Carver, 25 June 1918, box 5, Carver Papers, SBHLA.
42. McGlothlin, Diary, 8 Oct. 1919.
43. McGlothlin, Diary, 6 June 1919.
44. See Byron H. DeMent to William O. Carver, 19 Dec. 1903, box 4, Carver Papers, SBHLA.

same respect accorded the traditional disciplines. He also assisted Mullins by hearing students' recitations in systematic theology and assisted similarly in Hebrew. Mullins gave the class brilliant and engaging lectures. DeMent's job was to hear and grade their memorization of the assigned text. DeMent had been a successful teacher at Southwestern Seminary, but the dry and tedious nature of the recitation sections put him at significant disadvantage to Mullins. When students complained, Mullins, apparently supported by Robertson, tried to remove DeMent. They worked to have him called to a church. When the Greenwood, South Carolina, Baptist Church called DeMent, "Mullins advised that his colleague accept the call."[45] McGlothlin explained that "Mullins virtually told him that he ought to resign. It cost him a great deal of pain, but I think he goes without bitterness or resentment. DeMent is one of the most amiable and lovable men to be found anywhere. The students all loved him as a man but they were not satisfied with his teaching."[46] DeMent was humiliated and "suffered greatly during the negotiations," but he did as Mullins wished.[47] From 1917 to 1928, DeMent was the president of the New Orleans Baptist Bible Institute, which became the New Orleans Baptist Theological Seminary.

The president's relationship to the faculty would always be fraught with peril. Whitsitt reacted strongly against Boyce's authority, though Boyce was hardly domineering and was often unassertive. But Boyce had well-considered opinions on most matters. On many questions that came before the faculty, Boyce stated his opinion but also stated his readiness to support the will of the faculty. When consulting with Broadus on seminary business, Boyce frequently followed the same course and left the final decision to Broadus. But Boyce's views generally seemed better, and when he stated his opinions, he generally persuaded his hearers. His arguments were solidly entrenched, and his hearty commitment and daring were infectious. Above all, his career of wise leadership and sacrificial labors earned him considerable deference. He had proved his judgment over the years. Whitsitt seems to have been alone in his cynical appraisal of Boyce's leadership. The 1911 controversy and the resignations of McGlothlin and DeMent revealed that Mullins had rather less success than Boyce. But much had changed since Boyce's day. Seminary operations were larger in every way, the denomination had grown in size and complexity, and American religion had experienced dramatic change.

The most consistent sources of faculty alienation over the years were the president's exercise of executive authority, and salaries, especially when the

45. Carver, "Recollections," 84–86.
46. McGlothlin, Diary, 19 Dec. 1914.
47. McGlothlin, Diary, 7 Dec. 1914.

president's seemed to diverge significantly from the faculty's. Inman Johnson, who had been a student and professor during Mullins's presidency, reported that W. O. Carver once complained that "Dr. Mullins didn't consult me when he bought the property of the Beeches."[48] Salaries figured in other contests during Mullins's tenure. By the time of the nation's entry into the First World War, faculty salaries still lagged. Their buying power had been eroded by inflation. Some faculty were pressed to the limit of endurance. When they learned that trustees had raised Mullins's salary by $1,500 and that the YMCA was paying him an additional $2,000 for his leadership of their work in Camp Taylor, a rupture with Mullins was imminent. Several trustees took the initiative to vote raises for the faculty and defused the tension.[49] Jesse Weatherspoon, who was a trustee for some years during "Dr. Mullins' regime," reported that Mullins's executive authority regarding salaries provoked another crisis. "Up to that time Dr. Mullins decided salaries, and who was to get what. There was no salary schedule and Dr. Mullins wanted it that way." The board resolved the crisis by adopting a salary schedule.[50]

ECUMENISM AND THE 1914 EFFICIENCY COMMISSION

One of the great problems facing Southern Baptists between 1910 and 1920 related to the question of ecumenism, the extent to which the Southern Baptist Convention could cooperate or affiliate with other denominations. In 1913 the Southern Baptist Convention appointed the Efficiency Commission, an ad hoc committee with an omnibus commission to study all aspects of the convention's operations and make recommendations to "advance the fitness and efficiency of our organization." The commission, under the leadership of Mullins and James B. Gambrell, decided to address the question of ecumenical cooperation. This had practical bearings at the time with regard to Sunday school curricula, religious literature, and especially missionary operations. In China the mission board was operating schools jointly with the Northern Baptist Convention, but at the same time the Southern Baptist Convention was receiving Northern Baptist churches into the Southern Baptist Convention on the plea that the Northern Baptist Convention tolerated heresy. Most Southern Baptists felt that most other groups either tolerated heresy or taught serious

---

48. Inman Johnson, transcription of trustee interviews 28–30 Apr. 1958, 1:194.

49. See Carver, "Recollections," 10–11.

50. Jesse Weatherspoon, transcription of trustee interviews 28–30 Apr. 1958, 2:240–241.

errors. Cooperation with them would discredit and undermine Southern Baptist beliefs.

When the Efficiency Commission reported at the 1914 meeting of the Southern Baptist Convention, the burden of its report related to the question of cooperation with other religious groups. Mullins drafted its creedal section defining those Baptist doctrines most relevant to the question, and Gambrell drafted its section discussing the principles of cooperation. The report suggested that from a practical standpoint alone Southern Baptists could rarely expect to cooperate with other groups in religious endeavors in any meaningful way. The primary reason was that Southern Baptists disagreed with the scripture interpretations of most other groups, and they had a responsibility to promote their own interpretation. Nor could they with integrity receive money given for the promotion of Baptist views and spend any part of it in an effort that would promote other views. Commitment to orthodox Baptist doctrine was the main obstacle to ecumenical alliances. Gambrell praised Mullins's delineation of the New Testament doctrines that Baptists would not compromise by such alliances: "The doctrinal statement simply put up the Baptist front to a disintegrating movement affecting our work.... Our missionaries abroad have the Baptist answer to the unionizing appeals made to them." The creed was necessary for protecting the doctrinal integrity of Southern Baptist institutions and missionary endeavors.[51]

Most Southern Baptists recognized that in adopting the report they were adopting a creed and bearing testimony to their doctrinal convictions. They cheered the fact that the convention had drawn the lines clearly and repudiated all cooperation that threatened to diminish their testimony to scripture truth. J. F. Love, president of the Foreign Mission Board, used the report to end all arguments in favor of Southern Baptist cooperation on the mission field. Southern Baptists' sense of the stewardship of sound doctrine led them to oppose entangling alliances. When some Southern Baptist missionaries in China petitioned Love in favor of cooperation with other groups in theological education or other endeavors, he answered that the adoption of the 1914 report represented a clear conviction against it: "Sentiment in the Southern Baptist Convention, therefore, is overwhelmingly against alliance with those who so disregard our traditional faith."[52]

51. James B. Gambrell, "Editorial Notes and Comments," *Baptist Standard*, 4 June 1914, 4; Gambrell, "A Well Placed Interrogation Point," *Baptist Standard*, 11 June 1914, 8; Gambrell, "The Uses and Abuses of Creedal Statements," *Baptist Standard*, 18 June 1914, 1, 32.

52. J. F. Love to Charles R. Shepherd, 23 Sept. 1916, Charles R. Shepherd folder, box 54, Missionary Correspondence, Foreign Mission Board Papers, SBHLA.

Some of the more progressive leaders demurred, however. R. H. Pitt, editor of Virginia Baptists' *Religious Herald*, for example, expressed disappointment that Southern Baptists had closed the door on kingdom cooperation. Privately, Mullins believed that the report actually provided significant ground for cooperation: "It formally and decisively declares for cooperation with other denominations wherever it is possible." Mullins believed that the committee's report was the least restrictive position that Southern Baptists would approve: "In my judgment, a much more objectionable deliverance would have been made if this had not been prepared beforehand."[53] Mullins even claimed that the report committed Southern Baptists to cooperate with other bodies: "The convention has formally committed itself to the principle of cooperation, the first time it ever did so in its history."[54] Mullins agreed with the denomination's conservative position at most points, but he tried also to prevent the convention from driving off the progressives.

Mullins himself seemed satisfied with the statement's creed and position on cooperation. Cooperation in religious endeavors necessarily required agreement in the evangelical fundamentals of the Bible. No less important, such cooperation could not occur if it threatened to compromise any area of scripture truth. Baptists were in basic agreement about what the Bible taught, and it would do good to stipulate among themselves and publish to the world their interpretation of the Bible. Regarding cooperation, Mullins felt that the statement was progressive, for although it acknowledged the firm boundaries restricting Southern Baptists from many kinds of cooperation, it also acknowledged the propriety of cooperation under some conditions.[55]

In 1920 Mullins composed another creed for the same purpose. It had eight articles and was part of a "Fraternal Address." Liberals within and without the denomination protested, but the convention adopted it in order to communicate to Baptists around the world the doctrinal commitments that constituted the basis of union and cooperation.[56] Mullins and other leaders wanted the convention to appoint a committee in 1922 to devise a statement of faith jointly

53. Edgar Y. Mullins to William J. McGlothlin, 16 June 1914, Letterpress Copy Book 43, 1913–1914.

54. Edgar Y. Mullins to William J. McGlothlin, 24 June 1914, Letterpress Copy Book 43, 1913–1914.

55. Edgar Y. Mullins to James B. Gambrell, 2 June 1914, Letterpress Copy Book 43, 1913–1914.

56. "Fraternal Address of Southern Baptists to Those of 'Like Precious Faith with Us' Scattered Abroad, Beloved in the Lord," *Baptist Standard*, 26 Feb. 1920, 5, 20, 24; James B. Gambrell, "Can Northern and Southern Baptists Hold Together," *Baptist Standard*, 12 Feb. 1920, 5.

with a committee from the Northern Baptist Convention, for adoption by both conventions.[57] If they could accomplish it, Southern Baptist progressives would have a platform to promote closer cooperation with Northern Baptists, especially on the mission field. It would also serve as an argument against receiving any more Northern Baptist churches into the Southern Baptist Convention on the complaint that Northern Baptists were liberal—the two would now have the same official doctrinal commitments. Mullins suggested to Livingston Johnson that someone should make the motion when the topic came up in the executive committee report.[58] But Mullins and the others decided to make no motion at all on the matter. They rightly judged that "there were too many delicate and difficult things" in the way. Northern Baptists erected a formidable obstacle to this initiative when they rejected the adoption of a creed at their 1922 annual meeting.[59]

MULLINS, CREEDS, AND THE BAPTIST FAITH AND MESSAGE

In 1925 Mullins led Southern Baptists to adopt an official denominational confession of faith for the first time. It was a strange accomplishment for one who said that there was insufficient cause for Southern Baptists to adopt a creed at that time. The whole affair was stranger than history has remembered it. Mullins was not enthusiastic about the idea of the Southern Baptist Convention adopting a confession. He supported the convention's right to do so and thought that at another time it might be justified, but he did not support adopting a confession in 1925. The affair represented well one of Mullins's approaches to denominational statesmanship. He took leadership of an effort he generally opposed in order to make sure that it took the least objectionable form possible.

Mullins did not seek the job of chairing a committee to prepare a creed for the convention. When the convention appointed the committee, it was done, Mullins said, without the committee members' prior knowledge or consent. And a majority of the committee initially opposed making any kind of doctrinal statement. Some opposed doing so because "they did not think such statements were Baptistic." Others opposed it because "they thought enough had already been said about doctrine in recent years." When the Southern Baptist Convention voted to form the committee, it charged it to report to the

57. Edgar Y. Mullins to Lee R. Scarborough, 20 Apr. 1922, box 26, Mullins Papers.
58. Edgar Y. Mullins to Livingston Johnson, 8 May 1922, box 27, Mullins Papers.
59. Edgar Y. Mullins to Curtis Lee Laws, 29 May 1922, box 27, Mullins Papers.

convention "whether or not a creedal statement was necessary." Considered strictly, the convention did not authorize the committee to draft a creed for the convention's adoption. The committee asked the convention president whether the convention had authorized it to propose a confessional statement. He said, in Mullins's words, "the motion meant that we should report on the expediency of a doctrinal statement and submit such a statement if we concluded that it was expedient." [60]

American religion had experienced a high state of agitation for several years as fundamentalists pressed for the removal of liberals from denominational posts and from the ministry. The agitation was less intense in the Southern Baptist Convention than in several other denominations, but many Southern Baptists considered the threat of liberalism to be the top issue facing the convention. The committee recognized that this was the state of mind of the convention on the matter, Mullins said, and it wanted to be responsive to it. It knew that some Southern Baptists opposed adopting any statement of faith whatsoever, on the basis of their "aversion to all creeds but the Bible." Others, like Mullins and most of the committee, believed that Baptist churches and conventions could legitimately adopt confessions from time to time, but they were doubtful that this was the right time. But many others believed that "there ought to be a statement at the present time because of the menace of naturalism," and they had been agitating for several years "in favor of a doctrinal statement." The committee "waived their own personal judgment about it, and decided that they would revise the old New Hampshire Confession of Faith." [61]

The committee also recognized that this was the most expedient course of action, because the opponents of adopting creeds were a minority of the convention and could not prevent the majority from adopting one. The only question was whether it would be a good creed or a bad one. So the committee decided to submit a creed because it believed that the majority of the Southern Baptist Convention wanted one. If it did not submit one, the convention would appoint another committee to do the work, and Mullins's committee feared that "in all probability a much more radical and drastic series of articles would have been submitted than was presented by the committee who handled the matter." [62] Although Mullins did not explain what he meant by drastic and radical, he probably feared that the committee would include a statement rejecting all forms of evolution and would seek to exclude persons whose theology inclined toward liberalism.

60. Edgar Y. Mullins to J. W. Mitchell, 23 Feb. 1926, box 34, Mullins Papers.

61. Edgar Y. Mullins, Speech to the Southern Baptist Convention concerning the Baptist Faith and Message, 15 June 1925, box 33, Mullins Papers.

62. Edgar Y. Mullins to J. W. Mitchell, 23 Feb. 1926, box 34, Mullins Papers.

The committee also feared that a different committee might propose its "drastic articles submitted in a form which would become virtually a creed binding upon the convention and others." So the committee determined to submit a doctrinal statement that was moderate in its doctrinal substance and without operational relevance to convention agencies. It decided "to adopt a revised statement of the New Hampshire Confession" in order to "give the least opportunity for division." It determined also to draft a "preliminary statement" as a part of its report in order to "safeguard the [confessional] statement from any tinge of ecclesiastical authority." Mullins summarized: "Our committee were convinced that the greatest service it could render to the denomination was to submit a moderate restatement of Baptist beliefs along with an introduction which would protect that statement from any false inferences as to the assumption of ecclesiastical authority." [63] Mullins did not favor the use of creeds to exclude. He indeed felt that the true "Baptist conception of truth" was so broad and great that it would be chiefly inclusive rather than exclusive. [64]

The Baptist Faith and Message committee was dominated by leaders with close ties to Southern Seminary. Mullins was chairman. William J. McGlothlin, president of Furman University, was a former professor, as was Edwin C. Dargan, chief editor of the Sunday School Board. Z. T. Cody, editor of South Carolina's *Baptist Courier*, and R. H. Pitt, editor of Virginia's *Religious Herald*, were trustees. Other members were Lee R. Scarborough, president of Southwestern Baptist Theological Seminary, S. M. Brown, editor of Missouri's *Word and Way*, and C. P. Stealey, editor of Oklahoma's *Baptist Messenger*. Mullins drafted the confession and sent it to the committee members. He received their criticisms and suggestions, revised his draft, and sent the revision to the committee for adoption on May 11, 1925, just prior to the meeting of the Southern Baptist Convention. [65] The convention adopted it overwhelmingly.

The confession did not please progressive Southern Baptists, but it expressed its commitments with sufficient indefiniteness to prevent the exclusion of most progressive Southern Baptists. It expressed traditional evangelical commitments in muted Calvinist strains. It expressed also Southern Baptists' commitment to traditional Baptist practices.

Of the faculty Carver was the most opposed to adopting the confession. In a serious breach of protocol, he wrote an article urging Southern Baptists to oppose the recommendation of Mullins's committee, but the *Western Recorder*

63. Edgar Y. Mullins to J. W. Mitchell, 23 Feb. 1926, box 34, Mullins Papers.

64. Edgar Y. Mullins to W. W. Landrum, 19 June 1922, box 27, Mullins Papers.

65. Edgar Y. Mullins to C. P. Stealey, 6 May 1925, box 33, Mullins Papers.

did not publish it.[66] Carver also tried to convince Mullins of the "futility and danger" of leading the convention to adopt a creed. Carver understood that Mullins believed that conservatives in the convention would assuredly adopt some kind of creed, and that therefore he was trying "to make the best of a miserable situation." Carver was nevertheless critical of the proposed action and of Mullins's role in it. At the 1925 convention Carver voted against every proposal involving "this abomination of creed-making." [67]

But Mullins believed that the confession included ample protection for progressive Southern Baptists. He had wanted to lead the effort to draft and recommend a confession of faith for the convention because he felt he could lead the convention to adopt one with desirable limits and protections. He wanted first of all to ensure that the convention made no dogmatic pronouncements regarding scientific knowledge and advocated no strictures on scientific research. He wanted also to guarantee protection of the individual freedom of professors in Southern Baptist seminaries and colleges. He achieved moderate success on both counts.

Mullins established these protections in the confession's preamble. Its final sentence asserted that the confession reflected only a consensus of "religious convictions" and that it was "not to be used to hamper freedom of thought or investigation in other realms of life." By means of a characteristic paradox, Mullins presented a confessional statement sufficiently robust to please the conservative majority, but in the preamble he established a principle of toleration that offered protection to progressives and contradicted the convention's motive for adopting one in the first place.

But in practice the protections and limits Mullins placed on the confession in the preamble had their own limits. They erected a new barrier to the imposition of the convention's views on teachers in denominational schools and established a precedent against making pronouncements about science. But these barriers only shifted the argument from debates about the content of the confession to debates about its role in denominational life. Most Southern Baptists wanted teachers in denominational seminaries and colleges to pledge formally their agreement with the confession's doctrine. They viewed the confession as a minimum requirement of acceptable belief among denominational teachers and officials. And they held that the convention was entirely unencumbered in imposing doctrinal requirements in addition to those explicitly advanced in

66. Victor I. Masters to William O. Carver, 9 May 1925, box 6, Carver Papers, SBHLA.

67. William O. Carver to Livingston Johnson, 13 Aug. 1925, box 6, Carver Papers, SBHLA.

the Baptist Faith and Message. They did not read the preamble in the way that Mullins had hoped.

The inclusion of the preamble therefore did little to reassure the minority of liberals in the convention. They would have to wait until the 1963 Baptist Faith and Message committee revised the preamble to establish a stronger principle of toleration. But the 1925 preamble did reassure the convention's minority of theistic evolutionists, because the confession made no attempt to address scientific matters, that is, evolution.

MULLINS AND THE EVOLUTION CONTROVERSY

Mullins and the committee accomplished another paradoxical design. They acknowledged that the impetus for adopting a confession derived primarily from the convention's desire to exclude belief in evolution. But Mullins convinced the messengers to adopt a confession that said nothing at all about evolution.

Mullins and the committee acknowledged that they decided to recommend the adoption of the confession from "consideration of the general denominational situation." The most immediate consideration was that the denomination wanted one. But the broader issue was the growing acceptance of biological evolution. The committee acknowledged its awareness of this concern in the introduction to its recommendation to the convention: "The present occasion for a reaffirmation of Christian fundamentals is the prevalence of naturalism in the modern teaching and preaching of religion." Southern Baptists, like American evangelicals broadly, recognized that evolution threatened Christianity's place in society. It did so because it discredited one of Christianity's most basic truth claims, that God directly created the world and all living things, human beings above all.

Mullins told the convention that the committee was quite deliberate in avoiding any statement on science or evolution. To introduce a statement on evolution into the creed would introduce a source of division, Mullins said, since some would strongly favor including it and others would strongly favor omitting it. Such disagreement threatened division of the convention and imperiled the convention's missionary and educational work. Mullins explained, "All of us felt of course that if it were possible, we should find a common standing ground for all Southern Baptists in this doctrinal statement."[68] But Mullins opposed

---

68. Edgar Y. Mullins, Speech to the Southern Baptist Convention concerning the Baptist Faith and Message, 15 June 1925, box 33, Mullins Papers.

it also for epistemological reasons. Science and religion operated in distinctly different spheres and dealt with distinctly different matters. They should not be mixed or confused. As he explained, "Science pursues its own method in arriving at truth in the natural realm, and religion its method in arriving at truth in the religious realm.... An atom is a very interesting thing, but you might search an atom to the end of time, and you wouldn't find sanctification and regeneration and the new birth, would you?... It is common sense. The two things don't belong together." These considerations, Mullins said, formed the basis of the committee's insistence "that we keep statements about science out of a confession of faith." [69]

But Mullins also argued that article 3 of the confession emphatically contradicted the theory of evolution. Article 3 said that "man was created by the special act of God, as recorded in Genesis." To affirm this, Mullins said, was to deny that man came by evolution: "When you affirm that a thing came into existence by special creation you thereby affirm that it was not evolution." The variations found in cats, dogs, and other domestic animals, Mullins said, are "not evolution in the technical sense." Mullins averred that the committee did "not believe in evolution" and that the third article "can not be harmonized with evolution." [70]

Challenges to the adequacy of the confession began immediately. C. P. Stealey, editor of Oklahoma's *Baptist Messenger* and a member of the Baptist Faith and Message committee, presented a minority report asking the convention to amend the proposed confession by adding an explicit rejection of evolution. Mullins's carefully prepared response convinced the convention to reject the amendment.

After the convention adjourned, Stealey began a spirited campaign to persuade Southern Baptists to adopt some measure to prevent evolutionists from teaching in Southern Baptist schools. The controversy had been brewing for several years. At the 1922 meeting of the Southern Baptist Convention, William Jennings Bryan, the popular leader of American's antievolution crusade, addressed the Southern Baptist Convention on the dangers of belief in evolution. At the 1923 Southern Baptist Convention in Kansas City, Bryan again addressed the gathered messengers, speaking for about thirty minutes on prohibition and ninety minutes on evolution. Z. T. Cody, editor of the *Baptist Courier* and a Southern Seminary trustee, reported that Southern Baptists approved

69. Edgar Y. Mullins, Speech to the Southern Baptist Convention concerning the Baptist Faith and Message, 15 June 1925, box 33, Mullins Papers.

70. Edgar Y. Mullins, Speech to the Southern Baptist Convention concerning the Baptist Faith and Message, 15 June 1925, box 33, Mullins Papers.

the speech: "Ninety-nine persons out of every hundred present endorsed the positions that the Great Commoner took in his speech. It was a defense of the Bible, and was an arraignment of evolution only in so far as evolution is being used for the overthrow of established facts of the Bible and the undermining of the evangelical faith."[71]

Southern Baptists had hoped that adopting a confession of faith would exclude belief in evolution and thus resolve the question of whether to tolerate evolutionist teachers in Southern Baptist institutions. Mullins believed that the Baptist Faith and Message accomplished this by its implicit rejection of naturalistic evolution in the article on creation. Stealey argued that it was entirely inadequate. He claimed that the committee that drafted the confession wrote the statement on creation in such a way as to include room for theistic evolution. He was probably right, at least in the case of Mullins, though some committee members denied it. Stealey claimed that when he asked the committee whether this was its intention, it answered that it was and that such theistic evolutionists such as A. H. Strong, James Orr, and F. H. Kerfoot demonstrated that great Christian leaders have held the view.

The statement on creation did seem to leave room for belief in theistic evolution. It affirmed that the world was created "by a special act of God." Such language excluded belief in naturalistic evolution, but the claim was plausible enough that theistic evolutionists could affirm this statement by arguing that evolution itself was God's special act in bringing living things into their current forms. Only one committee member afterward recalled any discussion of theistic evolution or of the men who held it. Most committee members denied that they intended to make room for theistic evolution in the statement.[72]

Mullins too rejected Stealey's claim. He testified that he "said repeatedly in the committee that the phrase in article three 'by special act of God' negated, and was intended to negate every evolutionary implication or assertion." Mullins evaded the thorny question of theistic evolution by asserting that the only two consistent positions are creation by God's direct action or naturalistic evolution: "Evolution is defined by its scientific votaries as inherently and essentially in opposition to special creation. Special creation and evolution do not mix any more than oil and water will mix."[73] This statement may have been accurate in theory, but it was not in practice. Many, perhaps most, American evolutionists mixed special creation and evolution.

71. Z. T. Cody, "The Kansas City Convention," *Baptist Courier*, 31 May 1923, 2.

72. Edgar Y. Mullins, "Dr. Stealey and the Committee on the Baptist Faith and Message," typescript, box 33, Mullins Papers.

73. Edgar Y. Mullins, "Dr. Mullins Replies," 26 May 1925, typescript, box 33, Mullins Papers.

But Mullins had elsewhere defended the acceptability of Christian forms of evolution. Christian evolutionists, Mullins explained, did not reject the Genesis account of creation. They merely argued that the six days of the Genesis creation narrative represented extended periods of time, but employed the language of appearances rather than that of science. And since God was immanent in the creation and development of the world, "he lifted the process of evolution to a new level whenever it was needed." This theistic evolution, Mullins wrote, was "consistent with belief in God, and the Bible, and miracles, and the atonement, and all the vital truths of Christianity.... it presupposes and requires them." Mullins cited such trusted leaders as A. H. Strong, James Orr, Abraham Kuyper, and F. H. Kerfoot as theistic evolutionists who were also "staunch defenders of the orthodox religion."[74]

Most Southern Baptists wanted a definite stand against evolution. They wanted the convention to take a decided stand. They did not want evolutionists teaching in their colleges and seminaries, and they wanted to require the schools to hire none. So in 1926 the Southern Baptist Convention overwhelmingly adopted a statement written by George McDaniel: "This convention accepts Genesis as teaching that man was the special creation of God and rejects every theory, evolution or other, which teaches that man originated in, or came by way of a lower animal ancestry."[75]

The denomination's theistic evolutionists may have blanched at the statement, but they apparently found it acceptable enough. They believed that God directed evolution, and that human beings were perhaps created directly by God. When W. O. Carver came under attack at this point, he said that all the seminary's professors agreed with the McDaniel statement and "hold that view."[76]

Most Southern Baptists were satisfied with the statement, but they wanted some assurance that the colleges and seminaries agreed with it and would abide by it. Lee R. Scarborough, president of the Southwestern Baptist Theological Seminary, announced to the convention that he would require all faculty to agree with the Baptist Faith and Message and with the McDaniel statement. At the 1926 convention's last session messengers adopted "the Tull resolution," requesting the faculty, administration, and trustees of other Southern Baptist schools to follow Southwestern Seminary's example.[77]

74. Edgar Y. Mullins, "Evolution and Belief in God," box 39, Mullins Papers.

75. See Z. T. Cody, "The Convention and Evolution," Baptist Courier, 27 May 1926, 2–3.

76. William O. Carver to J. G. Davis, 3 June 1926, box 6, Carver Papers, SBHLA.

77. Z. T. Cody, "That Second Action," Baptist Courier, 3 June 1926, 2.

Mullins regretted Scarborough's action. He had labored hard to avoid this very thing and had argued against it earlier. In his 1922 presidential address to the Southern Baptist Convention, Mullins urged that teachers in Baptist schools be treated justly. Southern Baptists should not "curtail unduly their God-given right to investigate truth in the realm of science." But Mullins warned that scientific investigation gave teachers no right to reject the orthodox interpretation of the Bible: "We will not tolerate in our denominational schools any departure from the great fundamentals of the faith in the name of science falsely so-called."[78] He sent an article to the Baptist newspapers interpreting the actions of the 1926 Southern Baptist Convention meeting as bringing an end to controversy over evolution. The McDaniel statement was adopted unanimously and should "prove satisfactory to everybody." But Mullins took a different approach than Scarborough or the convention intended. He interpreted the Tull resolution not as a requirement that faculty subscribe to the Baptist Faith and Message and the McDaniel statement but merely as a request for information. On behalf of the faculty Mullins affirmed that "we of the seminary faculty are, as in the past, in harmony with" all four of the convention's recent pronouncements on evolution, including the McDaniel statement.[79]

Theistic evolutionists believed that God occasionally interfered supernaturally in the evolutionary process. Mullins did not believe that theistic evolution was a consistent position. The very essence of the idea of the evolution of species, he said, was naturalism. "So-called Christian evolution, allowing for the gaps and breaks and for the supernatural," Mullins concluded, was "not really evolution."[80] Mullins's conclusion that theistic evolution was "not really evolution" proved rhetorically useful. This meant that such members of his own faculty as Carver and Gardner, who were theistic evolutionists, were "not really" evolutionists. Mullins could therefore declare emphatically that "there are no evolutionists on our faculty."[81]

Carver thought that Mullins's approach was unhelpful. He considered it a capitulation to the tyranny of the majority. He wanted Mullins instead to take a stand for freedom and toleration toward evolutionists.

During the debate on Stealey's amendment at the 1925 Southern Baptist Convention, Mullins read a prepared statement on the relationship of science

78. Edgar Y. Mullins, "Southern Baptists at a Crucial Hour," 5, box 39, Mullins Papers.

79. Edgar Y. Mullins, "The Houston Convention and the Kingdom," typescript, box 35, Mullins Papers.

80. Edgar Y. Mullins, "The Evolution Issue: What Is It," typescript, box 34, Mullins Papers.

81. Edgar Y. Mullins to A. J. Holt, 30 Apr. 1926, box 35, Mullins Papers.

and religion. Evolution had to do with science and science only, Mullins felt. Science and religion examined entirely distinct aspects of reality.[82] It was impossible that they should contradict each other therefore, so whatever the scientists concluded about evolution was irrelevant and could not have any effect on religion. "The issue over evolution," Mullins wrote in 1925, "does not involve anything vital for Christianity."[83]

He hoped that this distinction would put an end to the agitation on the evolution issue by affording each sphere freedom from the interference of the other. The convention adopted Mullins's statement as reflecting its views, but it had no intention of tolerating evolutionist teachers. Presumably it felt that because evolution contradicted the Bible, it could not be true science.

Although Mullins seemed to advocate charity and toleration of theistic evolutionists, he claimed that he rejected the theory. He told L. L. Gwaltney, editor of Alabama's Baptist newspaper and a committed evolutionist, that "personally I reject the evolutionary hypothesis. I do not believe it has been or ever will be proved."[84] But he also did not believe that religious bodies should make pronouncements about science. "I do not believe man is descended from lower animals, nor that it will ever be shown that he is. But I believe most emphatically that modern Christians should refuse to dogmatize in their organic capacity in conventions on scientific matters."[85]

Faculties of Southern Baptist colleges were widely convinced of evolution by the 1930s. William L. Poteat, president of Wake Forest University from 1905 to 1927, was the most prominent and respected evolutionist in the Southern Baptist Convention. He argued that evolution was scientifically true. Such convention leaders as Z. T. Cody, editor of the South Carolina newspaper, thought evolution false but argued the toleration of teachers in Baptist schools who believed in evolution as long as they otherwise "held to our evangelical faith."[86] In 1925 most Southern Baptist newspapers printed objections to Poteat. Livingston Johnson, the progressive editor of North Carolina Baptists' *Biblical Recorder* and a Poteat supporter, estimated that 75 percent of North Carolina Baptists would vote "to have the teaching of evolution excluded from all of our schools." The only reason they did not do so was because "many of those who

---

82. See, e.g., Edgar Y. Mullins, "Fellow-Workers with God," *Baptist Courier*, 11 Feb. 1926, 6–7.

83. Edgar Y. Mullins to R. H. Pitt, 23 Dec. 1925, box 34, Mullins Papers.

84. Edgar Y. Mullins, "Statement on Science and Religion," insert in Mullins to L. L. Gwaltney, 24 June 1925, box 39, Mullins Papers.

85. Edgar Y. Mullins to George W. McDaniel, 24 July 1925, box 33, Mullins Papers.

86. William L. Poteat, "Evolution," *Baptist Courier*, 11 May 1922, 1; Z. T. Cody, "Evolution Again," *Baptist Courier*, 11 May 1922, 4.

oppose evolution do not attend the convention."[87] Poteat came under severe criticism for his belief in both evolution and liberal theology. He survived several attempts to force him out of office. Livingston Johnson gathered sufficient information on Southern Baptist colleges to conclude that "every college in the South teaches the kind of evolution that is taught at Wake Forest."[88] The number of evolutionists varied from college to college and department to department. But as long as professors taught theistic evolution, a kind of evolution designed and directed by God, and were content to do so cautiously and with reverence toward the Bible, they rarely came under attack after the 1930s. Those who did suffer attack generally believed other errors that gave greater offense.

For several years Stealey kept up considerable agitation on the matter. The Oklahoma Baptist Convention voted to withhold funds from the Southern Baptist Convention unless Southern Baptist institutions would subscribe explicitly to a statement rejecting evolution.

After the 1920s Southern Baptists weakened little in their disagreement with evolution, but the agitation against teaching it in Baptist colleges slowly diminished. They gave up the broad campaigns of the 1920s. Subsequent agitation generally focused on individual evolutionists who added to the offense by rejecting various traditional doctrines. Even in the case of Poteat, so outspoken in advocating evolution, the power of the opposition was due as much to his liberal views on the atonement and Christianity generally as to his teaching evolution.

B. F. Condray, a professor at Arkansas Baptists' Ouachita College, suggested in 1925 that even if the Southern Baptist Convention required professors at denominational colleges to reject evolution, "they cannot force out of the faculties of the schools all those who believe in evolution." He believed that although some faculty members would choose to resign, most would rationalize subscription to any required antievolutionary statement: "The majority will lie about their beliefs, and hold to their opinions and their positions."[89] When the convention adopted such a requirement in 1926, few evolutionist teachers left their posts.

Southern's faculty was rather thoroughly committed to theistic evolution by the 1930s. They argued that Christians did not have to reject evolution.[90]

87. Livingston Johnson to William O. Carver, 8 Sept. 1925, box 6, Carver Papers, SBHLA.

88. Livingston Johnson to William O. Carver, 8 Sept. 1925, box 6, Carver Papers, SBHLA.

89. B. F. Condray to Edgar Y. Mullins, 24 July 1925, Mullins Papers.

90. W. W. Barnes to William O. Carver, 2 June 1926, box 6, Carver Papers, SBHLA.

John R. Sampey rejected naturalistic evolution: "I have never been a Darwinian evolutionist."[91] He apparently rejected the theistic theory as at best unproven, but he was generally unconcerned about a teacher's scientific views as long as there was an explicit affirmation of the inspiration of the Bible. W. O. Carver and Charles S. Gardner, it was widely recognized, believed in theistic evolution.[92] Carver was the more outspoken of the two. He believed in evolution, he said, because science and scripture were equally God's revelation. "God speaks to me in the rocks as truly as in Romans; in geology as in Genesis."[93] Carver suggested that the six days stood for geological ages. The "day and night" of verse 5 may continue for "days, centuries, or ages." Carver clearly believed that they had continued for ages—he called day five an "epoch." The fact that in the Genesis account evening always preceded morning suggested a cycle with a period of quiet and then a "wonder-working movement," perhaps for as many ages as the geologists can find strata in the rocks. Regarding humans, Carver suggested that as biological beings, they originated through the process of divinely guided evolution like other living things. But they became persons, spiritual beings, when God breathed the breath of life into them, as recorded in Genesis chapter 2.[94] In this way he could believe that in their animal characteristics, humans evolved from lower biological forms, but in their truly human characteristics, they were the special creation of God.

But Carver also held that the natural process of evolution was God's special work. He tended to dismiss the notion that species developed by a slow, uniform process in favor of sudden bursts of creative activity, according to natural laws directed by God and fulfilling his plan for the ages. God was just as integral to the gradual and uniform process of evolutionary creation as he was in any creative acts.[95] God was immanent in evolution.

Most other professors at the seminary seem to have agreed more or less with Carver's views. By the 1940s, it is unlikely that a faculty candidate who rejected evolution could have gained election to the faculty for most positions.

91. John R. Sampey to J. Frank Norris, ca. June 1926, box 25, Sampey Papers.

92. James H. Wiley to William O. Carver, 6 June 1925, box 6, Carver Papers, SBHLA.

93. William O. Carver, "Characteristics of the Creation Story in Genesis," revised version, ca. 1925 or 1942, typescript, p. 10, box 1, Carver Papers, SBHLA.

94. William O. Carver, "Characteristics of the Creation Story in Genesis," *Western Recorder*, 13 Oct. 1921, 1–3. Carver revised this article on at least two occasions, in 1925 and in 1942. All three versions survive in the Characteristics of the Creation Story in Genesis folder, box 1, Carver Papers, SBHLA.

95. William O. Carver, "Characteristics of the Creation Story in Genesis," revised version, ca. 1925 or 1942, typescript, p. 9, box 1, Carver Papers, SBHLA.

Edgar Y. Mullins at a gathering during construction of the new campus

A NEW CAMPUS AT THE BEECHES

In 1909 trustees adopted plans to move from downtown Louisville at the earliest possible date. The student population had grown steadily, and the downtown campus had become cramped. As the business district crowded in around them, there was no room to grow there. Many considered the living conditions unhealthy. Soot and smoke at times grew quite dense. Mullins had already moved his home to the suburbs east of downtown seeking cleaner air for his wife's health.

But the main consideration was overcrowding. By 1915 the seminary's downtown quarters were filled to overflowing. The largest classrooms of Norton Hall could not accommodate any more students in the seminary's largest courses. "It is really a great emergency," Mullins warned, "and it would be a disaster if it is not taken care of." [96] Downtown property was too expensive to expand the campus there. They had to move out of the city.

Baptist leaders in Atlanta made a bid to relocate the seminary there. They promised to raise $1 million for the purpose, but trustees decided to build a

96. E. Y. Mullins to R. H. Pitt, 6 Mar. 1920, Letterpress Copy Book 56, 13 Oct. 1919–7 Dec. 1920, 460M.

Norton Hall

new campus in the vicinity of Louisville. The seminary initially acquired forty-four acres several miles east of the city on Brownsboro Road for the purpose. Trustees approved a plan to raise $1 million for the construction of the new campus. The stringencies of a wartime economy delayed plans to move. When the war ended in 1918, the board planned to begin raising money immediately in order to move the seminary as soon as possible.

But before construction could begin, Mullins found a more attractive property on Lexington Road and led trustees to acquire the fifty-acre parcel, about five miles east of the downtown campus. Mullins secured the renowned Olmstead firm of Brookline, Massachusetts, to design and landscape the campus and chose New York architect James Gamble Rogers to design the buildings. Rogers fittingly chose to pattern the buildings after the style at the University of Virginia.[97]

The new campus's design would be anchored by Norton Hall, a ranging two-story brick building facing Lexington Road and the property's namesake beech grove. Norton Hall accommodated classrooms, faculty and administrative offices, the library, a student lounge, and the chapel. Across a broad lawn would stand the other anchor, an equally ranging three-story brick dormitory initially called New York Hall. Trustees changed the name to Mullins Hall before construction was completed.[98] Both buildings were impressive and tasteful. Norton Hall, with its elegant clock tower and magnificent columns, drew praise from the public and the press.[99]

97. Unattributed, "Baptists to Start $3,000,000 Seminary Construction," *Louisville Courier-Journal*, 6 Apr. 1923, 1; Edgar Y. Mullins to William O. Carver, 17 Apr. 1923, box 6, Carver Papers, SBHLA.

98. Edgar Y. Mullins to William O. Carver, 17 Apr. 1923, box 6, Carver Papers, SBHLA.

99. Edgar Y. Mullins to John R. Sampey, 9 July 1925, box 25, Sampey Papers.

Mullins found raising the money to pay for the campus more difficult than he had imagined. The denomination effectively blocked his way by adopting a joint denominational budget that made no provision for the cost of the new campus. And since it was a joint "cooperative" budget, other leaders opposed wildcat fund-raising efforts by individual institutions, unless an institution could convince everyone else to endorse the effort. The new joint budget approach was called the Seventy-Five Million Campaign, an ambitious plan to raise $75 million between 1920 and 1925 for all Southern Baptist institutions. The seminary expected to receive a portion for the new campus. When Southern Baptists adopted the plan at the 1919 meeting of the Southern Baptist Convention in Atlanta, Mullins presented a motion that the budget of the Seventy-Five Million Campaign include $1 million for Southern Seminary's new campus. The convention adopted it overwhelmingly.[100] Mullins knew that it would be impossible to raise any money for a single institution while the whole denomination was bent on raising an ambitious general fund. Unless the cost of the new campus was included in the Seventy-Five Million Campaign, the seminary's move would be postponed indefinitely.

But the proposed budget adopted by the convention's executive committee in 1920 omitted funding for the new campus. Mullins and the trustees were shocked.[101] Seminary leaders felt betrayed by the executive committee's recommendations and by the state convention leaders who took it upon themselves to determine the appropriations of their states to each Southern Baptist Convention object. Many of them gave little to the seminary building fund. "The orders of the convention," A. T. Robertson observed, "were sidetracked and the seminary got practically nothing out of the Seventy-Five Million Campaign for the building fund."[102]

Texas Landmark leader James B. Gambrell led the opposition to including the seminary's building fund in the distribution of the funds of the campaign. Indeed, many leaders throughout the denomination felt some jealousy concerning the seminary. Its leading graduates seemed to rise almost automatically to denominational leadership. The most influential churches generally felt loyalty and affection for the seminary and repeatedly called seminary graduates to their pulpits. And for all the seminary's great need for constructing its new

100. E. Y. Mullins to R. H. Pitt, 6 Mar. 1920, Letterpress Copy Book 56, 13 Oct. 1919–7 Dec. 1920, 460K–460L.

101. E. Y. Mullins to R. H. Pitt, 6 Mar. 1920, Letterpress Copy Book 56, 13 Oct. 1919–7 Dec. 1920, 460L.

102. Archibald T. Robertson, "The Seminary and the Present Emergency," ca. Jan. 1925, box 33, Mullins Papers.

campus, the seminary had a significant endowment and some valuable property. By comparison, many leaders felt, the Southwestern Baptist Theological Seminary and the New Orleans Baptist Bible Institute had much greater needs. And although the three schools generally maintained good relations and cooperation, intrinsic rivalries and differences kept suspicion high and erupted into accusation and conflict frequently enough.[103]

But the seminary's leaders and alumni felt that denominational leaders handicapped Southern Seminary because of its success and effectiveness, the very reasons that it deserved full support. Everett Gill, seminary alumnus and missionary leader, summarized this sentiment in 1925: "The other sections of the country are jealous of our seminary and do not wish her to get what is justly hers."[104] Some leaders said that the seminary could pay for its new campus by the sale of its downtown property. But appraisers told Mullins that the downtown property was worth about $500,000, when the new campus would cost at least $3,500,000.[105] The Foreign Mission Board and the Home Mission Board, however, agreed to loan the seminary money out of their receipts from the Seventy-Five Million Campaign.

Because the seminary was left out of denominational fund-raising during the critical construction phase, it was forced to borrow heavily as the bills came in. All Southern Baptist institutions entered into an understanding that during the Seventy-Five Million Campaign their fund-raising efforts were exclusively for that campaign. They worked together to solicit gifts for the common fund and refrained from efforts to raise money for their individual institution. But as soon as the campaign ended, Mullins lobbied denominational leaders to give him their endorsement of a special seminary campaign. Such endorsements had always been necessary, since opposition from other Southern Baptist leaders could guarantee the failure of the campaign. Mullins secured the endorsement and sent letters to hundreds of pastors asking them to take up a special offering for the seminary's building fund and requesting names of wealthy individuals to whom he could make individual requests.[106]

The seminary observed a groundbreaking ceremony for the new campus on October 31, 1923.[107] It invited the Baptist churches of Louisville to attend a later

103. For a fine example of this suspicion and conflict, see Jeff D. Ray to Archibald T. Robertson, 1 Apr. 1925, box 4, Robertson Papers; Ray to Robertson, 7 Apr. 1925, ibid.

104. Everett Gill to William O. Carver, 9 Mar. 1925, box 6, Carver Papers, SBHLA.

105. Edgar Y. Mullins to Archibald T. Robertson, 26 Nov. 1923, box 4, Robertson Papers.

106. For an example of the circular letter to the pastors, see Edgar Y. Mullins to John R. Sampey, 10 Jan. 1925, box 25, Mullins Papers.

107. Unattributed, "Baptists Dedicate Seminary Site," Louisville Herald, 1 Nov. 1923.

Norton Hall

groundbreaking ceremony for the new Norton Hall on May 28, 1924.[108] Initial plans to construct a separate chapel, a president's home, and faculty houses on the new campus proved too ambitious. The cost of construction material was high, and revenues did not match expectations. In some respects the plans did not match denominational realities. Rogers designed an imposing $75,000 home for the president. Mullins recognized that the president's home could not cost so much and was prepared to recommend that trustees approve a $55,000 home. Sampey explained to architect Rogers why Mullins wanted a less costly

108. Edgar Y. Mullins to Archibald T. Robertson, 24 Nov. 1923, box 4, Robertson Papers.

home: "He knew the psychology of our Southern Baptist people and that it would make a bad impression if it should be known among them that the president of the seminary was occupying a home costing such a large sum of money, while his distinguished colleagues of the faculty were living in homes costing from $12,000 to $22,000 each. Our Baptist people are a democratic people." [109] Mullins then concluded that the president's home should not be located next to Norton Hall, and he bought two of the new spacious lots in Cherokee Gardens across Lexington Road and gave them to the seminary for the president's home. After Mullins's death, his successor Sampey thought that the president's home should be more modest still, costing perhaps $30,000 or $40,000. As he explained in a letter, "The psychological effect of making such a very great difference between the president's home and the homes owned or occupied by the different professors would not be good either within the immediate seminary circle or among the general Baptist public." [110]

The seminary moved from its downtown property to its new campus at the Beeches in March 1926. The seminary now had a fabulous campus with a spacious physical plant suited to its needs in every way. But it also had a fabulous debt. With the onset of economic depression in 1929, Sampey placed the original plans for a chapel, faculty homes, and a president's home on hiatus. Sampey's presidency was dominated by the challenge of servicing the seminary's debt during the scarcity of the Great Depression.

109. John R. Sampey to James Gamble Rogers, 28 June 1929, box 2, Sampey Papers.
110. John R. Sampey to Joshua Levering, 18 Jan. 1929, box 1, Sampey Papers.

8

ORTHODOXY, HISTORICAL CRITICISM, AND THE CHALLENGES OF A NEW ERA

John R. Sampey and Ellis A. Fuller presided over the seminary in an era of terrific challenge and rapid change. The Great Depression brought fiscal crisis that threatened to sink the school under the heavy debt load it amassed to build its campus at the Beeches. The crisis of war, the youth revival, and the return of prosperity launched a massive wave of new students into ministerial training and began an era of rapid expansion at the seminary. As the faculty expanded to meet student enrollment, a generation of young scholars reshaped the character of the school. They took the premises and methods of historical criticism for granted, and they embraced postwar reformist impulses that made them less patient with the constraints of realist denominational relations.

After Mullins's death on November 23, 1928, trustees appointed Old Testament professor John R. Sampey as acting president and began looking for Mullins's successor. Joshua Levering, chairman of the board of trustees, was surprised that so few persons seemed to have definite opinions concerning the matter.[1] I. J. Van Ness, a trustee who kept up many contacts throughout the convention in his position as president of the Sunday School Board, reported that Southern Baptist leaders and preachers had formed no clear conviction about it. Some proposed William J. McGlothlin.[2] Others thought Sampey the obvious choice.[3]

There was an obvious objection to electing Sampey—he was sixty-six years old. Sampey was willing to serve if the trustees thought it best, but he recommended

1. Joshua Levering to I. J. Van Ness, 6 Dec. 1928, box 18, Van Ness Papers, SBHLA.
2. I. J. Van Ness to Joshua Levering, 8 Dec. 1928, box 18, Van Ness Papers, SBHLA.
3. See, e.g., Byron H. DeMent to John R. Sampey, 5 Apr. 1929, box 1, Sampey Papers.

that they find a younger man "in the prime of life."[4] But by the time the board assembled for its annual meeting in May 1929, most trustees seem to have concluded that Sampey was the best choice. There was no opposition and no other nominations. Trustees elected him unanimously.[5]

FINANCIAL CHALLENGES

When Mullins died, he left the seminary with a beautiful new campus and an enormous financial challenge. The seminary's debt stood at $992,000.[6] Even before the stock market crash of 1929, Sampey decided to delay plans to build a chapel, a president's home, and homes for professors, and used funds already borrowed to reduce the debt by nearly $200,000.[7] When the Depression began, Sampey made it his first priority to reduce the seminary's debt. He first led trustees to get the best return possible on the downtown properties. The trustees voted in 1929 to raze New York Hall and sell the lot.[8] But the property fronting Broadway, where Norton Hall stood, he leased at very favorable terms. Although he had to renegotiate and reduce lease payments during the Depression, it is hard to see how the seminary would have survived without them.

Sampey also pressed Southern Baptist leaders to make sure that the seminary received its equitable share of Southern Baptist gifts. This was distressingly difficult. Every Southern Baptist agency was deep in debt. Each had increased expenditures dramatically in the early 1920s based on the expectation of receiving a share of the $92 million that Southern Baptists pledged in their Seventy-Five Million Campaign. When Southern Baptists gave much less than they pledged, Southern Baptist agencies borrowed heavily in order to meet their expanded obligations. With heavy debts still on their books when the Depression began, many agencies faced foreclosure at various times throughout the 1930s. In that atmosphere, every agency pressed its desperate claims for larger shares of the shrinking revenues from church contributions. Because Southern Seminary had a sizable endowment and valuable property in downtown Louisville, its needs appeared less urgent. Sampey, like Mullins before him, judged that Southern Seminary was being treated inequitably in this regard.

---

4. John R. Sampey to Joshua Levering, 1 May 1929, box 1, Sampey Papers.

5. Minutes, Board of Trustees, Southern Baptist Theological Seminary, 8 May 1929.

6. John R. Sampey to Herschel H. Hobbs, 5 Dec. 1941, box 15, Sampey Papers.

7. John R. Sampey to Joshua Levering, 27 Dec. 1930, box 1, Sampey Papers.

8. John R. Sampey to Joshua Levering, 18 Jan. 1929, box 1, Sampey Papers.

John R. Sampey

The Depression diminished the ability of churches to give, and they gave less each year to the Cooperative Program, which was the new annual funding arrangement for all Southern Baptist entities. The competition for the pool of funds was fierce, and the seminary's receipts from southwide funds were insufficient for the seminary to meet expenses throughout the 1930s.

Sampey pressed Southern Baptist leaders to support a special fund-raising effort to extinguish the debt of Southern Baptist agencies. The result was a campaign initiated in 1933 and called the Hundred Thousand Club. Its initial aim was to enlist 100,000 Baptists to pledge one dollar per month, with the receipts divided among Southern Baptist institutions. Southern Seminary got 10 percent of the gifts. Sampey and his wife took ten memberships and kept paying monthly for more than eight years, contributing more than $1,000 in all. With the campaign's success, and with the careful planning of Sampey, treasurer Dobbins, and the financial board, at the time of Sampey's retirement in 1942 the seminary's debt stood at only $215,000.[9] The seminary had to economize.

9. Minutes, Board of Trustees, Southern Baptist Theological Seminary, 16 May 1942. See also John R. Sampey to Herschel H. Hobbs, 5 Dec. 1941, box 15, Sampey Papers.

It reduced staff and distributed the work to Sampey and to the faculty. It reduced everyone's salary by 20 percent. Sampey struggled to refinance the seminary debt at a lower rate. The seminary had paid nearly $800,000 of the debt Sampey inherited.

SAMPEY, FULLER, AND HISTORICAL CRITICISM

Sampey and Fuller took rather similar approaches to the historical criticism of the Bible. They both followed Mullins's pietist approach. Sampey was an accomplished scholar, conversant with the latest trends in Old Testament historical criticism. Fuller never completed his dissertation and felt unqualified to evaluate most of the latest claims of historical criticism on their own terms. Both believed that the seminary should pursue the highest scholarly achievement. And both were confident that none of the conclusions of careful scholarship could diminish the authority of the Bible.

They believed that the faculty should aspire to the most advanced scholarship. This was part of the original vision of Boyce and Broadus, and they meant to encourage it. Sampey held to the scholarly standards he had learned under Broadus, Manly, and Riggan. Fuller's mentor was A. T. Robertson, and he shared Robertson's understanding of scholarship. They recognized that questions of authorship and date were fundamental to correct interpretation, but their conclusions on such matters were largely traditional.

Sampey and Fuller generally resisted the conclusions of historical criticism when those conclusions contradicted traditional interpretations of important doctrines. But in some cases they concluded that reasonable historical-critical scholarship rendered traditional interpretations uncertain. In such cases, they still felt that somehow, no matter what scholarship should prove, it affected only the superficial or external aspects of the Bible. It could not diminish the Bible's intrinsic truth, power, and authority. And it could not overturn the doctrines of traditional orthodoxy. Whatever concessions Sampey and Fuller were willing to make privately to historical-critical scholarship, its real value was for scholarship rather than for the church. It had little value in the training of preachers.

The biblical and theological scholarship that derived from the historical criticism was just emerging in the days of Boyce and Broadus. Biblical scholarship in the era of the founders meant first mastering the languages and literature of the ancient Near East, and second becoming familiar with textual criticism. The linguists, grammarians, and text critics set the bar of theological scholarship. The new scholarship was historical criticism. It included the linguistic and textual scholarship of that earlier era, but it included much more. It required reconstructing the historical context and determining the author's intentions and the text's meaning based on that historical reconstruction.

By the 1930s most biblical and theological scholars took it for granted that the biblical documents were not what traditional Christianity thought they were. Many were not written by their ascribed authors. They were written in a different historical context than the one traditionally supposed. And even when the named author was correct, their documents should be read not as simple history but as a confession or a polemic cast in historical garb.

Sampey and Fuller largely rejected the critical scholars' reconstruction of biblical history, though they admitted the force of some of the arguments. Sampey, for example, concluded that the last twenty-seven chapters of the book of Isaiah may have had an author other than Isaiah as most critics believed. Fuller seemed to admit that such conclusions were legitimate matters of scholarly investigation. But neither man wanted such conclusions taught in seminary classes. To do so ran the risk of destroying the ministerial effectiveness of the seminary's young preachers and would place the seminary in an untenable position in the denomination. Such methods and conclusions had little genuine relevance to the Christian faith and life. Regardless of who actually wrote Leviticus or Daniel, Sampey and Fuller believed, the authors wrote under the full inspiration of the Holy Spirit. Whether the book of Jonah was a parable or historical, its religious meaning was the same. It was important for the seminary's professors to know the scholarship and investigate such matters, but it had little relevance for preparing preachers and was best left out of the classroom. But the faculty of the 1930s and 1940s found it increasingly difficult to accept this restriction. They began to feel that it stifled their effectiveness and stultified pastors and their churches.

HISTORICAL CRITICISM AND THE TRAJECTORY OF THEOLOGICAL SCHOLARSHIP

Harold W. Tribble succeeded Mullins in the chair of theology and taught the course along the same lines. He used Mullins's *Christian Religion in Its Doctrinal Expression* as his textbook and supplemented class reading with a heavy dose of leading personalist theologian A. C. Knudson, along with such liberal theologians as William Newton Clarke and H. N. Wieman.[10] Tribble agreed broadly with Mullins's personalist theology. Tribble seems, however, to have been less

---

10. Harold W. Tribble, "SBTS Theology Lecture Notes (2)," 3/400, Tribble Papers, WFU. See especially notes on the first class meeting.

certain about many of Mullins's traditional conclusions. In his little book *Our Doctrines*, Tribble defined many traditional points of theology with remarkable vagueness.

Tribble was, however, cautious in teaching contrary to traditional orthodox conclusions. He let Mullins's textbook serve as the stackpole on which his more conservative students could rest. Like most of his like-minded colleagues in the 1940s and 1950s, he could not positively assert his disagreement with most aspects of traditional orthodoxy nor his agreement with some aspects of liberal or neo-orthodox theology. In the readings and classroom discussions on many topics of theology, he kept the various positions on a more or less level playing field. Some of the "better" students would be won over—and some of them had already been won over by their religion professors in college.

Tribble differed from Mullins by integrating into this thought some of the emphases of neo-orthodoxy. Like many of his colleagues, he found Emil Brunner's brand of neo-orthodoxy more persuasive than Barth's. Southern Seminary's postwar faculty cautiously adopted aspects of neo-orthodoxy. They were wary of Barth's radical disjunction between the creator and the creation. Barth left no room for revelation through human experience or the natural world. Brunner did. Many of Southern Seminary's faculty thus found a way to retain much of their experientially oriented liberalism and at the same time advocate such neo-orthodox emphases as the gravity of human sinfulness and the centrality of the Bible.

Their experience differed somewhat from that of many American theology professors, whose liberal views underwent more significant readjustment through the influence of neo-orthodoxy, but the result was in many respects similar. Southern's faculty, like their liberal colleagues at other seminaries, did not give up their liberalism in response to Barth's critique. They, rather, accepted the critique at certain points and admitted that they may have swung too far from orthodoxy in some ways. Barth's critique thus meant not the rejection of liberalism but its adjustment to more "realistic" analysis of human sin and culture.[11]

Neo-orthodoxy thus reinforced some of the emphases that Southern's faculty had largely retained under the influence of Mullins's mediating theology and their conservative constituency. They were conservative liberals who had all along emphasized the gravity of sinfulness and the centrality of the Bible. But neo-orthodoxy was still a long way from the old orthodoxy. Neo-orthodox scholars accepted broadly the same historical-critical conclusions on which

11. See the twelve contributions to Edwin Lewis et al., "How Barth Has Influenced Me," *Theology Today* 13 (1956): 358–375.

liberals relied. And Southern Seminary's faculty still yearned to teach the historical-critical conclusions openly in order to lead the churches into the light of modern Christianity. But it was not getting any easier for them.

In the 1930s Jesse B. Weatherspoon, professor of homiletics, wanted to introduce Southern Baptists to some basic matters of Old Testament historical criticism. He had written his dissertation on Hebrew meter in the book of Isaiah and taught Old Testament at the Southwestern Baptist Theological Seminary from 1913 to 1918. In 1934 the Sunday School Board published his *Book We Teach* as a study course textbook for Sunday school teachers and cautiously included some historical criticism.

Progressive Southern Baptist leaders, like their northern counterparts, sought to raise the "intelligence" of the laity. Some progress could be expected from an intelligent and educated ministry, but solid progress would depend also on developing an enlightened laity, especially Sunday school teachers. Sunday school literature needed to introduce the methods and findings of historical criticism if the teachers were going to be able to answer the tough questions raised by modern infidelity.

Southern Baptists had fallen behind the other denominations. Northern Baptist scholars, for example, were producing such material for Sunday school teachers as *The Bible for Home and School*, the commentary series edited by Shailer Mathews to which A. T. Robertson contributed. It aimed to place the "results of the best modern biblical scholarship at the disposal of the general reader." The recent rapid progress of "biblical science" required new literature for the "needs of intelligent Sunday school teachers," whose labors would "stimulate the intelligent use of the Bible in the home and the school." [12] Southern Baptists had similar needs. Weatherspoon and other progressive leaders sought to move Southern Baptist Sunday school literature in this direction.

Weatherspoon sought to introduce the premises of historical criticism under the aegis of "progressive revelation." For conservatives, the idea of progressive revelation meant only that God did not reveal the entirety of his plan of redemption until the time of Jesus and the apostles—it was a cumulative process, like adding pieces to a puzzle or erecting a building. Once completed, it did not change. But for liberal scholars, progressive revelation meant that as civilization progressed, the people of God experienced more accurate and complete revelation. It was not cumulative as much as evolutionary—fuller revelation came as civilization advanced, and it corrected and displaced the inferior and defective earlier forms of revelation. The ideas and practices suitable to an earlier period

---

12. Shailer Mathews, "General Introduction," in Loring W. Batten, *A Commentary on the First Book of Samuel*, The Bible for Home and School (New York: Macmillan, 1919), v.

of God's revelation were not suitable to later periods. In primitive eras, for example, Israel held that polygamy, easy divorce, "blood revenge, hatred of enemies, and cruel slaughter" were consistent with "the standard of righteousness." But as "God's light grew," their "ideas advanced to a law of love and forgiveness" that corrected and displaced these notions.[13] Even Jesus at times accommodated his teaching to the "sinful prejudices" of Israel and commanded the disciples "on the basis of their capacity and their understanding."[14] Such "unideal commands" were necessary steps in the moral progress of civilization.[15]

Weatherspoon also sought to introduce Southern Baptists to the distinction between the divine revelation itself and the human record of the divine revelation. This was a necessary presupposition of progressive revelation. God's revelation, Weatherspoon wrote, was "in creation, history, individual experience, in Jesus Christ, and his redemptive work." The Bible did not make Weatherspoon's list. It was distinct from the revelation. It was "the literary record of his revelation."[16]

But the most important presupposition of progressive revelation was the liberal understanding of inspiration. Weatherspoon avoided a detailed discussion of the doctrine but asserted its most important element: the Bible's religious element alone was inspired, and its scientific, historical, and even ethical elements were subject to correction. Weatherspoon stressed that "the Bible is a book of religion" in order to resolve questions about its "unscientific" statements relating to creation and the history and character of the earth. The fact that the Old Testament was unscientific posed no difficulty, Weatherspoon said, if the religious element only constituted the Bible's inspired matter.[17]

Weatherspoon introduced readers to two basic conclusions of the historical-critical reconstruction of the Bible's history, the question of the multiplicity of sources composing the Books of Moses, and the question of the authorship of Isaiah 40 through 66. Weatherspoon said that critical scholars were agreed that Moses contributed at most a limited core of materials for the five "Books of Moses," that they derived primarily from four sources composed long after Moses' death, and that they were redacted into a cohesive five-book set in around 500 B.C. Weatherspoon separated the question of sources from the

13. Jesse B. Weatherspoon, *The Book We Teach* (Nashville, TN: Sunday School Board of the Southern Baptist Convention, 1934), 27–28.

14. Weatherspoon, *The Book We Teach*, 29. "At one stage he said to them 'Go only to the lost sheep of the house of Israel' while even then his heart was burning to say what he later did say, 'Go ye into all the world.'"

15. Weatherspoon, *The Book We Teach*, 29.

16. Weatherspoon, *The Book We Teach*, 33. See also ibid., 23.

17. Weatherspoon, *The Book We Teach*, 21, 23, 29–30.

question of later authors. He wrote that Moses used many sources then existing for such topics as the creation and the history of the patriarchs. And he subtly suggested that Moses relied on Hammurabi's Code, apparently implying that he borrowed from it in composing the Ten Commandments.[18]

The Pentateuch had the same religious value no matter who wrote it, Weatherspoon believed, and the additions of later authors did not change the fact that Moses was the "essential" and "responsible" author of the material. Weatherspoon then prepared Southern Baptists for the most characteristic element of modern Pentateuchal criticism, the idea that the cultic aspects of the law were composed latest of all the parts of the Pentateuch: "If scholars find laws in Leviticus which bear evidence of a later date, we need not feel that any falsity henceforth attaches to the term 'Laws of Moses.'"[19] Regarding Isaiah 40–66, he merely stated in passing that the section was a comfort to Jewish exiles, "whether he [Isaiah] lived in Jerusalem in 740 B.C. or in Babylon in 540 B.C."[20]

When some Southern Baptists criticized these statements, the Sunday School Board's P. E. Burroughs asked Weatherspoon if it would not be wise to amend the objectionable passages. Weatherspoon was adamant that the passages should not be removed. Southern Baptists were ignorant of modern scholarship on the Bible, he said, and they could not afford to "shut the door to investigation." His aim in these objectionable passages was to prepare Southern Baptists for the notion that the Bible was trustworthy as scripture regardless of whether Moses wrote the Pentateuch or Isaiah wrote the last twenty-seven chapters of the book attributed to him. Without these advances in the knowledge of current scholarship, nothing would be gained "for a proper understanding of the Old Testament."[21]

All editions of the book since 1935 nevertheless omitted the objectionable passages. Burroughs and the board removed the passages on the sources and authorship of the Pentateuch, on the authorship of Isaiah 40–66, and on the "unscientific" character of the Old Testament.[22]

---

18. Weatherspoon, *The Book We Teach*, 10–11. "The laws of Hammurabi (Amraphel, Gen. 14:1), with whom Abraham warred, were written 500 years before Moses, and evidently were known to him." Of course, the only evidence that Moses knew Hammurabi's Code was the similarity between it and the Ten Commandments.

19. Weatherspoon, *The Book We Teach*, 11.

20. Weatherspoon, *The Book We Teach*, 61.

21. Jesse B. Weatherspoon to P. E. Burroughs, 28 Dec. 1934, Box 30, Corr., J. B. Weatherspoon, I. J. Van Ness Papers, SBHLA.

22. Weatherspoon, *The Book We Teach*, 10–11, 29, 61; Jesse B. Weatherspoon and Gaines Dobbins, *The Bible and the Bible School* (Nashville, TN: Broadman Press, 1935), 14, 33, 65. This last title combined Weatherspoon's *The Book We Teach* with Dobbins's *The School in Which We Teach*.

CONTROVERSY

Sampey opposed liberalism personally, but he also recognized that the seminary could not afford to promote liberalism in any way. As Mullins had done before him, he made sure that the faculty knew the limits that a realistic and constructive relationship with the Southern Baptist Convention imposed. In the late 1930s and early 1940s, a series of controversies spread the perception that the seminary promoted liberalism. Unsurprisingly, most of them involved missions professor W. O. Carver. On two occasions Sampey opposed Carver directly. The last episode provoked Sampey to such a degree that for a time he repudiated their fifty-five-year friendship.

In 1932 Carver nominated Quaker mystic Rufus Jones to give the Norton Lectures that session. Carver's own thought was "in many ways" indebted to Jones for his "progressive evangelical thinking." The faculty elected him, and Jones agreed to give the lectures in the spring of 1933. But Jones's beliefs were unacceptable to most Southern Baptists. Jones was a modernist and a favorite of Harry Emerson Fosdick, the great liberal preacher of New York's Riverside Church. And he played an important role in issuing *Rethinking Missions*, a 1932 report by a committee of progressive Protestants critical of traditional missionary motives and methods. When the seminary announced Jones as the lecturer, some Southern Baptist pastors raised strong objection. Sampey advised the faculty to recall their invitation, and they did. An embarrassed Carver relayed the news to Jones and considered it "the most disagreeable task I ever had in connection with the seminary."[23]

Carver also led the faculty to invite Toyohiko Kagawa to deliver the Julius Brown Gay Lectures at Southern Seminary in March 1936. Kagawa, a Japanese Christian whose work among the poor earned him wide fame, gave four lectures at the seminary as part of an American lecture tour promoting his vision of social Christianity. Kagawa's opposition to doctrine in general, his cosmological idealism, and his message of the universal kingdom of God did not seem quite orthodox to most Southern Baptists. The fundamentalist *Sunday School Times* and the Baptist newspapers in Kentucky and North Carolina published articles severely critical of Kagawa for his modernist beliefs. Alarmed Southern Baptists wrote Sampey and Carver expressing their concern.[24] Kagawa's humility, genuineness,

---

23. Carver, "Recollections," 111–112. On Jones, see Gary Dorrien, *The Making of American Liberal Theology: Idealism, Realism, and Modernity, 1900–1950* (Louisville, KY: Westminster John Knox Press, 2003), 364–371, 432.

24. William O. Carver to J. M. Brown, 16 Feb. 1936, box 23, Carver Papers, SBHLA; A. O. Moore to William O. Carver, 21 Apr. 1936, ibid.; B. P. Mitchell to William O. Carver, 3 June 1936, ibid.

and life of personal sacrifice for the sake of the poor convinced Sampey that he was a sound Christian teacher. Sampey and Carver wrote letters and articles defending their selection of Kagawa and did not rescind the invitation.

For Southern Baptists, the invitations extended to Jones and Kagawa afforded the most substantial evidence in twenty years that the faculty sympathized with liberalism. But the evidence was at best suggestive rather than probative. The invitations nevertheless deepened the suspicion of the seminary.

PREMILLENNIALISM

In 1940 Carver wrote some articles in the *Pastor's Periscope*, a denominational quarterly, criticizing a popular form of eschatology known as "dispensational premillennialism." In these and in subsequent articles and letters defending his views, Carver explained that premillennialists were too pessimistic about human society. The Bible called on Christians to establish a worldwide Christianity and a just society, but premillennialists held that biblical prophecy taught that such a thing could not occur until Christ returned at his Second Coming. Carver suggested that premillennialists had given up on Christ's commission to the church to "save" the world. But Carver misrepresented premillennialists by using the word "saved" in a rather different sense than they did. Carver used it in a social sense that required individual salvation but aimed beyond that to the salvation of human society. Premillennialists actively sought the salvation of individual sinners and established dozens of missionary agencies and missionary training schools to accomplish the task, but they did not believe that efforts to ameliorate society would have lasting effect, and so they tended to place little faith in such efforts.

Many Southern Baptists had come under the influence dispensational premillennialism in the previous generation, and they made known their displeasure with Carver's rather dismissive criticism. The *Western Recorder* in particular kept its columns open for months to premillennial Baptists who wanted to respond to Carver.[25] The controversy alienated many Southern Baptists from the seminary and sowed additional suspicion of its unsoundness.

25. William O. Carver, "Into the Clouds," *Western Recorder*, 25 Apr. 1940, 4–5; L. A. Daniel, "A Maryland Pastor Replies to Dr. Carver's Article," *Western Recorder*, 16 May 1940, 6; Jonathan Robinson, "This Present Evil Age," ibid., 9 May 1940, 12–13; William B. Riley, "Professor W. O. Carver on the Second Coming," ibid., 16 May 1940, 10–11; Carver, "What Is My Offense," ibid., 30 May 1940, 10–11; William B. Riley, "Dr. Riley's Answer to Dr. Carver," ibid., 20 June 1940, 5.

THE DAS KELLEY BARNETT CONTROVERSY

The episode that most seriously damaged the seminary's claims to orthodoxy was the Das Kelley Barnett controversy in 1941. Controversy erupted when W. O. Carver, as editor of the seminary's *Review and Expositor*, published an article by Barnett in which he called on Southern Baptists to relinquish their old theology for the new modern theology.

Barnett had an impressive record at the seminary and the faculty invited him to give one of the commencement addresses. The faculty had great confidence in Barnett's abilities and had appointed him a fellow in the theology department. There were nineteen fellows in all at the seminary.[26] They assisted professors in grading assignments and examinations, and hearing recitation on assigned reading.[27] His commencement address contained many of the liberal views expressed in the article. A fellow student also commended liberal views in his address. Sampey took the unusual step of telling the commencement audience that he "expressly disavowed" Barnett's and the other student's views and that "they did not represent the attitude of the seminary."[28]

Barnett's article elaborated the theme of his address. It was a cautious plea for modernism. He criticized severely Southern Baptists' preferences for traditional views and urged the advance of progressive thought. He called their beliefs "provincial, dogmatic, apocalyptic, and institutional," imposed upon people by "self-appointed guardians of the Baptist faith." But the most troubling element for most Southern Baptists concerned his criticisms of their traditional views of the Bible. Most Southern Baptists held that the Bible was itself a revelation, and was God's complete revelation to humanity. Barnett held that Bible was not itself a revelation at all, but a "record" of God's revelation, especially a historical record of Jesus Christ, who revealed God to humanity most fully. "God did not entrust his revelation to a book," Barnett said, "but to a historical process."[29] Southern Baptists did not understand how a theology fellow and commencement speaker could write what Barnett wrote.

Virginia's *Religious Herald* defended the article and some of the state papers stood aside, but several Baptist newspapers published extensive criticism of Barnett and Carver. William B. Riley, one of the most influential northern fundamentalists,

26. John R. Sampey, "The Southern Seminary after Fifty-Six Years," *Western Recorder*, 30 Oct. 1941, 12.

27. See Sampey description of the work of seminary fellows, John R. Sampey to L. E. Barton, 24 Oct. 1941, box 13, Sampey Papers.

28. John R. Sampey to W. D. Lester, 2 Oct. 1941, box 13, Sampey Papers.

29. Das Kelley Barnett, "The New Theological Frontier for Southern Baptists," *Review and Expositor* 38 (1941): 264–276.

criticized the seminary sharply for publishing Barnett's article.[30] Kentucky Baptists' *Western Recorder* carried the debate the longest.[31] Carver wrote an extensive explanation and apology.[32] Sampey wrote an article reaffirming the orthodoxy of the seminary.[33] The faculty issued a statement defending Barnett's freedom of expression and the right of the seminary journal to publish articles of divergent points of view.[34] Barnett published an article defending his views but announcing his resignation as a fellow.[35] Carver's apologies, Sampey's endorsement of the faculty's soundness, and Barnett's resignation satisfied most of the critics.[36]

It is surprising that Carver published Barnett's article in the first place. Carver knew that Sampey had already disavowed Barnett's views on behalf of the seminary. He also knew that Sampey was very sensitive about the seminary's reputation. Sampey's policy was to require his endorsement for the publication of any article in the *Review and Expositor*, but Carver did not submit Barnett's article for Sampey's review. He pleaded afterward that his own and Sampey's travel schedules prevented him from sending it to Sampey in time to get the journal into print, and that he had read the article hurriedly and did not notice its many problems. Neither plea is particularly plausible, since he knew

30. Reuben E. Alley, "Your Young Men Shall See Visions," *Religious Herald*, 16 Oct. 1941, 10–11; William B. Riley, "Professor Carver's Defense of Barnett," *Western Recorder*, 30 Oct. 1941, 4–5; William B. Riley, "The King Bolt in Baptist Creeds," *Western Recorder*, 1 Jan. 1942, 1.

31. Victor I. Masters, "Statement of the Seminary Faculty," *Western Recorder*, 9 Oct. 1941, 9; John D. Freeman, "Is the Attack Unfortunate," *Religious Herald*, 20 Nov. 1941, 12–13; L. E. Barton, "The Barnett Case and Baptist Freedom," *Western Recorder*, 4 Dec. 1941, 1; William W. Stout, "Concerning an Adventure in Misunderstanding," *Western Recorder*, 12 Feb. 1942, 4–5; T. E. Smith, "Observations in Connection with the Barnett Issue," *Western Recorder*, 26 Feb. 1942, 1–2; John D. Freeman, "Who Misunderstood What," *Western Recorder*, 26 Feb. 1942, 4–5, 12; William W. Stout, "Wait a Minute," *Western Recorder*, 12 Mar. 1942, 4–5; T. E. Smith, "An Issue Which Must Not Die," *Western Recorder*, 2 Apr. 1942, 4–5; Gordon Hurlbutt, "Prime Issue in the Barnett Case," *Western Recorder*, 2 Apr. 1942, 6, 23.

32. William O. Carver, "Concerning an Article in the Review and Expositor," *Western Recorder*, 9 Oct. 1941, 10–11.

33. John R. Sampey, "A Word from President Sampey," *Western Recorder*, 9 Oct. 1941, 12; John R. Sampey, "Safeguarding Doctrinal Soundness of Southern Seminary," *Western Recorder*, 13 Nov. 1941, 1.

34. Faculty of Southern Baptist Theological Seminary, "A Statement by the Seminary Faculty," *Western Recorder*, 9 Oct. 1941, 12.

35. Das Kelley Barnett, "Mr. Barnett Resigns Seminary Post," *Western Recorder*, 27 Nov. 1941, 6.

36. John R. Sampey to Louie D. Newton, 17 Nov. 1941, box 13, Sampey Papers; Sampey to J. E. Skinner, 18 Nov. 1941, ibid.

of Sampey's sensitivity concerning unsound views and his specific opposition to Barnett's speech. Carver too had heard the address and knew that Barnett planned to base his article on it.

E. D. Solomon, editor of Florida's *Baptist Witness*, wrote Sampey privately that the appearance of Barnett's article injured the reputation of Sampey and the seminary among Florida's Southern Baptists: "I have heard in Florida some most unfavorable criticism of you because of this article.... Unless this thing can be remedied our seminary will lose the ministerial students from Florida. I have also heard expressions that you should resign, all of which is very painful to me." Solomon thought that Sampey was orthodox and saw him as a "hero." But the appearance of the article suggested to many that Sampey kept and defended unsound men on the faculty.[37]

Sampey replied that Carver and the other professors were sound and orthodox: "As far as I can see, we have no modernism in our faculty and very little in our student body. The seminary has tried through all the years to be thoroughly conservative of all the Baptist faith and of the entire teaching of the Bible." He nevertheless suggested that the seminary allowed freedom for the promotion of progressive ideas. From his experience in the Whitsitt controversy he insisted on the faculty's freedom. He justified the seminary's course by appeal to Boyce and Broadus: "They were progressive conservatives."

Naturally considerable ambiguity attached to the progressive part of "progressive conservatives." For Sampey and other traditionalists, it meant primarily that the church will continue to grow in its understanding and application of the Bible. Careful study would reveal new depths of meaning. And the church would gain new insight about applying that truth to its social context. But the Bible's statements were true at every level of meaning, and were stable and unchanging in their meaning. They were largely satisfied with the old theology. But progressives understood the progressive part of the phrase as validating the replacement of old theologies and practices with new ones. It permitted more radical change in understanding the Bible and religion.

The controversy placed tremendous strain on Carver's relationship with Sampey. Sampey felt keenly how the article put the seminary in a deeply embarrassing situation before the denomination. Carver apologized to Sampey and Sampey accepted Carver's explanation and apology. He believed that Carver would never knowingly publish such views: "It was not very carefully read by Dr. Carver, and I am sure that some of the objectionable sentences did not register with him or he would have modified the article or rejected it."[38]

37. E. D. Solomon to John R. Sampey, 30 Sept. 1941, box 13, Sampey Papers.
38. John R. Sampey to Warren Payne, 7 Oct. 1941, box 13, Sampey Papers.

Sampey was not naïve about Carver's liberal sympathies, though he apparently underestimated their full extent. He knew that Carver "had sufficient sympathy with some things in the article to let it be published." But Sampey knew also that Carver was generally the very picture of circumspection in such matters and trusted his explanation that this episode represented an unfortunate lapse in judgment. He defended Carver and urged that "this slip on the part of my colleague will not seriously interfere with his standing in our Baptist brotherhood."[39]

But when Carver signed on in 1945 as a member of the advisory board of Barnett's *Christian Frontiers* newspaper, a paper designed to lead Southern Baptists into enlightened and modern views of religion, Sampey changed his mind about Carver's role in publishing Barnett's article in the *Review and Expositor*. He became convinced that Carver's explanation had not been fully honest. He saw that Carver was bent upon leading Southern Baptists in a more liberal direction and had published the article to this end. Sampey felt betrayed and he repudiated their long friendship. Carver and other faculty members apparently convinced Sampey to be reconciled.[40]

The Barnett controversy marked the beginning of a new era for the seminary. Until this time the seminary had maintained its reputation for orthodoxy in the denomination. Southern Baptists had been convinced of the orthodoxy of Mullins and Sampey, and had trusted their responses to any accusations of unsoundness. The only constant critic had been notorious fundamentalist leader J. Frank Norris, and he was not a reliable indicator. The Barnett episode however struck a chord that resonated for some time. Some Southern Baptists were not quite convinced by the explanations and apologies. A minority of pastors, especially in Kentucky, began regularly to criticize the seminary as unsound. Many of the faculty elected in the 1940s and 1950s adopted liberal and neo-orthodox ideas, and gave the critics more frequent occasion to complain.

SAMPEY AND THE ORTHODOXY OF THE SEMINARY

Sampey believed that part of his duty as president was to ensure that the faculty taught in accordance with traditional orthodoxy. This meant fidelity to the Abstract of Principles and to the ideas of Boyce and Broadus.

He characterized the seminary's position as Mullins had, as representing "progressive conservativism." For Sampey, this meant nearly the same thing

39. John R. Sampey to James C. Sinclair, 8 Oct. 1941, box 13, Sampey Papers.
40. John R. Sampey to William O. Carver, 20 Mar. 1946, box 10, Carver Papers, SBHLA; Sampey to Carver, 25 Mar. 1946, ibid.; Carver to Sampey, 23 Mar. 1946, ibid.

that it had for Boyce, Manly, and Broadus. But Sampey was far more comfortable with many of the progressive conclusions of historical criticism of the Bible than the founders had been. Boyce and Broadus felt that historical criticism had direct bearing on doctrine. Sampey managed to separate them.

But Sampey did not tolerate liberal theological conclusions on his faculty, however much he might tolerate progressive historical-critical conclusions. For the most part he seemed to feel that he knew his faculty well and that their whole approach to the Christian faith could not possibly entail liberal views. But when accusations arose, he examined the faculty concerning their theological beliefs.

Carver felt that Sampey grew increasingly troubled by liberal trends on the faculty: "Dr. Sampey, as he grew older, tended to grow more conservative in his scholarship and in his Baptist orthodoxy," Carver said, and expressed vigorous "antagonism toward some who he thought were introducing erroneous and dangerous ideas." [41] Sampey's growing conservatism was in part a response to the growth of liberalism in the seminary and in the denomination.

When the Das Kelley Barnett controversy erupted in 1941, Sampey wanted to know whether Carver, who published Barnett's article in the seminary's journal, agreed with Barnett. Carver satisfied Sampey by saying that the article had many unfortunate expressions that he could not endorse. Sampey was sufficiently shaken by Carver's decision to publish Barnett's article to wonder whether other professors may have had liberal sympathies. He interrogated theology professor Harold Tribble concerning his beliefs and concluded that he held the gospel "as Boyce and Broadus interpreted it." [42] Sampey was unable to detect Tribble's liberal views, but Tribble was accomplished at circumspection. Sampey and his successor Fuller trusted the piety and scholarship of the faculty, but the necessity of a careful investigation of their views began with the Barnett controversy. And from this time, for the next fifty years, answering accusations of the faculty's heresies became a regular part of the president's duties. This role was a source of deep antagonism between the faculty and presidents Fuller and McCall.

Sampey in fact undertook to examine the soundness of all members of the faculty. He apparently had no grave suspicion of any, but it gave his defense of the faculty greater credibility. He told L. E. Barton, one of the chief critics of Barnett's article, that "I am satisfied as to the doctrinal soundness of each one of my colleagues in the Faculty. I am talking freely with them in private interviews

41. W. O. Carver, "Recollections and Information from Other Sources concerning the Southern Baptist Theological Seminary," typescript, 1954, Archives and Special Collections, SBTS.

42. John R. Sampey to J. H. Anderson, 28 Oct. 1941, box 15, Sampey Papers.

and find everything in satisfactory shape. I do not believe any one has any plan to shift the seminary from its position of a progressive-conservative institution."[43] Sampey was thus assured that "all members of my faculty are earnest evangelical Christians and orthodox Baptists," and he was therefore "prepared to defend them to the limit."[44]

FRANK POWELL AND THE POWER OF THE PRESIDENT

Sampey's vision of the presidency was that of Boyce and Broadus—he thought that the faculty should function as democratically as possible in the operation and administration of the seminary. This was a deliberate reversal of some of Mullins's approach to leadership. An important representation of Sampey's new democratic regime was his approach to his salary. Mullins permitted the trustees to pay him considerably more than the full professors. Sampey did not. His salary was $6,500, the same as Carver and Robertson received.[45]

But this approach was no longer tenable. The seminary needed a president with executive authority. The trustees apparently wanted Sampey to exercise the authority, but he was reluctant. The faculty, student body, and operations of the seminary had grown too large to be administered by faculty committee. But there were two other reasons. The first was that the president needed to exercise strong leadership in hiring and evaluation of faculty. Trustees wanted assurance that the seminary would hire faculty who were sound in doctrine and acceptable to Southern Baptists, and who were effective teachers. So when Sampey became convinced that church history professor Frank Powell was an ineffective teacher, trustees expected Sampey to exercise his authority to dismiss Powell.

Jesse Weatherspoon said that Sampey and Powell had long been in personal conflict. Powell had little respect for Sampey. Sampey endured it for years. As Weatherspoon explained, "Dr. Sampey said that he had not handled it a long time before because he didn't have authority, individual authority." Trustees told him that someone must have authority.[46] When he made up his mind to take action, he consulted every other professor "concerning the value of Dr. Powell to the seminary."[47]

43. John R. Sampey to L. E. Barton, 10 Nov. 1941, box 13, Sampey Papers.
44. John R. Sampey to R. H. Satterfield, 15 Dec. 1941, box 16, Sampey Papers.
45. "Salaries in the Seminary," ca. 1940, Southern Baptist Theological Seminary folder, box 24, Carver Papers, SBHLA.
46. Jesse Weatherspoon, transcription of trustee interviews 28–30 Apr. 1958, 2:211.
47. Jesse Weatherspoon, transcription of trustee interviews 28–30 Apr. 1958, 2:241.

In March 1940 Sampey met with Powell and discussed his "faults." In Powell's written resignation five days later, he suggested that the faults consisted in ineffectiveness in the classroom, lack of fellowship with other faculty, and an unsatisfactory example in the Christian life.[48] Trustees accepted his resignation effective May 1941.

The seminary needed an executive president also in order to deal effectively with growing suspicion of the faculty's unsoundness. Some Southern Baptists believed that Powell was theologically unsound.[49] There is no evidence that Sampey thought this, but as such accusations were becoming common, the president needed authority for establishing and enforcing policies to protect the seminary from criticism. Carver's actions in publishing Barnett's article and in joining the editorial board of Barnett's liberal journal damaged the seminary's reputation in the convention. The president needed authority to make it easier to persuade the faculty to take a more realistic approach in denominational diplomacy.

Sampey retired as president in 1942. In previous years, when he had spoken of his retirement to trustees, they refused to hear of it. As Sampey approached his eightieth birthday, however, he insisted that it was time to step down. He had completed his mission—he had preserved the seminary intact through economic crisis and modernist errors. He died on August 18, 1946.

THE ELECTION OF ELLIS A. FULLER

The board planned to elect a new president in May 1942. Many observers expected the trustees to elect theology professor Harold W. Tribble, who was successor to Mullins in the chair of theology and an impressive and capable figure. He was one of the most liberal teachers on the faculty, but he was also realistic in his approach to denominational relations. He was extraordinarily circumspect even in private correspondence with trusted friends. Others favored the election of Old Testament professor Kyle Yates, an impressive preacher who had won the affections of many in the convention. In February 1942 he became pastor of Louisville's Walnut Street Baptist Church but continued his teaching duties. Yates tended to be more conservative and pragmatic than Tribble in his approach to theological education. Sampey wanted to avoid campaigning among the seminary's faculty and friends and warned against holding the election in Louisville.

48. Frank M. Powell to John R. Sampey, 23 Mar. 1940, Personal Correspondence File, Sampey Papers. See also John R. Sampey to Dick H. Hall, 23 July 1940, ibid.

49. See E. Godbold to John R. Sampey, 3 Nov. 1939, box 24, Sampey Papers.

Ellis A. Fuller

Outside of Louisville, Ellis A. Fuller became the favorite candidate among convention leaders. Fuller was pastor of the large and influential Atlanta First Baptist Church, had served as an evangelist with the convention's Home Mission Board, and was among the convention's foremost preachers. By 1929 Fuller had become one of Southern Baptists' most trusted leaders. When the board met in San Antonio in May 1942, only Fuller and Walter P. Binns received nomination. Trustees elected Fuller unanimously.[50] The day after his election, he preached the "convention sermon" to the messengers at the Southern Baptist Convention and left no doubt about his conservative theological convictions.

Many trustees preferred Fuller because they wanted him to shore up the seminary's flagging reputation for orthodoxy. Victor I. Masters, editor of the *Western Recorder*, had grown anxious about the seminary's orthodoxy in recent

50. Minutes, Board of Trustees, Southern Baptist Theological Seminary, 15 May 1942. Trustees elected Fuller over Binns by a majority on the first vote and by subsequent vote made the election unanimous.

years, but he was confident that Fuller would not tolerate liberalism in the seminary.[51] Anna S. Pruitt, a retired Southern Baptist missionary, approved the election of Fuller because he could "destroy the insidious poison" of the seminary's recent "unsound teaching" and prevent it from following the path of the Northern Baptists' Crozer and Rochester seminaries.[52]

Fuller faced enormous challenges. The most urgent demand was to expand the school's faculty and physical plant to meet the demands of an exploding student population. Fuller was an energetic and visionary leader, an irrepressible soul. He seemed precisely the right man for job.

RELIGIOUS EDUCATION AND THE MUSIC SCHOOL

As many urban churches grew to many hundreds of members, they developed elaborate programs of music and religious education with extensive lay involvement. Churches began to hire laypersons as full-time music or religious education assistants. But the demand was greater than the supply, and few had the requisite education in theology, music, and religious education. Fuller led the seminary to develop degree programs to answer the need for both music and religious education leaders.

In early 1943 Fuller sketched out his plans. To train leaders in religious education, he wanted to create a two-year program consisting of basic courses in the Bible, church history, and theology, as well as specialized courses in religious education, church administration, and church finances. Gaines Dobbins was teaching these subjects to pastors, but Fuller wanted a new degree program so that men could "fit themselves to serve as educational directors and financial secretaries or general assistants to pastors."[53] As pastor of Atlanta First Baptist Church, Fuller had been frustrated at his inability to find a qualified and able man to assist him in these areas of church work. Fuller quickly led the faculty to expand the religious education program and placed it under the guidance of Gaines Dobbins, who had taught the subject at the seminary since 1920. The seminary established a distinct school of religious education in 1953.

His plans for training ministers of music were similar, but in this case he established a separate school of music within the seminary. He wanted a two-year program with the same courses in Bible, church history, and theology, but with specialized courses in teaching and leading a broad church music program.

51. See Victor I. Masters to Ellis A. Fuller, 25 May 1942, box 9, Fuller Papers.

52. Anna S. Pruitt to Ellis A. and Mrs. Fuller, 13 June 1942, box 9, Fuller Papers.

53. Ellis A. Fuller to Walter P. Binns, 30 Jan. 1943, box 6, Fuller Papers.

He wanted as professors graduates of the Westminster Choir College, the school founded in 1920 by John F. Williamson that set the standard for training in church music and effectively invented the professional "minister of music."[54] At Atlanta First Baptist Church, Fuller had hired Westminster Choir College graduate Donald Winters as minister of music and was delighted with the results.

The music school opened in 1944 with about twenty students, almost all women, since students in this program were not exempted from military service. In 1943 Louisville trustee V. V. Cooke bought the beautiful and spacious Callahan home across Lexington Road and gave it to the seminary as the new home of the music school. The following year the owners of "the old Seelbach house," a stately mansion on five acres contiguous to the Callahan home, donated their property to the seminary, and it became a women's dormitory for music school students.[55] The buildings became Cooke Hall and Barnard Hall, respectively. Fuller secured Winters to be the founding dean but had to wait until he was discharged from the army. Frances Winters, his wife, opened the school and taught music. Donald Winters assumed his duties after his discharge in 1946.

PRESIDENTIAL AUTHORITY AND FACULTY ALIENATION

Throughout Fuller's tenure, tensions with the faculty remained high. One source of tension concerned the president's authority, whether he was a peer of the faculty, *primus inter pares*, or had executive authority over them. In 1943, on the night Fuller arrived in Louisville, Hugh Peterson recalled, "the faculty talked all night" about the right of faculty members to choose new faculty and to control promotions. They said that "nobody was going to come in and be in charge of them."[56]

The trustees took a different view. W. O. Carver recalled that the trustees "expected him emphatically to be president." Trustees took advantage of the opportunity of choosing a president to redefine the role and elevate his official administrative authority. Trustees appointed a special committee in 1942 to define the president's functions and responsibilities. The report, adopted by the board in 1943, declared the president "the executive head of the institution, with the authority and responsibilities usually pertaining to such an office." Trustees explicitly charged the president to "select and nominate new teachers" to the board and to recommend to the board the dismissal or retirement of faculty

---

54. Ellis A. Fuller to Walter P. Binns, 30 Jan. 1943, box 6, Fuller Papers.

55. Ellis A. Fuller to Charles S. Gardner, 29 June 1944, box 11, Fuller Papers; Ellis A. Fuller to J. Clyde Turner, 29 June 1944, ibid.

56. Hugh Peterson, transcription of trustee interviews 28–30 Apr. 1958, 2:262.

members. The report seemed to place the entire seminary program under his authority, except that the expulsion of students required faculty action.[57]

Fuller read the report to the faculty, and they understood that trustees had defined the president's role as being "responsible to trustees and the denomination for the total seminary make up and administration." Fuller inadvertently deepened the tension with the faculty when he told them that he had no intention of using this authority unless necessity required him.[58]

The tension increased because the faculty believed that Fuller administered the seminary like a hierarchical business rather than like a democratic church. In some ways Fuller did run the seminary like a business. The faculty felt that Fuller did not consult them enough or let them participate fully in important decisions. Fuller did consult the faculty by letter and by group discussion concerning hiring new faculty.[59] Tensions grew and gained notoriety among convention leaders. Duke McCall said that when he was the executive secretary of the Southern Baptist Convention executive committee (1947–1952), "the seminary faculty had a general reputation for strife, conflict, name-calling, etc." The state of affairs stimulated "disgust" among alumni and denominational leaders.[60]

Fuller also relied heavily on the counsel of the local trustees, most of whom were successful businessmen, and his administration reflected their influence. Theron Rankin, one of Fuller's closest friends, reflected afterward that a significant factor in the difficulties Fuller had in "securing the cooperation and support of the faculty" was that the "administration of the seminary had been absorbed by a group of business men." Fuller relied heavily on the counsel of the executive committee of the board of trustees, almost all of whom were businessmen. V. V. Cooke was perhaps the most influential. Rankin believed that under the influence of these men, Fuller administered the seminary too much like a secular business, placing too much value on money and property and too little on scholarship and spirituality. As a result, "members of the faculty had the impression that they were being dealt with as employees" rather than as highly trained professionals.[61]

His attention to expanding the seminary's physical plant gave this impression. With burgeoning enrollment, existing campus facilities had become

57. "Duties and Responsibilities of the President," in Minutes, Board of Trustees, Southern Baptist Theological Seminary, May 1943.

58. Carver, "Recollections and Information," 12–15. Carver incorrectly remembered that the report was never officially adopted.

59. See, e.g., Wayne Oates, transcription of trustee interviews 28–30 Apr. 1958, 3:354.

60. Duke McCall, statement to faculty, 27 Mar. 1958, in Hugh Wamble, "Conflict between Authority and Conscience," electronic typescript, 5:81.

61. M. Theron Rankin to Duke K. McCall, 28 Aug. 1951, SBTS—Call folder, McCall Papers.

Cooke Hall, home of the new music school, and later the President's home

inadequate. Fuller therefore initiated an ambitious building program. The most prominent parts included a large dormitory for married students, a spacious chapel, and a new classroom wing. The material growth of the music school engendered resentment also. Fuller was proud of the school and gave it wide publicity. He secured donations of organs, pianos, and equipment. The school of theology represented the central mission of the seminary and accounted for most of its students, but Fuller doted on the music school. "We have an enrollment of 951 theological students," Professor Wayne E. Oates observed in 1951, but the music school was like the "tail that wagged the dog." [62]

By the fall of 1950 the alienation of many on the faculty and the president appeared irremediable. Oates felt that a "cold isolation separates the faculty from the administration." [63] He saw no hope of reconciliation. Many on the

62. Wayne E. Oates to Olin T. Binkley, 1 Oct. 1950, Letters '50 Sabbatical folder, box 13, Binkley Papers, WFU.

63. Wayne E. Oates to Olin T. Binkley, ca. 15 Sept. 1950, Letters '50 Sabbatical folder, box 13, Binkley Papers, WFU.

Barnard Hall, a dormitory for women in the music school

faculty had arrived at a "settled aversion." [64] The younger faculty in particular felt that Fuller was unconcerned with their problems.

LIBERALISM, FUNDAMENTALISM, AND MEDIATING PIETISM

Fuller believed that the seminary should be committed to the highest scholarship and to producing effective gospel preachers for Southern Baptist churches. These goals were growing incompatible. To raise the level of scholarship on the faculty, the seminary was recruiting younger men who studied under liberal and

64. Wayne E. Oates to Olin T. Binkley, ca. 15 Sept. 1950, Letters '50 Sabbatical folder, box 13, Binkley Papers, WFU.

neo-orthodox scholars at leading universities. The churches did not approve of some of the conclusions of this scholarship. The first priority was that the seminary should equip pastors for effective service in the churches and on the mission field. Critical scholarship seemed of little use to this end.

Many on the faculty had a different vision. They believed that the premises and results of critical scholarship were fundamental to effective church ministry. Critical scholarship arrived at truth, and this truth was essential to the advance of a relevant gospel in the modern world. Fuller saw that this would not work. If the faculty openly promoted such conclusions, the churches would react in vehement indignation and denunciation. They would demand revolution or sever all ties and support. They would prefer dissolving the seminary to sustaining it in teaching error.

Fuller and some of the older faculty were concerned about the tendency of some of the younger professors to disregard the values and wishes of the convention at large. Harold W. Tribble concluded that the "future of the seminary" depended on the "younger group on the faculty," but he worried that their disregard of the churches' desires would endanger the enterprise: "Perhaps the greatest danger there at Louisville lies in the attitude of self-sufficiency." They needed rather to labor under the difficult restraints imposed by the reality of the churches' beliefs and expectations for the "cause of producing a better trained ministry." [65]

Clyde T. Francisco, who taught Old Testament at Southern Seminary from 1945 to 1981, taught the essential correctness of the historical-critical reconstruction of Israel's history, its view of the authorship of the Pentateuch and of Isaiah. But these conclusions played no effective role in how he taught students to interpret and preach the Old Testament. He felt also that this approach suited the seminary perfectly because the school occupied the middle ground between biblicism and criticism, between evangelicalism and liberalism: "Southern must continue to communicate with those on both sides of our mediating position." [66] This was a kind of pietist approach. Criticism and faith operated in different spheres.

But many students and many of the younger faculty judged this pietist approach to be obscurantist and outdated in the current state of scholarship. It was well enough that some like Fuller and Francisco had made their peace with historical-critical scholarship and felt no need to update their theology. But the time had come for the seminary to begin teaching an approach to the historical

65. Harold W. Tribble to Hugh Cantrell, 18 Apr. 1949, Tribble Papers, WFU.

66. Clyde T. Francisco to Duke K. McCall, 20 Nov. 1961, Clyde T. Francisco Papers, Archives, Campbellsville University, Campbellsville, Kentucky.

criticism that would be credible to the intelligent students who had already come to terms with the approach through their undergraduate education. This was a rather straightforward modernist approach. Criticism shaped true faith.

Some of the men Fuller hired to teach at the seminary agreed with his pietist approach to the historical criticism, and others held a more modernist approach. All accepted the validity of criticism. The only question was its role in teaching theology.

Fuller hired a lot of faculty. During his tenure from 1942 to 1950, he presided over the most dramatic change in the character of the seminary in its first hundred years. The student body nearly doubled from 520 to 1,009 and the seminary's budget grew from $213,000 to $584,000. Faculty size grew as dramatically, from eleven to twenty-seven in the same period. But the more significant change was not in the number but in the character of the faculty. Many of the new faculty abjured the pietist approach to historical-critical scholarship.

Fuller seemed to wish that he could find some faculty who rejected the historical criticism, but he found none. When he hired neo-orthodox theologian William Mueller from Colgate-Rochester Theological Seminary, many questioned why he chose someone from that liberal school. He told one pastor that Mueller was "strictly conservative" but then confessed that he had to make some allowances: "No one will ever know how difficult it is to find men for a theological faculty. Some day I will sit down and talk to you about it. I have had to reverse some of my original convictions, but we are going to build a great faculty." [67] He hired historical critics who seemed pious and who seemed sound in their theological convictions.

Fuller had to adjust his criteria to allow the conclusions of historical-critical scholarship. He accepted critical scholars who could persuade him that they held to the traditional doctrines, even if they reconstructed biblical history. But it was not easy to tell if candidates who accepted the latest historical-critical scholarship were still sound in their theological beliefs. Fuller sensed the danger that historical-critical conclusions posed to orthodoxy, but he was not sure where to draw the line between sound and dangerous.

For example, Fuller wanted to call Nat H. Parker of Toronto's McMaster University to replace Sampey as head of the Old Testament department. Parker rejected Mosaic authorship of the Pentateuch, taught that the book of Jonah was satire, and held that the book of Daniel was written in the second century B.C. and its prophecies were ex post facto.[68]

---

67. Ellis Fuller to J. P. Brandon, 24 Mar. 1948, Faculty (Prospective) folder, box 17, Fuller Papers.

68. Nat H. Parker to Ellis Fuller, 4 Feb. 1944, box 11, Fuller Papers.

Fuller did not agree with these conclusions and was not entirely comfortable with tolerating them, but he had no principled objection to them if accompanied by commitment to the full inspiration of the Bible and an evangelical outlook. Fuller believed that such questions of history as authorship had no necessary bearing on the fact of inspiration. He thought it "strange" that "some men tie in the idea of Mosaic authorship with inspiration itself." [69] As long as inspiration was presupposed, historical criticism posed no real threat to believers. Fuller judged that Parker taught the Old Testament in a positive way that deepened faith, and that this was the crucial qualification.

Historical criticism dealt in the realm of empirical fact, but theology dealt in the realm of spiritual truth. The professor pursued historical facts as a scholar but pursued spiritual truth as a theologian. To be effective, a professor had to exercise the proper "attitude, spirit, judgment, and tact" to promote confidence in the fundamental spiritual realities of the faith. This was necessary "to deal factually with his subject and at the same time preserve himself in the confidence of the people." [70]

But Fuller held that some of the scholarly facts were not worth the injury caused by disputes over them. He held that questions of date and authorship were akin to splitting hairs. This was because such questions did not affect the meaning. In such matters there is no wisdom in "denouncing the traditional orthodox view" because the "message" remains "unchanged." The wise teacher, then, should emphasize the "message and purpose of a great book like Jonah . . . regardless of which side wins the debate as to its historicity." [71] Jonah might be true or false as history, but inspiration related to the religious message, not to historical statements. Fuller, like Mullins and Sampey, apparently believed that the Bible's historical statements were reliable, but he refused to make this a fighting point. Unity on the religious truths of scripture was sufficient. Men like Parker who rejected the historicity and those like Fuller who affirmed it shared the "same great principles of the Christian faith" and "the conviction that we have got to give the Christian message to the world." [72]

But Parker disagreed. He held that the meaning of scripture depended on a correct understanding of its actual historical context. It was "impossible to interpret an Old Testament document" without gaining sympathy for the author's historical viewpoint. Questions of history determined religious

69. Ellis Fuller to Nat H. Parker, 11 Feb. 1944, box 11, Fuller Papers.
70. Ellis Fuller to Nat H. Parker, 11 Feb. 1944, box 11, Fuller Papers.
71. Ellis Fuller to Nat H. Parker, 11 Feb. 1944, box 11, Fuller Papers.
72. Ellis Fuller to Nat H. Parker, 18 Mar. 1944, box 11, Fuller Papers.

meaning: "One cannot separate introduction from interpretation."[73] Fuller decided not to invite Parker not because Parker's views were objectionable to him but because they would incite criticism and involve the seminary in injurious controversy.

Many of the young faculty members agreed with Parker. They felt that the questions of historicity were important to the Christian faith and to effective ministry. They held that the religious meaning of any passage in fact depended on the resolution of the historical questions. This meant reinterpreting the Christian faith.

REALISM AND HISTORICAL CRITICISM

Wayne Oates, who afterward became one of the most recognized professors at the seminary, was horrified that Southern Seminary's professors taught the traditional approach to the Bible and ignored historical-critical scholarship. He had learned to interpret the Bible based on historical criticism at Wake Forest College. Most of Southern Seminary's courses, Oates said, served the students "canned putrefaction." But a few professors sought to enlighten their students. He singled out Tribble, Weatherspoon, and Dobbins as progressive thinkers who were trying to teach students to think critically. But Oates thought that it was a losing battle because Fuller repressed efforts at reform. Requiring professors to sign the seminary's creed symbolized the seminary's distrust of the faculty's independence. And although Tribble was doing "wonderful work," he had to "blast away old conceptions" before he could teach the scientific approach to the Bible. "He is trying to sweep the ocean back with a broom," Oates concluded.[74]

Bob Lasater, another Wake Forest graduate, felt the same way. He complained that he was dissatisfied with the "dogmatism and closed minds" at Southern. He believed that Tribble and Weatherspoon were "doing their best to overcome the faults elsewhere." He acknowledged that Dobbins was trying also, but he had "to veil his thought over with so much generalization and introduction that most of the students miss the point altogether." Lasater wanted to transfer to Yale Divinity School.[75] Lasater and Oates stayed at Southern largely because

73. Nat H. Parker to Ellis Fuller, 11 Mar. 1944, box 11, Fuller Papers.
74. Wayne E. Oates to Olin T. Binkley, 26 Sept. 1943, Correspondence folder, box 37, Binkley Papers, WFU.
75. Bob Lasater to Olin T. Binkley, 17 Oct. 1943, Correspondence folder, box 37, Binkley Papers, WFU.

Faculty in 1944–1945: (front, left to right) Jesse B. Weatherspoon, Gaines S. Dobbins, J. McKee Adams, Sydnor L. Stealey, J. Leo Green. (back, left to right) Olin T. Binkley, Charles A. McGlon, Harold W. Tribble, H. Cornell Goerner, Edward A. McDowell, R. Inman Johnson

Wake Forest Professor Olin T. Binkley joined the faculty in 1944, and they concentrated their efforts on classes under Binkley, Tribble, and Weatherspoon.[76]

One of the costs of Southern Seminary's realist policy was the loss of progressive students to northern seminaries. Binkley was committed to promoting progressive views in the Southern Baptist Convention, but he was not always optimistic about the short-term prospects. In 1939 he recognized that the ministerial students coming out of Wake Forest were liberal and would find little encouragement in Southern Baptist institutions. He predicted that their stronger students would increasingly get their theology degrees from Yale, Colgate-Rochester, Crozer, and Duke.[77]

76. Wayne Oates to Olin Binkley, 20 Mar. 1944, Binkley Papers, WFU; Bob Lasater to Olin Binkley, 3 Apr. 1944, Binkley Papers, WFU; Wayne Oates to Olin Binkley, 4 Apr. 1944, Binkley Papers, WFU;

77. Olin Binkley to Kenneth Clark, 26 Feb. 1939, 1939 folder, Binkley Papers, WFU.

But this had advantages for progressive reform. As such Northern Baptists as Shailer Mathews had learned, Binkley and other Southern Baptist progressives understood that they could not reform the denomination by open agitation in favor of their views. They would succeed by changing the denominational mind gradually, by calm pedagogy rather than by direct confrontation. The conservative prejudices of people and of their demagogues would prevent progressive ideas from gaining a fair and unbiased consideration in the denomination. Binkley was distressed and embarrassed by the conservative "attitudes and utterances" of Southern Baptist leaders, but he saw "rays of light and hope" in the fact that gifted ministerial students were getting a progressive education: "We now have ministerial students who are going from our churches in this state to Yale, Union, Colgate-Rochester, Andover-Newton, Harvard, and Hartford for their theological training and then come back as pastors of some of our churches and exhibit Christian attitudes and become centers of infection for intelligent religious living."[78]

H. Cornell Goerner, who taught missions at the seminary from 1938 to 1957, explained the strategy in 1943 to alumnus Paul L. Stagg. Stagg had complained that the seminary was failing to produce preachers who could speak relevantly to the modern world, because the professors pretended to be more conservative than they were in order to please "a reactionary and socially backward constituency." Stagg cited the fact that the professors were not teaching openly the "assured findings of criticism" in Old Testament classes, and that publicly they showed less enthusiasm for the ecumenical movement than they did in their classrooms.[79]

Goerner answered that his approach on ecumenism was a deliberate strategy of small steps by which Southern Baptists could be educated gradually. "Prudence and policy" argued for keeping silent regarding "the most extreme convictions which one has." Sometimes he felt that "one should cast caution to the winds and boldly declare what he believed about controversial matters, regardless of the consequences." But to publish such views would "defeat the whole plan." Instead, Goerner wrote, "I am pursuing the path of education rather [than] revolution."[80]

Olin Binkley declined election to Southern Seminary's faculty in 1943 largely due to the fact that he would not be free to teach the historical approach to

78. Olin Binkley to F. E. Johnson, 3 May 1939, 1939 folder, Binkley Papers, WFU.

79. Paul L. Stagg to H. Cornell Goerner, 31 Aug. 1943, box 16, Henry Cornell Goerner Papers, SBHLA.

80. H. Cornell Goerner to Paul L. Stagg, 18 Sept. 1943, box 16, Henry Cornell Goerner Papers, SBHLA.

biblical interpretation. He apparently told Ernest R. Groves, his former colleague at the University of North Carolina, that he declined because he would have had less freedom at Southern than he had at Wake Forest.[81] Bob Lasater, Binkley's former student at Wake Forest, congratulated Binkley for rejecting Southern Seminary's invitation, since at the seminary "you do not have freedom to teach as you please."[82] Binkley explained to Yale's Luther Weigle that at Wake Forest he could still teach large numbers of ministerial students, and he would have the freedom within the "liberal tradition here at Wake Forest."[83]

When Binkley changed his mind and accepted a position at Southern Seminary, he recognized the necessity of the realist policy, but he longed for freedom to teach critical views openly: "I have often prayed in lonely hours for the privilege of studying and teaching in a school which provided freedom and fellowship and encouragement to achieve a vital union of critical intelligence and religious devotion." He found the necessary limitations on his freedom so onerous that he planned to leave the seminary. He wanted to escape the "resistance to Christian scholarship" he endured at Southern Seminary.[84] But Southern Seminary's faculty saw the necessity of a "constructive" approach. In order to have a hearing among the churches, and perhaps to retain their position on the faculty, they could not afford to arouse the opposition of conservatives. Their strategy entailed gradual advance.

THE ASPIRATIONS OF PROGRESSIVE THOUGHT

Most of the younger faculty wanted to modernize the curriculum, that is, they wanted to introduce modern scholarship into the ordinary teaching course. They felt that pastors needed to be educated in the latest scholarship, which meant interpreting the Bible according to the canons of historical criticism. The current curriculum introduced almost none of the methods and conclusions of modern scholarship and emphasized the memorization and transmission

81. Ernest R. Groves to Olin T. Binkley, 3 June 1943, Important Letters folder, box 39, Binkley Papers, WFU.

82. Bob Lasater to Olin T. Binkley, 17 Oct. 1943, Correspondence folder, box 37, Binkley Papers, WFU.

83. Olin T. Binkley to Luther A. Weigle, 17 May 1943, Important Letters folder, box 39, Binkley Papers, WFU.

84. Olin T. Binkley to Everett C. Herrick, 23 July 1945, Important Letters folder, box 39, Binkley Papers, WFU. Herrick, president of Andover-Newton Theological Seminary, wanted Binkley to teach there. Binkley also found the large student-faculty ratio burdensome.

of traditional orthodoxy rather than independent thinking and creative leadership.

They wanted greater freedom of expression. Unless they had some opportunities to advance progressive ideas, however cautiously, Southern Baptists would be relegated to fighting rearguard actions of increasing irrelevance in a culture that was progressing in education, science, and social relations. Southern Baptist churches would sacrifice their influence in society and miss their God-given opportunity to lead the South into a more just and equitable society.

During Fuller's tenure some faculty members began introducing historical criticism into the classroom but in measured doses and with great caution because Fuller opposed their doing so. When Clyde Francisco, for example, taught a course on the historical criticism of the Pentateuch, Fuller evidently told him in no uncertain terms that the seminary should not be offering such a course. He never offered it again. In his other classes afterward, he treated historical criticism cursorily.

Harold Tribble tried to convince Fuller that the seminary faculty needed to be free to teach modern scholarship, to expose students to its conclusions, in order that they might learn to think independently and become responsible and creative leaders in the denomination. Under Fuller's administration, the school operated as a promotional program of the convention, Tribble felt, rather than as a "graduate school committed to the ideals and techniques of true education." He urged Fuller to grant "freedom on the part of the faculty to do a creative job." Only this approach would produce the "courageous and creative leadership" that the Southern Baptist Convention desperately needed. But Fuller refused. Tribble believed that he was interested primarily in preserving the seminary's popularity with the convention at the expense of the truth and of effective theological education.[85] But Fuller believed that historical criticism was irrelevant to effective preaching, teaching, and pastoral ministry. He also felt that it was unrealistic to expect Southern Baptists to support a seminary that taught historical-critical premises and conclusions as true.

The older progressives like Tribble, Binkley, and Weatherspoon did not disagree with the policy of denominational realism. They recognized the practical impossibility of any professor teaching openly that such miracles as the virgin birth of Jesus or his walking on the water were not exactly the historical facts that the Bible claimed they were. There were similar obstacles to teaching that Moses did not write the Pentateuch or that Daniel was actually written in the second century before Christ rather than the sixth. But they wanted freedom

---

85. Harold Tribble to Wayne Oates, 14 Dec. 1953, Wayne Oates folder, box 26, Binkley Papers, WFU.

to teach their students to grapple with such possibilities. And they wanted to relieve such conclusions from the prejudice of being labeled heretical. This would at least provide for progress.

But unlike Fuller, they wanted to move the denomination toward acceptance of modern historical-critical scholarship. They believed, with the older liberals generally, that the way to reform the denomination was not by sudden revolution but by gradual teaching. Students instructed properly in modern scholarship would go out into the churches and exercise leadership in the gradual reformation of the denomination. For this reason progressive faculty urged the establishment of a stronger research doctoral program, in which a select cadre of gifted students could be trained in modern scholarship. Such a program would provide Southern Baptists with leaders capable of influencing the churches in a more progressive direction. When Tribble realized that Fuller would never permit such freedom, he left Southern Seminary for the freer atmosphere of Andover-Newton Theological Seminary in Massachusetts, and then of Wake Forest University, where he had opportunity to "give leadership in directing the thought life of our state through our graduates."[86]

Fuller required the faculty to conform to the theological beliefs of the more conservative wing of the denomination, most faculty believed, and required the faculty to restrict their expression of their ideas, with the result that the seminary could only mirror popular beliefs rather than lead and shape them. When Jesse Weatherspoon lobbied trustees regarding Fuller's successor, he emphasized three characteristics that the new president needed to have, reflecting his understanding of the problems they experienced with Fuller. The new president should be able to work with the faculty "with freedom of expression all around"; he should lead the seminary in such a way as to represent "all and not a segment of our constituency"; and he should "lead the seminary in setting the pattern for theological and ethical thought among Baptists."[87] What Weatherspoon and the faculty wanted was a president who shared their progressive ideas and who would administer the realist policy in such a way as to advance progressive ideas rather than stifle them as Fuller had done. They wanted a president who could negotiate the tension between the denomination's commitment to traditional orthodoxy and the faculty's commitment to progressive ideas in a way that promised ultimate success. They needed a president like Mullins.

86. Harold Tribble to Wayne Oates, 14 Dec. 1953, Wayne Oates folder, box 26, Binkley Papers, WFU.

87. Jesse Weatherspoon to Olin Binkley, 16 Nov. 1950, Answered Letters '50–1 folder, box 13, Binkley Papers, WFU.

When faculty resisted Fuller's insistence on the realist policy, he tended to remind them that the trustees invested him with executive authority. Under different circumstances perhaps this would not have mattered, but it provoked and irritated many on the faculty, some of whom had shared administrative authority with Sampey and others of whom held to the principle of shared authority. Inman Johnson later judged that Fuller "made the mistake of letting the faculty know he had it [authority], and letting them know it too frequently."[88]

ACCUSATIONS OF HERESY AND THE OSCAR GIBSON EPISODE

Several members of the young faculty appointed in the early 1940s proved too progressive for many students, who complained to Fuller and to trusted pastors that some professors were not orthodox. By the late 1940s the complaints became widely known. Fuller confessed in 1949 that "fear and uneasiness concerning the seminary" was higher than he had ever known it.[89]

A recent graduate told Fuller in 1949 that he did not wish to spread information about some of the liberal teachings at Southern, and when people asked him direct questions about the faculty's liberalism, he "endeavored to evade," but he would not feign ignorance or lie if pressed. He quoted Professor William Morton as saying that "no one but a few narrow-minded and uninformed Southern Baptists still believe in the historical nature and value of the first eleven chapters of Genesis." He said that Dale Moody taught that Moses "could not possibly have instituted the complex sacrificial system attributed to him." Another professor taught that the sixth-century prophet Daniel could not have written the prophecies in chapters 7 through 12 of the book attributed to him.[90]

But T. C. Smith provoked the most complaints in the late 1940s. Smith taught New Testament as instructor beginning in 1947. Instructors were on trial, for the faculty scrutinized them and often selected new professors from the ranks of instructors who passed the trial. Smith impressed the faculty with his scholarly ambitions, but students expressed such dissatisfaction with Smith that Fuller kept him on trial as an instructor for an additional third year.[91]

---

88. Inman Johnson, transcription of trustee interviews 28–30 Apr. 1958, 2:195.

89. Ellis A. Fuller to T. C. Smith, 21 Feb. 1949, Gibson folder, box 18, Fuller Papers.

90. F. M. Wood to Ellis Fuller, 31 Oct. 1949, Criticism folder, Box 17, Fuller Papers. Wood did not identify the teachers by name. Fuller inserted the identifying names.

91. Ellis A. Fuller to J. Clyde Turner, 8 Sept. 1949, box 18, Fuller Papers. Smith was elected as an assistant professor in 1950.

Students reported that Smith rejected the historicity of many passages in the Gospels. They said especially that he questioned the account of the virgin birth of Christ. A Georgia pastor wrote Fuller in 1949 that when a seminary student visited him recently, "he alarmed me with some startling statements quoting from Dr. Smith...in which Dr. Smith impugned the veracity of various portions of the Bible, particularly the record of Matthew."[92]

Fuller liked Smith, trusted his piety, and believed that he held promise to become a great New Testament scholar. But one of Fuller's duties as president was to ensure the orthodoxy of all current and prospective faculty. A number of students complained that Smith disparaged the virgin birth of Jesus, miracles, and the inspiration of the Bible. Fuller conducted six interviews with Smith concerning his views. He also asked for a written statement—"a full and frank interpretation of yourself in regard to your faith and Christian convictions"—on the virgin birth, miracles, the cross, the resurrection, the inspiration of the scriptures, and the deity of Jesus. Fuller reminded Smith that the seminary faculty must pledge to teach in accordance with the Abstract of Principles and not contrary to it, and that any professor who departed from it should resign.[93]

Smith gave terse responses clearly intended to affirm orthodoxy, though he did not explain how students could have misunderstood him so often.[94] He answered several questions by merely quoting the Abstract of Principles. His answer regarding inspiration implied that he held a liberal view. He said that the Bible was an inspired "record" of God's revelation. His answer regarding atonement was vague and avoided traditional terms of definition: "There is a saving efficacy in the crucifixion." He said that he accepted the virgin birth of Jesus "as given in the Gospels of Matthew and Luke" and that he believed that the "miracles which are given in both the Old Testament and New Testament are true." He apparently held some private interpretation of "as given" and "true," for he was uncomfortable with the traditional interpretation of many miracle accounts.

Smith remained similarly cautious in advancing historical-critical conclusions long after he left Southern Seminary in 1958. In his 1970 commentary on Acts for the denomination's *Broadman Bible Commentary* set, he sometimes explained miraculous acts of God as natural occurrences. He suggested, for example, that God did not kill Ananias and Sapphira in Acts 5:1-11, and that he did not kill Uzzah in 2 Samuel 6:6-7. "In ancient times," Smith explained,

92. E. C. Sheehan to Ellis Fuller, 31 July 1949, Criticism folder, Box 17, Fuller Papers.
93. Ellis A. Fuller to T. C. Smith, 21 Feb. 1949, Gibson folder, box 18, Fuller Papers; Fuller, "The Gibson Affair," 1949—T. C. Smith folder, box 18, Fuller Papers.
94. T. C. Smith to Ellis A. Fuller, 3 Mar. 1949, Gibson folder, box 18, Fuller Papers.

"when a person knowingly violated a taboo, the shock was so great that sometimes it brought death." In other miracle accounts, Smith merely stated that the participants understood the event as a miracle. He said, for example, that the people "became superstitious and believed" that Peter's shadow or items of Paul's apparel could heal miraculously. He said in other places that "so far as Luke understood his source" or "according to the author of Acts," God performed a miraculous act. He apparently believed that Luke was mistaken in depicting these occurrences as miracles, just as he was wrong in claiming that the prophet Agabus's prediction of a worldwide famine occurred during the reign of the emperor Claudius.[95]

In 1949, in any case, Smith's answers assured Fuller of his orthodoxy, though many Southern Baptists remained unconvinced. For many students, and for many more pastors, Fuller's defense of the faculty's orthodoxy was not persuasive. They rallied around Fuller publicly, but privately they urged him to be vigilant.[96]

Suspicions of the faculty's orthodoxy created a sense of crisis among them in 1949. That spring Oscar Gibson, a Southern Baptist pastor in Louisville, began buying advertisements in the *Louisville Courier-Journal* in which he accused the seminary faculty of promoting liberalism. Gibson preached against the faculty's heresies in his church, published the accusations in his church's monthly newspaper, the *Informer*, and immediately became a favorite of fundamentalist leader J. Frank Norris. Gibson soon received invitations to preach widely in fundamentalist churches and deliver his addresses advancing accusations against the seminary.

Fuller invited Gibson to meet with him and with some of the faculty, but Gibson felt that the seminary's leadership was unable to deal with the problem. He aimed to bring his accusations before the Southern Baptist Convention meeting in Oklahoma City in May 1949. At the convention, Gibson moved that the convention president, conservative stalwart Robert G. Lee, appoint a committee "to investigate the charge that modernism now exists in the Southern Baptist Theological Seminary." Convention leaders were prepared for Gibson's motion. Immediately John J. Hurt moved that Gibson's motion be referred to the seminary trustees. The convention constitutionally charged trustees with governing the seminary, so that referral of concerns to the trustees was

95. T. C. Smith, "Acts," in *Acts–1 Corinthians*, vol. 10 of *The Broadman Bible Commentary*, ed. Clifton J. Allen (Nashville, TN: Broadman Press, 1970), 43, 44, 111, 77, 79, 74.

96. See, e.g., W. O. Vaught to Ellis A. Fuller, 24 May 1949, V Misc. folder, box 18, Fuller Papers.

the appropriate course. But given the prevailing suspicions of the seminary's soundness, Gibson's motion had a fair chance of success if the floor had opportunity to vote on it. Then Gibson would have opportunity to present some of his accusations in defense of his motion. Hurt intended to rob Gibson of the opportunity. When the convention voted in favor of Hurt's motion to refer, Gibson recognized, as all experienced hands did, that it meant the defeat of Gibson's purpose, since the trustees were unlikely to share Gibson's evaluation of the faculty.[97]

The trustees appointed a committee of five to investigate Gibson's charges. In July the committee invited Gibson to appear before it, and he read at length his list of charges. The trustees already knew them, as Gibson had been giving them wide publicity for months. Most of the charges consisted of guilt by association and were at most merely suggestive. He charged the faculty with taking additional studies at such modernist schools at Union Theological Seminary in New York, studying under such heretics as Emil Brunner, inviting modernists to lecture at the seminary, requiring students to read books written by modernists, participating in ecumenical efforts, and teaching students to doubt such fundamental doctrines as the Bible's inspiration, miracles, and the virgin birth. He charged, for example, that William Mueller was a modernist because he formerly taught at Colgate Rochester Divinity School, and no orthodox teacher could consent to teach there. Such associations raised conservatives' understandable suspicions but were justifiable in the premises.

Gibson said that he wanted to present to the committee his full evidence, including witnesses, at a later meeting. When the committee invited him to do so in August, he refused to appear, pleading that he would not break his prior preaching engagement on that date. Fuller nevertheless investigated the charges on behalf of the committee and reported to the trustees that the faculty was sound and innocent of Gibson's charges. Upon concluding its investigation, the committee reported to the full board that the faculty were orthodox and their teaching "has not deviated from that of the founders of the institution." They did not justify the faculty's choices for past lecturers, but suggested that the faculty would "exercise due caution in the selection of the men who are invited to speak at the seminary, and will invite only those who are loyal to the truths of evangelical Christianity." They placed their ultimate trust, however, in the orthodoxy and vigilance of Fuller himself: "We have the utmost confidence in

97. Gibson believed that his motion would have passed, since at least fifty persons seconded his motion and since Hurt's motion barely passed. See Oscar Gibson, "The Truth about the Southern Baptist Convention," 5 June 1949, transcript, box 24, W. O. Carver Papers, SBHLA.

the wisdom, consecration, and doctrinal soundness of our president. He never recommends one for the faculty until he has been thoroughly convinced of his soundness in the faith." [98]

REALIST POLICY AND DEMAND FOR CONFORMITY

During the late 1940s the faculty's alienation from Fuller deepened. His demand that they conform their teaching to a realistic policy irritated them increasingly. They generally recognized the necessity of the realist policy, but they became deeply dissatisfied with it. Some of the faculty believed that historical criticism was essential to proper interpretation of the Bible, and that without it, the Bible's real message was significantly obscured or even perverted. Tribble, Weatherspoon, McDowell, and Binkley worked toward the day when such matters could be taught freely in Southern's classrooms. [99] But they were also firmly committed to the realist policy, for there was no safe or effective alternative. Reform and freedom would come only gradually in the Southern Baptist Convention. But the fact that the realist policy practically prohibited the teaching of historical criticism produced frustration, especially for some of the newer faculty.

Some of the faculty felt keenly the tension between authenticity and authority, between honesty and orthodoxy. Nat Parker, who taught at McMaster University in Toronto, had the freedom for which they longed. Parker wanted to teach at Southern, but he would have to teach the historical criticism, and he knew that Southern Baptist pastors would crucify him for it. When Fuller suggested that Parker could omit such matters, since they were not essential to the Bible's message or the seminary's task of training preachers, Parker disagreed. To keep these convictions hidden, Parker said, would be dishonest and inauthentic: "I hate superficiality, barrenness, evasion, and insincerity. If I cannot be honest I must be dumb. And I would follow the truth as I see it if it looked as though it were leading me to the devil." [100]

Traditionalists held that if an idea led to the devil, this was sufficient to discredit it. But some of the seminary's faculty shared Parker's viewpoint and grew

98. Report, Committee to Investigate Modernism at Southern Baptist Theological Seminary, in 1949—G Misc. folder, box 18, Fuller Papers; Oscar Gibson, untitled, *The Informer*, ca. Sept. 1949, clipping in 1949—Gibson folder, box 18, Fuller Papers.

99. In 1943 Wayne Oates singled out Tribble, Weatherspoon, and Dobbins as the only ones who sought to introduce current historical and scientific criticism. Wayne Oates to Olin T. Binkley, 26 Sept. 1943, Correspondence folder, box 37, Binkley Papers, WFU.

100. Nat H. Parker to Ellis Fuller, 11 Mar. 1944, box 11, Fuller Papers.

restive under the constraints of the realist policy. They resented Fuller's efforts to enforce the policy. They criticized him for his role in the Gibson investigation, believing that he should have ignored Gibson's charges. They were indignant that they should be subject to harassment at the hands of such troublemakers. They recognized that Fuller was using the episode as leverage to press the faculty anew to conform their teaching to denominational orthodoxy. They thought his repeated warnings were bullying and demeaning to their station. They considered the trustee investigation a medieval inquisition.

The faculty members who were in Louisville in the summer of 1949 discussed the trustee committee investigation at length. They naturally found the entire affair disconcerting, from Gibson's accusations to the convention action to the trustee investigation. But their deepest concerns related to Fuller. The faculty wondered, as Wayne Oates reported, "whether the Chief will use this as an opportunity to put the fear of the administration and the convention in all of us—especially for the benefit of the young men. I have a feeling that some of the older men may be taken as 'whipping dogs' to be an example for the younger ones." [101]

As suspicion of the seminary's orthodoxy spread, Fuller urged upon the faculty the necessity of wisdom and caution in their classroom statements. He suggested that they needed to make sure that they taught in such a way as to produce effective preachers and instill denominational loyalty. He reminded T. C. Smith of these things in 1949: "We must remember that this seminary was founded for the purpose of training leaders for our own people. It is mighty easy for us to lose patience with them at times and feel commissioned to go ahead and leave them behind. We may even feel so deeply our disapproval of certain dispositions and practices that we may develop unwittingly an unwholesome attitude toward them. They are our people. We must work through them and prepare men to serve them." [102] The faculty heard these sentiments as rebukes and found them demoralizing. In the context of public accusations, interviews with the president, and trustee investigations, many faculty felt threatened. They felt that Fuller was not defending their academic freedom but restricting it. Fuller was in fact seeking to preserve the school.

Fuller's approach was similar to Sampey's. Neither wanted the seminary to become a liberal school like Crozer or Rochester, never mind Chicago. Neither saw genuine virtue in leading Southern Baptists to adopt a more modern theology. Mullins before them and McCall after them urged the policy but sought to promote progressive thought in the seminary and in the denomination. But

101. Wayne E. Oates to Olin T. Binkley, 25 July 1949, Binkley Papers, WFU.
102. Ellis A. Fuller to T. C. Smith, 21 Feb. 1949, Gibson folder, box 18, Fuller Papers.

Sampey and Fuller urged the realist approach without any design to advance modern views. They tolerated the progressive men on the faculty because they believed that their historical criticism had not changed their theology. Some of their beliefs were perhaps troubling, but they were minor blemishes. The faculty nevertheless needed to be careful to keep their historical-critical beliefs and their blemishes from public view, lest the seminary lose its reputation for orthodoxy and lose support throughout the denomination.

Fuller, for example, was deeply troubled by T. C. Smith's views on the virgin birth. But in the end he retained Smith. He trusted Smith's affirmations of the fundamental doctrines of the faith, but he knew that something was askew, or students would not complain of his unsoundness with such frequency. Smith and some other professors sometimes said unwise things in the classroom, Fuller thought; he attributed it to their immaturity. "We have a faculty of young men," Fuller explained privately to the *Western Recorder*'s editor, "but we believe in them. Fundamentally they are sound."[103] Fuller seemed to hope that he, the trustees, and other faculty, perhaps, could help stabilize Smith's views and teaching approach. He believed that Smith represented the highest standards of scholarship. He confided in trustee J. Clyde Turner that if Smith "comes through, he will come nearer being an A. T. Robertson than any young man in that department."[104]

Despite Fuller's repeated warnings to the faculty, accusations against them multiplied, and Fuller grew increasingly concerned about the seminary's growing reputation as a liberal school. When Fuller interviewed Edwin Osburn for an assistant librarian position in early 1949, he wanted to know Osburn's theological views. Osburn had studied three years at Southern Seminary but "was not satisfied" with the teaching there and transferred to Crozer Theological Seminary in Pennsylvania, the favorite northern seminary of progressive Southern Baptist students. Fuller invited his secretary to take down the conversation and asked Osburn his views on "biblical inspiration, miracles, and especially the virgin birth." He "flunked" the test of his orthodoxy, and his Crozer degree was problematic. Osburn said that his faith had been "heightened and enriched" by his acquaintance there with the "historical and critical approach" to religion.[105]

As accusations against the seminary spread, Fuller insisted on the realist policy more strenuously. Fuller recognized that the faculty was growing restive

103. Ellis A. Fuller to R. T. Skinner, 8 Sept. 1949, Gibson folder, box 18, Fuller Papers.
104. Ellis A. Fuller to J. Clyde Turner, 8 Sept. 1949, J. Clyde Turner folder, box 18, Fuller Papers.
105. Edwin Osburn to Olin Binkley, 24 Mar. 1949, Binkley Papers, WFU.

in response to his demands for theological orthodoxy. Three faculty members participated in Osburn's interview, but Fuller, no doubt in view of the faculty's restiveness, dismissed them before raising the questions about Osburn's orthodoxy.[106]

As a result, the faculty began to resist Fuller's leadership openly. They blamed Fuller for the trustee investigation and openly censured him. They argued that Fuller and the trustees should have ignored Gibson and that the trustee committee should not have been appointed, overlooking the fact that the Southern Baptist Convention action required trustees to investigate and report. The faculty noticed that trustees had more confidence in Fuller's orthodoxy than in their own, for the "trustees made a stronger statement about the president than they did about the faculty," and the faculty took great offense. Some of the faculty felt that Fuller was becoming a "fundamentalist" like convention president R. G. Lee.[107] They refrained, however, from precipitous action and followed Binkley's advice: "Sit tight until they call us on the carpet."[108]

Fuller tired of the constant need to answer critics. He generally paid little attention to the fundamentalist critics who attacked everything related to the Southern Baptist Convention and its programs. But he felt a duty to answer loyal Southern Baptists who had concerns. He acknowledged that they had good reason for vigilance. He in fact agreed with them in principle: "In fairness to those who have fears concerning the seminary I must admit that our past experiences with some seminaries and our present observations of some others give reasons for fears and concern. Vigilance is not only the price of liberty but also of the purity of faith in academic circles. I would rather see this seminary die than for it to join the ranks of those which devitalize the faith of their students."[109]

In the spring of 1949, as Fuller prepared to depart for the annual meeting of the Southern Baptist Convention in Oklahoma City, he called the faculty together to urge again the necessity of restraint in their teaching. Fuller knew that Oscar Gibson intended to press his charges of heresy against the faculty from the floor of the convention. He feared that the faculty had been careless in promoting progressive views and that he would not be able to win the battle: "I shall go down in defeat—so will we all—at the hands of just and warranted

---

106. Edwin Osburn to Olin Binkley, 24 Mar. 1949, Binkley Papers, WFU. The faculty apparently did not know that Fuller would examine Osburn on his doctrine—Binkley said that the news came as a "distinct surprise" to him (Binkley to Osburn, 18 May 1949, ibid.).

107. Ellis A. Fuller, Statement to Faculty, 1950, in 1950—Faculty folder, box 19, Fuller Papers.

108. Wayne Oates to Olin Binkley, 25 July 1949, Binkley Papers, WFU.

109. Ellis A. Fuller to T. C. Smith, 21 Feb. 1949, Gibson folder, box 18, Fuller Papers.

criticism." Their only strong defense was innocence: "Our task and our problem is to be right in what we teach and how we teach."[110]

The faculty, Fuller said, had to teach in such a way as "to preserve and promote the great body of truths" that made Southern Baptists who they were. Their teaching should tend to "establish faith in these truths and not to destroy them." They were failing in this respect, Fuller suggested. Students were learning how to criticize the people rather than learning how to win their hearts. "Our young men must first get the confidence of the people in that realm of truth where there can be no quibbling—and that is the big area of truth—and then they can show the people some interesting truths they have discovered in this 'den of antiquity' and in the peripheral fields of truths."[111]

The "new bits of truth" the professors kept digging up in their scholarly research were interesting and helpful, Fuller said, but they did not compare to the "main body of truth in the perfect revelation of God in Jesus Christ." If they taught their scholarship in such a way that it undermined confidence in traditional gospel truths, then they were guilty of arrogance and careless haste. Fuller elaborated, "We may spread the Pentateuch out before us as an old fashioned quilt, and with the agility and the dexterity of finished scholars point out the seams which hold together a multiplicity of documents. We may turn the pages of Isaiah's prophecy and find all through the book pictures of different Isaiahs. There may be genuine convincing evidence to support these and many other modern theories about the Old Testament. Even when we know that these are true, it will still be necessary to be wise and harmless in teaching them lest we lose more than we gain."[112]

Fuller was not comfortable with the historical-critical methods and conclusions but felt that he had to grant the faculty some freedom to follow their research. He acknowledged that "it is right for the professors to have absolute freedom in their studies both within and without the bracket of revealed truth." But he insisted that if the faculty was going to teach modern historical-critical methods and conclusions, they must do so in a way that sustained traditional biblical beliefs: "Under no conditions should acquired scholarship be given precedence over revealed truth."[113] Fuller was asking the faculty to be realistic.

In late 1950 Fuller addressed Southern Baptists in Texas, New Mexico, Arizona, and California on behalf of the seminary. As he traveled, he found "a good deal of skepticism about our seminary." His own confidence grew: "I

110. Fuller, "Statement to the Faculty," 1949, 1949 Faculty folder, box 17, Fuller Papers.
111. Fuller, "Statement to the Faculty," 1949, 1949 Faculty folder, box 17, Fuller Papers.
112. Fuller, "Statement to the Faculty," 1949, 1949 Faculty folder, box 17, Fuller Papers.
113. Fuller, "Statement to the Faculty," 1949, 1949 Faculty folder, box 17, Fuller Papers.

believe in the seminaries as never before and deplore the tragedy of doubts concerning them."[114] He was confident of the faculty's essential soundness and sought to remove the widespread suspicions concerning them. He would not, however, grant the faculty theological carte blanche. He saw himself as the guardian of the seminary's orthodoxy. His investigation of insinuations and charges against the faculty were thorough and frequent enough to provoke their resentment. He wanted to know what they believed and taught, and did not intend to tolerate unsound views.

His faculty became more liberal nevertheless. When recommending new faculty to the board of trustees, Fuller relied heavily on the faculty's recommendations. He had broad familiarity with scholarly trends but could not match the faculty's attainments or judge adequately the breadth of scholarship of most candidates. And the crop of qualified teachers was relatively small. Candidates had to be loyal Southern Baptists and demonstrate scholarly abilities and attainments. This limited the field almost entirely to those who graduated from Southern Seminary. The faculty in this era typically took their bachelor of divinity (later known as master of divinity) and their doctor of theology from Southern. Some did their doctoral work elsewhere, and most others took at least some doctoral work elsewhere. It is not surprising that Fuller relied on the faculty's recommendations.

Fuller was impressed by their scholarship, but he was also basically satisfied with their orthodoxy. Fuller, like Sampey, took a pietist approach to the historical-critical conclusions of the faculty. He was very conservative in his own views of the Bible. He gave faculty members considerable benefit of the doubt, however, when it came to their specific views, because he believed that their piety was genuine. But their commitment to the modern historical-critical approach sustained denominational suspicion.

Fuller did his best to preserve intact the theological orthodoxy of the faculty, but the liberal convictions and affinities of the faculty were sufficiently discernible to provoke the denomination's suspicions. This was quickly becoming the seminary's most critical problem, and Fuller could not solve it. When he died on October 28, 1950, from a heart attack suffered while he was preaching in San Diego, he bequeathed it to his successor.

---

114. Ellis A. Fuller to H. C. Goerner, 25 Oct. 1950, box 5, Henry Cornell Goerner Papers, SBHLA.

9

DUKE K. MCCALL AND THE STRUGGLE FOR THE SEMINARY'S DIRECTION

McCall entered office knowing that he would face a struggle over the seminary's direction. A dissident faction of the faculty sought effective control of the school and were leading it toward the values and ambitions of the "non-denominational seminaries of the Northeast." Trustees and other faculty members opposed the dissidents' aims. Trustees vested in the president the authority to determine the direction of the seminary, and they expected the seminary to serve the needs and beliefs of Southern Baptist churches, not of New England divinity schools. McCall hoped that he could lead the school jointly with the faculty while keeping his executive authority theoretical. But as the dissidents gained a working majority on the faculty, McCall saw that his first job was to prevent the institution from being governed by a "self-perpetuating faculty" and secure the denomination's control. He also realized that sooner or later this state of affairs would probably result in a painful clash and that he might be forced out because of it. Before his election he told his friend Herschel Hobbs that "only a fool" would accept election as Southern Seminary's president. He accepted anyway and seven years later faced a catastrophic faculty rebellion.[1]

ORTHODOXY AND TACT: THE ELECTION OF DUKE K. MCCALL

Duke McCall was the obvious candidate to succeed Ellis Fuller. He understood and valued scholarship and was sufficiently progressive in his thought to fit

1. Duke McCall to Herschel Hobbs, 25 July 1958, box 20, folder 10, Herschel Hobbs Papers, SBHLA.

in with the faculty. He was an alumnus, having earned his Th.M. and Ph.D. at Southern. He knew the previous two presidents well. He wrote his dissertation under the direction of John R. Sampey and served as his fellow. He came to know Ellis Fuller while McCall was pastor of Broadway Baptist Church in Louisville from 1940 to 1943, during Fuller's first two years. He had experience, having served as president of the Baptist Bible Institute (later, New Orleans Baptist Theological Seminary) from 1943 to 1946. And he understood denominational structure and politics, serving as president of the executive committee of the Southern Baptist Convention from 1946 to 1951.

No less important, McCall had the confidence of the great mass of Southern Baptists. He earned their confidence by his remarkable skill and tact in denominational leadership and by his power in preaching and public speaking. Above all, he had their confidence because of his reputation as a champion for orthodoxy.[2] Floyd Looney, editor of the *California Southern Baptist*, had been worried about liberalism at the seminary, but he had confidence in McCall's soundness: "If I had ever entertained any such thoughts as its being unorthodox, your going as president would remove such an idea."[3]

McCall had recently declined nomination to be the first president of the newly created Southeastern Baptist Theological Seminary.[4] He discouraged his nomination to succeed Fuller and declared himself "out of the picture."[5] He knew that many on Southern's faculty opposed him as a candidate—they had told him so. Fuller's strengths had been promotion and denominational leadership, and many on the faculty had resented it. They viewed McCall as cast in the same mold and rebelled at the prospect of a McCall presidency. McCall knew the faculty's mood and predicted that whoever succeeded Fuller would have, as Louie Newton put it, "plenty of headaches."[6]

The faculty wanted trustees to choose a president from the faculty. Many favored Gaines Dobbins, the longtime religious education professor who had

2. See, e.g., Charles W. Pope to J. Clyde Turner, 29 Nov. 1950, SBTS—Call folder, McCall Papers.

3. Floyd Looney to Duke K. McCall, 9 Aug. 1951, SBTS—Call folder, McCall Papers.

4. See Duke K. McCall, *Duke McCall: An Oral Memoir*, with A. Ronald Tonks (Brentwood, TN: Baptist History and Heritage, 2001), 93–96; W. Perry Crouch to Duke K. McCall, 14 Sept. 1950, Southeastern Seminary Presidency folder, McCall Papers; Duke K. McCall to W. Perry Crouch, 30 Nov. 1950, ibid.

5. Inman Johnson to Duke K. McCall, 25 Jan. 1951, and 23 July 1951, SBTS—Call folder, McCall Papers.

6. Louie Newton to Duke K. McCall, [30 Nov. 1950], Southeastern Seminary Presidency folder, McCall Papers; dated November 31.

Billy Graham and Duke K. McCall

been serving as interim president since Fuller's death.[7] When the faculty learned that the trustees preferred not to elect someone from the faculty, they wanted trustees to elect Theron Rankin, president of the denomination's Foreign Mission Board. They knew that sentiment across the denomination favored McCall, but the "total climate of opinion" on the faculty opposed his election.[8] Homiletics professor Jesse Weatherspoon in particular lobbied aggressively for Rankin and against McCall.[9] Trustees courted Rankin seriously, but Rankin

7. See, e.g., Edward A. McDowell to Olin T. Binkley, 15 Jan. 1951, Answered Letters '50–1 folder, box 13, Binkley Papers, WFU; Olin T. Binkley to Edward A. McDowell, 23 Jan. 1951, Answered Letters '50–1 folder, box 13, Binkley Papers, WFU.

8. Wayne Oates to Olin Binkley, 25 Nov. 1950, Answered Letters '50–1 folder, box 13, Binkley Papers, WFU.

9. Jesse Weatherspoon to Olin Binkley, 16 Nov. 1950, Answered Letters '50–1 folder, box 13, Binkley Papers, WFU; Wayne Oates to Olin Binkley, 25 Nov. 1950, Answered Letters '50–1 folder, box 13, Binkley Papers, WFU.

decided that he wanted to remain at the mission board and withdrew his name from consideration.[10] Trustees turned back to their first choice, McCall.

Although the position must have had its appeal for McCall, he did not relish the prospect. Apart from the faculty's disfavor, McCall knew that the next president would face many of the problems that Fuller had not resolved. Fuller resolved the need for space, housing, equipment, and teaching personnel, but he had not achieved unity among the faculty or between the faculty and the administration. The source of division had to do with the aims of theological education—what type of education best prepares ministers for effective service, and how the seminary should relate to the denomination.

Many of the school of theology faculty were concerned that the seminary threatened to become a kind of factory for making preachers, emphasizing the mastery of skills and the implementation of programs geared toward the production of predictable church growth. Among those skills was the employment of the rhetoric of traditional orthodoxy. Southern Baptists placed high value on orthodox doctrine. Those who preached in that vein would better win the confidence of Southern Baptists, gain election at prominent churches, and attain standing in denominational meetings.

The faculty of the school of theology believed, however, that this approach would end in disaster. If preachers reinforced the dogma of the past, they were effectively relegating the churches to irrelevance. The world would move forward—its science, culture, and methods would advance through schools, newspapers, radio broadcasts, books, professional organizations, and other institutions of cultural progress. As the world embraced new ideas, those churches that doggedly refused to admit new light and new ideas would be discredited. The young especially would abandon the churches in droves.

The answer, many faculty believed, was to educate preachers in such a way that they might adapt the essential Christian truths to the changing conditions of culture. The churches needed not regimented programs but the power and consolation of spirituality, not rote skills but the ability to adapt the word of God to the needs of the day. Preachers needed to understand the Bible and how it applies to the science, philosophy, and social conditions of the times. What they needed was education in advancing knowledge, not indoctrination in the old dogmas. What the churches needed above all was theologians, not technicians.

McCall knew that the faculty had concerns along these lines and had criticized Fuller for neglecting the spiritual and academic aspects of the seminary's life. Fuller had discussed some of the seminary's struggles with him. He also

10. See Inman Johnson to Duke K. McCall, 5 Feb. 1951, SBTS—Call folder, McCall Papers; J. B. Weatherspoon to Duke K. McCall, 4 Aug. 1951, ibid.

knew many trustees and members of the faculty. Inman Johnson, a professor of speech who favored McCall's candidacy, explained the faculty's perspective to him in some detail. Immediately before McCall met with the trustees, Johnson sent him a detailed letter on the faculty's view of the seminary's problems and needs. Johnson wrote that the faculty wanted a president who would develop the seminary "spiritually and academically." The faculty felt that under Fuller scholarship's value for the church's mission had been discounted. Johnson concluded, "We do not want another promotional executive." [11]

McCall agreed to meet with the trustee board in Louisville on August 1, 1951. When the trustees elected him unanimously, he told them that he would not accept if even one faculty member opposed him. He knew that the result was uncertain, since they had been opposed to him. But Johnson had been lobbying on his behalf. And to reject him openly after the trustees had elected him would appear tasteless and obstructionist. He refused to give an answer until he had consulted the faculty.

The eight faculty members who were in Louisville—Theron Price, Dale Moody, Wayne Oates, Vernon Stanfield, Findley Edge, Inman Johnson, Charles McGlon, and Hugh Peterson—gathered together in the basement of the Faculty Center to meet with him. He explained that the trustees had just elected him president, but he would not accept if any of them objected. He explained also that his chief interest was not in administration and promotion but in developing the spiritual and academic aspects of the seminary. He said that he wanted to relate to the faculty "as friends" and that he needed to learn from them. [12] The faculty liked what they heard. "Your statement of a scholarly and spiritual purpose is welcome," wrote Professor J. Estill Jones. [13] His refusal to accept without their support showed the faculty "respect and all due regard," professor Wayne Oates wrote. [14] The effect was impressive. Each one affirmed his support of McCall's presidency.

McCall was rather surprised by the outcome. They supported him in part because he told them what they wanted to hear—that he would support their vision for theological education, though he did not emphasize the limits on that support, which later became a source of tension. They supported him also from a realistic assessment of the situation. By June the faculty had recognized, as Edward A. McDowell recounted, that the "signs began to point in his direction,"

11. Inman Johnson to Duke K. McCall, 28 July 1951, SBTS—Call folder, McCall Papers.

12. Wayne Oates to Olin Binkley, 3 Aug. 1951, Letters '50–1 folder, box 13, Binkley Papers, WFU.

13. J. Estill Jones to Duke K. McCall, 15 Aug. 1951, SBTS—Call folder, McCall Papers. Jones learned of McCall's speech afterward.

14. Wayne Oates to Duke K. McCall, 11 Aug. 1951, SBTS—Call folder, McCall Papers.

and they realized that "Duke was out in front" of most of the potential candidates.[15] They feared that the trustees would choose a fundamentalist president commissioned to root out modernism from the seminary. Although McCall was favored by fundamentalists in the denomination, he was not one. The faculty made a realistic assessment and concluded that McCall was better than the alternatives. "My own feeling is that this man is the best man our trustees were capable of electing," Oates reflected. "He has delivered us from the possibility of getting a man like Ralph Herring, Herschel Hobbs, or worse."[16] The faculty's endorsement impressed McCall as an indication of God's providential leading, and he accepted the position.

WHAT THE FACULTY WANTED

McCall announced a platform designed to please the faculty and published it in the seminary's magazine, the *Tie*. The faculty liked what they heard. W. O. Carver sent McCall a note to "express my appreciation and approval of your statement concerning your idea, ideals, and approach to the functions of the presidency of the seminary. These seem to me to be quite in line with what I would wish and with what I understand to be the concepts and hopes of our faculty."[17] Preaching professor Vernon L. Stanfield concurred: "The faculty members with whom I have talked greet your election with a sense of real satisfaction."[18]

Veteran New Testament professor Edward A. McDowell wrote McCall confirming the unanimity of the faculty in supporting McCall's election. McDowell's letter, however, held a portent of the problems that would soon arise. The faculty were happy with McCall because they felt that he understood and agreed with their vision for the seminary and their role in achieving that vision, which was that the seminary would promote "leadership in progressive thinking, scholarship, and spiritual advance." And there must be real mutuality and equality between the president and faculty. If McCall would hold to these two commitments, all would be well. As McDowell wrote, "There is no reason at all that the old tensions should return, and there is every reason for your administration to begin and continue in this spirit of fraternity and good will.... Just this we shall ask of our president, as any self-respecting group of men would ask: that

15. Edward A. McDowell to Syd Stealey, 3 Oct. 1951, E. A. McDowell Jr. folder, Binkley Papers, WFU.

16. Wayne Oates to Olin T. Binkley, 3 Aug. 1951, Letters '50–1 folder, box 13, Binkley Papers, WFU.

17. W. O. Carver to Duke K. McCall, 8 Aug. 1951, SBTS—Call folder, McCall Papers.

18. Vernon L. Stanfield to Duke K. McCall, 28 Aug. 1951, SBTS—Call folder, McCall Papers.

he treat us as men and brothers. I believe that you know this and that you will gladly accord to us this one basic expression of a principle upon which we can work together in Christian love."[19] McCall deliberately distanced himself from Fuller. "He appears to be headed in a direction opposite to that taken by his predecessor," observed McDowell, "and doubtless will profit by his mistakes."[20]

The honeymoon was brief. It quickly became apparent that the faculty's acceptance and support depended on how faithfully McCall lived up to his initial commitment to their vision. On the day that the McCall family arrived in Louisville, McCall and his wife attended a faculty dinner at which he endured public instruction on how to keep the faculty's favor. Professors Theron Price and Estill Jones, as well as Alice Carver, W. O. Carver's wife, all gave McCall an earful. There was no open hostility, but the message was clear: McCall would find the faculty to be loyal and supportive as long as he minded his own administrative business and heeded the faculty's counsel in matters of curriculum, hiring, and promotion.[21]

CONFORMITY, FREEDOM, AND ACADEMIC IDEALISM

McCall's realist diplomacy was not new but had developed out of the experience of the Whitsitt controversy. Whitsitt and his champions took an idealistic stand for truth. They refused to compromise and yield to popular sentiment— the seminary's freedom had to be maintained at all costs. The campaign failed, student enrollment plummeted, and Whitsitt resigned. This experience helped convince the seminary presidents and professors that a realistic diplomacy produced better results. They would relate to Southern Baptists as they really were and would be cautious in advancing progressive thought. By patiently exposing students to more progressive views, reform would surely come.

This approach had mixed results. The seminary had relative peace and generally held the confidence of most Southern Baptists during the first half of the twentieth century. The faculty's progressive ideas, however, made little headway among the churches. Many on the faculty grew impatient at the lack of progress. They wanted greater freedom to promote their views. As the faculty became increasingly progressive in the 1940s and 1950s, this aspiration became increasingly important to the faculty.

19. Edward A. McDowell to Duke K. McCall, 3 Aug. 1951, SBTS—Call folder, McCall Papers.

20. Edward A. McDowell to Syd Stealey, 3 Oct. 1951, E. A. McDowell Jr. folder, Binkley Papers, WFU.

21. See Duke McCall, *Duke McCall: An Oral History* (Brentwood, TN: Baptist History and Heritage, 2001), 105–107.

The solution to these problems, the faculty held, lay in serious biblical study and theological thinking. The old orthodoxy rendered good service in its day, but its day was now past. To cling to the tired dogmas of former generations would be to lose the opportunity for effective service in the present day. Current needs demanded fresh interpretation and application of the Bible to the churches and society in their modern context.

The denomination's churches and leaders also had aspirations for the seminary. For many pastors and churches, the characteristic most greatly desired was orthodoxy. As the faculty became increasingly progressive, Southern Baptists grew increasingly insistent on this point.

McCall aimed to secure the faculty's freedom to teach their progressive views, and at the same time he aimed to reassure Southern Baptists that the faculty was sound in doctrine. McCall referred to this as achieving "balance between freedom for progressive teaching and the need to keep the critics quiet."[22] This was the only realistic approach to the seminary's relationship with the denomination. A great deal of McCall's efforts went toward keeping the faculty within the limits of this policy of denominational realism.

Church history professor Theron Price led a caucus of six or seven professors who disagreed with McCall's vision for the seminary and who consistently opposed McCall's initiatives. Under Price's leadership some professors sought to transfer all the practical courses into the new school of religious education. Homiletics, which had an important place in the traditional theological curriculum, alone was excepted. It was a strategy to exile these interlopers on the body of divinity, to cast them outside the walls of the theological curriculum and isolate them within the religious education curriculum. They wanted especially to isolate Wayne Oates and his courses there. On this basis the majority supported establishing the new school of religious education, which began in 1953 under the leadership of Gaines Dobbins. Dobbins and the religious education professors wanted Oates with them, no doubt because he was talented and popular. But Oates resisted this effort to neutralize his influence in this way and lobbied McCall and other faculty to prevent this. The professors fought it out in faculty meetings. When the issue came to a vote, the majority sided with Oates. The school of theology curriculum would include religious psychology and pastoral counseling.[23]

22. Duke K. McCall to Olin T. Binkley, 25 Jan. 1952, O. T. Binkley folder, McCall Papers.

23. Wayne Oates, "Personal Reflections on the Controversy and Crisis at Southern Seminary," 24 June 1958, 3, Faculty Controversy 1958—Corr. with Faculty and Staff folder, McCall Papers.

The fundamental divide in the faculty concerned the purpose and character of a theological seminary. Beginning in the 1940s many of the faculty members chafed under the limitations imposed by the policy of denominational realism. They grew restive under McCall's efforts to keep them within the policy's boundaries. As suspicion of the seminary grew in the 1950s, McCall tightened the reins. Nearly half the faculty pursued a program of resistance. They viewed McCall's advocacy of diplomatic discourse as flattery to gratify the conservative reactionaries and the ignorant. What was needed was truth, not flattery. They saw McCall's realistic diplomacy as little less than duplicity.

In this respect the seminary's experience reflected the divisions of postwar theological education in America. The growing popularity of the practical courses in the curriculum of most seminaries provoked resistance on the part of those who thought that the most effective and practical education of ministers involved the purest scholarship. True ideas, not skills, had power to change society and advance the kingdom of God, they believed. A seminary best served Christ, therefore, by advancing the purest scholarship. Practical courses had ancillary value, but they should not diminish an overwhelming emphasis on scholarship. The greatest sin at Harvard Divinity School, G. Ernest Wright complained to his faculty colleagues in 1962, was "to be unscholarly." [24]

DIVINITY SCHOOL OR DENOMINATIONAL SEMINARY

McCall knew from the beginning that the faculty was divided concerning the character of the seminary. Price and ethics professor Guy Ranson promoted an ideal of theological education as a community of scholarly pursuit free from the restraints of the popular traditions and superstitions current in the churches. The institutions that best embodied this ideal were such northeastern divinity schools as Yale or Harvard. Many faculty found this vision compelling. But McCall and other faculty promoted an ideal of theological education as scholarship in the service of the church. Southern Seminary was not a divinity school but a denominational seminary. It pursued scholarship as a means, not as an end. It was owned and controlled by the churches of the Southern Baptist Convention, and its scholarship was intended for promoting the fidelity and effectiveness of ministry among them. Price and his sympathizers believed that McCall subordinated truth to the popular will of the denomination. McCall

24. Quoted in Clyde T. Francisco to Duke K. McCall, 19 Feb. 1962, Clyde T. Francisco 1952–1969 folder, McCall Papers.

and other faculty believed that Price's vision of the pursuit of truth without denominational support was quixotic.[25]

McCall recognized that Price's approach to theological education—freedom to criticize denominational beliefs and practices, and freedom to promote the historical-critical approach to the Bible—would not be tolerated by most Southern Baptists. So he pleaded with the faculty to apply themselves in a way that "will serve Southern Baptists" by producing preachers who will be acceptable to the churches. Price and his fellow dissidents pleaded that their approach to theological education was in fact better suited to serving Southern Baptists than his, because McCall's vision doomed Southern Baptists to conserving their irrelevant traditionalism. McCall told them that they received their approach from such places as Yale and that "it runs counter to what Southern Baptists want and need."[26]

Naturally it was a Yale professor who wrote the book on theological education. H. Richard Niebuhr, the prominent Yale theologian and ethicist, cast a vision for theological education in *The Advancement of Theological Education*, which appeared in 1957. Niebuhr was not sympathetic toward Southern Baptist expectations or to McCall's vision. Southern Baptists expected their seminaries to preserve and defend their view of scripture truth, and they expected the president and trustees to exercise careful guardianship in this regard. Niebuhr believed that such an approach denied the faculty their Christian liberty and constituted "thought control." It was "coercion."[27]

Price's group used the book against McCall. Henry Turlington led a discussion of the book for the seminary's Faculty Club in 1958 and read from it in the March 13, 1958, faculty meeting in order to enforce his opposition to McCall. He read the section on "one-man rule," with its "remarks about low morale

25. Duke K. McCall, "Excerpts—President's Address," *Tie,* Mar. 1952, 3, 7.

26. Guy Ranson (describing McCall's position), transcription of trustee interviews 28–30 Apr. 1958, 1:90.

27. H. Richard Niebuhr, Daniel Day Williams, and James M. Gustafson, *The Advancement of Theological Education* (New York: Harper and Brothers, 1957), 43–44. Niebuhr represented a group in the American Association of Theological Schools who found Southern Baptists' denominational approach to theological education deplorable. Another group in the association endorsed the denominational approach. Others still seemed content that both models coexisted. These three impulses can be seen in the minutes of the 1960 American Association of Theological Schools debate over the role of a proposed statement on academic freedom (American Association of Theological Schools, *Bulletin of the American Association of Theological Schools,* 24 [1960]: 98–104). See also Ernest C. Colwell, "The Theological Seminary and the Church, in ibid., 108–116. See also H. Richard Niebuhr, *The Purpose of the Church and Its Ministry: Reflections on the Aims of Theological Education* (New York: Harper and Brothers, 1956).

in insttutions in which the president bore too much authority."[28] The section delineated the various ways in which an executive president demeaned the abilities and gifts of the faculty. As Turlington read it, the dissenters meant it to be heard as an indictment of McCall.

Price argued that the purpose of a theological seminary was to "make possible the exercise of Christian truth in Christian freedom in Christian community." In this way "the objectives of theological education could be realized."[29] Truth required open debate of issues by all the "responsible" members of the community, "a constant meeting of minds in a constant reexamination of positions."[30] This meant freedom to criticize ideas, plans, persons, and the denomination. Central to the role of a theological professor, Price held, was this freedom to criticize.

The fundamental source of the controversy was disagreement concerning the role of the seminary in the denomination. Oates, Francisco, and speech professor Charles McGlon believed that preliminary to resolving faculty divisions, they had to agree on their vision for theological education: "What about the basic differences as to what kind of school the seminary should be and what of its relation to the Southern Baptist Convention?" They said that they did not want to remain at the seminary if Price and the dissenters were to continue to press their vision of theological education and oppose the vision held by McCall and the trustees.

AUTHORITY AND CONTROL

The disagreement over vision was not a theoretical issue. Implementing the vision required authority and control. Theology professor Wayne Ward summarized well the division within the faculty over the seminary's task as a conflict over "how we are to relate our work to our Southern Baptist constituency, to the lines of authority that operate over us, and especially whether or not the faculty shall have the final voice in determining that goal by selection of faculty members, promotion of them, addition of curricula, courses, and so forth."[31]

By 1957 the dissenters were winning the battle. They had driven some faculty members to seek positions elsewhere and had blocked faculty candidates who

28. Morris Ashcraft, transcription of trustee interviews 28–30 Apr. 1958, 2:253.
29. Theron Price, transcription of trustee interviews 28–30 Apr. 1958, 1:66.
30. Theron Price, transcription of trustee interviews 28–30 Apr. 1958, 1:76
31. Wayne Ward, transcription of trustee interviews 28–30 Apr. 1958, 3:419. See, similarly, Findley Edge, transcription of trustee interviews 28–30 Apr. 1958, 4:454–455.

did not measure up.[32] Most of the professors came into their orbit. Professors like Clyde Francisco recognized the fact: "My particular cause has been steadily losing, both in the student body and in the total picture of the institution."[33] The faculty was changing in the direction of Price's vision. They recruited men who shared their vision and drove away those who did not. Francisco said that the dissenters had driven away Edward McDowell, who told Francisco, "I am tired of fighting this battle." They drove away Cornell Goerner, who was a leader of the faculty who opposed Price's vision. And they drove away Ralph Elliott, said his doctoral supervisor, Clyde Francisco, because Elliott tired of the harassment of the dissenting faculty.[34]

The dissenters had attained a tenuous majority of the faculty, but they needed more help. They knew that Southern Baptists were not likely to support their vision, and more important, neither were the trustees. They needed concessions from McCall but he did not share their vision. They needed to have effective control over faculty hiring and promotion so that they could recruit more like-minded faculty. If McCall had all authority, Heber Peacock told trustees, then he had control "not only of who teaches but ultimately of what is taught."[35] For this reason above all others the dissenting faculty wanted the governance of the school in the hands of the faculty, at least in matters of hiring and promoting faculty.

Theron Price was the most influential leader of the young dissenters.[36] He was scholarly, self-assured, idealistic, persuasive, and a popular teacher. He cast the vision for modern Baptist theological education and persuaded many of its correctness. McCall's proposals and decisions supported a different vision, and Price opposed them openly. As Oates saw it, "Theron is bent on ruling or ruining the seminary."[37]

The dissenters made life difficult for those who did not make the grade. Francisco was miserable under assault of slights and attacks. The dissenters

---

32. E.g., Ralph Herring, who had a reputation as a denominational loyalist and a conservative, told J. D. Grey that when he was invited to become professor of New Testament at the seminary, Estill Jones, T. C. Smith, and Henry Turlington told him he was not welcome—his scholarship was inferior to theirs, and yet he would have higher faculty rank. See Ralph Herring to J. D. Grey, 12 Feb. 1959, folder 56, J. D. Grey Papers, SBHLA; J. D. Grey, manuscript notes from presidents' committee meetings, 4, folder 56, J. D. Grey Papers, SBHLA; S. L. Morgan to Harold Tribble, 7 Feb. 1948, Tribble Papers, WFU.

33. Clyde Francisco, transcription of trustee interviews 28–30 Apr. 1958, 3:396.

34. Clyde Francisco, transcription of trustee interviews 28–30 Apr. 1958, 3:407–408.

35. Heber Peacock, transcription of trustee interviews 28–30 Apr. 1958, 1:150.

36. See Hugh Peterson, transcription of trustee interviews 28–30 Apr. 1958, 2:283.

37. Wayne Oates to Olin T. Binkley, 11 May 1958, 1958 Correspondence folder, Box 40, Binkley Papers, WFU.

Theron D. Price

attacked the views of their colleagues openly. They told students, for example, that "Francisco is intellectually dishonest because if he were honest he'd take a different stand."[38] When he approached the seminary on his return from frequent preaching trips, he felt an oppressive pall come over him. He found the dissenters' repeated expressions of disrespect so demeaning that he accepted a position at Southwestern Seminary and changed his mind only when the situation changed dramatically.[39] Wayne Oates endured the same for many years. In 1960 he confided to Henlee Barnette that "this is the first year I have ever been in Louisville when somebody didn't bash somebody's else head in, professionally that is. It's a great relief to walk around without somebody knifing you in the back daily."[40]

Price and the dissenters treated men like Oates, Ward, and Francisco with some contempt. They ostracized them and told them that they were "traitors" to the "faculty."[41] Those who did not share their ideals were not truly members of the faculty. "Unless you are with this group in their concept of theological education, which essentially is purely academic with no relationship to the life

---

38. Clyde Francisco, transcription of trustee interviews 28–30 Apr. 1958, 3:403.
39. Clyde Francisco, transcription of trustee interviews 28–30 Apr. 1958, 3:393–394.
40. Wayne Oates to Henlee Barnette, 24 Apr. 1960, Barnette Papers, WFU.
41. Wayne Oates, transcription of trustee interviews 28–30 Apr. 1958, 3:362–364.

of the denomination or to the reality of pastoral ministry, you are not scholarly, you are not academic."[42] Oates believed that they hated him.[43]

Guy Ranson, who taught ethics, established a reputation as Price's protégé. The two of them frequently spoke at length in faculty meetings, urging their colleagues to support the policies that advanced their ideals. But frequently they were speeches about their educational ideals and were thinly veiled attacks on the views of those who differed from them. Old Testament professor William Morton also exercised leadership of the faculty on behalf of their ideals and had wide confidence among the faculty. Differences and conflicts of interest existed within the faculty, and each considered himself independent in his decisions, but the majority sympathized with Price, Ranson, and Morton on most issues.

Hugh Peterson, dean of students, explained to trustees that Price, Ranson, and Morton held deeply the conviction that the seminary had to have freedom to lead the denomination in its theology and practices. But they could not exercise leadership unless they could control the direction of the seminary: "The control of the seminary ought to be with these people who are enlightened and who really know what the story is, they ought to have control of the seminary so that they will be able continually to prepare a leadership that is above the theological and ecclesiological...structure of the day."[44]

By the spring of 1958, Inman Johnson said, the attacks on McCall were severe enough that "faculty meetings have gotten that it's uncomfortable to go to them."[45] Eric Rust said that there were times in faculty meetings, when certain professors spoke, that "I've been ashamed of being there."[46] Guy Ranson told trustees that the dissenters merely wanted a "democratic spirit" in which the faculty's judgments carried more weight.[47] McCall "has been unwilling for us to assume what is proper academic responsibility."[48]

But in 1957 McCall began to change the way he administered the institution, away from more democratic methods of decision making toward a more hierarchical structure. He created the position of dean of the school of theology and strengthened the authority of the deans of the three schools. The faculty of the school of theology reorganized its departments into three divisions and exchanged its many department chairmen for three division chairmen

42. Herbert Jackson, transcription of trustee interviews 28–30 Apr. 1958, 4:442.

43. Wayne Oates, transcription of trustee interviews 28–30 Apr. 1958, 3:358–359.

44. Hugh Peterson, transcription of trustee interviews 28–30 Apr. 1958, 2:263, 275.

45. Inman Johnson, transcription of trustee interviews 28–30 Apr. 1958, 2:193.

46. Eric Rust, transcription of trustee interviews 28–30 Apr. 1958, 3:317.

47. Guy Ranson, transcription of trustee interviews 28–30 Apr. 1958, 1:85.

48. Guy Ranson, transcription of trustee interviews 28–30 Apr. 1958, 1:91.

Guy H. Ranson

who exercised considerable influence in faculty affairs. Although the young dissenters saw some advantages to these changes, they believed that McCall would use the new structure for more effective control of the faculty by more direct control of hiring, promotion, policymaking, and curriculum.

Such fears gained momentum in the spring of 1957. McCall considered proposing regulations on how often faculty could preach on their own time, and perhaps how much of the money earned from such extracurricular speaking they could keep.[49] Faculty salaries were inadequate to support faculty members with families, and virtually all felt the necessity of preaching at revivals and conferences, and of accepting interim pastorates, in order to supplement their income.[50] Some faculty established such reputations as preachers that they were constantly in demand and could earn significant income in this way. Others felt that God called them to be scholars more than preachers and resented both the necessity of such labors and their small earning power compared with such popular preachers as Francisco and Ward. When Theron Price took out

49. See Duke McCall, memo to faculty, 27 Feb. 1957, Barnette Papers, WFU.

50. See Hugh Peterson, transcription of trustee interviews 28–30 Apr. 1958, 2:273. It was the same at all the seminaries. Southwestern's Ray Summers told John Newport that the faculty there were all going hungry, since no one could get pulpit supply work at that time (Ray Summers to John Newport, 17 Sept. 1958, Ray Summers Papers).

the mortgage to buy a home, he joked sardonically that in order to pay for it, perhaps "the Lord will lead me into evangelistic work."[51] And they felt it was inequitable to them and damaging to the seminary's mission for the faculty to consist of men who devoted their nonclassroom time to preaching rather than to research and writing. McCall was looking for a way to ameliorate the inequities but ultimately imposed no restrictions.[52]

More disconcerting still was the fact that McCall retained Booz, Allen and Hamilton, the nation's premier management consulting firm, to study the seminary's operations and recommend a more efficient organization. McCall believed that the firm's analysis would be sensitive to the school's unique mission and its denominational context, but the faculty interpreted it as a ploy to consolidate the president's power. The faculty believed that the reason McCall called in a business consulting firm was because it naturally would recommend a top-down approach to institutional authority based on the business model. Price and many other professors believed that a Baptist seminary should incorporate the democratic principles of the Baptist tradition. They did not trust business consultants to preserve Baptist principles.[53]

In 1957 the trustees implemented important recommendations of the Booz, Allen and Hamilton study. Trustees reaffirmed the president's duty to recommend new faculty to the trustees, but it added the duty to nominate deans and the power to appoint faculty to nonpermanent positions for a period of no more than three years.[54]

Another recommendation of the study was to establish a more objective procedure for determining salaries, raises, and promotions. For some years McCall had relied on the recommendations of an annual meeting of the full professors to determine which professors received promotion. These meetings sometimes became rancorous affairs, as the promotion of an individual might become a proxy for various intramural conflicts. The professors who wanted a more scholarly faculty wanted to promote those of like vision and keep back professors who did not seem scholarly enough. McCall implemented, as one of the recommendations of the Booz, Allen and Hamilton report, an instrument for evaluating faculty based on "performance criteria." Each dean asked the members of the faculty to rate one another based on eight criteria. The faculty

51. Theron Price to Olin Binkley, 4 Oct. 1950, Answered Letters '50–1 folder, box 13, Binkley Papers, WFU.

52. Hugh Wamble, "Conflict between Authority and Conscience," electronic typescript, 3:43–44, SBTS.

53. See Hugh Peterson, transcription of trustee interviews 28–30 Apr. 1958, 2:286.

54. Minutes, Board of Trustees, 1957.

feared that this instrument would be used in a prejudicial way to rationalize the decisions of the president and his deans.[55]

By 1957 many on the faculty viewed McCall's every move with suspicion. They vetted his every proposal for its hidden agenda so that they could counter it effectively. The proposal with the most serious ramifications for control of the faculty related to the office of dean of the school of theology. If the man elected to this office was loyal to McCall, the faculty would have little chance of countering McCall's efforts at control. If the new dean was, however, loyal to the faculty majority and shared their vision of theological education, the balance of power would tilt favorably in the direction of the faculty.

Allen Graves, dean of the school of religious education, believed that the dissenters wanted the faculty to have the "privilege of choosing faculty members and the privilege of promotion of faculty members."[56] It was essential to establishing the school according to Price and Ranson's vision. If the president named new faculty members, the school would not go in the direction they desired.[57] Wayne Oates agreed. They needed to have the right to determine who came on the faculty in order to implement their vision.[58] Trustee chairman Wade Bryant recognized that in their battle for control "they will have to have help from the dean."[59]

BATTLE OVER THE DEAN

McCall had trouble filling the new position, and ethics professor Henlee Barnette served as acting dean for two years while the search continued. The men he wanted were unacceptable to the dissident faculty; the men they wanted were unacceptable to him. McCall wanted a dean who understood Southern Baptists. For many reasons he had to be more sympathetic to Southern Baptists than to the academy of scholars. The dean would help McCall defend the faculty before the denomination and defend the denomination before the faculty.

The dissidents recognized that McCall would likely choose a dean who would be unsympathetic to their vision. They worried that he would impose on them someone from outside the school, a large-church pastor or denominational

---

55. Wamble, "Conflict," 3:44–45. McCall did not dispense with the full professors meeting but no longer felt obligated to accept their recommendations.

56. Allen Graves, transcription of trustee interviews 28–30 Apr. 1958, 3:343.

57. Allen Graves analyzed the matter this way (Allen Graves, transcription of trustee interviews 28–30 Apr. 1958, 3:348).

58. Wayne Oates, transcription of trustee interviews 28–30 Apr. 1958, 3:362.

59. Wade Bryant, transcription of trustee interviews 28–30 Apr. 1958, 2:228.

official who placed denominational loyalty above academic freedom. "If some man from outside our framework in Louisville were to be in the deanship," Old Testament professor J. J. Owens wrote, "there would be great fear."[60]

McCall and the dissidents struggled over the selection of the dean because the choice would in large measure determine the future character of the faculty. The dean's vision of theological education would generally determine his recommendations, and his recommendations would be hard to frustrate. Clyde Francisco noted that the conflict escalated into open war when McCall announced that he was going to appoint a dean, for "the kind of man the dean was would determine the whole future of the seminary."[61]

Olin Binkley, who taught sociology at the seminary from 1944 to 1952, seemed the obvious choice. He encouraged intellectual freedom and would have pleased the faculty, but he also understood the limits to freedom imposed by the Southern Baptist Convention and would have aided McCall in sustaining realist policy. McCall invited him to become dean, and many faculty urged him to accept, but Binkley seemed unconvinced that there would be sufficient freedom and declined.[62]

At the end of the faculty meeting on March 13, 1957, McCall elicited discussion of the selection of a dean for the school of theology. He announced that he was open to the possibility of selecting someone from the faculty. It does not appear that McCall had anyone in mind or was trying to direct the faculty's thinking at the time. McCall often thought through difficult decisions by talking them out with faculty members in faculty meetings and in informal conversations.[63] McCall did not anticipate what transpired next. It set in motion a two-year conflict that nearly cost him his job.

The dissenting caucus had discussed in advance their strategies for selecting a dean. Clyde Francisco believed that they feared he would select Cornell Goerner, who had openly opposed their vision for the seminary. They met, Francisco said, "in a little caucus and agreed on the man they wanted for dean to forestall Goerner ever coming."[64] They decided they would recommend William Morton. When McCall announced that he would consider faculty

60. J. J. Owens to Olin T. Binkley, 26 Feb. 1956, 1956 Letters folder, box 40, Binkley Papers, WFU.

61. Clyde Francisco, transcription of trustee interviews 28–30 Apr. 1958, 3:400.

62. See, e.g., Wayne Oates to Olin Binkley, 27 Feb. 1956, Misc. folder, box 26, Binkley Papers, WFU.

63. McCall suggested to Hugh Wamble a few days later that Morris Ashcraft should be considered but less than two weeks later selected Cornell Goerner. See Wamble, "Conflict," 3:46–47.

64. Clyde Francisco, transcription of trustee interviews 28–30 Apr. 1958, 3:411–412.

members for the position and opened the discussion, Guy Ranson seized the opportunity. He asked McCall if recommendations were in order. McCall, perhaps caught by surprise, let him continue. Ranson immediately recommended Morton. Several faculty members spoke enthusiastically in favor of the idea. Wayne Oates alone raised questions, though he did not oppose Morton's nomination directly. McCall asked the faculty to think it over for two weeks until their next meeting.[65]

Sometime prior to Ranson's nominating Morton, McCall had considered and rejected him as a candidate. He had explained to Morton privately that he did not want Morton as dean.[66] McCall had probably concluded that Morton shared Price and Ranson's vision for the seminary and that he would turn the school more toward Niebuhr's model of detached scholarship.[67] Because Morton knew these things, McCall felt, he should have withdrawn his name from consideration. But Morton left his name in nomination. If McCall allowed it to go to a vote, Morton would probably have received a nearly unanimous endorsement from the faculty. They had no authority to elect the dean, but their endorsement would back McCall into a corner. If he then rejected Morton, he would alienate the faculty further and give Price more recruiting leverage. He finally decided to preempt the vote on Morton by announcing his own nominee before a vote on Morton could take place.

McCall concluded that the best candidate was Cornell Goerner, professor of missions and comparative religion since 1938. He had previously spoken to various faculty members concerning their opinion of Goerner's fitness for the job and knew their general opinion of him.[68] At the April 2, 1957, meeting of the school of theology faculty, McCall announced that he had reconsidered the faculty's role in selecting a dean. It was properly his responsibility. After much thought and prayer he had decided to nominate Goerner as dean. McCall then adjourned the meeting without further discussion.[69]

Faculty members outside the Price-Ranson constellation looked favorably on Goerner's candidacy. They recognized, as Old Testament professor Ralph

---

65. See Wamble, "Conflict," 3:46–47.

66. Duke McCall, "Report to the Trustee Subcommittee on the School of Theology in Session Tuesday, April 29, 1958," in Wamble, "Conflict," 6:119.

67. Wade Bryant, trustee chairman, assessed the rejection of Morton this way, undoubtedly based on his conversations with McCall (Wade Bryant, transcription of trustee interviews 28–30 Apr. 1958, 2:229). See, similarly, Hugh Peterson, transcription of trustee interviews 28–30 Apr. 1958, 2:276, 278–279.

68. Duke McCall, "Report to the Trustee Subcommittee on the School of Theology in Session Tuesday, April 29, 1958," in Wamble, "Conflict," 6:119.

69. See Wamble, "Conflict," 3:48.

Elliott told Goerner, that Morton's nomination was the result of the Price caucus's "planned strategy." Elliott disagreed with Price and Ranson's vision of the seminary's purpose and thought that Goerner was the "logical choice for dean." He told Goerner that "the men who have what I consider to be the right perspective of the purpose of our institution are behind you."[70]

Many faculty were surprised by McCall's abrupt reversal concerning the faculty's involvement and by his sudden nomination of Goerner. But none was more surprised than Goerner himself. McCall made the announcement before he had spoken with Goerner about it. This proved a blunder with serious ramifications.[71] Goerner was caught unprepared, which put him in a difficult situation. The Foreign Mission Board was actively recruiting him for the position of secretary for Africa, Europe, and the Near East. McCall knew that Goerner was considering the position and perhaps rushed his decision to get ahead of the mission board's offer. Goerner gave no immediate answer and went to Richmond to interview with the mission board. On April 10 the board elected him to the secretaryship, and he accepted. Afterward Goerner worried that his rejection of McCall's nomination had been a mistake: "I have had the terrible feeling that things began to deteriorate then."[72] And indeed they did.

On April 9, 1957, one week after McCall nominated Goerner, the faculty met, and Ranson and Price chastised the president for exercising power without due regard for the faculty's wishes. Ranson indicated the direction the meeting would take when he moved to add to the minutes of prior meetings explicit statements that the faculty expressed its approval of Morton and that McCall had allowed no discussion of Goerner. After the motion passed, McCall asked if anyone objected to Ranson's maneuvers, and a heated debate ensued. Ranson and Price pressed McCall for a rationale for ignoring the faculty's wishes. McCall replied that the faculty's role was to provide advice and counsel, not to dictate. Hugh Wamble asked if this meant that McCall would no longer consult them when hiring new faculty members. McCall answered that he had the responsibility for nominating new teachers, but that he would consult with

70. Ralph Elliott to H. C. Goerner, 2 Apr. 1957, box 5, Henry Cornell Goerner Papers, SBHLA.

71. McCall later called it "the major blunder of the last six and a half years" (Duke McCall, "Report to the Trustee Subcommittee on the School of Theology in Session Tuesday, April 29, 1958," in Wamble, 6:119).

72. Cornell Goerner to Duke McCall, 8 Feb. 1959, Cornell Goerner folder, McCall Papers. See also H. Cornell Goerner to H. I. Hester, 27 May 1957, box 7, Henry Cornell Goerner Papers, SBHLA; Foreign Mission Board, Minutes, 10 Apr. 1957; Cornell Goerner to Duke McCall, 9 Apr. 1957, 15 Apr. 1957, and 8 Feb. 1959, Cornell Goerner folder, McCall Papers.

the faculty in advance. Price wondered if the faculty's advice counted for anything, since McCall had not acted consistently with it. McCall said that he had
already considered Morton as dean and had concluded against the idea before
the faculty recommended him.[73] McCall complained that Price and Ranson had
formed a clique and intimidated all opposition in faculty meetings to accomplish their ends. Price bristled at this and insinuated that professors who gave
McCall advice in private were hypocrites for saying nothing in open faculty.[74]

After the meeting McCall suggested that Ranson start looking for a position
at another school. According to caucus member Hugh Wamble, Ranson told
his colleagues in April 1958 that McCall called him into his office shortly after
the April 9, 1957, faculty meeting and confronted him regarding the disrespectful and unprofessional manner in which he opposed McCall in the meeting
and criticized McCall to his colleagues.[75] McCall then suggested that Ranson
find a position elsewhere.[76] This raised the stakes and deepened the dissenters'
distrust of McCall.

The struggle over the selection of a dean laid bare the deep tensions between
McCall and the dissident faculty members. But more important, it gave Price
and Ranson something tangible on which to build a durable party of opposition. In the wake of the deanship conflict Price's caucus fomented further dissatisfaction with McCall's administration and attracted new members. In the
spring or summer of 1957, T. C. Smith said that twelve men "were quite close to
signing a pact to resign."[77] In June 1957 he told Binkley that fifteen professors
were "thoroughly dissatisfied."[78] Over the next twelve months the civil war grew
more intense until trustees fired thirteen of the dissident faculty.

REALISM AND THE DEFENSE OF THE FACULTY

The realist policy existed because the beliefs and aims of the seminary faculty
differed in significant ways from those of Southern Baptists generally. Since the

73. Wamble, "Conflict," 3:49–50.
74. Wamble, "Conflict," 3:50.
75. Wamble, "Conflict," 3:51–52.
76. Wayne Ward remembered a meeting in McCall's office about this time in which
McCall gave Ranson the same advice for writing a letter to trustee Edwin Gheens criticizing Wayne Oates and Wayne Ward as unscholarly.
77. Cited in Robert Alley, typescript of diary excerpts, p. 3, box 1, Theron D. Price
Papers, Special Collections, James B. Duke Library, Furman University.
78. T. C. Smith to Olin T. Binkley, 6 June 1957, 1957 Letters folder, box 40, Binkley
Papers, WFU.

1940s especially, the faculty had become broadly liberal in their theology and progressive in their social views. The realist policy was a means of preventing the differences between the faculty and the denomination from degenerating into open hostility. McCall's job was to persuade the denomination that the seminary was orthodox and worthy of the denomination's trust and support, and to persuade the faculty that the denomination was worthy of their loyalty and respect. He expended considerable energy in the 1950s attending to these two tasks. In 1957 and 1958 the tensions between the faculty and the denomination were high. Waves of accusations against the faculty crashed upon the seminary and kept McCall busy mending the fences.

On September 16, 1957, an ordination council set in motion a series of events that culminated in the dismissal of the thirteen. Hargus Taylor, a doctoral student in church history, sought ordination at Broadway Baptist Church. The pastor, Ed Perry, invited the members of the Louisville Baptist Pastors Conference to examine Taylor's qualifications. Taylor professed a progressive view of the inspiration of the Bible and defended the practices of open communion and receiving alien immersions as valid baptisms. Some voted against recommending him, and others abstained. As a result of the opposition Perry delayed more than a year before asking the church to ordain Taylor.[79]

When the candidate was a seminary student, ordination councils often had more to them than met the eye. Some pastors used them not merely to test the candidate but to try the seminary. Such ordination councils afforded an opportunity to investigate the faculty's teaching. More than two generations earlier, a minister questioned carefully John R. Sampey for an hour not because he doubted Sampey's soundness but because "I just wanted to get at Boyce, to see what he had been teaching the young fellow."[80] The 1957 council asked questions of Taylor designed to detect faculty heresies. What it found was troubling.

Taylor's views of the Lord's Supper and of alien immersions caused grave concern to the more conservative pastors, but his view of inspiration evoked the greatest concern.[81] One of the pastors reported that Taylor "did not believe

---

79. Wayne Oates, transcription of trustee interviews 28–30 Apr. 1958, 3:373–374.

80. John R. Sampey, *Memoirs of John R. Sampey* (Nashville, TN: Broadman Press, 1947), 36–37.

81. T. C. Smith claimed afterward that only Lewis Ray "gave any serious objection" to Taylor's statement on scripture, and even he was "partially convinced." The real objection, Smith said, was to Taylor's belief in open communion and the validity of "alien immersions." Smith seems to have misinterpreted the extent to which many of the pastors were troubled by Taylor's statements on the Bible. See T. C. Smith, transcription of trustee interviews 28–30 Apr. 1958, 3:335–337.

in the Bible as the inspired Word of God without many qualifications."[82] Taylor refused to say simply that the Bible was the Word of God. Taylor acknowledged that the Bible was authoritative for matters of faith, but he held that it was the Word of God only in a qualified sense. It was a witness to the central revelation of God in Jesus Christ, who was himself the true Word of God. The Bible, then, was not in a strict sense revelation, but a witness of the true revelation of God in the person of Jesus. When two faculty members on the council, Guy Ranson and T. C. Smith, agreed with Taylor's views, the concern deepened.[83] After the adjournment of the council some members stayed and discussed the troubling implications of what they had heard.

The view that the Bible was not the Word of God had become common among professors at Southern Baptist seminaries. Frank Stagg, who taught New Testament at New Orleans Baptist Theological Seminary and later at Southern Seminary, wrote in 1957 that he was careful in his teaching to avoid confusing the Bible with the word God: "It is customary to speak of the Bible as the Word of God, but we must not forget that the Bible itself calls Jesus the Word."[84] Harold Tribble, who taught theology at the seminary from 1925 to 1947, in his 1960 convention address more artfully declared that the Word of God was "not primarily a written word....It is the living word in Christ." The Bible's validity was in its faithful witness to Jesus Christ, the true Word of God.[85]

Several Louisville pastors paid Duke McCall a visit the following week to voice their concerns about heresy at the seminary. In subsequent months Louisville pastors kept up their pressure on McCall. Some faculty heard a report that the pastors would introduce a motion to the 1958 annual meeting of the Southern Baptist Convention asking the administration to dismiss five professors.[86]

Suspicion of the seminary's soundness had been growing for years. Trustees had repulsed Oscar Gibson's 1949 attack, but renewed attacks from many quarters kept alive nagging suspicions. The standard proof of the seminary's liberalism was the fact that the faculty invited Nels Ferré, professor of theology at Andover Newton Theological Seminary, to deliver its Julius Brown Gay Lectures in 1947. For more than twenty years the seminary's critics mined Ferré's publications for heretical statements that they could pin on the seminary as punishment for having invited him in 1947. E. S. James, editor of the

---

82. A. W. Walker to Louie Newton, 25 Feb. 1959, folder 56, J. D. Grey Papers.

83. See Robert S. Alley, typescript of diary excerpts, p. 1.

84. Frank Stagg to Clifton Allen, 10 June 1957, folder 10, box 2, Stagg Collection, Samford University.

85. Harold Tribble, "Address to the Southern Baptist Convention: The Word and the Way," Tribble Papers, WFU.

86. Wamble, "Conflict," 10:201; Alley, diary, 11 Mar. 1958 and 22 Apr. 1958.

Texas Baptist convention's *Baptist Standard*, informed McCall in 1955 that "no week passes in which I do not get a letter from somebody criticizing the seminary for inviting Dr. Nels F. S. Ferré to come before the student body there."[87] It was the most rhetorically powerful criticism, and perhaps the least accurate. President Ellis Fuller was embarrassed by some of Ferré's statements, and at the close of one of Ferré's lectures, Fuller addressed the audience and expressed his disagreement.

Another common argument adduced the fact that the faculty assigned reading from liberal books in their classes. Critics were especially concerned that in theology classes professor Dale Moody had substituted textbooks by the neo-orthodox theologian Emil Brunner in the place of the traditional textbook by E. Y. Mullins.[88] The parallel argument noted that they had studied under liberal professors. The fact that Dale Moody studied with Brunner in Germany and lived in his home for a year gave the argument credibility. Many Southern Baptists wondered why so many of the seminary's professors wanted to study with such men as H. Richard Niebuhr, Reinhold Niebuhr, Paul Tillich, or Emil Brunner unless they found their ideas attractive. They also attacked the seminary for its defense and promotion of the new Revised Standard Version, which translated several passages in ways offensive to orthodox views.

Much of the criticism came from persons outside the Southern Baptist Convention, especially from John R. Rice's immensely popular *Sword of the Lord*, from the Bible Baptist Fellowship's newspaper, the *Bible Baptist Tribune*, and from the *Sunday School Times*. Many Southern Baptists read these newspapers. McCall received many letters from Southern Baptist pastors seeking answers. "Some of our men get John R. Rice's paper *The Sword of the Lord*," a Mississippi pastor explained before asking if the charges were true.[89] Other Southern Baptists received such articles from helpful friends or relatives.

Such criticism received a boost when Raymond Waugh published his *Mythical Book of Southern Seminary* in 1954. Waugh attended the seminary in 1952 and 1953, but the faculty expelled him for "distortion and misrepresentation" of the seminary faculty in articles he wrote for a Kentucky fundamentalist newspaper. The book enumerated the errors of such theologians as Ferré and Brunner

87. E. S. James to Duke K. McCall, 29 Nov. 1955, Criticism of the Seminary folder, McCall Papers. James trusted that the seminary "was perfectly sound in the faith" but wanted information in order to answer such letters.

88. See, e.g., Duke K. McCall to L. E. Barton, 26 Mar. 1954, Criticism of the Seminary folder, McCall Papers.

89. Charles W. Clinton to Duke K. McCall, 18 Jan. 1955, Criticism of the Seminary folder, McCall Papers.

at length and strapped their errors on the faculty because they assigned their books and invited them to give lectures. The book got wide circulation and provoked much doubt about Southern's orthodoxy.[90]

But many Southern Baptists were just as critical. They too read the fundamentalist criticisms, and though they often doubted their accuracy, they were sufficiently disturbed to request explanations. Many Southern Baptists became convinced that two or three professors were heretics, and they too criticized the school, though usually in personal conversation or in small groups.

In 1954 Ramsey Pollard, a prominent Southern Baptist pastor, suggested to a conference audience that Southern Seminary was more liberal than Southwestern Seminary and that one of its faculty members rejected belief in the virgin birth of Christ.[91] L. E. Barton, a denominationally involved layman from Alabama, wrote McCall wondering why Moody assigned his theology students to read Emil Brunner's books instead of Mullins's textbook.[92]

Many pastors who discounted the accusations of fundamentalist newspapers believed the accusations of students. Many students told their experiences privately to trusted pastors or denominational leaders. Tom Dillon, a third-year student, complained to McCall in 1954 that the faculty were not loyal to the denomination and did not adhere to the Abstract of Principles. Theron Price and the religious education faculty, he said, took a critical stance toward the Southern Baptist Convention. He said that William Morton, Henry Turlington, Estill Jones, and J. J. Owens rejected the inspiration of the Bible, that Eric Rust rejected the eternal punishment of the wicked, and that generally the seminary promoted open communion and acceptance of alien immersions.[93] Whatever the source of the doubts, uncertainty about the seminary's soundness was spreading throughout the convention in the 1950s.

Pastors tried to shore up public confidence. A Colorado pastor tried to quell the fears of one of his leading laymen after he read Waugh's book. The man was a "highly educated chemist," a "consistent tither," and a supporter of the Southern Baptist Convention. "If I fail to answer to some degree of satisfaction

90. See, e.g., Joe May to Duke K. McCall, 25 Apr. 1954, Criticism of the Seminary folder, McCall Papers; McCall to Guy L. Prather, 13 July 1954, Sunday School Times Criticism folder, McCall Papers.

91. Duke K. McCall to Ramsey Pollard, 8 Sept. 1954, Criticism of the Seminary folder, McCall Papers.

92. L. E. Barton to Duke K. McCall, 21 Mar. 1954, Criticism 1951–1956 folder, McCall Papers.

93. Duke K. McCall, "Tom Dillon," ms. notes, 1954, Criticism of the Seminary folder, McCall Papers.

his statements, there is danger of his giving us some trouble." [94] There would be trouble because so many Southern Baptists found the thought of contributing to the salaries of professors who weakened faith in the Bible and its gospel message to be unconscionable. Because a portion of their offerings went to the Southern Baptist Theological Seminary, by their gifts they "partake of their evil deeds" and would have to give an account for this at the judgment seat of Christ. [95]

Many pastors nevertheless had questions concerning the soundness of the faculty. W. O. Vaught Jr., a prominent pastor in Arkansas, felt relief in McCall's election, because "I believe in your kind of Christianity." He felt that McCall would not tolerate false doctrine at the school: "All across the South there have been question marks placed around some of the professors there at Louisville.... With the message which you can deliver over the South, we can erase some of these questions in the minds of many of our preachers." [96]

Most Southern Baptists felt that the seminary was generally worthy of their trust, but they were troubled by the criticism. It shook their confidence in the seminary. And the seminary's reputation was critical to the entire Southern Baptist denominational program. Southern Baptist churches gave to the Cooperative Program, Southern Baptists' pooled funding channel, chiefly to finance evangelism in the United States and abroad. But most held that orthodoxy was a prerequisite of their support. It is not surprising, then, that when the Southern Baptist Convention adopted the Cooperative Program in 1925, it also adopted a confession of faith. If Southern Baptists doubted the orthodoxy of a cause, they lost interest in contributing to it. And many Southern Baptists found the criticisms of the seminary so troubling that they joined churches affiliated with the fundamentalist critics. In other instances, churches voted to withdraw from the Southern Baptist Convention because of the liberalism of the seminary. But most urged Southern Baptist leaders to protect the orthodoxy of their schools. Like hundreds of other Baptists, William D. Bowen, a retired preacher, urged McCall to "weed out modernistic teaching from the seminary," for "at least one modernist is a member of the faculty." [97]

94. E. J. Speegle to Duke K. McCall, 13 May 1957, Criticism of the Seminary folder, McCall Papers.

95. Clarence A. Pippin to E. J. Speegle and Rev. Stanton, 18 Mar. 1957, Criticism of the Seminary folder, McCall Papers.

96. W. O. Vaught Jr. to Duke K. McCall, 4 Sept. 1951, SBTS—Call folder, McCall Papers.

97. William D. Bowen to Duke K. McCall, 3 Sept. 1951, SBTS—Call folder, McCall Papers.

Southern Baptist Convention leaders recognized that the denomination's seminaries—since 1958 there have been six—played a critical role in the convention. The fortunes of their organizations were bound together with that of the seminaries. If Southern Baptists lost confidence in one denominational agency, it weakened the giving to all of them. But the seminaries had a special place. They had vast influence, for their graduates took pulpits in the leading churches and held positions of denominational leadership. Southern Baptists expected them to be bulwarks of orthodoxy and were especially sensitive to apparent departures, since any error introduced there would spread downstream to the churches.

McCall spent untold hours writing letters and meeting with pastors defending the seminary from the attacks of its critics. He assured Southern Baptists that the school was orthodox. He always explained that the orthodoxy of the professors was guaranteed by the fact that every professor signed the Abstract of Principles and agreed to teach in accordance with it. He generally argued that the quotes adduced as evidence of heresy were taken out of their context in ways that distorted their real meaning. He argued that Nels Ferré's views were far to the left of the seminary. He defended Moody's preference of Brunner over Mullins. In sum, McCall worked hard to distance the seminary from its growing reputation for liberalism.

McCall knew that it was critical that Southern Baptists have confidence in his own orthodoxy, and he repudiated any sympathy with liberalism. "There are too many liberal preachers in the Southern Baptist Convention," he said in 1957, "not many, but too many." [98] He declared that such liberal leaders as Harry Emerson Fosdick were unsound: "Fosdick should not be labeled an evangelical Christian." [99]

McCall pledged that he would not tolerate professors who held liberal views. He told outsiders that any professor who "rejected the virgin birth of Jesus" would be dismissed: "Anyone who should deny the virgin birth would cease to be a member of this faculty. The bodily resurrection of Christ is fundamental." [100] And in language that apparently reflected what he told faculty members, he wrote conservative pastor Ramsey Pollard: "To put it bluntly, any member of this faculty who does not believe in the virgin birth of Jesus of Nazareth will be fired." [101]

---

98. Duke K. McCall to Nelson E. Spinks, 22 Apr. 1957, Criticism of the Seminary folder, McCall Papers.

99. Duke K. McCall to Nelson E. Spinks, 22 Apr. 1957, Criticism of the Seminary folder, McCall Papers.

100. Duke K. McCall to A. S. Croom, 28 Feb. 1957, Criticism of the Seminary folder, McCall Papers.

101. Duke K. McCall to Ramsey Pollard, 8 Sept. 1954, Criticism of the Seminary folder, McCall Papers. See also Duke K. McCall to Mrs. Howard Jarvis, 26 Dec. 1957, Criticism of the Seminary folder, McCall Papers.

When a group of Louisville pastors asked McCall to meet with them at the offices of the Long Run Baptist Association in 1957, and presented him with a list of charges against several faculty members, he would not accept a copy of the charges. The pastors demanded that he initiate a trustee investigation of the teachings of the accused. He refused. He told them that "I had no intention of starting a heresy trial, that I would stake my job that every member of the faculty, whether I agreed with him theologically or not, was within the boundary of a legitimate Southern Baptist Theological Seminary professor's position." [102]

DEFENDING THE DENOMINATION BEFORE THE FACULTY

McCall could not persuade Southern Baptists of the seminary's orthodoxy without the faculty's help. The more faculty publicly criticized traditional orthodoxy and advanced liberal theology, the less effective were McCall's efforts. In the late 1950s, with the seminary besieged by critics, McCall repeatedly pleaded for the faculty's cooperation. Guy Ranson explained that in faculty meetings and chapel messages McCall "has repeatedly told us that there are various people who are bringing charges of heresy against us." [103] McCall tried to communicate to the faculty the importance of taking a more realistic and cautious approach to teaching progressive views. But the more he urged it, the more rebellious the dissenting faculty became.

McCall's efforts to persuade the faculty to be more cautious in teaching their views deepened the alienation of the dissident faculty. When McCall told them about accusations of heresy against the faculty, they told him that it was his job to refute them. When McCall advocated the use of more diplomatic language in teaching their views, they accused him of advocating doublespeak. When he explained how such accusations made the seminary's work more difficult, they thought he was threatening to dismiss them for failure to conform their teaching to accepted Southern Baptist views. Dissenting New Testament professor T. C. Smith explained that when McCall discussed such accusations of heresy, many faculty felt that they were being muzzled. They understood it as an implicit "threat to us if we didn't change the direction of teaching." [104]

102. Duke McCall, transcription of trustee interviews 28–30 Apr. 1958, 4:497–498.

103. Guy Ranson, transcription of trustee interviews 28–30 Apr. 1958, 1:96–98. Hugh Wamble said that McCall talked about outside criticism at half the faculty meetings in 1956 through 1958 (Hugh Wamble, Guy Ranson, transcription of trustee interviews 28–30 Apr. 1958, 2:175.

104. T. C. Smith, transcription of trustee interviews 28–30 Apr. 1958, 3:335. See also Hugh Wamble, transcription of trustee interviews 28–30 Apr. 1958, 2:175.

All this resulted in low morale among many of the faculty. Hugh Wamble, another dissenting professor, reflected later that McCall undermined faculty morale because when he received accusations against the professors' beliefs, he would "comment in faculty meetings about unspecified complaints on unspecified grounds against unspecified professors."[105] He was trying to make them understand the importance of their words. The seminary's reputation for orthodoxy was eroding seriously. If it continued, the faculty's position in the convention would be untenable.

Many professors also found these reminders demeaning to their standing as scholars. McCall, they believed, was infringing their freedom to teach scriptural truth when it differed with the majority opinion. They were the experts. They had studied the scriptures in the original languages, mastered sophisticated theological works, and studied with the world's great scholars. McCall's pleas seemed effectively to subordinate their studied conclusions to the untrained and unsophisticated opinions of Southern Baptists generally.

But the problem was larger than dealing with accusations that the faculty taught heresy. Some professors regularly criticized the programs and ethos of the denomination with that scornful superiority that is the occupational hazard of academics. Some students adopted the same critical attitudes. When McCall urged the faculty to be careful in their criticisms of the denomination, they felt that he was again demanding conformity to denominational beliefs and practices. Just as objectionable to them was the implication that they were disloyal to the denomination.[106] They protested their loyalty and stood on their vocational duty and the "Baptist" right to criticize. "Some members may have been rather free in criticizing some of our denominational programs or plans," church history professor William Lumpkin explained, "but we think that's the right of a theological faculty.... We reserve the right to dissent. That's a good Baptist point too, and we hold to it very dearly."[107]

On February 19, 1957, the faculty had a meeting with Courts Redford, president of Southern Baptist's Home Mission Board, during which some members of the faculty gave him a rough time.[108] Apparently they accused the board of conforming its policies to the popular sentiments of the Southern Baptist masses. Hugh Wamble criticized the Home Mission Board and the Illinois Baptist State

---

105. Wamble, "Conflict," 20:726.

106. Guy Ranson, transcription of trustee interviews 28–30 Apr. 1958, 1:96.

107. William Lumpkin, transcription of trustee interviews 28–30 Apr. 1958, 1:55. See, e.g., Guy Ranson, transcription of trustee interviews 28–30 Apr. 1958, 1:90.

108. Robert Alley, typescript of diary excerpts, p. 3. Alley recorded that T. C. Smith told him that Baker Cauthen, president of the Foreign Mission Board, was also present.

Association for requiring home missionaries to agree to close communion.[109] In McCall's March 1, 1957, chapel address, he rebuked the careless way in which unnamed persons criticized denominational agencies. Wamble understood McCall as demanding that faculty criticism of the denomination be "muzzled," and as accusing anyone who criticized established denominational ideas as disloyal to the denomination.[110]

McCall tried to explain that the faculty needed at least to have some respect for the beliefs and practices held by common Southern Baptists. When they advanced ecumenism, liberal theology, and the historical criticism of the Bible, and criticized Billy Graham, W. A. Criswell, or the mission boards, McCall observed, you "don't represent grassroots Baptists."[111] McCall recognized that since grassroots Baptists paid the piper, they had the right to call the tune.

At the May 22, 1957, school of theology faculty meeting, McCall again urged faculty to take a realistic approach and be more cautious and diplomatic. He said that Southern Seminary's reputation was tarnished in the convention. In the ensuing discussion, loyalist faculty sustained his concerns. Wayne Ward pointed out that such trustees as Warren Rust of Tennessee were disturbed by reports of unsound doctrine, especially relating to the New Testament faculty. Other faculty members worried about the criticism some faculty aimed at the Southern Baptist Convention. As a result, Allen Graves said, students develop a sneering attitude toward denominational agencies.[112]

In the fall of 1957 McCall intensified his efforts at persuading the faculty to follow the realist approach. The Hargus Taylor ordination council was the proximate cause, for it created a great deal of criticism from local pastors. In October McCall tried to explain in his chapel address the proper approach to the denomination. He criticized faculty and students who said publicly that the Bible was not the Word of God, because Jesus alone was the Word of God, as Hargus Taylor had said in his ordination council, and as another student had recently asserted in a sermon at an associational meeting. McCall said that "when you say in a public meeting of Baptists, 'The Bible is not the word of God,' you have communicated a lot of things that you didn't mean to communicate."[113] For most Baptists, to deny that the Bible was the Word of God was

---

109. Hugh Wamble to Courts Redford, 20 Feb. 1957, Wamble, Hugh folder, McCall Papers; Hugh Wamble to Noel Taylor, 20 Feb. 1957, ibid.
110. Wamble, "Conflict," 2:38.
111. Guy Ranson, transcription of trustee interviews 28–30 Apr. 1958, 1:99.
112. Wamble, "Conflict," 2:39.
113. Duke McCall, transcription of trustee interviews 28–30 Apr. 1958, 4:539.

heresy. If students or professors believed the Bible was God's revelation, McCall said, they should be able to communicate that fact clearly. McCall's point, doctoral student Robert Alley reported, was that anyone "who could not communicate that the Bible is the Word of God is a fool." [114]

Some faculty and students recognized that McCall was responding to the way that Hargus Taylor, T. C. Smith, and Guy Ranson had expressed their views at Taylor's ordination council. They judged that he had unkindly scolded the faculty in public. Theron Price and the dissenting faculty thought that he was threatening to fire them if they did not conform their teaching to popular Baptist orthodoxy. In the days after McCall's chapel address, Ranson reported that the faculty's controversy with McCall had grown critical. Price gave a chapel address the following week answering McCall's address. [115]

On November 6, McCall raised the subject again at a lunch with several faculty members. He criticized Taylor and urged the importance of learning how to communicate one's beliefs in a way that did not provoke suspicions of the school's orthodoxy. [116] In the faculty meeting later on the same day, he told the faculty that a group of local pastors had organized a group and made accusations of heresy against several faculty members. [117] McCall said that he wanted to know what they believed so that he could know how to answer the critics. He urged the importance of standing together on their common beliefs. But the faculty felt that McCall was siding with the critics, and they told him that his job was to defend the faculty against such heresy hunters. They felt also that he was unjustly demanding that they conform their speech to the beliefs of the Southern Baptist masses, whether speaking to students or church groups. [118] When James Smart visited the campus to deliver a set of lectures on religious education in March 1958, he told Robert Alley that he was "shocked by what he saw as oppressive demand for conformity at the school." [119]

The dissenters felt that the seminary president alone was responsible for public relations. They would do their job, proclaiming truth, and the president should do his, protecting the seminary from its foes. They did not therefore concern themselves with attacks on the seminary's orthodoxy. On April 28, 1958, as McCall was burdened by explosive faculty tensions, he felt beset by "incessant calls" charging faculty members with heresy. When he mentioned

114. Robert Alley, typescript of diary excerpts, p. 2.

115. Robert Alley, typescript of diary excerpts, p. 2.

116. Robert Alley, typescript of diary excerpts, p. 2.

117. Hugh Wamble to Duke McCall, memorandum, 7 Nov. 1957, Wamble, Hugh folder, McCall Papers.

118. Robert Alley, typescript of diary excerpts, p. 2.

119. Robert Alley, typescript of diary excerpts, 5 Mar. 1958.

this to Hugh Wamble, Wamble was unsympathetic. He told McCall not to tell the faculty about it, for in his view McCall was "solely responsible" for dealing with critics of the seminary.[120]

When McCall summarized for trustees the dissenters' objections to his leadership, this was one of his main conclusions. The professors expected him "to defend the faculty against various charges brought by Southern Baptists," but they took offense when he raised objections "to anything a faculty [member] says in or outside of the classroom, regardless of the import of the statement to the public relations of the seminary." They interpreted such actions as a "dictatorial" imposition of presidential authority.[121]

Allen Graves similarly judged that the dissenters' disregard of denominational realism was the central cause of the faculty conflict. When Hugh Wamble asked him how he thought the conflict between the dissenters and McCall could be solved, Graves urged them to conform better to denominational values. They "should come to the position where they could agree with what Southern Baptists are trying to do at the seminary." They positioned themselves against the denomination, Graves continued, and their persistent criticism made many students cynical toward the denomination's beliefs and practices. Wamble of course rebuffed Graves's advice.[122]

Many faculty members accepted the necessity of the realist approach. Clyde Francisco had yielded to Fuller's counsel on this point and was careful not to push the limit of denominational toleration. He appreciated the president's role in protecting the faculty from its critics. He told a student that "McCall is the best friend the thirteen men [the dissenters] have, but [they] don't realize it."[123] Herbert Jackson, professor of missions, recognized the "amazing degree of academic freedom" that McCall's efforts secured for the faculty. He felt that McCall had exerted himself far beyond the call of duty "to protect faculty members against attacks from the outside." If he had not so exerted himself, the trustees would long since have insisted that some of the dissenters "be given the 'freedom' to resign."[124]

The realist policy rested in the hope that gradual progress could be achieved by educating a cadre of cautious but progressive leaders. Progressive principles would spread slowly, but one day the denomination would be prepared to

---

120. Wamble, "Conflict," 5:90.

121. Duke McCall, "Report to the Trustee Subcommittee on the School of Theology in Session Tuesday, April 29, 1958," in Wamble, "Conflict," 6:122.

122. Wamble, "Conflict," 6:131.

123. Wamble, "Conflict," 7:143.

124. Herbert Jackson, Statement of May 6, 1958, in Wamble, "Conflict," 7:149.

listen to progressive ideas and arguments. The dissenters, however, were restive under constraints and tended to feel that gradual change was capitulation to the dominance of ignorance and error. They were not at all confident that gradual change alone could prevail over denominational ignorance.

THE PENDENNIS CLUB LUNCH

When McCall saw that many professors were growing restive, he invited eleven of them in February 1958 to lunch at the renowned Pendennis Club, a traditional spot for occasional seminary meetings.[125] The meeting lasted five hours. The main topic of conversation revolved around McCall's question, "What is the duty of the seminary as you understand it?"[126] The professors shared their opinions, and McCall shared his. There was an obvious difference of views.[127]

The majority, Hugh Wamble noted two days afterward, held that the seminary should serve the denomination by unfettered pursuit of truth. It was their duty to pursue truth even if it led the seminary to oppose traditional Southern Baptist views. Because the seminary would "always be out in front of the general thinking," it would sometimes have a critical posture toward the denomination. If the seminary refused its duty of critical pursuit of truth, it abandoned education for indoctrination.[128]

McCall sought to instruct the professors in the protocols of realist diplomacy. He told them that the seminary held promise as the most powerful long-term influence on the denomination. It was "the center of real power" in the Southern Baptist Convention. But if the seminary assumed a critical posture toward the denomination, it would destroy its long-term influence.

But the professors took issue with the implications of McCall's argument. They held that what McCall was suggesting was that they stifle dissent from denominational views. This, they said, would only aid the trend toward the centralization of power in the convention. They apparently saw McCall's administration as a part of the trend, for they began to recite the problems at the seminary in terms of McCall's exercise of executive power. They wanted

---

125. The eleven were Morris Ashcraft, Ralph Elliott, Tom Hall, Herbert Jackson, Estill Jones, John Lewis, J. J. Owens, Heber Peacock, Henry Turlington, Hugh Wamble, and Wayne Ward. All except Elliott, Jackson, and Ward were among the thirteen dismissed on 12 June 1958. See Wamble, "Conflict," 3:55.

126. Wamble, "Conflict," 3:55.

127. See Wayne Ward, transcription of trustee interviews 28–30 Apr. 1958, 3:417–418.

128. Wamble, "Conflict," 3:55.

democratic procedure to prevail—McCall should take his cues from the will of the majority expressed in faculty meetings.[129]

McCall objected that the dissenters had derailed democratic process. Price was usually the heavyweight in faculty meeting discussions, and Ranson and Smith gave him strong support. Some professors had stopped voicing their dissent from Price, either intimidated by Price's influence or discouraged by the heavy fire and "harsh floor tactics" they had to endure.[130] He made it clear that the seminary was not a democracy and that he would exercise executive authority. He would communicate in advance which way things would go. Anyone who refused to get aboard and who challenged the direction after it was set would "get hurt."[131] McCall was trying to say that a "man must accept responsibility for the freedom he exercises."[132] The dissenting professors thought that McCall was threatening to dismiss those who did not censor themselves.

INTEGRITY, PLAGIARISM, AND THE CENTENNIAL HISTORY

In the fall and winter of the 1957–1958 session, the conflict between McCall and the dissenting faculty turned personal. In March 1954 the trustees had appointed McCall to write a complete history of Southern Seminary to be published in conjunction with its centennial observance in 1959. McCall asked William Mueller to "help with research and some of the drafting of the material."[133] He asked Loulie Owens, head of the South Carolina Baptist Historical Society, to do the same. McCall wanted them to submit their materials by the summer of 1957.[134]

Instead of gathering and organizing research for McCall, Mueller started producing a full manuscript. The more he worked on it, the more he viewed it as his own project. He began to complain to other faculty that McCall wanted

---

129. McCall apparently insinuated that Price, Ranson, and Smith could administer rough discipline in floor debates (Wamble, "Conflict," 3:57).

130. These are McCall's words from the Pendennis Club lunch, speaking of "unfair" floor debate in faculty meetings, and understood by those present to refer to Price, Ranson, and Smith (Wamble, "Conflict," 3:57).

131. Wamble, "Conflict," 3:56.

132. Wayne Ward, transcription of trustee interviews 28–30 Apr. 1958, 3:416.

133. Duke McCall to Loulie Latimer Owens, 22 Oct. 1956, Mueller History of the Seminary folder, McCall Papers.

134. For McCall's account of the affair, see Duke McCall, transcription of trustee interviews 28–30 Apr. 1958, 4:482–494.

Norton Hall (foreground), Fuller Hall (back left), and Mullins Hall (back right)

to put his name on Mueller's work. Tension between Mueller and McCall mounted during the fall of 1957.[135]

The seminary's centennial committee tried to mediate.[136] When Mueller insisted, however, that the book should be his own, McCall saw no alternative but for the seminary to relinquish responsibility for the book. Trustees agreed and formally reassigned the book to Mueller.[137] Broadman Press editor William Fallis edited the manuscript extensively and composed additional material before releasing it in 1959.

Throughout the fall and winter of 1957–1958, Mueller poured out his anxieties regarding McCall and the book to his colleagues. Many on the faculty believed that McCall treated Mueller unjustly and that McCall wanted Mueller to ghostwrite the book for him.

135. Herbert Jackson, chairman of the seminary's centennial committee, viewed it this way. Herbert Jackson, transcription of trustee interviews 28–30 Apr. 1958, 3:384–385.

136. Minutes of the Joint Chairmen of the Centennial Committees, 17 Dec. 1957, Mueller History of the Seminary folder, McCall Papers.

137. Minutes, Executive Committee of the Board of Trustees, 21 Jan. 1958. McCall wrote a detailed statement of his and Mueller's differences on the book ("Statement," 19 Dec. 1957, Mueller History of the Seminary folder, McCall Papers).

Other faculty had a similar experience. They accused McCall of plagiarizing the work of several professors in a set of Sunday school lessons titled *Broadman Comments*. The Sunday School Board of the Southern Baptist Convention invited McCall to write a weekly lesson for its 1958 curriculum. He accepted with the knowledge that he would ask some faculty members to assist him by doing background research and presenting ideas for each lesson. John Lewis, professor of Old Testament, initially agreed to do the job. When Lewis realized that he could not do it all himself, McCall asked other faculty members to help.[138] Some submitted rough research, but most submitted finished prose. When McCall wrote the final copy, he sometimes incorporated the finished material with little or no revision.

When the faculty saw the published product in December 1957, they recognized places where McCall had incorporated their work wholesale. McCall gave no notice anywhere in the volume that he had relied on their research or incorporated their writing. He had not promised them that he would give them credit, nor did he promise that he would not incorporate their work word for word, but some of the professors felt that he had no right to do so, since he had indicated that it was his intention to take their rough work and rework it with his own material and ideas. The faculty were effectively ghostwriters for significant portions of the material.[139] This was troubling as a basic matter of honesty—McCall claimed credit for writing what was only partly his. For faculty in higher education, publishing was a fundamental criterion of job performance and professional success, and it was assumed to reflect one's own analysis and composition. By scholarly standards, it appeared a straightforward instance of plagiarism.

McCall afterward acknowledged that he acted unwisely in this matter. He was less certain that he acted unethically. He felt that he and the professors had voluntarily entered a mutually beneficial agreement—he paid each man fifteen dollars per lesson, about two-thirds of what the Sunday School Board paid him. He was sure, however, that if it was wrong for him to buy and incorporate the faculty's work, it could hardly have been right for them to sell it to him.[140] It was not scholarship but popular Sunday school literature and could not be plagiarism. Here, as elsewhere in the controversy, so much hinged on how one viewed its character. The faculty viewed it by the standard of the academy. McCall viewed it by the demands of denominational effectiveness.

138. See, e.g., Duke McCall, memo to Henlee Barnette, 9 Jan. 1957, Barnette Papers, WFU.

139. John Lewis, transcription of trustee interviews 28–30 Apr. 1958, 3:303–312.

140. For McCall's interpretation of the events, see Duke McCall, transcription of trustee interviews 28–30 Apr. 1958, 4:462–481.

THE 1958 FACULTY REPORT

In January 1958 doctoral student Robert Alley summarized the conflict between McCall and the dissenting faculty in terms of eight "basic disagreements." Alley had unusual access to information. He was the manager of the Faculty Center, a two-story home converted to provide housing for campus guests. The basement hosted many faculty and trustee meetings. Alley's responsibilities afforded unusual opportunity to converse with the denominational leaders, trustees, and faculty who frequented the center. His responsibilities also kept him within earshot of luncheon conversations and basement meetings. And dissenting professors T. C. Smith and Guy Ranson kept Alley and several other graduate students informed of the group's thoughts and plans. His father, Reuben Alley, editor of Virginia Baptists' *Religious Herald*, became involved in the conflict and included his son in his conversations with trustees and faculty. As the crisis deepened, he was something of an information broker for many of those involved.

Alley's list of eight disagreements resolved into three basic issues. First was McCall's effort to persuade faculty to embrace a realist approach to denominational relations, which they interpreted as a demand for conformity to approved denominational views. Alley placed the "demand for conformity" first on his list. Two other items related directly to the matter of conformity, the Hargus Taylor ordination and McCall's chapel talks. A second basic issue was that of control of the seminary—two items related to faculty appointments and one to the authority of the deans. Finally, two items referred to a third basic issue, the issue of McCall's integrity—the 1958 *Broadman Comments* matter and the centennial history authorship.[141]

In the twelve months since McCall rejected Ranson's proposal of William Morton as dean, the dissenting faculty had become a coalition unified around a shared dissatisfaction with McCall's leadership. Its leaders were Theron Price, Guy Ranson, and T. C. Smith, but the group solidified with little deliberate planning. Discussions in the faculty lounge, where professors gathered several times a day for coffee breaks, became natural caucuses of opposition to McCall. Here they vented their complaints, shared the latest news, voiced their fears, and discussed the seminary's future. There was no membership list, only a profound sense of shared persecution, concern, and purpose.

Many in the group had resolved to resign as soon as they could get a position elsewhere. But as they discussed the alternatives, they concluded that their duty to the school and the denomination required them to inform the trustees of the

141. Robert Alley, typescript of diary excerpts, p. 5.

critical nature of the problem. If trustees did not act, then they would feel free to resign. Theron Price, for example, convinced William Lumpkin in the fall of 1957 that they should seek help from the trustees before resigning.[142] Their hope all along was that the trustees would either direct McCall to give the faculty more control or dismiss him.

They appealed for trustee intervention in March 1958 in their annual faculty report to the trustees. The report complained of low faculty morale and implied that it was due mainly to McCall's refusal to include the faculty in decision making.[143] It effectively invited trustees to investigate the source of the problem. The three who wrote the faculty report, William Lumpkin, Morris Ashcraft, and John Lewis, were members of the dissenting group. Before drafting the report, they asked faculty members to submit their concerns and recommendations. When they presented their draft to the theology faculty on March 10, 1958, the faculty adopted the report after some discussion and some revision. They persuaded all but two to vote for it.[144] The faculty could generally agree that morale was low, but they disagreed on the source of the problem. The dissenters saw the president as the problem; many other faculty members saw the dissenters themselves as the main problem.

The faculty report reflected the conundrum that the dissenters faced. They needed to gain more power for the faculty without asking for it directly and without protesting the president's official powers. The trustees had made it clear that they insisted on an executive president. The dissenters, Theron Price said later, hoped to gain either "some kind of restraints set" to limit McCall's authority or else McCall's removal.[145] If they explicitly said what they wanted, they would get no hearing from the trustees.

The report paid its respects to executive authority but made it clear that the faculty should have a share in governing such matters as faculty hiring and selection of a dean. The selection of the dean "should be a joint effort of administration and faculty." Such decision should be mutual, "made in closest cooperation with the faculty." The report asked for the faculty's effective control over the seminary's academic programs without directly challenging McCall's executive authority.

142. Robert Alley, typescript of diary excerpts, p. 3.

143. The report also complained of inadequate salaries, but the main issue was McCall's governance of the school.

144. Hugh Wamble and T. C. Smith remembered that the two were Wayne Oates and Herbert Jackson (Wamble, "Conflict," 3:60).

145. Theron Price, transcription of trustee interviews 28–30 Apr. 1958, 1:80. See also John Lewis, transcription of trustee interviews 28–30 Apr. 1958, 3:295–296. For statements relating to McCall's removal, see below.

Most trustees and interested observers recognized that whatever objections the dissenters had to McCall personally, they objected strongly to the seminary's structure of authority. Wayne Oates correctly observed that despite their denials, Price and Ranson in particular aimed to overturn the president's exclusive authority and that they believed that "it is a part of their Christian calling to try to change it." [146] McCall reported that Price's many arguments with him concerning the legitimacy of his authority always resolved into one point: "As long as you have authority to veto faculty recommendations, this is a matter of Christian conscience with me, that this is something that has to be altered." [147]

The faculty report did not please McCall, who urged the faculty not to adopt it. He objected to its harsh tone, its complaint of low morale, and its strictures on administrative policies. McCall viewed its specific complaints in light of the long faculty struggle against his executive power. He pleaded with the faculty to revise the report at these points and warned that if the faculty adopted this report, they were throwing down the "gauntlet," and he would have to pick it up. [148]

THE TRUSTEE MEETING

When trustees gathered on campus for their annual meeting, a committee of six professors from the school of theology met with the trustee committee for the school and submitted the faculty report. McCall told trustees that the tensions existed because some professors would not accept the authority structure investing the president with executive power. They were unrealistic. They pursued truth relentlessly and felt that truth, not the principles of business management, should rule in all seminary affairs. They were "not conformists to traditional patterns." They resented and opposed "any restraint which would hinder them in their pursuit" of truth. This was the reason, McCall explained, that they tended to view McCall's exercise of authority as a restraint on their calling to promote truth. [149]

And the dissenting faculty, McCall wrote, held that truth would prevail only in a spiritual environment in which Christian scholars could argue their ideas

---

146. Wayne Oates, transcription of trustee interviews 28–30 Apr. 1958, 3:376–377.

147. Duke McCall, transcription of trustee interviews 28–30 Apr. 1958, 4:550.

148. Wamble, "Conflict," 3:60.

149. Duke McCall, "Special Report on the Faculty of the School of Theology," in Wamble, "Conflict," 4:64–65.

freely as equals. With open expression and argument of ideas, the truth would prevail and the seminary would find its way to make its proper contribution to the kingdom of God. They held that an unequal distribution of authority created "organizational barriers to the creation of Christian fellowship" and open communication. They believed that it prevented them from becoming a truly "Christian" faculty, since an administrative hierarchy and an executive president hindered the free pursuit of truth and thwarted the seminary's vocation. That vocation, the dissenters held, was to serve the denomination "by being a critic" of the denomination's theology and practices. They believed that McCall obstructed the seminary's vocation because he was anti-intellectual and a denominational loyalist.[150]

The dissenting faculty held that an executive president exercising unilateral authority was inconsistent with the Christian faith. Dissenting church history professor William Lumpkin hoped for "some alteration in the structure affecting our relationship between administration and faculty," and for "less authority in the hands of the president." He explained that a Baptist seminary, to be "true to our Baptist concepts," should have more "democracy."[151] William Morton told trustees that there are "studies" that demonstrated that the seminary's structure was not the best one. He had in mind apparently Richard Niebuhr's *Advancement of Theological Education*. He suggested that their conflict could be resolved in the light of "such things as are set forth in that very well known and highly regarded Niebuhr report on theological education."[152]

When the matter came before the full board on March 12, McCall explained the situation at length. Robert Alley overheard his comments: "He said things were bad on the faculty and would not get better till some members left, that he had tried to give the faculty a hand in choosing faculty and they made a mess, that the professors who went to Yale were the chief troublemakers,... that the New Testament department had broken with the spirit of A. T. Robertson and was making a mess,... that the faculty did not care whether new members

---

150. Duke McCall, "Special Report on the Faculty of the School of Theology," in Wamble, "Conflict," 4:67–68.

151. William Lumpkin, transcription of trustee interviews 28–30 Apr. 1958, 1:52–53, 46, 53–54.

152. William Morton, transcription of trustee interviews 28–30 Apr. 1958, 1:12–14, 24–25. The transcriptionist rendered the line on pp. 24–25 as "such things as I set forth in that very well known and highly regarded legal report on theological education." The context makes it clear that Morton had reference to the Niebuhr report. He had already commended it to the attention of trustees to illuminate issues of authority. Morton had published nothing on the matter.

were loyal to the SBC."[153] The full board passed a motion instructing the trustee committee for the school of theology to meet the six-member faculty committee to communicate clearly that the board saw no need to alter the authority structure or to give instructions to the president. They were also to inform the faculty that the board had full confidence in McCall's leadership and vision of theological education. The board sided with the president: "We solicit the cooperation of the members of the faculty of the school of theology."[154]

This was not the response that the dissenters wanted, but they made the best of it at the March 13 faculty meeting. The trustee statement affirmed "the principle of counsel between the administration and faculty," and Price interpreted it as the controlling idea of the trustee response.[155] McCall interpreted it as a reaffirmation of the president's authority. The meeting became contentious. Theron Price's speeches contradicting McCall's interpretation set the tone of the discussion. Price first noted that the faculty had not asked the trustees to change the administrative structure, and so there was no occasion for reaffirming it—the trustee response could not mean what McCall indicated. Ironically, Price then began to criticize the administrative structure: "Too much authority must not be allowed, and a good board would not have given it to the president. As Lord Acton said, 'Power corrupts and absolute power corrupts absolutely.' It is not good for the president to have such power, such complete power, for it will harm him spiritually." Baptists, Price continued, believed in democracy: "They have distributed power among the members of the community." Because of sinfulness in human nature, Price said, "no man can wield great power without threat to his soul, and we should share some of the president's responsibility for his own good." When McCall pointed out that Price's statements related directly to the seminary's authority structure, Price acknowledged that he thought the "structure itself is deplorable."[156]

McCall left the faculty meeting convinced that if the trustees' reaffirmation of the seminary's structure would not deter Price and his followers from making war on his authority, nothing would. It was a refusal to cooperate constructively with the trustees and the administration. It was rebellion.

153. Robert Alley, typescript of diary excerpts, 12 Mar. 1958.

154. Minutes, Board of Trustees, 13 Mar. 1958.

155. Theron Price told the trustee theology committee on 8 May 1958 that their 12 Mar. 1958 response to the faculty letter rebuked the president's exercise of authority: "It appeared that you advised the president to work problems out with counsel." Price, cited in Wamble, "Conflict," 8:168.

156. Theron Price, quoted in Wamble, "Conflict," 5:74–75. See also Duke McCall's description of the speech in Duke McCall, transcription of trustee interviews 28–30 Apr. 1958, 4:511–512.

THE SUPPLEMENTARY REPORT

In the days following the March trustee meeting, the dissenters were disconsolate. They began making their plans to find employment elsewhere. Lumpkin told his graduate seminar good-bye. Henry Turlington said that he wanted to take a church. T. C. Smith told another graduate student that the faculty was on the verge of resigning. Price expected that "they might all resign" in the spring of 1959.[157]

When McCall seemed to be laying plans to fire Price and Ranson, the dissenters decided to make a more pointed appeal. On March 27, 1958, McCall again made a long statement to the faculty explaining his interpretation of the trustees' response to the faculty. The trustees, he said, had reaffirmed their understanding that the president will decide seminary issues, not the faculty. This was the baseline, and the trustees would not change this. The time was long past that the faculty should accept this. Resistance of the president's authority had kept the seminary in crisis. It must cease. McCall continued, "If you feel constrained of conscience to be a rebel warring against the organization and constituted authority (administration, trustees, and denomination) of the seminary, you are requested to find a more compatible place than this, that you may be happy and that we may get on about our task without repeated crises. I hope that we can each and all find fulfillment of our Christian calling here, but the welfare of the whole is more important than any of its parts."[158] Price and Ranson would either stop fomenting rebellion or they would find employment elsewhere.

McCall was determined to have a resolution of the tensions that had long plagued the school, and on April 15 he met with Price. Price reported to his colleagues afterward that McCall told him to stop criticizing McCall's administration. If Price refused, he would have to resign or face dismissal. Price reported that he made no concession. On the contrary, Price said that he warned McCall "not to force this issue."[159] Ranson believed that he too faced dismissal.[160] McCall reported that he told Ranson, "You will have to cease to use invectives in discussing the president and give some evidence that you are

157. Robert Alley, typescript of diary excerpts, 12 Mar. 1958, 14 Mar. 1958, 17 Mar. 1958, and 11 Apr. 1958.

158. Duke McCall, "Statement to the Joint Faculty," in Wamble, "Conflict between Authority and Conscience," electronic typescript, 6:98.

159. Duke McCall, transcription of trustee interviews 28–30 Apr. 1958, 4:502–503, 508; Theron Price, quoted in Wamble, "Conflict," 5:86.

160. Wamble, "Conflict," 6:99.

not, as interpreted by a number of colleagues, trying to discredit and displace the president."[161]

The dissenters took alarm. On April 16 Ranson was "desperate" and went to see Robert Alley for more information. He wanted to know if Alley had heard what McCall told the trustees in the March 12 meeting. Alley recounted everything, including McCall's statement that the Yale men were the chief troublemakers and that the situation would not improve until some faculty members left.[162]

On April 23 Alley informed Ranson and others that Wade Bryant, chairman of the trustee board, believed that Price was the main troublemaker and that he must go.[163] The same day the faculty learned that the trustee committee for the school of theology was returning to campus on April 28 and 29 and that the trustees might want to speak with various members of the faculty and staff.[164] McCall had already informed Price that he should keep his calendar clear on April 28. The only reasonable conclusion was that McCall would use the committee's investigation to dismiss Price and Ranson.[165]

As the day of the trustee investigation neared, the news of the installation of recording equipment in the Faculty Center conference room spread rapidly and deepened the sense of the gravity of the proceedings. The impending inquisition electrified the dissenting faculty, who felt themselves bound together by a common fate. They had to do something to avert Price's martyrdom. They decided to compel the committee to turn their meeting into an inquisition against McCall.

On April 18 seven professors, Theron Price, Guy Ranson, T. C. Smith, Hugh Wamble, William Morton, Morris Ashcraft, and John Lewis, met in Smith's home to discuss their course of action. They considered resigning en masse but felt that they had a duty to the trustees to inform them of the causes of

---

161. Duke McCall, transcription of trustee interviews 28–30 Apr. 1958, 4:528. See also Wayne Oates, "Personal Reflections on the Controversy and Crisis at Southern Seminary," 24 June 1958, 14, Faculty Controversy 1958—Corr. with Faculty and Staff folder, McCall Papers. See, similarly, Henlee Barnette, "The Crisis at Southern Baptist Seminary: An Interpretation," ms., 1, Barnette Papers, WFU.

162. Robert Alley, typescript of diary excerpts, 16 Apr. 1958.

163. Robert Alley, typescript of diary excerpts, 22 Apr. 1958 and 23 Apr. 1958.

164. Wamble, "Conflict," 5:92.

165. Duke McCall, "Report to the Trustee Committee on School of Theology of the Southern Baptist Theological Seminary," in Wamble, "Conflict between Authority and Conscience," electronic typescript, 6f:96, 98–99. Wamble recorded in contemporary notes that McCall recited this explanation of his strategy at a meeting with seven of the thirteen on 12 May 1958 (Wamble, "Conflict," 9:184).

the seminary troubles. They considered asking the trustees to dismiss McCall but concluded that this was unrealistic. Trustees would dismiss McCall only if they understood the full extent of his "arbitrary, abusive, oppressive, vindictive, and manipulative exercise of presidential prerogatives." They decided to draw up a list of grievances and present it to the trustees, "hoping that the trustees would exercise their legal responsibilities for the seminary's well-being," that is, that they would restrain or dismiss McCall. They called their petition "A Supplementary Report to the Trustees of Southern Baptist Seminary."[166]

They knew that there were six other professors who would want to partic-ipate in drafting and submitting the statement of grievances: Tom Hall, Estill Jones, Henry Turlington, J. J. Owens, William Lumpkin, and Heber Peacock. They considered approaching three others, Wayne Ward, Vernon Stanfield, and Jesse Weatherspoon, but for various reasons chose not to ask them.[167] Some of these thirteen men did not share completely Price's vision for theological edu-cation, but they all interpreted the current crisis as he did and shared his view of McCall's actions and his fear of McCall's executive power of appointment, promotion, and dismissal of faculty. And there was an additional motive: self-preservation. Those who did not join the dissenting group would be left on the outside and marginalized if Price succeeded in removing McCall and restoring faculty rights.[168] Those who joined the winning side would be the leadership in the new seminary order.[169]

They "crossed the Rubicon" on April 28, 1958.[170] The thirteen met that morn-ing and subscribed to the final version of their "Supplementary Report." The trustee committee, as yet unaware of the thirteen's efforts, had gathered at the Faculty Center and were organizing and planning their interviews. William Morton presented the document to the trustee committee and invested the act

166. Wamble, "Conflict," 6:100–101.

167. Wamble, "Conflict," 6:102. Ward remembers that some did ask him to join with them, as did Hugh McElrath (David N. Carle, "A History of the School of Church Music of the Southern Baptist Theological Seminary, 1944–1959," D.M.A. diss., Southern Baptist Theological Seminary, 1986, 152).

168. Clyde Francisco believed that two of his Old Testament colleagues received this impression. Clyde Francisco, transcription of trustee interviews 28–30 Apr. 1958, 3:395. Some of the thirteen said this to Wayne Ward (Wayne Oates, "Personal Reflections on the Controversy and Crisis at Southern Seminary," 24 June 1958, 9, Faculty Controversy 1958—Corr. with Faculty and Staff folder, McCall Papers).

169. Wayne Ward, transcription of trustee interviews 28–30 Apr. 1958, 3:430.

170. They used this metaphor a number of times to refer to their action. See, e.g., Wayne Ward, transcription of trustee interviews 28–30 Apr. 1958, 3:429; Wamble, "Conflict," 8:169–170.

with all the nobility of Martin Luther's unyielding stand before the Holy Roman Emperor Charles V at the 1521 Diet of Worms. Robert Alley recorded the event: "At about 3:50 Dr. Morton arrived with the faculty statement. He spoke briefly to us and movingly stated the faculty position. In a voice emotion ridden he spoke about the necessity to take a stand, God help them, they could do nothing else. I doubt we will ever forget the moment."[171]

The "Supplementary Report" was a bill of indictment. In it the thirteen made a number of charges against McCall and supported each charge with specific words and deeds. They charged him first with making threats against faculty members as a means of quashing dissent from his views. They charged second that McCall was deceptive in inviting faculty to participate in such decisions as promotion and hiring when he regularly decided these issues apart from or contrary to faculty advice. They charged third that his methods of leadership were manipulative and duplicitous, utilizing political tactics and insincere speech to get his designs accomplished. They charged him finally with plagiarism in his *Broadman Comments* volume.[172]

Regarding the fundamental charge, McCall insisted that it was ultimately his responsibility to decide such matters as promotion and hiring recommendations, and he resolved that he would not be bound by faculty recommendations. He nevertheless often followed faculty counsel, sometimes against his own preferences. He had hired Guy Ranson largely on Price's recommendation and against his own better judgment.[173] Many of the loyalist faculty indeed faulted McCall for tolerating Price and Ranson so long. Herbert Jackson, professor of missions, thought that McCall had been too "democratic and lenient."[174]

The "Supplementary Report" set the terms of the discussion. The trustees would now have to investigate the thirteen's accusations against the president instead of his accusations against Price. The trustee committee did as the thirteen expected and investigated the charges against McCall. On April 28, 29, and 30 they interviewed McCall, twelve of the thirteen signers of the "Supplemental Report," and ten other faculty. The thirteen had put McCall on the defensive—he was no longer setting the agenda. Smith reported a few days afterward that he thought McCall was scared.[175] Robert Alley wrote that

171. Robert Alley, typescript of diary excerpts, 28 Apr. 1958.

172. Morton et al., "A Supplementary Report to the Trustees of Southern Baptist Seminary," in Wamble, "Conflict," 6:108–115.

173. Duke McCall, "Report to the Trustee Subcommittee on the School of Theology in Session Tuesday, April 29, 1958," in Wamble, "Conflict," 6:120.

174. Jackson, statement, in Wamble, "Conflict," 7:149.

175. Robert Alley, typescript of diary excerpts, 4 May 1958.

T. C. Smith told him about the meetings at his home and described the thirteen's approach as a "plan to threaten resignation unless McCall is fired.... either the faculty or McCall must go." [176] Wayne Ward remembers Price warning him that McCall would soon be gone: "We are going to hang McCall from the highest pole in the SBC." [177] They had determined that either McCall had to leave or they would, and they preferred to stay.

But they knew that their bid was risky. It was easy to predict that trustees would rally to McCall's support. All except Owens agreed that they were willing to lose their jobs if the trustees did not take action. [178] Guy Ranson wrote Carlyle Marney on April 23 predicting that he would soon lose his job and asking for help finding a church position. [179]

The trustees indeed proved unsympathetic to the thirteen's point of view. On May 8 the trustee committee returned again to campus and met with eleven of the thirteen. The professors pleaded with the trustees to take decisive action. They tried to make it clear that they could not remain unless there was radical change in the administration. But the majority of the trustee committee agreed with McCall that the real source of controversy was the thirteen's unwillingness to accept the president's authority. The thirteen found the trustees' response disappointing and "unsatisfactory." They felt that the trustees "failed to perceive the gravity of the situation." They speculated, however, that the trustees were privately pressing McCall to amend his behavior. Their only hope, however slight it may have been, was to convince the full board of trustees to see McCall as they saw him. [180] So they resolved to appeal over the heads of the trustee committee and take the matter to the full board. They sent copies of the "Supplementary Report" to every trustee in advance of the board's scheduled meeting on May 23, 1958, in Houston, Texas. [181]

At the Houston meeting, the board of trustees adopted the school of theology committee's report reaffirming the board's establishment of the president as the "executive head of the institution with the authorities and responsibilities usually pertaining to such an office." The seminary's recent experiences "demonstrated anew the necessity for vesting in the president of Southern Baptist Theological Seminary full administrative authority and responsibility. In administering both the administrative and academic affairs of the seminary

176. Robert Alley, typescript of diary excerpts, 22 Apr. 1958.

177. Wayne Ward, oral history, 4 Oct. 2005, 3, SBTS.

178. Wamble, "Conflict," 6:103.

179. Guy Ranson to Carlyle Marney, 23 Apr. 1958, box 38, Carlyle Marney Papers, Rare Book, Manuscript, and Special Collections Library, Duke University.

180. Wamble, "Conflict," 9:190.

181. Wamble, "Conflict," 8:178–179.

the president is expected, at times, to consult with faculty and staff members to secure their counsel." The trustees recommended that persons who were "in rebellion against the policies adopted by the board" should "seek a climate in which they can work happily for our denomination." They concluded that "consistent and continued disagreement indicates a basic disharmony which makes cooperation impossible." [182]

The dissenters continued the fight because they had come to conceive of their struggle in stark moral terms. T. C. Smith told McCall that "he was not a Christian and that he was a blasphemer when he used the Bible." [183] In a letter to a colleague, Wamble likened McCall's play for power to that of Hitler. [184] It had become a battle between good and evil. When their prospects of success dimmed after May 8, Wamble urged them to continue united in their struggle: "More and more, I have the feeling of conscience that we are here because God brought us to this hour." Conscience compelled them to drink the "painful cup" in order to vindicate "the biblical truths, Christian faith, Baptist principles, and Christian and ethical ideals" upon which they took their stand. [185]

Consequently, the thirteen judged those who did not support them in the worst light. Those who supported the president had "sold out to McCall," had some hidden agenda, or were duped. They did not believe that rational persons would defend McCall's actions. The reason that the trustee majority supported McCall's view through it all was because the president "had every meeting rigged" to prevent examination of the "real issues." [186] Ranson told trustee chairman Wade Bryant that trustees had plunged the seminary "into almost total destruction" because "you permitted McCall to trick you." Trustees had not yet approached the problem "courageously and intelligently." [187] He expressed it with yet more condescension to liberal pastor Carlyle Marney: "The trustees sure are dumb." [188] Hugh Wamble told trustee Norman Shands that "you and other trustees have been hoodwinked by the president." [189]

182. "Report of the Committee on the School of Theology to the Full Board of Trustees," in Minutes, Board of Trustees, Southern Baptist Theological Seminary, 23 May 1958.

183. Robert Alley, typescript of diary excerpts, 17 Apr. 1958.

184. Hugh Wamble to Dale Moody, 23 June 1958, in Wamble, "Conflict," 12:312, n. 156.

185. Wamble, "Conflict," 9:188.

186. Hugh Wamble to J. Newton Rayzor, 15 Nov. 1958, in Wamble, "Conflict," 20:611.

187. Guy Ranson to Wade Bryant, 6 Apr. 1959, Guy Ranson folder, McCall Papers.

188. Guy Ranson to Carlyle Marney, 7 Apr. 1959, box 38, Carlyle Marney Papers.

189. Hugh Wamble to Norman Shands, 5 July 1958, in Wamble, "Conflict," 13:364. See also Norman Shands to Hugh Wamble, 2 July 1958, in Wamble, "Conflict," 13:361.

THE DISMISSAL OF THE THIRTEEN

The thirteen planned to resign if the trustees at the Houston meeting adopted the theology committee report sustaining McCall's leadership.[190] They prepared a letter to the board announcing that "if we receive no specific proposal from the board of trustees, you may expect to receive our resignations."[191] When the trustees rejected their pleas in Houston, however, they still did not resign. Some trustees agreed with the thirteen and encouraged them to continue the fight. They still hoped that soon McCall "would be cooked."[192] Trustees scheduled a meeting of the full board in Louisville for June 12 to consider appropriate action.

Trustees understood the "Supplementary Report" as "an ultimatum that either they will go or McCall will go." Southwestern Seminary professor Ray Summers rightly predicted that the trustees would stand behind their president and that the affair would "bring lasting hurt to the school, to all our seminaries, and to Southern Baptists."[193] Most trustees viewed it the same way. Trustee Norman Shands explained to Hugh Wamble that for this reason the thirteen's position was "hopeless" from the start: "The only alternatives left for the trustees were to support your charges and dismiss the president or to support him and accept your resignations."[194] Many observers saw this also. Wayne Oates predicted on May 11, 1958, that "these men will stick to a resolution to resign unless McCall capitulates. He will not capitulate because of the principle involved in letting a clique of the faculty plow the whole interests of the seminary under except as they permit them to be expressed."[195] George Cornell, a career religion reporter for the Associated Press who covered the controversy, wrote that sources at the American Association of Theological Schools agreed that the thirteen "put the administration in an untenable position by threatening to resign en bloc if changes weren't made."[196] By making their public appeal as they did, the thirteen forced the trustees to fire either McCall or them. The thirteen, however, could not see this. "All we did was make a report," Hugh Wamble protested.[197]

190. Wamble, "Conflict," 9:193.

191. Wamble, "Conflict," 9:196.

192. Wamble, "Conflict," 11:219–211.

193. Ray Summers to John Haldeman, 5 May 1958, Ray Summers Papers, SWBTS.

194. Norman Shands to Hugh Wamble, 25 June 1958, in Wamble, "Conflict," 13:355.

195. Wayne Oates to Olin T. Binkley, 11 May 1958, 1958 Correspondence folder, box 40, Binkley Papers, WFU.

196. George Cornell, "Row at Baptist Seminary," *Louisville Courier-Journal*, 12 Dec. 1958.

197. Hugh Wamble to Norman Shands, 5 July 1958, in Wamble, "Conflict," 13:366.

McCall wanted to dismiss Price and Ranson, but he wanted to retain the other eleven. He concluded unrealistically that if, however, the trustees fired them all, most would be willing to be rehired. He therefore recommended the dismissal of all thirteen but also recommended the reinstatement of those who pledged to work cooperatively with the administration.

McCall presented his recommendation at the June 12 meeting of the board. The motion recited various charges against the thirteen, but the chief complaint was their failure to relate cooperatively and constructively with the administration. The recommendation then took a surprising turn, proposing not to fire the thirteen but to accept their resignations, interpreting the thirteen's letter of May 15 as a resignation letter. McCall presented a thorough case for their dismissal but moved merely to accept their resignations.[198]

It was an artful ambiguity designed to secure the reinstatement of all but Price and Ranson. But trustees wanted no ambiguity—there would be no resignations. They amended the recommendation to remove the language about resignation and voted to dismiss the thirteen by a vote of thirty-two to nine.[199]

Trustees narrowly adopted McCall's reinstatement scheme and had misgivings about it. As they saw it, the men had made their choice and now had to live with it. It was time to move on without them. Local trustees especially seemed to want nothing more to do with the men. The reinstatement effort failed in any case. Old Testament professor J. J. Owens alone took advantage of it.

"THE MASSACRE ON LEXINGTON ROAD"

The dismissals precipitated a new crisis. The press, both within the denomination and without, unleashed a torrent of criticism of McCall and the trustees. There were rumors that several more faculty members were about to resign. Students chose to matriculate elsewhere. The American Association of Theological Schools appointed a committee to investigate the school, and many observers expected it to lose its accreditation. Many persons across the convention called for McCall's resignation, and a minority on the board of trustees agreed and agitated for his dismissal.

The media excoriated the trustees and McCall. The *Western Recorder*, Kentucky Baptists' news weekly, was unrestrained in its horror—it called the dismissals the "massacre on Lexington Road." Other papers, especially Virginia's

198. Minutes, Board of Trustees, Southern Baptist Theological Seminary, 12 June 1958.

199. Minutes, Board of Trustees, Southern Baptist Theological Seminary, 12 June 1958.

Religious Herald, followed suit. Louisville's *Courier-Journal* sympathized with the professors. The *Christian Century*, mainline Protestantism's popular weekly, defended the professors.

The mood on campus was grim during the 1958–1959 school year. Many students were angry. T. C. Smith in October reported that more than 400 students "have dedicated themselves to seeing him dismissed." Some faculty were angry also. Smith heard that six more professors were "about to band together as we did." [200]

Some of the remaining faculty in fact sought positions elsewhere. Vernon Stanfield and William Mueller were the most prominent professors to resign in the wake of the dismissals, taking positions at New Orleans Baptist Theological Seminary in 1960. Dale Moody, who criticized some of the actions of the thirteen, was nevertheless profoundly dissatisfied with McCall and was now his most outspoken critic on the faculty. He thought of going to Midwestern Baptist Theological Seminary in Kansas City and recruited Stanfield and Mueller to go to New Orleans and pledged to go with them. He told a special Southern Baptist committee that "if Dr. McCall is here when school opens next fall I will not be here." [201] Moody remained nevertheless.

Even some "loyalist" faculty felt that McCall had failed. [202] Barnette felt that McCall disrespected the "loyal" faculty by not including them in any discussions of reinstatement of the thirteen: "Had some of the men been reinstated without our approval others would have promptly resigned." [203] Only their dismissal dissuaded Clyde Francisco from leaving to teach at Southwestern Seminary.

Many students opted to matriculate at other schools. Dean Hugh Peterson recognized in September 1959 that enrollment would not turn up for some time: "We are facing a terrific recruitment problem.... It will be a long time before the tide turns and we begin to build back up again." [204] Enrollment fell steadily over five years by one-third, from 1,548 students in the 1957–1958 school year, to 1,035 in the 1962–1963 year.

200. T. C. Smith to Frank Stagg, 15 Oct. 1958, box 3, folder 3, Stagg Collection, Samford University. The six professors he had in mind probably included Dale Moody, William Mueller, Vernon Stanfield, and Eric Rust. See also Carlyle Marney to Jack Kilgore, 21 Nov. 1958, box 27, Marney Papers; and Edward McDowell to Carlyle Marney, 20 Nov. 1958, box 32, Marney Papers. Rare Book Manuscript and special collections Library, Duke University.

201. J. D. Grey, notes of meetings of presidents' committee, folder 56, J. D. Grey Papers, SBHLA.

202. J. J. Owens to Hugh Wamble, 27 Mar. 1959, in Wamble, "Conflict," 15:471.

203. Henlee Barnette, "The Crisis at Southern Baptist Seminary: An Interpretation," ms., 2, 5, Barnette Papers, WFU.

204. Hugh Peterson to Henlee Barnette, 9 Sept. 1959, Henlee H. Barnette Papers, WFU.

The seminary's accreditation was in jeopardy. The controversy and dismissals raised natural questions about the school's stability, the adequacy of its teaching staff, the fairness of its governance, its academic freedom, and its teaching environment. Many observers believed that the committee would recommend rescinding accreditation. The committee's chairman was Luther Weigle, dean of Yale Divinity School, and a friend of Theron Price and Guy Ranson, who shared much of their vision of theological education and academic freedom. Ten of the dismissed professors appeared before the American Association of Theological Schools committee in the November meeting in Louisville. The committee suggested that it would sustain the thirteen in its report and conclude that their dismissal was unjust and McCall should resign.[205]

Dissenting trustee William Link hoped that the committee's visit would awaken local trustees to the necessity of McCall's resignation, but it instead irritated them. Many trustees saw little advantage to belonging to the American Association of Theological Schools in any case. They bristled at any thought of surrendering the denomination's freedom to govern and administer the school to an organization whose membership was in large measure committed to liberal theology. When the American Association of Theological Schools investigating committee suggested that if the trustees rescinded the dismissals, and if McCall resigned, the seminary could preserve its accreditation, the local trustees were "incensed," and the conversation "ended in complete breakdown."[206]

If the seminary lost accreditation, it was likely that the Southern Baptist Convention would have demanded that their six seminaries withdraw from the American Association of Theological Schools altogether. Many denominational leaders favored withdrawal. "There was a great deal of talk going on in Nashville about our seminaries withdrawing from the American Association of Theological Schools," Herschel Hobbs reported after the American Association of Theological Schools report in December.[207] Hobbs judged that the trustees did "the only thing that they could have done," and that "it wouldn't matter at all" to him if the seminaries withdrew from the American Association of Theological Schools.[208] W. R. Pettigrew, a local trustee and pastor of the Walnut Street Baptist Church, brusquely told the investigating committee that "the

205. William Lumpkin to Hugh Wamble, 17 Nov. 1958, in Wamble, "Conflict," 20:607. Local trustee Farris Sampson suggested to the committee that there was "collusion" between the dissident trustees and the committee (Wamble, "Conflict," 20:601).

206. William Link, notes of meeting, 10–11 Nov. 1958, in Wamble, "Conflict," 20:601.

207. Herschel Hobbs to Howard Spell, 22 Dec. 1959, box 20, folder 11, Hobbs Papers, SBHLA.

208. Herschel Hobbs to Howard Spell, 22 Dec. 1959, box 20, folder 11, Hobbs Papers, SBHLA.

business of the seminary was to turn out preachers of the gospel and that academic accreditation was a matter of no real concern to this business."[209] The majority of the board valued accreditation as long as it served institutional goals, but they would not surrender the independence of denominational control in order to remain accredited.

The investigating committee reported its findings to the American Association of Theological Schools Commission on Accrediting on December 5, 1958. It concluded that the dismissals did not "conform to reasonable standards of dignity and due process of law" but recommended that the decision on removing Southern Seminary's accreditation be deferred for one year while the seminary took "adequate measures" to remedy its problems.[210] The following year the commission imposed four "notations" of deficiency on the seminary but did not revoke accreditation.

A group of about ten trustees strategized to force McCall out and to restore some of the professors. On October 30, 1958, seven of them met in Nashville in a secret caucus to devise a strategy for expressing their dissent. They considered publishing a "minority report" but took no action.[211] Trustee W. W. Finlator held a public meeting of alumni and friends to rally support for the dismissed professors. On their own initiative four of the dissenting trustees met with the American Association of Theological Schools investigating committee to defend the thirteen and to convince local trustees to seek McCall's resignation.[212] The board took strong exception to these activities, especially asking the investigating committee to find fault. Trustee Norman Shands felt that it was absurd for trustees to seek "to secure an unfavorable report concerning an institution we are supposed to serve." Their action constituted a "serious breach" of fellowship with the board.[213] Most trustees stood by McCall.

209. William Lumpkin to Hugh Wamble, 17 Nov. 1958, in Wamble, "Conflict," 20:608.

210. "Statement from Local Trustees," 8 Dec. 1958, cited in Wamble, "Conflict," 20:623–624.

211. Wamble, "Conflict," 14:439, 441.

212. Wamble, "Conflict," 20:600–601. The board majority were apparently displeased with the dissidents' behavior. The board choose not to reelect two of them when nominated to a customary second term (Jack Gritz and W. W. Finlator) and refused another when nominated for a term from another state (Roy McClung). One, Herbert Howard, resigned in 1960 in protest of the majority's actions in dealing with the thirteen. See Wamble, "Conflict," 14:445–448.

213. Norman Shands to W. W. Finlator, 20 Jan. 1959, in Wamble, "Conflict," 20:604. See, similarly, Norman Shands to J. Newton Rayzor, 6 Feb. 1959, in Wamble, "Conflict," 20:605.

Above all else, what saved McCall was the fact that most Southern Baptists interpreted the dismissals as an overdue purge of liberal theology at the seminary. McCall and the faculty on both sides insisted that it was not a conflict over theology, which was largely true, inasmuch as professors on both sides were committed to the same historical-critical approach to understanding the Bible and accepted many of the premises and conclusions of the broader liberal scholarship.[214] The major theological difference had to do not with theology per se but with how to relate a progressive theology to the churches of a conservative denomination. Southern Baptists nevertheless viewed the dismissals as a purge of liberalism. Several of the thirteen had reputations as the most liberal men on the faculty. And the men who had the strongest reputation as sound conservatives, Wayne Ward and Clyde Francisco, were not among the thirteen.[215]

Some of the remaining faculty in Louisville felt that there was in fact a theological element—some of the dismissed men had ventured too far and seemed nearer Rudolf Bultmann than Mullins. McCall's statement to the board that the New Testament department had departed from the spirit of A. T. Robertson reflected this sense. McCall did not dismiss them for their theological views, but their theology required him to practice strenuous oversight to keep them within the bounds of acceptable public statements. W. A. Criswell, Southern Baptists' best-known preacher, applauded the dismissals because they would "help stop this creeping modernism that gradually takes away one bastion of Christ after another."[216] Most Southern Baptists were unconcerned that the *Christian Century* or *Time* magazine criticized the dismissals. Their concern was saving the faith.

Denominational liberals interpreted the firings as a profound setback to enlightenment and progress among Southern Baptists. Harold W. Tribble, president of Wake Forest College, concluded that whereas the seminary had exerted "progressive leadership" in the denomination in the past, the current trustees "have closed the door on light and learning for many years to come."[217]

214. Clyde Francisco told trustees that he saw very little difference between his "theological orientation" and that of the thirteen, and that "it was not a battle between liberal and conservative" (Clyde Francisco, transcription of trustee interviews 28–30 Apr. 1958, 3:397–398).

215. They tried to persuade Wayne Ward to join them, and Ward got the impression that they wanted him largely because it would forestall accusations that the group was liberal (Wayne Ward, transcription of trustee interviews 28–30 Apr. 1958, 3:431–432).

216. W. A. Criswell to Herschel Hobbs, 3 July 1958, box 20, folder 10, Hobbs Papers, SBHLA.

217. Harold W. Tribble to Olin T. Binkley, 3 July 1958, 1958 Correspondence folder, box 40, Binkley Papers, WFU.

Most Southern Baptists, however, interpreted the conflict as a rebellion against legitimate authority by a group of liberal and disloyal professors.[218] Herschel Hobbs's assessment prevailed widely: "This was Southern Baptist Theological Seminary's finest hour as she stood in the breach and said to modernism and its kind that it shall go no further in Southern Baptist institutions and life."[219] McCall's purge had saved the school and the denomination from liberalism. The orthodox soon discovered, however, that it was not a case of once saved, always saved.

218. Wamble, "Conflict," 10:200–201.

219. Herschel Hobbs to Duke McCall, 26 May 1959, Southern Baptist Theological Seminary—Dale Moody Affair folder, Hobbs Papers, SBHLA.

10

LOSING TRUST

Liberalism and the Limits of Realist Diplomacy

The fact that most of the denomination viewed the dismissal of the thirteen as a purge of liberal theology gave McCall solid ground from which to pursue the realist policy successfully. The faculty largely followed his counsel. They focused on the basic gospel beliefs and Baptist distinctives that they shared with their constituency, and advanced progressive views with caution and respect. When critics raised the alarm of heresy, McCall pacified them. In the 1960s and 1970s McCall provided a relatively safe haven for Southern Seminary's progressive faculty.

THE PRAGUE SPRING

Ironically, the dismissal of the dirty dozen at Southern seemed to create something of a Prague Spring for the denomination's liberal intellectuals for two or three years after the firings. When the fall term began in 1961, the seminary was embroiled in a controversy with Southern Baptists in Oklahoma regarding statements made there by Professors Dale Moody and William Adams. McCall sought to assure his faculty he would protect the seminary's leadership role in denominational progress. Thus in McCall's September 14, 1961, convocation address he asserted the seminary's "right and responsibility" of denominational leadership. He arranged the school's history into a powerful mythology in support of freedom for progressive thought. The seminary was not bound by the limits of the popular beliefs of the churches. It claimed the "same right to speak to the issues of the day" as any other group in the denomination.[1] Having earned his fundamentalist credentials, McCall could now promote freedom.

This was not an abandonment of the realist diplomacy. It was, rather, evidence of its successful operation. The dismissal of the thirteen assured Southern Baptists of McCall's orthodoxy and afforded more freedom for the seminary to provide leadership in denominational progress. As long as the seminary's reputation remained sound, its position would be strong enough to offer cautious and constructive criticism of Southern Baptist beliefs and practices, and to promote more progressive theology.

The realist constraints remained, and one careless act of theological aggression could upset the entire arrangement. But as long as faculty minded their diplomatic manners, McCall gave them freedom to develop and promote their modern theology.

Since McCall's purge, Southern Baptists seemed to have renewed trust in the soundness of the seminaries, and liberal professors throughout the convention felt a relaxing of constraints. At New Orleans Baptist Theological Seminary, New Testament professor Frank Stagg was pleasantly surprised in 1959 to discover that President Leo Eddleman stood for freedom: "Eddleman has dispelled the fears that many of us had, and he is proving to be the best champion for freedom and scholarship we have had in a long time. He has shown understanding and given new courage to some of the men here who for too long have been badgered by the defenders of a borrowed 'faith.'"[2] In the same year New Orleans Baptist Theological Seminary professor Ted Clark published *Saved by His Life*, an interpretation of the Christian faith along neo-orthodox and Tillichian lines. Clark argued that belief in an infallible or inerrant Bible—"when the Bible is looked upon as the very Word of God"—was "a form of idolatry." He argued also that the church had distorted "the Jesus of history" into the "myth" of "Jesus the son of God" and second person of the Trinity. He rejected the doctrine of eternal punishment in favor of annihilationism and argued that early Christians gave "undue prominence" to the cross.[3]

In 1961 Ralph Elliott, professor of Old Testament at Midwestern Baptist Theological Seminary and formerly at Southern Seminary, published *The*

1. Duke K. McCall, "Southern Seminary and Southern Baptists," typescript, Convocation Addresses folder, McCall Papers.

2. Frank Stagg to C. Earl Guinn, 14 Aug. 1959, box 3, Frank Stagg Collection, Samford University.

3. Theodore R. Clark, *Saved by His Life: A Study of the New Testament Doctrine of Reconciliation and Salvation* (New York: Macmillan, 1959), 74, 125-126, 143-144, 176. See Fisher Humphreys, "Theodore R. Clark," in *Dictionary of Heresy Trials in American Christianity*, ed. George H. Shriver (Westport, CT: Greenwood Press, 1997), 88-93.

Message of Genesis, in which he relied on historical-critical premises to discount the historical reliability of such accounts as the creation, the flood, the sacrifice of Isaac, and Joseph's interpretation of dreams, in favor of their ostensible spiritual meaning. Also in 1961 the Southern Baptist Convention's Pastors' Conference, the premier venue for Southern Baptist preachers, gave great hope to Southern Baptist liberals as the presence of Dale Moody and Carlyle Marney made it the most progressive and controversial lineup in memory. At about the same time Southeastern Baptist Theological Seminary hired three New Testament professors, R. C. Briggs, Harold Oliver, and William Strickland, who taught their subject in close sympathy with Rudolf Bultmann's demythologizing approach. It seemed a new day for progressive scholarship in the Southern Baptist Convention.

"OUR DENOMINATION IS HEADED FOR DISASTER": PURGING THE SEMINARIES

But the Prague Spring did not last long. Conservative leaders soon called for a crackdown. Clark and Elliott had neglected the language of realist diplomacy and had awakened Southern Baptists to the fact that a few more liberals had infiltrated the seminaries. Many feared that unless there was another purge, "our denomination is headed for disaster." [4]

The seminary presidents generally wanted to support their faculty's freedom, but pressure from the churches forced them to purge a few liberal professors. Eddleman fired Clark in 1960. After a year of intense denominational controversy, Midwestern trustees fired Elliott in 1962. And after several years of intramural controversy, Southeastern trustees forced out their Bultmannians in 1965. Some wanted McCall to fire Dale Moody and Eric Rust, but McCall had already earned his stripes and received less pressure.

The seminary faculties supported the theological perspective of their martyred colleagues but chalked it up to incautious language. Frank Stagg, perhaps the most liberal professor in the denomination, faulted Clark for failure to follow the realist approach: "I am for freedom, but surely we must be somewhat realistic about the people with whom we work. One cannot say all that he wants to say and be able to keep on talking." [5] Bill Hull, who taught New Testament at Southern Seminary, felt similarly about Elliott. He affirmed Elliott's "general

---

4. Mrs. Clyde Morris to Herschel Hobbs, 8 Aug. 1961, folder 2, box 22, Hobbs Papers.
5. Frank Stagg to Malcolm Tolbert, 25 Mar. 1960, box 3, Frank Stagg Collection, Samford University.

(Left to right) Professors Clyde T. Francisco, Penrose St. Amant, William E. Hull, and Joseph A. Callaway

framework of judicious scholarship" as the prevailing approach in the seminaries—nearly "all the SBC biblical men are in this general tradition." Elliott's historical-critical approach, Hull felt, was "wholesome" rather than injurious. To dismiss Elliott, in light of this fact, was practically a "denial of present reality."[6] But Hull felt that Elliott was unwise in how he expressed his ideas and that his unguarded openness was "a bit naïve."[7] Most faculty thought the Prague Spring outbursts foolish and kept to the tried-and-true realist approach.

They could still promote progressive theology. Progressive Southern Baptists, for example, subscribed to Southern Seminary's quarterly journal, *Review and Expositor*, and knew to watch the book review section for messages intended for the cognoscenti alone. When Bill Hull, for example, wanted to make some suggestions about the best means for advancing New Testament scholarship free from the gaze of Southern Baptist anti-intellectualism, he placed his comments in the latter half of a book review on modern French and Belgian New

6. William Hull to Duke McCall, 27 Oct. 1962, William Hull 1959–65 folder, McCall Papers.

7. William Hull to Duke McCall, 27 Oct. 1962, William Hull 1959–65 folder, McCall Papers.

Testament scholarship. He told McCall, "I often like to 'bury' such comments in material that will be read only by those who need to see it."[8]

The seminary faculties duly noted the strong reaction to Elliott's views across the denomination and the fact that Midwestern's president and trustees supported his dismissal. Duke McCall responded in 1962 that he heard on every hand warnings of "the necessity of great caution in what the professor says," and laments that "no theological professor will feel free to publish in the future."[9] They could all identify with Louisiana College president G. Earl Guinn's observations after the crackdown began: "I can appreciate better than ever the old proverb, 'Better is a live dog than a dead lion.' Many times, I am sure that even a dog must have trouble living with himself."[10] They chafed under the restrictions of the realist policy, but it was their only safety.

The new purge in the seminaries ended the liberals' Prague Spring. Herschel Hobbs told fellow pastors that professors like Clark needed to be fired—they could not permit the seminaries to "continue to teach heresy."[11] And at the 1960 annual meeting of the Southern Baptist Convention, convention president Ramsey Pollard warned the seminaries in his convention sermon that Southern Baptists would not tolerate liberal teachers. C. C. Warren, pastor of the First Baptist Church of Charlotte, North Carolina, and leader of conservatives in the state, did not understand why the seminaries resisted anchoring themselves to traditional orthodoxy. "In the light of what we have gone through at Southern Seminary," it was incredible that seminary professors should still promote the results of their "creative thinking." It was time for some leaders "to make an effort to stem the tide which seems to be running against basic principles and tenets for which our forefathers verily gave their lives."[12]

Southern Baptist seminary presidents renewed their insistence that professors follow a realist policy in writing, teaching, and preaching. The dismissals of Clark, Elliott, and Southeastern's Strickland, Oliver, and Briggs brought

---

8. William E. Hull to Duke K. McCall, 12 July 1966, William E. Hull 1966–1969 folder, McCall Papers.

9. Duke McCall to William Hull, 20 Dec. 1962, William Hull 1959–65 folder, McCall Papers.

10. G. Earl Guinn to Frank Stagg, 9 Dec. 1960, box 3, Stagg Collection, Samford University. Guinn had in mind the controversy in Louisiana over desegregation of the public schools, but he and Stagg recognized that the same dynamic was at work in striving for racial progress as for theological progress.

11. Herschel Hobbs to W. Douglas Hudgins, 1 Mar. 1960, box 21, Hobbs Papers, SBHLA; Hobbs to Hudgins, 5 Apr. 1960, ibid.

12. C. C. Warren to Herschel Hobbs, 17 Aug. 1961, Southern Baptist Theological Seminary—Dale Moody Affair folder, Hobbs Papers, SBHLA.

the lesson home. Moody told McCall that many Southern Baptist professors wanted to enter a discussion of traditional Southern Baptist views, but they refrained because either they would have to resign on account of their beliefs or they would have to abandon them in order to be popular with the churches and retain their positions: "They are restrained by the pressures that prevail when one attempts to maintain his position in an institution and his reputation as a scholar."[13]

Some of the denomination's most progressive leaders abhorred the realist approach as much for its lack of progress as for its compromises. They felt that the answer to the problem was to make a clean breast of it and bring Southern Baptists up to date. Duke McCall reported in 1962 that some leading pastors responded warmly to recent faculty presentations at conferences in various places: "A summary of the comments made to me by men like Perry Couch of Asheville would be, 'Why don't you let all Southern Baptists know what you are doing and its implications. This would solve our problems.'" McCall thought that this was too optimistic, but he judged that professors could teach the "new perspective" successfully, if given sufficient time and a "half-way open-minded" audience.[14] But this was just another way of saying that professors needed always to assess realistically their audience and the limits of toleration. And the faculty who survived the purge of the early 1960s agreed.

DALE MOODY AND THE OKLAHOMA CONTROVERSY

At least most of them did. Dale Moody, who taught systematic theology at the seminary for forty years, had trouble minding the limits of realist diplomacy. Time after time he went down into the Baptist assemblies and criticized their backward theology and ecclesiology. Seminary professors had some freedom to do this in more progressive areas like Virginia, or at such eastern colleges as Wake Forest or Furman, and little criticism ensued. But Moody pursued the same course in Oklahoma and Arkansas as in Virginia. McCall responded by telling Moody in no uncertain terms that such aggressive tactics were out of bounds. Moody would then step back and help McCall to calm the waters. Moody's most serious breaches of realist policy involved his opposition to the

13. Dale Moody, "The Tension between Scripture and Tradition in Baptist Thought," typescript, ca. 3 Aug. 1961, Moody—Oklahoma Bible Conference folder, McCall Papers.

14. Duke McCall to William Hull, 20 Dec. 1962, William Hull 1959–65 folder, McCall Papers.

traditional Baptist belief in the doctrine of perseverance. Southern Baptists held that persons who genuinely had been born again, whose sins had been forgiven through repentance and faith in Christ, could not be lost and condemned to hell. God's grace would preserve them in faith, and if they fell into sin, God would work repentance in them and they would return to righteous belief and behavior. Any persons who fell away from their profession and finally died in apostasy were never truly saved. They had never experienced the new birth and had never been forgiven of their sins.

Moody battled the traditional view as early as his student days. For nearly one year from 1940 to 1941, Moody was pastor of the Calvary Baptist Church in Mexia, Texas. He preached with earnestness, passion, and power, and 133 new members joined the church in that period. As the time approached for him to leave the church to matriculate at Southern Seminary, he announced that one of his last sermons would be on apostasy. Everyone seemed to know that Moody's views diverged from those of his denomination, and perhaps everyone knew that Moody had one deacon in particular in mind as the object lesson apostate. The large congregation that gathered overflowed the meetinghouse, and many listened to the sermon on the lawn through open windows.

In the sermon Moody affirmed the possibility of apostasy—that true believers can lose their salvation: "To abandon faith after once having been saved is to commit a sin so serious that God can never restore such a one. . . . The Bible teaches that saved people can so sin as to be lost. . . . People who have sinned so as to be lost after once being saved are hopeless and helpless." Preaching "can never help them," Moody said, repentance "can never restore them," and prayer "will do them no good." [15]

The moderator of the association to which the church belonged aimed to refute Moody's errors and restore the church to correct views. He also notified seminary president John R. Sampey of the fact that the seminary had a student who taught these objectionable views.[16] Sampey assured the moderator that Moody was in error and encouraged him to restore the church to the "true Baptist position" that those who fall away "have not been really born again. None of God's children will be forever shut out of the Father's house." [17]

---

15. Dale Moody, "Apostasy Is Topic for Rev. Moody Sunday," *Mexia (TX) Daily News*, ca. 1 Sept. 1941, clipping in box 16, Sampey Papers. Moody sent the copy to the editor, who published it unchanged (William N. Sealy to John R. Sampey, 18 Sept. 1941, box 16, Sampey Papers).

16. William N. Sealy to John R. Sampey, 18 Sept. 1941, box 16, Sampey Papers.

17. John R. Sampey to William N. Sealy, 23 Sept. 1941, box 16, Sampey Papers.

When Ellis A. Fuller appointed Moody as a tutor in 1945, J. B. Tidwell, a professor in Baylor University's Bible department, similarly sounded a warning about Moody's doctrine. According to Tidwell, Moody withdrew from Baylor "several times only to return and declare that he was no longer antagonistic toward our denominational principles. And then later would seem to go astray again." Tidwell was especially concerned that Moody had recently been "openly antagonistic of Baptist views, especially on the security of saints."[18]

Moody maintained the main contours of this perspective throughout his career. In the summer of 1961 he preached a series of messages at a Bible conference at Oklahoma Baptist University and told the gathered pastors and laypersons that the traditional Baptist belief in the perseverance of the saints was unbiblical. Attendees reported that many persons were shocked, distressed, and angry.[19] Oklahoma pastors in several organizations adopted motions condemning Moody's views and suggesting in no uncertain terms that Moody had no right to teach at a Southern Baptist seminary.

It was bad enough that Moody assaulted a beloved doctrine of the denomination to such an extent that pastors were demanding his resignation. It made matters worse that Moody contradicted the seminary's confession, the Abstract of Principles. Professors pledged to teach "in accordance with and not contrary to" the Abstract, and "a departure from which principles" was grounds for their "resignation or removal." Article 13 of the Abstract stated that all persons who had been regenerated or born again by the work of the Holy Spirit "shall certainly persevere to the end" and be saved. And should regenerate persons fall into sin, the Abstract continued, "they shall be renewed again unto repentance" and salvation. Moody argued that Baptists derived this doctrine from their Calvinist tradition rather than from the Bible, since "as soon as Baptists were born, they were wrapped in swaddling clothes and laid in the cradle of Calvinism." Hebrews 6:4, Moody said, taught the opposite, that "it is impossible to renew them again unto repentance." Most Baptists, like other traditional Calvinists, argued that the apostates of Hebrews 6 had never in fact been regenerated by the Holy Spirit. They made an outward profession of faith without the inner reality. But Moody held that article 13 was "the most shocking statement in the abstract," since it "stands in plain contradiction to scripture." Article 13 and the Bible could not be reconciled: "The choice must be made between the scripture and the Calvinistic tradition transmitted through the confession."[20]

18. J. B. Tidwell to Ellis A. Fuller, 12 June 1945, box 13, Fuller Papers.

19. See, e.g., E. J. Kearney to Duke K. McCall, 8 July 1961, Moody—Oklahoma Bible Conference folder, McCall Papers.

20. Dale Moody, "The Tension between Scripture and Tradition in Baptist Thought," typescript, ca. 3 Aug. 1961, Moody—Oklahoma Bible Conference folder, McCall Papers.

McCall felt that his responsibility as president left him with no choice but to submit charges against Moody to the school of theology committee of the board of trustees, in order that they might investigate their merit.[21] Moody's official response to the investigation was ambiguous. He stated that he took the Abstract's article 13 to mean "moral lapses" rather than apostasy, and so he could affirm the article and scripture. But he implied that a contradiction still existed, for he was concerned that the Abstract made the scripture's negative assertion that "it is impossible to renew them again unto repentance" into a positive assertion that "they will be renewed again unto repentance." The trustee committee concluded nevertheless that Moody interpreted the Abstract "in harmony with what seems to us to be the obvious intent and purpose of the framers of the Abstract of Principles" and recommended "no further action should be taken." After a long and grave discussion in which a number of trustees censured Moody's rancorous spirit if not his beliefs, trustees voted to adopt the committee's recommendations and closed the investigation.[22]

MARTIN LUTHER KING JR. AND RACIAL SEGREGATION

In 1961 the faculty at Southern Seminary contributed to the Prague Spring by inviting Martin Luther King Jr. to address the seminary with his message of racial equality. The seminary's faculty held progressive views of race relations as an essential element of their theological progressivism. Enlightened views of theology and progressive social ethics were parts of the same program. Southern Baptists needed to be brought up to date in both areas.

When the seminary moved to Louisville in 1877, the city's black pastors requested the privilege of attending lectures as auditors. The faculty wanted to offer theological instruction to black preachers, but they would not integrate the school even for auditors. The faculty instructed black Baptist preachers under the rules of segregation. John Broadus privately tutored C. H. Parish, black pastor of Louisville's Calvary Baptist Church, in New Testament Greek.[23]

21. Duke K. McCall to Dale Moody, 11 Jan. 1962, Moody—Oklahoma Bible Conference folder, McCall Papers.

22. See Minutes, Board of Trustees, Southern Baptist Theological Seminary, Mar. 1962; Norman Shands to Dale Moody, 5 Apr. 1962, Moody—Oklahoma Bible Conference folder, McCall Papers; "A Chronicle of Events and Discussions related to Professor Dale Moody's View on Apostasy and the Abstract of Principles," 1–2, Dale Moody folder, President's Office, SBTS.

23. A.D. Muse, in T. T. Martin, *Viewing Life's Sunset from Pike's Peak: Life Story of T. T. Martin* (Louisville, KY: A. D. Muse, n.d.), 213–214.

Since the early 1900s the faculty taught courses at Simmons College, a black Baptist college in Louisville.

By the late 1930s President John R. Sampey and the faculty were anxious to end segregation at the seminary. Sampey admired Robert E. Lee and the glory of the old South, but he abhorred segregation, especially in Christian institutions. Southern Baptists might raise objections, and some students from the Deep South had already expressed resentment on occasions when blacks had been invited to eat in the seminary dining room, but the kingdom of God had no race barriers, Sampey said: "I can well understand that in most sections of the South it would still be unwise to attempt coeducation of the races, but in the theological seminary we ought to be able to rise above all racial prejudice."[24]

Sampey initiated an effort to recruit and admit a "limited number" of black students, but the Kentucky attorney general advised the seminary that it would violate Kentucky's so-called Day Law, which enforced the segregation of whites and blacks in the state's educational institutions by threatening heavy fines against violators. The faculty worked around the Day Law. In 1940 the seminary started a program it called the Negro Extension Department and enrolled the seminary's first two black students. Professors taught the curriculum to black students in faculty offices.[25] Black students could fulfill all requirements for the seminary's regular degrees in this way.[26] Seminary trustees expressed their "hearty commendation of this phase of the seminary['s] work."[27] In the spring of 1944 Garland Offutt became the seminary's first black graduate to receive the Th.M. degree; in September 1948, he earned the Th.D.[28] Offutt served as dean and professor at Simmons College.

In 1950 trustees considered anew the admission of black students into integrated classrooms. They received and studied a careful report prepared by a committee of students. The report pointed out that the state legislature had recently amended the Day Law to permit blacks to enroll in programs unavailable to them at the state-supported black college, Kentucky State College in

24. John R. Sampey to Blanche Sydnor White, 20 Sept. 1940, box 13, Sampey Papers.

25. John R. Sampey to T. O. Fuller, 20 Apr. 1940, box 13, Sampey Papers; John R. Sampey to Blanche Sydnor White, 27 Aug. 1940, box 13, Sampey Papers; John R. Sampey to Marshall A. Talley, 31 July 1941, box 13, Sampey Papers.

26. See also Minutes, Executive Committee, Board of Trustees, Southern Baptist Theological Seminary, 16 Aug. 1940; ibid., 6 Feb. 1941.

27. Minutes, Board of Trustees, Southern Baptist Theological Seminary, 14 May 1941.

28. See Ellis A. Fuller to E. P. Alldredge, 17 Sept. 1943, box 6, Fuller Papers; Fuller to Alldredge, 29 Apr. 1944, box 20, Fuller Papers; Edward A. McDowell to Harold W. Tribble, 24 July 1947, Harold W. Tribble Papers, WFU.

Lexington. Because the school did not offer theology degrees, blacks could legally enroll at Southern Seminary if the trustees approved it.[29]

The students also conducted an extensive survey of seminary students to determine their views on the matter. Of 754 students polled, 95 percent indicated that they were "willing for a few qualified Negro college graduates to be admitted to our seminary classes on a non-segregated basis." Only 1.7 percent expressed unwillingness, and 3.6 percent indicated that they had no opinion.[30] The current Negro Extension Department was inefficient, and professors were duplicating regular lectures. And it would discredit the gospel if a Christian seminary retained "the practice of discrimination and segregation."[31] Fuller and most trustees supported the idea, and in 1951 trustees voted to end segregation at the seminary.

On April 19, 1961, Martin Luther King Jr. addressed the seminary community in a packed chapel. The faculty invited King to give his address as the seminary's Julius Brown Gay Lecturer. King challenged the seminarians that the church had a central role to play in ending segregation. The church should teach the equality of all races and the destructive character of racial segregation. It should counter the racists' inflammatory rhetoric and assure white society that the "basic aim of the Negro is to be the white man's brother and not his brother-in-law." As true followers of Jesus Christ, they should be "maladjusted" to the "evils of segregation and discrimination" and lead their churches to "move out into the realm of social reform." It was King's familiar message, but no one missed the significance of its being given at the oldest seminary in the largely segregated Southern Baptist Convention.[32]

After chapel King addressed the students of the seminary's ethics classes, though so many other students attended that the class had to be held in the chapel. The students gave King a standing ovation. King also addressed the faculty in a more casual session. He afterward met with Louisville's mayor and his committee on integration, carrying a petition signed by more than 200

29. Davis C. Hill et al., "Statement Regarding Admitting Negroes to the Seminary Made to the Trustees of the Southern Baptist Theological Seminary, April 11, 1950," 1, SBTS—Report on Admitting Blacks folder, box 24, Carver Papers, SBHLA.

30. Hill et al., "Statement," 1–2.

31. Hill et al., "Statement," 3, 5.

32. Martin Luther King Jr., Address Given by Martin Luther King at SBTS, Martin Luther King Jr. folder, McCall Papers. This copy was transcribed from the audio recording of the chapel address.

(Left to right) Jim Austin, Allen Graves, Wayne Ward, Martin Luther King Jr., Hugh Peterson, Nolan Howington, G. Willis Bennett, 1961

Southern Seminary students urging the mayor to complete the desegregation of Louisville businesses.[33]

Although some Southern Baptist leaders praised the seminary for inviting King, most thought it unwise.[34] Herschel Hobbs, for example, thought it only aggravated an explosive situation.[35] Ramsey Pollard agreed.[36] The Baptists newspaper editors were divided. Chauncy R. Daley, editor of Kentucky's *Western*

33. Ora Spaid, "Dr. King Says 'Segregation Is Dead,'" *Louisville Courier-Journal*, 20 Apr. 1961; Henlee H. Barnette to Martin Luther King Jr., 26 Apr. 1961, Barnette Papers, WFU; Barnette to Wayne Oates, 27 Apr. 1961, ibid. Spaid said that the petition had 151 signatures, but most other sources indicated 251 signatures.

34. John Havlik to Duke K. McCall, 27 Apr. 1961, Martin Luther King Jr. folder, McCall Papers.

35. Herschel H. Hobbs to Mrs. William O. Carver, 5 June 1961, folder 8, box 21, Hobbs Papers, SBHLA.

36. Ramsey Pollard to Duke K. McCall, 28 Apr. 1961, Martin Luther King Jr. folder, McCall Papers.

Recorder, defended King's visit, but other editors found one way or another to register disagreement.

The most serious damage was the alienation of churches and the loss of donations. Some Southern Baptists, mostly in the Deep South, were outraged. The leader of an Alabama Baptist laymen's group demanded McCall's dismissal.[37] Some associations passed resolutions censuring the seminary. Many churches decided to withhold their Cooperative Program funds from Southern Seminary. The Dothan, Alabama, First Baptist Church, for example, voted overwhelmingly to withhold funds from the seminary because of King's visit.[38]

Martin Luther King Jr.'s visit in 1961 did not represent a sudden shift in the seminary's approach to racial segregation and injustice. The faculty was more progressive on racial issues than most white southerners, and they generally followed the rule of diplomatic realism in this area no less than in theology. But in inviting King and defending his visit, McCall and the faculty took a more aggressive approach than usual, and represented in a public way the seminary's sympathy with the fundamental aims of the civil rights movement. And the seminary paid the price by alienating many Southern Baptist churches.

The year 1961 proved a difficult one for the seminary. The criticism of the visit of Martin Luther King Jr. and opposition to Dale Moody put the seminary on the defensive. And before these controversies had eased, *Redbook* magazine published the results of a survey of the students of eight seminaries, including Southern Seminary, which showed that seminary students held traditional beliefs in surprisingly small numbers. Only 29 percent, for example, "believe there is a real heaven and hell."[39] In response, the seminary produced its own survey of its students, showing predictably much higher rates of belief in traditional orthodoxy.[40] But Southern Baptists were no longer sure what to believe.

37. Unattributed, "Duke McCall Ouster Called Improbable," *Louisville Times*, 24 May 1961.

38. "First Baptist Bulletin," First Baptist Church of Dothan, Alabama, 13 July 1961, in folder 57, J. D. Grey Papers, SBHLA; Alton Cumbus, "In Protest over King Invitation Six Baptist Churches Withhold Seminary Funds," news clipping, in Martin Luther King Jr. folder, McCall Papers.

39. Jhan and June Robbins, "The Surprising Beliefs of Our Future Ministers," *Redbook*, Aug. 1961, 107. See also Ora Spaid, "Baptist Seminary Takes Lumps, Moody—Oklahoma Bible Conference," *Louisville Courier-Journal*, 14 Aug. 1961.

40. Duke K. McCall, "Thinking Aloud," *Tie*, 7 Sept. 1961, 2, 8; "Survey of Summer School Students," Redbook Magazine Article folder, McCall Papers.

INSPIRATION, REVELATION, AND BIBLICAL INTERPRETATION

As the seminaries settled again into realistic diplomacy, many faculty concluded that the prospects of achieving freedom to advance modern scholarship were poor. The seminaries did not have sufficient freedom to teach progressive ideas, and the denomination was too conservative to permit the seminaries such freedom. The churches could exert too much control over the seminaries for the seminaries to get out in front of the churches. If the denomination was going to become more progressive, someone other than the seminaries would have to bring it about.

Some progressive Southern Baptists began to put their hope in the state colleges. H. C. Garwood, dean at Florida's Stetson College, made this point in an effort to persuade Henlee Barnette to remain at the college rather take a position at Southern Seminary: "Too many ministerial students lose their liberal ideas under the restraining influences of denominational pressures after they get out into the ministry. The intense conservatism of our denomination will likely persist for a long time to come and the only thing that will change it will be liberalism on the part of the laity." [41] By the 1960s many Southern Baptist colleges had hired the progressive graduates of doctoral programs in Southern Baptist seminaries, and they found more freedom to teach historical-critical views of the Bible.

Other progressives placed their hope of reform in the denomination's Sunday School Board. The board accepted the challenge and produced a twelve-volume commentary on the entire Bible. The commentary's editor, Clifton Allen, envisioned a scholarly work that would introduce Southern Baptist pastors and Sunday school teachers to a more intelligent approach to interpreting the Bible, one fully informed by scientific and historical-critical scholarship. Progressive Southern Baptists had long complained that the churches remained mired in their traditionalism because progressives had not exercised the courageous leadership necessary to bring them to more intelligent views. Clifton Allen made the venture.

The commentary series represented the views and historical approach of Southern Seminary. The commentary set, Southern Seminary professor Eric C. Rust observed, "is the product largely of our faculty and of the men whom we have trained at Southern." [42] More than 45 percent of the contributors taught at Southern Seminary at one time or another, and nearly 60 percent of the

---

41. H. C. Garwood to Henlee Barnette, 21 June 1951, Barnette Papers, WFU.

42. Eric C. Rust, "Alumni Address, Washington, D.C., 1973, Eric C. Rust 1970–present folder, McCall Papers.

contributors earned their doctorates there. But the historical-critical approach was not unique to Southern Seminary. The faculties of the other seminaries, not to mention the Southern Baptist colleges, shared its premises. Southern, Southeastern, and Midwestern seminaries promoted the approach more openly, however, than did Southwestern, New Orleans, or Golden Gate.

Most contributors seemed to understand the doctrine of inspiration as many of the older liberals and mediating theologians had, as meaning that the Bible was inspired with regard to its religious meaning only. Its statements regarding history, geography, or science reflected the beliefs of the authors' cultural context and were liable to error. Others understood the Bible's inspiration along neo-orthodox lines in which the Bible was the arena of divine encounter and salvific experience, rather than of propositional truth, and held a similar view of the Bible's historical statements.

The contributors generally held that the events recorded in the Old Testament had a genuine historical basis. A real historical event occurred that constituted the kernel upon which various writers overlaid their interpretive elaborations and additions. The historical accounts in their current form reflected the historical interests of the various redactors, who shaped their accounts to address the issues of their own times. The additions and layers obscured the precise character of the original historical event, but the obscurity did not impair God's revelation. The theological meaning of the text was the same regardless of what actually happened. The authors nevertheless generally omitted the more controversial historical-critical conclusions and ventured rather timidly the more palatable.

The result was unsatisfying to both the liberal minority and the conservative majority in the Southern Baptist Convention. The convention's liberals recognized that the commentary writers could do little more than try to remove the stones from the field and that until this work was done, Southern Baptists would not tolerate seminary professors teaching unadulterated historical-critical methods. But they regretted the necessity and longed for the day when they could promote modern scholarship with freedom. The convention's conservatives could tolerate the scholarship because it offered little direct challenge to traditional interpretation, but many were dissatisfied with the commentaries for what they implied more than for what they said. In many places the writers raised doubts about the historical reliability of the passage and expressed uncertainty before alternative conservative and liberal interpretations. Such uncertainty concerning the literal meaning suggested a liberal view of inspiration and a rejection of the doctrine of inerrancy. The implications went beyond the commentaries. Most of the contributors taught at Southern Baptist seminaries. These suspicions received corroboration when the Genesis commentary, by English Baptist scholar G. Henton Davies, interpreted Genesis

Professor Clyde T. Francisco teaching in 1968 in the Norton Hall "map room," while professors Harold Songer and Joseph Callaway sit behind

in much the same way that Ralph Elliott had done. When messengers to the 1970 Southern Baptist Convention meeting adopted a resolution requiring the volume to be recalled and rewritten from a conservative perspective, some seminary professors defended Davies's approach. Included among them was Southern Seminary's Clyde T. Francisco, who accepted the invitation to rewrite the volume, explaining, "My acceptance of this assignment does not imply my rejection of the previous work of G. Henton Davies, for whose doctrinal integrity I have the greatest respect." [43]

The commentaries, though they advanced progressive scholarship, did so cautiously and observed the strictures of self-censorship imposed by the realist approach to denominational relations. It took skill, however, to avoid inciting rebellion. Davies did not have an ear trained to the Southern Baptist constituency. Even Southern Baptist professors sometimes misjudged, as Ralph

43. Clyde T. Francisco, quoted in "Francisco Named to Write Genesis Portion of Broadman Commentary," *Baptist Courier*, 7 Oct. 1971, 5.

Elliott did in his *Message of Genesis*. But such men as Roy Honeycutt and Clyde Francisco, who interpreted the Old Testament much the same way as Elliott and Davies did, avoided nevertheless provoking outright rebellion as Elliott and Davies had done.

At the 1972 meeting of the Southern Baptist Convention in Philadelphia, a messenger introduced a motion to cease the publication and sale of the Broadman Bible Commentary. Convention leaders spoke forcefully against the motion, which mustered no more than 20 percent of votes cast. The fact that convention leaders persuaded at least 80 percent to continue the publication of the commentary set alarmed conservatives. Harold Lindsell, editor of evangelicalism's flagship monthly, *Christianity Today*, interpreted the vote as the triumph of liberalism in the Southern Baptist Convention.

STUDENT ACTIVISM AND UNREST

The late 1960s and early 1970s brought a series of challenges for the seminary. Students grew rebellious and disrespectful. They had expressed widespread discontent with the seminary's leadership on two prior occasions. In 1923 the student body divided over the moral character of secret student clubs and petitioned the faculty to abolish them. In the 1940s many students complained bitterly of their difficult living conditions due to the housing shortage on campus and in the city at large. The bitterness grew in response to scarcity—a lack of adequate student housing—and to the fact that the president seemed to be living on a scale that did not reflect sensitivity to the students' privations.

In the late 1960s and early 1970s many students distrusted institutions and established leaders and saw little value in the customs of respect toward them. They preferred a more casual and egalitarian relationship with their teachers and administrators. At various times in the 1970s, their restiveness produced acts of defiance and protest. Dissatisfaction with the Vietnam War was a strong source of student unrest, and like most seminaries in the decade, Southern Seminary attracted its share of draft dodgers. The name of the students' unauthorized newspaper captured the mood—it was called the *Gadfly*. Many students took such pride in challenging traditional orthodoxy that some boasted of their atheism.[44] McCall became sufficiently concerned at the rebelliousness of many students that he asked trustees to grant him power to declare a state of emergency that would permit him to expel students at will. Trustees granted his

44. Duke K. McCall, *Duke McCall: An Oral History* (Brentwood, TN: Baptist History and Heritage Society, 2001), 285.

request. McCall believed that the students' knowledge that he had this power prevented him from ever having to use it.[45]

A group of students organized the Southern Seminary Peace Movement, sponsored by ethics professors Henlee Barnette and Paul Simmons, and New Testament professor Frank Stagg. In October 15, 1969, they agitated in favor of a moratorium on the war in Vietnam, in which they led two chapel services on peace and reconciliation, wore black armbands in protest of the war, stood in the foyer of the main administration building, Norton Hall, and spent the day reading the names of Americans killed in Vietnam.[46] Students also picketed in front of the chapel while Rear Admiral James Kelley spoke in chapel; they repeated the episode when another military chaplain visited the campus.[47]

Barnette, who had one son serving as an officer in Vietnam and another son who had fled the country to avoid the draft, encouraged a good deal of the student activism. In 1977 Barnette brought peace activist Phillip Berrigan to give a public lecture and to speak in a number of classes. McCall and many trustees were incensed, not least because Barnette arranged for Berrigan's lectures without faculty or administrative approval.[48]

Other students opposed the rebellious mood of their fellows and were distressed by the impiety and worldliness they discovered in many of them. They respected their teachers and quietly attended to their studies. Many accepted pastorates in the area and preached three times a week, made hospital visits, conducted funerals, and led business meetings. They looked to the day of graduation, when their ambition to become pastor of a great First Baptist Church might begin its march. Southern Seminary had long attracted many of the brightest ministerial students in the denomination. Many aspired to become great preachers, denominational leaders, and scholars. One group of these students in particular came to represent the highest denominational ambition—a secret society of twelve students known as Dodeka, after the Greek word meaning "twelve." Other students heard rumors of the club's existence and resented the idea of a club that seemed to thrive on elitist appeal.

45. McCall, *Duke McCall*, 290–291.

46. See "Support, Opposition to Moratorium Displayed," *Baptist Courier*, 30 Oct. 1969, 14–15; Henlee H. Barnette to John Bennett, 8 Oct. 1969, Barnette Papers, WFU; Barnette to Harry Hollis, 20 Oct. 1969, ibid.

47. Henlee H. Barnette, "Protests," Barnette Papers, WFU.

48. Henlee H. Barnette, "Schedule for Father Philip Berrigan," Barnette Papers, WFU; Duke K. McCall, Memo regarding Philip Berrigan Lecture, Philip Berrigan folder, McCall Papers; McCall, "Draft of Letter to Eleven Local Trustees," ibid.

THE RESIGNATION OF WAYNE OATES

Wayne Oates was the seminary's most widely recognized professor. He was one of a few theological educators who established the field of pastoral counseling as a regular component of American theological education. At Southern Seminary he fought long and hard to gain a place for this new discipline as an integral part of the curriculum. He published books in rapid succession, many of which gained wide use in theological education. He coined the term "workaholic" and himself represented well the affliction.

Oates had declined several attractive offers to move from Southern Seminary. Union Theological Seminary in New York tried for several years to lure him away in the 1960s. McCall pulled out all the stops to retain him and acceded to a number of special requests to do so. In May 1973 Oates wrote and thanked McCall: "I do indeed appreciate greatly the support you have shown all of us and to me personally."[49] Oates, however, never seemed to feel satisfied for long with his work arrangements. Oates told McCall and Bill Hull, dean of the school of theology, that he deserved a "lighter teaching load in recognition of my role as a writer and a research man."[50] When McCall refused, he decided to leave. In November 1973 Oates accepted election to the faculty of Southeastern Baptist Theological Seminary in Wake Forest, North Carolina. He resigned from the faculty of Southern Seminary effective in July 1974.[51]

Oates had always been in some respects on the margin of the theology faculty, both because many viewed his field as involving insubstantial scholarship and because he was a political operator and rather a prima donna. Oates knew that he could not expect special privileges to come through faculty votes, but rather through McCall's graces. McCall had acted before to protect and aid him. When Southeastern Seminary offered Oates a position with everything he was seeking, Oates met with McCall to make one last plea for McCall to match the offer. McCall refused.

McCall thought that on principle Oates should not be given privileges unavailable to other faculty members. The only alternative was the establishment of a new category of faculty. Given institutional realities, McCall acknowledged, the entire faculty would have to agree to establishing such a category and to appointing Oates to it. McCall refused to make a "private agreement" with

49. Wayne Oates to Duke K. McCall, 11 May 1973, Wayne E. Oates 1970–1981 folder, McCall Papers.

50. Wayne Oates, quoted in Steve Pressley, *The Gadfly*, 13 Nov. 1973.

51. Wayne Oates to Duke K. McCall and William E. Hull, 2 Nov. 1973, Wayne Oates 1970–1981 folder, McCall Papers.

Wayne E. Oates

Oates to "isolate him from the responsibilities of a full professor." McCall did not wish to negotiate directly with Oates in any case, since that was Hull's job as dean. Hull knew McCall's position and seemed hesitant to resolve the matter. He gave Oates no answer and no encouragement. Oates felt that by ignoring his requests, McCall and Hull had belittled him: "I'm a combat officer—a bird colonel, yes. I'll be doggone if I'll be treated like a buck private."[52]

Upon his resignation, Oates took the opportunity to publish a withering critique of McCall, Hull, and the seminary's administration. He claimed that the administration saddled the faculty with increasing duties—January classes, classes for the new D.Min. degree, a prejudicial method of calculating faculty loads—and did not provide sufficient faculty or administrative resources to help professors with the increasing demands. The fundamental problem, Oates believed, was that McCall and the administration made decisions without faculty input and with more concern for their own reputations than for the faculty's welfare or the school's academic integrity.[53]

52. Wayne Oates, quoted in Steve Pressley, *The Gadfly*, 13 Nov. 1973.
53. Wayne Oates, quoted in Steve Pressley, *The Gadfly*, 13 Nov. 1973.

When Oates discovered Southeastern Seminary's trustees were interviewing Hull with a view to his election as president there, he got cold feet. Some of his colleagues at Southern Seminary tried to persuade McCall to rehire Oates, but McCall was sure that Oates's resignation was best for the seminary. He told Binkley, president of Southeastern Seminary, that "we do not want him back" and that his presence at Southern Seminary had become destructive: "He damages persons and schools."[54] Oates wrote letters to trustees and administrators at Southeastern Seminary in an effort to sink Hull's candidacy. Hull ultimately refused election as president. But when Southeastern's trustees officially elected Oates to the faculty, he changed his mind and rejected his election. He then publicly and privately criticized Southeastern's trustees because, Oates said, they were operating like McCall and Southern's trustees, making their decisions without sufficient faculty input and favoring practical training above scholarship.[55] In 1974 Oates accepted election as professor of psychiatry and behavioral sciences at the medical school of the University of Louisville; he taught there until retirement in 1991.

FACULTY CRISIS OF 1973

Other faculty disagreed with some of the particulars of Oates's critique, but many had their own reasons for discontentment.[56] McCall seemed unaware of the looming crisis. In the fall of 1972 he felt that the relationships among administration, faculty, and students was the healthiest it had ever been: "The student-faculty-administration relations are the best I remember." There was "grousing," he acknowledged, but he judged that the complaints were minor, "fourth-rate issues."[57]

One of the issues related to the school of religious education, which McCall wanted to merge into the school of theology. In 1972 the religious education faculty presented a formal statement in the seminary faculty meeting raising questions about the merits of the proposed merger. Professor J. J. Owens reported that McCall responded badly to the statement. McCall said that if the religious education faculty did not wish to merge, "he was not going to have a shotgun

54. Olin T. Binkley, notes of telephone call with Duke McCall, 1 Mar. 1974, box 5, Binkley Papers, WFU.

55. Wayne Oates to Olin T. Binkley, 30 Mar. 1974, box 5, Binkley Papers, WFU.

56. W. Morgan Patterson to Wayne Oates, Wayne Oates 1970–1981 folder, McCall Papers.

57. Duke McCall to Hugo Culpepper, 13 Sept. 1972, Hugo Culpepper folder, McCall Papers.

wedding." After much heated discussion, education professor Findley Edge made a motion to form a faculty committee to study the matter. McCall told the faculty that if they appointed the committee, it would have to recommend merger. Owens reported that McCall insisted on this point and gave the faculty the same kind of ultimatum that had helped provoke the 1958 crisis: "You will be happy with your decision, or you will find a place to serve where you could be happy." The faculty chose not to elect Edge's proposed committee. But discontent with the administration deepened.[58]

Since the 1950s the number of staff in the seminary administration had grown much faster than the faculty, as it had at virtually all institutions of higher education. Seminary operations were more complex in nearly every way. McCall wanted to bring the seminary's administrative offices together in one place to make seminary procedures more efficient for students, faculty, and administration. He decided to transform the original classroom space at the center of Norton Hall into a second-floor administrative office suite. For the faculty, the new administrative suite symbolized their loss of influence in the seminary. It became a focus of their resentment of the administration's prerogatives. It reinforced the faculty's belief that McCall could find money whenever he needed it for administration's wants, but rarely for the faculty's needs. They called the office suite the penthouse.

McCall apparently misjudged the state of affairs. Within a few months the entire faculty effectively voted that they had no confidence in his leadership. As late as October 1973 he felt confident that "everything seems to be going pretty well on campus at the moment."[59] But when the Faculty Affairs Committee issued its annual report in November 1973, it reported that faculty morale was very low. The committee attributed the problem to ongoing efforts of trustees and administration to diminish the faculty's power in the seminary's academic concerns, especially in the area of faculty selection.[60]

Faculty selection had been a source of profound difficulty in the institution since the earliest days of Fuller's presidency and was one of the underlying tensions in the 1958 controversy. Since the late 1950s, the school of theology was divided into three divisions, each of which held the primary responsibility for nominating new faculty in their division. But in 1972 McCall adopted a procedure by which a dean-appointed committee would have the primary

58. J. J. Owens to Henlee H. Barnette, 1 Mar. 1972, Barnette Papers, WFU.

59. Duke K. McCall to Lamar Jackson, 2 Oct. 1973, Lamar Jackson folder, McCall Papers.

60. "Addendum to the Report of the Faculty Affairs Committee," 26 Nov. 1973, folder 6, box 16, Frank Stagg Collection, Special Collections, Samford University Library.

Duke K. McCall

responsibility.[61] Faculty members reacted badly to this change. They interpreted it as a further erosion of their faculty prerogatives and further centralization of authority in the administration.

McCall mulled his response to the faculty report. One alternative was to fire William Hull as dean, making him the scapegoat and raising hopes that a new dean would improve the situation. But McCall "concluded the price is too high from a number of different directions for me to try to provide a scapegoat solution." It would have afforded only a temporary cessation of hostilities in any case. The fundamental issue in the faculty statement was its objection to the centralization of administrative authority. McCall recognized that in order to "avoid a face-off between the trustees and the faculty," he had to find a way to address this point. Otherwise, McCall concluded, "the challenge to

---

61. "Addendum to the Report of the Faculty Affairs Committee," 26 Nov. 1973, folder 6, box 16, Frank Stagg Collection, Special Collections, Samford University Library.

administrative style and philosophy in the document adopted last Monday will turn into a challenge of the administrative style and philosophy adopted by the trustees in 1942." [62]

McCall recommended that the faculty elect an ad hoc committee to discuss matters with the faculty and advise him on resolving the issues of difference between the faculty and the administration. [63] The faculty elected seven members, and Hugo Culpepper served as chairman. The committee discovered about a dozen common concerns and polled the faculty to determine which were the most significant and to solicit solutions. [64] The primary concern of faculty was little different than it had been for the previous thirty years—they felt that McCall aspired to erode the faculty's role in seminary decisions as much as possible. McCall responded that the faculty often did not participate in the decisions even when they were supposed to be officially involved—by indifference and absenteeism the administration was forced to make some decisions without the faculty's assigned role.

As discussions proceeded, it became clear that the faculty's dissatisfaction with salaries and the promotion process contributed to low morale at least as much as questions of faculty involvement in administrative decisions. When McCall entered office in 1951, there was no procedure in place for setting salaries. The president set salaries and decided on promotions, which he recommended for trustee approval. McCall introduced a fixed salary scale and a procedure by which the faculty's full professors recommended junior faculty for promotion. McCall initially refused to recommend a promotion unless at least two-thirds of the full professors recommended it. The recommendations included rating professors on various areas of professional competence. McCall, however, did not feel obligated to follow the full professors' recommendations and in a minority of cases went against them. The full professors' meetings were confidential. This secrecy, and its occasional and partial breach, spread considerable anxiety among the assistant and associate professors. Many on the faculty viewed the promotion process with fear, uncertainty, and suspicion. [65]

62. Duke K. McCall to William E. Hull, 30 Nov. 1973, William E. Hull 1972–1974 folder, McCall Papers.

63. Duke K. McCall to Trustees, 17 Dec. 1973, Wayne Oates 1970–1981 folder, McCall Papers; Minutes, Ad Hoc Advisory Committee, 13 Dec. 1973, Ad Hoc Advisory Committee folder, McCall Papers.

64. Ad Hoc Advisory Committee to Joint Faculty, 13 Dec. 1973, Ad Hoc Advisory Committee folder, McCall Papers.

65. Duke K. McCall, "Southern Seminary's Faculty Scale, 1951–1974," Ad Hoc Advisory Committee folder, McCall Papers.

McCall in fact had led the trustees to raise the salary scale considerably over the years, had added considerable fringe benefits, and had introduced a system of "extra pay for extra service," affording opportunities for faculty to earn additional income. By 1974 McCall doubted that the seminary could ever afford to pay enough to meet the faculty's expectations. All the administration's "heroic efforts" to raise professors' salaries had "resulted only in complaints," McCall concluded.[66] He received sufficient complaints in 1973 that he asked how many wanted to volunteer to return their salaries to the old scale and keep it that way. He expected no takers.[67] McCall observed that he received more expressions of gratitude from the faculty of the other Southern Baptist seminaries, which had raised their salaries also to try to keep pace, than from his own faculty. McCall finally considered the faculty's needs "insatiable and efforts to improve morale through salary futile."[68]

The catastrophe that struck the campus in the spring of 1974 may have helped reduce tensions and draw all parties together in a common effort. If nothing else it caused a "lengthy interruption" in the work of the ad hoc committee. On April 3, a tornado ripped off the slate shingles that covered campus roofs, destroyed the cupolas on Mullins Hall and Fuller Hall, downed the stately columns of Fuller Hall, and removed the roof of Foster Hall. The homes of a half dozen professors suffered extensive damage, and a thousand campus trees were lost.[69,70]

In any case, the 1973 controversy ended in a whisper. After a semester of intense scrutiny of the current process and consideration of alternatives, the ad hoc committee recommended a system of promotion and tenure very similar to the existing one. The committee similarly recommended a process of faculty selection that resembled the current one.[71]

66. Duke K. McCall, "Southern Seminary's Faculty Scale, 1951–1974," Ad Hoc Advisory Committee folder, McCall Papers. See also Paul Simmons to Duke K. McCall, 4 May 1973, Paul Simmons 1970–1983 folder, McCall Papers; Simmons to McCall, 30 May 1973, ibid. Simmons complained that his nearly 5 percent raise was inequitable because some professors would benefit more than others from the seminary's matching funds program for retirement contributions. "Equity" required him to request an additional 14 percent.

67. Duke K. McCall to the Faculty, 8 May 1973, Faculty Advancement and Promotion 1970–1974 folder, McCall Papers.

68. Duke K. McCall, "Southern Seminary's Faculty Scale, 1951–1974," Ad Hoc Advisory Committee folder, McCall Papers.

69. Duke K. McCall to Gaines S. Dobbins, 26 Apr. 1974, Gaines S. Dobbins 1970–1979 folder, McCall Papers.

70. *Biblical Recorder*, 13 Apr. 1974, 5.

71. Minutes, Ad Hoc Advisory Committee, 14 Feb. 1974, Ad Hoc Advisory Committee folder, McCall Papers; Minutes, Ad Hoc Advisory Committee, 22 Mar. 1974, ibid.; Minutes, Ad Hoc Advisory Committee, 29 Apr. 1974, ibid.

WILLIAM HULL AND THE INSPIRATION CONTROVERSY

But another crisis was already building. Nearly a hundred years after the inspiration controversy provoked by the dismissal of Crawford H. Toy, Southern Baptists embarked on a new inspiration controversy. And though its roots were broader than the nineteenth-century episode, this one too was provoked by Southern Seminary faculty, when New Testament professor Bill Hull criticized the traditional view of inspiration and inerrancy.

When the Southern Baptist Convention adopted the revised *Baptist Faith and Message* in 1963 in response especially to Ralph Elliott's *Message of Genesis*, it reassured conservative Southern Baptists that the convention's leadership was committed to traditional orthodoxy and would not permit the spread of theological liberalism in convention agencies. It reassured them largely because its first article affirmed inerrancy. But it had another interpretation. Its preamble emphasized the soul's competency before God, freedom of conscience, and the priesthood of the believer to reassure denominational progressives that they would not be forced to agree to inerrancy. In the 1972 debate over terminating the Broadman Bible Commentary, Herschel Hobbs appealed to this part of the preamble to save the commentary. Divergent interpretations of the Baptist Faith and Message meant the confession could not unite the denomination. And beginning in 1969 a number of events renewed the controversy over liberalism in the convention's agencies. The controversy convinced many Southern Baptists that liberalism was firmly entrenched in the agencies and that the denomination's leadership stubbornly refused to remedy the problem. The growing evidence of the persistence of liberalism at the seminaries, despite the crackdown of the early 1960s, was the chief ground of this conviction. More and more Southern Baptists were emboldened to question the plausibility of the progressives' claim to believe in the inspiration of the Bible and of their claim to the protection of freedom of conscience.

In 1969 the convention's Sunday School Board published *Why I Preach That the Bible Is Literally True*, by W. A. Criswell, president of the Southern Baptist Convention, pastor of Dallas First Baptist Church, and the most influential leader of conservative pastors in the denomination. The book provoked a storm of protest from the professors of religion in Southern Baptist colleges and universities, who formed the E. Y. Mullins Fellowship specifically to counter the influence of Criswell's conservatism and to promote greater freedom for liberal views in the denomination.

The following year, at the annual meeting of the Southern Baptist Convention in Denver, conservative messengers voted to instruct the Sunday School Board to recall the first volume of the Broadman Bible Commentary set because of its historical-critical interpretation of Genesis. They also threatened to abolish the convention's Christian Life Commission for its apparent promotion of liberalism. And messengers made several attempts to pass motions requiring all denominational teachers to sign a statement affirming the Bible's complete inerrancy and infallibility. It was everything the moderate leaders could do to prevent full-scale popular revolution against denominational leadership.

And as if rank-and-file conservatives were not already sufficiently provoked, later in the summer of 1970 William Hull, professor of New Testament and dean of the school of theology at Southern Seminary, preached a sermon entitled "Shall We Call the Bible Infallible?" and published it in the denomination's monthly, the *Baptist Program*. In the sermon Hull argued that the Bible was neither infallible nor inerrant. The Bible did not claim either, Hull said. The majority of Christian history and Baptist history opposed the doctrine. The doctrine, he said, led to perverse interpretations of scripture in support of such things as polygamy and slavery. He argued also that an infallible Bible would have limited practical value, since no original copies of the Bible had survived, and even if they had, human translators and interpreters would introduce errors. Hull concluded that the Bible was perverted "if we glibly assume that everything in the Bible is to be taken as absolute truth." The Bible was both divine and human, Hull said, and "distinguishing between the human and the divine" was "absolutely essential."[72]

Hull's arguments were hardly new. They had long before been answered to the satisfaction of most conservatives. Basil Manly had answered them in his *Bible Doctrine of Inspiration* (1888). Hull nevertheless argued implausibly that even when Baptists had called the Bible infallible or without error, what they really meant was that the Bible's message carried sufficient power to save sinners: "The reference is always to the saving knowledge of God mediated by the Bible, never to the historical accuracy of the date and place of every event and saying in the Bible.... The primary intent of our confession is to insist that one may rely completely on the message of the Bible to lead men to God." Conservatives were astonished that a Southern Seminary professor who claimed to agree with the Abstract of Principles, which called the Bible infallible, and with the Baptist Faith and Message, which described the Bible as having "truth without mixture of error" for its matter, could make such statements.[73]

Georgia pastor Raymond Johnson had the same reaction to Hull's sermon that many other Southern Baptists had. He was "simply bewildered and

72. William E. Hull, "Shall We Call the Bible Infallible," typescript, 5, Archives and Special Collections, SBTS.
73. William E. Hull, "Shall We Call the Bible Infallible," typescript, 4, Archives and Special Collections, SBTS.

mystified" how anyone could "write an article attempting to prove that the Bible is a fallible book, at the same time believe that the Bible has 'truth, without any mixture of error for its matter,' and be an honest man."[74] It motivated many Southern Baptists to write letters of protest to denominational leaders. Some associations voted their opposition. Many talked of leaving the Southern Baptist Convention.

Hull afterward said that he preached the sermon in an effort "to reduce the doctrinal polarization that has divided our ranks."[75] It did the opposite, especially after the Baptist newspapers published it.[76] For many years Hull's sermon remained notorious among conservatives. It was "exhibit A" in the charge that the seminaries were liberal, and it convinced many Southern Baptists that the seminaries needed theological renovation. It thus played an important role in the emerging conservative campaign to overhaul the Southern Baptist Convention and its agencies. Most Southern Baptists felt strongly that professors who held Hull's views of the Bible had no right to teach in a denominationally supported school. Hull's sermon motivated them to do something about it.

Hull perhaps did not recognize the extent to which the doctrine of inspiration played the central role in denominational conflict because it acted as a wedge issue. Such moderates as McCall and Herschel Hobbs represented denominational beliefs as a bell curve. At the center was a vaguely defined conservatism, and most Southern Baptists kept close to that center. The tapered right end represented a small number of fundamentalists; the tapered left represented a similar number of liberals. The conservatives who challenged the moderate denominational leaders represented denominational beliefs rather as a bowl-shaped graph. They believed that one's position on the doctrine of inspiration tended to drive a person either to a consistent orthodoxy or to a consistent liberalism. The positions represented by the center, a progressive view of inspiration combined with traditional doctrine, represented an unstable mix, and most persons could not hold the two together for very long. The conservatives therefore viewed the doctrine of inspiration as a continental divide that drove persons either toward a liberal understanding of the meaning of the Bible as a whole or toward a traditional understanding. They saw the denomination as divided into two parties based largely on their disparate views of inspiration.

74. Raymond Johnson to Duke K. McCall, 14 June 1972, William E. Hull 1972–1974 folder, McCall Papers.

75. William E. Hull, "Commentary on 'Shall We Call the Bible Infallible?'" *Baptist Program*, Apr. 1971, 11, 14.

76. Between September 1970 and January 1971 the sermon was published in the *Religious Herald, Alabama Baptist, Christian Index, Baptist Message, Baptist Program, Atlantic Baptist,* and *Baptist Bible Tribune.*

Moderates were partly right. Most Southern Baptists operated cooperatively, in concert, and few placed themselves apart. But the bonds of union that held Southern Baptists together at the center had become sociological and functional as much as doctrinal. And the doctrinal bonds were loosening noticeably. This helps explain the sense in which conservatives also were right. The doctrine of inspiration in fact operated effectively as a wedge idea. It functioned as a precommitment with wide ramifications for the methods and results of biblical interpretation.

INSPIRATION, INERRANCY, AND DENOMINATIONAL CONFLICT

The experiences of the 1970s combined to muster Southern Baptist conservatives for a revolution against the moderate denominational leadership. The denomination's theology and religion professors had harshly attacked W. A. Criswell's beliefs. The Sunday School Board had not only published the highly objectionable first volume of the Broadman Bible Commentary but initially resisted the convention's motion to recall and rewrite the volume. The fact that subsequent volumes advanced similarly objectionable interpretations added fuel to the fire. Some conservatives organized the Baptist Faith and Message Fellowship in 1973 to publicize the spread of liberalism in the denomination's agencies, to enlist pastors and laypersons to eliminate it, and to prevent conservative churches from leaving the denomination. Denominational leaders had been effective in the past in convincing most Southern Baptists to dismiss accusations of liberalism in part because the accusations came from the newspapers of independent fundamentalists, who were outsiders and who opposed the entire Southern Baptist program. The Baptist Faith and Message Fellowship's newspaper, however, gained credibility with many Southern Baptists. Its supporters and contributors were insiders, Southern Baptists who promoted the denominational program. Its editor was a career employee of the denomination's Home Mission Board.

One outsider, however, did play an important role in galvanizing conservatives for revolution, *Christianity Today* editor Harold Lindsell. Although he was ordained by a Southern Baptist church, Lindsell was one of the early leaders of the postwar neo-evangelical movement associated with Billy Graham, Carl Henry, Fuller Theological Seminary, and *Christianity Today*. When Southern Baptists ordered the recall of the first volume of the Broadman Bible Commentary in 1970, Lindsell thought that it represented the reinstallation of inerrancy as a fixed denominational commitment. When, however, Southern Baptists voted against recalling permanently the entire commentary series in 1972, Lindsell interpreted it as a "watershed" in the convention's history representing the denomination's shift toward liberalism. His *Battle for the Bible* (1976) and its sequel, *The Bible in the Balance* (1979) documented the spread of liberalism in American evangelicalism. He devoted a chapter in each book to the spread of liberalism in the Southern Baptist Convention, especially at Southern Seminary. Lindsell's prominence as an evangelical leader, and the books' publication by a major evangelical publisher, provided Southern Baptist conservatives with plausible substantiation of their claim that liberalism had infested the denomination's seminaries and leadership.[77] When the second volume came out in the weeks ahead of the 1979 annual meeting of the Southern Baptist Convention, it proved a valuable boost to conservatives who that year initiated their successful campaign to expel liberalism from convention agencies.[78]

One piece of evidence in particular added credibility to Lindsell's claims and greatly embarrassed efforts to refute them. In 1976 Noel Wesley Hollyfield Jr. completed a Th.M. thesis at Southern Seminary analyzing the persistence of traditional orthodoxy among the seminary's students. His survey of Southern students revealed that barely half of M.Div. students believed in the historical accuracy of the biblical miracles, including the virgin birth of Jesus and the account of Jesus walking on water. Barely one-third of Ph.D. students believed in them. Between 20 and 30 percent of M.Div. students were uncertain of the deity of Christ and the existence of God. Nearly 40 percent of Ph.D. students had the same doubts.[79] The seminary could not quite evade the troubling implications of the thesis. It was the work not of an outsider but of a student, and was approved as creditworthy by the three professors who made up his thesis committee. Conservatives repeatedly cited the statistics of Hollyfield's thesis as prima facie evidence of the spread of liberalism in the Southern Baptist Convention.

Many Southern Baptists were deeply troubled by these developments in the 1970s. Some attended convention meetings to offer or support motions designed to halt the spread of liberalism. Others drastically reduced their Cooperative Program giving or redirected it away from the liberal seminaries and colleges. Gwin Turner, pastor of the Mar Vista First Baptist Church in southern

77. See, e.g., Joel Moore to Henlee Barnette, ca. 25 Feb. 1980, Barnette Papers, WFU; Barnette to Moore, 1 Mar. 1980, ibid.

78. Harold Lindsell, *The Battle for the Bible* (Grand Rapids, MI: Zondervan, 1976); Lindsell, *The Bible in the Balance* (Grand Rapids, MI: Zondervan, 1979). For Duke McCall's response, see McCall, *Tie*, June 1976, 10.

79. Noel Wesley Hollyfield Jr., "A Sociological Analysis of the Degrees of 'Christian Orthodoxy' among Selected Students in the Southern Baptist Theological Seminary," Th.M. thesis, Southern Baptist Theological Seminary, 1976; Lindsell, *Bible in the Balance*, 172–174.

California, for example, led his church in 1973 to withhold contributions from the seminaries and redirect them to other Southern Baptist work. "We can no longer in good conscience support financially our seminaries.... We base our decision principally upon what our professors have written in the Broadman Bible Commentary, study course books, and William Hull's Baptist Program article, 'Shall We Call the Bible Infallible?'...Too many of our professors have taken a very vocal stand against the verbal inspiration of the Bible, and have contradicted Jesus Christ Himself with reference to the authorship of many Old Testament books."[80]

Vast numbers of pastors and laypersons were prepared to take action. What they needed was leadership, with a strategic plan for a revolution that would restore orthodox views of the Bible and its fundamental doctrines to the seminary classrooms, Sunday School Board publications, and the other denominational enterprises. And in 1978 Paul Pressler, a Texas judge on the state appellate court, and Paige Patterson, president of Criswell Bible College in Dallas, formulated such a plan and solemnly committed themselves to leading it. Their energetic efforts to enlist pastors in the cause led to the election of the conservative renovators' candidate, Adrian Rogers, as president of the Southern Baptist Convention in 1979. Rogers was the pastor of Memphis's Bellevue Baptist Church, one of the most influential megachurches in the convention. Rogers's leadership and counsel throughout the next fifteen years proved invaluable to the conservative cause.

Rogers's election in 1979 sent shock waves through denominational leaders. It served notice that the days of their leadership were numbered unless they could fight back effectively. Duke McCall urged fighting back. By the time his successor, Roy Honeycutt, heeded the call, it was too late.

With the dismissal of the thirteen, the question of the president's authority was settled. Also settled was McCall's policy of denominational realism. He gave the faculty freedom to pursue and promote progressive ideas in their disciplines, and he pledged to defend their soundness before denominational critics. But he expected them to accept realistic limits to the freedom. Responsible use of their freedom meant advancing their views in winsome ways that did not jeopardize the seminary's reputation for sound doctrine.

Over the next twenty years the policy succeeded remarkably well. The suspicions and criticisms still continued, and in several instances produced wide controversy. But the faculty spoke and wrote with sufficient care and caution that McCall could defend their views persuasively enough to forestall serious crisis.

80. Gwin Turner to Duke McCall, 30 May 1973, William E. Hull 1970–1971 folder, McCall Papers.

Perhaps it succeeded too well. By the 1970s the postwar faculty had trained a cadre of theologically progressive pastors, denominational leaders, and college and seminary professors who took for granted the historical-critical scholarship, the liberal view of inspiration, and progressive social views. And many faculty began to believe that Southern Baptists had finally embarked on the road to a more enlightened religion and relegated fundamentalism to the margins of the denomination. The progressive character of denominational leadership misled them into believing that the rank and file supported their vision of the faith. Most Southern Baptists did not. The spread of progressive views throughout denominational leadership ultimately provoked the Southern Baptist people to support revolution against the progressive denominational leadership, especially against Southern Seminary, the headquarters of the denomination's progressive wing.

But by the end of McCall's tenure in 1982, the realist diplomacy was failing. The evidence of the liberalism of the faculty was too great to deny plausibility. And at the same time, Southern Baptists like many Americans, were more willing to fight for conservative values.

11

DECLARING HOLY WAR

Roy L. Honeycutt and Popular Control

McCall had entered office knowing that his job was to change the direction of the seminary. Honeycutt entered office a generation later knowing that his job was to prevent change. By the time of Honeycutt's installation as president in February 1982, Paul Pressler and Paige Patterson had initiated a movement designed to dislodge denominational leaders and seminary professors who endorsed liberal theology and replace them with persons who held orthodox views. They formed a coalition of conservative Southern Baptists who convinced majorities at the 1979 and 1980 Southern Baptist Convention meetings to support their platform and their candidates for convention president. Southern Seminary was in the bull's-eye. As the conservative insurgency gained successive victories, the threat to the seminary's progressive faculty and administration grew. The conservative majority in the Southern Baptist Convention wanted a seminary of a very different sort. If Honeycutt and other denominational leaders could not find a strategy to stop them, the seminary that they had labored to establish would cease to exist. Honeycutt resisted the control of the popular majority. And when resistance failed, he obstructed.

In the search for McCall's successor, Honeycutt was apparently the frontrunner from the start, favored by both faculty and trustees.[1] Honeycutt had earned his doctorate at Southern and taught as an instructor in Old Testament for two years. In 1959, after serving two years as pastor in Princeton, Kentucky, Honeycutt began teaching Old Testament at Southern Baptist's newest seminary,

---

1. See E. Glenn Hinson, "A Word From...," *Review and Expositor* 102 (2005): 577.

Midwestern Baptist Theological Seminary in Kansas City. In 1971 he became dean there. When Hull resigned in 1975, McCall and his counselors quickly came to consensus that Honeycutt was the right choice. He served as provost and dean of the school of theology until he became president on February 2, 1982.

DALE MOODY, APOSTASY, AND THE ABSTRACT OF PRINCIPLES

Honeycutt's presidency got off to a difficult start. In April 1983 the board of trustees voted to adopt Honeycutt's recommendation not to renew the teaching contract of widely respected theology professor Dale Moody. Moody had retired in 1980, but McCall and Honeycutt wanted him to teach on five one-year contracts until he reached seventy, and Moody was delighted at this arrangement. The refusal to renew his contract was in response to pressure from Arkansas Baptists, who held that Moody's doctrine was fundamentally flawed.

Moody's latest trouble began in 1979 when Duke McCall asked the faculty if they wished to propose any revisions of the Abstract of Principles. Moody alone did so.[2] In a long letter on February 8, 1980, he explained the points at which many articles did not agree with the Bible. He said that articles 6 and 8, on original sin and regeneration, had errors, but he found article 13, on the perseverance of the saints, the most objectionable. Here, he said, "the Calvinistic tyranny of tradition still twists scripture." This article contradicted article 1's assertion of the primacy of scripture, because it was "contrary" to scripture, and his conscience was captive to the truth of article 1. He felt that "the contradictions with scripture in the Abstract of Principles" should be corrected.[3]

Since every professor had to sign the Abstract of Principles, McCall asked Moody to sign again for his contract as a senior professor. He signed it with this addendum: "With the understanding of my letter of 2–8–80."[4] McCall warned Moody of the gravity of the problem. The trustees would not grant Moody a contract as a senior professor "if you define yourself" to stand outside the historical understanding of the Abstract. If Moody was "absolutely convinced" that article 13 contradicted the Bible, "I hope you will take the initiative

2. Duke McCall to Dale Moody, 1 Mar. 1980 (originally 25 Feb.), Dale Moody 1982–1986 folder, Honeycutt Papers.

3. Dale Moody to Roy Honeycutt, 8 Feb. 1980, Dale Moody 1982–1986 folder, Honeycutt Papers. Moody submitted to McCall a draft of a complete revision of the Abstract, moving it decidedly away from its explicit Calvinist elements. Moody preferred, however, to use scripture as a standard, not a creed.

4. "Abstract of Principles," 1 Mar. 1980, in Dale Moody 1982–1986 folder, Honeycutt Papers.

in activating your normal retirement."[5] McCall had long warned his faculty that if they placed themselves outside the Abstract by stating their disagreement with it, then he would have a legal obligation to secure their removal. McCall nevertheless approved Moody's teaching contract in 1980 and 1981.

Moody was a colorful figure. He began teaching theology courses as a "tutor" at the seminary in 1945 and was elected to the faculty in 1948. He had a prodigious memory and seemed to be able to quote any verse in the Greek New Testament by heart. He was relentless and unyielding in argument. He insisted on his theological positions with pugnacious dogmatism. And he could be withering in his response to student questions. His colleagues respected his intellect and humored his dogmatism.[6]

Moody's objections to the doctrine of perseverance were part of his struggle against Calvinism. He saw the history of doctrine at Southern Seminary as a gradual liberation from Calvinism. Boyce held to five-point Calvinism, Moody said, his successor Kerfoot to three points, Kerfoot's successor Mullins to one point. Moody saw his role as finishing the job—he held to none.[7]

Moody had publicly repudiated the traditional Calvinist understanding of perseverance many times. He held that it contradicted scripture. But in the past, when controversy grew hot, he was content to imply that he understood the doctrine the same way everyone else did. But he did not, and in 1980 he wanted to make sure that he communicated his position clearly.[8]

Moody first provoked controversy by publicly rejecting perseverance in his 1941 sermon on apostasy in Mexia, Texas. He provoked a much greater controversy in 1961 when he argued for his views on apostasy before a group of pastors in Oklahoma. Moody got safely through that controversy in part because McCall sent him out of the country to keep him quiet on the matter, and because Ralph Elliott's *Message of Genesis* became the focus of conservatives' concerns.

5. Duke McCall to Dale Moody, 1 Mar. 1980 (originally 25 Feb.), Dale Moody 1982–1986 folder, Honeycutt Papers.

6. See E. Glenn Hinson, "Dale Moody: Bible Teacher Extraordinaire," in *Perspectives on Scripture and Tradition: Essays in Honor of Dale Moody*, ed. Robert L. Perkins (Macon, GA: Mercer University Press, 1987), 3–18.

7. Dale Moody, Oral History Interview, "Appendix: Dale Moody's Doctrine of the Atonement," in Walter Draughon III, "A Critical Evaluation of the Diminishing Influence of Calvinism on the Doctrine of Atonement in Representative Southern Baptist Theologians: James Petigru Boyce, Edgar Young Mullins, Walter Thomas Conner, and Dale Moody," Ph.D. dissertation, Southwestern Baptist Theological Seminary, 1987, 246.

8. Moody was antagonistic and unapologetic in the press. See Dale Moody, "Reply to the Arkansas Baptists," Baptist Press, ca. 26 Nov. 1982, in Dale Moody 1982–1986 folder, Honeycutt Papers.

Dale Moody

Moody reopened the controversy when he published his systematic theology textbook, *The Word of Truth*, in 1981. His chapter titled "Salvation and Apostasy" criticized Southern Baptists' Calvinist understanding of the doctrine.[9] The traditional Calvinist view held simply that persons who fell away demonstrated thereby that they were never authentically saved. James P. Boyce, for example, taught that of all persons in a state of grace, who had been born again, "not one will finally apostatize or be lost." God kept believers from apostasy by his special mercy and grace. Those persons who professed faith in Christ and followed him for a season before falling away were never truly saved, never born again, never in fact forgiven of their sin. They "did not fall from a state of grace and salvation" into perdition.[10]

Moody rejected the Calvinist view. He taught that those who fell away were truly in a state of grace before they fell. He wrote that "the possibility of

9. Dale Moody, *The Word of Truth: A Summary of Christian Doctrine Based on Biblical Revelation* (Grand Rapids, MI: Eerdmans, 1981), 348–365.

10. James P. Boyce, *Abstract of Systematic Theology* (Philadelphia: American Baptist Publication Society, 1887), 426, 431, 436.

apostasy" is "ever present between immaturity and maturity in the life of faith." It was indeed "possible for believers who do not press on to maturity to commit apostasy." Before their apostasy, apostates possessed eternal life: "No one can retain eternal life who turns away from Jesus."[11]

ARKANSAS BAPTISTS VERSUS DALE MOODY

In 1981 David Miller, the director of missions of the Red River Association in Arkansas, and Bill Williams, a pastor and moderator of the association, protested the employment of Moody at the seminary in view of his teaching on apostasy. Miller and Williams sent a more formal indictment with substantiating documentation the following year. When Honeycutt did not appear to take any administrative action against Moody, they decided to take the issue to the Arkansas Baptist Convention.[12]

David Miller offered a recommendation to the Arkansas Baptist Convention's executive committee proposing to appoint a committee to meet with the seminary administration to urge Moody's removal and "eliminate this heresy." A majority passed a milder substitute motion asking Moody to clarify his views on apostasy.[13] Moody was defiant. He responded that he found it difficult to discuss his views with his opponents, because whereas "I follow the infallible scripture alone," his opponents appealed to "infallible dogma" in the form of the Abstract of Principles and the Baptist Faith and Message. He had in any case fully explained his views on apostasy in his *Word of Truth*, and he invited the Arkansas Baptist newspaper to publish an entire chapter.[14] When the paper did so, Honeycutt prepared for the inevitable storm of criticism. Two additional Arkansas associations passed motions protesting Moody's views.

Seminary policy required Honeycutt to investigate the charges. He wrote Moody a letter in which he delineated the various possible outcomes of the investigation. Honeycutt initially took the position that Moody remained within the Abstract's boundaries, a charitable construction of Moody's statement that he

11. Moody, *Word of Truth*, 348, 355, 356.

12. For a concise overview of the course of events relating to this controversy, see Roy Honeycutt, "Chronicle of Events and Discussions Related to Professor Dale Moody's Views on Apostasy and the Abstract of Principles," 10, typescript, 6 Dec. 1982, in Dale Moody 1982–1986 folder, Honeycutt Papers.

13. Bob Allen, "Executive Board OK's Southern Baccalaureate Request; Takes Action on Moody Censure," *Arkansas Baptist Newsmagazine*, 2 Sept. 1982, 8–9.

14. Dale Moody to J. Everett Sneed, 16 Sept. 1982, Dale Moody 1982–1986 folder, Honeycutt Papers.

"could live with" the Abstract as it stood.[15] Honeycutt recommended in October 1982 that trustees take no action with the understanding that the matter was not closed and should "be left on the president's agenda."[16]

Moody seemed to feel that he was being judged by a new standard. His objections to the Abstract were not new. He had stated them in detail in a 1962 letter to Dean Penrose St. Amant defending himself against heresy charges at that time. The board of trustees at that time judged him to be within the boundaries of the Abstract, and his views had not changed: "My view now is precisely what I stated [to St. Amant] January 3, 1962."[17] Since trustees exonerated him at that time, Moody argued, there was no basis for a new investigation.

Honeycutt disagreed. Moody's aggressive posture toward those who disagreed with the traditional view gave him little choice. He had several meetings with Moody to discuss the matter.[18] In 1960 trustees had instituted the policy for dealing with accusations of violating the obligation to teach "in accordance with and not contrary to" the Abstract. The policy required the president to learn whether the matter justified recommending an investigation by the trustees. Ordinarily, professors under accusation had explained that the accusation was based on a misunderstanding of the professor's meaning or on a partial reading of the professor's entire statement on the matter. And every professor had pledged continued commitment to teach in accordance with the Abstract. The standard was not terribly high, since both McCall and Honeycutt deferred to the professor's own judgment. If a professor claimed to teach within the boundaries of the Abstract, that claim was probative.

Moody could not make that claim. After several meetings with him, Honeycutt concluded that Moody was "not committed to 'teach in accordance with and not contrary to' Article XIII." Honeycutt "had a responsibility clearly imposed by the charter and bylaws to recommend appropriate action." Under the circumstances, Honeycutt urged Moody to "consider seriously" resignation.[19]

15. Roy Honeycutt, "A Statement on Some Issues Related to the Arkansas Baptist Convention's Resolution re: Professor Dale Moody."

16. Roy Honeycutt, "Report of Officers of the Board of Trustees with Reference to Professor Dale Moody," 21 Oct. 1982, in Dale Moody 1982–1986 folder, Honeycutt Papers.

17. Dale Moody to Roy Honeycutt, 19 Apr. 1983, Dale Moody 1982–1986 folder, Honeycutt Papers.

18. Roy Honeycutt, "Chronicle of Events and Discussions Related to Professor Dale Moody's Views on Apostasy and the Abstract of Principles," 10, typescript, 6 Dec. 1982, in Dale Moody 1982–1986 folder, Honeycutt Papers.

19. Roy Honeycutt to Dale Moody, 1 Nov. 1982, Dale Moody 1982–1986 folder, Honeycutt Papers.

Roy L. Honeycutt

By the time the Arkansas Baptist Convention met in November 1982, the public controversy was at full boil. The Arkansas Baptist Pastors' Conference issued a special invitation to Moody to preach on the doctrine of apostasy on November 15, 1982, immediately before the convention opened.[20] He accepted and defended his views. When Jimmy Milliken, a professor at Mid-America Baptist Theological Seminary, responded with a sermon in favor of the doctrine of the perseverance of the saints, the conference erupted in a "resounding ovation."[21] When the convention met two days later, messengers rejected the executive committee's tepid motion reaffirming the doctrine of perseverance for a stronger one asking the seminary's trustees "to consider the termination of Dale Moody and any other professor or teacher or assistant who advocates apostasy as true doctrine."[22]

20. See Roy Honeycutt, "Report of Officers of the Board of Trustees with Reference to Professor Dale Moody," 21 Oct. 1982, in Dale Moody 1982–1986 folder, Honeycutt Papers.

21. "Messengers Ask for Dismissal of Southern Seminary Professor," *Arkansas Baptist Newsmagazine*, 25 Nov. 1982, 7.

22. "Messengers Ask for Dismissal of Southern Seminary Professor," *Arkansas Baptist Newsmagazine*, 25 Nov. 1982, 6; "Resolution No. 2 on Apostasy," in Dale Moody 1982–1986 folder, Honeycutt Papers.

Honeycutt knew that the seminary had to respond, and Moody's belligerent defense of his views left Honeycutt little basis for defending him. He recommended that trustees relieve Moody of classroom duties at the end of the spring of 1983 but grant him a one-year leave of absence at full salary. Trustees adopted the recommendation. Because Moody would no longer be teaching in the seminary, the trustees made no investigation of his views and rendered no ruling on his fidelity to the Abstract.

Moody's dismissal represented the outer limit of dissent from the Abstract of Principles. McCall and Honeycutt could tolerate nearly any construction of its statements, but they could not tolerate avowed opposition. Like McCall before him, Honeycutt defended every professor who professed to teach in agreement with the Abstract.

Moody's dismissal was a gift to Honeycutt, giving him credibility and power for effective leadership. When conservatives accused Honeycutt of failing to enforce the Abstract, he replied that he had enforced it in 1982. When they charged that he did not take the Abstract seriously enough, he replied that he took it so seriously that it cost him a valued friendship. And it reminded the faculty to guard carefully their heresies. The faculty knew the limits, Honeycutt said: "I don't think anyone in our faculty has any question about the seriousness about which we take the Abstract. That has been nailed down clearly since 1982." [23]

MODERATES AWAKE

In 1979 conservative leaders began their political effort to wrest control of denominational entities from moderate leadership. They made no effort to keep their strategy or their organizing activity a secret. Their strategy consisted in electing conservative Southern Baptist Convention presidents who would make committee appointments of inerrantists only. These committees could then secure the nomination of seminary trustees who would insist on belief in inerrancy and orthodox theology when hiring new faculty. The action plan consisted almost entirely in publicity, talking to pastors all over the convention to convince them of the need to send their full quota of messengers to the annual meeting to vote for inerrancy candidates.

Most moderate leaders watched all this warily but without deep alarm. They knew that throughout the history of the denomination such conservative movements arose with regularity, fueled by reactionary sentiment and populist protest, but none had accomplished much. For a year or two they might sway

23. Transcript, Annual Meeting of the Board of Trustees, Southern Baptist Theological Seminary, 13 Apr. 1988, tape 7, p. 7, Southern Baptist Theological Seminary.

a popular majority to elect a sympathetic president and pass some resolutions with backward and outdated ideas. But the moderate leaders were confident in their own security, in large part because they believed that the majority of Southern Baptists held to a moderate, middle-of-the-road theology. This proved a grave miscalculation.

McCall and a few others urged an aggressive response to the Pressler-Patterson movement, but few denominational leaders agreed. They dismissed his concerns as alarmism.[24] They were slow to perceive the threat because they believed that Pressler and Patterson represented a reactionary minority. As late as 1988, moderates remained convinced of this. Henry Huff, a trustee at Southern Baptist Theological Seminary, felt that the conservative takeover "is not representative of what a majority of Southern Baptists desire." They won successive elections, Huff said, because of their superior organization.[25]

After the 1983 Southern Baptist Convention annual meeting in Pittsburgh, when the conservative revolution won its fifth consecutive victory, a number of moderate leaders decided that it was time to start pushing back. Roy Honeycutt and Russell Dilday, president of Southwestern Baptist Theological Seminary, used their positions and institutional sway to urge Southern Baptists to fight aggressively against the Pressler-Patterson effort. They asked moderate Southern Baptists to make every effort to send their full complement of messengers to the 1984 annual meeting in Kansas City to defeat the inerrantist candidate. Moderate leaders felt that these efforts would muster 8,000 votes, which they believed would be sufficient to win.

The moderate cause, however, suffered a rout at Kansas City. Moderates mustered fewer than 7,000 messengers. Messengers elected inerrancy candidate Charles Stanley of Atlanta First Baptist Church by a 52 percent majority. Convention majorities passed resolutions declaring that the Bible restricted the office of pastor to men, seeking to prohibit abortion, and declaring that creation science should receive equal time with evolution in public schools. Moderates complained that the conservatives had been better organized. They arranged for buses to carry conservative messengers to the convention so that they could vote in the presidential election and then go home—persons for whom the expense of travel and lodging involved in convention attendance would otherwise have been prohibitive. Whatever truth there may have been to the charge of busing in commuter messengers, moderates lost nearly every contested vote on every day of the convention.

24. McCall, *Duke McCall*, 391–392, 405.
25. Henry Huff and William Thurman, "Friends of SBC Cooperative Missions," Mar. 1988, in SBC Issues 1988–89 folder, Honeycutt Papers.

THE HOLY WAR SERMON

The humiliation of the moderate cause in Kansas City galvanized moderates for action. Honeycutt and Dilday again shouldered leadership responsibility. On August 28, 1984, in his formal convocation address opening the new academic session, Honeycutt hoisted his colors in defiance of protocols of bureaucratic neutrality, and of professions of denominational inclusivity. He declared that the struggle with conservatives for control of denominational agencies was a "holy war." In doing so, he also abandoned all vestiges of the realist policy.

In the sermon he placed the conservatives beyond the pale—they were not authentic Southern Baptists but "independent fundamentalists." They were "unholy forces," "Judaizers" like those Paul anathematized and excluded from the grace of God. They sought "autocratic and dictatorial control" by the dishonest and manipulative methods of "political bosses and demagogic tyrants." If they succeeded, they would destroy gospel freedom, undermine authentic biblical authority, and coerce the conscience. Honeycutt urged true Southern Baptists to heed the "call to arms" and "raise a denominational battle cry" against the conservatives' tyranny.[26]

Honeycutt too believed that the conservative political effort represented a minority, and he aimed to awaken the majority to their peril. The call to "holy war" seemed to make sense in this light. The trial that the convention was facing, Honeycutt said, was the result of the convention having fallen "into the hands of a small group."[27] The "fundamentalist" perspectives on the inerrancy of the Bible and the sinfulness of abortion were opinions of "subgroups."[28]

But the inerrantists were not a minority in the denomination. Social scientist James Guth's 1980 survey of Southern Baptist pastors showed that 86 percent believed that "the Bible is without errors in its original form."[29] Nancy Ammerman's 1985 survey showed similarly that 85 percent of Southern Baptist

26. Roy Honeycutt, "To Your Tents O Israel," in *Going for the Jugular: A Documentary History of the SBC Holy War*, ed. Walter B. Shurden and Randy Shepley (Macon, GA: Mercer University Press, 1996), 125–128, 132.

27. Roy Honeycutt to Rumsey Taylor Sr., 13 May 1981, Trustee Correspondence—General, 1982–84 folder, Honeycutt Papers.

28. Roy Honeycutt, in Transcript, SBC Peace Committee Meeting, 9–10 Jan. 1986, tape 4, pp. 39, Honeycutt Papers.

29. James Guth, "Southern Baptist Clergy: Vanguard of the Christian Right," in *The New Christian Right: Mobilization and Legitimation*, ed. Robert C. Lieman and Robert Wuthnow (New York: Aldine, 1983), 119. Guth's randomly selected survey included 453 Southern Baptist pastors.

pastors and lay leaders professed belief that "the scriptures are the inerrant word of God, accurate in every detail." [30]

In this light, Honeycutt's holy war address was a treachery. It exposed, a Tennessee layman wrote, "the gulf expanding between the majority of Bible-believing Baptist laymen and the educational establishment." The seminaries, he continued, should not expect financial support when they tolerated and promoted "liberal interpretations of the scripture." [31] A Texas pastor warned that no denominational employee supported "by Cooperative Program money has the right to declare war on those who pay his salary." [32] Bill Crowley, a pastor in Decatur, Georgia, said that his church gave 18 percent of its budget to the Cooperative Program, the denomination's revenue stream, and they were deeply troubled by Honeycutt's address. "It is disconcerting to be castigated and vilified as 'myopic and uninformed...independent fundamentalists...sincere but naïve individuals...Southern Baptist Judaizers.'" His church was reconsidering its Cooperative Program giving.[33]

The executive committee of the board of trustees defended Honeycutt's address. In October 1984 it unanimously passed a resolution affirming that the president of Southern Seminary had an obligation to exercise denominational leadership and that the committee concurred with his "assessment and response to the political issues addressed in his 1984 convocation address." [34] When the full board took up the resolution, the new conservative members opposed it. The moderate majority passed the resolution, but the twelve conservatives moved that their names be recorded as voting against it.[35] The battle was now joined.

30. Nancy Ammerman, *Baptist Battles: Social Change and Religious Conflict in the Southern Baptist Convention* (New Brunswick, NJ: Rutgers University Press, 1990), 74. Ammerman's randomly selected survey included the responses of more than 400 pastors and nearly 600 lay leaders (ibid., 287–288).

31. Robert G. Hall to James L. Monroe, 28 Nov. 1984, Trustee Correspondence—General 1982–84 folder, Honeycutt Papers.

32. Ed Ethridge to James L. Monroe, 20 Nov. 1984, Trustee Correspondence—General 1982–84 folder, Honeycutt Papers. Honeycutt's address the trustees' affirmation of Honeycutt provoked many such letters, encouraged by the conservative *Southern Baptist Journal.*

33. Bill Crowley to Roy Honeycutt, ca. 17 Mar. 1985, Alan Culpepper, 1973–1989 folder, Honeycutt Papers; ellipses in original.

34. "The President and Denominational Leadership," Attachment D, in Board of Trustees, Southern Baptist Theological Seminary, *Minutes*, 15–17 Apr. 1985.

35. Minutes, Board of Trustees, Southern Baptist Theological Seminary, 15–17 Apr. 1985, p. 9.

THE DALLAS CONVENTION, THE PEACE COMMITTEE, AND SOUTHERN SEMINARY

Moderate leaders throughout the denomination responded to the call for holy war and organized a massive effort to turn back the conservative revolution at the 1985 meeting of the Southern Baptist Convention in Dallas. The presidents of the six Southern Baptist seminaries pledged their support. Honeycutt made several extensive speaking tours seeking to rally pastors and churches to enlist in the cause. Honeycutt also used the seminary's resources in more direct ways. He urged seminary faculty, staff, and students to attend and nearly doubled seminary subsidies of travel expenses for faculty and staff. For the meetings of the convention from 1979 to 1984, the seminary on average subsidized the attendance of forty-nine persons at an average total cost of $21,469. For the 1985 Dallas convention, the school subsidized the attendance of seventy-four persons at a cost of $40,116.[36] Conservatives suspected that the seminary was supporting the moderate effort in this way, and thought it unseemly at best. The moderate counteroffensive succeeded in mustering a remarkable 20,000 votes for moderate candidate Winfred Moore, but the effort still failed. Conservative candidate Charles Stanley won reelection by nearly 5,000 votes as over 45,000 messengers flocked to Dallas to make it the largest convention in Southern Baptist history.

Moderates were discouraged but vowed to continue the fight. Honeycutt was undeterred. The only way to "counter this movement," Honeycutt said, was by a "frontal assault" against the "'heretical' character of the inerrantist position."[37]

One action of the Dallas convention had lasting consequences for the seminary. The convention established a "Peace Committee" authorized to "determine the sources of the controversies in our convention and make findings and recommendations" with a view toward ending the conflict. When the Peace Committee decided to investigate the seminaries, it opened a new front on which Honeycutt would fight the seminary's battle against the conservative revolution.[38]

The committee consisted of equal numbers of conservatives and moderates. Conservatives saw that it would give them opportunity to legitimate their concerns about doctrinal error—they would have the stamp of a blue-ribbon

---

36. "Southern Baptist Convention Expenses and Attendance by Cost Center," 1979–84, John Michael 1984–89 folder, Honeycutt Papers; "Southern Baptist Convention Expenses by Cost Center," 1984, ibid.

37. Roy Honeycutt to Robison James, 28 Oct. 1985, SBC Peace Committee 1985–86 folder, Honeycutt Papers.

38. See "SBC Motion to Establish a Peace Committee," in Shurden and Shepley, *Going for the Jugular*, 175–176.

committee. And perhaps they would have opportunity to look behind the curtain and discover new problems at convention agencies. Moderates hoped that their participation would result in wider toleration of moderates in denominational service and would afford them opportunity to prevent the committee from adopting a prejudicial report and recommending extreme measures. At worst, it would perhaps de-escalate the conflict for a year or two and give moderates more time.

The Peace Committee appointed subcommittees to visit each seminary and investigate the merits of the complaints of false teaching made by conservatives. On January 9–10, 1986, the subcommittee for Southern Seminary met with Roy Honeycutt and a trustee committee. The subcommittee included two conservatives and two moderates. The conservatives were William Crews, pastor of the Magnolia Avenue Baptist Church in Riverside, California, and Adrian Rogers, pastor of Memphis's Bellevue Baptist Church and one of the most influential preachers in the conservative movement. The moderates were Winfred Moore, Southern Baptist Convention vice president, and Cecil Sherman, pastor of the Fort Worth, Texas, Broadway Baptist Church and the chief strategist of the moderate political effort. Representing the seminary in the meeting were Honeycutt, trustee chairman Ben Murphy, trustee vice chairman Perry Webb, and retired local trustee and seminary counsel Joe Stopher.[39]

The conservatives on the subcommittee were surprisingly ill prepared. The Peace Committee had already written the seminary and officially raised concerns about six professors. Adrian Rogers unexpectedly raised concerns about two more and raised additional concerns about the original six. Rogers based his concerns on a set of photocopies of articles and books by Southern professors, but he had received the set only the night before and, "by his own statement, he had not read the documents." Rogers did not want to close the opportunity to raise concerns about other professors, and the parties agreed to extend the period for raising concerns one more month. Rogers afterward registered concerns about six others, making a total of fourteen professors under scrutiny.[40]

Rogers was, however, already familiar with some of the issues and studied others late into the night of January 9. He presented a large number of concerns that he felt represented the concerns of most Southern Baptists, based on specific statements of Professors Joseph Callaway, Eric Rust, Kenneth Chafin, Alan Culpepper, Roger Omanson, Glenn Hinson, Molly Marshall-Green, Paul Simmons, and Honeycutt himself. Rogers was convinced that the problem

39. Roy L. Honeycutt to Board of Trustees, 13 Feb. 1986, Trustee Correspondence—General 1985–1988 folder, Honeycutt Papers.

40. Roy Honeycutt to Peter Rhea Jones, 22 Apr. 1986, SBC Issues 1985–86 (13-09 A) folder, Honeycutt Papers.

Adrian Rogers in Alumni Chapel

started with a basic dishonesty concerning what the faculty believed and ended with the faculty's unsound interpretations of the Bible. He wanted the subcommittee to help Honeycutt understand that this was at the heart of the objections raised by Southern Baptists. Rogers therefore pressed first on the contradiction between the faculty's professed belief that the Bible has "truth without mixture of error for its matter," and their belief that many scripture statements were false. Honeycutt raised multiple obstacles to a straightforward answer, but Rogers would not be turned aside. Honeycutt finally explained that it was necessary to "distinguish between different kinds of truth." [41] Genesis 1–11, for example, Honeycutt suggested, did not reveal historical truth but nevertheless revealed "ultimate truth," or "theological truth." [42] Honeycutt explained that the biblical references to Adam and Eve were symbolic and represented the experience of every human. He said that the faculty believed that "Genesis created a description of your experience and my experience,...that Adam is you, that you have a garden, that you are the first man." He told Rogers that most of the faculty probably saw "Adam and Eve as a representative of man." [43]

41. Roy L. Honeycutt, quoted in Transcript, SBC Peace Committee Meetings, Jan. 9–10, 1986, tape 2, p. 18, Honeycutt Papers.

42. Honeycutt, in Transcript of Peace Committee Meetings, tape 2, pp 19, 37.

43. Roy L. Honeycutt, in Transcript of Peace Committee Meetings, tape 2, pp. 32–34.

Rogers explained that such beliefs—denying the historicity of a literal Adam and Eve, of the destruction of the Canaanite city of Ai as described in the Bible, and of the tabernacle described in Exodus—angered the Southern Baptists who supported the seminary with their money. He asked also for an explanation of faculty support for abortion rights, of rejection of Peter's authorship of the letters of 1 and 2 Peter, and of statements suggesting that persons could be saved apart from conscious faith in the gospel of Jesus Christ.[44]

THE SEMINARY'S RESPONSE

Honeycutt took all the accusations and information provided by the subcommittee and delivered them to the dean, Willis Bennett, who forwarded them to the appropriate professors and solicited their responses. Each professor wrote a formal response addressed to the dean, after which Honeycutt and Bennett met individually with most to discuss the concerns. Honeycutt and Bennett prepared a detailed response to the accusations to present to the trustees as the institution's formal response to the Peace Committee's concerns.

The document defended the faculty's soundness and had several recurring elements. It first asserted the unqualified orthodoxy of the faculty. It said that they believed the Abstract of Principles and the Baptist Faith and Message, and in the inspiration of the whole Bible. It said that they believed that the Bible had truth without mixture of error for its matter.

The document claimed that the charges were based on misunderstandings and failure of communication. The accusers took the authors' words out of context and did not make sufficient allowance for the use of the technical argot of the experts—such words as "myth"—which untrained laypersons naturally misunderstood. Nor did they make allowance for the fact that the writings were intended for a scholarly audience rather than a popular one.

The document claimed third that whatever differences may have existed represented areas of legitimate academic freedom, since all faculty believed in the inspiration and authority of the Bible. Southern Baptists needed to recognize freedom for individual interpretation, and that such differences fell within the sphere of acceptable diversity.

The document claimed finally that the faculty's use of criticism in their scholarship was no different that what conservatives did. Many differences were based on text criticism—Honeycutt frequently strained a point here—that was

44. Rogers, in Transcript of Peace Committee Meetings, tapes 2–5.

less radical than that advocated by leading conservative pastor W. A. Criswell in his *Criswell Study Bible.*

There was considerable casuistry, but overall it was masterfully done. In many instances conservatives made exoneration simple enough because of the clumsy way in which they stated their charges. Many conservatives, for example, charged Molly Marshall with universalism, although she explicitly affirmed the likelihood that some kind of hell was a reality. Her actual position was hardly more acceptable to conservatives, since she refused to accept what conservatives believed to be a clear teaching of the Bible. But because she did not in fact say what conservatives accused her of saying, Honeycutt could refute the charge soundly. He felt no obligation to aid conservatives in making their charges.

CONSERVATIVE TRUSTEES AND THE PEACE COMMITTEE REPORT

When Honeycutt's report came before the full board of trustees, the new conservative trustees believed that Honeycutt's report was a whitewash. They were deeply dissatisfied that he characterized faculty beliefs as sound and orthodox. They believed that Honeycutt had evaded discussion of some errors and had recast others implausibly as scripturally valid. Among the conservatives, John Michael took the initiative to contest the report's conclusions. Michael, a young businessman and member of Louisville's conservative Highview Baptist Church, came on the board in April 1985.[45] Although some conservatives were active in less confrontational political maneuvering, for several years Michael was the most vocal and persistent trustee in pressing the conservatives' cause in direct confrontation of the moderates on the board.

The Academic Personnel Committee had met to discuss Honeycutt's report in March 1986. At the April meeting of the full board, the committee recommended that the board adopt the report and commended Honeycutt for "the fairness, openness, and thoroughness" with which he investigated the concerns raised by the Peace Committee. They concluded that after an "extensive and intensive review of all concerns," all the faculty members cited in the concerns of the Peace Committee were orthodox and taught "in accordance with and not contrary to the Abstract of Principles."[46] They also concurred with the report of

45. Michael was nominated by the Southern Baptist Convention in June 1984 and elected by the trustee executive committee the same month. The board met once annually at that time, so his first board meeting was in April 1985.

46. Minutes, Board of Trustees, Southern Baptist Theological Seminary, 8 Apr. 1986.

(Left to right) Professor Frank Tupper, trustee Wayne Allen, and Professor Bill
Leonard, 1986

the board's officers that Honeycutt's own writings were "in accordance with and
not contrary to the Abstract of Principles."

After comments by Honeycutt, John Michael raised an objection. He believed
that the president's report had not dealt fairly with the accusations against Molly
Marshall and Glenn Hinson. Michael gave a brief explanation and read a few
quotes from Marshall and Hinson, to which Honeycutt and former trustee Joe
Stopher made brief replies. Michael wanted a full discussion of his objections,
but the majority of trustees were satisfied and approved the report by a vote of
41 to 11.[47] The conservatives voted against it. Michael attempted to reintroduce
discussion of faculty beliefs at other times during the meeting. The board denied
Michael's request to present a "minority report" as an alternative to Honeycutt's
report, since he was not a member of the committees involved.[48]

Honeycutt later asked the board officers and the ad hoc committee on denominational relations to meet with John Michael to evaluate the validity of his
charges against Honeycutt. When they met three weeks later to hear Michael's
complaint, he presented each of them with an extensive notebook explaining
and documenting his concerns. They felt that they had already addressed these
issues. They predictably concluded that Michael's charges were unsubstantiated

47. Minutes, Board of Trustees, Southern Baptist Theological Seminary, 8 Apr. 1986.
48. Minutes, Board of Trustees, Southern Baptist Theological Seminary, 9 Apr. 1986.

and commended Honeycutt for his management and for his faithful handling of the Peace Committee's concerns.[49]

Michael then took his concerns to the Southern Baptist public. He submitted the materials that he had prepared for the trustee committee to the editors of the *Indiana Baptist* and the *Western Recorder*. David Simpson, editor of the *Indiana Baptist*, published an editorial supporting Michael's charges about Molly Marshall's beliefs.[50] Michael sent copies also to the new trustees elected in 1986.[51] This was a breach of trustee protocol for it expressed an unwillingness to cooperate with the board and abide by its rules and decisions. Michael sent copies to Honeycutt and the board chairman. Such wildcat actions reflected the deeply divided character of the board, though some conservative trustees thought such actions harmed their efforts.

GLENN HINSON

The conservative trustees certainly had a point. Honeycutt had not dealt entirely openly and fairly with conservative concerns regarding the faculty's beliefs. This was clear in his treatment of the four faculty whose beliefs attracted a disproportionate share of criticism: church history professor E. Glenn Hinson, theology professor Molly Marshall-Green, ethics professor Paul Simmons, and evangelism professor Ken Chafin.

Glenn Hinson joined the faculty in 1962 and by the 1980s seemed to provoke more criticism than anyone on the faculty. Hinson's understanding of Christianity drew heavily on mysticism, but it remained within the sphere of personalist-oriented liberalism. He believed that hell was the "deprivation" of God's love, in which persons rejected God's love and "never reach full personhood."[52] He held that God forgave some sinners apart from conscious faith in Christ, and Christians, he explained, were not the "exclusive people of God in the world." Mahatma Gandhi, though a Hindu and not a professing Christian, surely had a "personal, saving relationship with God."[53]

---

49. Perry Webb Jr. to Fellow Trustees, 6 May 1986, John Michael 1984–89 folder, Honeycutt Papers.

50. David Simpson, "Simpson Says," *Indiana Baptist*, 27 May 1986, 2.

51. John Michael to Larry L. Adams, 9 Sept. 1986, John Michael 1984–89, Honeycutt Papers.

52. E. Glenn Hinson, "My Faith Is Paradoxical," in *What Faith Has Meant to Me*, ed. Claude A. Frazier (Philadelphia: Westminster Press, 1975), 93.

53. E. Glenn Hinson to Chuck Kelley, 1 Apr. 1985, School of Theology 1982–86 folder, Honeycutt Papers.

E. Glenn Hinson in Alumni Chapel

No less offensive to conservatives were Hinson's views of the Bible. Hinson held that the gospel records were not historically reliable throughout. Their existence reflected the fact that some important historical events had occurred, but they were not exactly history. They had to be examined carefully to discover what they might reveal of actual events. Hinson concluded, "In the case of the gospels one can safely conclude that a kernel of historical fact underlies the early church's handling of the material." After critical evaluation of the Gospels, Hinson wrote, a fundamental "historical event" stood firm: the truth that "the man Jesus of Nazareth" lived and proclaimed a message of the kingdom of God.[54] But the Gospel writers fashioned their narratives for polemical purposes, Hinson said, and the fact that they were inspired did not assure their credibility. He viewed such matters as the place of Jesus' birth, the characterization of John the Baptist, Peter's confession that Jesus was the Messiah, Jesus' triumphal entry into Jerusalem, and the cursing of the fig tree as historically doubtful.[55] The account of Jesus' temptation by Satan "may have been the creation of the evangelists or their sources," especially since they portray the event in "mythological terms."[56] Hinson believed that the evidence that Jesus had a "healing ministry" was impressive, but the accounts of miraculous healings should be somewhat

54. E. Glenn Hinson, *Jesus Christ* (Wilmington, NC: Consortium Books, 1977), 57.
55. Hinson, *Jesus Christ*, 60–62, 71, 74.
56. Hinson, *Jesus Christ*, 64.

discounted "for embellishment."[57] He concluded that although Jesus' followers altered his words, they nevertheless "preserved a credible core of Jesus' own words," at least to the extent that "the main lines of Jesus' thought can be determined even now."[58]

His psychologizing of Jesus as uncertain of his mission shocked conservatives. He held that when Jesus sent the disciples on the preaching mission recorded in Mark chapter 10, he expected the act to bring about the consummation of the kingdom of God: "It is difficult to avoid the conclusion that Jesus expected the return of the Son of Man and the consummation to occur within his own lifetime." When the preaching mission "ended in failure," it "doubtlessly caused Jesus to ponder more deeply than ever what his mission was." Jesus' "error," Hinson said, was due to his own sense of urgency that God ought to consummate his kingdom immediately.[59]

Hinson's responses were not well calculated to satisfy conservative objections. He reiterated his belief that "Jesus expected the consummation within his own lifetime" and that the historical Jesus did not command his followers to repeat the Lord's Supper, but the Christ of faith did: "The real command for its repetition, however, comes from the Risen Christ."[60] He held to a Christian Platonism akin to the Logos theology of Clement or Origen. He suggested that persons could accept the revelation of God in Christ without conscious faith in Jesus, and that in fact everyone was already accepted by God:

> I prefer to look at God's saving work as a work he has chosen to do through his divine Logos who became incarnate in Jesus. This Word, now risen, reveals God everywhere among all persons (as Matt. 25:40, 45 imply). The urgency of our task is one of waking people up to his presence with them and in them.... some persons do not get the help they need to make an open acknowledgement. Mahatma Gandhi, for instance, lived Jesus' teachings better than any Christian I have known but could not become a confessing Christian because of the way Christians had treated him as an Indian in South Africa. Persons of similar experience are legion....Yet I can't believe God the Father, Creator and Redeemer and Eternal Lover of humankind, will give up on that. Indeed, I only hope I know him as well

57. Hinson, *Jesus Christ*, 67.

58. Hinson, *Jesus Christ*, 79.

59. Hinson, *Jesus Christ*, 70, 76.

60. E. Glenn Hinson, "Dr. Willis Bennett re Concerns of the Peace Committee," Meeting of Academic Personnel Committee, Trustee Officers, Seminary Ad Hoc, Mar. 20–21, 1986 folder, Honeycutt Papers, pp. 18, 20.

before I die as Martin Buber and Abraham Joshua Heschel, Conservative Jewish rabbis, have known him.

Hinson did not reject the possibility that some persons would experience some kind of alienation from God, for if God saved persons against their will, "this would be denial of freedom of choice." [61] Remarkably, Hinson saw no reason for conservatives to object to his views. He claimed that he came down "on the conservative side of the scale in every case." [62] Bennett and Honeycutt apparently agreed with his assessment, but they recognized that conservatism was in the eye of the beholder. They omitted these self-indicting passages from their report to the trustees and to the Peace Committee. [63]

MOLLY MARSHALL

Molly Marshall came under attack for statements in her 1983 dissertation on the "question of the possibility of salvation outside Christ and the church." Marshall completed her M.Div. and Ph.D. at Southern Seminary, and Honeycutt hired her to teach theology in 1984. She argued for "Christian inclusivism" and concluded that persons could be saved outside the church but not outside of Christ. [64] Persons who "do not know Jesus" could be included in the kingdom of God if they showed mercy to others or by following the light of nature. [65]

God bestowed mercy based on "the intentionality of one's heart." Sincere intentions rather than correct knowledge constituted the "criterion" of God's

61. E. Glenn Hinson, "Dr. Willis Bennett re Concerns of the Peace Committee," Meeting of Academic Personnel Committee, Trustee Officers, Seminary Ad Hoc, Mar. 20–21, 1986 folder, Honeycutt Papers, pp. 22–23.

62. E. Glenn Hinson, "Dr. Willis Bennett re Concerns of the Peace Committee," Meeting of Academic Personnel Committee, Trustee Officers, Seminary Ad Hoc, Mar. 20–21, 1986 folder, Honeycutt Papers.

63. E. Glenn Hinson, "Dr. Willis Bennett re Concerns of the Peace Committee," Meeting of Academic Personnel Committee, Trustee Officers, Seminary Ad Hoc, Mar. 20–21, 1986 folder, Honeycutt Papers, p. 17; Roy L. Honeycutt, Report to Trustee Committee on Academic Personnel, 42–65; SBC Peace Cmt. Meetings folder, Honeycutt Papers.

64. Molly Marshall-Green, "No Salvation outside the Church? A Critical Inquiry," Ph.D. dissertation, Southern Baptist Theological Seminary, 1983, 257–259. Marshall was known as Marshall-Green at this time.

65. Marshall-Green, "No Salvation," 272.

judgment. Those who responded to Christ without knowing him therefore received grace from "the unknown object of their faith."[66]

She rejected the doctrine of universal salvation. God would not coerce individuals to spend eternity in fellowship with him involuntarily. So hell might indeed exist.[67] Her position, though not quite affirming universalism, hardly pleased conservatives. The Bible asserted the reality of hell. Southern Baptists expected seminary professors to teach what the Bible taught, not a mere acknowledgment that its assertions may possibly be true.

Marshall responded that she rejected universalism but held that salvation by Christ extended to many of those who had never heard the gospel.[68] Like Hinson she advanced a Logos-theology as the basis of the central role of Christ in redeeming humanity. Although persons could come to God apart from conscious knowledge of Christ or the gospel, Marshall said, Christ's role was essential. Christ was the Logos, the word of God and the pervading basis of all human reason. The activity of the Logos was thus "universal" in humanity. The Logos operated through "human reason" and through "all movements of the [human] spirit toward God." Marshall concluded therefore that "the Christ-event was not the only point in the fabric of human history where God was working for the reconciliation of humanity."[69] Through his incarnation, Marshall concluded, Christ "bound himself to all of humankind, not just to Christians."[70]

Honeycutt refuted at length the accusation that Marshall believed in universalism, but he ignored the problematic belief that persons could be saved apart from conscious faith in Christ. "Her teachings and writings are within the Abstract of Principles," Honeycutt concluded, and her "dissertation is creative but not extreme."[71]

PAUL SIMMONS

Paul Simmons joined the faculty in 1970 and was repeatedly the object of the complaints of conservative trustees for his views on abortion and homosexuality. Simmons sought to relax or perhaps abolish Christianity's traditional prohibition

---

66. Marshall-Green, "No Salvation," 270–271.

67. Marshall-Green, "No Salvation," 282–283.

68. Molly Marshall, "Edited Response to Indiana Baptist Editorial of May 27 1986," typescript, John Michael, 1984–89 folder, Honeycutt Papers.

69. Marshall-Green, "No Salvation," 259.

70. Marshall-Green, "No Salvation," 279.

71. Roy L. Honeycutt, Report to Trustee Committee on Academic Personnel, 19–22, 24–25, SBC Peace Cmt. Meetings folder, Honeycutt Papers.

of homosexual behavior. He claimed that the various condemnations of homosexuality in the Bible did not in fact condemn homosexual activity. The sin for which Sodom and Gomorrah were condemned, he said, was not homosexuality but "inhospitality."[72] Later interpreters, like the New Testament author Jude, incorrectly interpreted their sinfulness as relating to homosexuality.[73]

Such passages as Leviticus 18:22 and 20:13 did not forbid homosexual activity but sexual activity connected with religious worship. The real concern "of the Priestly writer," Simmons wrote, involved "regulations for religious ceremonial purity." In 1 Corinthians 6:9 and Romans 1:26–27, Simmons wrote, Paul condemned not homosexual acts but pagan religious ceremonies and a "lifestyle obsessed with overindulgence."[74] Most Southern Baptists, including many moderates, found his exegesis outrageous.

Simmons implied that homosexual activity was not necessarily sinful. The Bible did not settle the question for him: "As for the problem of homosexuality, I have a great deal of uncertainty as to the moral parameters of this matter."[75]

Conservative Southern Baptists were outraged also that Simmons advocated abortion rights. Simmons asserted that "God is pro-choice." God sided with abortion rights, he explained, because personal meaning and value inhered fundamentally in the freedom to choose. Before birth, the fetus did not have the value of human personhood. The critical distinction in value was between "the personhood of the woman" and the child in the womb, who was not a person.[76] Most Southern Baptists, however, believed that a child in the womb was a person, no matter how small. A child was a human person from the time of conception.

Honeycutt was apparently troubled by Simmons's responses and offered little defense of Simmons's views. He merely concluded that he found "no cause for concluding that by so expressing his convictions he has violated the Abstract of Principles."[77] The Abstract of course did not address abortion and homosexuality directly. Honeycutt omitted Simmons's admission that God did not command

---

72. Paul Simmons, "Sexuality in Christian History," *Campus Minister* 4 (1981): 67.

73. Simmons, "Sexuality in Christian History," 68. The reference was to Jude 7.

74. Simmons, "Sexuality in Christian History," 68–69.

75. Simmons to Willis Bennett, 11 Mar. 1986, Meeting of Academic Personnel Committee, Trustee Officers, Seminary Ad Hoc, Mar. 20–21, 1986 folder, Honeycutt Papers.

76. Simmons to Willis Bennett, 4 Feb. 1986, Meeting of Academic Personnel Committee, Trustee Officers, Seminary Ad Hoc, Mar. 20–21, 1986 folder, Honeycutt Papers.

77. Roy L. Honeycutt, Report to Trustee Committee on Academic Personnel, 30–35, SBC Peace Cmt. Meetings folder, Honeycutt Papers.

Israel to kill the Amalekites and that Satan is not a personal being, but "Satan is the biblical way of speaking of the power of evil in the world."[78]

KEN CHAFIN

Ken Chafin came to Southern Seminary in 1965 after having served for many years in the Billy Graham Evangelistic Association. He became well known in the Southern Baptist controversy as one of the most vocal opponents of the conservative takeover. With Cecil Sherman, he tried to mobilize moderate leaders to oppose the conservatives. He was responsible for some of the small number of moderate victories in the early years of the controversy. In 1982 and 1983, for example, he successfully moved the Southern Baptist Convention to replace several fundamentalist nominees to trustee boards with moderates.

Chafin's theology came under attack when he denied the exclusivity of salvation by faith in Christ on *The Phil Donahue Show* in June 1985. He and Paul Pressler appeared together. A member of the audience said that she was not a Christian but sought to follow the moral requirements of various religions, and asked whether she was doomed or was going to heaven. Conservatives believed that sinners must repent of their sins and trust consciously in Jesus Christ in order to be saved from eternal punishment for their sins. Pressler answered in this vein. He replied that all persons were sinners and had to follow God's solution to the problem of sin—he wanted to talk to her after the show. Chafin, like some other moderates, however, believed that Jesus would save good-hearted persons with or without conscious faith in Jesus Christ. Chafin said: "Jesus said to love the Lord God and to love your neighbor as yourself, and that sums it all up." He said that his friend, a retired rabbi, who evidently rejected faith in Christ, would be in heaven, "probably because of what God has done in Christ."

Like Hinson and Simmons, Chafin had difficulty providing Honeycutt with the answers he needed to defend Chafin's orthodoxy. Honeycutt made his own editorial changes to Chafin's statement and then asked Chafin to approve them. Honeycutt's revisions made Chafin suggest that conscious faith was necessary to salvation and that there was no other way of salvation, but the wording was carefully ambiguous and did not require such a reading.[79]

78. Paul Simmons to Willis Bennett, 4 Mar. 1986, Meeting of Academic Personnel Committee, 3.20–21.1986, Paul Simmons section, Honeycutt Papers.

79. Honeycutt's emendations marked in Kenneth Chafin, "An Open Letter to Southern Baptists," 10 Mar. 1986, in Meeting of Academic Personnel Committee, Trustee Officers, Seminary Ad Hoc, Mar. 20–21, 1986 folder, Honeycutt Papers. For Chafin's adoption of Honeycutt's changes, see Chafin, "An Open Letter to Southern Baptists," 12 Mar. 1986, ibid.

LIBERALISM, TRUTH, AND ABSTRACT OF PRINCIPLES

Adrian Rogers said that the crux of the Southern Baptist conflict was the apparent dishonesty of the professors. The seminary presidents and denominational leaders said that the professors all endorsed the Baptist Faith and Message and agreed with its statement that the Bible has "truth without any mixture of error for its matter." But the professors taught that Adam and Eve did not exist literally, that the destruction of the city of Ai as recorded in Joshua did not occur, and that the tabernacle described in Exodus did not develop until centuries afterward. The professors claimed to believed that the Bible had truth without mixture of error for its matter, but they taught that many of its historical claims were false.[80]

Honeycutt argued that it was legitimate to believe that the Bible contained errors and to believe that it had "truth without any mixture of error for its matter." He claimed that Paul's teaching on the return of Christ in 2 Thessalonians was distinctly different than what he taught in 1 Thessalonians, that the gospel writers differed on the inscription that the soldiers placed on the cross, that their reports of Jesus' commands in sending out the disciples contradicted each other, and that John and Luke contradicted each other regarding whether or not Judas participated in the Last Supper. But such errors, Honeycutt said, did not "detract from the infallibility of scripture" or prohibit "saying that scripture is truth without mixture of error."[81]

Honeycutt pleaded for some flexibility "when you say truth without mixture of error." It could not be held "rigidly" when "John says one thing and Luke says another" about whether Judas was present at the last supper. Honeycutt affirmed that as a matter of history "either Judas ate the supper or he didn't." But he also affirmed that the two passages were not "contradictory" because "the truth of that passage is something more than whether Judas was or wasn't there." And when the gospel writers disagreed about what Jesus said, it was historically "incorrect" and an "inconsistency," but it was not an "error." False history could make true doctrine. Such historical errors did not therefore prevent him from affirming that the Bible had truth without mixture of error.[82]

Honeycutt acknowledged that his argument depended on how he defined truth. One had to distinguish "scientific truth," what the text said in its literal

80. Transcript, SBC Peace Committee Meeting, 9–10 Jan. 1986, tape 1, pp. 32–35; tape 2, pp. 7–8, 12, 15–16, 31–34, Honeycutt Papers.

81. Transcript, SBC Peace Committee Meeting, 9–10 Jan. 1986, tape 1, pp. 40–43, Honeycutt Papers.

82. Transcript, SBC Peace Committee Meeting, 9–10 Jan. 1986, tape 5, pp. 47–48, Honeycutt Papers.

sense, from "ultimate truth," which was the theological and spiritual sense of the text.[83] The Bible's literal statements contradicted each other in many places and contradicted science in other places.[84] But the Bible's theological meaning was coherent and deeply relevant: "There is a larger truth in that passage [on the] supper than whether Judas was or wasn't there."[85]

Honeycutt and the faculty made a similar distinction regarding the definition of "matter" in the Baptist Faith and Message's statement that the Bible had "truth, without any mixture of error, for its matter." The matter referred to a "certain kind of truth," to ultimate theological truth.[86] New Testament professor Alan Culpepper taught that the term matter here designated the Bible's "essential content" rather than its every statement. To affirm that the Bible had truth for its matter was to say that it taught truly "regarding matters of faith and doctrine." The statement made "no claims regarding other areas, such as science and history."[87]

Honeycutt held that the faculty's critical interpretations were explanations and elaborations of the ideas of the Abstract rather than exceptions and contradictions. In the wake of the Dale Moody crisis, Honeycutt explained to one trustee that despite Moody's rejection of the doctrine of perseverance, a doctrine explicitly stated in the Abstract, "he affirms the principles of the Abstract" and "is not in fundamental disagreement with the intention of that document." The principles and intention of the Abstract, Honeycutt held, consisted in a desire to represent the Bible's basic meaning in a way that is relevant to contemporary needs. Moody's letter in which he delineated all the errors of the Abstract, Honeycutt said, did not violate his commitment to its principles. It was, Honeycutt felt, a letter of "explanation" rather than a

83. Transcript, SBC Peace Committee Meeting, 9–10 Jan. 1986, tape 2, pp. 18–19, 21, 34, Honeycutt Papers.

84. Honeycutt cited as examples differing forms of the Ten Commandment in Exodus 20 and Deuteronomy 5, and differing numerical descriptions in Kings and Chronicles. Transcript, SBC Peace Committee Meeting, 9–10 Jan. 1986, tape 2, pp. 7–8, 20, Honeycutt Papers.

85. Transcript, SBC Peace Committee Meeting, 9–10 Jan. 1986, tape 1, p. 43, Honeycutt Papers.

86. Transcript, SBC Peace Committee Meeting, 9–10 Jan. 1986, tape 2, p. 20, Honeycutt Papers.

87. Alan Culpepper, "Jesus' View of Scripture," in The Unfettered Word: Confronting the Inerrancy-Authority Question, ed. Robison B. James (Waco, TX: Word Books, 1987; reprint, Macon, GA: Smyth and Helwys, 1994), 36–37. See, similarly, Duke K. McCall to Raymond Johnson, 19 June 1972, William E. Hull 1972–1974 folder, McCall Papers.

letter of "exception." [88] Not unlike some medieval scholastic theologians, who forced all the commentators to agree with each other no matter how strong the apparent contradiction, Honeycutt refused to admit that any teachings of his faculty contradicted the Abstract. The only way to violate the Abstract was evidently to say, "I am outside the Abstract." In light of McCall's and Honeycutt's dealings with Moody, however, even this did not necessarily suffice. Beliefs that appeared to contradict the Abstract were scholastic glosses on the Abstract—explanation, not exception.

GLORIETA STATEMENT

On October 22, 1986, the presidents of the Southern Baptist Convention's six seminaries released a joint statement affirming their belief in the "infallible power and binding authority" of the Bible. It became known as the "Glorieta Statement." In it the presidents affirmed their personal commitment to the "supernatural" character of Christianity, to the value of miracles, and to the Bible as "fully inspired" and "not errant in any area of reality." They also committed their seminaries to enforcing their confessional statements; "balanced" treatment of different theological views; respect for the theological convictions of all Southern Baptists; "fairness" in selecting faculty and lecturers; and promotion of personal piety, evangelism, and missions.[89] The most surprising affirmation of the statement was that "the sixty-six books of the Bible are not errant in any area of reality." All six presidents were "moderates." They rejected the doctrine of inerrancy and were leaders of the opposition to the conservative takeover. The Glorieta Statement, it seemed to most observers, represented broad capitulation to the conservatives' aims. It was outwardly capitulation. Direct opposition had failed. Honeycutt now adopted a strategy of obstruction. The Glorieta Statement was a part of that strategy.

Some moderates had urged Honeycutt to take this kind of initiative in order to placate conservatives. This became all the more appealing as the Peace Committee's response to Southern Baptist Theological Seminary and Southeastern Baptist Theological Seminary began to crystallize. Former professor Peter Rhea Jones urged Southern and Southeastern to take a "proactive approach." If they did not take steps to make themselves "acceptable to people

88. Roy Honeycutt to Julian Pentecost, 7 Jan. 1983, Julian Pentecost folder, Honeycutt Papers.

89. "The Glorieta Statement of the Seminary Presidents," in Shurden and Shepley, *Going for the Jugular*, 195–196.

who are poorly educated in many instances and who are anti-intellectual and have no critical faculties," moderates were going to "lose so many good things." The seminaries must somehow "appear more responsive to the grass roots." It was time, as Peter Rhea Jones put it, to assess "realistically the political realities." [90]

The political reality was that the Peace Committee was moving irresistibly toward indictment of Southern, Southeastern, and Midwestern seminaries for teaching liberalism. Cecil Sherman explained to Honeycutt at length how the Peace Committee had concluded in July 1986 that the seminaries' understanding of the Bible was far different from that of most Southern Baptists, and that the committee would recommend that the seminaries should adjust their faculties to better reflect the beliefs of the people. Conservatives on the Peace Committee targeted Southern and Southeastern especially. Moderates needed to recognize that the committee would certainly "raise the specter of liberalism and point at our seminaries." Sherman wanted Honeycutt and the other seminary presidents to recognize this "threat on the life of theological education among us" and to take it as "seriously as a threat on your life." [91]

Honeycutt believed that it was essential that the seminary take action ahead of the Peace Committee's report. The presidents produced the Glorieta Statement to forestall the imposition of rigid requirements to hire inerrantist faculty. The Peace Committee was prepared to recommend this in its report, and the presidents had to stop it.

The Peace Committee had become a dire threat to the liberal character of the seminaries. The committee had already found substantive theological differences within the convention and recognized that the seminaries were a major source of liberal beliefs in the denomination. The committee would likely recommend that the convention instruct the trustees to hire conservative professors, at least until they reached 50 percent of the faculty.

As the October meeting of the Peace Committee approached, the presidents took stock of their situation. The Peace Committee had "cleared" Southwestern, New Orleans, and Golden Gate seminaries from their list of denominational "concerns," but Southeastern, Midwestern, and Southern seminaries and some of their faculty remained under suspicion. The committee was in the process of drafting its final report to the convention. None of the seminaries could afford to have any of the others listed as "concerns" in that report. "This position was

90. Peter Rhea Jones to Roy Honeycutt, 25 Aug. 1986, SBC Issues 1985–86 (13-09) folder, Honeycutt Papers.

91. Cecil Sherman to Russell Dilday, Roy Honeycutt, and Randall Lolley, 1 Aug. 1986, SBC Issues 1985–86 (13-09) folder, Honeycutt Papers.

untenable," Honeycutt felt, "as we anticipated the final report of the committee and the possible action(s) of the convention."[92]

Conservatives were largely pleased with the Glorieta Statement, for it seemed to acknowledge the justice of their demand that the seminaries hire professors who believed in inerrancy. But they were not convinced that the presidents were truly inerrantists. And the faculties of the seminaries were hardly enthusiastic about the statement. Many felt that the presidents had betrayed them. Some denominational moderates shared the feelings.

Two items in particular troubled other moderates. The statement that the Bible was "not errant in any area of reality" appeared to define the Bible as inerrant in the same way that the conservatives did. And the commitment to "fairness in selecting faculty" appeared to be a pledge to hire conservatives who believed in biblical inerrancy.

Many moderates unsurprisingly felt betrayed by the statement. Cecil Sherman, the leading moderate on the Peace Committee, resigned in protest of the statement. He felt that the Glorieta Statement symbolized capitulation to the conservatives' agenda. He said the seminaries were already "conservative by any normal use of the word," but that the Peace Committee brought "pressure to bear" on them. He implied that the Glorieta Statement represented the presidents' best effort to deal with this pressure: "The statement made by the six seminary presidents sets a course for theological education in the Southern Baptist Convention for years to come. What fundamentalists have wanted, the Peace Committee has helped them get."[93] Many faculty members were similarly angered at the statement.

Capitulation, however, was the only choice short of losing total control. And it had the desired effect. As a result of the presidents' commitments in the Glorieta Statement, the Peace Committee "ceased its official inquiry" into the theological teachings at Southern, Southeastern, and Midwestern. The committee recognized that "unanswered questions and unresolved issues" at the three schools remained, but concluded that in light of the Glorieta Statement's commitments, the administration of each school could be trusted to resolve them.[94]

The Peace Committee gave greater credibility to accusations of liberalism at the seminaries, but it probably did not change the outcome. Conservatives

92. Honeycutt, "Glorieta Statement: An Interpretation," typescript, 3, Glorieta Statement folder, Honeycutt Papers.

93. Cecil Sherman, quoted in "Sherman Resigns from SBC Peace Committee," *Baptist Courier*, 30 Oct. 1986, 4.

94. "The SBC Peace Committee Report," in Shurden and Shepley, *Going for the Jugular*, 211.

had already defeated the moderates in the pitched battles at the 1985 and 1986 conventions in Dallas and Atlanta. But the Peace Committee's report helped ensure that conservative leaders would not be satisfied with halfway measures. It strengthened the resolve of Southern Baptists who might otherwise have been satisfied with partial victories. The Peace Committee report consolidated conservatives' commitment to total victory.

A RETURN TO REALISM

The Glorieta Statement represented a return to realism. But it was a different kind of realism. It was not the realism of cautious advance that had characterized so much of Southern Seminary's twentieth-century career. This was rather a realism of retreat. Honeycutt's call to arms had failed. He recognized that he would not succeed if he continued to press for freedom. So he returned to a realist policy.

The dynamics changed rapidly as the conservative revolution advanced. The realist approach had afforded some freedom for progressive theology as long as conservative opponents had no official authority. They could control the outcome of votes on the floor of the Southern Baptist Convention, but that power was more akin to a siege than to a coup. Consecutive victories, however, meant that conservative trustees were populating the boards that governed Southern Baptist institutions. They were turning their popular pressure into official power, and a coup was in the offing.

After the Dallas convention, some moderates realized that they could not win. Professor Alan Culpepper attended the convention and reflected on the difficulties moderates confronted. The Dallas convention convinced him that "moderates are the minority group in the Southern Baptist Convention," a point few moderates were willing to concede at the time. He thought it likely that the Peace Committee would strengthen the "fundamentalist attack on seminary faculties." He saw "no reason to believe that we will do significantly better in Atlanta [in 1986] than we did in Dallas." He recognized that as the minority side "our choices are limited." He recommended continued effort to "maneuver the Peace Committee process," to "define and contest issues before the SBC," and to protect Southern Seminary by efforts to "manipulate the trustee appointment process insofar as possible."[95] Such rearguard tactics sought to maintain some standing ground for moderates, especially in the seminaries. But as a rearguard

95. Alan Culpepper to Roy Honeycutt, 21 June 1985, Alan Culpepper, 1973–1989 folder, Honeycutt Papers.

action, its only hope of success was to stave off conservative reconfiguration of the seminaries as long as possible, in the hope that the battle would be called off before the moderates were completely driven out. Culpepper's assessment proved remarkably accurate, but moderates were unable ultimately to save Southern Seminary from a conservative renovation. About one year later Honeycutt arrived at a similar perspective.

In the fall of 1986 moderates were in a chastened mood. Honeycutt and the denomination's moderate leaders had called followers to execute a full-court press in 1985 to win back the presidency of the convention from conservatives, but they had failed by a considerable margin. Moderates repeated the effort for the 1986 annual meeting in Atlanta, but they again fell short. Honeycutt realized then that moderates could not win the battle from the floor of the Southern Baptist Convention. It would be pointless to try again at the 1987 convention in St. Louis. "I pull out all stops and go for Dallas, I pull out all stops and go for Atlanta, but if you can't do it in Dallas and Atlanta, why do you think you can do it in St. Louis?" he asked the seminary faculty in October 1986. The time had come for a different strategy of resistance. This is what the Glorieta Statement represented. As Honeycutt explained, "Now we are fighting at another level." Circumstances had reached a point that this "kind of movement was necessary." Direct opposition had failed. "You fight one battle one way and another, another." [96] The new way represented by the Glorieta Statement was conciliatory obstructionism.

Honeycutt called a meeting of the faculty and staff to explain to them the rationale and meaning of the Glorieta Statement. The widespread suspicion of the seminaries was the source of much of the conservative movement's power. If the seminary presidents could remove these irritants, perhaps they could rob conservatives of their cause célèbre in the conflict. They decided to make some concessions—or at least to promise concessions—in the hope that "we could pull enough people in the middle" that conservatives could not get majorities for more radical measures. "Our intention in the document was to try to gain ground from the middle" to strengthen support for the seminaries. They hoped, by moving toward the middle, to convince a majority of Southern Baptists to move on from the controversy, "to lay the issue to rest." [97] They recognized that unless they took some action, the delegates in St. Louis were likely to impose stiff new doctrinal tests on the seminaries. The Peace Committee invited the

96. Roy Honeycutt, "Glorieta Statement Faculty-Staff Meeting," 28 Oct. 1986, transcript, 5, SBTS.

97. Roy Honeycutt, "Glorieta Statement Faculty-Staff Meeting," 28 Oct. 1986, transcript, 7, 2–3, SBTS.

seminary presidents "to come and negotiate with us."[98] They knew that many on the committee wanted to commit the seminaries to a view of biblical inspiration that affirmed that the Bible was without error "in all matters including science, philosophy, et cetera."[99] Wayne Ward, professor of theology, felt that the Glorieta Statement saved the seminaries from the prospect that the St. Louis convention would impose on the faculties a requirement that they affirm "the inerrancy of the scriptures in all of its scientific, historical, philosophical references."[100] The seminary presidents could not afford to wait until the Peace Committee reported its concerns about the soundness of the seminaries. The committee was prepared to report on problems at the seminaries. The presidents created a new perception of the seminaries by a resounding affirmation of their commitment to orthodoxy. As Honeycutt explained, "Decisions are made by the convention on the basis of perception, however, and it was this that we sought to confront" in the Glorieta Statement.[101]

The Glorieta Statement represented a radical change in the seminary's public relations policy, but it represented virtually no change otherwise. The presidents had no intention, Honeycutt told the faculty, "to compromise consciously." The statement was a response to the fact that moderates could not win convention majorities. "You just fight on different levels and you try to hold the institution together." The goal was to keep the faculty "intact" and keep the institution "on main course." But the statement represented "no shift" and "no change of agenda" in Honeycutt's intentions for the character of the seminary.[102] The statement then was not a new departure, Honeycutt explained, but an affirmation of the way things already were: "The commitments are already operative in the several seminaries."[103] Honeycutt explained further that he had no intention of changing the way he would "enforce" the Abstract of Principles. He would defend the faculty as within the limits of the Abstract in the same way he had

98. Roy Honeycutt, "Glorieta Statement Faculty-Staff Meeting," 28 Oct. 1986, transcript, 3, SBTS.

99. Roy Honeycutt, "Glorieta Statement Faculty-Staff Meeting," 28 Oct. 1986, transcript, 7, SBTS.

100. Wayne Ward, "Glorieta Statement Faculty-Staff Meeting," 28 Oct. 1986, transcript, 4, SBTS.

101. Roy Honeycutt, "Glorieta Statement: An Interpretation," typescript, 4, Glorieta Statement folder, Honeycutt Papers.

102. Roy Honeycutt, "Glorieta Statement Faculty-Staff Meeting," 28 Oct. 1986, transcript, 7, SBTS.

103. Honeycutt, "Glorieta Statement: An Interpretation," typescript, 6–7, Glorieta Statement folder, Honeycutt Papers.

done before and would not require them to change their views on the character of biblical inspiration and inerrancy.[104] It was a dodge.

The part of the statement that most troubled the faculty and some denominational moderates was its affirmation that the Bible was "not errant in any area of reality." The presidents chose to use such strong language in order "to correct misperceptions" that the seminaries were "emphasizing the errors of the Bible."[105] They felt it was necessary to make a "simplistic statement," one that "would communicate to Southern Baptists the fact that by rejecting the theory of 'inerrancy' we are not thereby abandoning the high view of the Bible."[106] Honeycutt assured the faculty that he was not committing the seminary to uphold the doctrine of inerrancy. When the Peace Committee earlier asked the seminary presidents whether they could affirm that "the Bible is inerrant in all matters, including science, philosophy, cosmology, etc.," the presidents declined. The Bible was not about such things: "The truth of the Bible is 'religious' or 'theological' truth."[107] Honeycutt felt free to affirm that "the Bible is not errant in any area of reality because it is not the Bible's intended purpose to speak [to] areas of reality other than religious or theological issues."[108]

Honeycutt understood that the phrase "not errant in any area of reality" communicated at face value that the Bible had no errors. He was counting on it. Honeycutt hoped to divide the conservative voting bloc by satisfying the concerns of enough critics to convince them to vote in ways that supported the seminaries under current management. But using the phrase was risky. First, it would tend to alienate the seminary's more progressive supporters, who felt that Honeycutt had purchased peace at the price of the chains of slavery.[109] Honeycutt knew this but decided that the risk was worth taking. Second, conservative leaders would not be fooled by this. Honeycutt knew this also. The seminary presidents told the Peace Committee that the statement did not mean inerrancy. Honeycutt seemed to commit the faculty to inerrancy, but he told

---

104. Roy Honeycutt, "Glorieta Statement Faculty-Staff Meeting," 28 Oct. 1986, transcript, 1, 5, 7, SBTS.

105. Honeycutt, "Glorieta Statement: An Interpretation," typescript, 9, Glorieta Statement folder, Honeycutt Papers.

106. Honeycutt, "Glorieta Statement: An Interpretation," typescript, 10, Glorieta Statement folder, Honeycutt Papers.

107. Honeycutt, "Glorieta Statement: An Interpretation," typescript, 8, Glorieta Statement folder, Honeycutt Papers.

108. Honeycutt, "Glorieta Statement: An Interpretation," typescript, 10, Glorieta Statement folder, Honeycutt Papers.

109. See, e.g., T. J. Hill to Roy L. Honeycutt, 10 July 1987, Glorieta Statement 1986 folder, Honeycutt Papers.

the faculty that they had no obligation to hold or teach inerrancy. They would not be changing their views on the Bible.

The Glorieta Statement also committed Honeycutt to "fairness in selecting faculty, lecturers, and chapel speakers across the theological spectrum of our Baptist constituency." But Honeycutt pledged to the faculty that he was not about to make significant changes: "The lecturers—we are not going to be inundated by people any different than we have had in the past, but we are periodically going to have someone who is different." He was not about to change the selection of chapel speakers, which he considered diverse already.[110] Most important, he had no intention of hiring conservative professors. He rejected out of hand proposals to hire conservatives based on a system of quotas or parity. He refused suggestions that he "elect one fundamentalist for every department" or "elect two or three and save everybody else." His approach to hiring conservatives was only that "I will be fair." But "what fair means" depended on the circumstances. One thing was clear, fairness did not include hiring inerrantists. He believed that "the spirit of fundamentalism" would destroy "the ethos" of the school.[111] He concluded apparently that fairness to the current faculty and the character and aim of the seminary meant that he would hire no conservatives until he had no alternative. He sensed that others would not share his view of fairness in the premises: "Someone is going to look someday and say, 'What did you do about what you said about fairness on the faculty?' And they are going to ask me exactly what a pastor did here last year, 'Why can you find one kind of faculty member, but you can't find the other?' I didn't tell him that I didn't want to find them." The statement, Honeycutt said, simply had no implications for "what we do and how we function." It meant no internal change. "I can't see," Honeycutt assured the faculty, "that it's cost you anything."[112]

Honeycutt yielded in one respect only—he secured some inerrantist guest lecturers and visiting faculty for the short January and summer terms. Millard Erickson, professor of theology at Minnesota's Bethel Theological Seminary, and David Dockery, professor of New Testament at Criswell College in Dallas, taught in the summer of 1987.

But he balked at hiring even one inerrantist to the regular faculty, fearing that they would be antagonistic and damage collegiality. He wrote Peter Rhea Jones in October 1986 that he was "still in a quandary concerning the potential impact

---

110. Roy Honeycutt, "Glorieta Statement Faculty-Staff Meeting," 28 Oct. 1986, transcript, 6, SBTS.

111. Roy Honeycutt, "Glorieta Statement Faculty-Staff Meeting," 28 Oct. 1986, transcript, 2, SBTS.

112. Roy Honeycutt, "Glorieta Statement Faculty-Staff Meeting," 28 Oct. 1986, transcript, 6, SBTS.

of adding a person diametrically opposed to the institution to a tenurable or tenured position." Southern Baptist inerrantists, Honeycutt believed, tended to operate from an "obscurantist" position.[113] Honeycutt intended to resist popular control of the seminary by the denomination's obscurantist masses.

113. Roy Honeycutt to Peter Rhea Jones, 3 Oct. 1986, SBC Issues 1985–86 (13-09) folder, Honeycutt Papers.

12

THE CONSERVATIVE TAKEOVER

Moderate leaders knew that time was running out on moderate control of Southern Seminary. Efforts to elect a moderate convention president had failed. Before the 1988 annual meeting of the Southern Baptist Convention in San Antonio, Roy Honeycutt still hoped for a moderate victory to rescue the seminary from conservative control: "If Richard Jackson can be elected in San Antonio, then I am convinced that our board will escape complete domination by the fundamentalists. Should Jerry Vines or a candidate of like political theological convictions emerge as president, then the fundamentalists would move to majority position in the board by the annual meeting of 1991."[1] Conservative candidate Adrian Rogers was elected, and Honeycutt recognized the inevitability of conservative control. No help would come from the meetings of the Southern Baptist Convention. Nor had the Peace Committee's 1987 report offered any hope, even though it took a more conciliatory shape after the Glorieta Statement. It had served mainly to justify conservatives' concerns. Honeycutt and moderate trustees now looked elsewhere for rescue.[2]

---

1. Roy Honeycutt to William Henry Crouch, 6 Apr. 1988, SBC Issues 1988–89 folder, Honeycutt Papers.

2. In 1990 some Southern Baptist moderates and Southern Seminary faculty held serious discussions about taking the seminary into "exile" by founding a new school and moving the faculty there. Church history professor E. Glenn Hinson said that a group was planning to purchase the campus of the defunct Tift College in Georgia. When Hinson talked to a reporter about the idea, the publicity probably ruined its chances of success. Honeycutt officially declared the idea "premature." See G. Willis Bennett to

ALTERNATIVES TO THE CONSERVATIVE TAKEOVER

Some moderate leaders, apparently including some faculty and trustees, sought means for making the seminary independent of the Southern Baptist Convention. Southern Seminary seemed well positioned for such a move. Its faculty had a good reputation for scholarship in the convention. The ranks of its alumni pervaded the convention and would rally to support the school through state convention budgets and church budgets. It would lose funding from the denomination's Cooperative Program, but its endowment provided sufficient revenue that the Cooperative Program provided only about half of its annual revenues.

Many of the colleges belonging to Southern Baptist state conventions had successfully declared their independence. The seminary could do as they did. The board could declare its independence, refuse to recognize the trustees elected by the Southern Baptist Convention, and elect its own choices. The great obstacle here was the seminary's charter, which specified that the Southern Baptist Convention nominated the seminary's trustees. Trustees would have to change the charter on their own authority to cut out the convention's role, and trust that they could win the inevitable battle in the courts.

A more plausible strategy emerged around 1987 or 1988, when some moderate trustees argued that the board could control its own character without bolting the denomination. The board could merely vote to reject the persons nominated by the Southern Baptist Convention. By refusing to elect conservative nominees, the trustees could preserve a moderate majority and prevent a conservative takeover of the seminary's administration and faculty. One advantage to this plan was that it did not involve changing the charter. Under the charter, the Southern Baptist Convention merely nominated persons to serve as trustees at the school. The trustee board alone had the legal authority to elect new trustees from those nominated.[3] For some years, the convention had nominated one person for each open position, and the trustees had routinely elected them. The two-step process presumably implied that the trustees at the very least had authority to veto any person nominated by the convention.

SBTS Trustees, 21 Aug. 1990, Trustee Correspondence, General, 1990 folder, Honeycutt Papers.

3. The original charter provided that the Southern Baptist Convention would nominate "not less than three persons" for each vacancy. In 1928 this was amended to require two nominations for each vacancy, and in 1965 it was amended to require nomination of "one or more persons." After 1965 the convention nominated only one person for each vacancy.

Some trustees began pressing the idea in 1987. The trustees who supported this idea apparently hoped that a trustee initiative in 1988 would establish a mechanism for accomplishing this. In February 1988 the trustee executive committee discussed the "urgent need for trustees to be elected to the board who have a genuine interest in and loyalty to Southern Seminary." They approved a motion to appoint an ad hoc committee "for the purpose of developing guidelines related to the election of Southern Baptist Seminary trustees nominated by the Southern Baptist Convention, beginning with the 1988 San Antonio Convention." To conservative trustees, the move appeared self-evidently for the purpose of rejecting conservative nominees to the board. Moderate trustees naturally viewed the conservative trustees with suspicion and felt they had no legitimacy. They generally were not alumni of the school and promoted a platform of institutional change that was hostile to the generally accepted values and beliefs of the faculty, staff, and trustee majority. Moderate trustees therefore viewed the conservative trustees as persons who had no "genuine interest in and loyalty to" the seminary. Moderates appeared to be prepared to write the guidelines in such a way that most conservative nominees could be rejected.[4]

Because the seminary's charter did not require trustees to elect the persons nominated by the convention, this seemed an attractive option. The persons nominated by the 1987 Southern Baptist Convention to serve on the board came up for approval in April 1988. At the meeting of the trustee executive committee, two members voted against their election.[5] When their election came before the full board later the same day, several trustees spoke against accepting them. The board voted to elect them, but two trustees voted against doing so.[6] The two "nays" seemed to suggest that in principle a majority might defeat persons nominated by the convention.

Conservative trustees were alarmed by these events. John Michael said that executive committee chairman Sam McMahon confirmed to him that he wanted "to ensure that only trustees of the specified qualification are elected."[7] McMahon told him that "recently elected trustees were regarded as disloyal, incompetent, and inclined to destroy the seminary," and that some trustees were seeking legal counsel to make sure that their rejection of convention nominees had binding authority. If the Southern Baptist Convention withdrew funding

4. Minutes, Trustee Executive Committee, Southern Baptist Theological Seminary, 2 Feb. 1988.

5. Minutes, Executive Committee of the Board of Trustees, Southern Baptist Theological Seminary, 11 Apr. 1988.

6. Minutes, Board of Trustees, Southern Baptist Theological Seminary, 11 Apr. 1988.

7. John Michael to Roy Honeycutt, 7 Mar. 1988, John Michael 1984–89 folder, Honeycutt Papers.

in response to such a move, McMahon believed that individual churches and some state conventions could provide sufficient support.[8]

But most moderate trustees seemed to disfavor the plan. Perry F. Webb Jr., for example, urged caution. He wanted a "thorough evaluation of all that is involved." He feared that declaring their independence from the Southern Baptist Convention would "alienate us from our friends." He could not yet support such a move, in part because he still expected Southern Baptists to return the convention "back into the main stream." But he also worried that they would be unable to bear the inevitable loss of funding from the Southern Baptist Convention: "I do not believe there is enough money among our friends to provide the resources to carry on the work."[9]

Honeycutt was outwardly neutral, but he opposed the idea of making the seminary independent of the convention. Bill Hull, a member of the Peace Committee, summarized Honeycutt's views after a long conversation with him charting the seminary's options in light of developments on the committee: "Honeycutt felt that any 'distancing' or 'buffer' strategies to detach Southern Seminary from the SBC family would ultimately prove disastrous. In his view, the seminary is totally Southern Baptist by heritage, identity, and purpose, and could not survive meaningfully as a 'semi-independent' institution." Hull reported that Honeycutt "would not support legal moves" to place the seminary in a relationship more independent from the Southern Baptist Convention.[10] Honeycutt's opposition to the plan undermined trustee support for it.[11]

The ad hoc committee commissioned to develop trustee qualification guidelines ultimately commended deference to the Southern Baptist Convention's nominations to the board. It reported that "legally the seminary has no option other than to elect duly qualified persons nominated by the Southern Baptist

8. John Michael, "Controversy at Southern Seminary," *The SBC Cause*, June 1988, 16. Michael and McMahon discussed the matter by telephone on 29 Feb. 1988, and Michael wrote a letter with further discussion a week later (John Michael to Sam McMahon Jr., 29 Feb. 1988, John Michael 1984–89 folder, Honeycutt Papers).

9. Perry F. Webb Jr. to Roy Honeycutt, 15 Oct. 1987, Perry F. Webb Jr. folder, Honeycutt Papers.

10. Bill Hull, memo to SBC Peace Committee file, 25 Feb. 1987, SBC Issues 1987 folder, Honeycutt Papers. The telephone conversation occurred on 23 Feb. 1987, in response to the Feb. 18–19 meeting of the Peace Committee.

11. Honeycutt wrote John Michael that "with regard to my position concerning the work of the ad hoc committee, I will reserve judgment on that until the committee has completed its work" (Roy Honeycutt to John Michael, 9 Mar. 1988, John Michael 1984–89 folder, Honeycutt Papers).

Convention." The convention's proposed guidelines for trustee qualifications were broad enough to apply to most conservative and moderate trustees.[12]

In 1990 the board voted to amend the seminary's charter to permit the Southern Baptist Convention to elect trustees directly.[13]

SAVING SOUTHERN SEMINARY BY COMPROMISE

Honeycutt nevertheless had no intention of delivering the seminary willingly to conservative domination. He delayed and obstructed conservative changes when possible. And when conservative trustees grew frustrated by the obstructionism and pressed for thorough change, he pushed through compromises that weakened the character of the change. He yielded to conservative demands only when he thought it absolutely necessary to do so. Honeycutt wanted to protect his moderate faculty and provide for the persistence of moderate principles for as long as possible. He also wanted to make the conservative renovation of the seminary a long and painstaking process. He cooperated with conservative trustees in order to control the takeover—to slow its progress, to limit the damage done to the institution's moderate heritage, and to ensure that the moderate faculty were well entrenched. He was remarkably effective. He aimed to save the seminary by compromise.

Peter Rhea Jones urged Honeycutt in 1986 to bargain with the leaders of the "far-right" in order to secure the safety of the seminary—"to keep the barbarians outside the walls." Some "proactive compromising now" would be better than waiting for "these people to ruin our seminary and make us bitter for life." He suggested that Honeycutt "develop some compromises where you would give up ten percent in order to save ninety." This would mean compelling Glenn Hinson, Paul Simmons, and Molly Marshall "to modify or moderate their positions," and it would mean hiring "two or three highly conservative scholars."[14] But Honeycutt would not bargain until forced.

Honeycutt was also optimistic in the longer view. Sooner or later Southern Baptists would reject domination by the Pressler-Patterson political faction. He aimed to hold on as long as he could and limit damage to the seminary

12. "Report of the Ad Hoc Committee of the Executive Committee on Guidelines for Trustee Election and Function," p. 6, n. 9, in Minutes, Executive Committee of the Board of Trustees, Southern Baptist Theological Seminary, 11 Apr. 1988.

13. Minutes, Board of Trustees, Southern Baptist Theological Seminary, 23–25 Apr. 1990, 7–8.

14. Peter Rhea Jones to Roy Honeycutt, 24 July 1986, SBC Issues 1985–86 (13–09) folder, Honeycutt Papers.

by conservative trustees. He was not discouraged because he was confident that at some point in the future the Southern Baptist Convention would swing back their way, and moderates could retake control. His strategy, Honeycutt told a moderate pastor, "focuses basically on what happens to us in the interim between this point and the collapse of the fundamentalist movement."[15] His compromises might preserve the seminary for that day.

Honeycutt's dedication to saving the seminary reflected not only the value he placed on its moderate faculty and heritage but his belief that the inerrantists would wreck everything he valued about the seminary. Like many moderates, Honeycutt was convinced that inerrantists were anti-intellectual boors who would profane and desecrate the sanctum of learning. Bill Tuck, pastor of Louisville's St. Matthews Baptist Church and former Southern Seminary professor, spoke for many moderates when he told his congregation that the inerrantists were heretics whose "philosophy is based on ignorance" and whose "beliefs are based on fear." They feared truth, Tuck said, demanded conformity, and "do not believe in real education but in indoctrination."[16]

In the fall of 1987 moderates won significant victories in several state conventions. Some moderate leaders took this as evidence that they could retake the presidency of the Southern Baptist Convention in June 1988 in San Antonio.[17] Honeycutt was guardedly optimistic that these victories would renew moderate morale and produce a large moderate turnout at San Antonio. Moreover, since there was no sitting president up for reelection, the Texas moderates were now well organized, and after nine consecutive conservative victories, the "desperate nature of the times" meant that moderate victory in San Antonio was "crucial." He therefore gave the alumni association president a seminary-paid credit card and urged him to work the phones "on our behalf" and, working with the other seminary alumni, "coordinate a massive level of support by our alumni for San Antonio."[18]

Moderates also had a new cause célèbre. In the fall of 1987, President Randall Lolley and Dean Morris Ashcraft of the Southeastern Baptist Theological

15. Roy Honeycutt to Norman Cavender, 24 July 1987, SBC Issues 1987 folder, Honeycutt Papers.

16. William Tuck, "Pastor's Paragraphs," in the Bulletin of Saint Matthews Baptist Church (Louisville, Kentucky), 26 Oct. 1987, typescript copy in SBC Issues 1987 folder, Honeycutt Papers.

17. Peter Rhea Jones to Roy Honeycutt, 23 Nov. 1987, SBC Issues 1987 folder, Honeycutt Papers; Jim Jones, "Baptist Moderate Sees Shift," *Fort Worth Star-Telegram*, 12 Nov. 1987, sect. 1, 21–22.

18. Roy Honeycutt to G. Todd Wilson, 30 Nov. 1987, SBC Issues 1987 folder, Honeycutt Papers.

Seminary resigned after conservatives gained a majority on the school's board of trustees. Many moderates hoped that the spectacle of Southeastern Seminary falling to the revolutionaries would finally convince Southern Baptists to vote them out of office at the San Antonio meeting.

In 1987 Honeycutt believed also that he could keep conservatives from gaining a majority on the trustee board for at least four or five more years. New trustee orientation had become a sort of moderate reeducation camp, and Honeycutt and trustee leaders worked hard to turn conservative trustees. Honeycutt had won over three or four trustees elected by conservatives, and his aim was "to win the support of enough trustees elected by fundamentalists to assure a continuing working majority" of the trustee board.[19] Bill Hull reported that Honeycutt had achieved such "good success in winning the loyalty of all but a few 'hardcore' ministerial fundamentalists" that Honeycutt calculated that in the most likely scenario "it might be six to eight years, or even longer, before fundamentalists would have overwhelming control" of the board.[20] In fact it would be only three.

TO HIRE AN INERRANTIST

At the April 1987 board meeting conservative trustees pressed Honeycutt about hiring conservative professors. He had pledged to do so in the 1986 Glorieta Statement, but he had done nothing. His response was conciliatory, and the following year he recommended a conservative for election to the faculty. But the rider he attached to the recommendation angered many conservative trustees.

Honeycutt did not want to hire inerrantist faculty and yielded only to the extent necessary to keep "the dream alive." Inerrantists would destroy collegiality, he believed, and divide the faculty. And he did not believe that genuine Southern Baptist scholars could hold the "narrow" fundamentalist theology of Southern Baptist conservative leaders. Most moderate leaders believed that an inerrantist scholar was an oxymoron, a practical impossibility since intelligent and informed persons could not rationally believe in inerrancy. Moderates furthermore held that inerrantists undermined the Southern Baptist commitment to soul competency through intolerance of other views of the scriptures. True Southern Baptists held the moderate understanding of soul competency.

19. Roy Honeycutt to G. Todd Wilson, 30 Nov. 1987, SBC Issues 1987 folder, Honeycutt Papers.

20. William Hull, memo to SBC Peace Committee file, 25 Feb. 1987, in SBC Issues 1987 folder, Honeycutt Papers.

Honeycutt therefore did not believe that he could find any inerrantists who were scholars and who were genuine Southern Baptists. Those who had strong Southern Baptist credentials had been schooled in the denomination's traditions of "soul competency and the authority of scripture by the individual" and did not belong to the "narrowly focused theological group"—the fundamentalists. To find Baptists with such a narrow theology, they had to look to northern evangelical schools like Trinity Evangelical Divinity School in Chicago. But Honeycutt had "major reservations" about their "limited Baptist experience." [21] They did not seem to be authentically Southern Baptist. Of course, by definition, authentic Southern Baptists could hardly have a narrow theology.

During the 1980s the seminary had a couple of inerrantist faculty members. Lewis Drummond was the Billy Graham Professor of Evangelism since 1973. Timothy George, professor of historical theology, came on the faculty in 1978 directly from doctoral work at Harvard Divinity School. The faculty received him as a credentialed liberal, but in the years after his hiring he returned to the conservative Southern Baptist faith he knew as a youth. Both professors resigned in 1988, Drummond to become president of Southeastern Baptist Theological Seminary, and George to become dean of the new Beeson Divinity School at Samford University. Another inerrantist, Phil Roberts, taught at the seminary from 1982 to 1984 and served later as president of the Midwestern Baptist Theological Seminary.

In April 1988 Honeycutt nominated his first avowed inerrantist, David Dockery. In order to recommend a candidate to the trustees, the president had to inform them of the faculty's opinion of the candidate. Faculty expressed their opinion by ballot after interviewing a candidate. Dockery was a strong candidate, and the faculty interview went well.

Dockery was young and was just completing his doctoral work, but he was impressive, intelligent, and well-spoken and had a good sense of humor. And he had already shown unusual promise as a scholar. He was a bona fide conservative, a convinced inerrantist with degrees from Grace Theological Seminary and Southwestern Baptist Theological Seminary, and a professor at the Criswell Bible College and on the pastoral staff of Dallas First Baptist Church. Perhaps most important, he was raised in Southern Baptist churches and was recognizably "Southern Baptist."

The faculty knew that Honeycutt wanted them to approve a conservative professor, since he had pledged that he would not even consider any other kind of candidate for this position. But the faculty's approval of any candidate could be an uncertain venture, and an inerrantist candidate fought an uphill battle.

<hr />

21. Roy Honeycutt to Herschel Hobbs, 4 Feb. 1988, SBC Peace Committee 1985–90 folder, Honeycutt Papers.

David S. Dockery

Candidates before and after Dockery suffered rejection by the majority. Dockery managed, however, to win them over. They voted 48 to 5 to recommend his election.[22] The trustees elected him without apparent opposition. Nine years after the start of the conservative effort to renovate Southern Baptist Convention entities, Southern Baptist Theological Seminary had its first "fundamentalist" professor.

Honeycutt interpreted Dockery's election as symbolizing the trustees' commitment to establishing a "centrist" seminary. Since 1986 he had repeated forcefully and passionately his pledge to hire conservatives. His moderate friends and allies criticized him for making such a commitment, and Honeycutt delayed. Hiring Dockery was a fulfillment of that pledge. Hiring Dockery gave credibility to Honeycutt's pledge to cooperate with the conservative trustees. It also gave him leverage to ask for protection for the moderate faculty. He had now gone halfway toward the conservatives. He asked them to meet him in the middle and commit themselves to a "centrist" seminary in which the moderate faculty had a legitimate place. He told the trustees that Dockery would be a "substantive

22. Roy Honeycutt, in Transcript, Annual Meeting of the Board of Trustees, Southern Baptist Theological Seminary, 13 Apr. 1988, tape 6, p. 8, SBTS.

symbol saying that this institution is a centrist seminary and that we can reach out with arms in the center in both directions."[23] Conservative trustees, however, did not accept Honeycutt's interpretation. They aimed to build a conservative faculty and were not interested in a half-conservative one.

Honeycutt asked for something in return for his support of Dockery. He wanted trustees to grant tenure to Molly Marshall. With tenure, Marshall would have considerable protection against efforts to oust her from the faculty. Without it, her contract would expire in a couple of years, and she would not be rehired. Honeycutt was seeking to encumber the ground that the conservatives would soon control. He was ensconcing the moderate faculty firmly in place in order that the problems entailed in removing them would be greater than those entailed in retaining them. "This will be one more area nailed down for a future" dominated by conservative trustees.[24]

Honeycutt knew that many trustees would object, since Marshall had been one of the chief targets of conservative criticism of the faculty. On the board of trustees, John Michael was convinced that she was a heretic and had been out-spoken in his opposition to her presence on the faculty. Honeycutt knew that if he delayed, the opposition to Marshall would grow stronger as the conservative faction on the board grew annually.

The trustee Academic Personnel Committee was dominated by moderates and voted unanimously to recommend granting tenure to Marshall after the "most extensive and thorough interview ever held with a faculty member" in chairman James Monroe's memory.[25] He told the board that although in the past accusations arose against Marshall based on her dissertation, the full board thoroughly investigated the charges and dismissed them in the 1986 response to the Peace Committee. He said that her dissertation would have remained "largely unread" and no controversy would have arisen if some of her opponents had not insisted on circulating copies of it. Her dissertation dealt with difficult questions "on the periphery" and did not find "final answers." Her "basic convictions and her teaching" were sound and in accordance with the Abstract of Principles.[26]

23. Roy Honeycutt, in Transcript, Annual Meeting of the Board of Trustees, Southern Baptist Theological Seminary, 13 Apr. 1988, tape 6, p. 10, SBTS.

24. Roy Honeycutt to William Henry Crouch, 6 Apr. 1988, SBC Issues 1988–89 folder, Honeycutt Papers.

25. James Monroe, in Transcript, Annual Meeting of the Board of Trustees, Southern Baptist Theological Seminary, 13 Apr. 1988, tape 6, p. 11, SBTS.

26. James Monroe, in Transcript, Annual Meeting of the Board of Trustees, Southern Baptist Theological Seminary, 13 Apr. 1988, tape 6, pp. 12–14, SBTS.

Trustee Mark Coppenger, executive secretary of the Southern Baptist state convention in Indiana, objected that Marshall believed that unredeemed persons yearned for God and were grasping for God, and that God would bestow grace in view of such yearning. He judged that she violated the Abstract of Principles article on the fall of man, which stated that all persons inherit a "nature corrupt and wholly opposed to God."[27] Trustee John Michael charged that Marshall held that persons could be saved without consciously believing in Jesus and that the intention of one's heart rather than explicit faith in Christ determined who received mercy. Michael charged also that she taught a postmortem opportunity for salvation and that Christ was working in non-Christian religions to save people apart from knowledge of the Christian gospel. He said that her affirmation that some people might be damned was an afterthought that was inconsistent with the thrust of the entire dissertation. He charged finally that she condemned evangelical missions as inadequate because they were based on a gospel that required explicit repentance and faith in Christ in response to the Christian gospel. These beliefs, he said, violated articles 10 and 11 of the Abstract of Principles.[28]

Moderate trustees urged that Marshall had answered all charges against her satisfactorily, that students loved her, and that they ought to trust the evaluation and recommendation of the Academic Personnel Committee. Honeycutt defended her views as placing Christ in the center of all of God's redemptive activity. He then defended her right to do research and to speculate on the fate of those who never heard the gospel: "Her thesis is filled with 'maybe' and 'perhaps' and concludes by saying 'we must leave that in hands of God.'"[29]

Ordinarily the trustees discussed matters of personnel behind closed doors in "executive session," but they voted to suspend the rule to permit the presence of the large audience of students, faculty, and reporters. The debate was long. The chairman had to warn the onlookers several times to refrain from expressing themselves during the proceedings.[30]

And then, as he often did on contested issues, Honeycutt made it personal. He construed the vote as a vote on his leadership. He urged that the trustees adopt the recommendations out of their belief in him and his integrity. He told

27. Mark Coppenger, in Transcript, Annual Meeting of the Board of Trustees, Southern Baptist Theological Seminary, 13 Apr. 1988, tape 6, pp. 15, 26; tape 7, p. 4, SBTS.

28. Transcript, Annual Meeting of the Board of Trustees, Southern Baptist Theological Seminary, 13 Apr. 1988, tape 6, pp. 22–23, SBTS.

29. Roy Honeycutt, in Transcript, Annual Meeting of the Board of Trustees, Southern Baptist Theological Seminary, 13 Apr. 1988, tape 6, pp. 30, 32, SBTS.

30. Transcript, Annual Meeting of the Board of Trustees, Southern Baptist Theological Seminary, 13 Apr. 1988, tape 6, pp. 16, 19; tape 7, p. 19, SBTS.

the trustees that the question before them was about more "than granting tenure to a faculty member." The vote was also about "whether or not you support me as president in the commitments that I have made to the alumni of this seminary…in a variety of different forums." He had asked the alumni to support the school because the board of trustees "can work together" despite their differences, and make Southern Seminary a "centrist seminary, where we can reach out in both directions."[31]

Honeycutt sought to strap the vote on Marshall's tenure to the vote to elect Dockery. By voting tenure to Marshall, trustees would declare to the whole world that "Southern Seminary is a centrist seminary." He construed it as a straightforward matter of fair play: "We have reached out with one arm to bring in a professor…from Criswell College, and I ask you to reach out with the other arm and bring Molly Marshall-Green to tenure."[32] He was living up to his half of the denominational bargain by hiring a conservative; they should in good faith meet him halfway and tenure Marshall. The two recommendations were a package deal.

Some conservative trustees were unmoved. Honeycutt had hired no avowed conservatives before now. Hiring one conservative did not make Southern a "centrist" seminary. Until Honeycutt hired a faculty that was at least 50 percent conservatives, the appeal to fairness had little force. Nor did they believe that Marshall taught within the boundaries of the Abstract of Principles, and they could not in good conscience vote to grant her tenure. In the end, the board voted 45 to 7 in favor of tenure.[33]

Two-thirds of the board's conservative trustees voted in favor of Marshall's tenure. They did so because the moderate trustees had already secured assurance that conservative trustees would not block the vote. The moderate trustees negotiated with Wayne Allen, the caucus leader for most of the conservative trustees. They told him that if he would urge conservative trustees to vote for Marshall's tenure, they would not block Dockery's election, and they would give conservative trustees two seats on the executive committee. These were small concessions. Honeycutt had unalterably committed himself to hire a conservative for the New Testament position, and two seats on the nineteen-member executive committee would accomplish little for conservatives.

31. Roy Honeycutt, in Transcript, Annual Meeting of the Board of Trustees, Southern Baptist Theological Seminary, 13 Apr. 1988, tape 7, p. 14, SBTS.

32. Roy Honeycutt, in Transcript, Annual Meeting of the Board of Trustees, Southern Baptist Theological Seminary, 13 Apr. 1988, tape 7, p. 15, SBTS.

33. There were also three abstentions. Transcript, Annual Meeting of the Board of Trustees, Southern Baptist Theological Seminary, 13 Apr. 1988, tape 7, pp. 19–20, SBTS.

When Wayne Allen gathered about a dozen of the conservative trustees for a premeeting caucus session, he urged them to accept the deal. They did not have enough votes to block Marshall's tenure, he said, so they would do better to accept the deal and get something out of it. They also needed to consider the denominational context. Conservatives were facing a very difficult contest for convention president two months later at the San Antonio Southern Baptist Convention. If they raised a hue and cry against Marshall's tenure, it might create enough backlash against the conservatives to lose the presidency in what promised to be a very close election.

CONSERVATIVE TRUSTEES TAKE CHARGE

Moderate denominational leaders met defeat in 1988 but made one final push to defeat conservatives at the 1990 meeting of the Southern Baptist Convention. When the convention met in New Orleans that year, messengers elected conservative candidate Morris Chapman by a large majority, and moderate leaders declared the battle over. They organized an alternative set of affiliations for disaffected moderates in 1991 known as the Cooperative Baptist Fellowship.

With the denominational outlook altered by the events of 1990 and 1991, Honeycutt reassessed his approach to leading Southern Seminary. Conservative control of the board of trustees would soon become a reality. He apparently considered joining other moderates and taking leadership in one of their alternative organizations. But in 1991 Honeycutt committed himself "to preserve as much of the wholeness of this seminary as possible." Victory was no longer a possibility; his objective now was "damage control." He felt responsible to "preserve as much of our heritage for as long as we can in this seminary."[34]

All parties looked toward the April 1990 meeting of the board of trustees with concern. Students, faculty, and the moderate trustees feared that conservatives might achieve a majority at the meeting and begin to impose their vision on the seminary in warp and woof. Conservatives feared that moderate trustees would somehow block their majority. When trustees gathered on campus, some 300 students wearing matching "Maintain the Vision" shirts crowded into the meeting room. When the students were asked to leave during executive sessions, trustees could hear them outside as they prayed and sang hymns, keeping vigil in protest of the conservative threat to the school's moderate character.[35]

34. Roy Honeycutt, quoted in Mark Wingfield, "Honeycutt Speaks to 'Set Record Straight,'" *Western Recorder*, 25 May 1993, 3, SBTS.

35. David Wilkinson and Pat Cole, "Conservatives Take Control of Southern Seminary Board," news release, Southern Baptist Theological Seminary, 26 Apr. 1990, in Board of Trustees, Apr. 1990 folder, Honeycutt Papers.

Trustee meeting, April 1990

Moderate trustees did indeed try to block a conservative majority by putting three new moderates on the board, but the conservatives defeated the effort and attained majority on the board, with striking results.[36] They immediately sketched out a new vision for the school.

The meeting began with a test of party strength. The board's moderate-controlled executive committee knew that conservatives might attain a majority at this meeting. They took advantage of the board's prerogative to elect trustees to seats that had been vacated between meetings of the Southern Baptist Convention and nominated for election to the board three moderate candidates, who were present at the start of the meeting. Conservative trustees successfully divided the slate and nominated alternative candidates. The conservative nominees won close votes, but the three could not be seated because they received less than the required two-thirds majority.[37] The initial voting revealed that the conservatives had about a six-vote majority of the fifty-eight members in attendance. Although the conservatives did not control the executive committee,

36. For accounts of the meeting, see Bill Wolfe, "Conservative Trustees Move on Baptist Seminary," *Louisville Courier-Journal*, 25 Apr. 1990, 1; James C. Hefley, *The Conservative Resurgence in the Southern Baptist Convention* (Hannibal, MO: Hannibal Books, 1991), 162–174.

37. Minutes, Board of Trustees, Southern Baptist Theological Seminary, 23–25 Apr. 1990, 2–3.

the chairman position, or most committees, they took effective control of the meeting and practically dictated its agenda.

In the first matter of new business, conservative trustee David Miller moved adoption of a resolution declaring the board's opposition "to any and all abortions except where the physical life of the mother is in danger." They additionally warned faculty and staff against publicly advocating the pro-choice position and urged them to work for legislation to eliminate abortion on demand. The conservative majority voted to make it a roll call vote to record the vote of each trustee. The resolution passed 32 to 26.[38] Conservatives also voted through a controversial policy to permit students to record lectures in seminary classes.[39]

Conservatives blocked a recommendation to affirm controversial professor Glenn Hinson. The Academic Personnel Committee recommended commending Hinson for his explanation and apology for publicly criticizing the conservative majority in the Southern Baptist Convention and recommending that churches stop sending funds to the denomination's Cooperative Program. The conservatives forced a substitute that required Honeycutt to communicate to Hinson the board's concern regarding his "intemperate comments about controversial issues which negatively affect the public perceptions of Southern Seminary."[40]

Conservative trustees similarly voted to replace the Academic Personnel Committee's commendation of Honeycutt's investigation of accusations against Paul Simmons. Honeycutt had concluded that no grounds for dismissal of Paul Simmons existed. The report of the moderate-controlled committee affirmed Honeycutt's conclusion but expressed "disappointment, disapproval, and deep concern" regarding Simmons's activities. The conservative majority, which disagreed that there were no grounds for dismissal, amended the report to remove exonerating language and to emphasize the board's disapproval of Simmons's activities "relating to abortion." They also added a warning: "His continued activities in this area may be considered sufficient grounds for dismissal."[41]

The conservative takeover of the board provoked considerable indignation. The *Louisville Courier-Journal* covered the trustee conflict extensively during and after the meeting. Local columnist Bob Hill suggested that the "intolerant"

38. Minutes, Board of Trustees, Southern Baptist Theological Seminary, 23–25 Apr. 1990, 3–5.

39. Minutes, Board of Trustees, Southern Baptist Theological Seminary, 23–25 Apr. 1990, 6.

40. Minutes, Board of Trustees, Southern Baptist Theological Seminary, 23–25 Apr. 1990, 13–14, 16–17.

41. Minutes, Board of Trustees, Southern Baptist Theological Seminary, 23–25 Apr. 1990, 16–17.

conservative trustees were ignorant, stupid, and vindictive.[42] The paper's editorial staff denounced them as "saboteurs" whose "witchhunt" threatened the seminary's future as a place of learning.[43] The faculty of the nearby Louisville Presbyterian Theological Seminary gathered in front of Southern Seminary's Norton Hall in academic gowns and read a statement expressing sympathy with the faculty and administration, and urging trustees to protect academic freedom.[44] Sympathetic alumni urged indignant Southern Baptists to get out the vote to elect Daniel Vestal, the moderate candidate, as president of the Southern Baptist Convention at its June 1990 meeting in New Orleans.[45]

Although Honeycutt and moderate trustees were appalled at the conservatives' actions, they had one important victory. Trustees elected as chairman of the board one of the leading moderate members, Sam McMahon Jr.[46] But both groups knew that McMahon would be the last moderate chairman for some time. Conservatives successfully challenged the nomination of two moderates to the executive committee and replaced them with conservatives.[47] And fully three-quarters of the new members elected to the board's executive committee were conservatives.[48] Conservatives now had a majority both on the board and on its critical executive committee.[49] It was a strategic victory toward achieving their ambition to remake the seminary. They soon discovered, however, that

42. Bob Hill, "Intolerance in the Name of Education," *Louisville Courier-Journal*, 28 Apr. 1990, Scene, 3.

43. Editorial, "Seminary Saboteurs," *Louisville Courier-Journal*, 28 Apr. 1990, 14A.

44. Bill Wolfe, "Presbyterian Teachers Give Support to Baptist Faculty in Dispute with Trustees," *Louisville Courier-Journal*, 15 May 1990, 1B.

45. See R. Albert Mohler, "Southern's Georgia Alumni Meet to Hear Honeycutt," *Christian Index*, 24 May 1990, 1, 3.

46. Some conservatives probably voted for him in deference to board tradition and to honor his generosity. McMahon was chairman of the executive committee and vice chairman of the full board, and trustees traditionally elected this officer as chairman of the full board the subsequent year. McMahon had given substantial gifts to the seminary. Six conservatives insisted that their vote against McMahon be recorded in the minutes. Minutes, Board of Trustees, Southern Baptist Theological Seminary, 23–25 Apr. 1990, 18.

47. David Wilkinson and Pat Cole, "Conservatives Take Control of Southern Seminary Board," news release, Southern Baptist Theological Seminary, 26 Apr. 1990, in Board of Trustees, Apr. 1990 folder, Honeycutt Papers.

48. Of the eight elected, six had voted in favor of the resolution against abortion. Minutes, Board of Trustees, Southern Baptist Theological Seminary, 23–25 Apr. 1990, 18.

49. Eleven of the nineteen members of the 1990–1991 executive committee voted in favor of the resolution against abortion. Minutes, Board of Trustees, Southern Baptist Theological Seminary, 23–25 Apr. 1990, Attachment E.

even with a trustee majority, they could achieve only limited success while Honeycutt remained president. There would be no additional major shift until trustees elected a new president.

THE "COVER-UP AT SOUTHERN SEMINARY"

The most surprising aspect of the 1990 trustee meeting was when freshman trustee Jerry Johnson publicly accused Honeycutt of colluding to hide from Southern Baptists the truth about the teaching at Southern Seminary. Johnson mailed a fourteen-page document titled "The Cover-Up at Southern Seminary" to all trustees the week before the meeting of the board. He sent a copy also to the conservative *Southern Baptist Advocate*.

In the document Johnson denounced the "doctrinal infidelity" found in the writings of Honeycutt, Marshall, and Hinson and indicted Honeycutt for tolerating such errors. He asked why Frank Tupper had not been fired for his repeated use of profanity in a course in 1983. He criticized Paul Simmons for his pro-choice views and his outspoken political activism to promote abortion rights, especially in view of the fact that the Southern Baptist Convention had repeatedly condemned abortion. He criticized Honeycutt also for his aggressive public rhetoric and behind-the-scenes activity in support of moderates' efforts to unseat conservatives from the convention presidency. Johnson asserted that Honeycutt and his faculty covered up their heresies by appeal to prerogatives of scholars and specialists to engage their own field on its own terms. They claimed that they were writing for a special audience, scholars or educated persons generally, and that their fundamentalist critics could not understand their writings. They covered up their heresies also, Johnson said, by granting the broadest possible construction of the Abstract of Principles.[50]

Honeycutt quickly produced a lengthy reply. He noted that Johnson's criticisms implicitly charged the trustees with collusion in the "cover-up," since the trustees had already investigated these charges in 1986. He pointed out also that after their investigation, the trustees had exonerated all the accused professors. There had been no cover-up.[51]

Most of Honeycutt's reply consisted of a reprise of his response to the concerns raised by the Peace Committee, in which he defended himself from the

---

50. Jerry Johnson, "The Cover-up at Southern Seminary," in Board of Trustees 1990 folder, Honeycutt Papers. The seminary administration admonished Tupper, who apologized.

51. Roy Honeycutt, "Response to 'The Cover-up at Southern Seminary,'" p. 2, in Board of Trustees 1990 folder, Honeycutt Papers.

charge of rejecting the historicity of miracle accounts and charged the conservative *Criswell Study Bible* with doing the same thing he did. Ironically, Honeycutt's response in places seemed to buttress Johnson's claims as much as to undermine them. Johnson claimed, for example, that Honeycutt accused Elijah of immorality for calling down fire upon fifty men as the Bible said he did. Honeycutt replied that he did not call the act immoral, he only questioned "whether anyone today would defend the morality of calling down fire from heaven upon groups of fifty men as Elijah did." He did not call Elijah's act immoral, he continued, but "I do reject that model as an appropriate response to one's enemy."[52] Or when defending the historicity of the narrative in which Elijah made a sunken axhead float, Honeycutt claimed that when he described such stories as "saga or legend," he did not deny "the historicity of an event." But he discounted the historical value of the details of the story—"what we have now is the barest, minimal account."[53] Johnson's accusations may have breached protocol and taste, but they seemed to have some basis.

Johnson's accusations increased the tension between conservative trustees and the rest of the seminary community. Sixty members of the seminary faculty endorsed a statement expressing their "moral outrage" at Johnson's accusations and called for his resignation from the board.[54] The board had to respond to Johnson's charges. The executive committee voted to hold a special called meeting of the board in September 1990 "to confer with trustee Jerry Johnson regarding his article."[55] At the meeting Johnson told trustees that he met Honeycutt earlier that day to apologize and ask his forgiveness. He then read a letter of apology for his "lack of judgment," his "ill-chosen and too harsh" expressions, and for expressing his concerns in public rather than through the board's internal processes. The board voted to accept Johnson's apology and affirm his standing as a member of the board.[56]

Johnson's "Cover-Up" encouraged conservative trustee John Michael to renew his complaint regarding Honeycutt's handling of the Peace Committee investigation. Michael defended Johnson's charges and used the opportunity to

52. Roy Honeycutt, "Response to 'The Cover-up at Southern Seminary,'" p. 14, in Board of Trustees 1990 folder, Honeycutt Papers.

53. Roy Honeycutt, "Response to 'The Cover-up at Southern Seminary,'" pp. 19–20, in Board of Trustees 1990 folder, Honeycutt Papers.

54. Bill Wolfe, "Irate Professors Want Seminary Trustee to Resign," *Louisville Courier-Journal*, 9 May 1990, 1.

55. Minutes, Executive Committee of the Board of Trustees, Southern Baptist Theological Seminary, 11 June 1990.

56. Minutes, Board of Trustees, Southern Baptist Theological Seminary, 24 Sept. 1990.

press anew for a thorough investigation to compare Honeycutt's explanations of the faculty's writings with actual copies of the writings. On May 3, 1990, Michael invited Honeycutt to take the initiative to correct his misrepresentation of faculty beliefs in his 1986 Peace Committee report and thus "save the seminary and your presidency from an embarrassing inquiry."[57] Honeycutt declined the invitation.

SURRENDER BY DEGREES: COVENANT RENEWAL AND PARITY

Honeycutt's goal of preserving the seminary's heritage became much more difficult once conservatives attained the majority of the board. His basic strategy changed little, however. When possible, he got out in front of the trustees in order to preempt their initiatives and secure a result more favorable to moderate concerns. In other cases he persuaded trustees to rescind their action in favor of a compromise proposal. But with conservatives dominating the board, Honeycutt had little choice but to make concessions that went much further toward the conservative vision than he had done before 1990.

Honeycutt had long recognized that conservative efforts to transform the seminary would concentrate on hiring new faculty. Conservatives wanted all faculty at all six seminaries to accept the inerrancy of the Bible, which, they believed, entailed understanding the Bible's statements as literally and historically accurate. But trustees faced daunting obstacles. Any efforts to impose such criteria on tenured faculty would likely fail or result in more resignations and the total collapse of student enrollment, Honeycutt predicted. Firing tenured faculty members would be legally difficult and politically damaging. Conservatives, Honeycutt told Bill Hull in 1987, would therefore focus their attention on the "employment of new personnel." They would seek to impose a "rigid fundamentalist understanding of inerrancy" for all new faculty.[58]

In the course of resolving the "cover-up" controversy, the trustee executive committee adopted a motion in September 1990 refusing to revisit the president's 1986 report responding to the concerns of the Peace Committee and the board's action adopting the report. But as part of the same recommendation, the executive committee adopted a measure of profound significance. It agreed that the "Findings" section as well as the "Recommendations" section of the

57. John Michael to Roy Honeycutt, 18 May 1990, Ad Hoc Committee—John Michael 1990 folder, Honeycutt Papers.

58. William Hull, memo to SBC Peace Committee file, 25 Feb. 1987, in SBC Issues 1987 folder, Honeycutt Papers.

Peace Committee report should "serve as a guideline for the employment of temporary and permanent faculty and the granting of tenure." [59]

The Peace Committee's 1987 report to the Southern Baptist Convention consisted of a section titled "Findings" and one titled "Recommendations." Honeycutt held that when the Southern Baptist Convention adopted the report, it did not impose the report's findings on the seminaries, but only the recommendations. Although he was technically correct, his dismissal of the findings section was antagonistic to the spirit of the report. Moderates objected especially to the discussion of what Southern Baptists meant when they characterized the Bible as without error. The committee found that when Southern Baptists said that the Bible was "truth without mixture of error," they meant that its statements were literally and facially true. The committee listed four specific examples to illustrate the point: "(1) They believe in direct creation of mankind and therefore they believe that Adam and Eve were real persons. (2) They believe the named authors did indeed write the biblical books attributed to them by those books. (3) They believe the miracles described in scripture did indeed occur as supernatural events in history. (4) They believe that the historical narratives given by biblical authors are indeed accurate and reliable as given by those authors." [60]

In 1988 Honeycutt had told the trustee board's executive committee that he would not hire conservatives who met the criteria of the findings sections of the Peace Committee report. Honeycutt assured trustee George Steincross, "I do not intend however (as I said in the meeting of the Executive Committee) to select faculty who are committed to the [Peace Committee's] report and more specifically the four examples within the report." [61] The new trustee policy would force Honeycutt to do just that. Faculty, in order to gain election or attain tenure, would have to affirm these interpretations. The full board adopted this recommendation at its September 1990 meeting. [62]

This new policy shook the seminary to its foundations. For most faculty, students, and administrators, it meant the seminary's devastation, since all new faculty would be extreme fundamentalists, obscurantists hostile to everything good in the seminary's heritage. It meant also that none of the untenured

59. Minutes, Committee of the Whole of the Board of Trustees, Southern Baptist Theological Seminary, 24 Sept. 1990.

60. "The SBC Peace Committee Report," in Shurden and Shepley, *Going for the Jugular: A Documentary History of the SBC Holy War*, 214.

61. Roy Honeycutt to George Steincross, 9 May 1988, George Steincross folder, Honeycutt Papers.

62. Minutes, Board of Trustees, Southern Baptist Theological Seminary, 24 Sept. 1990.

professors on the current faculty could qualify for tenure. It meant the end of Southern Seminary as they knew it.

The faculty and administration moved quickly, therefore, to overturn the policy. They gained considerable leverage in early February 1991 when they learned that the school's accreditation was at risk. William Baumgaertner, a staff member of the Association of Theological Schools, had conducted a preliminary investigation of the seminary and recommended that the agency's accrediting commission send a team to evaluate the situation and make recommendations relating to the school's continuing accreditation. Baumgaertner, echoing faculty feeling, felt that the new hiring policy was a "far-reaching all-inclusive action" that "seriously impaired" the school's integrity.[63]

In his report Baumgaertner raised a host of objections to the new hiring criteria, objections that echoed those of the faculty. He acknowledged "the right of the board to establish confessional standards," but the new restrictions severely limited the ability of the faculty to recruit new faculty and to gain promotion and tenure themselves. This seriously impaired the "integrity" of the school because it jeopardized the school's mission of providing quality theological education. The "general distress" the action produced in the seminary community also undermined the "institutional conditions and procedures" necessary to maintain a stable faculty. To jeopardize thus the school's mission raised the "question as to whether the board by this action has exercised fidelity to the [seminary's] charter."[64]

Honeycutt believed that the criteria imposed an official interpretation of the Abstract and thereby undermined it. The new criteria thus altered the seminary's confessional standard, the Abstract of Principles, thereby violating the seminary's charter. Honeycutt argued that "by adopting a new set of guidelines, some of which move beyond the confessional statement to interpret particular passages of scripture, the trustees have breached the charter's fundamental laws." Honeycutt claimed that since article 1 of the Abstract taught that the scriptures were the "only sufficient, certain, and authoritative rule," then any additional statements or interpretations of scripture constituted an additional authority and thus altered article one. "By introducing a set of guidelines foreign to the charter's specifications, trustees have failed to fulfill the charter's requirement that trustees 'preserve inviolable and maintain forever in the management and

63. Bill Wolfe, "Baptist Seminary's Accreditation to Be Examined," *Louisville Courier-Journal*, 8 Feb. 1991, 1A, 10A. See also David Wilkinson, "Trustees to Consider SBTS Covenant," *Western Recorder*, 2 Apr. 1991, 2.

64. William Baumgaertner, "Report of the Special Staff Visit Mandated by the Commission on Accrediting, November 18–19, 1990," 13–15, A.T.S. Report (Baumgaertner) folder, Honeycutt Papers.

President Roy L. Honeycutt and trustee Rick White examine the Abstract of Principles subscription book, 1989

control of this institution, the principles of the fundamental laws" established by its adoption in 1858.[65] Honeycutt essentially claimed that an official interpretation of the Abstract invalidated it. He argued that the imposition of a "required interpretation of the confessional statement and [of] particular biblical passages constitutes an abridgement of the Fundamental Laws as outlined in the seminary's charter." He certainly strained a point. In this view, the Abstract was apparently valid only when uninterpreted by the institution. Honeycutt left interpretation to the conscience of each individual who signed it, as McCall had also done.[66]

But Honeycutt's argument strained another point. It assumed that the charter's imposition of the Abstract as a criterion of faculty beliefs required that it be the exclusive standard. But the charter did not assert that, or prohibit trustees from considering other doctrines or interpretations when considering electing faculty. Honeycutt and the faculty argued that the adoption of the Abstract

65. Roy Honeycutt, "President's Report to Accrediting Commission Staff Reviewing Trustee Actions at the Southern Baptist Theological Seminary, Nov. 19, 1990," 11–13, A.T.S. Report (Baumgaertner) folder, Honeycutt Papers.

66. Roy Honeycutt, "President's Report to Accrediting Commission Staff Reviewing Trustee Actions at the Southern Baptist Theological Seminary, Nov. 19, 1990," 13, A.T.S. Report (Baumgaertner) folder, Honeycutt Papers.

meant that it was the exclusive criterion of acceptable belief—though it was also an uninterpreted standard.

Honeycutt argued also that the new criteria violated the accrediting standards of the Association of Theological Schools because they undermined the seminary's "integrity" by subjecting it to "destructive interference or restraints." The criteria also threatened "radical disruption" in the seminary, jeopardizing "institutional effectiveness and the ability to carry out the mission of the seminary." Any attempt to implement the new guidelines, Honeycutt said, would be "all but impossible," for it would create institutional "chaos." [67] The guidelines, Honeycutt claimed, also violated the contracts of faculty hired under different criteria and violated the seminary's policies of academic freedom. The new guidelines furthermore imposed a new institutional policy without revising the official rules governing academic personnel. [68]

Many conservative trustees were troubled by the violence of the reaction. In February 1991 the trustee executive committee appointed a special committee on trustee-faculty relations to review the board's adoption of the new policy. It consulted with Honeycutt and with seven faculty members appointed by Honeycutt. By the time of the April 1991 trustee meeting, Honeycutt and the two special committees had developed a document that aimed to provide a framework for harmonious relations among trustees, faculty, and administration. The document they presented to the full board for adoption was called "Covenant Renewal between Trustees, Faculty, and Administration." The board rescinded its 1990 adoption of the findings of the Peace Committee report as criteria for faculty hiring and tenure. It then adopted the Covenant Renewal document to guide hiring. This act averted the crisis.

The covenant document represented a compromise on both sides. The trustees wanted to hire a conservative faculty, and Honeycutt wanted to protect the moderate faculty and heritage of the seminary. Honeycutt promised to assist actively with the change the trustees desired: "We want to pledge to you that we will work with you toward achieving your goal of a more conservative direction, as you perceive it, than we have been." In return for support of this change, Honeycutt and the faculty wanted more latitude and flexibility than the 1990 hiring policy permitted. After considerable debate and several unsuccessful

67. Roy Honeycutt, "President's Report to Accrediting Commission Staff Reviewing Trustee Actions at the Southern Baptist Theological Seminary, Nov. 19, 1990," 13–15, A.T.S. Report (Baumgaertner) folder, Honeycutt Papers.

68. Roy Honeycutt, "President's Report to Accrediting Commission Staff Reviewing Trustee Actions at the Southern Baptist Theological Seminary, Nov. 19, 1990," 14–15, 20, A.T.S. Report (Baumgaertner) folder, Honeycutt Papers.

motions to amend or refer the document, trustees adopted the covenant 49 to 7.[69]

It was far too conservative a statement to please most faculty members. Glenn Hinson opposed it because it would "tilt the seminary toward the conservative, evangelical side."[70] But the document was not conservative enough for some trustees. Jerry Johnson tried to amend the document to include a requirement that new faculty agree that the Bible was inerrant on "such matters as miracles, history, and the declared human authorship." David Miller felt that the document's assertions were vague and relied too much on trust in the faculty and administration to evaluate candidates. Miller judged that they had not fulfilled past commitments to recommend conservatives—"I have about had all the trust I can stand."[71] Trustee Delton Beall, with some prescience, opposed it on the ground that it postponed rather than solved the problem: "I have a problem with this board putting a screen door on a submarine and expecting me to fix the leak in three or four years."[72]

Most trustees, faculty, administrators, and outside observers, however, held that despite the covenant's dangers and defects, it represented the best hope for continued cooperation between faculty and trustees, though it was, as Honeycutt described it, a "frail hope." Because it represented a mutually agreed upon process for hiring, there was a genuine basis for cooperation and for sustaining the seminary's "viability and mission." It was a frail hope indeed, but it was the "seminary's best hope."[73]

The covenant did provide a platform for trustees, administration, and faculty to work together for change. The change would be slower than what the conservative trustees wanted and greater than what the moderate faculty wanted. Without such compromise, however, a violent rupture such as had occurred at Southeastern Baptist Theological Seminary a few years earlier was likely, with deeply damaging results in enrollment, morale, and institutional effectiveness at every level. Such results would threaten accreditation and interrupt institutional

---

69. Minutes, Board of Trustees, Southern Baptist Theological Seminary, 8–10 Apr. 1991.

70. Glenn Hinson, quoted in Bill Wolfe, "Faculty Okays Compromise with Trustees at Seminary," *Louisville Courier-Journal*, 30 Mar. 1991, 14A.

71. David Miller, quoted in Bill Wolfe, "Seminary Board Passes Compromise on Hiring," *Louisville Courier-Journal*, 9 Apr. 1991, 12A.

72. Delton Beall, quoted in Marv Knox, "Seminary Covenant Renewal: Miracle or Mistake," *Western Recorder*, 16 Apr. 1991, 10.

73. Roy Honeycutt, "Report to the Association of Theological Schools and Southern Association of Schools and Colleges from the Southern Baptist Theological Seminary," 15 Nov. 1992, 9, ATS Report Re/Trustee Actions (1/91) folder, Honeycutt Papers.

momentum. Recovery from such a wrenching change would have been long and uncertain. The Covenant Renewal compromise established ground rules for less disruptive change. All parties covenanted to work together in a "spirit of mutual respect, cooperation, and effort." It was an effort to effect change that "will maintain the vitality, integrity, and mission" of the seminary.[74] They would preserve continuity in order to maintain institutional effectiveness.

THE COVENANT, SCRIPTURE, AND INERRANCY

The heart of the five-page covenant was the section on faculty selection. Although it addressed briefly seven other criteria, such as commitment to distinctive Baptist doctrines, and to evangelism and missions, its central concern was to define the boundaries of acceptable belief regarding the Bible. The document pledged all parties to seek faculty members who had a "clear evangelical orientation" in their view of scripture. Seven paragraphs explained what the evangelical orientation entailed.

The statement on the Bible was a curious mixture of evangelical and liberal affirmations, and affirmations ambiguous or obscure. It appeared to be a deliberate amalgamation of an inerrantist statement drafted by David Dockery at Honeycutt's request and non-inerrantist statements drafted by moderate faculty.[75] Awkwardness and ambiguity were probably unavoidable if both the trustees and the faculty were going to be able to sign it.

Some of the covenant's assertions emphasized traditional conservative affirmations. The Bible was "entirely and completely the Word of God." It was "recorded as God intended." The Holy Spirit's inspiration "guaranteed true and trustworthy utterances on all matters" such that the Bible "in its entirety is free from all falsehood, fraud, and deceit." God's "special revelation" was "propositional" as well as "personal."

But in other places the statement advanced less orthodox notions. It referred to the Bible as "the accounts and interpretations of God's revelation," rather than as revelation itself—a distinction that implied that God revealed himself by some act in history, and that the revelation was in the act, not in the human interpretation and record of the act. The document stated that "these acts of

---

74. "Covenant Renewal between Trustees, Faculty, and Administration of the Southern Baptist Theological Seminary," Attachment A, in Minutes, Board of Trustees, Southern Baptist Theological Seminary, 8–10 Apr. 1991.

75. Dockery's drafts and some of Honeycutt's editing of those drafts survive in Dockery Statement folder, Honeycutt Papers.

special revelation have been interpreted by God's prophets and apostles." The evangelical view was that the Bible was itself a special revelation of God.

Even where the covenant asserted that the Bible was "true and reliable in all the matters it addresses, whatever the subject matter," conservative trustees suspected that this fell far short of affirming the Bible's inerrancy, since they had heard moderate interpretations of such language before. And the document's assertions that the Bible was "to be interpreted in light of the centrality of Jesus Christ," that God revealed himself also in nature, history, conscience, and experience," that God's revelation was progressive, and that the Holy Spirit "leads believers today to recognize the authority of scripture" all had ambiguous meaning in the tortured history of interpretation of Southern Baptist confessions. No less striking was the fact that the document avoided any affirmation of inerrancy. The rejection of falsehood, fraud, and deceit could be interpreted as a rejection of deliberate or conscious falsehood. And the statement omitted the crucial sentence in Dockery's proposal that upheld inerrancy. Dockery had written that scripture was not only "free from all falsehood, fraud, and deceit," but that it was also free from "error in all matters relating to God and his creation, including such matters as miracles, history, and the declared human authorship of scripture."

Conservative journalist Robert Tenery warned that the document was "dangerously vague" in its terminology relating to scripture, for it used the term "authority" but avoided the term "inerrant." Tenery observed that most moderates believed that the Bible was authoritative but not inerrant. He argued similarly that the commitment to hire persons with an evangelical orientation toward scripture was imprecise, since the word "evangelical" was too broad to be useful. Southern Baptists were evangelical, but many evangelicals could not be Southern Baptist: "There are a number of evangelical scholars that Southern Baptists can not live with."[76] But most conservative and moderate leaders were cautiously optimistic and supported the document.

The covenant did not require current faculty to agree with its statement on scripture. It represented their pledge to support faculty candidates only who held such a view. Despite the ambiguities, the statement on scripture was very conservative. Its purpose was to indicate the kind of conservative scholars that the school would seek to hire for the foreseeable future. The faculty, except Dockery, were moderates and naturally wanted as mild a conservativism as they could get, but Honeycutt persuaded them to adopt a very conservative statement. Convincing the faculty to pledge this was nevertheless a formidable task, and Honeycutt played the crucial role. He edited and revised the document until it was strong enough to satisfy most trustees, and yet avoided those

76. Robert Tenery, "Dangers of the Southern Seminary Covenant," *Southern Baptist Advocate*, June 1991, 3.

trip wires that would provoke the faculty to reject it. He told the faculty that unless they pledged to adopt the Covenant Renewal's criteria, trustees would retain the hiring criteria they adopted in 1990. He asked the faculty to trust his judgment and leadership. They did—only five faculty voted against adopting the covenant.[77]

WHAT THE COVENANT ACCOMPLISHED

The covenant was a child of necessity. The trustees were acknowledging that pressing for immediate and whole-cloth change in the faculty was unwise. Conservative trustees sought to prevent the kind of meltdown that deeply injured the viability of Southeastern Baptist Theological Seminary. The sobering reality of Southeastern's experience showed the dire consequences of disruptive change. Trustees were therefore willing to consider a painful compromise. But the faculty had their own sobering reality. Moderate denominational leaders had given up all attempts to reverse the conservative leadership of the convention. The faculty could no longer look to them for rescue but would have to shift for themselves. They likewise saw the necessity of painful compromise and now reluctantly agreed to cooperate with change to a more conservative faculty.

Trustees had the upper hand. They supported the covenant agreement because there was no question concerning the seminary's future direction. It would be conservative. But by agreeing to cooperate with Honeycutt and the faculty, they prevented a "head-on collision" between trustees and faculty and averted institutional crisis.

Most trustees felt that they could accept slower progress toward their goal in exchange for the faculty's concession that the future of the seminary would be conservative. Without it, the trustees would not have adopted the covenant. With this concession, trustees expected that they could hire conservative candidates with the faculty's cooperation and goodwill rather than over their opposition and resentment. By adopting the covenant, the faculty committed themselves to accept the fact that "Southern Seminary is going in a new direction." That fact, conservative trustee leader Wayne Allen said, made it "a new day."[78] Trustees compromised to gain the faculty's cooperation.[79]

77. Transcript, Board of Trustees meeting, 8 Apr. 1991, tape 1, pp. 11, 14, 18, 33. The faculty vote was 38 to 5.

78. Wayne Allen, in transcript, tape 5, Meeting of the Board of the Trustees, 8 Apr. 1991, 44.

79. Rick White, in transcript, tape 5, Meeting of the Board of the Trustees, 8 Apr. 1991, 6.

But moderates gained important points also. Though born of necessity, the covenant turned out to be a brilliant strategy. In return for the faculty's support, trustees agreed to close finally all concerns raised in the course of the Peace Committee's work. It thus served to exonerate all faculty who had been investigated in the course of the Peace Committee. Honeycutt and the moderate faculty had to abandon the long-term goal of saving Southern Seminary as a moderate school. But it was effectively lost already. They now relied on the covenant to protect their interests. It was surprisingly effective. For four years it delayed the imposition of traditionalist interpretations as criteria of faculty selection.

The Covenant Renewal also resolved the most serious concerns of the accrediting agencies. By the time the agencies sent their team to the campus, the covenant was already in operation. The team's report noted the beneficial effects already apparent and recommended only that the seminary file semiannual progress reports for the next two years.

THE UNRESOLVED ISSUE OF BALANCE

The covenant stated that the "seminary will employ only faculty or instructors (whether temporary or permanent) or grant tenure to those who sign the Abstract of Principles and positively affirm this covenant." The covenant did not say how long it would be in force but only implied that it was temporary and stated that the faculty had to subscribe to it "until" the trustees determined that the "seminary has achieved faculty balance."[80] But the covenant left the key issues unresolved—it did not define what "balance" meant or what would happen once they achieved it.

Some trustees raised this issue in the debate before they adopted it. Morris Denman wanted to know what would happen when the faculty arrived at balance. Did the covenant mean that when they achieved balance, the statement on scripture was "no longer applicable to hiring faculty"?[81] If they did not make it clear at the time what would happen when the faculty achieved balance, "we're going to create problems down the road." Denman feared that

80. "Covenant of Renewal between Trustees, Faculty, and Administration of the Southern Baptist Theological Seminary," in Appendix A, Minutes, Board of Trustees, Southern Baptist Theological Seminary, 8–10 Feb. 1991, 4.

81. Morris Denman, in transcript, tape 4, Meeting of the Board of the Trustees, Southern Baptist Theological Seminary, 8 Apr. 1991, 26.

The Roy L. and June Honeycutt Campus Center

without defining "balance," the covenant would become a "stick of dynamite" in a few years.[82]

Wayne Allen replied that his main concern was to get beyond the "impasse." The lack of precise definition of balance "may be putting off some problems for a few years" when perhaps there would be more trust. Trustees at a later date would have to "determine balance at that time."[83] Trustees and faculty could avoid a devastating explosion now by this compromise. The covenant did in fact delay the resolution of the central problems. But perhaps trustees in the future would find a healthier context for dealing with the seminary's problems.[84]

Two schools of interpretation of the meaning of the covenant existed from the beginning. Honeycutt and the faculty viewed it as a permanent arrangement— or perhaps a temporary means for securing permanently a balanced faculty. They believed that the covenant committed trustees to preserving about half the faculty for moderates. The trustees, however, viewed the covenant as a temporary agreement by which the faculty agreed to bring in conservative scholars and prevent institutional collapse. But they were not committing themselves to perpetuating a moderate faction on the faculty.[85]

82. Morris Denman, in transcript, tape 4, Meeting of the Board of the Trustees, Southern Baptist Theological Seminary, 8 Apr. 1991, 29.

83. Wayne Allen, in transcript, tape 4, Meeting of the Board of the Trustees, Southern Baptist Theological Seminary, 8 Apr. 1991, 27.

84. Wayne Allen, in transcript, tape 4, Meeting of the Board of the Trustees, Southern Baptist Theological Seminary, 8 Apr. 1991, 29–30.

85. Tammi Ledbetter, "Southern Seminary Enters Covenant Arrangement on Hiring," *Indiana Baptist*, 23 Apr. 1991, 5.

The agreement seemed to be an explicitly interim arrangement. It committed the school's stakeholders to employ and tenure "only" persons who could agree with the document's statement on scripture and affirm the covenant. It would remain in effect "until" the trustees determined that the faculty was balanced. Its rules would guide the faculty and administration for the indefinite future. Conservatives saw it as a significant move in the right direction, but their long-term aim was not parity between liberalism and orthodoxy but entire orthodoxy. Moderates viewed it as a necessary concession but recognized that it might serve to justify the continued inclusion of moderates on the faculty and protect them from dismissal. Honeycutt tried to make the covenant durable. He urged that it was more than a "temporary, stop-gap measure." [86] He was attempting to commit the school for the foreseeable future to a diverse faculty of both conservatives and moderates. This is what he meant when he cast the seminary's identity as "centrist" and "inclusive." He placed the emphasis on the covenant's language of "balance."

Faculty leader Bill Leonard correctly interpreted the covenant as a starting point for continued negotiations: "The covenant gives faculty a *via media* between complete acquiescence to fundamentalist demands and rapid institutional collapse. At best, it will serve as a guide for further faculty-trustee negotiations." [87] The covenant's great success was in keeping all parties at the negotiating table for four years.

THE UNRESOLVED ISSUE OF ADDITIONAL CRITERIA

There was another unresolved issue—whether or not trustees could use criteria not explicitly stated in the covenant and the Abstract of Principles in evaluating persons nominated for election to the faculty. Faculty believed that in adopting the covenant the trustees bound themselves to consider no issues beyond those explicitly stated in the Abstract of Principles and the covenant. The covenant they felt represented exclusive criteria for selecting faculty—no additional criteria could be added.

During the debate over adopting the covenant, trustees were concerned with this possibility. Since the covenant replaced the Peace Committee's findings section as hiring criteria, would it place limits on the use of hiring criteria? They feared that adopting the covenant would preclude trustees from using the

86. Roy Honeycutt, quoted in Ledbetter, "Southern Seminary Enters Covenant Arrangement on Hiring," 5.

87. Bill Leonard, "Pragmatic Compromise at Southern Seminary," *Christian Century*, 1 May 1991, 478.

Peace Committee's findings statements in this way. Both Honeycutt and trustee leaders assured everyone that the covenant did not preclude trustees from raising any issue they wished with faculty candidates. With this assurance, trustees adopted it with only one dissenting vote.[88]

Julian Pentecost, chairman of the trustee ad hoc committee that drafted the document together with the faculty ad hoc committee, told trustees that they could still ask questions about such matters. His answer was perhaps carefully crafted to satisfy conservative trustees without antagonizing the faculty. The adoption of the covenant, he said, would not "preclude the possibility of someone raising the questions listed in the Peace Committee findings and recommendations."[89]

Executive committee chairman Wayne Allen, who also served on the ad hoc committee, was adamant that the covenant did not impose exclusive limits on questions trustees could raise in the faculty hiring or tenure process: "It has repeatedly been said and discussed in the fifteen member committee that this document in no way prohibits anybody from asking any question—that is, on the academic personnel committee or on the trustees—of any person coming before them. I would resist personally as a member of the Academic Personnel Committee anybody telling me what I can't ask or what I have to ask. There are a lot of things we want to ask.... Those questions [from the Peace Committee findings] will be asked. They were asked prior to the Peace Committee. Prior to September, last April, those questions were asked.... Now how the faculty will respond to trustees asking those four specific questions...I'll have to let the president say."[90] The covenant, Allen said, "isn't an all inclusive document. There's a whole lot of other things to consider in hiring somebody."[91] He told them that the faculty understood this: "The faculty understands that [the covenant] does not prohibit those questions or any questions."[92]

Honeycutt assured the trustee executive committee that the faculty had the same understanding. "The faculty shared precisely what we've heard this morning, namely, that any question is appropriate during a period of interview. So there was no question, no ambiguity about it. One might bring up any one of the

88. Transcript, Board of Trustees meeting, 8 Apr. 1991, tape 1, pp. 13, 25–30, 38.

89. Julian Pentecost, in transcript, tape 1, Meeting of the Executive Committee, Board of the Trustees, Southern Baptist Theological Seminary, 8 Apr. 1991, 13.

90. Wayne Allen, in transcript, tape 1, Meeting of the Executive Committee, Board of the Trustees, Southern Baptist Theological Seminary, 8 Apr. 1991, 26–27.

91. Wayne Allen, in transcript, tape 5, Meeting of the Board of the Trustees, 8 Apr. 1991, 17–18.

92. Wayne Allen, in transcript, tape 4, Meeting of the Board of the Trustees, Southern Baptist Theological Seminary, 8 Apr. 1991, 23.

four areas of the [Peace Committee] findings, one might bring up other issues, and adopting the covenant did not rule out bringing up any kind of question one felt appropriate for prospective members of the faculty."[93] He repeated it for the full board: "One could raise any one of the four questions or all of the questions. One could raise any other questions that you thought germane to the election of a faculty person. And so there were no limitations whatsoever in the matter of the kinds of questions that could be raise."[94] The trustee minutes included a truncated version of Honeycutt's verbal statement: "Any question is appropriate in the trustee-faculty interview process within the academic personnel committee."[95]

Wayne Allen appealed to three considerations in favor of adopting the covenant. First, the faculty's agreement that they would bring nominees who agreed with the covenant's statement on scriptures was a major step forward—a "milestone for us at the seminary." Second, the seminary was at a critical point in its history when open collision could be devastating to the institution. This was probably its only opportunity to secure a basis for cooperation between faculty and trustees and thus avoid the head-on collision. Allen appealed finally to the importance of trust: "The trust level of the covenant has to come into play."[96]

But the faculty disagreed with the trustees' interpretation. When the trustee executive committee discussed the proposed covenant, John Michael asked whether it would preclude asking questions about the interpretations enumerated in the Peace Committee report. Would it still be appropriate for trustees to use the "Peace Committee guidelines" in the "process of hiring" and of "granting tenure"? Michael said that he had learned that some faculty believed that under the proposed covenant neither the Academic Personnel Committee nor the full board could ask such questions. Raising such questions would betray the faculty's trust in the covenant.[97] Trustee Jerry Johnson called Bill Leonard, who was chairman of the faculty ad hoc committee, to confirm that this was the

93. Honeycutt, in transcript, Tape 1, Meeting of the Executive Committee, Board of the Trustees, Southern Baptist Theological Seminary, 8 Apr. 1991, 27.

94. Honeycutt, in transcript, tape 4, Meeting of the Board of the Trustees, Southern Baptist Theological Seminary, 8 Apr. 1991, 23.

95. Minutes, Board of Trustees, Southern Baptist Theological Seminary, 8–10 Apr. 1991, 4.

96. Wayne Allen, in transcript, tape 1, Meeting of the Executive Committee, Board of the Trustees, Southern Baptist Theological Seminary, 8 Apr. 1991, 31–33; and in transcript, tape 4, Meeting of the Board of the Trustees, Southern Baptist Theological Seminary, 8 Apr. 1991, 27.

97. John Michael, in transcript, Tape 1, Meeting of the Executive Committee, Board of the Trustees, Southern Baptist Theological Seminary, 8 Apr. 1991, 13, 26.

faculty's view. Leonard told Johnson that if trustees "consistently" applied the Peace Committee findings "as a litmus test" of faculty candidates, then the faculty would have a problem with that and would "cry 'foul.'" [98] When the faculty finally cried "foul" in 1995, it caused an explosion.

MOLLY MARSHALL, THEOLOGY, AND GENDER

The Covenant Renewal was effectively a grant of amnesty to the moderate faculty—at least to most of them. For those faculty whose offenses were greater, who strayed farthest from traditional orthodoxy—Simmons, Hinson, and Marshall—it afforded less protection. Several trustees continued to press for their dismissal. It did not help matters that the three kept adding to their offenses. In January 1992, for example, Marshall delivered two addresses on theology and gender at Averett College, a Southern Baptist school in Virginia. She argued that the use of exclusively male language about God in the Bible and in Christian history distorted correct notions of God, of women, and of men and produced damaging social and ecclesiastical patriarchies.

Exclusively male language about God promoted a "deformed image of God" and "impugned the dignity of women." The traditional view of scripture language raised questions about the justice and credibility of a God who was thus ordaining patriarchy and "authorizing sexism." It jeopardized the "retention of the Bible as a Christian canon." [99] The Bible's "predominantly masculine" language about God hindered a "proper theological understanding of the character of God." The Bible used this language because men were the ones who wrote the Bible and who subsequently interpreted it. They wrote in the "language of primarily male experience" and reflected the cultural context of their times. [100]

A correct theology of God and gender required abandoning "exclusively male categories" in "our thinking and speaking of God," and in the "way we translate and read the Bible." The Bible, "albeit inspired," reflected the patriarchy and exclusively male God-language of its original cultures. In order for the Bible to remain useful "for contemporary direction, insight, guidance, and

98. Bill Leonard, quoted by Jerry Johnson, in transcript, tape 4, Meeting of the Board of the Trustees, Southern Baptist Theological Seminary, 8 Apr. 1991, 41.

99. Molly Marshall, "Theology and Gender," lecture 2, 2–4, Attachment E (Keitha Brasler transcription), in "President's Report to the Committee on Academic Personnel," Honeycutt Papers.

100. Molly Marshall, "Theology and Gender," lecture 1, 6–7, 10, Attachment E (Keitha Brasler transcription), in "President's Report to the Committee on Academic Personnel," Honeycutt Papers.

formation of character," Marshall pointed to "less accentuated traditions" in the Bible that could serve to correct the "deformed image both of women and of God" in traditional interpretation.[101]

The Danville, Virginia, newspaper ran a story on Marshall's lectures and quoted her as saying that the "gospel has not been good to many women." Marshall actually said that the Bible's exclusively male language about God had not been good for women.[102] A group of conservative Southern Baptists in Virginia complained, as did two of Virginia's trustees. Seminary policy required Honeycutt to investigate.

The lectures were taped, and Marshall produced a transcript from the tapes. The administration also had transcripts made from the tapes. A comparison of the two sets of transcripts showed that Marshall omitted from her version several provocative statements. She omitted her discussion of her own experiences as a pastor. Remembering a course at Southern Seminary on Pentateuchal criticism, she reflected that "God was working in mischievous ways her wonders to perform." Talking about the personal character of God as revealed by Jesus, she said parenthetically, "I'm not equating Jesus with God." And in her address she said at one point that "human words applying to God and gender-specific language exclusively used of God distorts [sic] mightily." But in the set of transcripts she submitted, she changed it to "human words used of God in a sensitive and inclusive manner."[103]

The investigation by Honeycutt and by the Academic Personnel Committee resulted in a conclusion that no formal charges were warranted. Marshall had been accused of saying that the gospel had been unkind to women and that the gospel was a deformed image of God, and the trustees concluded correctly that she had not said those things. Trustees were nevertheless troubled by other things she said. They asked Honeycutt to investigate with regard to their concerns relating to the two lectures.[104] In August 1992 David Dockery interviewed

101. Molly Marshall, "Theology and Gender," lecture 1, 13, 7, and lecture 2, 10, Attachment E (Keitha Brasler transcription), in "President's Report to the Committee on Academic Personnel," Honeycutt Papers.

102. Unattributed, "Group Wants Professor Fired," *Baptist Courier*, 20 Feb. 1992, 14; unattributed, "Accusations against Professor Do Not Warrant Her Dismissal," *Baptist Courier*, 7 May 1992, 19.

103. Molly Marshall, "Theology and Gender," pt. I, 1, 8, 10, 17; pt. II, 1, in Appendix E, "President's Report to the Committee on Academic Personnel," 8 Apr. 1992, Honeycutt Papers. Marshall's version of the transcript appeared in appendix D of the same report (quote from pt. I, 9–10).

104. Minutes, Board of Trustees, Southern Baptist Theological Seminary, 27–29 Apr. 1992; Mark Wingfield, "Trustees Consider Concerns with Simmons and Marshall," *Western Recorder*, 5 May 1992, 8.

Marshall in order to provide clarification on matters of concern to the trustees.[105] Dockery recommended no formal charges were warranted. Marshall survived the investigation.

THE FIRING OF PAUL SIMMONS

Simmons, like Marshall, added new sins to old. On March 15, 1990, Simmons gave an address to the Charlotte, North Carolina, chapter of Planned Parenthood. He there affirmed his support for the U.S. Supreme Court's *Roe v. Wade* decision: "Those who desire to terminate a pregnancy should be able to do so, in the first stage of a pregnancy, without oppression or intimidation."[106] The Southern Baptist Convention and the seminary's board of trustees had passed resolutions opposing abortion. In order to defuse trustee anger, Simmons took the initiative, with counsel from Dean Larry McSwain, to promise to distance his personal views from those of the seminary and the Southern Baptist Convention, to refuse interviews with the media, and to "avoid inflammatory rhetoric."[107]

But trustees kept hearing new complaints conserning Simmons, Marshall, and Hinson. In 1992 the Academic Personnel Committee passed a motion instructing Honeycutt to issue formal warnings to Hinson and Marshall that they could be dismissed if they repeated their offenses. It was a compromise measure. Honeycutt recommended that no warning be issued, but he knew that trustees were likely to pass the motion and worked with John Michael on the wording of the warnings.[108] Preaching professor Raymond Bailey said that the trustees' action demonstrated that a new "dark ages" had arrived.[109]

At the April 1992 meeting of the board, Rick White appointed a committee to investigate the relevant issues concerning charges against Simmons to determine whether there was sufficient cause for bringing charges against him.[110] At Honeycutt's request, longtime seminary attorney and former trustee Joseph

---

105. David Dockery to Larry McSwain, 25 Sept. 1992, in Molly Marshall Notebook, President's Papers.

106. Paul Simmons, quoted in *Charlotte Observer*, 12 Mar. 1990. See also *Charlotte Observer*, 16 Mar. 1990.

107. Paul Simmons to Members of the Board of Trustees, 13 Apr. 1990, Paul Simmons 1990 folder, Honeycutt Papers.

108. Bill Wolfe, "Baptist Professor Gets 'Warning,'" *Louisville Courier-Journal*, 26 Feb. 1992, 1A, 5A.

109. Raymond Bailey, "An Embarrassment," *Louisville Courier-Journal*, 16 Mar. 1992, 6A.

110. Minutes, Board of Trustees, Southern Baptist Theological Seminary, 27-29 Apr. 1992.

Paul D. Simmons

Stopher had prepared a report relating to the legal grounds for dismissing Simmons. Apparently he advised against the attempt, since conservative trustees were sufficiently dissatisfied with it to request an opinion from a different law firm.[111]

Honeycutt spent enormous effort and money defending Simmons, but Simmons had at the same time been in negotiations with the administration and trustees, offering to resign for sufficient monetary incentive. But a majority of trustees either viewed this as rewarding heresy or judged it too expensive. Most Southern Baptists would have viewed the action as granting a golden parachute to a false teacher. At a called meeting of the board in Atlanta in December 1992, the Academic Personnel Committee recommended to the full board that they pay Simmons six years' salary, $362,000, to secure his resignation. The board overwhelmingly rejected the recommendation.[112]

111. Mark Wingfield, "Trustees Consider Concerns with Simmons and Marshall," *Western Recorder*, 5 May 1992, 8.

112. Bill Wolfe, "Baptist Seminary Board Won't Buy Out Professor," *Louisville Courier-Journal*, 16 Dec. 1992, 4B; Mark McCormick, "Baptist Professor Retires; Film Flap Just Part of Long Battle," *Louisville Courier-Journal*, 7 Jan. 1993, 1B.

Many trustees left Atlanta prepared to proceed to formal charges against Simmons. It appeared to be the only remaining avenue to resolve the issue.[113] But on December 15, 1992, Simmons showed a sexually explicit film in one of his classes. Although Simmons allowed students to opt out of viewing the film, which was intended for use in sexual therapy of persons with spinal injuries, seminary administrators unanimously concluded that the film was highly inappropriate and represented a serious failure of judgment. Simmons chose to take early retirement, with an undisclosed severance package, rather than face administrative discipline.[114]

THE COVENANT FACULTY

Honeycutt had pledged to recruit conservative professors in the 1986 Glorieta Statement. Some of the new faculty added since 1990 were rather conservative, but Honeycutt had prevented any significant incursion of conservatives on the faculty and had hired only one avowed inerrantist, David Dockery. The adoption of the covenant agreement forced Honeycutt to begin recruiting inerrantists—only Honeycutt did not recruit them, Dockery did. Honeycutt looked to Dockery to do the work of building a conservative faculty under the terms of the covenant. In 1992 trustees elected the first group of covenant faculty, all avowed inerrantists. A few months later, Honeycutt appointed Dockery dean of the school of theology.

Dockery taught for only one year before being called to Nashville as editor of the Sunday School Board's new conservative commentary on the Bible. The Sunday School Board had recently come under conservative control, and this new commentary was important to the credibility of the movement. From 1989 to 1991, Dockery led this project in Nashville, but at Honeycutt's insistence, he remained on faculty under a leave of absence. Honeycutt got the benefit of having hired an inerrantist without the expense of having him teach.

Honeycutt, however, found Dockery a congenial conservative. Dockery got along well with the faculty and administration, and students gave him high marks as a teacher. When Willis Bennett resigned as provost, Honeycutt promoted Larry McSwain from dean of the school of theology to provost. He would face considerable opposition from the trustees if he appointed a moderate as

---

113. Greg Warner, "Heresy Hearings Possible at Southern," *Western Recorder*, 5 Jan. 1993, 2.

114. Marv Knox, "Paul Simmons Suddenly Leaves Post at Southern Seminary," *Western Recorder*, 12 Jan. 1993, 1, 6; Mark Wingfield, "Video Showing Led Simmons to Final Seminary Conflict," *Western Recorder*, 12 Jan. 1993, 7.

dean. He appointed Dockery in the hope that he would serve as a moderating influence, tempering the zeal of the trustees impatient for wholesale change. As a bona fide conservative, Dockery would have the credibility with the trustees to be effective. But there was no mistaking the fact that the hiring of inerrantists had begun in earnest.

But the moderate faculty still played a central role in the hiring process, and they hoped to determine what kind of conservatives got elected. All candidates for election to the faculty originated from nomination by a faculty search committee. The faculty knew that they had to bring inerrantists on the faculty, but they recognized that inerrantists were not all alike—they differed significantly in their interpretation of the Bible.

If there was any doubt, trustees discovered in 1992 that inerrancy was not enough. In April 1992 the Academic Personnel Committee recommended several candidates for election to the faculty. They all professed belief in inerrancy, and they all opposed abortion. Trustees were thrilled. When trustees discovered that the candidates supported the ordination of women as deacons or as deacons and pastors, however, their joy turned to dismay. Although trustees in the end elected all by large margins, some trustees voiced their deep displeasure at having to hold their noses while they voted. David Miller urged Rick White, chairman of the Academic Personnel Committee, which brought the recommendations, to "find men who are consistent on every point" of trustee concern. "Why should we be satisfied with men who are 95 percent correct when there are hundreds of men who are 100 percent correct?"[115]

When a "100 percent correct" candidate came before the faculty, however, they rejected him. In 1993 the administration opened a search for a New Testament professor. The search committee recommended Scott Hafemann, a conservative evangelical who taught at Gordon-Conwell Theological Seminary near Boston. His scholarly credentials were impressive, with a doctorate from the University of Tübingen. His interpretation of the Bible differed sharply from that of most on the faculty. He held to the inerrancy of the Bible, opposed abortion, and understood the Bible in a generally Calvinist way. He held also that it taught a complementarian view of gender roles—the view that although men and women were intrinsically equal, God prohibited women from ordained ministry and required wives to submit to their husbands. This was the position of most Southern Baptist conservatives and many evangelicals. The vast majority of the faculty rejected these ideas, but since they had agreed to receive conservatives on the faculty under the covenant document, there was every reason to expect his election. The New Testament department supported his

---

115. David Miller, quoted in Mark Wingfield, "Six Elected to Faculty after Debate on Women," *Western Recorder*, 5 May 1992, 9.

candidacy, and the faculty search committee endorsed his candidacy by a vote of 8 to 0.[116]

Hafemann's interview before the full faculty, however, went badly. Hafemann recalled that for the first fifty minutes of his one-hour interview, faculty members asked him questions concerning his view of gender roles. At the end of the interview he answered a few questions regarding church polity and why he was a Baptist. His responses, that he was Baptist because of his interpretation of Jeremiah 31 and that he advocated plural eldership in the churches, were unconventional and alien to most on the faculty. After they dismissed Hafemann, many opposed him because they concluded that he "was not Baptist." The vote to recommend him for election failed 18–26. In accordance with seminary policy at that time, this negative vote ended his candidacy.[117] The unspoken objection, evidenced by the faculty's intense scrutiny of his views of gender roles, was his complementarian views of gender. This soured his candidacy for many faculty and made other objections more attractive.

Dockery was shaken by the result. He was mortified on Hafemann's account, but even more he worried about the trustee response and the storm that might follow. Within hours trustees across the country knew of the outcome. They felt that the rejection of Hafemann was a serious breach of the covenant. Years of obstructionism from Honeycutt and the faculty had worn their patience thin. They were ready for change. When Honeycutt announced his retirement in the fall of 1992, they began looking for a candidate who could lead them in the changes they believed in. Their candidate for change was R. Albert Mohler Jr.

116. David Dockery, oral history, SBTS. One committee member abstained.
117. Faculty Minutes, Southern Baptist Theological Seminary, 4 Feb. 1993.

13

R. ALBERT MOHLER AND THE REMAKING OF SOUTHERN SEMINARY

In the fall of 1992 conservative trustees set about finding Honeycutt's successor. Three leading candidates emerged. Bob Agee, president of Oklahoma Baptist University, was a trusted conservative and a proven administrator in denominational higher education. Conservatives admired his accomplishments as president of Oklahoma Baptist University. Agee, however, withdrew his name from consideration to allay concerns at the university. Richard Land was a loyal conservative with an Oxford University doctorate and was the first conservative president of the denomination's Christian Life Commission. Timothy George had emerged as an intellectual leader among Southern Baptist conservatives, had considerable familiarity with Southern Seminary, and had experience leading a seminary as the founding dean of Beeson Divinity School at Samford University.

Some hoped that trustees would elect David Dockery. Trustees would have put his name on their short list for final consideration, but Dockery recognized that if he lost, he would not have the president's full confidence and could not remain as dean. Dockery did not permit his nomination to be considered.[1]

Dockery and several others recommended R. Albert Mohler, the thirty-three-year-old editor of the *Christian Index*, the weekly newspaper of the Georgia Baptist Convention. He seemed too young and inexperienced to rival the other candidates, but he was interviewed because of the strong recommendations he received. When the committee members began to discuss their opinions after

---

1. Dockery had moved several times in the preceding years and wished to avoid moving his family again so soon.

interviewing Land, George, and Mohler, they quickly realized that Mohler was their consensus choice. Mohler's interview made a deep impression and there was need to prolong discussion.[2] The search committee nominated Mohler to the full board during a called meeting in Atlanta, March 25–26, 1993. The board then elected him the ninth president of the Southern Baptist Theological Seminary. Of the ten or eleven moderate trustees on the board, five voted against him.[3]

Mohler had deep affection for Southern Seminary, and the institution had a shaping influence on his life during the years in which he earned both his M.Div. and his Ph.D. there. During his doctoral studies, Mohler served six years in the seminary's development office, first as coordinator of foundation support and then as director of capital funding and assistant to President Roy Honeycutt.

For much of Mohler's student career at Southern, he identified with the denomination's moderates. As an adolescent in south Florida he had been impressed with the ideas and ministries of such evangelical leaders as Carl F. H. Henry, Francis Schaeffer, and D. James Kennedy. While completing his dissertation at Southern Seminary on the thought of Karl Barth and Carl Henry, his conservatism deepened. His friendships with Timothy George, David Dockery, and several other conservatives challenged him. He was a voracious reader and read widely the conservative scholarship. By the time he received his doctoral degree in 1989, his theology was thoroughly conservative.

In 1989 Mohler became the editor of the *Christian Index*. At the time of his election, he affirmed his belief in the inerrancy of the Bible and pledged the paper to promote "biblical evangelicalism."[4] Conservative leaders throughout the convention took immediate notice of his trenchant editorials defending conservative positions on such matters as inerrancy, substitutionary atonement, the exclusivity of the gospel, the sovereignty of God, abortion, sexuality, and gender issues.

The seminary community's reaction to Mohler's election was initially muted. Faculty and students had feared that the search committee would nominate Richard Land, whom they considered a hard-line fundamentalist. They hoped that the committee would nominate Timothy George, whom they considered the least objectionable. Few anticipated Mohler's nomination.

2. Mark McCormick, "Georgian, 33, Picked to Head Seminary," *Courier-Journal*, 23 Feb. 1993, 1A.

3. Wayne Allen to David Olive, 26 Feb. 1993, Search Committee—Presidential folder, Honeycutt Papers; Wayne Allen, Larry Adams, et al., to the Board of Trustees, 9 Mar. 1993, Trustee Correspondence General 1990–1993 folder, Honeycutt Papers.

4. "Georgia Names Mohler Editor of Christian Index," *Baptist Courier*, 23 Mar. 1989, 14.

Billy Graham, R. Albert Mohler,
and Carl F. H. Henry in front of
Norton Hall, 1993

Many alumni and faculty were surprised at his election because when they knew him as a student, he identified more with moderates than with conservatives. Henlee Barnette, professor of ethics, selected Mohler as his Garrett Fellow or teaching assistant in 1983. Barnette thought that "Mohler was a 'liberal' or a 'moderate' at that time."[5] Other faculty were horrified at Mohler's election from the start. Tim Weber, one of the evangelicals elected in 1992, noted that the news of his election sent shudders through the faculty. They knew that as editor of the *Christian Index* he had defended the positions of the conservative party.

Mohler did not receive a warm welcome from the Louisville community or from Kentucky Baptist leaders. The press identified Mohler from the start as a leader in the conservative movement in the denomination, "a hero of SBC

5. Henlee Barnette to William Mueller, 16 Feb. 1995, Henlee Barnette Papers, WFU.

conservatives."[6] The *Louisville Courier-Journal* quoted Jack Harwell, editor of the moderates' weekly *Baptists Today*, who identified Mohler as an "unquestioned fundamentalist" with proven "loyalty to the fundamentalist machine in the Southern Baptist Convention."[7] Marv Knox, editor of Kentucky's *Western Recorder*, was dismissive of Mohler's record and skeptical of his ability to lead the seminary successfully.[8] Local columnist John Ed Pearce identified Mohler with "Neanderthal beliefs" and suggested that the seminary's "extremism" was akin to that of the Branch Davidian cult, whose members had attacked federal agents at their Texas compound a month earlier.[9]

Some trustees and administrators resigned in response to Mohler's election. Three moderate trustees resigned at the end of the April 1993 board meeting in protest of the "hostile takeover of Southern Seminary."[10] They announced their resignations at the end of the meeting and excoriated the conservative policies of their fellow trustees.[11] Milburn Price, dean of the school of church music, and Bill Rogers, dean of the school of Christian education, resigned also in April 1993 in reaction to Mohler's election. Both opposed Mohler's conservative vision for the seminary, and Rogers cited especially Mohler's opposition to the ordination of women.[12]

But some faculty disagreed with the dire predictions and were cautiously optimistic. Mohler was the only candidate who had graduated from Southern Seminary. His doctorate from the school was nearly an imprimatur. Many persons believed that those who completed a degree at Southern, especially a doctorate, could not help being deeply formed by the experience in a way that went far beyond scholarship. It created identity. They seemed to believe that Mohler

6. Unattributed, "Mohler, 33, Nominated for Southern Presidency," *Western Recorder*, 2 Mar. 1993, 3. See also unattributed, "President-Elect's Opinions Expressed in Weekly Editorials," *Western Recorder*, 30 Mar. 1993, 9; and Mark McCormick, "Southern Baptists See Two Sides to New Seminary President," *Louisville Courier-Journal*, 25 Mar. 1993, 1B.

7. McCormick, "Georgian, 33, Picked to Head Seminary," 5A.

8. Marv Knox, "Can Mohler's Resources Offset Slim Experience," *Western Recorder*, Mar. 1993, 5.

9. John Ed Pearce, "Religious Extremism," *Louisville Courier-Journal*, 10 May 1993, 18A.

10. George Steincross, quoted in Mark Wingfield, "Three Moderate Trustees Quit Seminary Board in Protest," *Western Recorder*, 27 Apr. 1993, 2.

11. Mark McCormick, "Three of Seminary's Moderate Trustees Quit," *Louisville Courier-Journal*, 22 Apr. 1993, 1A, 7A.

12. Mark Wingfield, "Two Deans Stepping Down at Southern Seminary," *Western Recorder*, 20 Apr. 1993, 3. See also Mark McCormick, "Two Deans Resigning at Baptist Seminary," *Louisville Courier-Journal*, 22 Apr. 1993, 1A, 6A.

would not enforce rigid doctrinal boundaries or cause ruptures at the semi-nary. They knew that he was intelligent and thoughtful, which fundamentalists, most moderate faculty seemed to believe, were not. Theology professor Wayne Ward said that most persons had expressed to him their relief and satisfaction at Mohler's nomination. "There was a sigh of relief that you could hear all over the campus," Ward said. "He definitely is not a crazy, irrational fundamental-ist." [13] If they had to have a conservative, Mohler was the kind they wanted. And they knew that he understood and appreciated Southern Seminary's heritage. What they perhaps did not understand was that the heritage that Mohler most appreciated was not that of the post–World War II faculty but that of Boyce, Broadus, Manly, and Williams.

THE ABSTRACT OF PRINCIPLES

Mohler made it clear from the start that he intended to enforce the Abstract of Principles according to its original intent. He knew that many professors subscribed to the Abstract in full awareness that they disagreed with its literal assertions. Mohler sought to return to Boyce's understanding of the Abstract's meaning and use in the seminary.

For much of the twentieth century, Boyce's approach had been abandoned or neglected. His concern for exact agreement with the Abstract, "based upon no mental reservation, upon no private understanding," held sway until Edgar Y. Mullins became president in 1899.[14] Mullins granted some latitude for inter-preting the Abstract's statements according to its general spirit and allowed room for elements of progressive theology. The Abstract's articles, Mullins told a progressive faculty candidate in 1907, were "sufficiently broad and elastic to admit of freedom to any mature man who can accept them at the outset." [15] John R. Sampey was less accommodating to progressive theology than Mullins was, but he seemed to trust that the evangelical character of faculty members guaranteed their adherence to the Abstract. He seemed to give the matter little attention, with the practical effect that some latitude of interpretation existed.

Ellis A. Fuller aimed to enforce the Abstract strictly. At his inauguration he pledged to keep the seminary within the Abstract's teachings, for "the truths

---

13. Wayne Ward, quoted in Mark McCormick, "Reaction to Baptist Seminary Nominee Is Mixed," *Louisville Courier-Journal*, 24 Feb. 1993, 1B.

14. James P. Boyce, *Three Changes in Theological Institutions* (Greenville, SC: C. J. Elford, 1856), 35.

15. Edgar Y. Mullins to Charles S. Gardner, 4 May 1907, Letterpress Book 31, 1906–1908, 342.

contained in them are the rock upon which the seminary was built.... I have neither desire nor purpose to do anything except to hold the seminary in the straight course which my predecessors chose for it." [16] He expected the faculty to subscribe to it "free from all mental reservations and rationalizations." [17]

Like his predecessors, McCall was committed to enforcing the Abstract—it was after all an official duty of the president. But he rejected a strict constructionist approach. He granted, on the contrary, the broadest latitude of subscription. He agreed that he bore an obligation to dismiss any professor who departed from the Abstract, but he left it to the conscience of each professor to interpret its meaning. Any professor who declared that he or she was within the boundaries of the Abstract thereby was within. Practically the only way to go outside the Abstract was to declare oneself outside. McCall acknowledged the "freedom given to faculty members across the years in their interpretation of the document." [18] On this basis he had "accepted the footnoting of Dr. Moody's correct insistence that the Abstract of Principles must be judged by the Bible and not the Bible by the Abstract of Principles." [19]

Honeycutt's approach was similar to McCall's. He held that the seminary's presidents had "never interpreted the Abstract for a professor. Each person interprets the Abstract and indicates whether he or she is able to teach in accord with, and not contrary to, the 'principles' within the Abstract of Principles.... The implementation of the Abstract remains fundamentally dependent upon the conscience of the individual and the integrity of those who sign the document and the administration of the institution." [20] Honeycutt recognized that the professors' pledge to teach in accord with the Abstract constituted a "contractual obligation" that the president was "obliged to enforce." [21] But it is unclear how the administration could find a professor in violation of his or her private construal of the Abstract's broad principles. Honeycutt explained that "at Southern Seminary we have always emphasized

16. Ellis A. Fuller, "The Seminary Faces the Future," *Western Recorder*, 22 Oct. 1942, 3.

17. Ellis A. Fuller, "President's Statement," 1949, box 17, Fuller Papers.

18. Duke McCall to Dale Moody, 1 Mar. 1980 (originally 25 Feb.), Dale Moody 1982–1986 folder, Honeycutt Papers.

19. Duke McCall to Presnall Wood, 27 Dec. 1982, cited in Dale Moody to Roy Honeycutt, 19 Apr. 1983, Dale Moody 1982–1986 folder, Honeycutt Papers.

20. Roy Honeycutt, A Statement on Some Issues Related to the Arkansas Baptist Convention's Resolution re: Professor Dale Moody, Dale Moody 1982–1986 folder, Honeycutt Papers.

21. Roy Honeycutt, A Statement on Some Issues Related to the Arkansas Baptist Convention's Resolution re: Professor Dale Moody, Dale Moody 1982–1986 folder, Honeycutt Papers.

that the Abstract of Principles is an 'abstract' and does not say everything. It deals in 'principles' and not rigid legalisms." [22] It was not to be interpreted literally.

This appraisal was consistent with Honeycutt's view of the character of creeds. Honeycutt said that the Holy Spirit alone mediated an individual's interpretation of the Bible: "The only thing that should stand between the Baptist and the Bible is the Holy Spirit as he leads us to interpret scripture." This meant, he explained, that there was "no room for creedal statements adopted by anyone and imposed on an individual Baptist." He had to acknowledge the "propriety of theological statements such as our Abstract of Principles" as a norm for seminary professors. "But in principle, creeds have no place in Baptist life." [23] The seminary's creed, therefore, though ostensibly having a place in Baptist life, had to be interpreted in a noncreedal way.

Young professors sometimes asked their colleagues if they should have any qualms about signing the Abstract. They were told that it was a traditional statement of general Christian truth, though clothed in the historical forms of the nineteenth century, and that they should sign it and forget about it. A few professors may have signed it with a private understanding with the president, in which they declared in advance their differences with the Abstract. Dale Moody justified his subscription based on this approach. He claimed long afterward that he told Ellis Fuller of his conviction that article 13 of the Abstract contradicted the Bible, and that Fuller was satisfied nevertheless to nominate Moody for election by the trustees. Fuller probably did not understand it this way. He had no such intention in any case. He had long discussions with Moody, T. C. Smith, and perhaps others to investigate their orthodoxy. He was not entirely satisfied with Moody or Smith, but he evidently was finally convinced that they agreed with the Abstract interpreted strictly.

Most professors signed the Abstract based on a mental reservation or private interpretation. Frank Stagg, for example, signed the Abstract in accordance with his private understanding of it. He remarked that he had not read Boyce's writings until after his retirement: "I was told to read the Abstract and sign it as I understood it. When I signed the Abstract, I had not seen James Petigru Boyce's 1856 Inaugural Address in which he made clear his stance on the creedal nature of his proposed Abstract... and his mandate that it be strictly observed; and no one mentioned Boyce or his mandate to me." [24] Stagg recognized that

---

22. Roy Honeycutt, A Statement on Some Issues Related to the Arkansas Baptist Convention's Resolution re: Professor Dale Moody, Dale Moody 1982–1986 folder, Honeycutt Papers.

23. Roy Honeycutt to Rumsey Taylor Sr., 13 May 1981, Trustee Correspondence—General, 1982–84 folder, Honeycutt Papers.

24. Frank Stagg to Greg Warner, Jan. 1995, folder 43, box 33, Stagg Papers.

"through most of Southern Seminary's years, professors were permitted to sign the Abstract of Principles as they interpreted it, contrary to Boyce's demand."[25]

One candidate interviewed in 1987 or 1988 made the mistake of failing to honor the distinction between actually believing the Abstract and saying one believed it. In his interview before the faculty, the candidate said that he rejected the Abstract's doctrine of the eternal security of believers. But the candidate felt that his disagreement with the Abstract should pose no difficulty: "I know you play games with the Abstract, and I can too."[26] Such an explicit disavowal of the Abstract should have precluded any thought of hiring the candidate, and he lost significant support from the faculty and from Honeycutt. Surprisingly, 40 percent of the faculty nevertheless supported hiring him, and Honeycutt at first was still inclined to recommend him but ultimately did not.[27]

Moody charged that such a practice was hypocritical "double-speak," not because he supported requiring strict subscription but because most professors kept their disagreements with the Abstract private. Moody held that integrity required professors to tell the president their points of disagreement with it, and that they were dishonest when they secretly crossed their fingers and signed. But he also held that professors should be granted latitude for explicit disagreements with it.[28]

When Mohler became president, many faculty feared that he would interpret the Abstract literally and require strict subscription to its literal meaning. Some thought it hardly possible for an intelligent person to take this position. Mohler told trustees at the time of his election that he believed that some current faculty members were teaching in violation of the Abstract of Principles and that he intended to fulfill his duty to enforce the requirement that faculty adhere strictly to it. Five moderate trustees voted against him largely because of his pledge to require such strict adherence.[29]

The faculty had two basic concerns regarding the interpretation of the Abstract. Because Mohler understood the Bible to teach five-point Calvinism, they wondered whether he would interpret the Abstract as imposing five-point Calvinism on the faculty. Second, they felt that it was unjust that the president

25. Frank Stagg, "Abstract of Principles Smacks of Calvinism, Says Frank Stagg," *Baptists Today*, 19 Jan. 1995, 3.

26. Transcript, Annual Meeting of the Board of Trustees, Southern Baptist Theological Seminary, 13 Apr. 1988, tape 6, p. 8.

27. Transcript, Annual Meeting of the Board of Trustees, Southern Baptist Theological Seminary, 13 Apr. 1988, tape 6, pp. 7–8. The candidate had several other strikes against him—he was very conservative, and he did not belong to a Baptist church.

28. Dale Moody to Roy Honeycutt, 3 May 1983, Dale Moody 1982–1986 folder, Honeycutt Papers.

29. Mark Wingfield, "Mohler Cites Abstract as Seminary's Doctrinal Border," *Western Recorder*, 30 Mar. 1993, 9.

claimed official unilateral authority to interpret the Abstract. When the Faculty Committee met with trustees at their fall 1994 meeting, they raised these two concerns. Jim Chancellor, committee chair, reported to the faculty that the trustees told him that the Abstract insisted on three Calvinist distinctives: "election, total depravity, and perseverance of the saints." On the second point the trustees gave no satisfaction to the faculty. Chancellor reported only that the committee expressed the faculty's concern about the "difficulties, stress, and confusion in a system that empowers one single individual to be the sole arbiter of the meaning and interpretation of the Abstract."[30] They knew that if they lost the right of individual interpretation, most would suddenly find themselves outside the Abstract. They were not prepared to accept Boyce's original intent. Mohler was.

MOLLY MARSHALL

Most faculty and students were nevertheless shocked when Mohler acted in accordance with his convictions concerning the Abstract's strict construction and the faculty's strict subscription to it. On June 21, 1994, David Dockery informed theology professor Molly Marshall that Mohler had recently reviewed her writings and addresses and had concluded that her beliefs placed her in contradiction to the Abstract of Principles.[31] He intended to bring to the trustees a report formally charging her with violating the Abstract of Principles. On June 30, 1994, Dockery wrote a memorandum to Marshall in response to her query concerning the nature of the charges. Dockery speculated that Mohler would charge her with failing to relate constructively the Southern Baptist Convention and with violation of the Abstract of Principles, though Mohler's statements mentioned only charges for violating the Abstract.

The seminary's official procedure required the president to investigate all charges brought against professors in order to determine whether they possessed sufficient merit to warrant a formal investigation by the board of trustees. Over the years McCall and Honeycutt had reviewed hundreds of such accusations against various professors and found no basis for trustee investigation in any of them—Dale Moody's explicit rejection of the Abstract's statement on perseverance in 1962 was the lone exception. Mohler now concluded that Marshall's teachings merited a trustee investigation. It was his duty to bring the

30. Faculty Minutes, Southern Baptist Theological Seminary, 5 Oct. 1994.

31. Robison James, "Molly Marshall," in *Dictionary of Heresy Trials in American Christianity*, ed. George H. Shriver (Westport, CT: Greenwood Press, 1997), 243–244; Marv Knox, "Molly Marshall Resigns after Mohler Threatens Firing," *Western Recorder*, 23 Aug. 1994, 7.

Molly T. Marshall

charges before the trustees. He notified Marshall in advance of this step to give her opportunity to preempt an investigation by resigning.

Marshall, like her colleagues generally, felt that Mohler had no right to interpret the Abstract for the faculty. The interpretation of the Abstract, she said, "has always been left to the liberty of the conscience of the faculty member."[32] Marshall nevertheless chose to resign and take a monetary settlement rather than fight the charges. She resigned in part because she believed that she would not receive a fair hearing and that the trustees would certainly vote to dismiss her. She reasoned also that even if the board exonerated her, she did not desire to remain while Mohler was president: "I have no future here."[33] She was permitted to retain her office through the subsequent academic year and complete supervision of her doctoral students. In 1995 Marshall became professor of theology at Central Baptist Theological Seminary in Kansas City, Kansas. In 2005 trustees there elected her president.

32. Molly Marshall, quoted in Knox, "Molly Marshall Resigns after Mohler Threatens Firing," 7, 9.
33. Knox, "Molly Marshall Resigns after Mohler Threatens Firing," 8.

Mohler's move against Marshall provoked considerable anger on campus. Students held demonstrations and prayer vigils in sympathy with her. Faculty, with few exceptions, felt profound grief. By a vote of 44 to 8 the faculty passed a resolution in her support, effectively censuring Mohler. The resolution challenged Mohler's positions. It suggested that there was no substantive merit to Mohler's claim that Marshall was outside the Abstract: "In our opinion her theology is in accordance with and not contrary to the Abstract of Principles."[34] It suggested that Mohler had violated "both the letter and the spirit" of the Covenant Renewal agreement when it called on him to reinstate both. It implied that Mohler preferred obeying a creed to obeying Christ: "When absolute adherence to creedal formulations has eclipsed Jesus' clear teachings on justice and righteousness and genuine love…many of God's children have suffered terribly."[35] At the December 1994 commencement, many graduates pinned roses to their gowns, and friends showered Marshall with rose petals. It was, she felt, a fitting "ritual of death."[36] This was not merely grief at Marshall's resignation. The majority of the faculty immediately wondered who would be next. For at least forty years the seminary's presidents had permitted professors to sign the Abstract according to their own interpretations of its statements. Mohler, however, had pledged that he would interpret it according to its original meaning. Many on the faculty knew that if Marshall was outside Mohler's understanding of the Abstract, they probably were outside it as well. Most professors lived in anxiety, waiting for the next shoe to drop. Seven months later, it dropped in an alarming way.

DIANA GARLAND, THE ORDINATION OF WOMEN, AND THE CARVER SCHOOL

In March 1995 the seminary experienced the most traumatic crisis of the first fifteen years of Mohler's presidency. It began with the firing of a dean and ended with the closing of an entire school. It convinced many moderate faculty members that they could no longer hope that Mohler would compromise and cooperate with them. This induced many to seek employment elsewhere

34. Unattributed, "Faculty Opposes, Trustees Praise Marshall's Leaving," *Western Recorder*, 30 Aug. 1994, 2. Six faculty abstained (Faculty Minutes, Southern Baptist Theological Seminary, 26 Aug. 1994).

35. "Resolution No. 2," Faculty Minutes, Southern Baptist Theological Seminary, 26 Aug. 1994.

36. Molly Marshall, quoted in Dianne Aprile, "The Ghost Still Walking the Halls," *Louisville Courier-Journal*, 23 July 1995, 1H.

immediately. It made an early retirement offer attractive to many others. The result was a rapid transition from a faculty dominated by moderates to one dominated by inerrantists.

It began, like many conflicts in higher education, as a disagreement over faculty selection. Diana Garland, whom Honeycutt had appointed dean of the Carver School of Church Social Work in 1993, declared a faculty position open and initiated the formal search process. Garland wanted the search committee to recommend David Sherwood, director of the social work program at Gordon College, an evangelical college in Wenham, Massachusetts. Garland believed that Sherwood was the ideal candidate—he was conservative, scholarly, and a team player. The search committee agreed and recommended him to the dean for election. Garland scheduled Sherwood to meet personally with students, the faculty of the Carver School, and the president and created considerable momentum in favor of Sherwood's candidacy.[37]

The procedure for electing persons to the faculty was rather involved. The faculty, the administration, and the trustees each played a central role. This process began with the dean's appointment of a search committee of faculty members who built a list of candidates, interviewed top prospects, and made a recommendation to the dean of the school. The dean took the committee's recommendation to the provost and president, and if they decided to move forward with the candidate, they scheduled an interview before the whole faculty. The faculty interviewed the candidate and voted their recommendation. The dean, provost, and president, with the faculty's opinion in hand, decided whether to recommend the candidate for election to the faculty by the board of trustees. The president also had authority to hire faculty "on contract for a specified number of years," which did not require the involvement of a search committee, faculty interview and vote, or trustee interview. The president nevertheless had to report to trustees all faculty appointed under contract for their approval. For several years, until the faculty became dominated by conservatives, Mohler's ability to appoint conservatives apart from faculty search committees and faculty vote was critically important to the transition to a conservative faculty.

Sherwood felt that his interview with Mohler went well. Garland called afterward, however, to tell him that Mohler wanted Sherwood to write out his views on the Abstract of Principles and on four issues not addressed in the Abstract: homosexuality, abortion, women's ordination, and the exclusivity of the gospel as the means of salvation.[38]

37. Mark Wingfield and Marv Knox, "Mohler Fires Garland as Carver School Dean," *Western Recorder*, 21 Mar. 1995, 2.

38. Marv Knox, "Sherwood Says He Was Rejected over Interpretation," *Western Recorder*, 28 Mar. 1995, 7.

In his response Sherwood explained that he supported women serving as deacons and pastors, defending his views by appeal to relevant scripture passages.[39] After examining Sherwood's response, Mohler notified Garland that he would not support the nomination. Mohler's addition of the four criteria blocked Sherwood's nomination to the trustees.

Garland viewed the rejection as entailing apocalyptic consequences for the school of social work. She saw Sherwood's candidacy as a test case. She believed that he was the best-qualified candidate anywhere, and if he could not pass muster with Mohler, then none could. She did not recognize that Mohler graded in a different way than she did. She saw his doctrinal beliefs as one component of a basket of goods. He scored very high on every component and in the composite. But Mohler did not view a candidate's doctrinal beliefs that way. Many beliefs were nonnegotiable, including the Abstract and the four criteria. Garland protested Mohler's use of the four criteria and drew the entire seminary into the apocalypse.

Garland gathered the social work faculty and told them of Sherwood's rejection. She announced that if Sherwood was not qualified, then no one would be. The school would be unable to hire a new professor and would fail to meet accrediting standards for the minimum number of faculty. And if it lost accreditation, the school would have to close. Mohler's rejection of Sherwood meant the death of the school in whose unique mission they so deeply believed. Garland and the school's faculty began plotting their strategy to save the school. They met in the homes of faculty, discussed their options, including their resignations, and consulted attorneys.

Garland finally concluded that she would have to resign, but an attorney friend suggested that she should "fight for what you believe in." So she decided to fight. She called the faculty to her home on a Sunday and told them of her plan to make a public statement the following day at a scheduled student forum. She called the student body president and told him to get the message out that it was important for students to be present. "He heard the urgency in my voice." She expected to be fired.[40]

On Monday morning most of the school's 117 students were present. Garland read a prepared statement to the gathered students and released the document to the press. She related the events that led to the rejection of David Sherwood as a faculty candidate and concluded that she "could not find faculty that would satisfy the president's criteria." She predicted direly that within six months the Carver School of Church Social Work would be out of compliance with

---

39. David Sherwood, "Sherwood's Statement," *Western Recorder*, 28 Mar. 1995, 7.

40. Diana Garland, "When Professional Ethics and Religious Politics Conflict: A Case Study," *Social Work and Christianity* 26 (1999): 65–66.

accrediting standards. She suggested that Mohler's rejection of Sherwood had imposed a death sentence upon the school.[41]

She then called the gathered troops to action. She asked them to join her in the struggle "in seeking a future for our school and in asking that the administration follow the stated institutional policies." Students heeded her call and gathered en masse outside the president's office to keep vigil.[42]

Mohler first learned of Garland's statement when a reporter contacted him for his comments before he had arrived at the office. When he arrived at Norton Hall, he saw that the students had begun a "sit-in" in the long hallway outside his office. After Garland explained herself, Mohler asked for her resignation. Garland afterward said that Mohler fired her, though Mohler said and initial reports indicated that she had resigned.[43] In either case, Mohler and Garland both recognized that she could no longer serve as dean. Mohler then spoke to the gathered students to explain to them the situation from the administration's perspective. As the social work students followed Mohler to a classroom for the meeting, they sang "We Shall Overcome."[44]

Garland took the matter public in order to bring "pressure on the president and on the institution."[45] She was accusing Mohler of failing to follow stated guidelines, especially by imposing secret hiring criteria. She sought "redress for my school and my faculty colleagues" for Mohler's "abuse of power."[46] She evidently believed that if she publicly demonstrated the damaging character of Mohler's policies, trustees would compel Mohler to rescind all criteria beyond the Abstract of Principles.

The four additional criteria became the chief point of contention between Mohler and the faculty. Many faculty members felt that Mohler had been using secret hiring criteria. Garland charged that Mohler deliberately hid these criteria from the faculty and the public, though she said that all the deans were aware of them. Mohler said that there was nothing secretive about the criteria. When he was elected president, he declared that he would use them. He had done so since that time, and the provost and deans were aware of this. Faculty

41. Diana Garland, "What's Really Going on at Southern Seminary," *Western Recorder*, 18 Apr. 1995, 7; Diana Garland, "When Professional Ethics and Religious Politics Conflict: A Case Study," *Social Work and Christianity* 26 (1999): 67.

42. Garland, "When Professional Ethics and Religious Politics Conflict," 67.

43. Mark McCormick, "Dean Says Seminary Fired Her from Post," *Louisville Courier-Journal*, 22 Mar. 1995, 1A.

44. Leslie Scanlon, "Dean at Baptist Seminary Forced to Quit," *Louisville Courier-Journal*, 21 Mar. 1995, 1A, 9A.

45. Wingfield and Knox, "Mohler Fires Garland as Carver School Dean," 2.

46. Garland, "When Professional Ethics and Religious Politics Conflict," 66.

selection, Mohler said, required examining candidates regarding "a constellation of issues about which I have been quite candid." [47] The faculty evidently did
not expect that he would carry through on these commitments.

The appeal to the public was an act of desperation. It was a declaration of no
confidence in Mohler's leadership and functioned intrinsically as an ultimatum. The only ones who could come to Garland's rescue were the trustees, and
they were unlikely to do so for many reasons.

WOMEN, ORDINATION, AND SOUTHERN SEMINARY

Most Southern Baptists were "complementarians." This was a new name for
their traditional view of gender relations in the family and in the church. They
believed that when God established the family, he invested husbands with
authority and responsibility over the household, for the scriptures commanded
wives to "be subject to your husbands." They believed also that God called only
certain men to the office of gospel minister, for the scriptures permitted "no
woman to teach or have authority over men." [48]

The feminist movement challenged the traditional views. Some Southern
Baptists embraced the feminists' "egalitarian" vision of gender roles and ordained
women as preachers. Moderate and liberal Southern Baptists discounted the
complementarians' scripture passages as culturally delimited expressions of
ancient folkways. God did not intend modern folk to follow them. In 1964,
the Watts Street Baptist Church in Durham, North Carolina, ordained Addie
Davis as the first woman ordained to the gospel ministry in a Southern Baptist
church. By 1993 Southern Baptist churches had ordained about 900 women to
ministry roles (not including deacon ordinations). Of the 900, only 2 percent
were serving as pastors. Most had roles in chaplaincy, missions, social work,
and counseling. [49]

As egalitarian views spread in the denomination, the Southern Baptist majority adopted statements affirming the traditional view. The 1984 meeting of the
Southern Baptist Convention passed a resolution declaring the convention's
opposition to ordaining women to the ministry. In 1999 and 2000 the convention
adopted statements affirming extensive agreement with the complementarian

---

47. R. Albert Mohler Jr., quoted in Wingfield and Knox, "Mohler Fires Garland as
Carver School Dean," 6.

48. See Eph. 5:22; Col. 3:18; 1 Pet. 3:1; 1 Tim. 2:12.

49. Unattributed, "Who Are Baptist Women in Ministry," *Western Recorder*, 26 Jan.
1993, 7.

view. The strongest support for egalitarian views in the denomination came from the seminaries, especially Southern Baptist Theological Seminary.

WOMEN AT SOUTHERN BAPTIST THEOLOGICAL SEMINARY

Women had been attending classes at Southern Seminary since at least the early 1880s. In the session of 1882–1883 two women, Florence Blanford and Cynthia Morris, attended seminary classes in preparation for missionary service.[50] When the Southern Baptist Woman's Missionary Union established the missionary-oriented Women's Training School in Louisville in 1907, its female students took some of their classes in the seminary alongside the men. When the seminary moved to the Beeches in 1926, it was too far from the Women's Training School for its students to take classes there anymore. The seminary admitted also the wives of ministerial students from the early twentieth century. When Fuller introduced music and religious education programs for training laypersons, women especially enrolled in these programs. After the Women's Training School relocated on Lexington Road contiguous to the campus in 1941, female enrollment at the seminary jumped. In 1946, for example, the seminary enrolled 675 men and 300 women. In 1948 trustees voted to admit women to its regular B.D. and Th.D. degree programs. The first woman to enroll in the B.D. program was Helen Armstrong in 1949. Armstrong afterward enrolled also in the Th.D. program.[51] All the seminary's programs for women students complemented the denomination's beliefs regarding gender roles.

In the 1970s that changed. Some women in the school of theology felt called of God to pursue ordination and organized in support of their aspirations. Roy Honeycutt, who had become dean of the school of theology in 1975, supported women's ordination warmly. In 1975 he invited these women students to a

50. John A. Broadus, *Memoir of James Petigru Boyce* (New York: A. C. Armstrong and Son, 1893), 296; Minutes, Foreign Mission Board, Southern Baptist Convention, 5 Feb. 1883; ibid., 7 Dec. 1885; ibid., 6 Mar. 1882; ibid., 30 Apr. 1883; ibid., 15 Oct. 1883; Eliza S. Broadus to John A. Broadus, 8 May 1883, box 10, Broadus Papers; Minutes, Foreign Mission Board, Southern Baptist Convention; Edgar Y. Mullins, "WTS Statement," 5, box 39, Mullins Papers.

51. See John R. Sampey to Ruth Naomi Franklin, 6 Jan. 1937, box 11, Sampey Papers; H. Cornell Goerner to Paul Travis, 5 Oct. 1946, H. Cornell Goerner Papers, SBHLA; Carrie U. Littlejohn to Ellis A. Fuller, 31 May 1948, box 17, Fuller Papers; E. L. McDonald, "Personally Speaking," *Tie*, Oct. 1949, 2; unattributed, "Believe It or Not a Woman Is Now Fellow," *Tie*, 1953, 5. The B.D. was open to women who had an M.R.E. from the Women's Training School and who aspired to an educational ministry. Armstrong's training school sisters dubbed her "Brother Armstrong."

meeting in which he helped them to organize a "Women in Ministry" group to promote women's ministry among students at the seminary. Honeycutt wanted the group to encompass women in all the seminary's schools, but apparently the women in the religious education and music schools showed little interest. Most of the seminary's female students were in these two schools and did not aspire to the pastorate. The new organization chose therefore to call itself "Women in Theology." The group effectively promoted egalitarian views across the campus and in 1983 changed its name to "Women in Ministry."[52] Honeycutt supported its aim and promoted the ordination of women in many addresses and letters.

MOHLER AND COMPLEMENTARIANISM

When Mohler was a student at Southern Seminary, he assumed that the egalitarian position was the correct one. Mohler was "coordinator" of a committee organized by moderates, Concerned Southern Baptists, which in the summer of 1984 gathered signatures for a statement in opposition to the 1984 Southern Baptist Convention resolution opposing women's ordination. They bought a full page of Louisville's *Courier-Journal* to publicize the statement and the signatures.[53]

A few years later Mohler made a thorough study of the Bible's teaching on gender roles in the church. Mohler remembered walking across campus one day with Carl Henry as they discussed this question. Henry asked Mohler how he derived his position from scripture. This motivated Mohler to investigate the matter carefully. He concluded from his study that scripture prohibited women from the office of pastor or elder. He concluded that men and women "stand equal before God" but do not have exactly the same roles in the church. Women's ministry was critical to the church, and women were eligible serve in many ministry roles, Mohler believed, but the New Testament restricted the office of pastor to qualified men.[54]

52. See Roy Honeycutt to Valerie King, 2 June 1983, Women in Ministry— Correspondence 1983–84 folder, Honeycutt Papers.

53. Concerned Southern Baptists, "A Statement in Affirmation of Women," *Louisville Courier-Journal*, 4 Aug. 1984.

54. R. Albert Mohler, Oral Memoirs of R. Albert Mohler Jr., interviewed by Barry Hankins, 5 Aug. 1997 and 13 Aug. 1999, Baylor University Institute of Oral History, 15–16; R. Albert Mohler, quoted in Mark Wingfield, "Mohler Says He Changed His Mind on Women's Ordination," *Baptist True Union*, 2 Sept. 1993, 3.

This was perhaps the most critical issue for many faculty and students. It generated more passion than any other issue on campus. From the time of Mohler's election as president, students and faculty repeatedly challenged him on this issue. Just as repeatedly, Mohler explained his views on women's roles in the church. On April 8, 1993, Roy Honeycutt hosted a student forum to introduce Mohler to the student body. About 325 students gathered in Alumni Chapel to hear his responses to their questions. Fourteen students asked questions. Five addressed directly the question of women's roles in the church, and others did so indirectly. Mohler said that he "believed in women's ministry" with the exception of service as pastor: "It's a question of what kind of ministry. It is impossible for me to square the ordination of women to the pastoral ministry with what I see in the New Testament."[55]

William Rogers, dean of the school of religious education, resigned shortly afterward in protest of Mohler's views on the matter. Rogers said that he could not participate in an administration that "devalued" the gifts of women by opposing their ordination as pastors. "This issue," Rogers said, "is crucial, central, and pivotal."[56] The vast majority of the faculty, including many of the new conservative faculty, felt the same way and rallied strongly to Garland's cause. They chose to fight the president on this ground.

BLACK WEDNESDAY

On Wednesday, March 22, 1995, two days after Garland's resignation, the faculty gathered for its regular meeting. The mood was somber and tense throughout the two-and-one-half-hour meeting. Tim Weber, one of the new conservative faculty, set the tone of the meeting when he said that the institution's stand against women's ordination had brought the seminary to its current crisis because it placed the seminary on the "far right" of evangelicalism. If Southern Seminary wanted to be in the mainstream of evangelicalism, it needed to remain neutral on this issue. Weber urged "flex" on this issue. He wanted Mohler to compromise in order to hire highly qualified persons who supported women's ordination. Weber believed that the seminary would miss out on many of the best-qualified scholars and that the school could not become a premier evangelical school if it excluded them.

55. R. Albert Mohler, quoted in "Students Confront Mohler in Forum," *Western Recorder*, 13 Apr. 1993.

56. William Rogers, quoted in Mark McCormick, "Two Deans Resigning at Baptist Seminary," *Louisville Courier-Journal*, 17 Apr. 1993, 6A.

R. Albert Mohler

Weber also claimed the trustees had set the precedent for electing persons who believed in the ordination of women when they elected him and several other conservatives in 1992 despite their support for women's ordination. He understood the trustees to have stated formally that although they disagreed with the position, they would not make it a criterion in hiring. Now, three years later, Weber said, he had learned that he could not be hired under Mohler's new criteria. Weber felt personally betrayed by the new hiring rule.

Mohler reminded the faculty that his vision for the seminary had not changed since he was elected two years earlier. He acknowledged that the question was not a first-order matter of the faith but a matter that defined fellowship. Southern Baptists were almost entirely opposed to women's ordination, and the seminary had an obligation to bring the faculty into line with denominational expectations and realities. Mohler personally agreed with the Southern Baptist position.

Faculty left that meeting profoundly demoralized. Most faculty believed that Mohler had violated the 1991 covenant by adding criteria to the Abstract and the covenant. Mohler insisted that it had always been necessary to ask questions about all kinds of issues beyond the Abstract and the covenant. Faculty admitted that they recognized that women's ordination was a "critical issue" in hiring, but they were incensed because they did not know that it was a "litmus test" hiring issue.

The moderate faculty, and apparently including faculty hired under the covenant, wanted to view the covenant's hiring guidelines as placing strict limits on what questions trustees could ask candidates. The Abstract of Principles and the covenant statement should constitute the maximum standards for assessing the qualifications of any faculty candidate. Any criteria beyond these explicit guidelines were illegitimate.

But seminary presidents and trustees had never viewed the Abstract as an exclusive criterion for hiring. The addition of the covenant did not change this. Mohler announced at the time of his election that he would have criteria beyond the Abstract. Agreement with the Abstract of Principles was nonnegotiable, he said in March 1993, but it was not the maximum and exclusive standard for selecting faculty members. It was "the irreducible minimum," he said, but it did not address every issue relevant for the seminary's commitment to scriptural fidelity and effective denominational service. Mohler explained that prospective faculty members would probably face questions, for example, on such issues as abortion and homosexuality.[57]

The conservative trustees from the start intended to judge faculty candidates by additional criteria. At the same meeting in which the trustees adopted the covenant in 1991, trustees elected or tenured five faculty members. Trustees asked all five their views on the historical reality of Adam and Eve, the accuracy of the Bible's historical statements, the reliability of its accounts of miracles, and the accuracy of its statements on authorship. Several of them were asked also their views on homosexuality and on abortion. Marv Knox, editor of the *Western Recorder*, noted that adoption of the covenant "did not keep trustees from applying other tests to faculty candidates."[58]

WOMEN'S ORDINATION AND COVERT HIRING CRITERIA

The ambiguities of the covenant renewal agreement came to the surface in the Garland controversy. The covenant's burden all along had been to find a way to advance the agenda of the conservative trustees sufficiently to prevent

57. Mark Wingfield, "Mohler Cites Abstract as Seminary's Doctrinal Border," *Western Recorder*, 30 Mar. 1993, 9.

58. Marv Knox, "Was Southern Compromise a Miracle or Mistake," Associated Baptist Press Release, 11 Apr. 1991. The five were Leigh Conver, Craig Loscalzo, Jon Rainbow, David Stancil, and Rebecca Russell.

them from adopting radical measures, and to protect the hopes of the moderate faculty sufficiently to secure their continued constructive cooperation in the school's mission. The greatest challenge was in faculty selection, and the covenant promised a framework by which the moderate faculty could nominate persons who might be acceptable to the conservative trustees.

The 1995 controversy turned largely on divergent interpretations of what occurred in April 1992, when trustees considered the election of five persons as the first to come through a search process under the covenant. They included James Chancellor, Jack Cunningham, Tim Weber, James Nogalski, and Charles Scalise. The first four were recruited as inerrantist evangelicals, as "covenant faculty."[59] Scalise was already teaching under a non-tenure-track appointment. Trustees interviewed David Dockery for granting tenure at the same meeting.

The Academic Personnel Committee had asked them their views on women's ordination and recommended all five to the full board without any statement on their views of ordination. The full board had approved the first two recommendations granting tenure to Dockery and electing James Chancellor. During the discussion of the next candidate, Jack Cunningham, trustee David Miller asked about his views of women's ordination. Committee members answered that he endorsed women's serving as deacons but was uncertain about women serving as pastors. Miller strongly opposed electing Cunningham, since he held an "aberrant view of scripture" that only a tiny percentage of Southern Baptist churches accepted.[60] Such trustees as David Miller opposed ordaining women as deacons no less than pastors. He opposed electing the candidates because Southern Baptists would perceive the trustees "as endorsing women deacons." That, he said, "violates my conscience."[61] Other trustees echoed Miller's concerns. Rick White, chairman of the Academic Personnel Committee, explained that voting in favor of a candidate did not imply that trustees agreed with the candidate at every point. Trustees voted to elect Cunningham, though nine trustees voted against election.[62]

Members of the Academic Personnel Committee disclosed that Chancellor and Dockery also supported women serving as deacons. Motions to reconsider Chancellor's election and Dockery's tenure failed. The board then considered

59. Mark Seifrid, an evangelical New Testament scholar, was appointed later by Honeycutt under a nontenurable contract, and began teaching in the fall of 1992. Seifrid and the other four made up the first conservative evangelical faculty cohort under the covenant.

60. Mark Wingfield, "Six Elected to Faculty after Debate on Women," *Western Recorder*, 5 May 1992, 9.

61. David Miller, quoted in Wingfield, "Six Elected to Faculty," 9.

62. Wingfield, "Six Elected to Faculty," 9.

the committee's recommendation of Tim Weber. Weber, a committee member related, was "100 percent in favor of women in ministry as a deacon and pastor." Rick White and Dean Larry McSwain made impassioned pleas for Weber's election, which passed with only four dissenting votes. The following day similar debates occurred regarding electing James Nogalski and Charles Scalise, with the same result.[63] Trustee chairman Wayne Allen reflected afterward that "some of us were shocked that people with the same high view of scripture have held these views."[64]

The conservative trustees were in a bind. They had recruited these candidates as their first hiring effort with the board under their control. To reject them would signal a failure of their governance. It would also credit moderates' assertions that there were no intelligent and credible scholars who would agree with inerrancy or the Covenant Renewal statement on scripture. The conservative trustees wanted to prove that they could govern and that they would be able to recruit qualified scholars who also believed in inerrancy, so most voted to elect them despite their reservations.

But they were also opposed to ordaining women and made it clear that this was not precedent. They clearly did not want to elect persons who supported women's ordination. At the same meeting they adopted a resolution affirming "the commitment to the scriptures" of the recently elected faculty but repudiating any intimation that they would tolerate egalitarian views in the future. They resolved that "no action of this board shall be construed as an endorsement of women in the role of pastor or deacon."[65] Trustee Jerry Johnson told Jim Chancellor that they would elect no more egalitarians.

Honeycutt, however, interpreted the election as a precedent. He held that the majority of the trustees viewed the covenant as restricting them from imposing any doctrinal criteria beyond the Abstract and the covenant's statement on scripture. Honeycutt noted that "strong opposition" on the board arose when they learned that the five candidates up for election to the faculty in April 1992 supported the ordination of women. But the board voted to elect them, Honeycutt said in a report to the American Association of Theological Schools, because "the issue was not included in the covenant and to do otherwise would break faith with the covenant." By adopting the covenant, Honeycutt said, the trustees

63. Wingfield, "Six Elected to Faculty," 9.
64. Wingfield, "Six Elected to Faculty," 9.
65. Minutes, Board of Trustees, Southern Baptist Theological Seminary, 27–29 Apr. 1992. The resolution passed 23 to 14. See also Wingfield, "Six Elected to Faculty," 9.

restricted themselves from considering any criteria beyond the Abstract and the covenant.[66] Most faculty accepted Honeycutt's interpretation.

Honeycutt acknowledged that trustees adopted the covenant with a different interpretation of its implications. He told the accrediting commission in November 1992 that the "faculty are concerned that beyond agreement with the Abstract of Principles and the covenant, some trustees think additional limitations should apply." He said that he was helping the trustees recognize that the covenant played a "crucial role for the seminary's viability" and suggested that he was leading them to adopt the faculty's interpretation of the covenant's restrictions: "Trustee commitment to the covenant matures with growing experience of its implications."[67] Honeycutt represented to the accrediting commission that the faculty's interpretation of the covenant was controlling and that he was trying to get the trustees to recognize that. He failed to mention that he represented a different interpretation to the trustees at the 1991 meeting when they adopted it.

Seminary policy gave the faculty the responsibility of making nominations of candidates for election to the faculty. The covenant's statement on scripture restricted them to hiring evangelicals. Honeycutt noted that in the April 1992 nominations, the covenant had been "indispensable in guiding faculty to bring persons outside normal channels of faculty addition to include 'conservative-evangelicals' who could affirm the covenant."[68] But they believed that the covenant's silence on other issues prohibited trustees from imposing any other criteria on candidates.

But the faculty employed their own additional criteria in their searches. The most important criterion for the faculty was the candidate's view of women's roles in the church and in the family. When the faculty search committee interviewed Tim Weber, the first question they asked him concerned his beliefs on women in the ministry. He told them that he fully supported the ordination of women. When Weber asked how his views squared with the seminary's faculty, Molly Marshall said that "all the faculty would agree with you but probably

66. Roy Honeycutt, "Report to the Association of Theological Schools and Southern Association of Schools and Colleges from the Southern Baptist Theological Seminary, May 6, 1992," 6, ATS Report Re/Trustee Actions (1/91) folder, Honeycutt Papers.

67. Roy Honeycutt, "Report to the Association of Theological Schools and Southern Association of Schools and Colleges from the Southern Baptist Theological Seminary," 15 Nov. 1992, 6, ATS Report Re/Trustee Actions (1/91) folder, Honeycutt Papers.

68. Roy Honeycutt, "Report to the Association of Theological Schools and Southern Association of Schools and Colleges from the Southern Baptist Theological Seminary, May 6, 1992," 5, ATS Report Re/Trustee Actions (1/91) folder, Honeycutt Papers.

none of the trustees." [69] Jim Chancellor had a similar experience in his interview with the faculty search committee. So did Scott Hafemann. Support for women's ordination functioned for the faculty as an informal litmus test.

Diana Garland said that her "primary concern" was Mohler's criteria. To impose such criteria violated the seminary's official policy permitting academic freedom beyond the commitments enumerated in the seminary's confession, the Abstract of Principles: "Within the confessional guidelines of Christian faith and with a deep respect for one another's differing ideas, a seminary must be a place where persons can respectfully hold differing views and explore God's truth together." Garland therefore argued that it was inappropriate for Mohler to exclude candidates based on doctrinal criteria beyond the purview of the Abstract of Principles. He asked David Sherwood "his personal views on several issues that are not a part of the confessional guidelines of the seminary." [70]

She criticized Mohler also for keeping the criteria secret: "I had not been informed that the president could add criteria to the hiring process" outside established guidelines. [71] Garland conceded that "the president has every right to interview faculty candidates and ask them questions that shed light on how they will teach their classes and relate to our churches." But any "absolute criteria," she said, must be clearly stated in seminary policies. [72]

THE END OF ENTENTE

In fact Mohler had told the deans what criteria especially concerned him. Garland acknowledged that Mohler had a right to ask questions beyond the Abstract and the covenant, and apparently had a right to reject candidates based on such questions, as long as he did not reject everyone who failed the criteria. Her complaint was the same as that of the faculty generally. It hinged on whether Mohler would make exceptions to the additional criteria. It was the question whether opposition to women's ordination would be an ordinary expectation of candidates or whether it would be an unvarying requirement. At the Black Wednesday faculty meeting some professors acknowledged that they knew the president would apply the criterion of women's ordination, but they

---

69. Timothy Weber, "Oral Memoir of Timothy Weber," interview by Barry Hankins, 19 May 1998, 5, Baylor University Institute of Oral History.

70. Garland, "What's Really Going on at Southern Seminary," 7.

71. Garland, "What's Really Going on at Southern Seminary," 7.

72. Garland, "What's Really Going on at Southern Seminary," 7.

had not been informed that it was an "absolute" criterion. They did not know that the president had decided definitely that this was a nonnegotiable issue. The depth of anger, dismay, and disorientation by faculty revealed that a more serious issue was involved.

The deeper issue was the faculty's realization that their efforts to negotiate compromise over faculty hiring were over. The shock was so severe because the moderate faculty now saw the foreclosure of their hopes for preserving in some measure the moderate heritage at Southern Seminary. They had seen Honeycutt negotiate one compromise after another. They knew that Mohler and the trustees wanted to elect no more egalitarians. But they believed that they could force compromises, especially by arguing that the candidates were stellar scholars who passed muster on inerrancy. Larry McSwain had made this very argument in 1992 when trustees questioned whether they should elect Tim Weber, whose egalitarian views troubled many trustees. McSwain told trustees that Weber was "the best qualified candidate you will ever have a chance to elect to this faculty."[73] Diana Garland made the same argument regarding Sherwood. Weber pressed the point in the Black Wednesday faculty meeting. They expected Mohler to make exceptions.

The rejection of Sherwood's candidacy signaled the end of negotiation over the meaning of the covenant renewal document. The era of entente was over.

A SOUTHERN BAPTIST INSTITUTION

Most of the new evangelicals on the faculty experienced the same kind of shock as their moderate colleagues. As it turned out, their vision for the seminary was that of a moderate evangelicalism. They were not Southern Baptist moderates— they held to inerrancy and other evangelical commitments. But within broader evangelicalism, they were on the left side—though Tim Weber called his position mainstream evangelicalism. Weber said that "most evangelical seminaries" tolerated both views on their faculties. He pointed to Trinity, Gordon-Conwell, Bethel, and Denver seminaries. He felt that Southern Seminary's exclusion of candidates who endorsed women's ordination placed the school on the "far right." With Mohler's additional criteria, Southern was, he said, "not even in the mainstream" of evangelicalism.[74]

73. Larry McSwain, quoted in Wingfield, "Six Elected to Faculty," 9.
74. Marv Knox, "Faculty Warns of Hiring Restrictions' Chilling Effect," *Western Recorder*, 28 Mar. 1995, 9.

All parties at the seminary wanted to recruit a faculty of the highest standards of scholarship. But the new evangelicals felt that there were fewer nonnegotiable beliefs than the trustees and the president. They wanted to have the freedom to choose from a larger field of candidates. Refusing to hire egalitarians, Weber said, would exclude the "brightest, most devout conservative evangelical scholars."

This raised the issue of the seminary's larger mission and the criteria of its success. It valued scholarship, but measuring scholarly achievement was problematic. Many evangelicals, consistent with standardization in the professions generally, tended to measure success by the recognition achieved within the larger professional guild, among the universe of scholars.

For evangelical scholars, this was an uncertain venture. Many nonevangelical scholars in theology and religion thought it laughable that serious scholars could believe in the inerrancy of the Bible. Adherence to that belief alone discredited one's scholarship. Such evangelical overachievers as George Ladd and E. J. Carnell ran afoul of this difficulty. Others, especially such historians as George M. Marsden, Mark Noll, and Harry Stout, gained recognition in the larger academy. Marsden nevertheless criticized the academy's refusal to recognize evangelical scholarship, and Noll judged evangelicalism by the same refusal. For most evangelicals, it was the broad, ugly ditch that they could not cross.[75]

For moderates and for left-wing evangelicals, the rejection of women's ordination represented a similar kind of questionable scholarship. They argued therefore that the seminary could not hire the top scholars if it could not hire egalitarians. Refusing to hire egalitarians, Tim Weber said, would exclude persons who "would bring glory to this seminary" and would prevent Southern Seminary "from becoming the evangelical school we're longing to become."[76] Weber believed that Southern Seminary intended to define itself as a mainstream evangelical seminary. Mainstream meant egalitarian.

The trustees did not aspire to make Southern Seminary a mainstream evangelical seminary but an evangelical and Southern Baptist seminary. They did

75. See George M. Marsden, *Reforming Fundamentalism: Fuller Seminary and the New Evangelicalism* (Grand Rapids, MI: Eerdmans, 1987); Rudolph Nelson, *The Making and Unmaking of an Evangelical Mind: The Case of E. J. Carnell* (New York: Cambridge University Press, 1987); George M. Marsden, *The Outrageous Idea of Christian Scholarship* (New York: Oxford University Press, 1997); Mark Noll, *The Scandal of the Evangelical Mind* (Grand Rapids, MI: Eerdmans, 1994).

76. Tim Weber, quoted in Knox, "Faculty Warns of Hiring Restrictions' Chilling Effect," 9.

not aspire to become like Gordon-Conwell or Trinity. Their vision was the evangelical Baptist orthodoxy represented by the seminary's founders.

Among evangelicals the question of women's ordination was a wedge issue. The hermeneutical principles that influenced scholars' views on women's ordination influenced their perceptions of the plausibility of various other interpretations. No less important, evangelical institutions found it difficult as a practical matter to maintain neutrality on the question. They coalesced on either side of the question, which acted as something of a continental divide in evangelicalism.

Neutrality on the issue in faculty selection was difficult in practice because it was not just an interpretive issue—it was a personal issue. And egalitarians viewed it as a justice issue. They tended to view any support or accommodation of complementarian views as compromise with injustice. Their support of egalitarianism tended to become a moral principle that brooked no compromise. Complementarians similarly saw it as a question of obedience to God's revealed command and one that had practical consequences on which churches had to act one way or the other. Complementarians and egalitarians believed that the issue had profound significance beyond the church, as it had ramifications for the family and the social order.

Southern's faculty had not been neutral on the issue. The selection of post-covenant faculty ostensibly should have reflected the beliefs of conservatives in the denomination, since one of the stated agreements in the covenant was the restoration of balance on the faculty in reflecting Southern Baptist beliefs. But the elected faculty were egalitarians, with the exception of David Dockery, who held that women were ineligible to serve as pastors but might serve as deacons.

Mohler made it clear that Southern Seminary did not aspire to be a "mainstream" evangelical institution. "We are a Southern Baptist institution," he told the faculty, "and we are an evangelical institution." The Southern Baptist identity functioned to prescribe the character of the school, whereas evangelical identity could function only descriptively. Southern Seminary was broadly evangelical, but it was specifically Southern Baptist. "There's a qualifier on evangelical," Mohler explained. Southern Seminary was a "Southern Baptist-evangelical" seminary. It "would not, could not" define itself merely as a mainline evangelical institution. The school would remain loyal to the denomination and to its historical identity. Southern Baptists established, governed, and sustained the school and had every right to expect the school to support and strengthen the faith and practice of Southern Baptists. "We don't own this place," Mohler reminded the faculty, "we work here." Southern would not, indeed could not, be a generic evangelical school of any sort.

AFTERMATH

The Garland controversy became a defining moment in the seminary's life. The local press and the newspapers of Southern Baptist state conventions excoriated Mohler.[77] Threats against the campus disrupted chapel and classes four times during the week of March 20.[78] The student sit-in in Norton Hall continued for several weeks.[79]

After the Black Wednesday meeting, the seminary faculty and students rallied to Garland's cause. The faculty met on April 5 and passed a resolution in support of Garland and the school of social work. Some faculty apparently stayed away from the meeting, but of the forty-one faculty present, only two voted against it and two others abstained.[80] Two of the new inerrantist faculty, Tim Weber and Carey Newman, urged trustee chairman Rick White to dismiss Mohler and replace him with David Dockery: "You've got to fire this guy. He's ruining everything."[81] As institutional instability increased, this outcome became more plausible. But White told Weber and Newman that he thought it unlikely that recent events would convince the board that it was mistaken when it concluded just two years previously that it was God's will to elect Mohler.[82]

On April 18, 1995, more than 500 students and faculty gathered on the seminary's main lawn for a service of encouragement and grief. Molly Marshall, who still occupied her office in Norton Hall, told the crowd that Mohler and

77. See Bob Hill, "Seminary President's Dogma of Intolerance Is Intolerable," *Louisville Courier-Journal*, 23 Mar. 1995, 1B; Mark McCormick, "Some Want U of L to Cut Ties with Seminary," *Louisville Courier-Journal*, 25 Mar. 1995, 9A; Richard Bridges, "Baptist Oppression," *Louisville Courier-Journal*, 9 Apr. 1995, 5D; Dianne Aprile, "Saving Grace," *Louisville Courier-Journal*, 16 Apr. 1995, 1H; Paul Simmons, "Seminary 'Has Been Destroyed,'" *Louisville Courier-Journal*, 8 May 1995, 6A.

78. Mark McCormick, "Bomb Threat Disrupts Seminary Classes," *Louisville Courier-Journal*, 24 Mar. 1995, 15A.

79. Mark Wingfield, "Accrediting Agencies Likely to Investigate Seminary," *Western Recorder*, 28 Mar. 1995, 8; Mark Wingfield, "Carver School Students and Alumni Organize to Save School," *Western Recorder*, 4 Apr. 1995, 10; Mark Wingfield, "Mohler Reprimands Student Protesters," *Western Recorder*, 11 Apr. 1995, 13.

80. Marv Knox, "Seminary Faculty Supports Carver School, Garland," *Western Recorder*, 11 Apr. 1995, 12.

81. Timothy Weber, interview by Barry Hankins, 19 May 1998, p. 15, Oral Memoirs of Timothy Weber, Baylor University Institute for Oral History, Baylor University.

82. Rick White, quoted in Timothy Weber, interview by Barry Hankins, 19 May 1998, p. 15, Oral Memoirs of Timothy Weber, Baylor University Institute for Oral History, Baylor University.

the trustees usurped the place of God in their attitude toward women's ordination: "That is blasphemy."[83] She anathematized them as heretics who taught "not the gospel but another gospel."[84] Marv Knox, editor of Kentucky's *Western Recorder*, declared in the wake of these events that "Southern Seminary no longer is Baptist."[85]

TRUSTEE RESPONSE

At their April 1995 meeting, trustees adopted the "Statement on the Resignation of Dean Diana Garland," in which they expressed complete support for Mohler's handling of the matter and affirming Mohler's authority to evaluate faculty candidates based on the four criteria recently employed, or others he may think necessary. Trustees also adopted a policy requiring seminary employees to "support and relate constructively to the institution, its policies and administration."[86]

The faculty mistakenly believed that board chairman Rick White would support them against Mohler. He criticized Garland instead. Her offense, White wrote, was taking a public adversarial posture on what was properly an internal administrative matter and releasing a prepared statement to students, faculty, and the media. "Dr. Mohler took the reasonable course," White concluded, when he asked Garland to resign her position as dean.[87]

Trustees also affirmed his use of the additional criteria in faculty selection. They were acting consistently with their own convictions and with those of Southern Baptists generally. "We believe," White explained, "that new faculty members being hired should share that view held by the overwhelming

---

83. Molly Marshall, quoted in Melanie Childers, "Supporters of Seminary's Past Rally and Remember amid Changes," *Western Recorder*, 25 Apr. 1995, 11.

84. Molly Marshall, quoted in Mark McCormick, "Former Professor Criticizes Seminary's Leadership at Rally," *Louisville Courier-Journal*, 19 Apr. 1995, 4B.

85. Marv Knox, "We Need a New Seminary 'for Such a Time as This,'" *Western Recorder*, 25 Apr. 1995, 5.

86. Mark Wingfield, "Seminary Trustees Praise Mohler, Restrict Faculty," *Western Recorder*, 25 Apr. 1995, 8; Mark McCormick, "Baptist Seminary Board Curbs Faculty Influence," *Louisville Courier-Journal*, 20 Apr. 1995, 1A.

87. Rick White, "What's Really Going on at Southern Seminary," *Western Recorder*, 18 Apr. 1995, 6. Tim Weber suggested that this letter did not represent Rick White's true views and that he merely put his name on it out of party loyalty (Timothy Weber, interview by Barry Hankins, 19 May 1998, p. 15, Oral Memoirs of Timothy Weber, Baylor University Institute for Oral History, Baylor University).

majority of the denomination that supports the seminary."[88] The president had a responsibility, White wrote, to ask prospective faculty regarding "significant issues within the life of the church," including such matters as homosexuality and the ordination of women, where the values of American culture pressured churches to recast traditional beliefs, practices, and scripture interpretations. The selection of faculty was critically important, since persons elected would be shaping the beliefs of church leaders for thirty or forty years.[89]

Trustees also adopted an amendment to the school's faculty-staff manual designed to prevent faculty from sowing disaffection among students or in the churches. It was always a delicate and dangerous matter in times of controversy to balance individual expression and action against responsibility for the welfare of the institution and the denomination. In 1899 the trustees adopted a resolution requesting "that members of the faculty will refrain from *public* expression of their views on any issues in which the proper administration of the seminary may be involved, and on which Southern Baptists may be divided." They agreed additionally that this rule "shall not be given out for publication."[90] McCall had tried repeatedly to persuade the faculty to exercise the greatest tact and reserve on such matters. Conservative trustees beginning in the 1980s frequently expressed their concerns with professors who spoke publicly on issues that involved the seminary in controversy within the denomination. Official policy in fact already required faculty to relate constructively to the seminary's constituency. The 1995 amendment defined constructive relationship. It prohibited professors from using class time "for the purpose of undermining or obstructing the policies of this institution." It required faculty also to avoid acting "in ways that are injurious or detrimental to the seminary's relationship with the denomination, donors, or other constituencies within and without the seminary community."[91]

When the trustees expressed their strong support of Mohler, at their April 1995 meeting, Garland's and the faculty's last remaining hope of rescue vanished. With few exceptions the faculty descended into anger and despair. Some felt that the Holy Spirit had abandoned the seminary. Others just called it "evil."[92]

---

88. White, "What's Really Going on at Southern Seminary," 6.

89. White, "What's Really Going on at Southern Seminary," 6.

90. Minutes, Board of Trustees, Southern Baptist Theological Seminary, May 1899, 259–260.

91. Mark McCormick, "Seminary Rule Stifles Faculty, Many Say," *Louisville Courier-Journal*, 27 Apr. 1995, 10A.

92. Marv Knox, "Trustee Actions Bury Seminary Faculty in Despair," *Western Recorder*, 25 Apr. 1995, 11.

The American Association of Theological Schools investigated the seminary's problems in January 1996. It imposed a "notation" that the "general tone of the school impairs the capacity to provide significant theological education and ministerial training." When the agency visited the campus again in 1997, it found a transformed institution and voted to remove the notation.[93]

The Garland controversy also accelerated the accomplishment of the trustees' design to transform the seminary. Professors Anne Davis and Jim Chancellor urged Mohler to offer an early retirement plan and urged their colleagues to consider it favorably. They recognized that many faculty now wanted to leave, and they knew that the president and the trustees would welcome the retirements. The early retirement package offered one year's salary plus $500 for every year of service. To be eligible, a professor's age and years of service needed to equal at least sixty-five. Twenty-nine professors qualified under the terms of the offer. By June 1995, ten professors had accepted the offer of early retirement.[94] Almost as many accepted it later. The early retirement was a mutually agreeable resolution to the alienation of faculty and administration and eased the transition from a moderate to a conservative faculty.

The Garland controversy also precipitated a crisis for the Carver School of Church Social Work. It was barely ten years old, founded in 1984, but it claimed the heritage and endowment that attached to the older Woman's Missionary Union Training School and its successive transformations. The training school had closed in 1963 and transferred its assets to the seminary, and in return the seminary agreed to offer a social work track in its master of religious education degree. Mohler had questioned the wisdom of having a school of social work as part of a theological seminary before he became president. When Mohler entered office, he told Garland that part of her job initially would be to prove to him that the school belonged in a seminary whose primary mission was to equip pastors to preach, teach, and lead churches in faithful discipleship, evangelism, and missions. It did not seem to fit.

But there was another problem. The standards of the social work profession undercut some Christian ethical norms. Mohler held that "the culture of social work and the culture of theological education are not congruent."[95]

93. James A. Smith, "ATS Removes Notation from Southern Seminary," press release, 25 June 1997, Baptist Press.

94. Patrick Howington, "Ten More Professors Are Leaving Baptist Seminary," *Louisville Courier-Journal*, 17 June 1995, 7A, 10A.

95. R. Albert Mohler, quoted in Wingfield and Knox, "Mohler Fires Garland as Carver School Dean," 2.

If the rejection of Sherwood put the Carver School at risk, the ensuing controversy effectively ensured its demise. Faculty and students would flee and destroy its educational viability. The crisis led trustees to appoint a special committee to study the Carver School and prepare recommendations regarding its future. The committee recommended to discontinue the school and in 1998 agreed to transfer it to Campbellsville University, a college controlled by the Kentucky Baptist Convention.

CALVINISM AND DENOMINATIONAL DOUBT

Moderates were astonished to discover that Mohler advocated Calvinism and attacked him for it. Most conservatives in the Southern Baptist Convention rejected the doctrine of predestination but were little troubled by Mohler's views. Since the 1940s, Calvinism had grown in popularity in evangelicalism generally. London preacher Martin Lloyd-Jones influenced many evangelicals in the United Kingdom to embrace Calvinism through his preaching and his promotion of interest in the Puritans. A number of publishers reprinted Puritan writings to meet the growing demand. The writings of John Stott and James I. Packer popularized these emphases in Great Britain and in the United States. In the United States, such preachers and authors as R. C. Sproul, John Piper, and John Macarthur taught an explicitly Calvinistic understanding of the Bible. Francis Schaeffer and Carl Henry, whose writings spurred an intellectual renaissance within American fundamentalism and evangelicalism, also contributed greatly to the spread of Calvinism's popularity. Mohler had studied appreciatively the writings of many of these.

In the Southern Baptist Convention, Calvinism's popularity was spreading at the same time, drawing in part to the same influences. But many Southern Baptists were looking also to their own past and discovered there a rich stream of Calvinist evangelicalism. They reprinted and read the theological works of nineteenth-century Baptists, especially of such men as James P. Boyce. Some formed the Founders Ministries, an organization that produced a quarterly journal and hosted an annual conference dedicated explicitly to the promotion of "the doctrines of grace," as Calvinism was also known. Tom Nettles, professor at Mid-America Baptist Theological Seminary, published in 1986 an extensively documented history of Calvinism among Baptists, which served as an influential introduction to Calvinism for many Southern Baptists. Nettles joined Southern Seminary's faculty in 1997.

Convention moderates agreed with Mohler that Boyce and Manly were Calvinists, but they viewed Calvinism as part of an obsolete tradition of interpretation that included also the oppression of blacks and women. To "return to

Boyce and Manly," retired Southern Seminary professor Frank Stagg wrote, was to return to "slavery, silencing of women, the mean theology of Calvin." [96]

Other Southern Baptists were puzzled or troubled by Mohler's affirmation of Calvinism. At the 1995 meeting of the Southern Baptist Convention in Atlanta, two messengers questioned Mohler's Calvinism. One said that he could not find Calvinism in his Bible.[97] Mohler was disarmingly honest about his convictions. Most conservatives did not seem threatened by it even if they did not agree with him. He had never seen Calvinism as his cause. He wanted to promote the gospel of redeeming grace.

In the early twenty-first century some conservative leaders nevertheless began warning Southern Baptists of the apparent dangers of Calvinism. In 2008 two of the denomination's leading conservative preachers, Johnny Hunt, pastor of the Woodstock, Georgia, First Baptist Church, and Jerry Vines, retired pastor of the Jacksonville, Florida, First Baptist Church, held a conference that challenged the five points of Calvinism. All the evidence, however, indicated that Calvinism was spreading, especially among younger Southern Baptists, despite the warnings.

OF CULTURE WARS

Mohler was not well received by many in the Louisville area. He was the face of the Southern Baptist conservativism that wrenched the seminary from its customary place in the community. As he presided over the institution's near-complete turnover, the *Louisville Courier-Journal's* editorial pages expressed the grief of the former tenants for all to see. Those who took pride in the progressive character of the city found Mohler and the new seminary an embarrassment. The outrage was especially evident when Marshall resigned in 1994 and when Garland resigned in 1995.

His forthright expression of traditional Christian positions in theology and ethics provoked outrage also. When Mohler addressed homosexuality in a paper on Western culture's moral decay in 1995, the *Louisville Courier-Journal* considered it newsworthy, though it was given in a small seminar in North Carolina. Mohler said that Western civilization's rapid acceptance of the moral legitimacy of homosexuality showed "how far we have come from a biblical worldview." Homosexuality was an integral part of Western culture's rejection

---

96. Frank Stagg to Henlee Barnette, 5 Sept. 1995, Henlee Barnette Papers, WFU.

97. Mark Wingfield, "Mohler Declares His Beliefs in Line with Abstract," *Western Recorder*, 27 June 1995, 12.

of God's design for the family and for sexuality, which redefinition was pro-foundly destructive.[98]

The following day the *Louisville Courier-Journal*'s editorial board accused Mohler of inflaming public debate and intensifying the "assault on homosex-uals." They judged him based on their belief that the "leader of a venerable institution" should elevate public discourse and promote charity and tolerance rather than "compassionate hate." The editors suggested that Mohler's message of intolerance bred "persecution and violence."[99] Although Mohler continued to attract hostility from many in the public and in the media for his forthright defense of traditional orthodoxy, he gained national recognition of his lead-ership in this area. In 1994 *Time* named Mohler as one of the nation's top fifty leaders under the age of forty. In 1996 *Christianity Today* selected Mohler as one of the nation's top fifty evangelical leaders under forty. Mohler was a frequent guest on radio and television news programs. In 2001 he began hosting *The Albert Mohler Program*, a daily radio show devoted to engaging contemporary culture with biblical truth.[100]

THE NEW SHAPE OF SOUTHERN SEMINARY

Mohler's first major initiative was the establishment of the Billy Graham School of Evangelism, Missions, and Church Growth. He announced the initiative at his inauguration in October 1993. Billy Graham endorsed Mohler's vision for the new school and the attachment of his name to it. Graham preached at Mohler's inauguration service at Louisville's Freedom Hall arena. Graham's support gave the school credibility and momentum. A gift of nearly $3 mil-lion from A. P. and Faye Stone to endow the school set it on a strong financial basis, as did the transfer of several endowed chairs from the school of theology. Thom Rainer, pastor of Green Valley Baptist Church in Birmingham, Alabama, served as the school's first dean, built the school's faculty, cast the vision for the school's curriculum, and recruited the student body. The school opened in 1994, and enrollment grew rapidly.

98. R. Albert Mohler, quoted in Estes Thompson, "Seminary Chief Links Moral Decay and Homosexuality," *Louisville Courier-Journal*, 1 Mar. 1995, 3B.

99. "Compassionate Hate," *Louisville Courier-Journal*, 2 Mar. 1995, 11A. See also Martha Barnette, "Targeted for Hate—Without Reason," *Louisville Courier-Journal*, 12 Mar. 1995, 1D.

100. The program began as the weekly *Truth on the Line* in 2001, became daily in 2003, and began nationwide syndication in 2004.

The Billy Graham School also afforded Mohler the opportunity to recruit conservative scholars to compose the faculty of a growing school. The Graham School professors were an important counterweight to the faculty's moderate majority during the years of transition.

Mohler was recruiting a faculty committed to conservative orthodoxy. Many came from evangelical seminaries. From Bethel Theological Seminary came Marvin Anderson, Daniel Block, Robert Stein, and Tom Schreiner. Others came from Trinity Evangelical Divinity School, Western Conservative Baptist Theological Seminary, Gordon-Conwell Theological Seminary, Dallas Theological Seminary, and from such evangelical colleges as Taylor University, Bryan College, and Wheaton College.

They were all inerrantists. They all interpreted the Bible as teaching that conscious faith in Jesus Christ was the only means of salvation, that abortion was the unlawful taking of human life, that God declared homosexuality to be sin, and that God restricted the office of pastor or elder to qualified and called men. They all agreed with the teachings of the Abstract of Principles, not according to their own interpretation, but according to Mohler's traditionalist reading of it. Many of the new faculty did not have Southern Baptist backgrounds, but all were Baptists. Others came with a more traditional Southern Baptist background. They came from positions at such Southern Baptist colleges as North Greenville University and Baptist College of Florida or were newly minted Ph.D. graduates.

For Mohler personally, evangelical and Southern Baptist were two essential components of a single identity. For some faculty members, however, these two sources tended to engender distinct identities. Some felt that the seminary's exclusive commitment to serve the churches of the Southern Baptist Convention was objectionably parochial. Others felt that that the seminary was objectionably inclusive—too evangelical and insufficiently Southern Baptist in its character. The seminary, and Southern Baptists generally, had always struggled to find the right way on this question. The faculty nevertheless worked together with great harmony and common purpose and little strain. They blended proven scholarship and effective ministry.

SOUTHERN SEMINARY'S TRAJECTORY

When Mohler became president in 1993, enrollment at the seminary had been falling for nearly a decade. The transition in the character of the school and the controversies associated with it initially contributed to the trend. Southern Seminary's enrollment had peaked about 1985. Using the guidelines established by the Association of Theological Schools, Southern Seminary reported 2,335 students and 1,675 full-time equivalents in the session of 1984–1985. Enrollment declined for the next thirteen years, to a low in the 1997–1998 session of 1,350 students and 851 full-time equivalents. In 1998 the trend reversed. Enrollment grew rapidly in subsequent years. Not counting the new undergraduate program, it nearly doubled in ten years. In the 2007–2008 session, the seminary reported 2,562 students, the highest number in its entire history, and 1,411 full-time equivalents.[101]

The seminary faced new challenges. The revenues the school received from the denomination's Cooperative Program generally grew, but at a much slower rate than the growth of the cost of education. As a result, the Cooperative Program provided a diminishing percentage of the seminary's budget. The only feasible solution was to raise tuition. All six Southern Baptist seminaries experienced this trend.

Mohler's deep and genuine appreciation for Boyce shaped his vision. His agreement with Boyce's commitment to the precritical orthodoxy of the founding four shaped his approach to institutional policy. He viewed his role first as that of a steward administering the seminary in trust on behalf of the founders, donors, and above all the churches of the Southern Baptist Convention. He aspired to fidelity to the founders' commitment to evangelical orthodoxy, to Baptist principles and practices, and to denominational trust. Everything, from general vision to specific policy, had to rest on this foundation.

Boyce hoped that Southern Seminary would serve as a bulwark and defense against Arminianism and false teaching. The purpose of the Abstract of Principles and of a trustee board elected by the denomination was to preserve biblical orthodoxy. But these measures had not prevented the wholesale transformation of the theological character of faculty. They abandoned most of the Calvinism in the early twentieth century and promoted liberalism especially after the 1940s.

But Boyce's early vision and labors played an essential role in the recovery of orthodoxy beginning in the 1990s. The seminary could never quite get out from under the Abstract of Principles. Even though McCall and Honeycutt gave wide latitude of individual interpretation, it had a restraining influence. More important, the seminary could not get out from under the control of the denomination. The denomination's prevailing conservatism restrained the seminary's faculty from still greater divergence from traditional orthodoxy. Faculty had to be careful of teaching aberrant doctrine, and trustees looked to elect new faculty who could hold their progressive views in check. Denominational control

---

101. See Association of Theological Schools, *Fact Book on Theological Education* (Vandalia, OH: Association of Theological Schools, 1985; 1998; 2008).

finally provided the means by which the denomination could overthrow the liberalism there. And Boyce set the precedent for the overthrow. His leadership in the defense of inerrancy and the dismissal Crawford H. Toy in 1879 provided a reference point for conservatives in the conservative revolution in the 1980s and 1990s. Mohler embraced and embodied this vision as fully as any had.

Under Mohler's leadership, Southern Seminary was once again Boyce's seminary.

INDEX

abortion
  resolution opposing, 486
  Simmons, 458, 459, 488, 506
Abstract of Principles, 31–40, 122–123,
  213, 215, 545
  adherence, 375
  Committee on the Plan of
    Instruction, 34–35
  drafts, 33–34
  faculty commitment, 492–494, 501
  fundamental laws, and denominational
    control, 40–42
  liberalism, truth and, 461–463
  Marshall, 519–521
  minimum standard of orthodoxy, 134
  Mohler, 515–519
  Moody, 412, 413, 438–441
  Mullins interpreting, 237
  seminary professors accepting, 40
  Toy's views and, 130, 135
Abstract of Theology, virgin birth, 265
academic idealism, McCall, 357–359
accreditation, seminary, 401–402, 492
activism, student, of seminary, 421–422
Adam's posterity, responsibility for
  sin, 37
admissions, theological education, 18
alien immersion. See also baptism
  discussion, 100–102
  resolutions, 105–106
Allen, Wayne
  balance, 500
  covenant, 498
  hiring, 502–503
  photograph, 453

Alley, Robert, conflict, 387, 390, 395
American Baptist Flag, Landmarkism, 235
American Protestantism, Southern
  Baptists, 109
anti-intellectualism, opposition, 49–50
apostasy
  Arkansas Baptists vs. Moody, 441–444
  Moody, 411, 438–441
A Question in Baptist History,
  Whitsitt, 208–210, 216
Arkansas Baptists, vs. Moody, 441–444
Arminianism, alarming Baptist
  preachers, 92–93
aspirations, progressive thought, 338–341
atonement, article draft, 37–38
authority of Bible, Glorieta
  Statement, 463–466

Baconism realism, Toy, 122
balance, undefined in
  covenant, 499–501
baptism
  alien immersions, 100–102, 372–373
  A Question in Baptist History, 208–210
  Baptist beliefs, 39, 99
  controversy over historical
    practices, 198–202
Baptist colleges, theological
  education, 5–7
Baptist Courier
  Calvinist doctrine, 240, 241
  new view of inspiration, 126
  Whitsitt's controversy, 205
Baptist Faith and Message, Mullins,
  creeds and, 290–294